The OMAHA COMMUNITY PLAYHOUSE STORY
A Theatre's Historic Triumph

The OMAHA COMMUNITY PLAYHOUSE STORY
A Theatre's Historic Triumph

Warren Francke

omaha**community**playhouse
Omaha, Nebraska

©2014, Omaha Community Playhouse. No part of this book may be used or reproduced in any manner whatsoever without written permission except in the case of brief quotations embodied in critical articles or reviews. Any similarities to other intellectual works are either coincidental or have been properly cited when the source is known. Trademarks of products, services, and organizations mentioned herein belong to their respective owners and are not affiliated with Omaha Community Playhouse. The author and publisher shall have neither liability nor responsibility to any person or entity with respect to any loss or damage caused, or alleged to have been caused, directly or indirectly by the information contained in this book.

Photos in this book are courtesy of the Omaha Community Playhouse's archives, the *Omaha World-Herald*, Durham Museum, and *The Reader*.

For information, address the publisher:
Omaha Community Playhouse
6915 Cass St
Omaha, NE 68132
(402) 553-0800

Paperback:	978-0-9906828-0-6
Hardcover:	978-0-9906828-1-3
Mobi:	978-0-9906828-2-0
EPUB:	978-0-9906828-3-7

Library of Congress Control Number: 2014947860
Cataloging in Publication Data on file with Publisher

Publishing and Production: Concierge Marketing Book Publishing Services.
Printed in the United States of America

10 9 8 7 6 5 4 3 2 1

CONTENTS

Omaha Community Playhouse Chronology, 1924–2014 i

1   Founding a Little Theater, 1924–1925 1

2   First Full Season, None Better, 1925–1926 31

3   Coming of Age in "Temporary" Home, 1926–1935 47

4   Hard Times, War, But Show Goes On, 1935–1946 117

5   Postwar Prosperity Leads West, 1946–1959 175

6   New Theater Stages Musicals, 1959–1974 245

7   Charming Charles Brings *Carol,* Caravan, 1974–1977 317

8   Ten-Year Rise to No. 1 Theater, 1977–1986 345

9   Nation's Top Community Theater, 1986–2006 383

10   Living the Legacy and Looking Ahead, 2006–2014 467

90 Years of Theatre Productions 495

Acknowledgments 507

About the Author 509

Index 511

To all the players, on and off stage,
who brought their passion to the Playhouse.

Omaha Community Playhouse Chronology, 1924–2014

1924   Planned at September meeting, incorporated November 13.

1925   Variety show at Technical High School, February, *The Enchanted Cottage* in March, both star Dodie Brando. First full season opens with Henry Fonda in *You and I*.

1926-27 Plays at Cooper Dance Studio, 4012 Farnam.

1927   Fonda now director Greg Foley's assistant director/janitor for $100 a month.

1928   Playhouse, 40th and Davenport, built in 28 days; Bernard Szold replaces Foley.

1930   Fonda returns, paid $150 to star with Dorothy McGuire, age 13 in *Kiss for Cinderella*.

         First man of color, Donald Morton, in cast of *The Last Mile*.

1933   Grant Wood does design for *Brigham Young*; Mormon protest cuts 17 wives from cast.

1935	Edward Steinmetz Jr. replaces Szold; Emmy Gifford does sets, costumes.
1938	"Tired Old Horse" in *Raggedy Ann & Andy* played by Letitia Baldrige, standing 6 feet 1 at age 13.
1939	City threatens ban on *Yes, My Darling Daughter*; 100th show: *Our American Cousin* includes music. Land donor Sarah Joslyn's death leads to forgiven mortgage.
1941	First modern musical, *Knickerbocker Holiday*, with Julie Wilson in chorus.
	Mary Peckham on stage, hears news of Pearl Harbor bombing.
1942	Kendrick Wilson starts 25 years as director; World War II shortage of men so switch to such plays as *The Women*.
1946	Short on money, theater kept afloat by treasurer Clarence Teal.
1951	Elaine Jabenis makes debut; first full-time designer-technician Robert Soule.
1954	Infidelity in *The Moon Is Blue* brings second official Catholic protest.
1955	Fund-raiser for new theater with McGuire, Henry and Jane Fonda in *Country Girl*. Royal Eckert new designer; Studio Theater adds avant-garde.
1959	New theater opens at 6915 Cass with musical *Say Darling*.
1961	Peter Fonda in Venetian play, pranksters put catfish in tub for canal-dunking.
1962	Yvonne Johnson first African-American award winner for *Raisin in the Sun*.
1966	Mortgage burned; Bill Koll, Janet Wallace honored for *King and I*.
1967	Wilson, Eckert leave, replaced by Jim Cavanaugh and R. Thomas Casker.
1972	Junior Theater splits; Emmy Gifford leaves board.

1974	Gentleman from Georgia, Charles Jones, new director, brings designer Jim Othuse.
1975	Tornado rips roof from Playhouse in May.
1976	Robert Storz funds parking lot; Jones adapts Dickens's *A Christmas Carol*, starts Nebraska Theatre Caravan, hires 8 pros, including Bill Hutson and future Caravan manager Carolyn Rutherford.
1978	Caravan hires future leaders, Carl Beck, Susan Baer, Jim Boggess.
1979	Orchestra pit added; *Carol* national tours begin, later with three companies.
1986	Expands to 66,000 square feet, four plays added in what becomes Fonda-McGuire Series, now called America's largest, finest community theater.
1987	Staff up to 35, Hutson, Susan Baer Beck added as staff artists.
1988	*South Pacific* with guest star Greg Ryerson draws record 19,248; *Rocky Horror Picture Show* adds record 6,628 in smaller space later known as Howard Drew.
1990	Actors Procession sculptures by Milt Heinrich added to south brick wall.
1991	Jones suffers paralyzing stroke in November, returns for *Brigadoon* in May.
1992	Season ticket sales at 12,289, record high for all community theaters.
1994	Record musical and drama: *Joseph, Dreamcoat*, 19,677; *My Antonia*, 14,478.
1997	Carl Beck replaces Jones as artistic director.
2001	Tim Schmad becomes executive director.
2002	*Buddy* big hit with Billy McGuigan as Buddy Holly.
2005	National acclaim for Dick Boyd, retiring after 30 years as Scrooge in *Carol*.

2009	Belt-tightening dispute brings brief resignation of directors Beck and Susan Baer Collins, cancellation of play, protests, then forward-looking agreement.
2012	Edgy staged readings in "21 & Over" series leads to "Find Your Stage" concept opening with *August: Osage County*.
2013	*Les Misérables* wins raves, sells out theater with all-star cast.
2014	Beck and Collins retire, Hilary Adams hired as new director for 90th season.

CHAPTER

1

Founding a Little Theater, 1924–1925

Flapper Brando Calls for Fonda

They met in the Burgess-Nash Tea Room on Sept. 24, 1924. If someone moved and seconded a plan to create America's largest theater of its kind, no minutes record that ambition. They just wanted to put on plays.

The Omaha Community Playhouse was born at 16th and Harney that evening, and the next March its first star made her debut. Dodie Brando (few called her Dorothy, some called her Do) was "a flapperesque stenographer" in the first Playhouse performance, a variety show. Mrs. Brando, quite understandably, missed that tea room session where the incorporation papers were signed. Her daughters were ages 4 and 2, and her infant son was not yet six months old. But three youngsters didn't stop her from taking leads in O'Neill's *Anna Christie,* Shaw's *Pygmalion* and others as she became the leading lady of the new Playhouse.

Dodie would live through darker days before the magic night on Broadway when her boy Marlon opened as Stanley Kowalski in *A Streetcar Named Desire* and wowed those who wondered, "How can an actor like that come from Omaha, Nebraska?" In the summer of 1925, as the first full Playhouse season neared, his mother would phone another mother of three, friend and fellow Christian Scientist Herberta Fonda, and recruit her son to the Playhouse stage.

Henry Fonda had returned from two years at the University of Minnesota and worked weekends for Northwestern Bell. The phone message that launched a career was direct: "The company needs a juvenile." The lanky scoutmaster of the Dundee troop, age 20, recalled knocking on the second floor Aquila Court apartment "and a short red-headed man asked me in." Henry stared up at the first skylight he'd ever seen until director Greg Foley handed him a book and said, "Read Ricky."

He recited, "Ricky," then the line, "But why not?" and was stopped by the director, who explained that Ricky was the character in Philip Barry's *You and I*, not part of the dialogue.

Later, both Fonda and Mrs. Brando, among others, would get credit for bringing a third star, Dorothy McGuire, to the Playhouse. Actually, a less famous but more enduring figure in its history, Echo Guiou Ellick, may have played that role. Echo was born April 6, 1917, the day America declared war on Germany. Her mother, Genevieve Guiou, also had her hands full with three daughters in 1924, a year after the death of her husband, Arthur.

As head of the Omaha Drama League, she was an especially interested observer when the Playhouse was organized. A charter member of the League, she had shepherded two earlier efforts to start a community theater. Mrs. Guiou would serve as Playhouse president, a post later held by her daughter. And she bought stock share No. 19 in March 1925, to invest in the new corporation known as the Playhouse.

But she did not join Marguerite Beckman, Rex Morehouse, Alan McDonald, Mark Levings, the Mackin sisters and others at Burgess-Nash that night. Mrs. Guiou, class valedictorian of Vassar '01 and frequent European traveler, loomed large in the theater's future, but it began with Miss Beckman. She came to Omaha after dropping out of *The Gypsy Rover*, another failing road company, in Sioux City, Iowa.

So, just as the larger Little Theater movement grew from the decline in traveling companies, Omaha's theater began when a road dropout called a meeting. But that's its genesis only if you ignore all that came before.

Road Companies Fall, Drama League and Little Theaters Rise

Before the century's end, the community theater founded that evening in 1924 would grow to one of artistic stature, but, more measurably, to the top of its class with the largest staff and budget. What came before is more than the story of one theater company can comfortably contain: the long trail from dramatized liturgy in medieval cathedrals and the wailing songs of the Greek chorus.

Drama came to America, near Santa Fe in 1598, with a title, *Los Moros y Christianos,* that gained new meaning after Sept. 11, 2001. Drama surfaced at Harvard in 1690 and came to Omaha in 1857, if the promise of a faded playbill was realized, or in 1860 if the pioneer memory of businessman Byron Reed was correct.

Live drama thrived at the dawn of the twentieth century, but soon the old opera houses and legitimate stages were converted into movie theaters that advertised "photoplays." By the autumn of 1924, only sixty-seven legitimate theater productions were touring America, compared to 392 in 1900. Observers didn't agree on the exact year or all the conditions, but they concluded that a great tradition was dying.

Around 1915, "Commercial theatre began slowly and unobtrusively committing suicide in that rather inclusive portion of the United States known as the Road," wrote Kenneth MacGowan, the director who, with Eugene O'Neill, founded the Provincetown Players. "At the same time, a number of fanatical amateurs took to the notion that they might be Belascos and Barrymores without invading Broadway." Before long,

"20, 50, 200, 500 community theatres developed to feed a play-starved public." As the professionals withdrew, the amateurs emerged.

According to MacGowan, whose *Footlights Across America* was its definitive early study, the Little Theater movement began in 1912 with the Chicago Little Theatre and Boston's Toy Theatre. "Little" and "Toy" contrasted stages and buildings smaller than the grand opera and movie houses of the day with their plush lobbies and opulent décor.

Before 1920, the Provincetown Players were joined by two fabled Playhouses, Cleveland and Pasadena, founded when another touring company went broke nearby. Enough were emerging by 1917 to alarm a Broadway giant, David Belasco. With the Washington Square Players flourishing in New York, Belasco gave that city's *Herald* an earful. Yes, the theater has always suffered from "acting organizations devoted to false ideals, but never until this season have they been so vicious, vulgar, and degrading. They have multiplied alarmingly … this so-called new art of the theater is but a flash in the pan of inexperience. It is the cubism of the theater—the wail of the incompetent and degenerate."

Five years after his tirade against "the mere boys and girls" of the little theaters, he saw their light and began awarding the Belasco Cup to the winner of an amateur theater competition.

Another movement also paved the way for community theater in Omaha. The Drama League started nationally in Chicago in 1910 and came to Omaha in 1915, founded by Kate McHugh. An English teacher, she became the first woman to head a 2,000-student high school. Her Omaha High School became Central, alma mater of Mrs. Brando, Fonda and McGuire. McHugh's initial Drama Leaguers included U.S. Sen. Gilbert Hitchcock, founding publisher of the *Omaha World-Herald*; architect Thomas Kimball and two who later served on the Playhouse board, Mrs. Guiou and Rabbi Frederick Cohn.

The League offered a lending library and public lectures until 1919 when it began backing local plays by precursors of the Playhouse. From 1928 to the 1940s, the Drama League brought the Barrymores and other theatrical greats to the professional stages of Omaha.

Margaret Hitchcock Doorly, Others Precede Playhouse

Senator Hitchcock's daughter Margaret and architect Kimball's sister Arabell would object to beginning Omaha's theater story with either the Drama League or the Playhouse. They might not mind neglecting all the local efforts to perform pageants, festival plays and other sporadic activity. They knew that the Little Post Theatre popped up at Fort Omaha in 1892. The Knights of Ak-Sar-Ben, a powerful civic group, did elaborate men-only shows in its downtown "den" with such notables in the audience as presidents of the United States. The Junior League produced revues, and, as always since the dawn of drama, church and school plays were plentiful. In all likelihood, Margaret Hitchcock and Arabell Kimball would prefer to claim their Players Club as the most memorable predecessor of the Playhouse.

Arabell's brother Thomas gained more fame from designing the Cathedral, St. Cecilia's, just blocks away on 40th Street from the home, a decade later, of the

Henry Doorly (undated).

Mrs. Doorly and horse, 1920.

first Omaha Community Playhouse. But Kimball also built a grand house on St. Mary's Avenue for his mother and equipped it with "a complete Little Theater," where "she sponsored many amateur productions." Some thought the home theater compensated Arabell, victimized by the family's rejection of unsuitable suitors and her stifled dreams of acting on Broadway.

Arabell was the director when the Players Club presented Sheridan's *The Critic* in 1904. When her romantic leads were late for the final dress rehearsal, she waited tearfully, then quickly forgave Margaret Hitchcock and Henry Doorly when she heard their excuse. They were delayed by Margaret's acceptance of Henry's marriage proposal.

Henry would later run her father's daily newspaper, but Margaret Doorly would write plays and take acting roles in Drama League efforts to develop community theater. In 1919, the League founded the Folk Theatre, which lasted long enough to close the Boyd in 1920. Led by director-actor Oscar Wilder Craik, their farewell to the historic theater featured three one-act plays and such players as Rex Morehouse and Charles Docherty, later Playhouse performers. They won favorable reviews from the *World-Herald's* Keene Abbott, who could hardly complain about the selection of one-acts. He served with the League's Miss McHugh on the play-reading committee. Another 1920 effort by the Folk Theatre presented more one-acts with Playhouse founders Mark Levings and Morehouse, a butler in one play, director of another.

Three one-act plays weren't enough. "Between the second and third, Miss Ruth Harms offered her Egyptian dance, which showed careful training." Dance acts and the later inclusion of the West Sisters String Quartette forecast traits of the first Playhouse shows.

In 1921, the company's billing said, "The Omaha Drama League Presents The Craik Company," dropping Folk for the man named Oscar Wilder (not Wilde) Craik, a World War I veteran who'd worked in the Portmanteau Theater, another pioneer in the "little" movement. They then did local plays, among them *White Lies* by Mrs. Doorly.

In 1923, another League effort earned the headline, "Little Theater Movement Launched." Mrs. Guiou pushed it by trumpeting "the enthusiastic interest" Miss McHugh "feels in the movement." The plan called for two plays at the Brandeis supervised by the Misner School of the Spoken Word. Manager Ernest Misner was located in the same downtown building with W. Brace Fonda's printing business, an office visited by son Henry when he witnessed an infamous courthouse lynch mob. Misner would be responsible for casting and directing, while the League took the financial role—renting the theater, advertising, and other tasks.

His company appeared at the new Technical High School, described in a national study as having the best stage in Omaha, and it followed the pattern of the Folk-Craik productions. A musical solo aired during the intermission between plays. Each one-act was written by an Omaha woman, including two present in the tea room for the Playhouse founding—Henrietta Rees and Helen Masters, wife of then Central High principal J.G. Masters.

A half dozen in those casts would soon appear in Playhouse drama, but again the most prominent thespian was Mrs. Doorly, this time as a character in a Chinese restaurant scene. The playbill identified the program, a one-night stand, as "The Omaha Press Club Prize Plays of 1924," presented by the Drama League "under the personal direction of Ernest Misner."

If none of these theater companies lasted, they provided training for future Playhouse performers and board members and showed the need for credible backing—from Miss McHugh and the civic leaders of her Drama League. Their use of Tech High and musical interludes would soon be adapted by the Playhouse.

If Tech High had the best school venue, the Brandeis, built in 1910 at 17th and Douglas, made even larger claims. It seated 1,650, some in seats "of unusual size for big men." Its stage, 75 by 52 feet deep, was declared "bigger than the Belasco," and the Brandeis was billed simply as "the most beautiful theater in America."

Attending the memorial service of Emil Brandeis, lost as the *Titanic* sank in 1912, mourners passed under the Saturnalian procession that marked the entrance. Its central figure on a white charger was encircled by dancing Bacchantes who celebrated the rites of spring. The great stage would soon welcome Otis Skinner, Mrs. Fiske (Minnie didn't need a first name) and Ethel Barrymore (who did need one to distinguish her from her brothers). Mrs. Patrick Campbell, for whom an adoring George Bernard Shaw created leading roles, brought her *Pygmalion* to the Brandeis after a film run of D.W. Griffith's *The Birth of a Nation*. Such intermingling of media required ads warning, "This Is Not a Motion Picture."

So if The School of the Spoken Word didn't light their dramatic fires, would-be actors were promised the Brandeis. The Drama League venture, Mrs. Guiou said, "Will afford an opportunity for local talent to find itself. Anyone with dramatic ability in any walk of life is urged to try for a part. These ambitious ones will find themselves behind the footlights of the Brandeis Theater. You, the people of Omaha, must be the body and soul of this important movement."

The rest is history, but rather garbled history, in at least two cases. Eugene Konecky, advertising manager for WOW radio, wrote a telling portrait of the Playhouse for *Theatre Arts Magazine* in the 1930s. Unfortunately, he relied on memory rather than research to summarize earlier attempts. He may have hit the mark in calling the 1920 Folk Theatre "a pretentious theatricality" that failed due to "insufficient finances and clannishness," but he failed to mention its being sponsored by the well-established Drama League. He recalled the subsequent effort as "more promising ... under the vigorous initiation of the proprietor of a dramatic school, and with the half-hearted support" of the League.

Still, he brushed their work off as "mediocre one-act plays," competing with what he identified as "Craig's [sic] Little Theatre," which he termed "better and more courageous, but too exclusive to represent the community." Underline that earlier mention of those from "any walk of life." It becomes a recurring theme.

One can only guess at causes of Konecky's confusion, but at least he didn't come to the conclusion reached in a New York University doctoral dissertation. It botched the genealogy and the birth year of the Playhouse in a single sentence: "In 1927, with the help of a number of high school teachers, the Folk Theatre changed its name to what is now the nationally recognized Omaha Community Playhouse." The year and the roots were both wrong, though teachers clearly played a part.

It's also clear that theater enthusiasts active in the early 1920s with the Drama League and its ventures helped the Playhouse get started in 1924. Were they "the dowagers who took command," as one historian put it? Were they the "buxom, high-bosomed ladies" of a later slur?

Omaha, Broadway and the World of 1924

Actually, Marguerite Beckman who called that meeting in the Burgess-Nash Tea Room would become more famous for her comely ear than her lofty bosom. She later went to New York for a screen test and the director cast her left ear for a close-up symbolizing "gossip" in the movie *Love 'Em and Leave 'Em*. Her presence in the community after leaving the *The Gypsy Rover*, however, fit the trend: the fall of those road companies as the movies were rising.

John Barrymore was praised for his Hamlet in 1922, then left Broadway for film. Lee DeForest, the man from Council Bluffs who called himself "The Father of Radio," was experimenting with sound on film, and Al Jolson's *Jazz Singer* brought talkies just two years after the first Playhouse performance. And radio was fast becoming another threat to legitimate theater.

On the day the founders met, Sept. 24, 1924, the newspaper listed only three radio stations: WOAW was silent that day, WAAW promised only the 3 p.m. market report from the Grain Exchange Building, and KFNF in Shenandoah, Iowa, offered the only entertainment, a 7:30 p.m. band concert. But the next day's paper showed all three scheduling more music, such as the Omaha Nightingales from Roseland Gardens and other local talent. The first broadcasting networks, NBC and CBS, were born in 1926 and 1927. A month before the Playhouse debut in 1925, a British dramatist told an Omaha Drama League audience, "Radio in five years will have swept every stage, every newspaper, every book out of existence."

In short, the mid-1920s world was a fast-changing one. Prohibition was a pervasive fact of life, especially in a city where the longtime mayor, Cowboy Jim Dahlman, was less powerful than Boss Tom Dennison. The Boss was known early as "Pick-Handle Tom," later as "the Old Man," finally as "the Old Gray Wolf."

Dennison ran Omaha's politics, gambling and prostitution from the Budweiser Saloon until prohibition came in 1919, then from a bank office and the Cornhusker Cigar Store. Easily the most interesting character on the public stage, this weathered fellow with the cauliflower ear wore derby hat, tie and vest. He trained wire-haired terriers but walked a pair of Dalmatians, surveying the scene with what author Orville Menard described as his "steely blue eyes and narrow, whimsical smile." One photograph gives him the look of an impish John Gielgud.

Add the fact that Cowboy Jim Dahlman had shot a man in pre-mayoral Texas days—"I was pretty handy with a six-shooter then."—to the aromatic presence of the South Omaha stockyards, and it's not hard to see 1920s Omaha as something of a frontier cow town.

Yet it was a city that saw Broadway shows soon after they played the Great White Way. In 1924, Ethel Barrymore led the cast there of Pinero's *The Second Mrs. Tanqueray,* and she brought it to the Brandeis the next spring as the Playhouse gave its first performance. Ed Wynn did *The Grab Bag* on Broadway, then brought it to Omaha.

Pauline Lord preceded Tallulah Bankhead in *They Knew What They Wanted,* then Miss Lord headlined at the Orpheum in Omaha. Lou Holtz, the blackface comedian, starred in *George White's Scandals* in New York, then won top billing at the Orpheum that September.

Omaha remained a far cry from Broadway. Many of the stars made it to town from time to time, but the half dozen theaters offering live shows here might bring one top attraction a week while Manhattan displayed a dazzling array. No capsule can do justice to a theater scene blending O'Neill's early plays with Sophie Tucker in *Earl Carroll's Vanities*. Its unclad girl on a pendulum circumvented the rules against nudes moving on stage. Shubert's *Artists and Models* ran 261 nights with disrobed models in frozen poses.

Katharine Cornell played the crippled daughter of a surgeon. Walter Huston starred in *Desire Under the Elms* before heading for Hollywood. Fred and Adele Astaire, the Austerlitz siblings who left Omaha and first danced on Broadway in 1905, starred in *Lady Be Good* with music by Ira and George Gershwin.

Lunt and Fontanne played leads in Molnar's *The Guardsman,* while other shows featured Fanny Brice, Bea Lillie, Will Rogers, W.C. Fields, George M. Cohan, Noel Coward and Basil Rathbone. Humphrey Bogart and Shirley Booth debuted in 1924, and *I'll Say She Is* featured four brothers named Herbert, Leonard, Julius and Arthur. They'd be more famous as Zeppo, Chico, Harpo and Groucho Marx.

Minor roles went to Antoinette Perry, namesake of Broadway's Tony awards, and a chorus girl named Imogene Coca. George S. Kaufman wrote comedies with Marc Connelly and Edna Ferber. O'Neill shared the playwright spotlight with Maxwell Anderson, while Shaw and Ibsen joined Shakespeare as staples. Even the Gershwins, a few years after George wrote "Rhapsody in Blue," weren't alone in the musical limelight they shared with Irving Berlin, Cole Porter and Rudolf Friml whose "Rose-Marie" wailed its "Indian Love Call."

See Her Bathe, Exercise, Dress for the Street

As the founders met in September 1924, the biggest Broadway name in town was Pauline Lord. But she did a sketch, not a full play, as she shared the Orpheum bill with blackface Lou Holtz and Davison's Louisville Loons. The Brandeis offered a legitimate play, but it was a haunted house mystery with no headliner.

At the Empress, a live rural musical, *Hiram,* was billed as "the show that outlaughs them all," and it was paired with a film starring Laura LaPlante. The Gayety's comedian sounded less exciting than its

Theater Row, 1924, Empress, World, Rialto and Moon at 16th and Douglas.

Fast Steppers, touted as "faster than the Ak-Sar-Ben track's fleetest," and backed by the Humdinger Chorus and Princess Mysteria the Human Radio.

At the World, the pairing of motion picture and stage show may have reached perfection with the film *Flapper Wives* and "the Eternal Flapper, Edna Wallace Hopper, Still a Girl at 62." Her live, "lavish production" features her morning routine, showing how she bathes, exercises and dresses for the street. Add Adler's Syncopators, the eleven Maids of Melody, all for fifty cents.

Such was the sort of stage entertainment in Omaha that autumn with nary an O'Neill or Shaw in sight. At those movie houses where films didn't share billing with live shows, Rudolph Valentino's *The Sheik* played at the Muse, Norma Talmadge in *Secrets* at the Strand, and, among others, Tom Mix in *The Heart Buster* at the Moon.

The biggest advertisement heralded the opening of *Welcome Strangers* at the Sun, and its promotional language speaks volumes about these transitional days of movies derived from the stage: "It's a

Photoplay," the top line promises, "from the great Broadway play by Aaron Hoffman." The ad sells the film as local access to a Broadway hit: "Omaha will roar over the screen version the same as Chicago and New York roared over the stage success for two solid years."

If the visibility of a Cowboy Mayor and Boss Dennison exaggerated the cow town side of Omaha life in the mid-1920s, so did newspaper competition give more play to the sensational side. While many Omahans attended churches and supported the arts, such as the new Omaha Symphony, others supplied front-page headlines for Omaha's *Bee*, the *News* and the *World-Herald*.

Sample the week of that founding meeting that gave birth to the Omaha Community Playhouse:

"Mother Grief Stricken," a page one headline said, as "Girl, 25, Weds Man, 60."

Overcome with "nervous shock," the mother complained, "Cleo has disgraced us all by marrying a man so old," even if he was an inspector for the Council Bluffs water works.

A front-page brief was more optimistic: "Hugh Atherton's only leg, broken by an auto Sunday, may not have to be amputated as feared at first." The same day a twice-married 16-year-old girl named Marie, brought here on a train after being charged with robbery, "asked time to arrange her bobbed hair." If that seems an odd concern, note that an earlier story quoted the head of the Nebraska cosmetologists, returning from the East, to declare that the bobbed hair worn by New York women "is not becoming with evening dress."

The lead story another day told of a pharmacist who died after forty days of hiccoughing and left his estate to his ex-wife. Divorce stories fascinated the competing press. One case was headlined, "Judge Refuses to See Hopson's Damaged Toe. Air Mail Pilot Seeks to Show Where Wife in Temper Hit Him with Kettle." The pilot swore her addiction to parties and clothes, not to mention two attempts to shoot him, made him too nervous to fly. She testified that lingerie found in his car belonged to the other woman known by many as Mrs. Hopson

No. 2. Their son, Bobby, ten, preferred to stay with mom, saying he saw dad strike her after they saw him with the other woman.

The times were changing, warned an item quoting the parting words of a drummer in a Berlin jazz band: "The days of jazz music are gone and as there is nothing else for me to do, I have decided to hang myself."

The Playhouse founders wanted more sophisticated drama than the crude displays in the three dailies.

Meet the Founders: Did Dowagers Take Command?

In 1924, Mary Lane was already Omaha's version of Dear Abby, offering advice to the lovelorn as would various Marys for another forty years. Most of the news read that pleasant fall day by the Playhouse organizers was less lurid than the pilot's divorce trial. The school board wanted $2.5 million to build Benson High School, complete South High and add both auditorium and gymnasium to Central High. Readers learned that "Omaha leads the world with 28 telephones for every 100 persons." Minneapolis was close behind with 24 per 100, but Denver, Los Angeles, Chicago and others trailed with fewer than 20.

That Wednesday was a busy time for Ak-Sar-Ben with its annual Electrical Parade and its den show, "Bullfornia," a satirical offense to some Californians. Even news from its Wild West show was rather dramatic. Old Slim Jones, announcer and bronk buster, introduced a gray mustang called Plenty of Pep.

"I'll ride him myself," drawled the lengthy Jones, "and if anybody else can do it I'll give him $100 cash." If that was his standard come-on, nobody took him up on it after Jones "was thrown 20 feet over the head of an almost frantic horse last night, directly in the path of the rearing, snorting, pawing animal and rendered unconscious."

So it wasn't that Omaha lacked entertainment, but that "Bullfornia" and "the Eternal Flapper" weren't quite the cup of tea for Playhouse founders sipping at "Everybody's Store," as Burgess-Nash advertised.

Looking back at the national rise of community theater, an observer claimed, "The dowagers took command." He wrote of the ladies and the occasional "arty young misfit male" whom "the dowager assembled in her drawing room and over tea cups founded Little Theatre. The American matrons of that period, said Edith Wharton, 'Met culture in bands, since they were afraid to face it alone.'"

Yes, the founders met in a tea room, but, no, they neither fit the dowager slur nor the one in the 1930s. Then *Time* magazine identified Omaha Drama Leaguers as "buxom, high-bosomed ladies" in reporting their flap with an actor. *World-Herald* reviewer and columnist Keith Wilson defended their "admirably slender figures ... acquired through years of double duty as wives and mothers and as hard-working show promoters." He assured: "They are not buxom."

Measurements aside, few of the founders fit the matronly dowager mold.

Miss Beckman of the comely ear close-up left that *Gypsy Rover* company to do research for a Drama League exhibit. She lived downtown while teaching drama at the nearby College of St. Mary and directing children's theater. She'd met that summer of 1924 with Morehouse and others, paving the way for the September meeting when incorporation papers were signed and officers elected. Her founding role grew in the months ahead, but she took time to visit Broadway, catching shows and scoring a small part in *The Popular Sin*.

Rex Morehouse, the man elected temporary board president at that first meeting, poses some problems. While he's clearly no buxom dowager, he's also not a Creighton University student as identified in news coverage of the occasion. He was busy in those Drama League ventures and landed the title role when the Playhouse did *Liliom*. The city directory listed his occupation as "lumber," so perhaps Mrs. Guiou placed him in her lumber yard. A later news clipping credits his "state university" acting experience, apparently on the University of Nebraska boards in 1902 before joining the Players Club. After getting the Playhouse started, he pursued acting in San Francisco.

Presence of the Mackin sisters supports the proposition that teachers played a founding role. Clare Mackin, English department head at South High, and Marie Mackin, a Tech High teacher, signed those founding documents, and Clare served as the first membership chair.

Playwright and principal's wife, Helen Masters, signed then and responded 50 years later when the *Golden Follies* show celebrated a half century. "I remember that first meeting as generating enough enthusiasm to carry little theaters through all the Midwest."

Her Central High School friend, Lena May Williams, recalled: "There were so many ideas about what a community playhouse should be that I wondered if it ever would really get under way." That golden anniversary comment came from Mrs. Lester Herrick, but as Lena May she taught English and directed a Central cast of 500 in the huge "Nebraska" pageant staged at the Brandeis in 1921.

Perhaps another founder, Mrs. William F. Baxter, better fits the dowager mold. Her husband was president of Kilpatricks, which ranked with Brandeis and Burgess-Nash as the leading department stores. Board vice president Mrs. Walter Hixenbaugh Jr. was spouse of the junior partner in a family book business. And the stereotype misses a mile when it comes to Mrs. Mark Levings, board secretary.

Only Alan McDonald arguably played a larger founding role than Mark and Mary Levings. The square-jawed Mary was the woman's golf champ of Nebraska four times in the 1920s. The same news story that reported Morehouse as president, Mrs. Levings as board secretary and Miss Beckman as executive secretary, identified Mark Levings as director of the plays.

Just as Morehouse gave way to McDonald's presidency in January, Levings never functioned as director, turning the job over to Beckman for the March variety show and then to the first full-time director, Greg Foley, that spring. But Mark proved he could tackle any job, on or off stage, as early production credits and laudatory reviews would show.

While his wife golfed at the Field Club, Levings worked as an architect with George Prinz, whose spouse was a charter member of the Drama League. Accomplished in his own right, Mark Levings seemed overshadowed first by his parents and then by his wife. Mark's mother held a law degree from Northwestern, and the senior Levings, a route engineer for the Union Pacific, was a personal friend of poets Eugene Field and James Whitcomb Riley.

A big Sunday spread in the *World-Herald*, titled "Vacations Apart Make Happy Marriages," featured Mary the golf champ on the links and Mark at his drawing board doing etchings to illustrate fine books. They shared Playhouse service but not vacations or avocations. Two years later, their divorce made news, and Omaha learned that Mark Levings believed no marriage could be successful unless one partner was "a dub," as he described himself. Maybe *duffer* was a better word.

"He is no dub," Mary responded, "but I can't understand why he should be scornful of my bridge and golf associates." She told the reporter, "It would be small of me to suggest that his interest in golf declined as my prowess increased."

Both declared the other "a fine person" in a news story that began with, "Incompatibility is a grand word and it covers all my differences with my husband." Thus spoke Mary Levings on return from a European tour, rejoining her husband to play the victims of journalism that typified the Roaring Twenties. Mark Levings left another legacy. He was survived by his scrapbook preserving the first news stories of the Playhouse.

Men on Board: Architect, Reverend and Rabbi

After the September 24 incorporation meeting and formal filing on November 13, Beckman and Morehouse planned other events that provided occasion to promote the purpose of the group now identified as the Community Playhouse: "To encourage talented amateurs in all the dramatic arts, which include acting, playwriting, stage directing, lighting and costume design; to provide an outlet for community expression in the form of plays and pageants; and to offer an opportunity for the people of Omaha to see the best of the plays which would otherwise not be produced here." This elaborated on the incorporation statement that the Playhouse purpose was "to encourage and promote interest in the dramatic and allied arts."

News stories in two dailies, while identifying Beckman as executive secretary and Morehouse as president, made no attributions to sources as both reporters connected the founding here to roots in Europe and America. But a common source seems obvious when separate stories say Chicago's Maurice Browne "blazed the way so successfully." They also cite Cleveland, where "our own Frederick McConnell" was leading that theater to national prominence as he built their grand playhouse.

Omahans knew McConnell, the local high school graduate, earlier as the "First Omaha Boy Taken Prisoner by the Huns," then as a Drama League lecturer. Described by *Time* as "a diminutive person of perpetual vigor," McConnell kept Cleveland at the top for thirty-seven years before going to its chief rival for excellence, the Pasadena Playhouse. He trained at Carnegie Tech under Thomas Wood Stevens, the mentor there of the second Playhouse director, Bernard Szold.

Nothing special was said about the chosen name, the Community Playhouse, not yet modified by "Omaha." While *Little Theater* was a term still widely used, *playhouse* and *players* had become more common terms.

"No one person named it," Mrs. Masters recalled, "it was just a collective urge." And nothing more was said in the December stories about the founding call for fund-raising through the sale of capital stock at $10 a share. Memberships would take two forms: active members and those who wanted to give only support and encouragement. For purity sake, stockholders with professional ties to dramatic art could not be elected to the board of trustees.

Stock sales apparently began after the first annual meeting in January 1925 at the Colonial Hotel. In any case, a surviving share, No. 19 sold to Mrs. Guiou, is dated March 3, 1925. It bears the signatures of president Alan McDonald and secretary Mary Levings. Mary had also served under Morehouse since September, but McDonald had replaced him at the hotel meeting. McDonald and wife, Helen Scobie McDonald, would remain active leaders in the decades that followed.

If those fictitious dowagers were sipping tea, Alan McDonald and his father, John, were designing a museum for their neighbor, Sarah Joslyn. She lived in a castle across 40th Street from a pasture that would soon be transformed into their theater.

With prominent architects Kimball and Prinz involved in the Drama League, it isn't surprising to see another architect take the Playhouse leadership, even as he worked with the senior McDonald on the Joslyn Museum project. Commissioned in 1920, it would open in 1931. McDonald, 33, was no dowager, but he had disappointed one. Mrs. Joslyn watched him growing up at 509 N. 38th, across the street from her castle, and playing with her daughter Violet. She'd hoped he would return from Harvard to marry the girl. Instead, he wed Helen Scobie, the girl Mrs. Joslyn had hired as Violet's companion.

A talented linguist and subject of a youthful portrait by J. Laurie Wallace, Helen McDonald later served long as secretary of the Playhouse board. She was a familiar figure, often seen walking

Sarah Joslyn seated on the southwest lawn Joslyn Castle 1929. (Photo courtesy of Joslyn Castle Trust.)

Architect Alan McDonald plays pressman.

from her 38th Street home to the first theater at 40th and Davenport, a building still three years away.

The McDonalds had two sons, Donald and Wallace, who followed their father to Harvard. As board president at the time of the first two productions and then during the first full season, McDonald was often the voice that defined the Playhouse purpose in lofty terms. He said, "One of the great forces in the rise and fall of nations has been the theater. It must provide recreation, afford genuine relaxation, exercise the mind, and ennoble the feelings of the people."

A Unitarian, he likely brought the Rev. Ralph E. Bailey, First Unitarian minister, to the board. Clare Mackin and Mrs. Baxter chaired membership and program committees. Bank officer John Gamble was treasurer; Rabbi Frederick Cohn headed the play-reading committee.

If all were capable workers, the two clergymen were most intriguing. They would become a truth squad of sorts when critics later assailed the moral values of certain plays. Rabbi Cohn grew up in the fine arts, and Mr. Bailey would reach both literary and denominational heights.

Rabbi Cohn served Temple Israel, Omaha's oldest and largest synagogue, from 1904 until 1940. When the newspaper ran childhood photos of prominent Omahans, he was shown as a small boy with his violin, supporting the claim that his youthful interests were not sports, but drama, literature and music. He played in the Brown University orchestra at a precollege age and loved Emerson and Browning.

Wife Esther held a math degree and the reform rabbi made Phi Beta Kappa while earning two degrees from the University of Cincinnati. His Omaha activities ranged from the Drama League and Playhouse to the Red Cross and Chamber of Commerce. He faced Clarence Darrow at the Orpheum Theatre to debate "Does Man Have a Soul?" and he gave public lectures on topics ranging from anti-Semitism to the latest Playhouse drama. Edwin Markham dedicated a brotherhood poem to Rabbi Cohn, who was remembered as "a little man, full of poetry" and "a hypnotic teacher."

Bailey, 37 in 1925, was born in Georgia, raised a fundamentalist and educated as a Southern Baptist. He preached fire and brimstone when he baptized thirty-five people in a Kentucky creek one morning. Pastor Bailey served a big Baptist church in Cleveland, Ohio, where he regularly golfed with his most prominent worshipper, John D. Rockefeller. A liberal epiphany brought his Unitarian conversion, and a committee including Alan McDonald brought him to Omaha.

Before he joined the Playhouse board, he made headlines: "Bailey Flays Bryan," the *World-Herald* wrote in 1923, when he blamed William Jennings Bryan's role in the Scopes "monkey" trial for attacks on the scientific theory of evolution. Bailey also spoke in support of birth control.

As he rose to Playhouse board president in 1928, a call came from the East and McDonald declared it "an honor to be sending him to the church which is the final goal of any Unitarian minister: the First Unitarian Church of Cambridge, Mass.," the church of the Longfellows and the Eliots on Harvard Square. The intellectual credentials of the founders included Bailey's authoring a biography of Alexander Hamilton. He was ready and quite able to defend the Playhouse when a play selected for the first season sparked criticism.

First "Real" Play: Dodie, et al., in *A Vaudeville Entertainment*

Director Greg Foley was hired in late February 1925, but was not on hand for *A Vaudeville Entertainment,* as the March 4 program billed the ten-act variety show at the Technical High School auditorium. Fresh from Iowa University, Foley met with "Omahans interested in this new movement" on a Sunday and then returned to Iowa City.

The show went on, apparently under the direction of Miss Beckman.

The Sunday *Bee* called it "the first real show" by what was now identified as the Omaha Community Playhouse, or "Little Theater Group." The *World-Herald* ran the first photo showing Playhouse performers under the February 27 caption, "Will Take Feminine Roles in 'Trifles.'" Decked in hats, gloves and fur collars, Mrs. Dora Sass McGorrisk and Mrs. Klea Orschel Lewis smiled for the camera.

The program began with an overture by the Community Playhouse Orchestra, but then came the skit that brought the debut of Dorothy Brando, as she was listed in the program. She played Miss Parsley, "a flapperesque stenographer," opposite A.R. Groh as "a substantial businessman, Mr. Spitzengerberheim."

Abe Groh doubled as emcee, and if he made history by sharing that moment with Dodie Brando, contemporaries knew him as an ace reporter for the *Bee*. He predicted in a 1920 story that Omaha would reach a population of one million by 1980 and travel on a network of subways. Groh also looked to the future in 1929 when he moved that the disbanding Omaha Press Club leave the $80 in its treasury to build a monument to the city's newsmen. In 192 years, he argued successfully, interest would make the fund worth $3,642,880.

Reviewer Keene Abbott treated the one-act play *Trifles* as the dominant feature of the evening along with a dance by Adelaide Fogg. The cast included L.C. "Brick" Hawley, who would co-star soon with Mrs. Brando in the first full play.

As for Adelaide Fogg, Abbott couldn't have been kinder, calling her dance "quaintly exquisite, a lovely bit of fancy, full of whimsy" by this "veritable sprite." The *Daily News* gave a clearer picture: "Wee Adelaide Fogg was at her best as a porcelain clock figure which came to life."

Abbott would learn to know Mrs. Brando and praise her often in Playhouse roles, but now he called the mother of three "Miss Dorothy Brando" before noting that she "gave a lively and amusing characterization of a stenographer."

Others added to the evening: young attorney Edward F. Fogarty, whose brothers Hugh and Frank became prominent in newspapers and television, joined a colleague in a dialect skit on "clients and fees"; Francis Potter performed on four different instruments; and a costumed Scottish trio, with bagpiper William Henry Wallace, presented Harry Lauder's most popular pieces. As promised, the closing act was "a group of dances by pupils of Mary F. Cooper."

Their seven numbers might be ignored, but for their Dance of the Five Veils. Drawn from the choreography of the famed Ruth St. Denis, the dance would reappear in the first play, *The Enchanted Cottage*. Five Mary Cooper pupils would be pictured in the first full-page Sunday spread devoted to the Playhouse, and they would appear beside the West Sisters String Quartette, also part of the Tech High variety show.

Abbott gave them passing mention while raving that "the audience would gladly have held" Miss Fogg "longer than the one encore which she gave." Adelaide Fogg, however, would not supply a home for the next play. Mary Cooper would.

Greg Foley Goes to Work

The "vaudeville entertainment" was called "creditable" by Keene Abbott and "a success" by another journalist, whose closing line assured, "The little theater movement is still open to new members."

Perhaps that sounded more inviting than the formal statement on the cover of the program: "The Community Playhouse is a non-profit-making organization incorporated for the purpose of developing latent talent in the histrionic and kindred arts." The same words were attributed to Alan McDonald in an earlier news story announcing the hiring of Gregory Foley as director. The board president added, "The Playhouse cannot and must not make a profit."

More would soon be known, but then Foley was connected to the State University of Iowa and identified as former president of its theater, with other ties to the Northwestern University School of Speech and Chicago's North Shore Theater Guild. "As a teacher of makeup, stage design and stage craft, Mr. Foley brings to Omaha's new 'little theater' council invaluable in the production of plays of the best quality." Miss Beckman apparently made the contact that led to his hiring.

He returned in the second week of March and began immediately to prepare for two performances of Arthur Wing Pinero's *The Enchanted Cottage* on April 13 and 14. The author showed up in the top twenty when Kenneth MacGowan tallied those writers most staged in community theaters of the 1920s.

Greg Foley.

"I believe 'Enchanted Cottage' is an ideal play for a little theater as the many intimate passages lost in a large auditorium register in a smaller room." (The word *register* resonated, it seems. Abbott used it often in his reviews.) A later story said the endorsement of Rabbi Cohn's play-reading committee "had much to do with the selection of the premier production."

Just as news stories proclaimed the March event "the first real show," they now called *The Enchanted Cottage* the "first actual play." When Robert Martin Nelson wrote his doctoral dissertation, *History of the Omaha Playhouse from 1924 to 1963,* he interviewed Mrs. McDonald, Mrs. Guiou, Echo Ellick and the Teals, Clarence and Val. He doesn't indicate who told him the Mary Cooper Dance Studio was "the only auditorium available," and no explanation of that decision has been found.

Tech High would be used for Junior Theater plays in the future, and the Playhouse would turn to Benson High when the dance studio was sold. An advance story said, "The play will be given at the Mary F. Cooper studio theater which is nearing completion at 4012 Farnam Street." Barely two blocks south of the 1928 Playhouse building site at 40th and Davenport, the Cooper location certainly was convenient for president McDonald and others who lived nearby. But Foley lived downtown in Aquila Court, which also housed the Playhouse office.

The $1 tickets were sold there, with Mary Levings in charge, and at Matthews Book Store and Kilpatricks.

Between the March and April Playhouse productions, Marguerite Beckman joined Mrs. Doorly in the cast of her latest one-act play *The Mole,* a Women's Press Club event at the Orpheum Theatre. News coverage emphasized not only Beckman's cooperation as a Playhouse member and director of the children's theater, but that both the Playhouse and the Drama League would buy blocks of tickets for Mrs. Doorly's play.

Enchanted Before Opening

More lavish publicity preceded *The Enchanted Cottage,* a triumph for publicist E.L. Holland, an advertising man whose son, eighty years later, would became the name donor of the Richard and Mary Holland Performing Arts Center. On Easter Sunday, the Playhouse opening filled the front page of the society section. The largest photo featured the five girls repeating their veil dance. All in white tunics, four seemed to hold the fabric trailing from Virginia Holliday, who kneeled in a graceful pose.

The spread showed the two leads, Mrs. Brando as Laura Pennington and Brick Hawley as Oliver Bashforth, and others in separate head shots. The previous Sunday, a two-column portrait of the leading lady, Mrs. Brando, emphasized her bobbed hair and a Cleopatra necklace. Another photo showed Tech High students building the set under the direction of Robert Galt, who taught at the school with founder Marie Mackin.

Only Jayne Fonda (Henry's sister) and a few others missed seeing their faces in that Easter display above the headline, "Community

Playhouse to Make Bow to Enthusiastic Audience Monday." The 450-seat studio "will be taxed to capacity." The writer found "spiritual significance" in the opening a day after Easter for the story "of a crippled Englishman, injured in the war." He "considers himself an outcast from society until comes into his life the love of an unattractive village girl."

Another handful of advance stories listed the entire cast, and the *Bee* passed early judgment: "Five rehearsals are being held a week under the direction of Gregory Foley and the actors have attained extraordinary grasp of their parts, those who have witnessed the rehearsals say." That justified a lead predicting the play to be "one of the strongest ever given by amateur talent in Omaha."

The society page treatment was a little breathless in its hopes for Mrs. Brando, noting that "even conservative critics are making extravagant prophecies. Mrs. Brando's individual style, her voice of pleasing quality, and her experience in college dramatics, make her a real acquisition to the community players."

Dodie Brando.

In a city still blessed with live performances in the downtown theaters, the press drew a clear line between commercial and community theater. Miss Holliday, so gracefully posed with the veil dancers, gained special attention because she would also appear at the Orpheum with a "noted danseuse" from Council Bluffs. "The young dancer will have to divide her time Monday and Tuesday evenings between the professional and amateur stage."

The program listed Foley's production assistants as stage manager Kenyon Morris and costumer Marian Reed. The program also cited dances by the Cooper Studio and music by Mrs. Karl Werndorff at the piano and the West Sisters String Quartette. Best known of the foursome was Belle West, a local radio personality from 1922 to her Polly the Shopper role in the 1950s.

Cottage Delights Critic

Board member Harry Shedd pasted that Easter Sunday photo spread in the first of many scrapbooks that preserve the history of the Playhouse. He added a clipping with that striking portrait of Dodie Brando, a separate one of Lucy Updike. Then came the authoritative headline over Keene Abbott's review, "'The Enchanted Cottage' Has a Delightful Premiere."

Abbott, 49, would reign as the *World-Herald* drama critic for the next decade. Son of a pioneer doctor, he joined the paper as a police reporter in 1903 and married another writer, Avery, two years later. Keene wrote books and sold articles to the *Atlantic Monthly* and *Saturday Evening Post*; Avery could also claim books and journal pieces. As the Playhouse opened, he headed the new Nebraska Writers Guild, presiding over a membership with such literary lights as Willa Cather, John Neihardt and Bess Streeter Aldrich. His reviews were not easily brushed off as the work of a flattering hack.

The headline's "Delightful" preceded the muted praise in his rather formal lead sentence: "Credit is to be given the Community Playhouse for the attractive presentation of Pinero's appealing play in three acts,

Omaha World-Herald Reviewers

Keene Abbott

Keith Wilson

Jake Rachman

Denman Kountze

Jim Delmont

Bob Fischbach

'The Enchanted Cottage.' The pictorial stage setting; the well-chosen cast; the colorful lighting effects and the elaboration of the dances, both graceful and grotesque, much enhanced the effectiveness of the opening performance," the first play under "the capable direction" of Foley.

If Dodie Brando and Brick Hawley scanned for mention of their lead roles, they waited well into the review. Abbott began his more specific comments with the second act fantasy dances, seven by his count. "Particularly lovely is the dance of the veil performed by a quintet of lithesome misses. All in white, with floating scarfs, the girls displayed their agile and spirited graces with exceptional beauty."

Then he singled out Grace Lennon Conklin's Mrs. Minnett, a seeming minor role raised by her skill to "one of the highest points in the whole performance." Her brief climactic scene "carried the whole message of the play, and she gave it with real beauty and pathos."

He then praised Mrs. Brando's "sweet and gentle voice" as just right for Miss Pennington. "In fact, her whole personality was extremely well suited to the character. Her best scene was by the fireside," when describing "all she would have loved to have of beauty at her wedding."

The leading man then won comparable raves: "It was remarkable how convincing L.C. Hawley made the crippled and nerve-racked condition of Oliver Bashforth. He was delightful as a lover. The stage seldom sees a prettier scene" than he and Mrs. Brando "in the window seat before the fall of the curtain."

No wonder the headline hit on "delightful." After applying it to Hawley as a lover, Abbott awarded it to "a delightful comedy part" of Anne Johnston as Mrs. Corsellis and to the audience response to Lucy Updike's "delineation of a society mother with a nice degree of snobbishness." The Updikes were big in lumber, coal, grain and ranching. Uncle Nels owned the *Bee* and would combine it with the *News* in 1927, then sell the *Bee-News* to William Randolph Hearst. The story of a man disfigured in combat bore special meaning for Lucy Updike, who lost her intended in World War I and never married.

As for the now-famous family, he merely mentioned that "Jayne Fonda appeared briefly and creditably."

Enchanted Splendid in Fremont

Why they traveled to Fremont was not explained, but the play moved to the Midland College auditorium on Thursday. Such outings would seldom be repeated until the Nebraska Theatre Caravan was formed in the 1970s. The *Fremont Tribune's* headline said, "Omaha Players Give a Splendid Show in Fremont."

The writer found it "unfortunate" that more weren't on hand for "one of the best dramatic productions offered in Fremont in many years," professional or amateur. "Had the Omahans come to Fremont incognito with the ballyhoo of a regular professional production, the house might have been well filled by an audience that would have been well satisfied."

After summarizing the plot, it dubs Brando's Miss Pennington "an ugly duckling with a beautiful soul" and "one of the leading features" of the play, "her versatile ability, her expression and graceful movements being all that could be desired."

Hawley's interpretation of Oliver "was heart-gripping and impressive … a work of art as he actually lived the character he sought to depict in every moment of the drama." Supporting roles were praised before noting Lucy Updike's "unusual ability" in a difficult role.

Among those well satisfied with the first "actual" play was board president McDonald, pleased that it won "unusual praise." The board met a few days after the Fremont performance and "engaged" Foley to direct the full 1925–1926 season. The eight-play schedule was not set, but *Liliom* and others "of similar quality" were being considered. The new season admissions "probably will be confined to season ticket subscribers."

They planned to limit capacity to 300 reserved seats. Nothing was reported about problems with the 450-seat capacity claimed for *The Enchanted Cottage,* but the smaller number might have been a reaction to complaints. Nelson's dissertation interviews forty years ago led him to conclude, "Although the non-slanting dance floor" of the Cooper Studio "was to prove ideal for supper-dances during the subscription campaign for the coming season, it hardly provided advantageous sight lines for the audience."

Others could ponder sight lines on the dance floor at 40th and Farnam. Two days after *The Enchanted Cottage* played its one-night stand in Fremont, Greg Foley left for a month in New York City where he would "make arrangements for next season's plays."

CHAPTER 2

First Full Season, None Better: 1925–1926

Poem, Creed and Eight Plays

"I am the Community Playhouse," the poem began. "I am the home of all the arts, Haven for hungry souls, I bring color into the drabness of city life, a festival of sound and dance. I am the antidote for ugly streets." It was Whitmanesque but the Walt who waxed poetic was Hixenbaugh, the book dealer whose wife served on the board.

Now the theater with a variety show and one play under its belt had its own poem. Then there was the Playhouse Creed, borrowed from a community theater pioneer named Gordon Craig. It repeated the phrase "It believes in" before each item in a long list, "the Theatre Universal … the actor … actress … scenographers … dramatists," and more, before adding a localized conclusion: "Above all its workers believe in the Community Playhouse and pledge their best to the end that there may be realized in Omaha the finest artistic achievement of which such a theatre is capable."

With poem and creed, they lacked only plays, so eight were announced in September 1925, just a year after the founding meeting. A printed program termed it the "second season," giving vaudevillian variety and the Pinero play "season" status.

Mark Levings's line drawing of the Cooper Dance Studio decorated the announcement, which promised the lofty—"interesting and artistic" plays—and reported the mundane: "The curtain will rise promptly at 8:20 p.m." If seats were still available after holders of $5 season tickets made reservations, the nonmembers could attend for $1 per play. Among the surviving artifacts is an early membership list, numbering more than eighty names a few days before the first show. An April list grew to nearly a hundred, including Mrs. Guiou, Mrs. N.P. Dodge and Sarah Joslyn, but nary a Brando or Fonda. By autumn, 150 stockholders owned those $10 certificates.

Two news stories gave hints about play selection. The play-reading committee's Rabbi Cohn said, "We plan to present in our 'little theater' worthwhile plays which have attracted attention elsewhere, such plays as *The Devil's Disciple* by George Bernard Shaw, *You and I* by Barry, *The Show-Off* by George Kelly and others."

Another story cited twenty-five possible plays, including Molnar's *Liliom* and others eventually produced by the Playhouse. It explained that Foley, then in New York City, "is acquainted with many playwrights and plans to go directly to them for permission." The director was "affiliated with the year-old Amateur Directors Assn." and "has access to the best plays" from several agencies, including "Samuel French, which handles more plays than any other." Their director, they seemed to say, was an insider who called French "Sammy."

After road companies stop presenting a play "and it is no longer popular," a less upbeat comment added, "it is accessible for amateur production." Actually, as the road grew less traveled, more plays were available soon after Broadway runs. Royalties ranged from $50 to $100, with April's *Enchanted Cottage* costing just $50.

Who were the most popular playwrights of the mid-1920s? Kenneth MacGowan surveyed 475 community theaters and found

Shakespeare led with 35 productions, followed by a single Lula Vollmer play, *Sun-Up*, with 34, then Shaw and Kelly with 30 each. Close behind were George S. Kaufman (then writing with Marc Connelly and Edna Ferber before teaming with Moss Hart), A.A. Milne, Sutton Vane, J.M. Barrie, Frederick Lonsdale, Henrik Ibsen, Phillip Barry, Robert Sherwood and Eugene O'Neill. Then came Wilde, Sheridan, Noel Coward, Pinero and others, from Americans Clyde Fitch and George M. Cohan to the likes of Tolstoy, Chekhov, Moliere, Molnar, Strindberg, Rostand and Pirandello.

That 1925–1926 Playhouse lineup lived up to both the rabbi's teaser and MacGowan's popularity list. Opening with Barry's *You and I* followed by Shaw's *Devil's Disciple,* Molnar, Milne and Vane also made the list.

Only Shakespeare among the most popular writers wasn't produced during the first five seasons. That may explain why Margaret Hitchcock Doorly launched her own Shakespeare Company and took it to Estes Park, Colorado, in the early 1930s. The board had hoped to also continue the tradition of earlier Drama League groups and present one-act plays by Nebraskans, but those plans changed in the spring—another negative for the playwriting Mrs. Doorly.

Starting with *Liliom,* three plays by Ferenc Molnar made him the most-performed playwright in the first two seasons, and Shaw made the list each of the first three years.

You and I and Young Mr. Fonda

As August ended, the season schedule still hadn't appeared, but word spread that Foley would begin work September 1 at his "temporary headquarters," Studio Three, Aquila Court. A four-page flyer concluded with an invitation: "The director of the Playhouse will be pleased to meet by appointment anyone who is interested in stage activity and who may desire to participate in productions of the Community Playhouse." *Cottage* publicist Holland had been replaced by board member Harry Shedd, who jotted, "About a dozen appeared the first night to meet Mr. Foley."

Missing that 7:30 audition was 20-year-old Henry Fonda. The story of Mrs. Brando's phone call and Fonda's meeting with Foley unfolded in *My Life*, his "autobiography as told to Howard Teichmann," and was retold by other biographers in varying forms. (Sisters Harriet and Jayne told *Photoplay* magazine in 1941 that a board member, Mrs. Sam Burns, called for Henry. But Mrs. Burns wasn't involved with the Playhouse in the 1920s.)

Employed only part-time after his return from the University of Minnesota, Fonda had shown more interest in writing than in theater. In 1915, the year his home village of Dundee was annexed by Omaha, 10-year-old Henry won a writing contest, and his story, "The Mouse," ran in the neighborhood weekly. He studied journalism in Minneapolis and considered himself too shy to perform in public. (His sisters also disputed his claim of shyness.) He was still embarrassed over a local newsreel that showed "a close-up of my bare little 12-year-old bottom" as a loincloth-clad Henry and other boys headed down a trail at scout camp. He stuck with the Boy Scouts, rising to Eagle rank and becoming scoutmaster of the Dundee troop. So that was a tall Eagle Scout who shuffled into Foley's office and eyed the unfamiliar skylight.

As the anecdote goes, Foley hands him the script for Barry's *You and I*, orders him to "read Ricky," and the rest is history. Or, in the words of daughter Jane Fonda's biographer, "a cocky Cagneyesque redhead named Foley was desperate to find someone to play the part." Whether or not the director was a desperate Cagney, he cast Henry as Roderick White, the juvenile lead.

Omaha wasn't waiting breathlessly for young Fonda, and reviewer Abbott would pay more attention to the man who played his father, Lee Aitchison. Advance photos featured Aitchison and others. Virginia Holliday, that "lithesome" veil dancer who also hoofed professionally at the Orpheum, would play Henry's love interest, Veronica Duane.

"*You and I* is a most fitting play to open the season," Foley told the press, calling it "one of the best comedies by one of America's younger writers." It's the story of a businessman who gave up his art for the stability to marry his sweetheart, then sees his son facing the same choice. It's a choice between expediency and happiness that all face, as the title suggests.

The final dress rehearsal was not held in the Mary Cooper Dance Studio, where three public performances were set for late October. It was moved to the grand home of Mrs. T.L. Kimball at 2236 St. Mary Ave. The 94-year-old mother of architect Thomas Kimball, whose crowning work was St. Cecilia's Cathedral, couldn't attend the public opening but had "expressed such great interest" that board president McDonald arranged a Saturday performance in her mansion. Kimball bowed to his mother's love of drama by equipping the house with "a complete little theater" on the third floor, where she "sponsored many amateur productions."

Seating about eighty in front of its proscenium arch, the theater featured a raised stage with a rounded thrust. Some suggested that the theater compensated daughter Arabell, victimized by a family that rejected her suitors as unsuitable and thwarted her dreams of acting on Broadway. The architect's sister, who'd directed Margaret Hitchcock and Henry Doorly on the eve of their engagement, did not become a part of the new Playhouse.

It was a gala weekend for the arts in Omaha. Sandor Harmati, the new conductor of the Omaha Symphony, had arrived, and receptions honored the Hungarian who had won a Pulitzer Prize for his symphonic poem. Films were still billed as "photoplays," and news was still sensational. A banner headline proclaimed, "Bootlegger Queen Arrested, Louise and Pal Nabbed" with "two jugs of booze." Journalist Jake Isaacson, who later led Ak-Sar-Ben to horse racing heights, reported seven mustangs running loose in town. This transpired in Omaha "Where the West is at its Best," the *Bee* motto reminded daily.

Keene Abbott, though a St. Mary's Avenue neighbor of old Mrs. Kimball, reviewed the public opening, declaring it "an auspicious beginning" that left the audience "well pleased." Those "favorably impressed" with *The Enchanted Cottage*, he assured, "are sure to like the present attraction still better." Not that the acting "is better, but the play is, and the production," especially the settings and lighting. Most praise went to director Foley who was also the set designer.

Miss Holliday, who debuted in April with her veil dance, now did well enough in "the more frivolous scenes, but does not quite measure up to the emotional demands of the part" as Fonda's love interest in his first Playhouse role. Abbott couldn't claim great vision as he simply stated, "Henry Fonda does well in the juvenile role." Henry would muse much later, "I couldn't have been very good," but when the theater went dark and the stage lights came up, "I was hooked."

Inside *The Devil's Disciple*

The future star of stage and screen would earn even less mention as one of the unnamed soldiers in Shaw's *The Devil's Disciple*. But before it opened on November 10, less than three weeks after the Barry comedy, Omahans would get a look inside their new theater group and see Fonda in another light. Newsman George Grimes went to Foley and asked, "What the devil are you doing?"

He was painting some canvas stretched on a frame, "but how was one not initiated into the mysteries of little theaters to know that he was building an air castle? Foley let Henry Fonda keep at work, and relying on Mark Levings to come along and add an artistic daub or two, he talked." (After playing leading roles in *You and I,* another writer said, Fonda and Mark Levings were now "log cabin architects.")

Foley explained that the Playhouse was "not to make professional actors," but provide "a new experience, a chance to express themselves." It offers "a place for everyone with a bent along these lines ... a paper hanger, a cook, a bottlewasher or a bank president. There isn't a social line drawn here." Such sensitivity to the democratic side of theater would pop up throughout Playhouse history.

"As he talked, sewing women (Junior Leaguers) were stitching costumes in an adjoining room," with Mrs. I.W. Carpenter Jr. in charge. (Elizabeth Reed Carpenter, granddaughter of pioneer Byron Reed, would play leadership roles in both the League and the Playhouse.) Before the first curtain fell, "more than 50 people will have taken an active part." The writer wrapped it all up by urging, "If you are the suppressed blacksmith or housewife, or society bud or banker, you may find relief … as a toiler or a player for the Community Playhouse."

Another news story told how "precious heirlooms from Omaha homes will lend revolutionary atmosphere" to *The Devil's Disciple*. Social leaders loaned "a beautiful mahogany settee," an antique sofa, ancient andirons, a spinning wheel and "two highly-prized British flags." And the society page described Mrs. Carpenter's creation of twenty-five British military uniforms from the colonial period, noting, "The costume budget of $100 for these 25 and four hooped and bustled gowns … presented a nice economic problem." The costumer "solved it with the aid of her friends, two sewing machines and untold bolts of denim and sateen."

Meanwhile, Brando, Fonda and others appeared at the Brandeis in Robert Mantell's production of *Hamlet,* starring the touring producer as the melancholy Dane. And Dodie Brando handled props for the Shavian play, which again went on a minimal tour. Scenes from *The Devil's Disciple* and *Cottage* were performed in banker John Gamble's home on Happy Hollow, then a western outpost, as the Gambles hosted 150 Playhouse stockholders for a Sunday afternoon of tea and theater. Now a company in only its fourth production, the ambitious players had performed in a high school auditorium, a dance studio, two homes and a radio station.

Perhaps they were ready for the words of Myrtle Mason, reviewer for the *Bee*, who followed praise for "the most successful offering thus far" by concluding (drum roll, please), "In fact, one may say the Community Playhouse is established."

A third reviewer, Phil Mick of the *Daily News,* spotted the anachronism of a safety match and wondered whether the "wow" Spirit of '76 finish was "Shaw's satire or Playhouse patriotism."

All three praised Foley's direction and the five sets used in the three-act play. In two years, three reviews became two as the *Bee* and *News* were hyphenated into the *Bee-News,* and its demise a decade later left only the *World-Herald* in the daily field.

Opinions weren't confined to the three critics. After Abbott's review, the headline "What Others Think" added "comments on all sides" that the Playhouse "had established itself as a vital and necessary part of Omaha's life."

Armed with assurances of "permanent success," the busy group squeezed in a December dinner-dance before their next play. From Tech High acrobats to Randall's Royal Fontenelle Orchestra, the evening saw Foley perform with others in a satire on Playhouse activities.

Defending Lusty *Liliom*

Before *Mary the Third* opened at the Cooper Studio in mid-December, theater-goers learned about cast members:

—Marguerite Howes, a Tech High teacher playing Granny, "astonished Foley by having her lines letter perfect within 24 hours after she received her script."

—Charles Moore, a South High grad playing Mary's successful suitor, had a leading part in *Jiggers of 1923,* "the biggest amateur success ever presented in Omaha."

—Frank Barlow as Bobby was a young interior decorator who would later win fame for feuding with a Playhouse feline.

—Dorothy Davidson in the title role was an Ak-Sar-Ben princess, one of the season's debutantes. Her mother, Mrs. J.E. Davidson, "one of Omaha's most beautiful women," entertained a party for Dorothy's Playhouse debut.

That's more than they were told about earlier players, but they could not know that Dorothy Norton's role marked the first for a family name that would reappear for the next sixty years. The caption below her demure photo, pensively eyeing a bouquet, said, "young and pretty," Miss Norton "is known to come from a family talented in dramatic art. Her brothers, Kenneth and Rudyard Norton, have been great successes in the past in Junior League revues." Rudge Norton would appear in his first Playhouse role in 1926 and continue on the local stage into the 1980s. As for sister Dorothy, one reviewer dubbed her "a peerless little flapper."

Keene Abbott upped the ante again, claiming *Mary the Third* "wins a much heartier response than anything previously done" by the Playhouse. It was "compelling proof of why the enterprise deserves to prosper." Myrtle Mason of the *Bee* noted that opening night was sold out, and she seconded the idea that "the audience was the most responsive" to witness a play.

The often irreverent Phil Mick of the *Daily News* said, "Even the inclement weather could not mar the occasion." The Rachel Crothers play, which shows its title heroine in 1870, 1897 and 1925, was labeled ultra-modern and "brilliantly satirical," with special praise for Frank Barlow's young Bobby, who says, "Personally, I think parents are over-rated."

If *Mary the Third* won a hearty response, Molnar's *Liliom* sold more tickets in icy January. After a debate over its morality, an extra performance was needed to meet the demand, with the women's division of the Chamber of Commerce buying a block of seventy-six seats. Even routine advance stories billed *Liliom* as "sensational," the story of an outlaw merry-go-round barker (it later became the musical *Carousel*). But a *Bee* editorial unleashed a tirade, not just against Molnar, who "has no reverence for the higher and finer things in life," but against Eugene O'Neill and the rest of theater, "which has abandoned all sense of decency." More pointedly, "*Liliom* deals frankly and plainly with lust of the flesh."

Rabbi Cohn had lectured on the earlier plays at Temple Israel, but now his defense of Molnar made headlines. He promised the playwright's portrayal of "God's policemen will not easily be forgotten." Then "Cleric Defends Drama of Lust" featured Unitarian Reverend Bailey's view that *Liliom* was "not subversive of sound ethics." Instead, it "definitely strengthens the bases of morality" not vindicating the profligate title character but redeeming him.

Also chiming in was the new symphony director. Sandor Harmati praised the genius of his fellow Hungarian and commented on the writer's roots in Budapest. He mused that Molnar "does not wish to convince, so unlike Shaw, who compels one to swallow the sugar-coated pill willy-nilly. Molnar's aim is to offer a delicious bon-bon, which never fails to arouse the appetite for more." The board proved his point by adding Molnar's *The Swan* as its May bon-bon, replacing those promised one-act plays by such Nebraska authors as Margaret Hitchcock Doorly.

No play this season, board president McDonald told the press, "has attracted so much attention or caused so much discussion" as *Liliom*. May Robson, a Broadway star performing in Omaha, compared Foley's cast favorably to professional productions she'd seen. Dr. Olga Stastny, who provided costumes she'd imported from Budapest, had also seen the version starring Joseph Schildkraut, and she claimed that Rex Morehouse in the title role and Mrs. Brando as Julie matched the lead roles on Broadway. Advance photos showed Dodie with elbows akimbo in white peasant blouse beside a slouching Morehouse.

Founder Marie Mackin, the Tech High drama teacher, won acclaim in a large cast of notables, old and new. George McIntyre, who played the villainous Sparrow, had shared stages with Morehouse for more than 20 years, going back to their days with the Doorlys in the Players Club and continuing in those Drama League shows.

James Allison Flynn would grace many a cast as he worked for more than three decades as a *World-Herald* artist and designed Playhouse sets. Jess Thurmond, a future King of Ak-Sar-Ben, played two policemen, one terrestrial, one heavenly. The townspeople included Nelson Updike Jr. and Katherine Doorly. Their fathers would own all three Omaha dailies in the not-too-distant future. (Katherine married Richard Young and, after his death, W. Dale Clark, two men whose names would be remembered on a hospital and a library.)

Reviewer Mason called Henri Milan's sets "remarkable" work "very simple and very modern," while Mick identified Milan as "a local modernist artist" whose real last name was the more difficult Domshydte.

Jerry Hall, who acted in *The Devil's Disciple,* was credited in the program as stage director, but would serve as Foley's technical director for the rest of the season, a prelude to the hiring of Polly Robbins and then Henry Fonda as assistant directors.

Dodie Brando was emerging as the theater's leading lady, now with her third role in the first six productions. Reviews emphasized her poise and restraint. Referring to her "profoundly moving" death scene, Abbott said, "Many so-called stars would have spoiled that phase of the play by overdoing it. Mrs. Brando, with her reserve, gives you the effect of numbing sorrow."

Harriet, Florence in *Romantic Age*

If the enthusiasm in that first full season drifts easily into hyperbole, hard facts seem to justify a fair share of it. After the extra night added for *Liliom,* the February 1926 dinner-dance reached the 250-reservation limit so quickly that it required a second night. Credit the likes of Sarah Joslyn, who attended as McDonald's guest, then returned for the encore. Dinner at 7 with music, a one-act play *The Clod* directed by Foley and Levings, dancing at 9, an "operatic interlude" at 10 and dancing again to that Royal Fontenelle orchestra made a full evening.

That operatic interlude offered "Indian Love Call" by a couple with memorable names: Helen Nightengale and a "Mr. Louis Armstrong."

The post-holiday schedule went busily from *Liliom* in mid-January, to reelection of McDonald and others at the annual meeting, to this second dinner-dance, and on to *The Romantic Age* in mid-February, one of five plays in a four-month span, with still other dinner-dances and a final costume ball to cap the season.

The Romantic Age, a comedy by A.A. Milne of *Winnie the Pooh* fame, brought another Fonda, sister Harriet, to the forefront. She would become a Playhouse pillar as Mrs. Jack Peacock and then Mrs.

Zach Warren, but in 1926 her experience was connected to children's theater directed by Marguerite Beckman in pre-Playhouse years.

She's Melisande, the bookishly romantic princess of the story. Playing her parents are Lucy Updike and "Par Sam Reynolds, the golfing wizard," whose performance was also dubbed "par stuff." Known then for his golf titles, a later appointment gave him the title of U.S. Senator Reynolds.

Another Norton, Lewis J., veteran of Ak-Sar-Ben Den shows, won the most plaudits, and a child named Hudson Rose would appear. His brother Halleck Rose would later marry Echo Guiou, better known for her long Playhouse leadership as Mrs. Echo Ellick.

Harriet Fonda's role received the most attention, as Abbott found "the youth and pictorial elements of the personation especially appealing." Finally, he notes that Florence Taminosian "makes a coquettish maid." Her appearance in a minor role might not earn a special place in history, but for two facts: One, the Fondas, her neighbors across the street at 49th and Chicago, had asked her to fill in for an ailing dancer in *The Enchanted Cottage*, and two, as Florence Young, she remained a leading season ticket seller into her late nineties and became the living person with by far the earliest connection to the Community Playhouse when she celebrated her 106th birthday in 2013 before passing.

"Big Marlon" Manages, Dodie Sees Pasadena

Starting with *The Romantic Age* and continuing through the season, each playbill listed both a production staff for the play and "executive staff of the Playhouse." For Sutton Vane's *Outward Bound*, then one of the most popular plays in little theaters, L.W. Smetana designed the ocean liner setting. Employed by architect Thomas Kimball, Smetana built a model of the set for display in a downtown store. Marlon Brando helped "fashion hand-wrought boat lamps and other accessories." The show's stage manager, he was called Big Marlon to distinguish from son Bud, now nearly two, who made their shared name famous.

Grace Lennon Conklin, praised for her role in *The Enchanted Cottage*, was also an *Outward Bound* standout as a "dingy but spirited charwoman," and Mrs. Alfred J. Brown "never misses a point" as the snobbish lady. Another Drama League leader, Mrs. Brown would coauthor an unpublished *History of Drama in Omaha* with Mrs. Guiou.

Countering the Little Theater stereotypes of dowagers and debutantes, journalists played up male participation from all quarters of the community. Edward Thompson, "shoe salesman in a local store," played a member of the English parliament. "Robert Motherwell, in real life a young, ambitious insurance salesman, is a drunken ne'er-do-well," and J.F. Mead, "a very busy grain broker, became a quiet, earnest minister."

And then there was Chet Wynne, the Creighton University football coach, playing the Great Examiner and described as "St. Peter in golf knickers." His involvement so intrigued the *Daily News* that it told how he "turned out" for the part after lunchtime banter with friends, then promised his work "will be as effective and satisfactory" on the stage as on the football field.

While Big Marlon managed the stage, wife Dodie visited Southern California and saw another version of *Outward Bound* at the famous Pasadena Playhouse. "Altogether," she wrote director Foley, "you had a better cast. The new Pasadena Playhouse, however, is a little gem—too good to be true."

That phrase seemed fitting for the first full Playhouse season, which lacked only a permanent home. With no explanation, the scheduled one-act plays were replaced in April by the farcical *Captain Applejack*, and Molnar's *The Swan* was moved into its May slot.

A slick four-page playbill, predecessor of the Prompter, promoted the early May dinner-dance and proclaimed the success of the soon-to-be-completed season. Soon the players would branch out to prepare a production for the Nebraska Medical Association meeting, with young Fonda staging the event.

But first *Captain Applejack* would fill the Cooper Dance Studio with pirates and such motley characters as Lush and Poppy Faire, led by lawyer Brick Hawley as Ambrose Applejohn, the title captain. The farce, subtitled "An Arabian Nights Adventure," starts a bit like *Treasure Island* as nocturnal visitors in search of a pirate map involve the dull young Applejack in their escapades.

Hawley, it was reported, "made such a favorable impression" in *Cottage,* that he "has been held in reserve by Foley especially for this role." Sally Ann O'Rourke, "prominent in the high school set," played his sweetheart Poppy, just weeks before she was seriously injured in a fall from a horse. Henry Fonda, Big Marlon, attorney James English and contractor Bing Grunwald Jr. joined the ten-man pirate crew.

First Season's *Swan* Song Paid Its Way

Molnar's *The Swan* gave Katherine Doorly a chance to cross gender lines. She played a lad named George and was "thoroughly a boy," Abbott wrote, congratulating his employer's granddaughter on "just the shading of impishness" needed. Mrs. Alfred Brown was back as Princess Maria Dominica, and Jerry Hall was Prince Albert. Ever ready for humble duty, Henry Fonda, sporting a thin mustache, portrayed a footman and went unmentioned.

That original playbill, printed before the early May dinner-dance and *The Swan* dates, was bursting with pride and comparisons. The great Cleveland Playhouse showed to an audience of four thousand in its fifth year, and the illustrious Pasadena Playhouse failed financially its first three seasons.

But by mid-May, the Omaha Playhouse would count more than seven thousand theater-goers and more than 200 performers from "all walks of life," and boast that it was "perhaps the only organization of the kind which has paid its own way from the very start without organized appeal for support or outside help." The board was equally proud of its "ambitious" and varied program, "eight splendid productions for so small a sum as five dollars."

A rare ledger from the 1927–1928 season showed $500 monthly pay for Foley from September through May. Revenue included the income from dinner-dances, where even hat check tips went into the coffers. Later, the Playhouse leased the Cooper Studio space for the entire year and generated income by subletting it to other groups.

Playbill notes give insight into the mechanics of their dance studio home. "Patrons are cordially invited to visit the Playhouse workroom at the north end of the basement corridor, where an interesting collection of stage sets, scenery and theatrical paraphernalia is to be shown." Smetana's miniature of his *Outward Bound* set and Irving Benolken's seascapes for the same play were on display.

Bouquets filled most of page four with complimentary excerpts from reviews and supportive comments from the community. Otto Kahn, the business tycoon and president of the Metropolitan Opera Company, promised to visit the Playhouse in the fall, but the longest, climactic appraisal came from future board president Genevieve Guiou. She praised "the atmosphere of intimacy, the personal pleasure of finding so many of your friends interested." But, she added, "The democracy aspect of the audience is also interesting, for each play has become not only a rendezvous of fashion, wit and art for the city, but a common meeting place for those from all walks of life—critics, teachers, social leaders, business and professional men, the clergy, young people who are working in stores and offices, even children." It becomes tempting to title this story "All Walks of Life."

In a sense, though, the final word went to Rev. Ralph Bailey, the Unitarian preacher who continued on the board and would become its president. "It is believed," he concluded, "that no other art theatre, in a city of similar size, ever has done better in its initial year." He gave credit "largely to the fine abilities and indefatigable labors of our artist-director" Gregory Foley. "We would make Omaha outstanding among those cities in which, at low financial cost, the best of plays are ever being worthily rendered for all who appreciate and desire the ministry and beauty of dramatic art."

Any who feared these players were taking themselves too seriously could attend the costume party a few days after *The Swan* closed. Advertised as The First Annual Playhouse Masque, outfits ranged from Dr. Alfred Brown's Chinese mandarin, the top male costume with his pagoda hat and Fu Manchu mustache, to a woman's winner that one wishes had survived: Dodie Brando wearing a barrel. Well, not only a barrel. Suspenders, long johns and a prodigious black beard. What a way to end a wonderful beginning. But what they didn't know threatened to drive them from their home: Mary Cooper wasn't paying her bills, and a villain lurked in the wings.

CHAPTER

3

Coming of Age in "Temporary" Home, 1926–1935

Polly Joins Foley, But Where Will They Play? 1926–1927

Pride in its first season didn't mean the Playhouse was ready to stand alone for a summer announcement of the 1926–1927 schedule. A joint pamphlet advertised both the twelfth season of the Omaha Drama League and the "second regular season" for the Playhouse. Its "repertoire" of plays was paired with the League's lectures and information on board members of both groups. Cooperation meant saving fifty cents when paying a combined $7.50 for Drama League membership and the Playhouse season. Or you could become a Playhouse member for $2.50 and apply that to your $5 season ticket covering nine plays.

Most of the "possibilities" promised in the earlier playbill made the lineup. For Shaw's *Pygmalion,* the pamphlet crowed, "No Playhouse season is complete without a play by the brilliant author of *The Devil's Disciple.*"

The season would begin with Kaufman and Connelly's comedy, *Merton of the Movies*, followed by O'Neill's *Anna Christie*, called "a vivid, unconventional and singularly stirring drama by America's most distinguished living playwright."

Completing the schedule were Oscar Wilde's "most charming and delightful comedy *Lady Windermere's Fan*," and the season finale, Karel Capek's robotic *R.U.R.*, an impressionistic Czech play. It would get coverage in Nebraska's Czech language press serving an immigrant population second in size only to the state's Germans.

More historic than the nine-play program was the arrival of a second member of the Playhouse staff, "Miss Polly Robbins, Assistant to the Director." She would add the duties of "executive secretary." In short, she was Foley's only paid staff, with others cited as production staff working as volunteers. One writer gushed about Polly's "golden brown hair, winning personality and pleasing smile." A Central High and Nebraska University grad, Polly had taken charge of dramatics for a Minnesota summer camp, but she would not gain the fame of her successor who assisted Foley the following year, Henry Fonda.

"New talent" was needed, with dancer Virginia Holliday moving to Florida, founder Rex Morehouse to the Players' Guild in San Francisco and other "Playhouse artists" moving on, as they would in years to come. Foley and Robbins "will interview applicants" at the Cooper Dance Studio, the home base that was now in jeopardy. "Muny Playhouse Faces Prospect of Home-Seeking, Problems of Finance and Suitable Location Both Are Involved" the August headline had warned. Mary Cooper still managed the building, but a holding company foreclosed when she couldn't meet payments.

The unfolding melodrama lacked only a mustache-twirling landlord wearing a black cape. With the Playhouse rental contract expiring just days before the Oct. 4, 1926, opening of *Merton of the Movies*, the mortgage company demanded higher rent or purchase of the studio for $71,000.

The old Jewish synagogue at 24th and Harney and the Clark Barn on 35th Street were suggested as alternate sites for the Playhouse, but both would require $10,000 in renovations. A last resort would be the Tech High auditorium, an outstanding space but available only two successive nights for plays now scheduled for four-night runs.

"Whatever we do," president McDonald said, "we will make our own expenses as we go along. If we build, we will find some way to finance the project ourselves. We don't want to make the Playhouse a begging organization." That resistance to philanthropy would remain for nearly a half century.

In August, he counted 184 stockholders and 1,200 "subscription members." When "well-to-do men" made larger donations, $10 stock was issued and given to "worthy workers who could not afford to buy stock themselves." Whatever happens with the 40th and Farnam site, McDonald emphasized, "The season's program will be carried out … if we have to hold it in a tent."

As it turned out, they continued at the Cooper Studio. A new lease gave the Playhouse control, generating income by subletting to other groups. Dinners could be booked at $2.50 a plate. Then it was renamed the Playhouse Studio, which competed for rentals with former tenant Mary Cooper, now operating in a new location she called "Ye Old Country Club."

Foley Hides Bride, Directs Fonda as Merton

Maybe that rescue of the theater site, just before the season opening, kept Greg Foley from revealing his summer secret. He'd taught once more at the University of Texas but didn't mention that he'd also married one of his summer students. He waited until January at a dinner hosted by board members to introduce Evelyn Sarrell of Houston, whom the press labeled "a most attractive blond."

"This announcement comes as a complete surprise to Mr. Foley's friends," a news item explained. In other words, when he returned to direct *Merton of the Movies,* Foley tucked Evelyn away with his parents in Rock Rapids, Iowa. He completed half the season before unveiling his bride, and then "Mr. and Mrs. Foley refuse to disclose the date of their wedding or where the ceremony took place. They are admitting that they were married early last fall," it was reported.

Actually, they were married in August before his return to Omaha, and when she joined him in January, they shared an apartment in the Blackstone Hotel.

If such press attention seems odd, consider that Foley appeared in mid-January 1927 with his Chaplinesque mustache, combed-back hair and polka-dot necktie, on a full-page Sunday spread beneath a photo of the theater. The story gave an overview of Little Theater and the sudden rise of the Playhouse into community prominence. Readers were again reminded that "all walks of life" took part, not just the social elite.

The article described Foley's "system" of rehearsals beginning months ahead, frequently with three shows in rehearsal at a time. "He departs almost entirely from the traditional procedure," the writer said. Rather than "the old method" of taking the entire company through from first to last, he begins with the leads and may first rehearse "a big scene in the last act." Minor characters may not rehearse until the show "is nearly ready to go on the boards."

A less generic look at the Playhouse described *Merton* being "whipped into shape" on the stage proper while *Anna Christie* prepared in the Playhouse workroom. Elsewhere in the theater, workers were painting and building sets while still others were sending out a mailing. Last season's plays were scheduled for three nights, but then added a fourth date.

For the first time in *Merton*, young Fonda won more than passing mention. Much of Merton's appeal, reviewer Keene Abbott wrote, "is due to the sincerity and boyish dignity with which Henry Fonda plays his part. He makes the role the very embodiment of youth and beautiful dreaming" and he does so "without being sentimental."

This was the role that apparently caused Henry's first confrontation with his father. Foley called him at work, at the Retail Credit Company, and asked him to play the title role. The senior Fonda heard the news and said, "Absolutely not," arguing that his son couldn't do justice both to his job and the part.

When Henry threatened to move to the YMCA, Dad said, "Do that," but Mother mended the dispute and the episode ended with the family attending the play. After, sister Harriet seemed about to say something critical of Hank's performance when their father, in what became an oft-repeated anecdote, said, "Shut up. He was perfect."

Appealing as that story may be, it is suspect considering that young Fonda had toured Iowa and Illinois the previous winter, playing Secretary of State John Hay to George Billings's Abe Lincoln. Maybe father Fonda thought the tour would get this acting bug out of his son's system. In any case, Hank was back on the Cooper stage with such regulars as Mark Levings and James Allison Flynn, who would design scenery for the next play.

If an older and wiser Fonda recalled being "hooked" by his first flirtation with the footlights, he told a different story to the *Central High Register* after *Merton*. "I don't intend to make acting my profession. It is just my hobby. It was thrilling at first, but the glamour has worn off. From

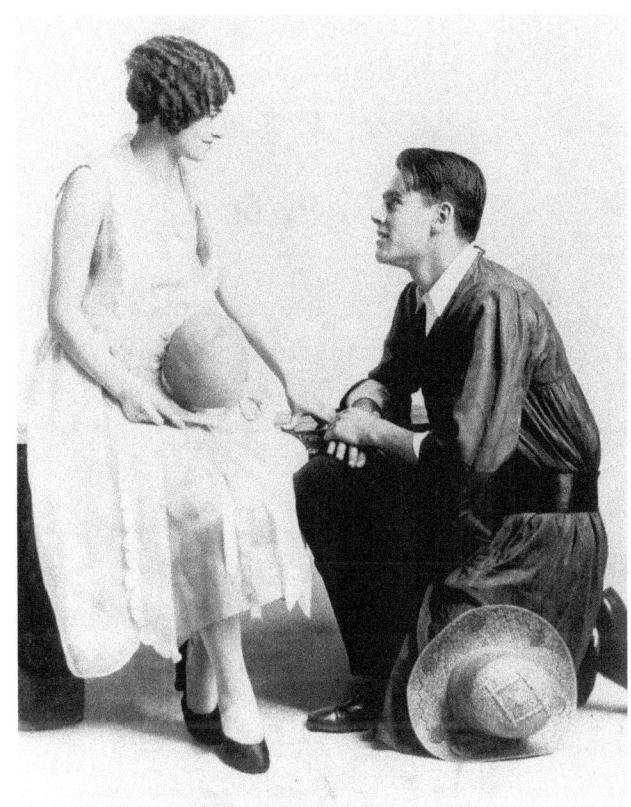

Henry Fonda as Merton.

7:30 a.m. to 7:30 p.m. I am a business man." That must have pleased both his father and his employers at the Retail Credit Company, no matter how eventually misleading.

Anna Christie Offends, *Youngest* Stirs Cat Fight

The second October play, *Anna Christie,* found O'Neill's use of profanity competing for coverage with the visit of Otto Kahn, an event so prestigious that a special matinee performance was arranged as the New York banker and opera patron passed through. Accompanied by Mrs. T.L. Kimball, now 96, Kahn was "amazed" by the cast, saying he noticed "not a single touch of amateurism." Before his arrival, a banner Sunday headline claimed, "Morals of 'Anna Christie' and Profanity Stir Omahans." Foley had warned that what he termed O'Neill's masterpiece was "a rough show" and its dialogue "may prove offensive to playgoers of superfine sensibilities." Bear in mind, he said, that it's the story of a barge captain, a prostitute and a steamship stoker.

Under that "profanity" banner, readers were told that the heroine explodes, "Men, I hate 'em. I hate 'em all, G— d— 'em!" Anna the title prostitute was played by Foley's favorite leading lady, Dodie Brando. An unsigned review complained that the "cursing probably wouldn't have been noticed at all, if some of the characters, unused to the harsh words, hadn't inhaled on the 'Gods' and the 'damns.'"

If people complain of the rough talk, Abbott observed, "Why should they?" Without it, "the characters could not be faithfully portrayed."

The only fight stirred by Barry's *The Youngest* starred a big yellowish cat named Fluffy. It seems Spunk, ingénue Dorothy Davidson's wire-haired terrier, was subbing for a tardy bulldog when the cat showed up and "started things," such as Fluffy scratching a props mistress. But that wasn't the half of it. Frank Barlow, the interior decorator from Dundee who played the title role, finally refused on Thursday to tote Fluffy on stage again. "That cat weighs 300 pounds, or maybe it's 15 pounds lighter. And it squeals. I hate a squealing cat. When I'm supposed to fondle it, I want to hurl it off stage and extinguish eight of its nine lives. I want a smaller cat."

To which Foley replied: "You'll carry that cat and none other. If you won't go on the stage, I'll shave off my mustache and take your lines myself. Or, I'll have Henry Fonda do it. Henry, begin studying up Barlow's lines." All this especially worried Miss Davidson, who played Barlow's sweetheart, and Ellinore Baxter, the current Queen of Ak-Sar-Ben, who played his sister Muff. Barlow ended up going on again with Fluffy, but said, "I'm promised a smaller cat for tonight." A headline proclaimed, "Playhouse Storm Subsides; Foley's Mustache Safe."

The December drama, Andreyev's *He Who Gets Slapped*, found all three Fondas sharing the circus stage with Henry as Tilly the musical clown and sisters Harriet and Jayne as troupers. Henry was lumped favorably with others, but Abbott wrote, "Polly Robbins possesses to an unusual degree the sylph-like lightness of the professional equestrienne," especially in her final scene when "she flutters out of life as a butterfly might."

Czechs Add Their Applause

Those days in September, when president McDonald said the show would go on, even if it took a tent, spurred talk about a building of their own when the board held its annual meeting early in 1927. No action was taken, but the architect would begin designing a theater that summer.

Just as the board worked closely with the Drama League, they cooperated with the Omaha Symphony. The five-day run of Wilde's comedy left Thursday open for the symphony concert, and later in the season maestro Harmati's wife would appear in Molnar's *The Guardsman*. More was made of newcomer H.A. Smith, identified as North High football coach and former director of dramatics at a college.

If most plays still received three reviews, *R.U.R*, did that one better. Narodni Pokrok, of the *Bohemian Weekly*, added his appraisal after a sixth performance for a heavily Czech audience. Its readers saw the play praised and learned that a Czech language production was promised later at the Sokol Auditorium. The title letters stand for Rossum's Universal Robots, the first use of that term, with Big Marlon Brando and James Allison Flynn among those cast as mechanical creatures.

The fast-changing program then added *March Hares* by Harry Wagstaff Gribble. McDonald announced the comedy as a light interlude between heavier offerings, and the Playhouse charged only seventy-five cents to attend opening night. The cast included William Dozier, whose fame came later in television, where he produced the campy Batman series.

Pride in *Pygmalion* and Building Plans

The first full season had been declared a great success, but the completion of the 1926–1927 program with Shaw's *Pygmalion* seemed an even greater coming of age for the young theater. Dodie Brando, now more clearly their leading lady, was Eliza Doolittle, the Cockney guttersnipe known later in the musical *My Fair Lady*.

Rudyard Norton, fresh from Yale drama school, became the third member of his family on the Playhouse stage. His portrayal of Professor Henry Higgins started a string of roles stretching across the next sixty years. With her old Players Club colleague, George McIntyre as Alfred Doolittle, Mrs. Henry Doorly made her Playhouse debut as the professor's mother, Mrs. Higgins.

Critic Abbott said the season, now brought "to a triumphant close," featured two great successes, *Anna Christie* and *Pygmalion*, both with Dodie in leading roles. "Those who have seen the London Cockney girl on her native pavement will realize how amazingly true to life is Mrs. Brando's delineation."

Norton marveled years later that her accent "was remarkably dead-on. Where she picked it up I never knew." Jocelyn Brando, now seven, watched her mother while sitting on usher Henry Fonda's lap. She kept two memories of that evening: "I think I am the only one of the children who ever saw my mother act," and regarding usher Fonda, "I was in love with him for years afterward."

Abbott gently assessed the daughter of his newspaper boss, Senator Hitchcock. "Mrs. Doorly's role as Mrs. Higgins gives her little opportunity to do more than be gracious, graceful and lovely to look at. In those qualities, she is thoroughly successful, and wherever she is upon the stage she is a charming picture."

Margaret Hitchcock Doorly would pursue two avocations, theater (she also wrote plays) and animals. Then she was known for raising Belgian horses, but more would remember her gift that started Omaha's now world-famous Henry Doorly Zoo. Line problems in the final act required young Mrs. Foley, described as "slight of build," to hide under a sofa to offer up-close prompting.

Staff, program and facilities soon evolved. Rather than Polly Robbins in her dual role as assistant director and executive secretary, Mrs. Margaret Quinlan was hired for the secretarial job at $125 a month and Henry Fonda joined as assistant director for $100 monthly, September through May. Summer also brought the Jack and Jill Playhouse, drama classes for children in cooperation with the Drama League. This proved to be a forerunner of Junior Theater in the spring of 1928 and the start of a half century of Playhouse involvement with children's theater.

The most dramatic development came when a July meeting got the ball rolling on a theater of their own: a foundation was formed, $5,000 was borrowed, and a 400-seat theater was planned "on a prominent West Farnam site," namely 38th Street. That plan quickly changed when McDonald's castle-dwelling neighbor, Sarah Joslyn, offered her cow pasture with its 111-foot frontage on Davenport and more on 40th Street.

The headline said, "Little Theater Site Is Donated," but a later news item said Mrs. Joslyn "has taken $15,000" of a $25,000 gold note issue. Eventually, those notes would be forgiven, making the site a gift as originally reported.

McDonald not only remained on the board but designed the building with his father, John. Their architectural work on Joslyn

Museum was still in progress toward opening in 1931. The Playhouse would not look like Alan's drawing that ran in the *Bee* that July, nor would it provide promised wide opera seats, and other extras, from motion picture booth to orchestra pit, would vanish in the coming financial crash. But that summer they were optimists, still reminding the world their Playhouse was the only one of its kind "to pay its own way from the start."

Short on Funds, Building Delayed: 1927–1928

The day before the mid-October opening of *The Potters,* the *World-Herald* revealed McDonald's new drawing for the northwest corner of 40th and Davenport. The 24-by-50-foot stage, housed in a brick building with slate roof, would be more than a third larger than the Cooper Studio. The best news was that construction would be completed by the January dates of the fourth play. Foley's doubled staff had assistant director Fonda working with a new house manager, the senior Brando, and Mrs. Quinlan handling ticket sales and studio rentals.

As *The Potters* began its Monday through Saturday run, they knew it would be followed by *Secrets* and Sheridan's *The School for Scandal* before the next great moment in their short history: Two more firsts, the premiere of the new theater and their first musical comedy *Mr. Pepys,* a London hit in its initial American presentation.

Neither happened. Money ran short, the building was delayed, *Mr. Pepys* was canceled, the Cooper Studio became a chicken joint, the director resigned, the board secretary moved to Ohio and its president, Reverend Bailey, headed for Harvard.

The only good news was that the bad news spread over the first five months of 1928, and the fall start of the third season went well. Maude Gerow, 70, won high praise for her Ma Potter, as did Fred Eckstrom as Pa Potter. Now a Playhouse staple, Eckstrom came from a musical and dramatic family. His brother and sister had performed on Broadway, and his nephew, Howard Hanson, was already rising to fame in the world of symphonic music. (The native Nebraska composer and conductor headed the Eastman School of Music for forty years.)

Abbott said J.P. McEvoy's *The Potters* delighted its audience, especially with a scene on a swaying trolley car. Complex scene changes wowed a visiting writer, Leon Edward Joseph of the *New York Herald-Tribune*. As its "The Big Little Theater" writer, he devoted his entire column to the Playhouse. Praising the entire production, he caught the contagious optimism and claimed, "They raised the entire $30,000 for building at two luncheon meetings, and so are adequately financed to go ahead."

Unfortunately, that wasn't quite the case. Though it was two years before the stock market crashed, money wasn't flowing in freely.

The mid-December *School for Scandal* run was sponsored by the Trinity Cathedral Guild, an innovation prompted by involvement of members Lucy Updike (Mrs. Candour) and Mrs. Sanford Gifford (Lady Teazle) in Sheridan's Restoration classic. Fonda again showed his talent for managing scene switches. Abbott remarked on "the celerity of changes for 14 scenes," calling Fonda's settings "simple, but striking and really beautiful."

Bad news came from board president Bailey. Citing low ticket sales and fund-raising, he said, "We have been attempting to do too much with too small a constituency." He made clear that Foley, "an artist-director of consummate ability," was not at fault. Saying "plans for the building are in abeyance," Reverend Bailey made no prediction for its completion.

Fast-Changing Program Moves to Benson

Certainly twenty-first-century hindsight would make one wish to see the first pairing of Henry Fonda and Dodie Brando in lead roles in O'Neill's *Beyond the Horizon*. Abbott noted Fonda's speeches in the last two scenes, as death approaches, "are beautifully done." Mrs. Brando "excels in the depiction of a mood of sordid and hopeless tragedy."

The *Bee* complained that O'Neill offers "the greatest panacea for the low in mind" by giving them characters "infinitely more unhappy than any person in the audience could possibly be."

That ended their stay at 4016 Farnam.

The lease on the Cooper Studio expired in February, and the board both searched for a new stage and juggled its schedule. Negotiations almost landed the Playhouse downtown in the Strand Theater, but instead they found another temporary home at Benson High School, with an auditorium "especially well-suited" for "the intimacy sought by little theater groups," McDonald noted. The McDonalds had designed the new school in then somewhat remote Benson, part of Omaha for barely a decade.

Seventeen made the Playhouse even more a family affair. Henry's dad, W.B. Fonda, played the father of Molly McIntyre, 12, and Damian Flynn joined brother James Allison Flynn on stage. While Allison remained a newspaper artist, Damian went on to Broadway and Hollywood. Frank Barlow, who'd once struggled with that 300-pound cat, was an "amusingly animated" Willie Baxter. But little Molly stole the show as his little sister, "peskiness personified."

Rip Van Winkle Wakes Up, Foley Departs

If the Playhouse needed a boost, they found one by combining with the Junior League to present *Rip Van Winkle*. The Friday matinee drew 800 school children while another "400 were turned away because of inadequate seating capacity." Perhaps the Junior League was better organized for marketing. For the first time, a twenty-page program was crammed with advertising, from a congratulatory *World-Herald* ad on page two to the Fontenelle Hotel on the back cover. Henry Fonda's wood cut of an awakening Rip enlivened the front cover. Nebraska Power took the center fold to say, "Oh, of course, modern women use electricity for everything," and Ernest Buffett, whose congressman son and billionaire grandson would exceed his fame, offered "Groceries and Meats of Quality."

John Swan played Washington Irving's title character, and a fifth Fonda, Henry's cousin Douw, joined a cast that included Junior Leaguers as the silent, bearded gnomes who play ten-pins.

"It stormed children," Abbott wrote, "there was a perfect avalanche of children." Those turned away were given street car fare. Thanks to the success of *Rip Van Winkle,* children's plays became a continuing part of the Playhouse schedule.

This chaotic season closed with Shaw's *You Never Can Tell,* despite earlier notice that a Civil War drama, *Secret Service,* would be added to the schedule. When Rudyard Norton was cast in the lead role of Mr. Valentine, Omahans were reminded that his recent Hollywood adventure led to bit parts in *Let 'Er Go Gallagher* and *The Leopard Lady.* As an aged waiter dispensing drinks, Fonda delivers the title line, "You never can tell."

The merged *Bee-News* now sported a critic with a show-biz name, Bobbie O'Dare, who called Norton's work "clever." Surprisingly, it played back in the Studio Theater, briefly available again after the Benson High interlude.

A packed house on Thursday and strong sales for the added Saturday performance spurred optimistic comments from treasurer Clare Mackin, who had recently traveled to observe business practices of the Pasadena Playhouse. Heavy attendance was "very heartening," she said, "especially after the rather difficult season just passed." A newspaper editorial said the year "has proven financially difficult for all cultural organizations," but the Playhouse "held its own."

Reverend Bailey resigned to accept the Unitarian pastorate on Harvard Square, and Genevieve Guiou, the longtime Drama League leader, replaced him as board president. Henry Fonda launched his larger career by joining a summer stock company on Cape Cod, and director Greg Foley said farewell. As he left for another Texas summer, he told the board he was weighing two other offers. Publicist Shedd felt he deserved a raise after three years, but admitted, "We hardly know what we shall do."

Word soon came from Des Moines, where Foley was revealed as the new director of its Community Playhouse. He would direct plays and conduct drama classes for a theater organized in 1919 that claimed four employees but only a $10,000 budget. Foley would stay there, nearer his Iowa roots, for just a few years and then go to New York City as a radio producer for NBC. He returned to Omaha in 1965 for the Playhouse fortieth anniversary and held a reunion with actors from his day. By then, Foley was running trotting horses in Highland Falls, N.Y.

If the departure of a director won headlines, other changes went unreported. Usually paid in one $500 monthly check, Foley received partial pay during those rough winter months. Henry Fonda banked his $100 each month until a final $50 covered his last two weeks.

One source figured the theater group was $2,600 in debt. These bookkeeping scraps didn't surface in the news, but they hint at the facts behind those vague "difficulties" and help understand why Foley headed for Des Moines.

Genevieve Guiou Takes Charge: 1928–1929

Only a reversal of fortune gave Playhouse backers the freedom to say how bad things were the past season. Buoyed by a new director, a new theater and other advances, the year before was now dubbed "a disastrous season which almost closed the books forever."

That new board member, suddenly thrust into the presidency, would be remembered for her role in its salvation. She appointed a committee to search for a director and promised to maintain "the high ideal of artistic excellence and dramatic quality." Selection of the season would await the new hiring. Mrs. Arthur Poundsford Guiou, had taken charge.

When she bought that nineteenth stock certificate in early 1925, the graceful calligraphy identified her as Genevieve Guiou. She was a Baldwin from Council Bluffs, which meant her grandfather Caleb became chief justice of the Iowa Supreme Court after founding the Baldwin and Dodge Bank with his brother John and the two

Dodges, General Grenville and N.P. Friends had to lure Caleb in his buggy on to a grain wagon scale, then weigh it without him to establish his weight at over 400 pounds.

Daughter of Union Pacific Railroad general counsel John Baldwin, Genevieve was born in 1879 and graduated first in her Vassar class of 1901. She traveled to Europe in 1904 with a friend and a chaperone. Though happy they didn't see the chaperone after leaving the ship, she felt her father was cheated out of the $50 she was paid. She apprenticed with a book-binder in Paris, lived on the Left Bank "and we were very arty." A handsome leather-bound book survives as evidence of her time running a bindery in Chicago.

Back in Omaha, she joined the Drama League as a charter member and led its short-lived efforts to produce local plays. She married Arthur Guiou and helped him become Ak-Sar-Ben king and organize its electrical and floral parades.

By the time she was called on to lead the Playhouse, she was known not only as vice president of her late husband's lumber yard,

Genevieve Guiou in later years.

but for work with the Creche and other civic activities. While she spearheaded the hiring of the director in the summer of 1928, she also took charge of a new women's department at the First Trust Company and advised women investors. She traveled regularly to Europe in the 1930s and lectured to Omahans on current events.

Known much later as a teacher at Brownell Hall, she was a remarkable leader not only in the days she "saved" the Playhouse. In the 1940s, she took the lead in hiring director Kendrick Wilson at the same time she headed the British War Relief Society, a role that won her a gold medal from the King of England. In short, a near-disaster at the Playhouse didn't faze her. If some wanted to give up, Mrs. Guiou was just getting started.

Bernard Szold: Eccentric All-American

In August, she introduced Bernard Szold, saying, "By all reports, our new director is a man of great experience as a producer, organizer and builder." Like Frederick McConnell, the Omahan then famous as director of the Cleveland Playhouse, Szold studied at Carnegie Tech under Thomas Wood Stevens, the acclaimed master of technical stagecraft. Szold was also schooled at Northwestern and trained with the great Maurice Browne in Chicago.

He came from five years at the Birmingham Little Theater in Alabama, where he was credited for growing membership and, most pertinent, building a new $75,000 theater. Of his Alabama work, the Birmingham press said, "Nothing that has ever happened to the Little Theater here could have been more fortunate."

In a history rich with names like Fonda, Brando and Charles Jones, Szold was the most colorful talent of all. If any yawned at the credentials reported on his arrival, they might perk up to hear he was a football all-American and that his home art studio often hosted such friends as Grant Wood. Add that he would paint a provocative Mae West in a downtown bar and then lose his car after the long night's work. And he would race an airplane from Lincoln to Omaha and impishly brush off bad press. That he would work in Hollywood with Al Jolson, Bob Hope, Jimmy Stewart and others.

Not enough? He was also the perfect stereotype of the temperamental artiste: Szold literally tore his hair out in aggravation at "insensitive acting." He would bang his head against the wall and then collapse in a heap, burying his face in his hands.

The press didn't yet know these vivid details, but a line under his photo referred to "the Greek-godlike physiognomy of Bernard Szold, 30." A more dramatic head shot with thrusting chin and noble brow came with this teaser: "Tall, bronzed, 30, and unmarried, Szold might have passed as an athletic coach." Track and football star at Northwestern, he'd served in World War I. Like playwright Molnar and the symphony's Harmati, his family came from Hungary, though his birthplace was less exotic Peoria.

"He was something new to Omaha," the *Theater Arts* profile said. "He had the typical appearance of the eccentric artist." Call him Greek god or eccentric artist, his face and his sketches preceded his plays.

Bernard Szold applying makeup.

One backlash from those "difficult" times: Szold started at $335 a month, less than Foley's $500. But Playhouse life began to get exciting, starting with Frederick Lonsdale's *Aren't We All?* a "sparkling comedy of English domestic life." The question was: Where would the Szold years begin?

Ground was broken October 2 on the long-awaited building, and its grand opening was promised in twenty-eight days. The Along Theater Row column said insurance man Harry Koch "in a reckless moment wagered a fair-sized silver certificate" that the new theater would not be ready in time. But the other party to the wager was the building's designer, Alan McDonald. Harry Rosenthal said Koch "was sure to lose because Alan is Scotch."

Born In (Less Than) Thirty Days

By October, McDonald had added a new title: president of the new Community Playhouse Building Association with W.B. Fonda as secretary and Rosenthal as treasurer.

Minutes of their first meeting spell out Mrs. Joslyn's offer of land and the two mortgages set up to pay her over time. They voted to borrow $10,000 and to employ the McDonalds as architects. The founding president never found time to lay out a complete blueprint for the job but made sure he was present each day to supervise the work.

One other statistic: the total amount for all contracts, including builder Oscar Olson's costs for the entire building "should not exceed $12,000." That meant Olson had from October 3 until opening, just four weeks, to put up a stage, a sloping floor, and all that went into the brick and stucco building and to keep the cost low enough to leave something for other fittings.

Perhaps he struck some good deals, at least from Guiou Lumber. The major expenses listed that fall were $9,987 to Olson and $3,500 for "oil burner."

The headline "Sets Building Record" ran above a photo of the results. An exclamation point followed the claim, "Two weeks and

First Playhouse, 1928, 40th & Davenport. This photo was taken during the last play in 1959.

four days of actual construction! That is exactly the time required by Oscar Olson, contractor, to erect the new Community Playhouse building." It was completed last Saturday, "except for minor details," at a cost now reported at $15,000.

"A curtain of deep rich red … has been ordered from an eastern theatrical supply house" and "is being rushed to Omaha by express." Clarence and Val Teal, who had just arrived in Omaha in 1928, became members that fall. At the Tuesday opening, Val would recall in her brief fiftieth anniversary history, "First-nighters had to wait a half hour as the last of the seats were bolted down and the debris swept out." The theater group that organized in the fall of 1924 and gave its first performance in March 1925 came home to its own building on Oct. 30, 1928.

The seating capacity, originally set at 400, now was reported variously but later fixed at 252. Officers made a virtue of cutbacks from the earlier plan, saying, "Elegance has not been possible nor desired." The *Bee-News* took the claim up a notch, suggesting its simplicity allows appreciation of drama "undisturbed by extraneous things."

Again, "intimacy" was seen as a "little theater" plus, with particular attention to the equipment. The stage remained 50 feet wide by 24 feet deep, and the proscenium arch 30 by 13 as first proposed. For the record, the Playhouse now had a 57-by-80-foot building on a 111-by-214-foot lot at 40th and Davenport, a far cry from its eventual facility farther west.

Sans frills, it would serve for the next thirty years and provide endless anecdotes about cramped dressing rooms and actors rushing through the cold night to make entrances on the opposite side of the stage. But nostalgia must wait; it was time for Bernard Szold's first play.

Grand Opening with *Aren't We All?*

Back in mid-October as the skeletal framework was rising across the street from the Joslyn Castle, Szold rehearsed a cast drawn from a record turnout for auditions. The arrival of an exciting new director and a new facility encouraged more than a hundred to try for parts in Lonsdale's *Aren't We All*. They rehearsed on 16th Street at Studio No. 2, Aquila Court, where Szold offered to "take a limited number of private pupils in expression and modern dramatic technique." Rival teams competed in ticket sales, with Sarah Joslyn "the first to sell her quota."

Leading characters in the English domestic comedy ranged from the familiar Rudyard Norton and Mrs. Alfred Brown to Ray Suber, recently a professional actor in Chicago. Another newcomer, Robert Ellick, was a good friend of the Fondas, and an uncle of lawyer Al Ellick who would marry Echo Guiou and head the Playhouse foundation.

Norton's Willie Latham kisses another woman as his wife comes home and the plot unfolds from there. When a character complains, "You called me a blooming bloody fool," another gives the title reply, "Aren't we all?"

Reviews understandably paid more attention to the theater-opening occasion than the nuances of performance. Abbott declared the audience "immensely amused," then focused on the new venue, especially its "excellent acoustics, excellent ventilation" and that "every seat is a good seat because the floor has the right cant."

Under the page-wide headline, "Playhouse Is Congratulated," the *Bee-News* wrote mostly of telegrams and women's furs. Mrs. Karl Louis wore a white ermine coat with a handsome collar of white fox. Mrs. Prinz wore beaver, and Mrs. Baxter's black velvet opera cape had a chinchilla collar. Szold took a curtain call, and telegrams were read from Henry Fonda and others.

In every way, the twenty-seventh production got the new director and the new home off to a start that made the past season's problems fade quickly into the background.

Szold "Knew What They Wanted"

An early look into the psyche of Bernard Szold came in a *Central High Register* interview. "In the South I was hampered a great deal by prejudices," he said, emphasizing his points "by quick gestures of his expressive hands." Praise for his Birmingham work had been well publicized, but only one small item reported that he had been ousted from his job then offered it back by a dissident group. He saw Omaha as a better opportunity in "a broader field." The reporter described the walls of his studio hung with his oil paintings, particularly "studies of Negroes." Szold explained, "In Birmingham it was easy to get colored people to pose, and I really enjoy this type of work."

Omaha learned more from an entire Sunday newspaper page the following spring. "He takes a full measure of exercise daily at the Y" and lives alone in his studio at Aquila Court where he conducts both drama and painting classes. There, "first you pull a bell rope to let him know you are there"; inside, "you are in the studio of a man who appreciates good things. Insult Mr. Szold and, with a mighty leap, he is at the fireplace" where "he snatches the sword that Richard Mansfield drew in *Monsieur Beaucaire*. Be so rash as to continue in the vein and he may run you through and then cover you with a signed cashmere shawl."

"A new system of casting" was attributed to Szold earlier, then spelled out more fully as he prepared *They Knew What They Wanted*. The title fit both Foley and Szold, according to the *Bee-News*. "Foley prided himself on his ability to step into a crowd of strangers a pick a person for the part." Cecil B. DeMille and others were said to follow this "type" school of casting.

"Read 'Em and Weep, Szold's System," claimed the headline with a photo showing the director hovering over an Aquila Court crowd at his "round-table reading." Szold "places the stress where Duse, the Barrymores and other exponents of the old school of acting placed it—on intonation, inflection and facility with the spoken word." Among the 110 hopefuls at the reading was Mrs. Brando, who was cast with many newcomers, including the director himself.

They Knew What They Wanted won the 1925 Pulitzer Prize for writer Sidney Howard. It's the story of Tony, played by Szold. He's an older Italian vintner who sends a younger man's picture to his distant bride-to-be, and a character well-known to fans of the derivative musical *Most Happy Fella*.

Rose Webber, another Brandeis player, was his bride Amy, who must reveal that Tony is not the father of her child. Abbott began his review, "It's all right for you to see the play. But you hadn't better let your grandma see it. Might shock her."

Grandmas no doubt joined the many who attended, including folks from Omaha's Little Italy who supplied shawls and other costuming. They saw the work of a new scenic artist, a versatile young woman named Ruth Medders, a tennis champ later known for gardening, cooking and camp directing. She wasn't the culprit who took the cherry pop for Szold's wine-drinking scene and substituted a sour wine that made his Tony gasp.

The season's third play, *Fashion*, made history, too. Promoted as "the first American comedy written by a woman" (Anna Cora Ogden Mowatt), it came close to being the first musical comedy offered by the Playhouse. Although identified as "incidental music arranged and directed by Mrs. Walter Pierpoint," the program listed fifteen "most popular ballads of the Early Victorian Era, selected and adapted by Madame Pierpoint." Add orchestral music by Eloise West McNichols, one of the ubiquitous West sisters, and a polka arranged by, who else, Adelaide Fogg, and *Fashion* went well beyond earlier musical touches.

Still, it wasn't the main reason that 1929 began by making history. The first Prompter appeared, the corporation was reorganized as a nonprofit organization, the "Workshop" or "laboratory theater" was established to produce original local plays, and the Playhouse soon hired a children's director and produced three junior plays.

The Prompter Peeks Inside Playhouse Life

The story of the Prompter, or playbill, born in January 1929 and continuing in the twenty-first century, deserves a book of its own. It started with the cast of *Fashion* and a whimsical account of its selection.

"We gave up musical comedies long ago," the writer said, and "we merely smiled coldly" when "Bernard Szold began to beam" about *Fashion,* subtitled "New York in 1840."

"'But,' someone argued, 'this is different.' We sniffed—what with the prevalence of post-Christmas colds and all. We even murmured 'go away,' but he wouldn't." More in the same vein promised the first six rows would be reserved for "ardent feminists," and concluded that "we have decided not to renounce musical comedies forever."

Who wrote the flippant piece? Most likely Julie Caldwell (Morsman) as in later issues, the lead article carried her byline.

Inside pages carried news items, general information—"published with each production"—and notes on the cast. Much in the manner that continued decades later, readers learned who was new, who was seasoned and so on. Mary T. Johnson was just back from the Pacific Coast where she'd appeared in movies and the Pasadena Playhouse. C.A. Sparks played vaudeville in Georgia, "often taking blackface comedian roles." William Dozier, whose Batman TV series later made his fortune, "is an old hand behind the asbestos curtain," and no one winced at "asbestos."

The fun with the Prompter carried over to the *Fashion* program. Like the production that revisited the good old days with tin reflectors on the footlights, it drew diction from yesteryear. "The Manager of the

House, Mr. Fonda, respectfully announces that no noise, disturbance or throwing of objects will be permitted. Owing to the Intricacies of the Plot, the audience is requested by Madame Guiou to be seated and give the most careful Attention to the Opening Scene, which will begin at the half hour past eight o'clock precisely."

Those fifteen "popular ballads" found the three-piece orchestra accompanying such chestnuts as "My Mustache" sung by Damian Flynn's villain, and "Why Did They Dig Ma's Grave So Deep" by Dozier. C.A. Sparks became the answer to a trivia question: Who sang the first song in a Playhouse musical comedy? Back in blackface again, his Zeke, "a coloured servant," opened the show with "Heav'n, Heav'n." Did this vestige of minstrel days delay the rise of musical comedy as a staple of much later seasons?

Bertha Greenhouse, who sang "Come, Birdie, Come," often performed with the Omaha Society for the Grand Opera in English. The Playhouse didn't "give up" musical comedies as the Prompter pretended, but had never attempted one. More than a decade would pass before they produced a modern Broadway musical. The "standing-room-only" sign went out for all nine performances, setting an attendance record that held for years.

Frances Fintel Directs Children's Theater

Soon more than a hundred children tried out for *Racketty Packetty House,* Harry Shedd won a playwriting competition, and the Workshop group prepared two plays. On the society page, the Fondas announced daughter Harriet's engagement to John Blanchard Peacock. Years later, their marriage was still solid enough to provide a college home for Henry's son Peter.

After the February comedy *Dear Brutus* by Sir James Barrie, that busy March started with the children's *Racketty Packetty House,* then the pair of Workshop one-acts and by mid-month *Aesop's Fables,* a single performance by the children of Dundee School. (Young Ralph

Kiewit, who played Aesop's Elephant, would join his brother Peter in founding one of the world's construction giants.)

The play involved about 40 of the 100 children who auditioned. Among the youngsters were four offspring of board presidents McDonald and Guiou, with Echo Guiou, age 11, as the villainous Duchess of Tidy Castle, her sister Sarah, Donald McDonald and Wallace McDonald, the future Harvard University librarian. Officially, Szold produced the play, assisted by Frances Fintel, but she apparently took charge.

Miss Fintel headed the children's theater, but no salary payments show up in 1929 ledger sheets. Still, news items make a distinction between her ongoing role as children's director and the work of volunteers. The daughter of a Methodist minister, Frances Fintel, just 19, had a lovely face that friends told her belonged in movies. She returned to Omaha from Denver, where she attended the university and performed in a stock company. She left in the 1930s for Los Angeles and was last heard from rehearsing there for Kaufman and Hart's *Merrily We Roll Along*.

Plans called for monthly plays with "young folk ages 3 to 14" in both cast and production roles. Adults such as Mrs. Brando helped by doing makeup.

With three shows seen by more than 1,000 attendees, "continuance of children's plays is assured for the rest of the season." *Raggedy Ann and Andy* was set for April, and the Playhouse would be associated with children's plays into the 1970s.

Season Draws Record Crowds, No Deficit

The adult plays, which started the season set for five-night runs, now needed eight dates "to accommodate the crowds." And the 1922 Broadway hit *The Torchbearers* meant the Playhouse could poke fun at itself with a satire on amateur theater.

With due respect to Abbott and his successors, *The Torchbearers* was reviewed by the most distinguished critic in Playhouse history.

Bess Furman later covered Eleanor Roosevelt for the AP Washington Bureau, worked for the *New York Times* and held a top World War II position with wartime publicity chief Elmer Davis. Now she wrote for the *Bee-News*, " 'My dear, was any artist ever adequately appreciated?' That's the theme. And it's a scream."

April matched the many activities of March. More than sixty children appeared in *Raggedy Ann and Andy,* and two other groups, St. Cecilia's school alums and the Standard Oil Dramatic Club, took the Playhouse stage before *Arms and the Man* closed the month. Lawrence Krell, later a juvenile court judge and a Playhouse regular, performed with the St. Cecilia's group. The cast surrounding the famed raggedy dolls featured such long-established family names as Barker, Ellsworth, Maenner, Sibbernsen and Skinner. Though prominent in Omaha, none gained the national fame of the tall girl in a later Playhouse *Raggedy*. But the story of Tish Baldrige must wait for the next chapter.

Shaw's *Arms and the Man* was publicized as the fourth anniversary of the Playhouse, but the usual Prompter piece irreverently quoted the author: "Professionals can't produce my plays; amateurs shouldn't; but go ahead—and God help your audience." The reviewers liked the cast, including the seasoned George McIntyre as a servant. Now nine artists were credited for scenery design and art posters, including Jayne Fonda.

Jayne's small part in *Grumpy,* the season-ending comedy, brought the comment that she "surely belongs to 'The Royal Family' of Little Theatre," with brother Henry playing *A Kiss for Cinderella* in a Washington, D.C., repertory company and father W.B. the man to call for Playhouse information. Miss Fonda "registers well" as she joined the pantheon of Playhouse maids. Joseph Eaton, credited with "an outstanding bit," worked as an announcer for WOW radio, heading a long line of broadcasters lending their talents to the theater.

The final Prompter carried a long list of plays each with a check box to allow playgoers to vote their choices for the next season. As summer took them separate ways, Szold headed for New York before his usual camp leader duties, and Jayne Fonda visited Henry to see him play *Merton of the Movies* in Washington.

When they tallied up the numbers for the 1928–1929 season, it was heralded as the first with no deficit after record attendance at the seven regular plays.

Dorothy's Debut, Pros Play Wilde: 1929–1930

The 1929–1930 season opened with Oscar Wilde, and then got wilder. *Ten Nights in a Bar-room* and O'Neill's *The Hairy Ape* sparked controversy, and the latter won national acclaim. Szold found a wife in the cast of *The Queen's Husband*, and the season ended with Henry Fonda's return to star with 13-year-old Dorothy McGuire in *A Kiss for Cinderella*.

Miss McGuire made her Playhouse debut at age 12 in October as Ermengarde in *The Little Princess*. The story unfolds at the boarding school run by Miss Minchin, with Echo Guiou, again chosen for the mature villain role. Echo and Dorothy, seventh graders at Columbian School, were called "splendid" and "credible" in a review by "drama editor" John Savage, who found later fame as a news photographer and founder of the modern Omaha Press Club.

Both *The Little Princess* and November's *The Wizard of Oz* offered "incidental music between acts." Betty Barr starred as Dorothy, with her dog Toto played by Rags, "who can be bribed by candy to do almost anything." Three munchkins did a "weirdly amusing" dance. Four more children's shows would complete Frances Fintel's season, now guided by its own board of directors.

Szold came back from his boys' camp work in West Virginia sporting a new mustache and still settling on the season as September began. The big news was that Hart Jenks and Beatrice Hoel, fresh from three years on the Chautauqua circuit, would play the leads in Wilde's *An Ideal Husband*. Jenks, later known as a broadcaster, made a splash on the University of Nebraska stage before doing classics with a New York company. So the Prompter ran his name as "guest artist" (Jenks was paid $50) in large type above the play's title. As Beatrice Hoel Farrell in 1942, his co-star would become the first woman to direct an adult production for the Playhouse.

Their presence, it was reported, spurred drop-in attendance at rehearsals. They were joined by Damian Flynn, now dubbed "the John Barrymore of the Playhouse stage," and Lucy Updike, who still handled all the ticket sales. Abbott felt the title role "rather too superficial" to give Jenks "much chance to display the best phases of his ability."

Beatrice Hoel won top billing again as Widow Cagle in Lulu Vollmer's *Sun-up*, the most popular Little Theater play of the period. She had played the role on the professional stage, and her Playhouse performance would be remembered as one of the great portrayals in the theater's history.

Abbott compared *Sun-Up* to *Anna Christie* and *Dear Brutus* as the best of the first thirty-five productions. Widow Cagle, a mountain woman, smoked a pipe, no easy trick for Beatrice, who said, "It was pretty terrible" until "by elimination I found a brand of tobacco that didn't make me quite so dizzy."

Protesting *The Curse of Drink*

Recalling the success of *Fashion*, the Playhouse in December attempted another musical melodrama, the temperance classic *Ten Nights in a Bar-room or The Curse of Drink*. Harold Felton won top billing as the drunkard singing "The Face on the Bar-room Floor," but another tongue-in-cheek program had more fun with Dodie Brando as the drunkard's wife. When she sings "The Little Rosewood Casket," "objects that will injure must not be thrown." During the dancing to "Ta-ra-ra-boom-de-aye," "gents" were asked not to use opera glasses "owing to the natural delicacy of the young women in the ensemble."

The man who became the financial backbone of the Playhouse, Clarence Teal, played Drover Stevens, "a truculent rascal." The future longtime treasurer sang "Little Brown Jug" in a show that closed with "Father, Dear Father, Come Home with Me Now." Later generations are left to wonder at "the Great Locomotive Scene," but the Union Pacific was credited for "the great monster of iron and steel."

Criticism came from the Women's Christian Temperance Union. Its leaders called the melodrama "a disgrace" and "the cheapest thing I ever saw."

Just one day into 1930 the children performed Maeterlinck's *The Blue Bird*, and Keene Abbott took his first notice of a future star. "Dorothy McGuire, in the dual role of the fairy and Madame Berlingot, is … to be congratulated for her effectiveness." A photo showed Dorothy daintily fanning out her skirt.

Mary Cooper, whose studio provided the theater's first home, directed dancing with Cora Quick, whose name was synonymous with dance for decades to come. (One of her students, Joanne Cady, would become the first full-time Playhouse choreographer in the 1970s.)

Three dozen boys dominated the February cast of *Treasure Island*, including future bank president Morris Miller. Abbott's "congratulations" went next to the young princess in Robert Sherwood's *The Queen's Husband*. The object of his praise, Elizabeth Woolworth, had studied in France. Her father, Colonel Gilbert Woolworth, was a cousin of film actor Lee Bowman. The Prompter noted her recent return from Paris but could not predict that her bio would become more interesting in August. That's when she married Bernard Szold, her director.

Szold made huge front-page headlines in February as a banner screamed, "Demands Racer's Arrest," when he raced fellow artist Auguste Dunbier from the Lincoln airport to Omaha. The wager: Szold could make the fifty-mile trip quicker in a car than Dunbier could in a plane. Both were passengers, not driver and pilot, but the head of the Nebraska Safety Council demanded Szold's arrest, indignant about "a hair-raising escape" involving "a hay truck clogging a flying passage of a narrow bridge."

Unrepentant, Szold mused that friends claimed his hour-and-eighteen-minute trip "was nothing at all," that they'd done it faster. In a photo, Dunbier and Szold shook hands between the car and plane.

The director lost the race and owed the artist one membership in the Dundee Golf Club.

But his great race wasn't the most unusual press for the Playhouse that winter. A letter to local lovelorn columnist Mary Lane asked "where can a young man of 27 with some intellectual leanings meet girls of my own mental caliber? I'd like painters, musicians or dramatic folks to hobnob with."

Mary advised, "Go up to the Community Playhouse … introduce yourself to Bernard Szold." Even if the questioner didn't land a role, it "would help to establish a contact with that very interesting and knowledgeable group up there."

Meanwhile, both old and new faces were cast in the episodic drama, *Escape*. Rev. Robert Crawford, rector of St. Barnabas Episcopal Church, had only to walk across 40th Street to play the village curate.

The Hairy Ape: Omaha's Coming of Cultural Age

No more memorable image survives from these early years than the photo of Szold as Yank the stoker, the title character of O'Neill's *The Hairy Ape*. Bare from the waist up, gleaming with sweat and coal dust, armed with shovel, he lunges toward a white-clad society woman who screams, "A hairy ape," and faints in the arms of the petty officer. Eugene Konecky, who played a labor organizer, added to this moment when he wrote for *Theater Arts Monthly* depicting the play as Omaha's coming of cultural age. He argued the drama "did things" to the 2,000 who witnessed it, "to the entire personnel of the Omaha Community Playhouse and to its deepest traditions."

He portrayed a city steeped in the agricultural West, long boasting its "Cowboy Mayor," a "commercially top-heavy" place where cultural development lagged. Konecky, recently the new publications editor for Woodmen of the World, told of "wealth from the soil," "Bible belt" beliefs and honest, sincere people who "know little or nothing of sweatshops, or labor struggles" and other urban problems.

Szold as *The Hairy Ape*.

He spoke as one of the players, a cast "assembled and fused" by Szold "into a splendid comprehending dramatic group."

The idea that this play marked a turning point was not just for national consumption in the theater monthly. The *Bee-News* believed the "drama of the under dog" was evidence the Playhouse "is not afraid of its audiences." Allison Flynn, in a design still seen on the Playhouse lobby photo wall, used silhouetting heavily in art deco settings.

It was not the first or last time the theater would face controversy, but Konecky's article recalled that in flaps over *Liliom* and *Anna Christie* the Playhouse "instead of standing on its own two feet" had "obtained the defense of a minister" on the board.

Fonda Meets McGuire in *A Kiss for Cinderella*

The April children's play *The Silver Thread* featured "princess" Myrtle Newbranch, whose father Harvey wrote the *World-Herald*'s Pulitzer Prize–winning editorial on the 1919 courthouse riot. But the

George McIntyre, McGuire, Fonda in *A Kiss for Cinderella*.

month's Playhouse headlines focused more on the return of Henry Fonda and the casting of Dorothy McGuire to perform with him in *A Kiss for Cinderella* by Sir James Barrie.

Oft-reprinted pictures would pair Henry's London bobby with Dorothy's heroic little janitress doing her part in the war. Omahans saw formal portraits of Miss McGuire, "Stage Genius at 13." The Prompter gave top billing to Fonda, "by arrangement with the University Players Guild of New York City" (he was paid a $150 "guest artist" fee).

Identifying Dorothy as "the youngest girl ever to be given a lead in the adult theater," her "natural instinct for the stage" was lauded by Szold. "I believe that her skill is more than a childish aptitude," he added, "and that she really feels the characters she portrays."

The venerable George McIntyre played the other key role (Mr. Bodie), and for the third consecutive time the cast included Miss Woolworth, Szold's bride-to-be. Rosemary Howell, a musician and later a fine arts media critic, became the latest to play a maid. Fonda came home early enough to design the sets, ranging from Bodie's studio to Cinderella's ball and a retreat for convalescing soldiers.

A Kiss for Cinderella marked the theater's fifth anniversary, its fortieth production and its single largest crowd. When the fifty-cent children's tickets quickly oversold Playhouse seats, the matinee was moved to Tech High School where 1,500 packed the place.

Abbott applauded Fonda's take on the serio-comic policeman who suspects the waif of being a spy. But he saved his fullest raves for Miss McGuire: "Only now and then, and that very rarely, it is given to a child of 13 to have a perception of emotions far beyond its years while it still retains the artless innocence of childhood. Such a gift has Dorothy McGuire. She may do something unusual with her gifts as the years go on, but Omaha will remember her as Barrie's adorable 'Cinderella.'"

Fonda joined Szold and the prescient Abbott in acclaim for the teenager. He would recall how he met Dorothy in varying versions over the years. In 1947, a reporter began, "Ever hear how Henry Fonda discovered Dorothy McGuire's acting talents?"

In this story, "Hank worked patiently with the company for days while they held tryouts for the all-important part of Cinderella." Hundreds auditioned, then "in the sea of faces bent intently over scripts, Fonda caught a glimpse of a girl, far in the back, perched on a high stool … drinking in every word. When her turn came, she walked up to Fonda rather shyly and explained that she didn't need a script; she knew the part by heart." They played the scene together. "When it was over, no one moved. The director finally stood up and called off the readings. 'The part is cast,' he said. And there were tears in Fonda's eyes when he thanked the little girl for playing the scene with him."

Fonda told his biographer a version adding dialogue.

Hank: "Well, she looks awful pretty to me."
Szold: "You think she's old enough?"
Hank: "She sure seems right to me."
Szold: "If that's what you want."

Then came the scriptless reading and, "There was no more contest. She was wonderful." He didn't mention the tears, but recalled persuading her parents to keep her in school rather than sending her immediately to New York City.

They did let her travel there briefly with Violet Heming, a Broadway star then playing at the Brandeis. She'd seen Dorothy's Cinderella and shared the excitement: "The child has the spark … that thing, whatever it is, that means everything for the theater." It seems they all discovered Dorothy—Echo Guiou, the classmate she joined in the children's plays; Fonda and Szold, Abbott and the actress.

Dorothy's memories of *A Kiss for Cinderella* started with affection for Fonda and stopped at her sizable feet. Her self-consciousness grew to quiet outrage when "a pair of rather roomy slippers were brought out" for her to wear. Fonda couldn't resist teasing about her feet. Art dealer Milton Darling collected autographs plus a favorite line from Katharine Cornell, Bea Lillie and many others, and now asked Fonda to sign his playbill. Henry signed his name and wrote, "What's all this nonsense about your feet?"

In the Black, Gaining Friends

The theater completed its six-play season in May with a cash balance of $500.

Another boost came with the publication of Kenneth MacGowan's *Footlights Across America* with its thorough look at community theaters. The author ranked the Playhouse among the best in the land and complimented its Prompter publication.

He had valued the Playhouse property at $35,000, using it as an example of theaters that built new homes at reasonable costs. His grouping of Omaha with the great theaters of Cleveland and Pasadena made it eye-opening to compare their budgets of $325,000 and $400,000 with the Playhouse budget of $12,000.

The next season's schedule was not determined, but Szold intended "to present one Shakespearean drama." That didn't happen then or in any of his remaining five seasons as Playhouse director, giving cause for

Margaret Hitchcock Doorly to start her own touring Bard's company with Hart Jenks as leading man.

A *World-Herald* editorial said the Playhouse "has won a constantly increasing hold on the affections of the Omaha public. It has done so by deserving it." The stock market had crashed, the Great Depression was setting in, but the Playhouse was in the black and gaining friends.

What went unnoticed, at least by the press, was the departure of its favorite leading lady, its Anna Christie, the star of Foley's first play and of nine in the first five years. Dodie Brando's last role as the drunkard's wife was the least memorable, though perhaps the most ironic. *Ten Nights in a Bar-room* finished last in both categories of that popularity poll, and both Dodie and her husband had drinking problems.

Goodbye Dodie, Big Marlon, Brando Kids

In June 1930, the Brandos moved to Evanston, Illinois, after young Marlon's kindergarten year at Field Club School. Omahans knew his mother as a fine actress, a crusader for her causes, and also as a bohemian, a bit wild. Many years later, a contemporary celebrating her one-hundred-first birthday quietly recalled that Dodie was "very fast." By then the life only glimpsed in the 1920s was an open book, bared by her son's fame.

Henry Fonda grew to steady fame, but Marlon Brando rode a rocket, flaming bright and crashing from time to time. Dodie saw him open on Broadway in *A Streetcar Named Desire,* the primal, sensual brute screaming, "Stella." She was there with Big Marlon as the standing ovation for their son's Stanley Kowalski and Jessica Tandy's Blanche Dubois roared on and on for thirty minutes. They partied at 21 as the reviews rolled in saying he'd "changed the face of American acting." And Dodie died in 1954, hearing forecasts that her son would receive an Oscar for *On the Waterfront.*

Then the book on her life opened wider, until she stood stripped of any postmortem privacy in 1994, the year Peter Manso told of Brando

Marlon Brando next to Mrs. Herbert Davis with his parents left and right.

in more than a thousand pages, and the year her son dictated, *Songs My Mother Taught Me.*

What was whispered in her Playhouse years grew louder in her son's words: "At first I was unaware of my mother's nipping from the bottle or the unhappiness of my father, who was also an alcoholic." Their son tells of coming home from school in Evanston, finding Dodie gone and the refrigerator empty, then of calls from a bartender demanding that someone fetch her home.

Even worse were the times, later in life, when she'd disappear from his New York apartment and wind up in a flophouse with the bum from the next bar stool. But even in their Omaha years her "fast" style sparked gossip. When musician and broadcaster Belle West ran into Dodie one weekend in Kansas City, Mrs. Brando gave her the impression she was meeting a man other than her spouse. With Dodie, who wore her offbeat lifestyle on her sleeve, one couldn't be sure whether she was cheating or just choosing to give that impression.

That's the sordid side in a nutshell. It wasn't all like that. A

Lincoln attorney remembers the Brandos visiting his parents, Lom and Fitzy Doyle. John (Dugie) Doyle became an attorney. Brother David Doyle was an actor known for his part in television's *Charlie's Angels*. Lom Doyle was a Nebraska University classmate of Big Marlon, and Fitzy had campaigned across Nebraska with Dodie in the 1920s, fighting child abuse, especially in the workplace.

When the Brandos stayed with the Doyles in the 1940s, "Both drank lots of coffee then, both were sober," Dugie recalled. He saw Dodie as "a good-looking, entertaining woman with lots of style. She was always clicking on all cylinders, and she always had a cause." Her fervent crusading led to some leg-pulling by Doyle, who rigged a friend to sell them on investing in his factory. He swore it was highly profitable thanks to working children long hours at low wages.

"You're a monster," Dodie raged, getting so angry "they couldn't tell her it was a joke." When she found out later, she sent the man a telegram threatening prosecution and signed it by Eleanor Roosevelt.

More relevant to her Nebraska ties, the woman born in Grand Island who graduated from Central High in Omaha did not forget her Playhouse connection when young "Bud" began showing acting talent. Her first thought on hearing praise from his high school drama teacher was to send him to study "with her old friend Bernie Szold."

That didn't happen, but this did: The psycho-biographies probed the roots of Marlon Brando's genius and his dysfunctional personality. Most often, they traced both back to Dodie. Rather than Elia Kazan or Stella Adler, the biographers would dig deeper and conclude that another woman, Dodie, was the greater influence, for better and for worse.

Those "songs my mother taught me" played on his mind. When he had money to invest, he named his company Pennebaker, Dodie's family name, then called his Nebraska ranch Penny Poke. And he took up his mother's causes, always finding underdogs to defend.

During her five eventful years with the Playhouse, Dodie Brando played lead roles, applied makeup for the children, helped Szold direct a festival, served on the board of the League of Women Voters, and crusaded for her causes when she wasn't doing lunches or taking sketching classes from Szold at his Aquila Court studio. She also, more or less, raised her son and two daughters.

Separating myth from reality grows most difficult when young Marlon's memories come into play. But sister Jocelyn seems a safer source, especially for the quite real relationship between the Fondas and the Brandos. She once came down with measles while spending the night with the Fondas and was quarantined there for days. When Jocelyn tried acting in New York, Henry helped her land the nurse's role in *Mr. Roberts,* while he played the title naval officer.

The Brandos left Omaha early in the history of the Playhouse, and they would not return the affection shown later by both Fonda and McGuire. But they were not forgotten. Even if Dodie had not played many roles that advanced the theater's coming of age, she would be remembered for phoning Herberta Fonda in the summer of 1925 and calling Henry to the Playhouse.

Szold's Summer Surprise: Marriage, Then Marionettes: 1930–1931

With Henry Fonda and Mrs. Brando gone separate ways, director Szold's enthusiasm focused on young Dorothy McGuire. Reaction to her *Kiss for Cinderella* performance was still buzzing when he began talking about casting her in Shakespeare's *Romeo and Juliet.*

She would play leading roles opposite Szold in the next two seasons, but not the star-crossed Juliet. When the season was announced, only the first three plays listed remained on the eventual program. Shakespeare's *Taming of the Shrew* and Ibsen's *Hedda Gabler* were announced then but not performed. These choices and others disappeared from the schedule with little or no explanation. Buyers of $5 season tickets got the plays promised for October, November and December but were kept guessing about February through May.

The September announcement had also promised "a season of marionette plays under the direction of Mrs. I.W. Carpenter, Jr."

She had created the puppets two years earlier under Junior League sponsorship, and now McDonald, chair of both children's and puppet theater, had constructed a suitable stage to present her *Pinocchio*. Before Mrs. Carpenter's seventeen costumed marionettes made their debut, her daughter Jane played the title role in the children's *Snow White and the Seven Dwarfs*.

Szold followed Foley's example in springing a surprise wife on the Playhouse. He didn't quite match his predecessor who kept his wedding a secret for months, but again the press put exclamation marks on the news: His August wedding to Miss Woolworth in New York "came as a surprise to most of their friends and those closely associated with the Playhouse."

Apparently Mrs. Joseph Lehman, a board member, was closer than most. She got news of the ceremony in a telegram described as "brief to the point of abruptness." It told of the next day's marriage followed by a honeymoon and a return to Omaha on September 2 after Szold completed duties as athletic director for Greenbriar Camp.

The new bride didn't turn up in the cast of *Cock Robin*, the season-opening comedy-mystery. Instead, Elizabeth Woolworth Szold was listed as prompter and she took Mrs. Brando's makeup duties with the children.

After a well-attended run, *Cock Robin* moved to Tech High, where teachers were treated to two extra performances. Mixed with this good news at the Playhouse was bad news for the symphony: Maestro Sandor Harmati, who had arrived in the city as the theater was founded, resigned as conductor.

Still starting at 8:30 p.m., plays now routinely ran Monday through Saturday, and "as much longer as the patronage demands," but typically at least two added evenings. It also continued to be common to present extra performances for special groups. Just as the state teachers meeting saw *Cock Robin,* Nebraska bankers saw their own performance of *Ned McCobb's Daughter.* Such events increased the already strong news and photo coverage of the Playhouse, and now the Sidelights of theater life were covered in a column by that name. And the Playhouse keepers of the scrapbooks also weren't confined to the mainstream.

When "Boss" Tom Dennison, 72 and still dominating city politics, married Nevajo Truman, 21, they clipped the item that credited her appearance in a Playhouse production. She played a countess in *An Ideal Husband*, the previous season. History does not record whether the "old gray wolf," just one of Boss Dennison's nicknames, saw her on stage, or was *her* ideal husband, but the marriage did not have an extended run.)

Defending Cultural Status, Touring the Boonies

Instead of Ibsen, playgoers got Martin Flavin's *The Criminal Code*. Instead of Shakespeare, Booth Tarkington's *Intimate Strangers*. But, no, that didn't reflect on Omaha's cultural status, which was earnestly defended in January 1931.

The city's "smart set" came under attack for failure to patronize a visit by the German Grand Opera company. Joseph Littau, the new conductor of the Omaha Symphony, countered, "It is up to great music to sell itself." Maybe many Omahans "simply couldn't afford" the opera, added a Creighton University literature professor. As for the Playhouse, president Harry Shedd said, "We're not complaining. The Playhouse has consistently chosen the better plays for its productions without thought of how successful commercially they might be." Yet the audiences keep growing, Shedd concluded.

January brought news that the Playhouse was spreading culture of sorts to the surrounding region. Mrs. Carpenter's marionettes had added *Jack and the Beanstalk* and *The Town Musicians of Bremen* to their repertory and now planned a spring tour of nearby Iowa and Nebraska towns.

Abbott saw *The Criminal Code* as "the most forceful drama that has yet been staged" by the Playhouse. Its February opening introduced Adolph Brandes, who played the warden in a "brutal penal system." He brought twelve years of professional stage experience on the road and in major cities. Catherine Flynn added to her acting credits while brother Allison again designed scenery. (Let's not keep mentioning James Allison Flynn without noting his first claim to fame: as a child, finishing second in a dance contest to another young Omahan named Fred Astaire.)

Comic relief came from the warden's sister, played by Emma Sprecher, a court reporter encountered by Szold on a street car. Seeming to contradict earlier claims that Szold, unlike Foley, didn't cast "types," an item headlined "Found ... on Tram Car" quoted the director, "I knew when I saw Miss Sprecher that she was just the person I wanted" for the hysterical, jumpy sister.

Dorothy Becomes Szold Co-Star

Frances Fintel's children had followed *Helga and the White Peacock* with *The Silver Thread* and then *Heidi*, but Dorothy McGuire wouldn't return to their plays after her *Kiss for Cinderella* triumph. Now 15 and a Central High freshman, her "promotion" was cited as "proof of the merit of the children's theater" as "a training school."

Publicity for the April production of *Death Takes a Holiday* claimed heavy advance sales and unprecedented discussion of the "fanciful continental drama still playing to large crowds on Broadway." The director would play *Death* with Miss McGuire in the leading feminine role of Grazia. She was "unforgettable," Abbott said, bringing "an ethereal quality which is exquisite."

Several more grads of the children's theater joined the cast of the season-ending play, Sir James Barrie's *Alice-Sit-By-the-Fire*. Abbott discounted the play as among Barrie's lesser comedies, though "quaintly amusing."

Ethel Barrymore, however, approved. She'd been advising Szold during her run of *The Love Duel* at the Brandeis. Meanwhile, the laboratory or workshop branch of the Playhouse was performing one-act plays at the Military Theater. Crippled children from the Hattie B.

Munro Home were guests for a special performance of *Heidi,* with its live goat and two puppies.

May's annual meeting declared the season the most successful, "both financially and artistically, that the Playhouse has known." An unsigned report gave insight into the age-old conflict in play selection. "As usual, attendance records reveal on the part of our patrons a greater desire for serious drama than for comedy … although the trustees are constantly importuned to present more comedies." Szold was retained as director "after nearly losing him to the Little Theater of Dallas, Texas."

Both Szolds were given celebrity treatment in the local news. Their bathroom, of all things, was subject of a feature story describing it as small but Park Avenue stylish. They had an interesting visitor in spring 1931. His artist friend Grant Wood stopped by, flush with acclaim and controversy for his American Gothic, the grim pitchfork farmer and stoic daughter that would become the iconic rural image of the twentieth century. Wood saw Szold's play and would return two years later to do a scenic design for the Playhouse when controversy would overshadow his presence.

Guiou's Loving Satire: *Of Them We Sing*: 1931–1932

The most memorable artifact surviving from the seventh season was created by Genevieve Guiou and presented at the May annual meeting. She put tongue-in- cheek and wrote *Of Them We Sing* and read it to the gathering.

"The Time: The year of the Great Depression, the Place: The Stage of the Omaha Community Playhouse, used for the moment, as a meeting place of the Board of Trustees." She had already introduced the characters. First: "The Men (Bless their hearts): Harry Shedd, our president … gentle and harassed; Alan McDonald, our treasurer … harassed but not gentle." And so on to Brace Fonda, "Impatience on a monument! And howling at Grief!" Her references, if obscure decades later, still reflect bonhomie on that early board.

So goes *Of Them We Sing,* a loving revelation of how the founders saw themselves after that season. Alan McDonald and vice president Henry Rosenthal sing duets, "We want money! We want money," as Shedd rises to say, "I am sorry, but I have a business engagement and I will have to be excused." Alan and Henry in unison say, "Well, the Playhouse must go on despite the Depression, else ... what would the Storz' dog have to bark about? And, Brace, what about the rubbish and ventilating system?" Brace Fonda notes "a great deal of criticism" about rubbish and ventilation, then "breaks down and sobs with his head upon his arm."

Nothing in all the archives looks so fondly at their early struggles.

Big Cast Squeezes into *Once in a Lifetime*

The reality of the season readily rolled over and submitted itself to broad satire. Indeed, as many would recall, the burly, deep-voiced dogs (Did they thrive on Storz beer?) would bark when actors, often scantily-clad in freezing weather, ran outside the building to make their next entrance. If they had exited on the opposite side when the full depth of the stage was used, they had no choice but to also quietly exit the theater then hurry around without disturbing the dogs.

"If aroused," Val Teal wrote, "they raised such a hullabaloo that the actors had to scream their lines to be heard." In large casts, some dressed at home. If not, they came early and conformed to strict schedules for use of the two seven-by-nine-foot dressing rooms. The tiny lobby was crowded, backstage even more cramped, and then there was the men's restroom, tinier than the women's though both served cast and audience. It also served as an overflow library and storeroom. A seven-by-eleven-foot Green Room quadrupled as director's office, makeup room, library and actors' lounge.

As for that final scene in *Of Them We Sing,* heaven knows what took place between those September announcements of the season's shows and the actual plays produced by the following May. As promised,

Berkeley Square and *Jealousy* opened in October and November. Not so the five plays scheduled from December through May.

No Sherwood and again no Ibsen. Yes, Barrie, but not the play first planned. Perhaps that shrieking scene where the board settles on *The Last Mile* to close the season was not such a satirical stretch.

The season that ended with Mrs. Guiou's Great Depression reference started with a ticket campaign that promised divertissement, defined as "the French for rising above the Depression." The marionette shows would continue, but the children's theater was replaced by plays performed at the Playhouse by the five high schools. Before the first curtain, however, Tech High and the Playhouse suffered the loss of Marie Mackin, the English teacher who helped found the theater. She died a dramatic death: her car overturned on the way home from a trip to Arizona.

The Jitney Players, a road company sponsored by the Drama League, took the Playhouse stage with Sheridan's *The Duenna,* and the first high school play, *Daddy Long Legs* by Central students, would follow. An earlier headline said Dorothy Gish was contemplated as guest star for the second Playhouse drama, *Jealousy,* but Szold cast Kathleen Comegys of the National Art Players opposite Damian Flynn in the two-person French drama.

Theater devotees had seen both often: Flynn at the Playhouse and Comegys at the Brandeis. They were shown in a close embrace, alone with "no support except for the telephone," said the photo caption, which repeated their two passions, "Love and jealousy, jealousy and love." It was Damian's best performance yet, Abbott said, though the characters were so unsympathetic that their troubles raised his indifferent, "Well, what of it?"

The fiftieth play, Omahans learned in November, would be the biggest show yet attempted, the "American Little Theater premiere" of Hart and Kaufman's *Once in a Lifetime*. Another guest star, Sue Garrett, who led a cast of forty, never fails to get "full value of fun or sarcasm" from every line, Abbott noted.

A long family tradition began when Mrs. Lesem Baer shared the costume designing for this show, then continued with costumes and properties. Her granddaughter, Susan Baer Collins, would become Playhouse associate director and a talented performer. Sam Greenberg, a businessman who became known as Mr. South Omaha, switched from backstage work to the part of the porter. And Mary Elizabeth Jonas, whose brother Carl became a novelist, had acted in an earlier show and now did scenic design. She would become legendary as M.E. and then Emmy Gifford, later a board member, costume designer, and namesake for a children's theater that would split from the Playhouse.

The satire on the movie business was "the most laughable comedy" yet at the Playhouse, Abbott decided. Adding to the fun, floodlights and a uniformed major domo greeted patrons with a Hollywood premiere atmosphere. No hint at how all this squeezed into those cramped quarters at 40th and Davenport.

Adding to the chaos, a character's illness brought an eleventh hour call to the director's wife. Betty Szold was "completely mistress of the situation," and "showed no evidence of lacking rehearsal."

For the first time that December, a form of *Christmas Carol* came to the playhouse stage. It was *The Birds' Christmas Carol* presented by Technical High School students. That wasn't the last news of 1931. Word came that Henry Fonda had married Margaret Sullavan in a Baltimore hotel on Christmas Day.

Vote Calls for Comedies, Not Ibsen

Hart Jenks again won star billing when he returned in January 1932, for Barrie's *What Every Woman Knows*. Then he guest starred in February as *Othello*, a University Players production that traveled after its Lincoln run for matinee and evening performances on the Playhouse stage.

Benson, South and Brownell Hall would contribute to the series of high school plays given that spring at 40th and Davenport. Mrs.

Carpenter was back with her marionettes, now adding *Aladdin and the Wonderful Lamp.*

Illness also hit *What Every Woman Knows*, which lost Jenks's co-star, Catherine Flynn. Her replacement, Mildred Cody, stepped up from the maid's role with only thirty-six hours of preparation to win praise. Her credits revealed another of the director's outside activities—Cody had performed in playlets given for luncheon clubs by Szold's Northwestern Bell Telephone acting class.

Mister Antonio gave Szold another chance to share the stage with his protégé, Miss McGuire, now a 16-year-old sophomore. Another young cast member, Creighton student Lawrence Forsythe, made his debut. He'd later try Broadway, then return for many major roles and honors as the theater's leading man. Szold's Antonio, based on the Biblical Good Samaritan, was apparently the best thing about the Booth Tarkington play, unless you count Capitano, the donkey given "100 in deportment" by Abbott. In other words, Capitano left no gifts.

Reviewers called Szold "gayly ebullient" and "irresistible" as "the swashbuckling, debonair, hurdy-gurdy grinder." "Lovely Dorothy McGuire is not so well cast as June, the kitchen drudge," Abbott said, "but she is always attractive." Both reviews praised Forsythe's mayor, the "sanctimonious, cowardly" villain. A full-page Sunday spread showed Szold applying makeup, Dorothy perched on a cart, and production chairman Erna Reed feeding the donkey.

The Royal Family, Kaufman's collaboration with Edna Ferber, featured Paul Reese as Tony Cavendish, spoofing John Barrymore and his theater clan. Reese's credits were impressive—from the Kit Kat Klub in London to eight years "as an R.K.O. headliner" and three as manager of the NBC station in Los Angeles.

The cast mixed troopers such as George McIntyre with such newcomers as Dana Bradford and Szold's niece Rosemary Carver, who came from Shanghai to attend Brownell Hall. Since Kaufman and Ferber had their theater royalty crossing swords, Shakespearean Hart Jenks coached the fencing. Insider tidbits on *The Royal Family* noted that the gift box given the grande dame Cavendish by her son "contains the very finest ruby Mrs. Baer could procure along the rue de la Woolworth."

A women's column gave plenty of ink to the season's final drama, *The Last Mile,* despite it being "a womanless drama." A large photo showed seven prisoners and four guards in a grim death row setting. The columnist made the most of the all-male cast by asking mothers how they felt about seeing sons "in their agony."

Abbott's review was headlined, "Powerfully Dramatic," and he gave first notice to a man of color. "It is difficult to see how the role of the Negro convict could be better done than the portrayal given by Donald Morton. The part played by this colored actor is not the stellar role; but the player makes the characterization stand out as the most vivid feature of the performance."

Morton, who sings a spiritual as convict Sonny Jackson, was pictured with all sixteen men in a *World-Herald* photo, but the Prompter made no mention of race. He was identified as a newcomer who "has played many roles in college, but his greatest was as a football star at Drake." Abbott followed with praise for "the convincing work" of Virgil Sharpe, a broadcaster, as convict Red Kirby.

Lest the audience wince at the language of the condemned men in *The Last Mile,* a note below the cast list asks viewers to "keep in mind" that "the vehemence of their blasphemies carries no tone of derision nor intended affront of the Almighty. They are subconscious last appeals to the Creator to help them in their extremity."

By the way, when a policeman walked on stage during rehearsal and pulled one "prisoner" from his cell, it was no joke. He summoned Frank Casey because his parked car broke loose and coasted three blocks down the hill. "You'll find it wrapped around a light pole."

Great Depression No Laughing Matter

The board could smile that May at Mrs. Guiou's satire, but the problems lampooned at their annual meeting were no laughing matter. When McDonald presided at a special meeting of trustees of the Playhouse Building Association in June, the financial picture was bleak.

The separate nonprofit Playhouse was supposed to pay $320 a month to the association. As it met, those payments had fallen behind. Worse, the theater was faced with "outstanding bills which must be paid," the trustees noted in a formal resolution. The solution? Building trustees kept bailing the theater by lowering both past due rent and the monthly rental charge. Both mortgages held by Mrs. Joslyn and Occidental Bldg. & Loan were in friendly hands that gave the trustees flexibility.

During the troubled 1932, Mrs. Joslyn received no interest payments, Occidental only $217, and less than $400 toward the principal. The following January the trustees again lowered the rental charge to $70 a month, and they bumped their loan up an additional $5,000. The Playhouse would continue to pay only $70 monthly through the 1930s.

They could recall the good old days when director Greg Foley was paid $500, assistant Henry Fonda $100 and secretary Margaret Quinlan $125. Now Szold was dropped to $300 a month paid September through May. Perhaps they threw in a free Prompter ad. It promoted the Wisconsin summer camp where he'd supervise drama and athletics.

Optimistic reports on attendance had continued in news items, but data on "memberships," the term used for season tickets told a different story: Sales had peaked at 1,646 for the 1929–1930 season, then dropped and would not surpass that number again until after World War II, more than a decade later.

The upcoming program would prove one to remember if only for the original play *Brigham Young.* Grant Wood's scenic design and a controversy over the Mormon leader's wives won national notice in *Time*. But it was also the first season with neither Fonda, Mrs. Brando or Miss McGuire. Dorothy would graduate from Central and go on to Pine Manor Junior College in Wellesley, Mass., with her friend Sally Johnston (Marshall). Damian Flynn of the Barrymore profile would be back only a short time before he headed for the Great White Way.

By 1934, Playhouse founders would feel like proud parents when Flynn in *Biography,* Hudson Shotwell in *Yellow Jack* and Fonda in *New*

Damian Flynn, set design by Allison Flynn.

Faces of 1934 were all appearing on Broadway. A few years further down the road their little Dorothy would win raves and a long run there with the title role in *Claudia*. And most of those founders would live long enough to see her in the film version of *The Enchanted Cottage*, the play that started it all for the Playhouse in 1925.

Competing Group Has Playhouse "Blessing": 1932–1933

Hindsight is 20-20, so it's easy to see two big surprises in the eighth season. One comes later when neither *Brigham Young* review mentions Grant Wood, the man acknowledged in the Prompter as the "internationally-known artist."

The earlier surprise is the contrast with the previous season when only the first two plays announced in September were eventually produced. The calendar named six plays plus an April appearance by the University Players from Lincoln. They stuck with the six, but Alice Howell's University troupe did *Romeo and Juliet* at Joslyn Museum, and the premiere of *Brigham Young* filled their April slot at the Playhouse.

Added to the schedule was *The Money-Changers* performed by the Council Bluffs Community Players, a group less than two years old.

The season announcement and the birth of a new theater group inspired two September editorials, which bowed to the changing world of theater. The first began, "Many cities lament the death of the drama and mourn the passing of the theater." That Omaha does not share the lament was then credited to the Playhouse, declaring its new season promised the plays "most of us would want to see."

The next editorial also noted how the professional road companies were going the way "of the dodo," then welcomed the new Prairie Playmakers, headed by Mrs. Henry Doorly. They were not intended to be "a rival of the Playhouse, but to occupy a unique field," doing drama by area authors, including their founder. "With Playhouse blessing," added a handwritten note below the clipping in the year's scrapbook.

The participants made that obvious. Their first play, *The Reluctant Lady* given at Creighton University, was written by Martin Chicoine, the Playhouse technical director. It starred such Playhouse stalwarts as Fred Eckstrom and Damian Flynn, not yet bound for Broadway. If that weren't proof enough of cooperation, the title lady was played by Mrs. Szold. The Prairie Playmakers concluded their season the following spring with a single performance at the Brandeis Theater.

The play was *Sanctuary* by Omaha's most prolific playwright of the past decade, Margaret Hitchcock Doorly. Mrs. Doorly starred opposite Hart Jenks who also directed a cast including Frances Fintel, now free of her duties with children's theater. Mrs. Guiou, now chairman of "junior activities," had named Benson High teacher Bernice MacLeod to direct children's plays, starting with *Aladdin*.

As the Playhouse prepared to open with *The First Mrs. Fraser*, rehearsal was visited by Eugenia Ong, who grew up three blocks from the Playhouse but now headed the Pasadena Playhouse School. The telegram alerting to her arrival said: "Look for a black silk suit and red scarf."

"Calamity in the Szold household," the press reported, as Bernie and the Mrs. moved to a different apartment in the Aquila Court. Under the impression Szold's painting were "junk," a worker sold them to "a shrewd junk man" who paid a dollar a piece. "Mr. Szold—who gets much more than that for a painting—is hunting around town to get them back."

Queen Elizabeth and President Gallagher

Before *The First Mrs. Fraser* opened in mid-October, Mrs. Baer captained a redecorating crew that spruced up the dressing rooms and other backstage spaces. Mabel Baer, who studied stagecraft at Nebraska University, also headed the costume team for the first show, and that became her continuing responsibility. An Irish Catholic, Mabel Mahoney, had married a German Jew, Lesem Baer, to give the Playhouse its own version of the longest-running Broadway show of the 1920s, *Abie's Irish Rose*.

Those early efforts to push the idea of an open door for "all walks of life" were undermined now and then by the latest headline promising "Society Stars in Playhouse Show" and picturing three "socially prominent Omahans" heading the cast. One of that trio, Frances Brown (Pyper), followed her mother, Mrs. Alfred Brown. Frances's son Walt Pyper would become mayor of neighboring Council Bluffs, Iowa.

Another whiff of the upper crust welcomed November's *Elizabeth the Queen* with "Society Is Flocking to the Playhouse Tonight for Opening." They would see royalty in Maxwell Anderson's historical tragedy played by actors seasoned on the professional stage. Sue Garrett, no longer billed as guest star, returned in the title role, and Lauren Gilbert (Sir Walter Raleigh) had recently done summer stock in Maine. Adolph Brandes, who would continue in leading roles, took time from his radio work for Boys Town to play the Earl of Essex, and Rudyard Norton was Sir Francis Bacon. Just as his prior roles followed a foray in Hollywood, this time Norton was back after two years in New York. Robert Brinkema served as art director for his second straight show and took a spear-carrier role on stage.

Mabel Baer.

Abbott proclaimed *Elizabeth the Queen*, with its cast of forty "the most picturesque" and "one of the best constructed" presented by the Playhouse. Even non-playgoers got a glimpse of what excited Abbott: newspaper photos of Norton and others in makeup and costumes were likened to works of the great masters.

Adding to the play's historic status, the press for the first time drew attention to the way Nebraska Cornhusker football competed for attention with the fine arts. A sizable news item explained that Mrs. Rachel Gallagher would accomplish a considerable feat—attending the Nebraska-Pittsburgh game and making it back for the final performance of the play and the cast party. As Playhouse president, she would host the party.

A very fashionable full-length photo of Mrs. Gallagher in an evening gown made it clear that she was capable of greater feats "because she is vice-chairman of the women's division of the Chamber of Commerce, past president of the Junior League, president of the Playhouse board; because, in the days of the Art

Institute of Omaha, she was one of its most ardent workers; because she is an able writer and a well-informed speaker; because she has won many a prize for book reviews and magazine articles."

In short, the theater once led by McDonald, then Bailey, Guiou and Shedd was again in good hands. That catalog of her accomplishments made no mention of her husband Paul's role in Paxton-Gallagher's Butternut Coffee, nor could the writer know that a later generation would identify her with beautification of the city and its parks.

A role in December's *The Devil Passes* went to Russ Baker, now "heard weekly over WOW in Padded Fists, the Playhouse broadcast." Mrs. Alan McDonald, who later became board secretary, played her first on-stage role, a minister's wife. Then a major loss brought 1932 to an end.

Harry Shedd, 56, died. An editorial credited "his zeal and intelligent devotion" to the Playhouse for much of its "enviable leadership among little theaters in this country." Identified as "a real estate man whose great desire was to write fiction successfully," Shedd was working on a novel when he suffered a heart attack.

Grant Wood Designs Sets for Friend Szold

Before the next play opened in late January, Szold and his players made a special appearance before the "gala premiere showing" of Eugene O'Neill's *Strange Interlude,* the film starring Norma Shearer and Clark Gable. Another innovation would follow when the Junior League took over sponsorship of the children's plays, which remained on the Playhouse stage when *The Steadfast Soldier* opened in March.

January's drama, W. Somerset Maugham's *East of Suez,* featured Damian Flynn as the Englishman who falls for the half-caste Daisy (Virginia Skinner). The newspapers still ran Szold's sketches of performers, highlighted here by his caricature of Adolph Brandes as a sinister Chinaman with a drooping Fu Manchu mustache.

The first five plays stuck to the schedule announced back in September, but now two additions brought original plays to 40th Street.

Szold and Fred Morrow, director of the Council Bluffs Community Players and a high school drama teacher, met "and reached an agreement" for the group from across the Missouri River to present *The Money-Changers*. Billed as a sociological view of events leading up to the crucifixion of Christ, it was written by Rev. J.R. Perkins, minister of First Congregational Church of the Bluffs. A prolific writer, he also penned *The Emperor's Physician*, a best-selling novel. His son William created the scenic design, but "the technical staffs of the two theaters will unite" for the production, the article said. Nels Hansen, later an Iowa office-holder, played the lead role of Pontius Pilate.

If the appearance of an original play and an outside cast was unusual, *The Money-Changers* would soon seem ordinary by contrast with the upcoming *Brigham Young*. The two plays had one point in common: both were primarily written by men from Council Bluffs. The front page of the Prompter announced the April 3 opening of *Brigham Young* as "the world premiere" and gave top billing to coauthors Szold and John McGee, plus "settings by Grant Wood." McGee, on leave as theater director of Purdue University, did the research and Szold adapted his manuscript for the stage.

Wood, who often visited Szold and other Omaha artists, served on the community theater board in Cedar Rapids, Iowa. The Prompter said he designed the sets "in deference to his warm friendship" for Szold. He was characterized as "the first American artist to capture the earth warmth and rhythm of the Midwest." His fame could be tracked in much more specific terms.

Five years before, in 1927, few had heard of Grant Wood. But Eugene Eppley (the same Eppley the Omaha airport is named for) liked his work and commissioned the Iowan to decorate the Corn and Pioneer meeting rooms of his new Chieftain Hotel in Council Bluffs. Its architect, E.P. Schoentgen, would become the father-in-law of Jayne Fonda. He and Eppley were prominent in news stories of the hotel's opening, but Wood's artwork went unmentioned.

Fame came to Grant Wood, though, before he agreed to design for the Playhouse. He painted Stone City in 1930, and Omaha Art

Institute patrons bought it for $300 and gave it to the just-opened Joslyn Museum in 1931. That's the year he created America's most familiar rural image, American Gothic. A *World-Herald* profile that March said, "Grant Wood, whose painting of Iowa farmers and their wives recently aroused a storm of criticism and praise, spent Monday in Omaha." The painting "shows farmers and wives as thin-lipped, leathery-faced dissenters," the reporter noted, making the common error that the woman in American Gothic was the farmer's wife.

Of more historic value, Wood told the writer he found "the germ of my style while researching" the Bluffs hotel's Corn Room. The story said the artist "visits Omaha often to drop in on his fellow painters," particularly J. Laurie Wallace and Bernard Szold. Wood returned in 1932 amidst new controversy over his latest grim Americans, Daughters of the Revolution.

Unfortunately, the two *Brigham Young* reviews said little or nothing about Wood's work. Abbott made no comment on any visual aspect of the play. Worse, the only photograph showing a scene reveals little of the set. How could it? It captures the Mormon leader backed against the wall by seventeen irate wives. And that swarm created a far greater stir than the artistry of Grant Wood.

Concessions: *Brigham Young* Sheds Fourteen Wives

On April 17, 1933, the Playhouse made *Time* magazine, and again Grant Wood got only passing mention. As *Time* put it, rehearsals for *Brigham Young* began with seventeen women playing the Mormon's wives. "The plot unhistorically showed other Mormon men trading wives." In the news weekly's version of the episode, church president Heber Grant, a director of the Union Pacific Railroad, and other Latter-Day Saints leaders got wind of the script and contacted UP president Carl Raymond Gray "about the slanderous play." In short, "Mr. Gray called in a lawyer and the Playhouse board of directors. The next day Brigham Young had only three wives."

Brigham and wives.

Then there was the Omaha press version. The play set in the Florence (north Omaha) "winter quarters" and the westward exodus to Utah first drew complaints from a church official in Council Bluffs, the place where Young was installed as Mormon leader. The official "heatedly objected" to the play's reference to Joseph Smith as a polygamist."

Szold replied, "We have only one such reference to Smith, and because we have definite authority to prove it, we aren't going to be bullied out of it." The same news story said Utah officials were concerned only about a scene with two elders "swapping wives, with one tossing in a pinto pony to seal the bargain."

The Mormon spokesman said, "I'm not really objecting to it … but I wouldn't have made them wife-swappers." The authors admitted to humanizing Young by showing "his failings as well as his virtues," but added, "It's impossible to keep sex out of a play like this."

A subsequent story told how a script was sent to the Mormon spokesman who then made suggestions, but the headline read, "Protested Scenes to Stay in 'Brigham Young' Play." Soon another headline referred to "Revising Play in Secret," and Szold expected "a report from the executive committee Friday as to what changes we ought to make." The changes won even bigger headlines just before the Monday opening.

"'Brigham Young' Takes 81 Per Cent Matrimonial Cut" cried the banner over that five-column photo of the seventeen wives backing one husband against the wall. "Only Three Wives Instead of 17" headed a story that began, "As a concession to conscientious objectors," authors "consented" to portray only three wives. "The change comes in the final scene of Act 1 when, after a pursuit, the 17 wives have just cornered Brigham," said McGee. The directors of the Playhouse "read the script and suggested we decrease the number of wives, so we are only going to show three wives pursuing Brigham."

The telling paragraph explained, "Objections to certain scenes were said to have been laid before the Playhouse executive committee by persons representing the Mormon church." Only three wives survived, but Omahans had already seen a costumed half dozen in one photo and all seventeen in that mob scene.

Adolph Brandes had changed radio jobs so his title credit added "courtesy of KFAB." The tall actor with the strong jaw made a striking Brigham Young in his hat and great coat. Szold played rival prophet Almon Long. If *Time* had a correspondent with the *World-Herald*, he was a harsh critic. *Time's* Names Make News item said the play "wavered between the religious and the farcical." The audience "liked little about it beyond Iowa artist Grant Wood's settings."

Reel and Abbott were kinder. "Sharp realism" and "an abundance of human feeling and a fine eye to character development" were cited by Reel. Abbott called it "the most effective drama by local authors that has yet been staged in Omaha," a comment that might have offended the oft-performed local playwright, Mrs. Doorly.

At the final curtain, McGee answered the call for "author" and made a short speech of thanks. Two decades later, Creighton University drama professor Harry Langdon saw it as proof of Playhouse strength. "A less secure group," Langdon wrote in his master's thesis, "could never have strayed as far from standard theatrical fare."

In retrospect, the May play, *Engaged* by W.S. Gilbert, would seem anticlimactic. But in the earlier style of *Fashion* and *Ten Nights in a Bar-room*, Szold added songs from the Gilbert and Sullivan operettas, and publicists claimed the director and cast were in stitches during rehearsals. Along with *Tit Willow* and *A Modern Major General*, Damian Flynn revived his "My Mustache" song by popular demand. Rudyard Norton in his third show of the season "convulsed the cast at rehearsal as "a conniving old codger."

Neither the likability of *Engaged* nor the controversy over *Brigham Young* caused a rush on the box office. The latter's 310 single admissions were about average for the year. It's not clear what if anything was paid Grant Wood or author McGee. No disbursement items mention them by name or category. Treasurer Alan McDonald tallied up the season and declared a $92 balance after expenses of $9,121. He also ruled that a forty-cent check issued to Mrs. Brando four years earlier was unlikely to be cashed.

Bozell Sells Tickets, Crowd Sighs at Togs: 1933–1934

While Szold conducted summer camp in Wisconsin, burglars hit the empty theater, stuffing a bag with money. It turned out to be stage currency. Their other disappointment came when they poured four glasses full of amber liquor found in a decanter. It turned out to be stale tea. That convinced Szold that nobody connected to the Playhouse was involved. They'd know better than to sample that "liquor."

Heading into the season, Leo Bozell, cofounder of Bozell and Jacobs, destined to become Omaha's largest advertising agency, joined the trustees along with an English professor from the new Municipal University of Omaha, no longer a Presbyterian school.

Bozell headed the ticket drive, issuing these marching orders: "Each trustee is counted upon to sell a minimum of 100 season tickets." Sell ten and get one free, but no more than two free tickets per worker.

A newspaper editorial welcomed plans for seven plays, but added a special request for *Uncle Tom's Cabin* or an old melodrama. "We want to see little Eva, bless her heart, ascend up into Heaven once again while those fiddles play." New board president John Stewart II thanked the

World-Herald for its support, and vowed in his letter to the editor to double membership.

Another published letter, however, griped about "the suburban theater," wondering why they Playhouse couldn't move to "the marble memorial" (Joslyn) or "the Jewish Center" downtown, two "fine auditoriums with modern seats." The writer claimed playgoers at 40th and Davenport fidgeted restlessly "due to the old-fashioned seats which seem to be stuffed with bricks."

The first Prompter had a happier outlook, reporting on Damian Flynn and Hudson Shotwell's Broadway prospects while Henry Fonda starred in *New Faces of 1934*. Leading man Harold Felton had moved to the West Indies as a government attorney, and Lauren Gilbert was going back to the professional stage.

The season opened in late September, not the usual October start, with Maxwell Anderson's *Both Your Houses*, the 1933 Pulitzer Prize play about pork barrel graft in Congress. Technical director Robert Brinkema did the settings, and his sister Bernice made a "piquantly amusing" private secretary in a cast that included Rudyard Norton and Clarence Teal.

June Moon meant more George Kaufman comedy in November. Coauthor Ring Lardner, who'd once named Szold to his all-American football team, wrote the original story about a country boy's adventures in Tin Pan Alley. The society section still added its take on costumes, noting "oohs and aahs at the good-looking togs" and "an audible sigh" when a Jean Harlow–type appeared "in delectable sea-green velvet lounging pajamas."

From Ibsen to Obscenity? "Was It Dirty?"

Oft-promised but never before performed, a Henrik Ibsen play finally was presented in December. The Prompter prepared its audience for *A Doll's House* by featuring a long essay on the drama and a short history of Ibsen. Szold cast himself as the loan-sharking Nils Krogstad, with Ben Stilphen, recently with the Pasadena Playhouse, as Torvald Helmer and Peggy Doorly as Nora. Then reigning Queen of Ak-Sar-Ben, Margaret's daughter would marry Ben Cowdery, who succeeded her father at the *World-Herald*. Recently she had appeared as Hamlet's Ophelia in her mother's Folio Shakespeare company, directed by Hart Jenks.

Abbott declared the story now "more than a trifle obsolete." The headline said, "Peggy Doorly Proves Convincing Actress." but Abbott's praise was faint. The *Bee-News* was more generous to the rival publisher's daughter, citing her Nora as "a spirited and plausible young wife," not the "doll" mistreated by her stern husband.

Stilphen, 26, must have been buoyed by two straight leading roles. He took a job tending cattle on a train to New York, where he planned to join Flynn and other Omahans on Broadway. The Playhouse stage was last used in 1933 by the Junior League's *The Golden Goose* two days before Christmas. Mrs. Carpenter of marionette fame directed, and a familiar face was back under a different name. The former Harriet Fonda, now Mrs. Jack Peacock, took charge of properties. If any thought an Ak-Sar-Ben crown and such roles as Nora and Ophelia went to Peggy Doorly's head, she didn't mind playing one of three penguins in *The Golden Goose*.

Springtime for Henry rather than Shaw's *Candida* started the 1934 portion of the season, promising a play "for laughing purposes only" and one making "sound morality" irrelevant. The caveat didn't keep Abbott from typing a review claiming the Benn Levy play "thumbs its nose at decent living." It also had "smutty jests, if you like them." The reviewer wondered, "What has happened to the good taste of the Community Playhouse?"

The *Bee-News* found no fault with the "sophisticated drawing room farce." A follow-up headlined, "Was It Dirty?" quoted Szold saying, "I don't think it's smutty," and the review saying so "ought to help business and maybe extend the run of the show." He needled Abbott by explaining that a character he criticized for going into a bedroom with another man's wife actually went offstage to the switchboard "well chaperoned by the electrician." He added, "I'm glad that Mr. Abbott doesn't spare us. It shows he takes us seriously."

Uncle Tom's Cabin, Done Right or Wrong

The children's theater revived *Racketty Packetty House,* its first play in the 1920s, then the Playhouse heralded "a spectacular revival of the historical American classic, 'Uncle Tom's Cabin.'" The play-reading committee had listened to that pleading editorial and brought back Harriet Beecher Stowe's story "in the old manner." And the editorial writer's niece, Nancy Newbranch, played Little Eva in a cast featuring Donald Morton as Uncle Tom.

Morton, the black convict in *The Last Mile,* was now identified as a fifteen-year veteran of vaudeville and concert tours. "You can kill my body, Massa, but yo' cain't kill my soul," the Prompter quoted his title character. Rudyard Norton didn't appear in the play, but later recalled Szold's distinctive staging and lighting, which harshly accented brutal slavery scenes with huge shadows.

Morton was criticized "by his own race" for lending himself to a play "in which objectionable terms are applied to Negroes." He replied, "The show must go on although my heart is somewhat heavy within me." He saw his selection for the role as "recognition of the talent and civic spirit that the race can contribute if given an opportunity to do so."

Szold and cast members suggested Morton's "talent should be a matter of great pride among the Negroes." A letter of support came from "a very large and progressive group of young Negroes." Szold also promised that "real bloodhounds will chase the footsore and harassed Eliza across the Ohio River ice." "No Phony Pooches," said the headline over a story that admitted that some offstage baying would come from two-legged hounds.

Abbott made history of a sort by panning a second straight play. Morton's baritone voice and persona was "deeply appealing," and the Jubilee Singers added atmosphere, but the headline said simply:

"Uncle Tom is Done Wrong." He objected to playing "chiefly for laughs, in the manner of the old 'rep' companies" And grumbled about "burlesque grotesquery." A letter writer disagreed, chiding Abbott for leaving "some good time" before the end of the show.

Mrs. Baer Acts, Miss Borglum Marries, *Brigham* Adds Wives

Counsellor-at-Law and *Three-Cornered Moon* completed the season on a more complimentary critical note, and local playgoers took pride in favorable reviews for Damian Flynn's lead role in *Biography* on Broadway. There and later in Hollywood, he reverted to the old family spelling of O'Flynn. Hudson Shotwell had a smaller part in *Yellow Jack*, also running in New York. With Fonda in the musical *New Faces*, the Prompter boasted, "Talent plus good training under B. Szold surely counts."

Mabel Baer left her costume corner to play the lead in *Three-Cornered Moon*. Her Mrs. Rimplegar flutters through life after that old "meanie" the stock

Morton played Uncle Tom.

market left her broke in the Depression with four children. The farce shows "how far an author can go with a set of loony characters," Reel wrote. Among the loonies, Allison Flynn tickled Abbott with his dreamy novelist, Jean Borglum scored laughs as the gawky maid, and Mrs. Baer played "the vapid mother divertingly."

Meanwhile, *Brigham Young* won a July tryout at Greenwich, Conn., and one headline had it headed for Broadway. Contrary to Omaha's cutting wives from seventeen to three, "the New York producers wanted more wives than the script contained."

The season ended with the director's contract renewed for a final year. It was an exciting summer for the Szolds as he flew back from that Wisconsin camp in July for the birth of their first child, Elizabeth Stephanie—or Queen Elizabeth II as one news item named her. He'd planned to fly home on a seaplane and land on Carter Lake, but weather led to a Chicago airliner instead.

Just as directors Foley and Szold surprised friends with their "secret" weddings, a summer headline said Jean Borglum "Became Secret Bride of Robert Brinkema Early Last Spring." So the scenic designer was already wed to Miss Borglum as she played that gawky maid in the final play. A gifted pianist, she assisted her uncle August, the *World-Herald* music critic, with his teaching. Perhaps the fact that her other uncle's masterpiece was years from completion explains why he wasn't mentioned in the *World-Herald*.

The *Bee-News* closed its story about the marriage of two "leading figures in the Community Playhouse" with this sentence: "She is also the niece of Gutzon Borglum, the sculptor." The year was 1934, and his work on Mt. Rushmore had started in 1927, but would not be finished until 1941. Borglum, in other words, was halfway through the blasting of presidential faces from the Black Hills granite. One can only wonder if Uncle Gutzon advised Bob Brinkema on Playhouse scenery, or if Bob climbed George Washington's nose with the great sculptor.

No Fight Over Plays, Leave Selection to Szold: 1934–1935

The opening of the tenth season competed with a visit home by Henry Fonda and press speculation about his trip to California where Margaret Sullavan was making a movie. "Henry bobbed up in Hollywood … accompanied to lunch by his famous former wife," sparking speculation by columnist Louella Parsons. Perhaps it meant a reconciliation, "a rewelding of the bright young romance which ended so abruptly and disappointedly," she suggested. Or maybe Fonda, "notoriously in love with his work on the stage before 'audiences that breathe,'" wanted her advice on switching to films.

The Playhouse closely followed its favorite son, pasting two full pages of his clippings to start that season's scrapbook.

After leading off with praise for backstage volunteers, president Stewart thanked "Mrs. Joslyn's great kindness in making it possible to have the Playhouse." And he reported a major change in the method of selecting plays. "It was the custom of the play-reading committee to meet during the hottest nights of the summer and read with … zeal some 15 or 20 plays." In a final meeting just before Szold's return, "after a good rousing fight seven plays would be selected." Not more than three of the ten would approve the choices, "leaving Mr. Szold as cool as the proverbial well digger."

So this year the play selection was left to the director, based on the thought that he was "quite as well qualified to pick plays as are architects, insurance men, school teachers, and even automobile dealers." Stewart claimed Szold's choices, billed as an "international program of plays," proved the board had made a sound decision. "The current Broadway success is noted for its complete absence."

Instead, Hungary, England, Germany, Holland and France were represented with two Americans. Stewart, a radio announcer, revealed what Mrs. Guiou suggested in her satire on the annual meeting. The trustees and the director didn't always see eye-to-eye on play selection, and for now the solution was to let Szold rule.

Rachel Gallagher wrote the program notes describing the seven choices, starting with Molnar's *The Good Fairy,* followed by the first play to be repeated by the Playhouse, Barrie's *Dear Brutus*. Now that matinees were built into the schedule, subscribers could choose between the usual $5 season tickets or $2.50 for the Saturday matinees. At thirty-five cents per show, that seemed a bargain even in the middle of the Great Depression.

The Good Fairy in Molnar's season opener is a well-meaning "glow worm," the usherette who lights the way to theater seats. Nonsmoker Mary Updike was also supposed to light up a cigarette in the role, but Szold deleted the business rather than afflicting her with a coughing spell. Reel rated Updike's performance among the theater's best, and she reminded Abbott of Puck, Ariel and Peter Pan. The title character is asked about her diet and explains: "There is one rule for every diet." "What?" "It starts tomorrow."

World Premiere of Play on Poet Keats

The return of *Dear Brutus* was explained in Lucy Updike's Prompter note as a response to its popularity in 1929 and its fit for the international flavor of the season.

The play goes into the midsummer woods to delve into "what might have been." A child was played by Mary Lee Wilson, home from California, where she "all but won" the much-publicized search for the title role in the film *Alice in Wonderland*.

The December play, Susan Glaspell's *Inheritors* departed from the international theme by dealing with the dreams of Iowa homesteaders. Educator Belle Ryan, later honored with a school bearing her name, characterized it for the Prompter as "not a soothing sedative, but a challenge for thinkers."

An advance photo featured five Flynns—Mrs. Catherine Flynn, now performing for the first time in thirty years, and her four acting offspring. Actually, seven Flynns graced the local stage. No relation to

Catherine and her clan, James R. Flynn played a state senator in *The Inheritors,* and his daughter Mary Emilie Flynn was in *Dear Brutus.*

Commenting on mother Catherine, Szold said, "It is easy to see where her children get their talent. Mrs. Flynn is one of the best character women I have had," and her pioneer roots in O'Neill, Nebraska, added authenticity to her role as the grandmother. Mrs. Carpenter's marionettes reprised *Aladdin and His Wonderful Lamp* to complete Playhouse activities for 1934, and the lone children's play that followed was also a repeat, *The Wizard of Oz* by the Junior League Players. The former children's director, Frances Fintel, was in Los Angeles rehearsing *Merrily We Roll Along,* a Kaufman and Hart comedy. Most parts in the Junior League's children's plays were now taken by adults.

The year 1935, however, opened on a more original note, the world premiere production of *A Thing of Beauty,* subtitled "An Exquisite Quest." The story of poet John Keats came with a condition. Author DeWitt Bodeen required that young Keats be played by his friend Thomas Kennedy, an Omahan who studied drama at Yale. Publicity featured a drawing of Kennedy, and Abbott's review said his personation was aided by the fact "he so looks the poet."

After teetering on the brink of film stardom, Mary Lee Wilson won acclaim as Fanny Brawne, the sweetheart who must bid adieu to the ailing Keats, both knowing he will not return. A dialogue sample in the Prompter summed up the title theme: Fanny asks, "John, what do you think is the most beautiful thing in the whole world?" and Keats replies, "Well, I don't know, dear. I suppose that's why we're on earth—to discover the most beautiful thing here."

Szold wasn't searching for beauty when he climbed to the fly floor 20 feet above the stage. He was rearranging scenery for the sold-out Saturday matinee when he slipped and fell, "wrenching his back severely."

Broadcasters in *Wet Paint,* Lawyers in *One Sunday*

A German adaptation of Ben Jonson's *Volpone* had been listed as the next play, but the January Prompter began plugging "a gala revival of 'East Lynne' produced in the old manner" with period songs. Perhaps they recalled that editorial that once pleaded successfully for *Uncle Tom's Cabin,* but also for *East Lynne* and other vintage plays.

News items added confusion by promising both *Volpone* and then *East Lynne* for February 25. Somewhere along the way, a French comedy retitled *Wet Paint* opened instead on March 11. As *Prenez Garde a la Peinture* (guard or be careful of the paint) by Rene Fauchois, it had been scheduled for May, so it was just a matter of moving it up when the other two fell through.

The French play was successfully adapted for American stage and screen as *The Late Christopher Bean,* but the Playhouse presented its own translation, *Wet Paint* by Bess Bozell and Elizabeth Szold. Both the sister of advertising's Leo Bozell and the director's wife had studied in France.

Again the cast was dominated by experienced actors, particularly those from radio. Ray Suber not only played roles in radio drama, still in its hey-day even at local stations, but did one-man shows on the air using eight or nine voices. Bea Chesebrough was famous for her Swedish monologues as Hilde on KOIL. Suber's doctor and Bea's maid appealed to both reviewers.

Nancy Mercer, playing the doctor's daughter Nanette, was a Londoner in Omaha for the winter with her father, Dr. Nelson Mercer. His father Samuel built the city's famed Mercer mansion, and a later generation played the central role in reviving downtown's Old Market area.

Theater-goers found other distractions beside the changing play list at the Playhouse. George M. Cohan starred for one night in O'Neill's *Ah, Wilderness!* at Tech High, and Szold's alums made more news. Damian O'Flynn landed in *The Eldest* at the Ritz Theatre, and

Hudson Shotwell considered it an honor even to be in a mob scene with Katharine Cornell's production of *Romeo and Juliet*.

Hank Fonda went from *The Farmer Takes a Wife* on Broadway to filming it in Hollywood. Brace Fonda lay ill in daughter Harriet Peacock's home, but a Fox executive shipped the film to Omaha. A projector was brought to 5205 Izard and father saw son on the screen. "He smiled as the final scene was shown with Henry and Janet Gaynor," the first leading woman to win an Oscar. So, the story said, Hollywood "proved that it has a heart."

A play from the Netherlands was replaced by *One Sunday Afternoon*. Its April run marked the tenth anniversary of the Playhouse, so the Prompter reprinted the cast of *The Enchanted Cottage* from 1925, and the editor did some summing up.

It was timely to remind again of their 1929 musical version of *Fashion*, which still claimed the longest run and largest single admissions of any show. Now *One Sunday Afternoon* would return at least a little of that flavor with intermission songs such as "In the Good Old Summer Time" and "Only a Bird in a Gilded Cage."

Frances Brown returned as the flirtatious target of village beaus in a cast that included Howard Fischer, whose nephew Tim Schmad would one day become Playhouse administrator.

Mrs. Baer and her costume crew came up with plenty of rustling taffeta, feather boas and big picture hats for the Gay Nineties theme. If radio personalities played the largest part in some plays, lawyers and law students ranked close behind. Two Creighton law students, Russell Blumenthal and Cappy Liberman had performed on campus but were Playhouse newcomers.

Szold Heads Down to New Orleans

The French play originally planned as the season finale had been presented earlier, so *Louder, Please* by Norman Krasna closed the season. Judge-to-be Lawrence Krell carried the burden of the comedy as a high-energy publicity man for a movie studio. He fakes the disappearance of starlet Polly Madison and farcical fun ensues. Polly was Mary Updike, fresh from playing the dog Toto in *Wizard of Oz*. One headline fashions her as a gentle soul, unwilling to slap Krell as the script demands.

Benson High student Miriam Tolle raced between afternoon rehearsals for her role in the school play and evening rehearsals at the Playhouse.

Trustees retained Bernard Szold as director, an action soon contradicted by the headline, "Director for 7 Years Quits Playhouse." The June 1935 story didn't quite catch the name of the theater that lured him from Omaha, calling it the New Orleans Petite Theater, an error repeated years later in his obituary. He went to the larger Le Petit Theatre du Vieux Carre, a French Quarter mouthful.

"The resignation came as a complete surprise to the Omaha group," although they knew of offers before from Dallas, among others. Neither Keene Abbott nor Jack Reel eulogized the departing director. Another scribe, Colonel T.W. M'Cullough, who would donate theater books to the Playhouse, commented in his Looking Things Over column that trustees "find themselves a bit perplexed. To discover a new director of the caliber of Bernard Szold is not such a simple assignment."

President Gallagher would introduce his replacement in the fall, but she took care to avoid any impression of disloyalty to Szold, "whose direction was a delight to us for seven seasons."

The portrait artist and football all-American, their "Hairy Ape" who banged his head against the wall and threw himself to the floor in frustration, left after the first year he won complete freedom to name his own plays. He went to a better-paying job in a bigger city. Bernie Szold would also remain loyal to the Playhouse, praising its graduates when he moved to Hollywood six years later. He did not coach the son of his star, but Mrs. Brando thought first of him when a teenage Marlon showed signs of talent.

No one proclaimed this the end of an era, but it closed a decade when the Playhouse dared Ibsen and O'Neill, when it risked unknown authors and braved the Mormons. Szold didn't find Fonda, but he brought Hank back and he kindled the spark in Dorothy McGuire. Bernie wasn't there at the birth, but he nurtured the adolescence. He was not the first director, but the first one larger than life, racing an airplane, painting a saloon all night and losing his car, falling from backstage heights and loving the theater he opened at 40th and Davenport.

Years later, a full page in the *World-Herald* showed him coaching Ann Miller and directing Forrest Tucker. It told of collaboration as a captain in World War II with Jimmy Stewart, and working with Jimmy Cagney and Bob Hope. Dorothy McGuire's recommendation helped him become Resident Director of the Actor's Company in La Jolla with Gregory Peck and Jennifer Jones. He wrote a play, *Tide's End,* with Tucker, who admitted the famed Szold temperament "still can go into high, to a degree which is almost frightening."

The intervening years brought changes that came home to him when his first cousin, David Lilienthal, was named head of the Atomic Energy Commission. Yet there was serenity in his San Fernando Valley home, where two Grant Wood paintings were prominently displayed. Mrs. Guiou had chosen well in 1928, and when Szold returned twenty years later to see Fonda and McGuire in *The Country Girl*, he still had the ready smile, a full head of hair, and nothing but kind words for the city and theater he had served for seven seasons.

CHAPTER 4

Hard Times, War, But Show Goes On, 1935–1946

Fonda Buys New Seats, Young Steinmetz Arrives

The business of hiring a new director gave way to the Playhouse board's pleasure in welcoming Henry Fonda home again. His *The Farmer Takes a Wife* was playing at the Orpheum, and Hank, after completing his next film, *Love Song* with opera star Lily Pons, took time off to be the toast of the town.

Board president Rachel Gallagher hosted an Omaha Club luncheon for Fonda, sisters Harriet and Jayne—now Mrs. Jack Peacock and Mrs. John Schoentgen—and the expanded twenty-one-member board. They'd hear the inside stories: how Charles Bickford failed to pull his punch and floored Fonda in a fight scene, and how Hank boasted about his cow-milking then tugged at Bossie in vain—not knowing she'd been milked an hour before shooting the barnyard scene. It wasn't all insider anecdotes. Fonda praised new "left-wing theater," singling out *Waiting for Lefty* by Clifford Odets as "the most exciting thing he ever witnessed."

Henry took a Friday train back to Hollywood, where *Trail of the Lonesome Pine* co-starring Joel McCrea would begin filming on Monday. That turned out to be the day William Brace Fonda died at the home of daughter Harriet, a year after the death of his wife, Herberta. (Henry regretted that his mother didn't live to see his name in lights, as she had foretold.)

In that time of slower travel, a trip home would have delayed shooting a week, so Henry didn't return for his father's funeral. Instead, he sent a gift of $500 to buy new Playhouse seats, replacing the ones that caused so many complaints when Brace Fonda was house manager. It came with a note: "When they catch up with me out here, I expect to come back and do scenery at the Playhouse. The enclosed is a bribe." Perhaps Henry persuaded his hosts at another dinner, the Junior Leaguers, to add their gift of $380 to pay for the rest of the chairs.

To put that money in perspective, season ticket sales totaled only $6,735 for the 1935–1936 season. It took gifts and $700 from students attending a spring tour of their first Shakespeare production to meet season expenses of $9,500. Ticket income came from fewer than 1,350 members, short of the 1,500 goal despite board action to boost sales of the seven-play plan.

Such were the facts facing Edward G. Steinmetz Jr., the man hired that summer from "scores of applicants." Turning the tables on the Iowans who lured director Foley from the Playhouse in 1928, the board took Steinmetz after two years at the Des Moines theater. He'd arrive after directing summer stock in New Hampshire. A Pennsylvanian with an undergraduate degree from Lehigh and Master of Fine Arts from Yale, Steinmetz was described as "a grave young man with a pleasant smile." A photo supported the claim that "he seems much younger than his 28 years."

But a profile view, as he sat with Mrs. Gallagher, revealed a thin face and pointy nose. Based on that photo, typecasting would make him the snooty butler, haughty heir or fussy elf. In other words, he looked nothing like Szold, the rugged football star and hairy ape who preceded him. But young women of that day remembered him years later as a handsome fellow. He preferred directing to acting, he told a reporter, but tended to play juvenile roles or such "character bits" as "the quaint old man." Steinmetz commented on casting policy: "If plays are well chosen, there shouldn't be an occasion to use an actor more than twice in one season."

Within months, he would face a challenge from actors who felt the Playhouse season, though expanded now to eight plays, limited their opportunities. His arrival came after the publicist sounded a familiar theme: "The Playhouse exists for no single group. There are no social or professional distinctions." Once more, the promise was democratic participation "from varied walks of life." Listed as possible productions were Fonda's favorite *Waiting for Lefty* and dramas by Sean O'Casey and Pirandello. Odets and the other two playwrights would not make the season schedule, but Shakespeare finally did.

Society Still Turns Out, New Critic Reviews Opening: 1935–1936

The October Prompter gave Mrs. Gallagher room to present Steinmetz "with a pride and a certainty of his ability." Just as the Playhouse once declared Foley a director with special access to plays, now she promised, "Through Mr. Steinmetz's influence and acquaintance with author and producers, the Playhouse is to be permitted to present Edward Chodorov's 'Kind Lady' while it is still enjoying its run in New York." She called the new ban on single tickets "the custom of more worldly little theaters," and added another new policy—admission to dress rehearsals "by written invitation only."

Tryouts for *Her Master's Voice* gave Omahans their first glimpse of Steinmetz at work. The *Bee* described an "almost packed" theater as the new director "called the first aspirant to the stage. With him sat Mrs. Joseph Lehman, in a chic black ensemble," taking names and noting "the abilities of all those who read." Among the onlookers were board members and Miss Dorothy McGuire "in a French blue wool," the sort of trivia to make feminists cringe.

They were already calling the new man "Ted," and Dot McGuire's pal, Sally Johnston, thought he was "pretty cute," a nice change from Szold who seemed "scary" to the coed. Once more a banner headline greeted opening night with "Society Turns Out", followed by such minutiae as a woman in "a black gown with brilliant clips at the neckline enjoyed a cigarette during intermission." One hopes she flicked no ashes on the patron in "a raisin-colored wool frock trimmed in bands of chinchilla with a cunning little hat of matching hue." Another item proclaimed, "The new cushioned seats, donated by Henry Fonda, truly were a joy." And, yes, there was a play reviewed by Keene Abbott's replacement.

The ailing Abbott had retired and a Creighton University graduate, Keith Wilson, left his apprenticeship as police reporter to become the new drama critic. He'd eventually become chief editorial writer. But he would write the stage-screen column and review plays into the 1940s. Two years later, he would become Omaha's only daily newspaper critic when the *Bee-News* went out of business.

One sign of changing times: Unlike Abbott, Wilson wore the title of "motion picture editor." While Abbott headed the Nebraska Writers Guild, Wilson was named to the board of directors of the Newspaper Film Critics of America.

Wilson began his first review with less formality than the usual Abbott style: "Act II, Scene II of *Her Master's Voice* takes about a quarter hour to play, but more merriment was packed in Tuesday night's presentation of it than has been heard in the Community Playhouse in quite some time." He predicted success for the season and the new director.

The new reviewer also praised Robert Brinkema's use of real leaves in the scenic design. President Gallagher hoped Brinkema would continue as technical director and scenic designer, but she would end up sharing him with the Junior League children's plays. Praise for Franklyn Judd included regret that the young actor was Hollywood-bound. Brinkema would do scenic design for two of the next three plays, winning special praise for creating copies of paintings by El Greco and Whistler as props for *Kind Lady*.

Seven Plays Too Few for New Actors Guild

A Tuesday appearance in Omaha by the great Katharine Cornell was apparently too much competition, so the December play opened on a Wednesday. David Belasco's *The Return of Peter Grimm* was a sentimental classic about an eccentric Dutch florist. The *Bee-News* claimed it gave "justification and meaning to the whole Community Playhouse purpose," calling it "a great old tear-compeller and reflection-inducer." Howard Fischer, the young lawyer with a half dozen Playhouse credits, played the title character, who haunts his house as a gentle ghost.

The early history of the Playhouse survives primarily in scrapbooks, started by Mark Levings and Harry Shedd, then maintained into the 1980s. Until December 1935, most photographs were gray newsprint. Then a stage-wide glossy photo of *The Return of Peter Grimm* appeared. Certainly the work of Clarence Teal, known for singing "Little Brown Jug," but making an even greater impact as photographer and then treasurer. The entire cast occupied the stage. This ordinary scene captured costumes, furnishings, even the faces of actors in the theater that was the Playhouse home for more than thirty years.

As 1935 ended, something was stirring on Sunday evenings. "Following the great enthusiasm for the round-table reading of 'Tobacco Road' last month," the Prompter said, a mid-December reading would be followed by more 8 p.m. Sunday play readings in January. This practice was revived in 2010 with the 21 & Over series of staged readings.

A group called the Actors Guild had also received permission to use the Playhouse on Sundays. Brinkema was identified as director of an experimental effort involving actors, workers and friends of the Playhouse. Apparently everyone wasn't on the same page. A three-page letter to the board, signed by four Guild organizers, made it clear that they had stepped on some toes. "Because of an unfortunate misunderstanding of terms by which we were to be permitted the use of the Playhouse, we canceled our Sunday meeting (Jan. 5, 1936) in deference to the Playhouse board," wrote the group chaired by Martin Chicoine. The letter listed Lawrence Krell as financial advisor, Brinkema as activity director, and others, all men.

Misunderstandings must have been resolved because the Guild again scheduled Sunday night "workshop theater" with improvisational sketches. (An earlier workshop had been motivated more by local playwrights or by Bernie Szold's hope of getting them off his back.) Much of that long Guild letter was devoted to declaring their loyalty to the Playhouse and explaining that their activities would keep restless thespians from turning away from the theater. Recall that Chicoine, after serving the Playhouse as technical director, was quite active in the short-lived Prairie Playmakers three years before.

The Guild's summary point was simple: a seven-play season provided only about seventy opportunities to be cast, and it was time for the Playhouse to expand through their group. "We are, and desire only to be, the experimental branch of the Playhouse."

Snowbound *Yellow Jack,* Irish *Far-Off Hills*

The February play, Sidney Howard's *Yellow Jack,* answered the Guild's complaint about scarce parts. A cast of twenty-four men and one woman, a nurse, told the story of Dr. Walter Reed's fight against yellow fever.

Broken into "a phantasmagoric succession of blackouts," seventeen scenes in Cuba, London and West Africa made it "by far the most ambitious presentation ever attempted by the Playhouse." They had help from President Roosevelt's New Deal with "settings constructed, painted and lighted by Federal Theatre Project No. 1 of Omaha, Works Progress Administration."

Wilson's review made no mention of the Playhouse debut by Glenn Cunningham, who gained more fame as Omaha mayor and then congressman. The young South Omahan would take other Playhouse roles and marry a makeup volunteer, Janis Thelen.

February weather added problems for the "most ambitious" play: Cast members coughed with colds, and the lone woman, Josephine Jelen, couldn't make it to the theater by cab or trolley. Mabel Baer, in her costumer's smock, had script in hand to play the nurse when Josephine arrived breathless after dashing up 24th Street to be rescued by a passing motorist. Playgoers inadvertently left cars parked on snow-buried streetcar rails and were summoned out by impatient conductors.

The weather had improved by mid-February when the Actors Guild presented a thirteen-part program, starting with improv "situations" and ending with *Bulldog,* an ironic one-act comedy by one of the four organizers. Perhaps this workshop, like the earlier one, was also motivated as an outlet for local writers.

In March, *The Far-Off Hills* by Lennox Robinson, was touted as the first Playhouse attempt at Irish dialect comedy. Made famous by the Abbey Players of Dublin. Bancroft School principal Stella Holmes, Agnes Krell and others delivered the Irish well enough for reviewers, though one found the dialect "pretty hard to manage at times."

Quickened Shakespeare: Comedy and Tragedy Tour

Shakespeare finally came to the Playhouse in April 1936, then hit the road to Creighton University and four high schools. The program first promised *As You Like It* and *Midsummer Night's Dream,* but the latter gave way to *Macbeth.*

The fall announcement called it "Shakespeare quickened into cinema tempo. Do not worry; no one will be permitted to tamper with the beautiful, precise language." That warning wasn't good enough for a local columnist. He huffed about the "tabloid form," an hour of *Macbeth,* thirty-seven minutes of *As You Like It.* To him, "It does suggest unpleasant thoughts," when well-rounded dramas are "worked over by moderns." Szold's mentor, the renowned Thomas Wood Stevens, was the modern who "quickened" the Bard.

Aesthetics aside, the 4,500 tickets sold on the student tour brought in $700, so Shakespeare was thanked for "practically obliterating the season deficit." The gate from the plays and the marionette *Alice in Wonderland* brought the Playhouse "closer to being out of the red than it has been for several seasons," a news item said.

The Junior League's *Pinocchio* saw young women, not children, playing roles directed by Mrs. Carpenter, with costumes and sets by Mary Elizabeth Jonas, soon to become Emmy Gifford. The cast included Peggy Doorly (Mrs. Ben) Cowdery and Harriet Fonda Peacock. Harriet played the band leader and half the "second donkey." She wasn't listed first, so she presumably performed as the donkey's hind quarters.

Mrs. Arthur Scribner must have been a good Gepetto because she won the lead in *Post Road,* the final play of the eleventh season. Steinmetz also cast a pair of Omaha policemen in the mystery-comedy. The director "received his money's worth" when he paid $1 and costs on a speeding charge, then went back to the station and recruited two of Omaha's finest. At least Steinmetz's driving seemed to be in Szold mold. Both reviewers treated *Post Road* as a play that "floundered a bit," but the board had given Steinmetz a new contract before the opening.

Steinmetz Survives "Disastrous" Complaint, Strikes Back

In his first year, Steinmetz, Mrs. Guiou concluded, proved quite as capable in the use of logical persuasion as Szold had been in utilizing emotional stimulus. In other words, Ted didn't pull out his hair or bang his head against the wall.

And he apparently didn't persuade Martin Chicoine, chairman of the Actors Guild. Steinmetz worked with most Guild members, but Chicoine wrote a bridge-burning Public Pulse letter. "The past season was the most disastrous in Playhouse history," he grieved.

If the new director was Chicoine's primary target, he defended himself by suggesting his critic was out of step with the Omaha audience. Steinmetz said, "I have never known a more able, conscientious" group of trustees with "more exacting standards." It's the board, he added, "which must listen to the half-baked opinions and ignorant proposals of such people as Mr. Chicoine."

As the summer ended, Chicoine left town. Identified as a freelance newspaper man, he became publicity director for federal theater projects in Ohio. He was hired by the assistant national director of federal theaters, John McGee, that *Brigham Young* author from Council Bluffs. And the Broadway-bound cattle train took two more Playhouse actors—Howard Fischer and Russell Baker, with Franklyn Judd close behind to share their New York apartment. Another bit of mid-September news: Henry Fonda surprised his friend Jimmy Stewart by revealing his engagement to Frances Brokaw, the woman who would become the mother of his two children, Jane and Peter.

Mrs. Carpenter: Puppeteer, Playwright, President: 1936–1937

Libby Carpenter, thirty-two, would lead the board for the twelfth and thirteenth seasons, but not at the expense of her other interests. She still managed a new marionette show, *Toyland Circus,* and directed her own children's play, *Goldilocks and the Three Bears.* Then she sold at least ninety-nine season tickets and kept hounding her hundredth prospect.

Granddaughter of pioneer Byron Reed, daughter-in-law of the founder of Carpenter Paper, and wife of Zeke who would assist John Foster Dulles in the Eisenhower State Department, Mrs. Carpenter had been crowned Queen of Ak-Sar-Ben and was a charter member of the Junior League. As she presided in the Aquila Court tearoom at a ticket campaign meeting, a society reporter noted her black crepe gown and elaborated on "her smart turban trimmed with two white feathers that met in front and formed a peaked brim."

Only three shows had been selected as Mrs. Guiou, still play-reading chair, commented on the upcoming season: The London courtroom drama, *Libel,* would open in October, followed by *The Senator's Husband,* a comedy by Nebraskan Fred Ballard, and Maxwell Anderson's poetic

Libby Carpenter.

tragedy, *Winterset*. The final three? "Many of the new and best plays are not yet released to little theaters," awaiting the schedules of road companies. When the dust settled, they picked *Personal Appearance,* debunking film star tours; an adaptation of Jane Austen's *Pride and Prejudice,* and another courtroom drama, Ayn Rand's *Night of January 16th.*

During the opening *Libel*, a backstage look featured Echo Guiou painting sets. A more memorable news photo in all the Chicago dailies snapped Echo aiming a long-barreled pistol while a young man held a bull's-eye target. It publicized a new women's rifle and pistol club at Chicago University where Miss Guiou starred in the freshman play. The space given her gun-toting photo is better explained by noting that the target-holder was Jay Berwanger, the first winner of football's Heisman Trophy.

Comedy Widens Missouri, Tragedy Barely Triumphs

Playwright Fred Ballard was not unknown in Omaha. The famous Mrs. Fiske once brought his *Ladies of the Jury* to the city. But now the Nebraskan's Washington satire, *The Senator's Husband,* would make its stage premiere at the Playhouse while Paramount shot the film starring Charles Ruggles in the title role. Wilson took notice of Dow Fonda (Henry's cousin had dropped the "u" from Douw), whose juvenile role "detracts nothing from the family's acting reputation." The play was "sprinkled with allusions to Omaha" and to widening the Missouri River channel, "big enough for ocean liners."

Maxwell Anderson's *Winterset*—a blank-verse tragedy in mid-December while the film played at the Brandeis—posed special problems. Wilson noted that "the Playhouse folk conquered" in their "tussle with blank verse," and "if their margin of victory was not great, the audience found it sufficient."

To the *World-Herald* critic, "One of the finest things about the production is the river bank set," giving the "astonishing" illusion of the Brooklyn Bridge stretching into the distance. Credit went to Jack Christiansen, who would continue in scenic design, and Bob Brinkema, who became the latest loss to the WPA theater projects. Brinkema moved to Cincinnati in time to help fight a flood.

The usual Fonda news was joined by word from other grads. When Rose Webber won attention in Hollywood, she was remembered as the youngest wife of their *Brigham Young.* Louise Fitch, after dramatic work with KOIL radio and many Playhouse roles, was cast in a CBS network serial, *Manhattan Mother,* and later spent years on the *Ma Perkins* soap opera.

But locals were more impressed to see Damian O'Flynn beside Bette Davis in publicity shots for *Marked Woman* with Humphrey Bogart. Word also came that Howard Fischer had landed a contract with the off-Broadway Subway Circuit and a part in *Waiting for Lefty.* Director Steinmetz was cool to the news that RKO would make its young contract players available to gain experience with community theaters. Hindsight might have warmed him to a list that included Betty Grable and Lucille Ball.

Echo's "Appearance," Then Jane Austen, Ayn Rand

The 1937 half of the season began with casting problems. Steinmetz couldn't find a Carole Arden, the sexy movie star lampooned in *Personal Appearance*. The Mae West screen role finally went to blonde Angeline Rush, credited in the Prompter with small movie parts before her Playhouse debut.

Advance publicity soon gave more attention to Echo Guiou, back from Chicago. Playing the small town fiancée of the bucolic lad being seduced by the blonde bombshell, Echo was shown in two large photos reflecting her image in mirrors. In one, she applied makeup, in the other she was dolled up over the line: "Miss Guiou has done considerable backstage work, but that, one can see with half an eye, is hardly fair to a beauty-loving public."

Clarence Teal played a Hollywood press agent with a heart, "if you can imagine" that, Reel quipped in his upbeat review. Miss Guiou, Wilson promised, "gave an excellent account of herself in romantic scenes."

Film stars Brian Aherne, Joan Fontaine with Echo Guiou (Ellick).

"Mrs. Gifford Paints Playhouse Costumes" alerted Omahans to her sketches of *Pride and Prejudice* designs. Not yet identified familiarly as Emmy, M. E. Jonas Gifford designed settings and costumes for the stage adaptation of Jane Austen's novel. Wilson confessed her "beautiful gowns are something the society department can describe better than I," adding, "The cast had something of a struggle to keep the play from being overwhelmed by its background."

The Playhouse was the first Little Theater given permission to present the famed story of Elizabeth Bennett, and both reviewers praised Mrs. Edward Rogers in the lead role. "Her Lizzie was the independent, spirited Lizzie of Jane Austen." Opening night took on added buzz with word that a Warner Brothers talent scout would be on hand to find the next Fonda or McGuire.

Reporters had not mastered the name of Ayn Rand, misspelled "Aryn" in one news story. But they found some familiar ones in the cast of *Night of January 16th*, her courtroom thriller that closed the six-show season in mid-April. Of all the radio personalities taking to the Omaha stage, none was better known than Foster May. "Take it away, Foster May" was the cue line for his popular WOW Man on the Street show. But the spotlight fell each night on Juliann Caffrey as Karen Andre, the secretary accused of killing her multimillionaire employer. A jury of twelve was drawn from the audience to decide her guilt or innocence.

Neither reviewer commented on the debut of Frances McChesney in a small role. Then a Central High School teacher and later drama professor at Omaha University, she became an important actor, director and Playhouse leader as Frances McChesney Key.

Wilson's review capped the season by concluding, "The Playhouse left its most exciting play till the last." A page-wide photo of one night's jury made a point of social history: "Nebraska women, barred by statute from serving on juries, are gaining some taste of one masculine prerogative still denied them in this state." The jury, including three women, acquitted the defendant and was rebuked by the judge.

For the first time, in April and May, the Playhouse used a slick brochure to promote acting classes. Szold had conducted classes, both in acting and painting, but at his Aquila Court studio. Now the Playhouse formally announced six-week courses in voice and diction, play production and directing in a four-page flyer.

Meanwhile, Mrs. Carpenter continued as board president as she wrapped up the children's season with three one-act plays including *Little Black Sambo,* not yet a source of racial controversy. Costumes and sets for all three were designed by Emmy Gifford, who would become a leading light of children's theater when it split from the Playhouse to be housed in a theater bearing her name.

Bee-News Dies, Big Apple Shrinks Debt: 1937–1938

Once more the play selection was incomplete when the season was promoted in a large two-color piece. "YOU HAVE BEEN CHOSEN," it emphasized, "because of your cultural interest in the Arts and Drama to membership in the 1937-38 season of the Community Playhouse."

The chosen were warned that, due to limited seating, sales "will be closed at 1,600 season tickets." Only 1,180 were actually sold, down from the year before, but the optimism of August came with enthusiastic endorsements by four journalists—Wilson of the *World-Herald*, Miles Greenleaf of the *Dundee News,* and two from the *Bee-News*, Jack Reel and Don Hollenbeck.

Unfortunately, Reel and Hollenbeck were about to be unemployed, and plays would no longer have two daily newspaper reviews. On Sept. 18, 1937, the *Bee-News* stopped publishing, bringing an end to daily competition in Omaha. Hearst had turned down a buy offer from employees, then sold the plant, equipment and circulation lists to *Herald* president Henry Doorly. The surviving daily could afford to pay more to kill it than the employees could scrape up to continue. Neighborhood weeklies, such as the *Dundee News,* would evolve and other media outlets would rise, but the lavish photo spreads in advance of Playhouse openings would decline.

In August, it looked like three one-act plays would open the season, then another choice, but finally Steinmetz got rights to *Excursion*, which features the last voyage of a Coney Island ferry captain who transports his humdrum passengers to an "Isle of Happiness."

For one last time, the *Bee-News* did a big spread as its "Roving Reporter" captured *Excursion* tryouts. Steinmetz put pencil to clipboard notes and Mary Strahl, 14, staged a tantrum to win a part. Another four-photo layout showed first-nighters in furs, Mrs. Carpenter being ushered in by a Sea Scout in dress blues and white cap, actors checking scripts and Agnes Krell touching up an actor's mustache. The Krell family of four all played passengers.

Van Wyck Benner's captain looked a bit regal to critic Wilson, who saved his kudos for Mark Levings, whose "exits and entrances were marked by frequent applause" as audiences rooted for the man who labeled himself a "dub" in that divorce item a few years before. As for the romantic lead, Dow Fonda, his "resemblance to Henry is startling in more ways than one," Wilson said.

Playgoers learned in the Prompter that Steinmetz doesn't like Shaw, reveres Robert Benchley and admires Frank Capra more than any other Hollywood director. When the director "smiles, we call him 'Ted,' but when he's busy being a director his dignity calls for Mr. Steinmetz." It made clear he was no Bernie Szold. "Because he doesn't rant and tear his hair or clasp his brow and soulfully hiss 'Ah, Art!' he is very difficult to describe." It was a breezy, flattering profile for popular consumption. One of his actors, Glenn Cunningham, later recalled Steinmetz as "stiff, brusque."

The Prompter insights were well-timed. The director took the leading role in his next play, *Night Must Fall*. Steinmetz cast himself as Dan, the murderous maniac played by the author on Broadway. He smothers an old woman on stage and hides the head of another victim. Wilson found it "the most interesting production the Playhouse has offered in the past three seasons." The mystery "is why or how the play failed to please Nebraska's teachers who saw it last week."

High Tor brought Maxwell Anderson's blank verse back for the second straight season, and again it proved "a tricky hurdle," according to the reviewer. At times actors clicked off iambic pentameter in a "school boy cadence."

The year ended with the Big Apple Ball at the Music Box. To publicize the fund-raiser, planners posed with Johnny Goodman, the Omaha golfer who was the first and only amateur to win the U.S. Open. The event featured a dance contest, judged by Goodman, et al., and two swing bands. The ball chairman brought her big German shepherd to meet bandleader Dusty Rhodes at the train station.

Headlines declared, "Society En Masse Glimpsed at Big Apple Exhibition," and "Benefit Dance Shrinks Debt." Some 600 paid $1.20 to see teenage dancers win cash prizes. They did "Truckin', peckin', posin' and the Susie Q." "Gum seemed to help," the reporter noted. "Long bobs flew with the wind. Plaid skirts blurred as they whirled by. A man on his toes bent back until his hands touched the floor, and from this position he churned his arms alternately through the air."

Then came a famous 1937 flap with Alfred Lunt. Lunt and Fontanne brought *Idiot's Delight* to Omaha, courtesy of Mrs. Guiou's Drama League, but he left muttering about the mayor and those censorious "high-bosomed ladies."

The real culprits were two *World-Herald* pranksters, Adolph Schneider, one of the Actors Guild leaders, and Keith Wilson. They planted a carefully underlined script in Mayor Dan Butler's office. He reacted with the expected indignation when he read references to hanky-panky at Omaha's fictitious William Jennings Bryan Hotel. The mayor demanded censorship of allegedly lascivious lines, and others began taking sides. The show not only went on, but the Lunts "overplayed" the controversial lines and "the audience loved it," Wilson said. It wasn't the last theatrical moment for Mayor Butler, whose censorious eye would later glare at the Playhouse.

Editor's Dog on Cue, *Stage Door* Disappoints Reviewer

"Smart and well-behaved" were the sole requirements for the title role in *Storm Over Patsy,* Steinmetz advised. A well-behaved dog, that is, "a little terrier-type mongrel" was needed for the January play.

The director found a Skye terrier named Poco, "the pride of the B.F. Sylvester children." In other words, the dog belonged to the terror of the *World-Herald* newsroom, city editor Ben Sylvester. The pooch played the storm center without missing a cue. Wilson placed the mild comedy in the Scottish tradition of James Barrie. A pompous provost locks up Patsy when his owner can't pay the dog tax. As usual when dialect was needed, "our linguist" Mary Murray took part.

Wilson now used his Spotlight and Reel column in the *World-Herald* to catch up with Playhouse alums. The usual suspects popped up in Hollywood, the New York stage, network radio and other places. Rudyard Norton's absence from the Playhouse was not so distant—he was doing radio in Lincoln. Director Greg Foley was managing a clothing store in Rock Rapids, Iowa, after a stint with NBC radio. Hart Jenks taught in the University of Nebraska drama department, and several were studying dramatics—Polly Robbins in California and Dorothy McGuire in New York. Later in 1938 she'd take a key role in *Our Town.*

In March, a cast of thirty-five for *Stage Door* ranked among the largest in the theater's thirteen-year history. George Kaufman's collaboration with Edna Ferber, however, was stung with the headline, "Disappointing to Reviewer." Wilson liked the movie, but called the play "dull and unexciting." Then he added, "Of course, I must be wrong," citing Broadway success. The twenty women in the cast included Ak-Sar-Ben Queen Elizabeth Ann Davis, later known as Libby Lauritzen, the banking matriarch whose passing would be mourned seventy-five years later.

Playgoers disagreed with Wilson's thumbs-down, and the *World-Herald* vented their views under the headline, "Drama Critic 'On Pan' for Criticism of 'Stage Door.'" One woman ranked it "the best, by far, that the Playhouse has ever done. There were about a dozen in our party, and they all felt the same way."

A professor matched wits with a gangster in the sixth and final play, *Blind Alley*. Clarence Teal's professor and Guy Bandle's mobster were upstaged, according to the headline: "Agnes Krell as Gang Moll Steals Show." A photo showed her standing with a pistol over Teal and others bunched on the floor.

Raggedy Returns, Director Departs

The main season behind him, the director drew on 600 contenders from week-long auditions to double-cast fifty-six grade schoolers in his version of *Raggedy Ann and Andy* and *The Camel with the Wrinkled Knees*. In March, the Junior League had presented *Sleeping Beauty* on the Playhouse stage with the usual cast of young women. But Steinmetz toured fourteen public and parochial schools on week days, then met all Saturday with any youngsters who were missed.

With dozens in the casts, inevitably some would find fame.

Tish Baldrige in 1985.

That was certainly true of Letitia Baldrige, who ended up as White House chief of staff for Jackie Kennedy and author of books and columns on manners. Tish Baldrige had grown to six feet one inch by age 13, so she was too tall for the title Raggedy Ann, but was game enough to play a Tired Old Horse.

Lenke Isacson started an acting career that would reach beyond Omaha. She dreamed of being a concert pianist, but a friend talked her into attending a mass audition. "We were all a little afraid" of director Steinmetz, who seemed "severe," Lenke recalled. He reprimanded her when "I peeked out to see who was in the audience." That *Raggedy Ann* audience included Mrs. Howard Buffett and children. Her husband became a four-term congressman, her son Warren a billionaire with a penchant for witty prose who gained Wall Street fame as "The Oracle of Omaha."

Summer brought the resignation of Ted Steinmetz after a three-year stay.

He accepted an offer from the Community Theater of Indianapolis. Rumors of his leaving began back in February. As a result, forty applicants already sought the job, and two had been interviewed by Mrs. Guiou's committee.

As Steinmetz departed, the inevitable comparisons followed: "A soft-spoken, reserved man, his methods were different from his dynamic predecessor, Bernard Szold." Wilson praised his knowledge of theater, and Dr. Langdon's M.A. thesis added this summary years later: Although Steinmetz "trod a rather quiet path at the Playhouse, the general consensus seemed to be that he was efficient, dedicated and thorough." So he wasn't dynamic, but he did the first Shakespeare, replaced Shaw with Maxwell Anderson's blank verse and "attempted to elevate aesthetic taste," the thesis said. Unlike Foley and Szold, he didn't hide a bride, but waited until 1939 to marry an Omahan.

Director Giffen, From Yale via Duluth: 1938–1939

The fourth director's hiring helped the first one return to theater. Gordon Giffen left the Duluth Little Theater, and the Minnesotans hired Greg Foley to succeed him. Giffen, like Steinmetz, arrived at age 28 with a master's degree from Yale. And he also arrived after directing summer stock in New England. But he was married and the Giffens had a son, Peter Thomas, age three months when Mrs. Carpenter met them on her vacation in Cape Cod. She had stepped down after two years as board president, and Mrs. A.D. Dunn now led the trustees. Her husband was on the Creighton medical faculty, and she wrote program notes for the Omaha Symphony and was a Tuesday Musical organizer.

Giffen would stay four years before asking McDonald to recommend him to Frederick McConnell, the ex-Omahan heading the great Cleveland Playhouse. Written in 1942 as Giffen was leaving, McDonald's letter also serves as an overview of the upcoming years. It points out that he had been welcome to stay, but chose to go. However, it also revealed that Giffen left Duluth after division on the board made continuing "inadvisable."

"An able director," McDonald summed up, whose plays "are well-directed and produced, and with few exceptions have been satisfactory to our board and to our audience."

"He has worked smoothly with everyone. As you know," he reminded the legendary McConnell, the Playhouse has had four directors, which he named. "Of these I think Gordon has been all around the most satisfactory. He does not have the technical ability of Foley nor some of the color which Szold had, but he is a good combination of the two." The occasion, a recommendation sought by a job-seeker, certainly colored McDonald's view. But the comparison with past directors gives insight as the Giffen years begin.

Gordon and True Giffen didn't have the spotlight to themselves at a welcome tea. Henry Fonda showed up with his mother-in-law and talk turned from the Giffens' young son to Hank's eight-month-old daughter, Jane. He joked about his urge to pass her baby pictures around the room.

Another update on Playhouse alums quickly acquainted the new director with a proud heritage. Bob Brinkema had an apartment just off Broadway as he worked on World's Fair exhibits. Dow Fonda was appearing with Walter Huston, and Julann Caffrey had joined the New Yorkers. Adolph Schneider, Wilson's co-prankster in the Lunt flap, now worked for NBC news, while Hudson Shotwell, Louise Fitch and others continued stage and radio careers. Soon Shotwell, whose mother still performed with the Playhouse, would head to Hollywood.

Omahans learned more about Giffen when Keith Wilson filled a page of the season's first Prompter. He put himself in a bit of a bind as reviewer by reporting high praise of the new director and adding his own upbeat predictions for success, all in advance of the man's first local production. Still, it was impressive to hear strong endorsements from his Yale mentor, Alexander Dean, and from Duluth.

Giffen came on board with only two shows selected to start the season: *Tonight at 8:30,* three one-acts by Noel Coward, and a royal tragedy, *Masque of Kings*. On the Saturday before the October opening, Gertrude Lawrence stopped by to see preparations for the plays in which she co-starred with Coward. She was in town for a luncheon talk. Her speech was delayed as she repaired a three-inch rip in the front of her dress. She "pushed and jabbed" the needle, muttering that she was "hooking everything underneath the dress, too. You'd almost think it was a Caesarian."

Tragedy, Comedy, Then Realism of *Street Scene*

Masque of Kings, another Maxwell Anderson heavyweight, arrived in November as did *Mayerling*, the Charles Boyer film of the same historical episode. Crown Prince Rudolph revolts against his father, Emperor Franz Joseph of Austria, in 1899. He also mistrusts his wife, ala Othello, and leads to their mutual demise.

Both major roles, Eldon Anspach as Rudolph and Virgil Sharpe as Franz Joseph, "were acted expertly." Wilson singled out Anspach, calling him "an actor" when "few in these parts deserved to be called so." Anspach, who had performed with the Prairie Playmakers and Mrs. Doorly's Folio group, would become the first scenic designer employed full-time by the Playhouse, using a talent he'd later apply as a television pioneer.

Meanwhile, Ray Suber, the character actor of the many voices, was making it so big with NBC in Chicago that an item about his "fairy tale" success boasted that he now earned "more than $200 a week" in such soap operas as *Backstage Wife: the Story of Helen Trent*.

Dorothy McGuire also played in a radio drama, *Big Sister*, but was preparing to leave New York and go on the road with *Our Town*. She was quoted saying, "I was petrified when I first came to New York" until Damian O'Flynn took her in tow. "Damian was very nice. He told me all the agents to go to."

Another Omahan, Tom Kennedy who played Keats at the Playhouse, tipped her to the search for an understudy for Martha Scott, and the rest was history. War clouds in Europe didn't make the scrapbook, but worries about Genevieve Guiou, her daughter Echo and friend Sally Johnston visiting Germany did.

"Dig as deep as you care to go," began the review for the amiable English play, *George and Margaret*, and "you'll find nothing but frothy, funny comedy." Wilson went on to declare it "the most laughable evening I have spent there since I began reviewing some 20 plays back." Clarence Teal "has never done a better characterization than the amiable, absent-minded yet understanding father," and Christel Pratt was a "screamingly funny maid" without uttering a line. As Christel Pratt Kent she would become an enduring figure in community theater and music.

Mabel Baer was back in town, winning "many laughs in a Billie Burkeish mother role." Add future politician Glenn Cunningham as the arty, blasé brother and it's clear that the critic loved this stage family.

In January 1939, a Playhouse-sponsored talk by "the great lady of the theater" Maude Adams won a full-page spread, "Society Goes to a Lecture," flush with furs on women named Storz, Diesing and Brandeis. Many remembered Maude Adams fondly as the first Peter Pan. She had asked them if they believed in fairies, and they had shouted back, "Yes, yes." (A very young Rudyard Norton saw her and feared the pirates.)

Her audience, Wilson noted, included retired art dealer Milton Darling, who has "more star-autographed playbills than any man in town." The new year also brought Mrs. Guiou and Sally Johnston back, but Echo had found a job at the Berlin embassy, where a former Omahan assured her mother that he'd "take care of her." Halleck Rose would divorce his wife and marry Echo, who spent part of the 1940s with him in the Lisbon, Portugal, embassy. Sally Johnston married Tom Marshall, a descendant of Chief Justice John Marshall, and retained haunting memories of pre-war Nazi Berlin.

The urban realism of Elmer Rice's *Street Scene* required a two-story brownstone apartment sturdy enough for a cast of seventy milling in and about it. Among the passers-by in this "granddaddy of slum realism" was the director's wife, True Compton Giffen. "Her ill-fitting print dress and omnipresent baby carriage" brought laughs and the writer's call for Giffen to award her a meatier role.

Darling Daughter Faces Ban on Stage

Yes, My Darling Daughter was described as the story of "an ultra-modern young woman" who persuades her intended to share a weekend in a cabin. As its March opening neared at the Playhouse, the National Council of Decency rated it "C" for condemned. Then Mayor Dan Butler's welfare board banned the movie in Omaha the day before it was set to open at the Brandeis. Wilson wrote that he'd never heard of such a thing and wondered if Omaha could retitle it *No, My Darling Voters*. Actually, he had heard of such a thing. In 1937, "Mayor Butler's 200 huskies" stopped a stage performance of Erskine

Caldwell's *Tobacco Road* at the Paramount. Then, you'll recall, the mayor fumed at Lunt's *Idiot's Delight*.

That was two years ago. Now the press rained headlines about "Ban on Stage" and "May be Out at Playhouse," plus "Welfare Board to View Play Before Making Decision." It was, after all, the job of that board "to decide what plays and what movies are fit for Omaha audiences to see," reminded a *World-Herald* editorial. But that "tremendous power … must be exercised with the most solemn discretion. To an adult free citizen, censorship of any kind will always be repugnant." The newspaper made it clear "their personal opinions aren't worth a dime," questioning the board's competence "to pass upon the moral values of films and plays."

Mayor Butler was indignant. He promised "a showdown fight" over the air, rebuking the editorial and a cartoon. "Thank God we have the radio," he said. The *Herald* wasn't through with him. Butler attended a civic dinner in Norfolk and found the walls plastered with posters advertising the banned film's arrival there.

That same evening his welfare board previewed the play. Some, the news story said, "were squirming under their duties as censors." But Dr. A.A. Klammer said, "The play is even worse than the movie. There was nothing in the picture as bad as that last speech which referred to seduction." Pictures of five board members spilled the width of a newspaper page.

Chairman James Patton said, "The first act was fine; the second made me sleepy. Wake me up if I drop off during the last one." For the record, neither film nor play puts the couple side by side in bed. McDonald had defended the play by quoting Robert Benchley: "The cleanest play on Broadway and the frankest." The board spokesman added, "It is a fact that there is not a vulgar word, a dirty or insinuating line in the whole production." One defense backfired. McDonald mentioned that thirty-two Duchesne High students were ticket holders, and school officials promptly barred their attendance. On the other side of the fight, Omaha University students threatened to phone their protests to Mayor Butler, hourly, day and night.

Our American Cousin, 1939.

When all was said and done, the movie was approved after a slight change and no action was taken against the play. It wasn't surprising to read "the place was packed on opening night," under the headline, "Darling Daughter Proves Big Wow."

Musical *Our American Cousin* for No. 100

A nice touch of fence-mending helped publicize *Our American Cousin* in April. Portly Dan Butler, under the headline "Mayor Aids Drama," was shown buying a ticket. Given his desire to ban the previous play, one suspects a little sarcasm when the newspaper wrote, "Mayor Butler continued his interest in the drama today."

The hundredth production was billed as a play, a musical comedy, an operetta and "a musical version of the old play" by Tom Taylor. *Our American Cousin* was best known for the worst reason: Abraham Lincoln was watching it the night he was assassinated in a much earlier April. A thicker Prompter, full of the fourteen-year Playhouse history, credited the lyricist and composers who "turned the play into an operetta," but listed no songs.

Readers of this history know that none of the first productions fit the modern idea of the Broadway musical, often traced to *Oklahoma* in 1943. An early Prompter poked fun at the resistance to musicals, but the closest they came to musical theater fell short of an integrated form. Old period plays, *Fashion* and the temperance melodrama *Ten Nights in a Bar-room,* added popular songs of the era.

So why didn't an audience that enjoyed Clarence Teal singing "Little Brown Jug" get musicals from the Playhouse and other community theaters? All the answers would bring this story to a halt, but a few are obvious. It wasn't because they weren't popular. From Friml's *Rose-Marie* to Gershwin's *Porgy and Bess,* some musical theater was high-brow, called opera and operetta.

When *Our American Cousin* opened in Omaha, *Hellzapoppin* was setting a Broadway record run for a musical, broken a few years later by *Oklahoma*. With slapstick comics, Olson and Johnson, *Hellzapoppin* was on the low-brow side of musical theater: raucous vaudeville.

But, between the high-brow and low-brow, the 1930s were full of wonderful shows, not only by Gershwin, but Irving Berlin, Cole Porter, Jerome Kern, Harold Arlen, Rodgers and Hart. Their *Babes in Arms* aired such standards as "Funny Valentine" and "I Wish I Were in Love Again." Porter's *Anything Goes,* Berlin's *As Thousands Cheer* and Gershwin's *Of Thee I Sing* featured songs still sung in the twenty-first century. However, rights to these great shows weren't readily available, and they were costly to mount.

When rights weren't the problem, they weren't done much in high schools and colleges because they required collaboration between two separate departments—music and drama. The music people did operettas, the drama teachers did plays. In the Omaha area, no local group was regularly presenting musical theater in the late 1930s.

In 1944, Dick Walter started the Civic Music Association in Council Bluffs. Better known in the 1950s as the man who brought *My Fair Lady* and other Broadway musicals to Omaha, Walter and his Civic

Music friends presented the likes of *Desert Song, Student Prince* and other operettas. Opera Omaha would later thrive in the future.

The Playhouse would stage Gilbert and Sullivan's *The Gondoliers* in 1940 and their first show billed as a musical comedy in 1941.

In spring 1939, however, the Playhouse was still a one-man band, no dance or music expert on the staff. Giffen went back to their roots for help with *Our American Cousin*. His musical director was Eloise West McNichols, one of the West Sisters String Quartette that accompanied both the variety night and *The Enchanted Cottage*, those first shows in 1925. Dances were credited to Rita Davlin and the director's wife, True Giffen. The most familiar cast member was Clarence Teal who left "the audience limp," the reviewer said, with his mournful rendition of "Tottering Toward My Grave." The minor role of Georgina "revealed that Christel Pratt has an unusually fine voice."

An old joke claimed John Wilkes Booth was actually aiming at the cast, so it wasn't surprising that Wilson called it "one of the corniest plays in the history of the American Theater. The entertaining quality of the show is due chiefly to the music." The villain, Fred Segur, was hissed when he delivered those immortal lines: "Heh, heh, heh, revenge is mine! Your daughter's hand or I'll foreclose the mortgage."

Many Playhouse newcomers were identified by their musical backgrounds. For example, Harold Clizbe had returned to Council Bluffs after singing for the Fibber McGee radio show in Chicago. As a drunkard, he "brings down the house with his comic waltz and his song, 'The Tears in the Eyes of Poor Maw.'" Clizbe would perform in those Civic Music operettas and continue in theater for the next half century.

So Giffen and company rolled them in the aisles to cap his successful first season.

Our American Cousin drew the largest audience, *Yes, My Darling Daughter* the smallest, despite its notoriety. In May, *Jack and the Beanstalk* came to the Playhouse stage. Then the trustees ruled that they could "no longer provide a production facility" for the Junior

League children's plays. The young players moved to Tech High where they continued in the 1940s.

That interesting year, with threat of a banned play and then the hundredth show, added excitement in May when John Barrymore came to town with Dorothy McGuire in the cast of *My Dear Children*. Otto Preminger was the director and Barrymore's young wife, Elaine Barrie, played his temperamental daughter. But she wasn't the problem. A generous reporter referred to Barrymore's fatigue, but others blamed booze for "the worst and most unpredictable performance of his life." Wilson's review said he ad-libbed his way through the play "with profanity and risque remarks." Mrs. Guiou told a reporter, "I considered it a perfectly disgraceful performance."

And what of Omaha's young Dorothy? She soon left the tour, which some described as Barrymore's "dramatic swan song." Before her Omaha performance, she gushed to a reporter that Barrymore "is the most wonderful person I've ever met. Positively dynamic." Begging exhaustion, Barrymore snoozed after the final curtain. On awakening, he returned her compliment: "I've never acted with anyone more completely enchanting … the most dextrous young person I've ever known."

If such an exchange smacks of show-biz schmoozing, Dorothy's answer to another question was simple enough:

Reporter: "Just how much do you think the Playhouse contributed to your success?"

Dorothy McGuire: "Why, everything!"

She had a question for the reporter: "Does the Playhouse still have that unique smell? I can still remember it."

He concluded, "I assured her it did. Seems that other grease paint and pine lumber doesn't smell the same to her." In a photograph, she was seen showing Barrymore her Playhouse scrapbook.

Our Town Opens, Shaw Returns: 1939–1940

The only more famous alum, Henry Fonda, filled an entire page of the rotogravure section with sepia pictures from infancy to *Kiss for Cinderella* and now as *Young Mr. Lincoln*. He had already been cast as Tom Joad in *Grapes of Wrath*. The play-reading committee, still headed by Mrs. Guiou, may have been influenced by Miss McGuire's recent Broadway success when they selected *Our Town* to open the fifteenth season. Giffen returned from summer stock in Connecticut to cast himself as the Stage Manager in the Thornton Wilder classic.

Mrs. Guiou had promised that *Our Town* would be "the most unusual and beautiful play ever produced by the Playhouse," and Wilson's review said it "equals or surpasses that rash estimate." Orchestrating it all was a pipe-smoking Giffen, "Giff" in Wilson's laudatory review.

The Dorothy McGuire role went to Eileen Zevitz, a South High girl, and Larry McNichols, 10, played her brother. The son of musician Eloise West McNichols first performed as Clarence Teal's son in *Blind Alley,* the last play directed by Steinmetz. At a tender age, McNichols could compare Giffen and his predecessor. His memories seventy years later? Steinmetz was a "taskmaster," Teal was "wonderful, like a father to me," and Giffen tolerated his precocious habit of prompting others' lines.

November saw Shaw return with *Candida*. Virginia Skinner Boyer won the title role with Lawrence Forsythe as Reverend Morell. Back from Broadway and network radio work, Forsythe had performed with the likes of Katharine Hepburn. A young Creighton professor, Donald Luttrell, took a role, the poet Eugene Marchbanks, that later would introduce Mrs. Brando's boy Marlon to Broadway.

They skipped the usual December show and scheduled four in the first months of 1940, starting with John Galsworthy's *The Roof* in January. "A stew-bum sets fire to a hotel for the fun of it" summarized the play previously seen only in London. Giffen did some rewriting and consulted technical experts on staging fire and smoke that chases the characters, floor-by-floor, until they flee to the rooftop. Advance teasers insisted that several actors looked like Hollywood stars—Allison Flynn "looks a lot like Errol Flynn," and so on. The return of Echo Guiou won some attention for her NBC radio experience with Jimmy Fidler and her job with the Berlin embassy.

Wilson called the smoke and fire effects "excellent," but added the needling notion that where there's smoke, there's also "the fragrance of roasted ham."

Another English play, *Bachelor Born,* had an unsympathetic headmaster known as "The Egg." Glenn Cunningham, then executive secretary of the Junior Chamber of Commerce, "played 'The Egg' without a trace of ham," said Wilson's latest food metaphor.

Edward Darnell caused the biggest stir. He was back from the West Coast, where he won roles in two films and the Pasadena Playhouse. His Sir Berkeley Nightingale tells the housemaster: "This rowing is a bit silly … eight boys in an insecure boat … all facing one way and progressing in another. They ought to be in government."

Sarah Joslyn's Final Gift: Mortgage-free Property for a Dollar

As February 1940 drew to an end, so did the life of Sarah Joslyn. Joslyn Museum closed the day of her funeral, which was held in her castle home across 40th Street from the Playhouse. John and Alan McDonald, who designed the museum, served as pallbearers. When death came to Mrs. Joslyn, she was still owed $15,000 by the theater's building association.

Her estate put the castle and the Playhouse mortgage in the hands of the Society of Liberal Arts, which directed the Joslyn Memorial museum. Family members were said to hope that her home would become a branch of the museum. As for the theater, "Playhouse officials say interest payments have been kept up to date," it was reported. No further public announcement was made about matters vital to the future of the property where cows once grazed.

Negotiations began in the summer of 1941 between the mortgage-holding Society and the building association, still headed by McDonald. The $15,000 note came due in 1941, and the Society of Liberal Arts didn't want to extend it. McDonald's board promised to replace the heating system and improve ventilation if the Society surrendered the mortgage.

The resulting agreement was not easily tracked when the Playhouse was ready to move in the late 1950s. But the deed was apparently delivered to the building board in August 1941. As Clarence Teal explained the transaction to a later historian, the $15,000 was forgiven and the property sold to the Playhouse Building Association for one dollar.

Meanwhile, two shows remained in the season: Robert Sherwood's *The Petrified Forest* and the musical *The Gondoliers* by Gilbert and Sullivan. "Giff," as Wilson continued to dub the director, was now sporting a beard, a "sensational Golden Spike Days beaver" described as a cross between "Orson Welles and the Man Who Came to Dinner."

Duke Mantee, the *Petrified Forest* movie's killer made famous by Humphrey Bogart, was portrayed on stage by Russ Baker. Gone four years to do ten Broadway plays and some network radio, he came back as dramatic director for WOW. The reviewer found Mantee "menacing as ever." Tom Kennedy was also fresh from Broadway and from Orson Welles Mercury Theater of the Air, famous for its War of the Worlds Halloween scare. Cast earlier as John Keats, he now played the "world-weary intellectual" who asks Mantee to kill him.

The comic opera *Gondoliers* closed the season in May, but not before Omahans learned that it required "a record amount of work" by volunteers. Emmy Gifford designed both sets and costumes.

For *Gondoliers* the *World-Herald* followed the usual Wilson review with the byline of music critic August Borglum, the half-brother of the Mt. Rushmore sculptor. (Before converting to Catholicism, their Mormon father wed two wives.) Wilson said Omaha was "starving" for Gilbert and Sullivan, and after this production "a good many will vote" to make their works an annual event. The staid Borglum determined that the performance "proved very convincing from the musical standpoint." He gave first mention to Kathleen Shaw Miller and Dorothy Haugh (Casilda and Gianetta) for "their beautiful velvety voices and high tones, which gave distinction and brilliancy."

Kathleen had appeared in that original Council Bluffs play, *The Money-Changers,* and taught music at Abraham Lincoln High School. Dorothy was a young soloist at Dundee Presbyterian Church. So Gilbert and Sullivan brought new blood to the Playhouse, including young Kermit Hansen. He would serve honorably in World War II, take a leading role in Ak-Sar-Ben coronations, and serve as a University regent.

Hesitant About Nazis, Then Toe-Stubbing: 1940–1941

A drama about Nazis in America posed some problems as it opened the season in autumn 1940. The director sensed that actors were hesitant to play Nazis, and an artist agreed to do a bust of Hitler, but secretly to avoid suspicion of disloyalty. Swastika flags proved hard to find.

Clare Boothe wrote *Margin for Error* before she married Henry Luce of Time-Life fame. Wilson added it to the director's successes, but the string broke in November. "For the first time since Gordon Giffen took over, the Community Playhouse last night stubbed its toe." Actors and the director "swung hard at some scenery-less, impressionistic drama and came up with something that can rate no better than a good try." If that wasn't clear, he also complained about "a distressing lack of entertainment."

The toe-stubbing also involved combining three works by distinguished playwrights: William Saroyan's *My Heart's in the Highlands,* Thornton Wilder's *Happy Journey* and *Air Raid* by Archibald MacLeish. Wilson blamed himself "as one who has shouted" for "more experimental drama." The evening of short plays was first planned to pair Saroyan with Wilder. But the Giffens had stayed in Omaha as True awaited the birth of their daughter in September. That gave the director time to direct a visual version of the radio play *Air Raid* at Omaha University in mid-August and later add it.

Lenke aka Lenka, Other Teens Win Honors

The December comedy put the Playhouse back on the entertainment track. *Rarely Fatal* by Florence Ryerson and Colin Clements earned seven curtain calls on opening night, and at season's end took all the acting honors for the first Fonda-McGuire awards.

Three Central High students wowed the crowd then and took home the trophies later. Russell Gast won for Chuck, too focused on making a glider fly to think about romance, and a tie vote honored both Mary Joan Evans and Lenke Isacson. Evans, "a pretty and vivacious little girl" made coherent "a flood of tumultuous adolescent chatter."

Wilson called Lenke "a Nordic miss with a flock of charm and an expressive face." She found acting fame later as Lenka Peterson. Casting the Irwin Shaw play *Gentle People* brought out the old "all walks of life" claim as the Playhouse called for any "butcher, baker and candlestick maker" to audition. The story dealt with two old men deprived of happiness by a violent racketeer. Veterans Mark Levings and Broadway trouper Lulu Nethaway joined such newcomers as Lyle DeMoss, a radio and then television pioneer who would later hire Johnny Carson at WOW-TV. "Incidental performances" by DeMoss, a bankrupt merchant sweating in a Russian bath, and others "stand out more impressively than those of the leads." Wilson complained, "We out front enjoy the play more if the actors know their lines."

Before the next play, the Playhouse-sponsored Cuban Fiesta, a fundraiser like their previous Big Apple, but this time a rumba contest at the Music Box. The press treated it as a major social event with photos of Echo Guiou dancing with Larry Forsythe. She joined in a conga line that wound around the dance floor after an exhibition by the Arthur Murray dancers.

First Show Billed as Musical Comedy: *Knickerbocker Holiday*

May brought more than flowers. Clarence Teal joined the board of trustees, starting a long run of offstage service, especially as treasurer. And for the first time the theater billed a production as a musical comedy.

Knickerbocker Holiday by Maxwell Anderson with music by Kurt Weill had no orchestra, just two pianists and a chorus directed by Fred Segur. He also played Washington Irving, the author whose tales of Dutch New York inspire the show. Some Weill music was unavailable, so original tunes for Anderson's lyrics were supplied by the Segurs and two Omaha brothers, Edward and Warren Berryman.

The first musical comedy deserved a guest star, Joy Hodges Doorly. She'd played the ingénue with George M. Cohan in *I'd Rather Be Right* on Broadway, then made "Baby Sandy" films and others in Hollywood. And she was married to Henry and Margaret Hitchcock Doorly's son Gilbert. She helped end a mixed season on "the upbeat," Wilson wrote. The production's "color and zest" are "sparked by Miss Hodges' singing, Ted Haas' Barrymorish mugging" and strong choral support.

Haas was Governor Stuyvesant, the autocratic Dutchman, and Donald Reisser played his rival, "the first American," Brom Broeck. Playwright Anderson expected audiences to sympathize with Brom, but Weill gave the aging Stuyvesant the most sympathetic number. "September Song" went on to become a standard, with everyone from Nelson Eddy to Jimmy Durante singing the "long, long way from May to December." Unnoticed was a 16-year-old high school student singing in the ensemble. She called herself Mary Lou, a name she adopted from a popular song. Using her given name, Julie Wilson, she became the cabaret star of the Oak Room at Manhattan's Algonquin Hotel and retold her Mary Lou story at age 69 during a Lincoln Center tribute shared with the likes of Rosemary Clooney, Judy Collins and Lena Horne.

A soldier in the cast would play a large role in the theater's future. Ed Owen would not only become a trustee, but with his wife, Dee, would bring financial and other support to the Playhouse.

Henry Fonda joined cousin Dow, who'd played in *Knickerbocker Holiday* on Broadway, during the rehearsals. That's when news spread that he'd sponsor those acting awards with Dorothy McGuire. The Fonda-McGuire awards went to "the best new actor and actress," which explains why young Gast won instead of the much-praised Lawrence Krell.

Clarence Teal proposed a one-act play competition, and an advertising man told the board many Omahans "are under the illusion the Playhouse is a 'social' affair." They don't realize tickets are "for sale to everyone." Board president Mrs. Loucks announced "a reversal of policy in that hereafter we will try to make a broader appeal to the Omaha public."

More ominous than the state of the Playhouse was the state of the world. Teal had written in the May Prompter, "In at least 12 European countries the theaters are blacked out." He urged readers to keep "drama alive in all its dignity" by backing his season ticket campaign.

Bombs Drop as *George Slept Here*: 1941–1942

The seventeenth season would bring the bombing of Pearl Harbor as Mary Peckham and others rehearsed *George Washington Slept Here*. Even while more young men left for war, the experimental Laboratory Group mounted a special production. And the season turned out to be the final one for Gordon Giffen, whose departure for the Dock Theatre in Charleston paved the way for a larger figure in the Playhouse story.

These eventful times followed what would be remembered as the last "normal" summer for years to come.

Perhaps the beating of war drums in September 1941 explains the headlines, "Light Plays Chosen" and "Comedies Will Predominate." For pure creature comfort, the biggest news as *The Male Animal* opened was the "new and more adequate heating and ventilating system" just completed as part of the deal that August with the Joslyn deed.

"The new system will give the actors a break also—being more quiet."

If *The Male Animal* by New Yorker cartoonist James Thurber wasn't light enough, November's *Brief Music* by Emmet Lavery was another college comedy with an all-girl cast, seven co-eds named Lovely, Drizzle, Spiff, Jinx, Rosey, Maggie and Minnie. As war neared, the men were off to boot camp, but others returned to Omaha. A backstage stalwart, Erna Reed Ayers, was home sharing costume duties with Mabel Baer while her husband, Lt. Philip Ayers flew for the Army Air Corps in England.

The Giffens co-directed Saroyan's *Jim Dandy*, the Laboratory Group's one-night stand to celebrate the tenth anniversary of the Joslyn Museum. The reviewer admitted, "I have very little idea of what Saroyan is getting at in 'Jim Dandy,' providing he is getting at anything." The actors included Daniel O'Connor, son of Omaha's fire chief. He'd marry Lenke (Lenka Peterson) Isacson and produce news for NBC television.

It's hard to imagine watching *George Washington Slept Here* the day after Japanese bombs fell on Pearl Harbor. At the final rehearsal on Dec. 7, 1941, Mary Peckham, a newcomer who became a Playhouse legend, exited the stage and heard a little news boy shouting, "We're at war. The Japs bombed Pearl Harbor."

But a review treated the opening as if nothing had overshadowed the bucolic comedy by Kaufman and Hart, an "old chestnut about the mortgage due on Tuesday." Mrs. Peckham was Annabelle, "a study in vitriol and molasses, a city matron with scorn for the simple life." She'd win the next Fonda-McGuire award, her first of many.

Green Grow the Lilacs Inspires *Oklahoma*

Although Wilson didn't mention World War II in his December 9 review, its shadow soon covered American life. Mrs. Carpenter, as divisional chairman of the Seventh Corps Area, promised to bring plays from community theaters in the Midwest to soldiers. "We all realize entertainment and recreation are an important part of the morale of the Army," she said.

Giffen publicized his next play, *Green Grow the Lilacs,* by suggesting, "What we need right now is material for all these soldiers, skits, novelty songs, dance material—anything that's good and in written form. We need somebody to fiddle these old tunes and call the dances. He doesn't have to be an Uncle Ezra type, but it would help."

It was a play about Oklahoma, he explained, "full of old songs and country dances." Just a year later the play became *Oklahoma* and started a nearly six-year run on Broadway, a landmark in the history of musical theater and the first of nine collaborations by Rodgers and Hammerstein. The Playhouse *Green Grow the Lilacs* introduced Omahans to Curley and Laurey, Aunt Eller and Ado Annie.

Reviewer Jake Rachman, later the replacement for critic Wilson, wrote, "Curley, a clean cowboy type, sang prairie songs, prodded hesitant dogies and finally married Laurey. Libby Davis Lauritzen does the moody young bride well … and Lenke Isacson contributes one of the best juvenile bits as Ado."

As Elizabeth Davis, "she served a full apprenticeship" in Junior League children's plays and on the Playhouse technical staff. The Davis and Lauritzen families led Omaha's largest bank, First National. Libby pleaded with her parents, "Please, wait until later in the week to come," so they saw the fourth performance on Thursday. Not yet the musical comedy that broke all the records, it already had dancing. "They did kind of a hoedown, square dance thing," Mrs. Lauritzen recalled.

Ed and Dee Owen, a couple that played a minor backstage role for *Green Grow the Lilacs*, took a more prominent part in the next play, *Mr. and Mrs. North*. The mystery-comedy found him as stage manager doubling as "medical examiner" while Dee co-chaired "hand properties."

"Our heavy spring dew with its slush and chill air" was blamed by Wilson for a small mid-March turnout, but "the scant audience forgot the dreary weather and laughed wholeheartedly." He gave a glimpse of the box office attendant, noting "Mrs. Tunnicliff was her usual cheerful self but she wasn't having much to do" after switching reservations all afternoon. The reviewer particularly enjoyed Dr. Cleveland Simkins, Creighton anatomy professor, as "the first bright police detective in the history of the theater." *Mr. and Mrs. North* was also performed at Fort Crook for soldiers stationed there.

War Threatens Playhouse, Director Giffen Departs

The season's final show would end Gordon Giffen's four-year run as director of the Playhouse. But before its April 27 opening, the trustees met to decide if plays should "discontinue for the duration of the war." A spokesman claimed "unprecedented interest" in the theater, but that was for public consumption. Only about 1,100 season memberships were sold. A letter from Genevieve Guiou, now board secretary, listed five suggestions from the executive committee from discontinuing plays for the duration of the war to operating part-time. These dramatic actions were not taken, but World War II would force other changes in the next season.

Meanwhile, *You Can't Take It With You* opened as the Prompter promised, "War or no war, people insist that the Playhouse continue its normal functions."

The cast included Penny Pennington, who played a xylophone, and such familiar actors as Christel Pratt and both Krells. Giffen played Paul Sycamore and Anspach, his technician, was the Russian ballet master. The review notes some dating, however. When Krell's Grandpa asks what the government does with his tax money, "Today he'd just explain about General McArthur needing planes, and let it go at that."

The Giffen family headed east in May, True and the two boys by train, Giff and the two dachshunds, Madchen and Willie, by car. They would return only to pack for Charleston, S.C., and the Dock Street Theatre. This was "good news to his thousands of friends here," Wilson said in his column, "and sad news, too, because it will be difficult to replace him." Good directors are scarce, he noted, especially with many of the younger ones in the military.

The new board president, Clarence Teal, had experienced help seeking a successor—Mrs. Guiou, as usual, chaired the search committee.

Kendrick Wilson Starts Record Run as Director: 1942–1943

The first full season with the world at war brought changes large and small. Fewer than 1,000 season tickets were sold and 100 were the half-priced student tickets. Single admissions were now available for all six plays. And soldiers were guests for Monday preview performances.

The new director had not arrived when a postcard announced tryouts for *Prologue to Glory,* dramatizing the young manhood of Abraham Lincoln. Kendrick Wilson was expected in from Minnesota, and casting of forty-four men and ten women was scheduled.

"Echoing the sentiments of young ladies," a news story said,

Director Kendrick Wilson.

director Wilson asked, "Where can you find 44 men in times like these?" He called a quick conference with the board and the play was changed to *Ladies in Retirement.* So he was welcomed with this lead sentence: "Kendrick Wilson is in Omaha looking for a man who can act like a heel, six talented woman and a place to live." In fact, five plays announced earlier were all dumped for shows with fewer male roles, such as Clare Boothe's *The Women.*

The "breathless abruptness" of his hiring was the first Omahans had heard of the new director. Wilson would stay, after an absence for military service, until 1967, serving longer than his four predecessors combined. Playhouse workers and audience would come to know him well, but the immediate message focused on the decision that "left Mr. Wilson himself fairly gasping."

He told a reporter, "This is faster than I've ever seen it done before." President Teal was all business. "Mr. Wilson liked us. We like the things he has done. So we decided to team up," he said. Mrs. Guiou "nodded assent."

Among the things he'd done was share an alma mater, the University of Minnesota, with Teal. Though only 32, Wilson claimed twelve years' experience. At age 19, he toured with a tent company, and at 20 he began directing the St. Paul "Y" Players. At 25 while courting his future wife, Leslie, he landed a summer job in Itasca Park, and that became their honeymoon. He'd been on the university theater staff and directed summer stock and industrial films.

During the 1940–1941 season, he directed the St. Paul Little Theater. "One season, successful though it was," was enough, said the October Prompter. "Too many strangling influences made his directorship a hollow thing." The item concluded, "He is very even-tempered, an artist with common sense, a fine director—but one who hates to talk about himself. You can take my word—I know him quite well. You see, I've been married to him for seven years." With that revelation, no byline was needed to identify the profiler as Leslie Wilson. She served as makeup artist for the opening play.

Ken Wilson wasn't shy about making demands. He not only changed plays on his first day on the job, he complained about the "filthy condition" of the theater after being closed all summer. The next day he saw a scrub woman mopping away. He took advantage of her willingness and "gave her orders all day," he told a reporter years later. "At the end everything was spick and span. By that time she was exhausted and pretty dirty and her hair was falling down over her face." But the cleaning woman said she'd return when needed.

"Just then a big, black, shiny limousine pulled up. A chauffeur got out and opened the door, and my 'scrub woman' got in." She was Mrs. Phillip Ayers, a new addition to the Playhouse board. "That's the kind of cooperation I've had," he noted.

No scenic designer was credited for *Ladies in Retirement*, but cast member Mary Peckham recalled, "In the first play he did just about everything himself. I remember that the fireplace in one set didn't suit him. So the night before our opening he didn't go to bed at all in order to repaint every brick."

As for his wife's word on temperament, the later article with the anecdotes on the scrub woman and the fireplace said, "Though even-tempered, when something displeases him beyond endurance he emits an anguished groan and follows with an exaggeratedly calm explanation of what the actor did and what he is supposed to do. It's the kind of dressing down a mother gives a naughty 3-year-old."

Ladies, *Women*, Then Wilsons Take Stage

Then Frances McChesney, Central High drama teacher and the future Mrs. Key, played "the grim Victorian spinster who sneaked up behind her employer on strangulation bent," the reviewer wrote of *Ladies in Retirement*. "And the soldier boys who saw Miss McChesney appear out of the shadows to give Mrs. (Virginia) Ashburn the rope treatment last night" witnessed a "magnificent" scene, as critic Wilson found director Wilson's first effort "unquestionably entertaining."

When Wilson rehearsed *The Women*, the press warned, "Not one man will dare show his face on the Playhouse stage for a solid week." Photos presented many of the forty-four in its cast: One was receiving a manicure. A "home-wrecker deluxe" held a phone in her bubble bath, two shared a bed and three faced a mirror in "the climactic powder room scene." Author Clare Boothe was now Mrs. Luce and a congresswoman from Connecticut. Her play's cast ranged from dowager and debutante to negligee model and cigarette girl, from Playhouse newcomers to such veterans as Mrs. Alfred Brown and Beatrice Hoel Farrell.

The review was headlined, "Glossy Felines, Obstetrics and Sex," hinting that Mrs. Luce and her women proved too much for Keith Wilson in his last review before moving to the editorial page. "I think the audience couldn't believe its ears at first. Never has sex been discussed so much nor has the Playhouse been the obstetrical clinic it was last night." Now Omahans who'd seen the film were seeing in person "a particularly revolting breed of glossy feline."

Recall that this reviewer defended the Playhouse against the mayor's censors, but now was being more narrowly male than prudish. He felt the audience adjusted to the obstetrics and laughed often, though not when the marriage of the lead woman was being destroyed.

His last Spotlight and Reel column took a titillating look at blonde Beverly Wiechel in that bathtub. On stage, she "was giving voice to Clare Boothe's lines and concealing, as far as a bathtub will permit, her own." He praised her bathing scene, and quoted Beverly: "Suddenly I began to feel chilly. I knew something must be wrong. It was. I'd kicked the plug out." She heard technician Anspach whisper hoarsely, 'Quick, somebody bring me a mop.'" She finished her phone call and the curtain came down before the stage was flooded.

The next play scheduled was *Broadway,* but the director dropped it. The newspaper noted "casting difficulties," but Ken Wilson was candid in the Prompter: It was evident after four sessions of readings, he said, "that I was not going to obtain a top-notch cast." So he sold the play-reading committee on *The Dark Tower,* a "gory melodrama."

Both Wilsons, the director and wife Leslie, also took roles. Her Hattie the maid "got a particularly fine audience response," the new reviewer wrote. "Kendrick Wilson's playing of the play producer ... made him a versatile personage around the Playhouse." Reviewer Jake Rachman said, since the victim is an abusive Svengali, "You feel glad about the murder."

Rachman, a bachelor devoted to his widowed mother, was a stoop-shouldered, rumpled fellow, no fashion-plate. Already known for his Town Tattler column, he would cover show business and write reviews until his death in 1952. Then, an official of the movie operators union said, "The word 'critic' in connection with Jake just does not sound right." Hedda Hopper called him "one of the kindest men in show business." A tireless worker who "could never be persuaded to take a vacation," Rachman would spare the Playhouse any references to "toe-stubbing."

Wilson's Honeymoon Over, *Family Portrait* Offends Catholics

Family Portrait earned its place in Playhouse history for more reasons than the controversy over its portrayal of the family of Jesus Christ. The press had fun with the presence of the entire Teal family—Clarence, Val and the three boys, John, Peter and Topper, the youngest at age five. His mother was played by Joan McCague, a teenager in her first Playhouse performance. She would appear on local stages over the next sixty years, primarily as Joan Hennecke, but in February 1942, she was identified as "another of Miss Mac's pupils." That is, a student of Frances McChesney at Central High. Her teacher played Mary Magdalene, and her friend Lenke Isacson joined the cast.

"At least five Catholics dropped out of the cast," Mrs. Hennecke recalled, "and they came and got us—Lenka and me" and three others. Not every Catholic quit after the archdiocesan newspaper declared, "The Omaha Community Playhouse has forfeited all rights to expect Catholic support." Catherine Flynn stayed.

The complaint, as expressed by Bishop Ryan's official publication, the weekly *True Voice,* centered on the play's "theory that Mary, the Mother of Christ, was not a virgin and that she had other children besides Our Lord." This was termed "manifestly offensive to every Catholic," and to non-Catholics as well. The editorial pointed out that rehearsals began five days before Christmas, that Playhouse president Teal was told on January 6 that the play was "sacrilegious in the eyes of Catholics," and that many "courteous protest" letters followed from priests and institutions. The writer suggested that all this came early enough to stop production, but the board waited until January 26 to meet and go ahead with the February 2 opening. "In so doing they have grossly and consciously outraged the religious sentiments of Omaha's 60,000 Catholics."

Among the offended must have been the Playhouse publicist, Hugh Fogarty, who resigned as trustee. He had still handled publicity for the season's earlier plays, but was replaced by Beatrice Farrell starting with *Family Portrait*. Fogarty, later managing editor of the *Herald*, then worked in public relations for Creighton University, a source of one of those protest letters. He most likely wrote that letter and informed the Catholic response, which showed inside knowledge of board decision-making.

Teal had mailed a letter "To the Reverend Gentlemen of the Clergy," and ministers had attended two rehearsals. "Pastors Give Play Approval" headed a story about endorsements "from numerous Protestant pulpits" and a support letter signed by eight ministers led by Dr. Elwood Rowsey of Dundee Presbyterian Church. Teal's mailing urged the clergy to promote attendance as "an honest story of mother love."

The Prompter cover cited scripture from St. Mark, and an announcement next to the cast listing said, "It is regrettable that a controversial interpretation of the Bible forms the basis about which the play revolves, but patrons of the Playhouse know that our productions are presented solely from the standpoint of dramatic entertainment." After noting that the play did not necessarily reflect the beliefs of board members, it concluded, "We sincerely hope no offense is taken since, certainly, none is intended."

"Nonsense," snapped the Catholic weekly. "This is an offensive play and offense is taken." Teal was "called on the carpet" at Northwestern Bell, his son John recalled, but later received an apology. Tom (Topper) Teal said his parents even talked about leaving Omaha, and a few Catholic friends stopped speaking to them.

Jake Rachman's review stayed out of the fray. "Aside from any controversial aspect of this play, which we are reporting solely as drama, it seems that director Kendrick Wilson has achieved a remarkable effect, one of the best that we have witnessed at the Playhouse." He focused on Mary Peckham, who "plays Mary with a simple reverence." While Christ never appears, "you feel His presence. It is a remarkable piece of dramaturgy, splendidly and intelligently acted and directed."

When all was said and done, *Family Portrait* drew nearly 400 of the $1.50 single admissions, the largest total for the season.

Wartime Bataan to *Punkin Creek* at 1:30 a.m.

Perhaps the wartime theme of the next play, Maxwell Anderson's *The Eve of St. Mark*, turned down the heat on the Playhouse. Certainly the war's impact could be seen again in the casting.

Three more of Miss Mac's protégés from Central High, including Lenke Isacson, played older characters. And elderly Charles Docherty, who'd acted for all five directors, brought his forty years of experience to the role of a rugged sergeant. Charles Gray, the next Playhouse performer to try Hollywood, played a soldier stricken with malaria. He's aided by America Pilkington, the Puerto Rican wife of Colonel George Pilkington. She was in Omaha while her husband served overseas.

It's already apparent that Rachman will accentuate the positive. He praises many, but notes of Lenke only that she "makes an extremely youthful fiancée." *The Eve of St. Mark* ran an extended eight performances at the Playhouse, then once more for the soldiers at Fort Crook, which had supplied uniforms and equipment.

If patriotism didn't dim the memory of controversy, the closing play would only offend those with small appetite for corn. *Aaron Slick from Punkin Creek* was billed as the most-produced play in America, rustic and royalty-free, a bucolic comedy as clean and virtuous as any Toby show of the nineteenth century. Apparently, a good time was had by all.

David Majors, a fixture in Omaha music circles for the next half century, directed a nine-piece orchestra that accompanied vaudeville acts. Wilson was no fan of musicals, but his first season was ending in Giffen's style with variety acts tacked on. Walt Graham did magic, and Scampy Quigley sang "Alice Blue Gown." Beverly Weichel, the blonde home-wrecker of *The Women,* added accordion-playing to her bathtub-posing, while cast as "a sweet young thing." *Aaron Slick* became the answer to a trivia question: What play was performed at 1:30 a.m.? Why? To entertain the swing shift from the Martin Bomber Plant, a nearby factory that assembled military aircraft including the famous Enola Gay.

Wilson's first season ended with an upbeat news story. Single admissions helped leave a $375 balance. Trustees decided, "If conditions are no worse in the fall, the new season will start as usual." They wanted Wilson back, "but he may enter armed service."

Uncle Sam Gets Ken, Beatrice Subs at Eleventh Hour: 1943–1944

Summer once more brought good and bad news. The world premiere of *Claudia* came to Omaha with the film's title star, Dorothy McGuire, repeating her Broadway role. She invited all seven Fonda-McGuire award winners as her guests, but Dorothy herself couldn't make it—she and other Hollywood figures were busy with a savings bond drive. Many from the Playhouse joined Governor Dwight Griswold and the star's grandparents, Mr. and Mrs. Andy Trapp, at the premiere. The

Claudia showing sold out, raising about $3,000 for the *World-Herald*'s Smokes for Service Men fund.

So the good news was that proceeds would buy 1,320,000 cigarettes, "enough for a smoke for every other American overseas." Stifle that cough. As for Dorothy's first big film role, Jake Rachman assured her Playhouse friends that "any misgivings" about her transition from stage to screen "may be calmed. All the charming naiveté, the piquancy and relish" of her character survived. Adding to the good news was word of Miss McGuire's marriage to John Swope, son of the president of General Electric and a buddy of Henry Fonda. Capt. Jimmy Stewart was best man.

The bad news that same August was reported in blunt terms: "Uncle Sam Got Him," and probably won't let Kendrick Wilson go "until the end of the war." He would soon leave for Ft. Leavenworth in Kansas.

The season was set to open with the detective story *I Killed the Count*, and with a new director, Kenneth W. Turner. He met with the board in late August, came to Omaha in early September and quit before the season opening. This latest and short-lived Ken "resigned to re-enter educational work," president Teal said. What started as a swift, smooth transition instead became years of rapid turnover until Wilson's return from World War II.

Beatrice Hoel Farrell took over *I Killed the Count* in rehearsal "at the eleventh hour." The first woman director was always remembered for her remarkable Widow Cagle in *Sun-Up*, the hit of the 1929 season, but her Chautauqua and Lyceum Circuit experience preceded her Playhouse roles. She had directed community theater on Chicago's North Side after earning a degree at Columbia University. Mrs. Farrell, the Prompter reported, indulged in one superstition—a huge amethyst ring. "She wore it the night of her first dramatic appearance and still wears it at all occasions involving the theater." It seemed to be lost on opening night, but "just as the curtain was rolling at 8:30, it turned up in the pocket of a makeup smock" she'd worn while applying grease paint.

Shows now ran from Tuesday through a Sunday matinee. "The war finally caught up" with the Playhouse, a news item said, and the production staff "will be composed entirely of women for the first time in history." (An exception: Cliff Donnell remained the paid technician-janitor.)

Rachman's review credited Mrs. Farrell "for working out such a tricky story with three flashbacks" and other complications. His references to "tricky" soon became as common as his byline.

Papa Is All in November completed the 1943 portion of the season with only two rather than the usual three plays. Prompter notes described Mrs. Farrell "shuttling between painters and actors, making like twins." Clarence Teal in his twentieth show played the tyrannical Papa in the story of a Mennonite family, a six-character play for this time of shortages. The other two men were teenagers.

Two for Palmer Brink, Then More New Directors

Mrs. Farrell "found that she could not devote the necessary time to the Playhouse work," the *Dundee News* reported during *Papa Is All* rehearsals, "but will finish production of the current play." Then the longtime box office attendant, Minette Tunnicliff, left for California, but planned to return. Instead, she was hired as resident manager of the Motion Picture Country House, a rest home operated by the Motion Picture Relief Fund, whose board included Mary Pickford, Basil Rathbone and Sam Goldwyn. President Teal would try Ethyl Rogers as her replacement. Ethyl was better known by her stage name, Mary Murray, that grand gray-haired matron of many roles.

So 1944 began with a new box office manager and a new director. One item identified Palmer Brink with the optimistic phrase "permanent director." Nothing was very permanent those days. The announcement of his hiring said his first play would be Shakespeare's *Twelfth Night* and then they tried for *Rebecca*, but ended up with *Let Us Be Gay*, a well-known comedy by Rachel Crothers.

A profile view of Brink, pipe poised in his hand, appeared on the cover of the Prompter. He'd gone from Broadway to CBS radio to a season as director of the Tulsa, Okla., Little Theater, before working in Omaha as production manager of KBON. He would last for only two plays, though news clippings gave no hint of problems.

He started The Community Playhouse of the Air, a weekly series of fifteen-minute radio dramas, which he would write and produce on KOWH. A photo showed Brink and a half dozen others, including Clarence Teal, huddled around a microphone with scripts. Teal seemed to be smiling then, but years later explained that trustees were not satisfied with Brink's technical competence. "The job was too much for him," a historian was told. He resigned after directing two plays, both applauded, of course, by the upbeat Rachman.

Let Us Be Gay wasn't all smooth sailing. The original leading man, radio's Ed Morgan, was transferred to Fort Benning, Ga., leaving the part to a youngster. An intriguing program note involved newcomer Jane Dressler, who had trained for two years with Madame Maria Ouspenskaya, famed for her Gypsy woman speech about the full moon and the wolfbane blooming in *The Wolfman* with Lon Chaney Jr.

Brink followed with a revival, *The Guardsman* by Molnar. Teal played The Critic, so the question of Brink's competence was studied at close hand by the board president. The reviewer, who had dubbed the previous play "a tough and tricky modern comedy," said Brink and cast accomplished "no mean trick to play this comedy as light as it is."

Palmer Brink was rehearsing the next play, *Janie*, when he resigned four days before it was to open. He was replaced by Larry Forsythe and Anspach, who continued with the same cast. The Prompter blamed "wartime conditions which make casting difficult" for the delay.

World War II hit home many ways: board vice president and Prompter editor Cecil Slocum was training at Camp Dodge. Emmy Gifford replaced Jean Kelly as production chairman while she worked at a Red Cross rest center in England. Word came from Ken Wilson in California, from Bernie Szold somewhere in Europe and from Frances McChesney, now Mrs. Walter Key with her husband stationed in San Antonio.

It was the third straight play termed "tricky" by Rachman. He liked Virginia Huston, a Duchesne student who won the title role in competition with fifty-five girls.

The season's sixth and final play suffered an even longer postponement "due to difficulties of casting and a delay in obtaining direction." Captain Key was still stationed with the surgical group at Fort Sam Houston, but wife Frances came home for a visit and stayed to direct *Dark Eyes*. Rachman called the story of "three Muscovite gals in an American capitalistic household" the "best Playhouse effort in years." A backstage look showed one worker "enjoyed a succulent chicken leg, forgetting that it was a prop to be eaten by one of the Russians." As the Russian Natasha, the reviewer wrote, Jane Dressler "is not only the star of this piece, but … she does the standout bit of the season."

The season was reported "a financial and artistic success … despite war and handicaps."

Berne Enslin's "Stock Company": 1944–1945

The twentieth season seemed to bring stability to the director's job and started an upward swing in attendance. U.S. troops had landed on Omaha Beach in Normandy on June 6, 1944, and would wade ashore in the Philippines soon after the Playhouse season opened. The G.I. Bill was passed that summer, paving the way for troops to come home to college and to launch the baby boom when the war ended the following year.

Meanwhile, Mrs. Farrell commanded a committee that searched old talent files and made 1,171 calls to recruit actors. They found many still in the service or moved from Omaha. "Last season," Mrs. Farrell said, "some of our best talent was discovered because wartime difficulties made it necessary to draft people into casts."

So the war rhetoric was still in place as the Playhouse welcomed another new director, Berne Enslin. The war reality came home once more with word that Kendrick Wilson had suffered wounds while serving in "the hottest sector of the front in France." Shot first in one leg, he was crawling to safety when hit in the other.

An Iowan with a degree from Iowa City, Enslin arrived with his wife and three-year-old daughter, Merrily Ann. After college work in South Dakota and community theater in York, Penn., he had most recently directed the University of Nebraska theater. The war was winding down, and the Playhouse would soon face another skirmish over the director's job.

Enslin began well enough, promising "good shows" that would "increase the box office with a better product." He did that from the start, as measured by Rachman's review and packed houses for *Suspect*. He also sang the old song about players from "both sides of the tracks," emphasizing "community" in contrast to "little theater groups which are not so composed." His late season conflict with the trustees, however, focused on his alleged "stock company" repetition of the same actors rather than drawing on a broad base of talent.

Suspect featured a cast of eight including Clarence Teal. Rachman raved about the leading lady, Evelyn Paeper Arthur as Mrs. Smith. "Out of this suspenseful, somewhat weird murder mystery ... emerged a player so competent and dramatic" that he placed her "among the leading lights of the Playhouse for all its career." He told his readers to "go prepared for jolts," such as the apparently innocent Mrs. Smith viciously swinging an ax "with a face hate-filled and exuding venom."

Noel Coward's *Hay Fever.* brought a new twelve-page Prompter, with more information and much more advertising. Along with such standbys as Northrup Jones and Updike Lumber and Coal, the inside cover said: "It's a woman war, too. Join the Navy WAVES." The Nebraska Power Company proclaimed, "After the War, Everybody's Going All-Electric."

Evelyn Paeper Arthur returned for *Hay Fever,* and Rachman's column claimed her two performances had movie scouts calling

Ax-wielding Evelyn.

for photos. Because it opened on November 7, election night, voting results were passed on to the audience during intermission. Not that the third term for FDR was a great surprise.

Enslin had directed *The Little Foxes* at the University and now brought Lillian Hellman's classic to the Playhouse in December with the much-acclaimed Mrs. Farrell as Regina Giddens.

Deloris Chapman played Birdie Hubbard. Other Hubbards plot greedily with sister Regina in Lillian Hellman's classic drama. Mrs. Farrell "caught nicely the woman with sharp claws beneath velvet paws." Rachman also liked Doreene Holliday as Addie the maid. Perhaps the first African-American woman on the Playhouse stage, she served on the board of the Urban League, where she also appeared in plays.

None of the nine cast members of *The Lady Who Came to Stay* had appeared before this season, and most were playing their second, third or, in the case of Deloris Chapman, fourth role. One newcomer, Betty Rhodes, had been Enslin's student in Lincoln.

In short, Enslin was developing his own group of players and audiences were seeing fewer faces from past seasons. Thanks to sound effects and lighting by Fred Segur and young John Teal, the ghost story's audience was treated to "apparitions, eerie sounds, half-lights, storms and moaning winds." The reviewer concluded, "Better take somebody with you."

Early End to Enslin Era: Not Drawing on Broad Base

Beatrice Farrell described Enslin's directorial style in the Prompter. "You think he's left the auditorium and can't possibly hear the rehearsal when suddenly like a dagger his voice pierces the muddled reading of a line. From high in the loft or back of the set ... he gives the speech, word perfect. But slow cues are more nerve-wracking to him than incorrectly spoken lines." She portrayed him as "this tense man, completely absorbed in his work. He is the taut wire, the sharp blade, the soft-spoken word."

The *Pursuit of Happiness,* a romantic comedy set in the Revolutionary War, would end Enslin's brief stay with the Playhouse. Clarence Teal had returned to the board presidency, and his As We See It commentary in the March Prompter dealt indirectly with casting questions. After a general reference to casting problems, blaming the war again, he noted that the Playhouse has never resisted "repeated participation during a season," but "frowned on repeated participation in leading roles."

In any case, *Pursuit of Happiness* brought back such familiar players as Earl Braddock and Mary Lou Starr, now the daily newspaper's church editor. The play "never fails to throw the audience into a shocked, hilarious mood because of the bundling scene," Rachman wrote.

That was March. In April, Teal told the press that the Playhouse "jealously guarded" its nonprofessional status. "It became evident that Mr. Berne Enslin's program for a semi-professional theatre and our policy of maintaining an amateur theatre could not be reconciled." Sans compromise, Enslin and trustees "agreed to terminate our relations."

Enslin countered by filing incorporation articles for a nonprofit Civic Theatre Guild of Omaha. It "threatened to give the Playhouse its first major competition in its twenty-year career." The group planned a three-play season at Sokol Auditorium "at prices lower than those of the Playhouse." Civic Guild signers had been cast by Enslin in several plays. "Talent alone should determine lead roles and less emphasis should be placed on 'social aspects,'" Enslin told a reporter.

The ousted director claimed he had been ordered to cast two specific persons in the principal roles of *Over 21*, the season's final play. In his absence, those two roles went to Teal and Mrs. Key, who co-directed the comedy with Beatrice Farrell and Larry Forsythe. Teal's version of the conflict focused also on Enslin's request for summer stock and an acting school, a plan the board opposed due to lack of air conditioning.

To make a long story short, the Civic Theatre Guild lasted for one play. Audiences voted *Over 21* their favorite play of the season.

While the short-lived Enslin era and disagreement on casting was historic for the Playhouse, it was overshadowed by other events. Within a month after the death of President Roosevelt, the Germans surrendered. In August, the first atomic bombs fell on Japan, and World War II soon ended.

Two or More with Wess Densmore: 1945–1946

Teal handed the presidential gavel to Fred Segur who had worked both on and backstage at the Playhouse. In *Knickerbocker Holiday*, the first musical comedy, he played Washington Irving, directed the chorus and co-wrote one of the added songs. He'd become known as the "premiere impresario" for organizing special Playhouse events.

Word came that Lenke Isacson would tour Europe with the comedy *Kiss and Tell*, and the Playhouse family was pleased that Dorothy McGuire would star in *The Enchanted Cottage*, a film version of their first play. Joan McCague had returned to Omaha as Mrs. Robert Hennecke, and Leslie Wilson was reported staying at the Blackstone

Hotel while looking for an apartment, "an indication that Ken Wilson will be back from the wars."

As Pfc. Wilson told the story, he set some kind of record for the shortest combat experience. Two hours into battle near the French-German border, a German sniper shot him in the hip. "I got that temporarily fixed up and was crawling to our reforming point. As I was going through the last hedgerow he nicked me in the right shin." While convalescing, he wore a leg brace and awaited bone-grafting operations. Wilson would return wearing special "space" shoes, as he called them.

But that return would not come in time for the 1945–1946 season. Wess Densmore, "slight and white-haired at 38," was the new director. A letter from Segur to the trustees qualified his status: "He will be with us for at least two shows and longer if Ken Wilson is not able to take over."

Born in Maine, another Carnegie Tech student like Szold, he came from Hollywood and claimed credits from East and West coasts and Europe. His photograph looked much older than 38. In fact, Densmore resembled a weary Marlin Perkins, Mutual of Omaha's *Wild Kingdom* host. More impressive was word later that Densmore and his assistant, Joe Hembree, would spend Christmas in California with Glenn Ford and his wife, Eleanor Powell. Hembree was reported to live with Densmore at the Blackstone.

Young Joan Hennecke hung on Densmore's every Hollywood word. "He was full of stories," she later recalled, but she felt uncomfortable with what seemed to her a lifestyle of drinking and dissipation.

He couldn't have arrived at a better time. Nearly 12,000 would attend the six postwar plays, almost doubling attendance just two seasons before. Teal again led the season ticket campaign, and his wife, Val, was again the sales leader. This time the total reached 1,700 by opening night, topping the total sold back in 1929 and never approached until the past season.

With only 252 seats and planned six-day runs, an extra Monday show became routine starting in October with Hugh Herbert's *Kiss and Tell.* It's the teen comedy about Corliss Archer that inspired the network radio show bearing her name. Benson High junior Patty Willard played Corliss, and Joan Hennecke as the crusty kitchen maid won laughs simply by walking across the stage.

In November, Sidney Howard's *The Silver Chord* presented Mary Peckham as a cruel widow controlling her sons. No longer confined to teenagers and older men, the cast had two men home from the Army Air Corps as the sons.

Plans Drawn for New, Larger Theater on Old Property

Ken Wilson returned as guest director for Thornton Wilder's *The Skin of Our Teeth,* and both Wilsons joined the cast of thirty-two on stage. Rachman struggled to review "some of the screwiest situations ever devised," and couldn't resist noting that Wilson "will probably survive this week but it will be by the skin of his teeth."

Densmore returned from his California trip to direct *Old Acquaintance,* the story of two women writers by John Van Druten, a playwright better known for *I Remember Mama.*

The trustees used the Prompter to reveal that "plans have been drawn up for an addition on the north end of our property." This would bring "a new, larger theater," making the present auditorium for tryouts, rehearsals and classes. "It is also hoped that a 'down-to-earth' Laboratory Group can be organized." Perhaps previous lab groups were floating a bit free of the old terra firma. After citing "a great need," the Prompter item closed by asking, "Would you help to finance such an addition?" Nothing came of these plans until they later took a much different form.

In March, word came that "ill health has caused the resignation of Wess Densmore," and Kendrick Wilson would finish the season. He'd direct John Patrick's *The Hasty Heart,* and he wasn't the only reason it seemed like a homecoming. Lenke Isacson was back from the South Pacific to play the British Army nurse, and six of the nine cast members had served in the Armed Forces. The military convalescent ward was all too familiar a setting for Wilson who had spent twelve months in hospital recovery.

The photographers loved Lenke, who was featured in at least five news photos. One showed Larry Forsythe as Lachie the kilted Scot proposing to the white-capped Lenke. Forsythe's doomed character is cheered by the other convalescents who soften his hard heart. Lenke's nurse was full of "fresh and stimulating cheer, radiating optimism and light in that bamboo hospital shelter." No comment was made on an actor who would play dozens of roles over the next decade—an Iowan named Milo Green, fresh from five years of service.

Green wasn't ignored when he appeared again in the season's final play, the "salty, political" *First Lady*. Green had gone from British colonel to a publisher, "a blatant press agent type bubbling with schemes to elect his man."

First Lady included Beatrice Farrell and Frances Key, plus Daniel O'Connor. Now "he gave an earnest feeling to the young Senator," but he first caught Lenke Isacson's eye in that workshop play, *Jim Dandy*, and was still her husband in the twenty-first century.

Hard Times Behind, Stability Ahead

The May Prompter reported Wilson's hiring for the next season, and he soon left for the Plantation Playhouse at White Bear Lake, Minn. Milo Green and others joined him there for a summer season that opened with *The Hasty Heart*. Time would tell that the directorial merry-go-round had stopped. Wilson would stay for more than two decades and see the "temporary" theater at 40th and Davenport replaced by a new building beyond the wildest dreams of the founders.

The Playhouse had turned the financial corner. They'd survived a ten-year span marked by crisis after crisis, a time when the agenda of more than one board meeting called for consideration of closing the theater. But now the Depression years when director Steinmetz was paid $1,800 for the season were behind them. Wilson had started at $3,000 and returned for $5,400 in 1946.

Those booming ticket sales brought in double the income of the early war years. Receipts for 1945–1946 totaled over $15,000, and, when all the counting was done in May, left a balance of $1,518—a small fortune compared to the previous fifteen years.

One source of satisfaction that sustained the Playhouse family in hard times remained a pleasure as the good times began. The keepers of the scrapbooks still clipped the stories of their "graduates" gone on to Broadway and Hollywood. The glamorous Virginia Huston, 20, went from the title role in *Janie*—"Some of the boys fell for her pretty hard," Teal noted—to steal Robert Ryan from Joan Bennett in the film *None So Blind*. She got regular shipments of cod liver oil, supplied and prescribed by Mary Pickford, who took a shine to Virginia. Lois Fitch still played on radio's *Ma Perkins,* and Julann Caffrey, like Lenke Isacson, had joined the USO.

And a name missing from the Playhouse press for fifteen years resurfaced. Dodie Brando's leading roles were remembered when her son Marlon, a one-year-old when she played her first part, was cast as a young poet on Broadway. Supporting Katharine Cornell in Shaw's *Candida,* young Marlon "achieved a believable, love-sick introvert by playing very quietly. His intensity was within him where it should be."

Somewhere, someone must have said, "You ain't seen nothin' yet." Not with Brando, not with the Omaha Community Playhouse. If the show went on during the Great Depression and World War II, what might postwar prosperity bring?

CHAPTER 5

Postwar Prosperity Leads West, 1946–1959

Season Ticket Boom Requires Two-Week Runs: 1946–1947

Kendrick Wilson still wore a leg brace when he returned from White Bear Lake, and he was happy to hear about support of another sort.

Clarence Teal was leading the membership campaign to heights beyond the old, unreachable goals. Postwar prosperity raised attendance and income, but didn't bring stability to season planning. A pocket-size flyer, a drawing of Your Intimate Theatre on the cover, confirmed only the opening play, *Holiday* by Phillip Barry. A list of "best possibilities" began with *The Late George Apley*. *Holiday* was put aside and *Apley* opened the first of twenty-one consecutive years with Wilson as director.

Old reliable George S. Kaufman helped John P. Marquand turn his Pulitzer Prize novel about the Apleys into a stage comedy of Boston manners. When the woman cast as Mrs. Apley had to drop out, Wilson paired Mary Peckham with Rudyard Norton as the title character.

Mary Peckham, Rudyard Norton as seated Apleys.

The cast ranged from dapper newcomer Morey Landman and Leslie Wilson to venerable Mary Murray and Charles Docherty, who "confided his greatest ambition is to play as many Playhouse roles as Jim Flynn." The class-conscious Apleys, Harvard Bostonians, fear their daughter may marry a Yale man, and, worse, their son falls for a girl from Kansas City.

The historic pairing of Peckham and Norton was followed by another memorable return for *My Sister Eileen*. Echo Guiou Rose, back from Portugal with her son Charles, coached six men playing Brazilian Admirals to speak passable Portuguese. Another appearance by Milo Green hinted he might challenge Flynn and Docherty for most roles. And a "satisfying performance" marked the first appearance by Jack McBride, who became a pioneer in public television.

December's *Soldier's Wife* sees a soldier come home to a wife (Anabel Shotwell Adler) who has grown quite self-sufficient in his absence. Anabel had been in New York City with her brother Hudson, Douw

Fonda and Damian Flynn when all the ex-Omahans were painting furniture for Dorothy McGuire's small apartment there.

Frances McChesney Key, now teaching play production at Omaha University, took the lead in monthly Playhouse Forum sessions. It was the start of an educational role that grew to include acting and other classes.

Premiere for *Joan of Lorraine* Brings Longest Run

The Time of Your Life by William Saroyan gave hints that learning about the language of diversity was under way in 1947. The February Prompter identified the role of Wesley as "a colored boy who plays a mean and melancholy boogie-woogie piano." A news story headlined "Acting Variety Playhouse Need" did not refer to a boy but "a colored man." Rather than colored boy or man, Rachman's review mentions Robert Floyd playing Wesley, "a Negro lad." Times and terms were a changin'.

Ethnicity abounded in Saroyan's play, from Italian and Armenian to a cop named Krupp (played by Sebi Breci, later a *World-Herald* photographer). Larry Forsythe's lead character, "an enigmatic Irishman," hangs out at Nick's Saloon on the San Francisco waterfront.

Ingrid Bergman was starring as *Joan of Lorraine* on Broadway as Wilson prepared for its community theater premiere in March. He discovered there were no stage directions in the Maxwell Anderson script, so the board sent Wilson to New York. He not only saw the play twice, but picked up a prompt book with "cuttings, directions and other valuable aids." And he met Miss Bergman, already well established in films, and declared her "more beautiful in person than on the screen."

Seen for the first time in the Midwest, *Joan of Lorraine* was a success, the review claimed. Harriet Walker, a radio personality with professional stage experience, won praise as Joan of Arc, arguing with the director/inquisitor played by Dan O'Connor, teaching drama at Creighton University a year before marrying the Omahan who'd become Lenka Peterson on Broadway.

Unusual advance interest in the premiere led to its opening on Friday, not the usual Tuesday. The run covered three weekends, and more than 3,400 attended, compared to an average of 2,500 for the season's other shows. Perhaps this Prompter note best captures the enthusiasm for the occasion: "Very seldom are we privileged to see a Broadway success while it is still playing in New York. No wonder that we rejoiced when we learned that we were the first community theater … to be granted the rights to 'Joan of Lorraine.'"

Then *I Like It Here* featured an immigrant handyman, a professor and his shrewish wife, played by Eleanor Mooberry whose architect husband would a decade later design a new Playhouse. Director Wilson headed north again for summer stock in Minnesota. With record season membership and a record run and attendance for *Joan of Lorraine,* he could enjoy the cool breezes on White Bear Lake with few worries.

McDonald's Death "The Greatest Loss in 23 Years": 1947–1948

That annual gathering took place at the Legion Club, so the festivities were pictured in the *Douglas County Legionnaire.* Young John Teal was shown in a vocal act; Ken Wilson danced with Miss Walker, his award-winning Joan; and Mrs. Farrell congratulated a smiling Rudyard Norton, cigarette dangling from his hand.

All these photos seem poignant enough more than a half century later, with most of the participants gone. But it's most touching to see Alan McDonald, the founding president, smiling as he leans over a table full of his friends. He would die later in 1947 at age 56, survived not only by wife and children, but by his parents. He had still lived on North 38th Street, near the Playhouse. While the obituary headline cited architectural work on the Joslyn Museum, Mrs. Farrell called his passing "the greatest loss the Playhouse has suffered in the 23 years of its existence."

The board president emphasized that "many Omahans do not realize to what extent Mr. McDonald contributed to the cultural life of this city." She noted the Joslyn and his many services to the Playhouse, from founding president to designing and supervising construction of the theater, through his continuing service as box office chairman. "Up to within a few days of his death," he "worked faithfully on the play-reading committee."

Mrs. Farrell added, "Far beyond these many loyal services, Mr. McDonald fought unwaveringly for the true community theater spirit." She concluded, "Unanimously and sincerely, the board says that no one can ever take Alan McDonald's place." He lived to see the first 150 shows, only missing number 151 before he died.

In September, trustees stuck to their plan of limited memberships, cutting off sales at 2,200 season tickets. Dean Morrill, who had designed and constructed scenery at Central High and Omaha University, received the new title of technical director. Another innovation: Coca-Cola was now available at intermission.

Oscar Wilde's *Earnest* Marks Milestone Production

The 150th production in late October was Oscar Wilde's *The Importance of Being Earnest*. A Milestone Mailbox appeared in the lobby for fund-raising, and the first contributor was Alan McDonald, still active six weeks before his death.

It was the twentieth season in the "temporary" building, and the Prompter made a milestone promise: "We had hoped to erect a more adequate theater long ago. We hope to do so soon." Looking ahead, they anticipated celebrating the twenty-fifth anniversary in "a new Playhouse, spacious, air-cooled, with every facility for actors and audience."

They hadn't done a Wilde play since a pair back in the 1920s. Now *Earnest* was presented as "a play befitting such a memorable occasion … as gay and scintillating a comedy as the years have produced." Director Wilson deserved a deep bow because "it is no easy matter to end acts effectively when the script calls for nothing more exciting than a character seating himself in a chair."

With Ruth Gordon's *Years Ago,* the story of her ambition to become an actress, Morrill had been replaced as technician by Harold Dergen as each Prompter listed Playhouse staff separate from volunteer "production personnel."

Another sign of change came when the Playhouse Forum met at Creighton University for a television demonstration. A few days before the end of 1947, Mrs. Key and others saw a television experiment conducted by the Rev. Roswell Williams, S.J., Omaha's pioneer in the medium. He helped WOW-TV prepare to go on the air with KMTV in 1949, giving Omaha two stations well before most major Midwestern cities had even one. If films and radio had made an impact on theater, what would TV bring?

The Many Roles of Milo Green, Plus Marlon and Lenka

A Christmas party was followed by the second annual Twelfth Night Costume Party—come as "the person, real or fictional, that you would like to have been." Libby Lauritzen must have mastered the refreshment duties because she took charge for both events. New trustees included Helen McDonald, replacing her late husband. Groups could buy out a performance for $200, and one was sold in advance of the January play.

A psychological thriller, *Uncle Harry,* opened the 1948 half of the season with a newcomer in the title role. Jack Reeves, from KFAB radio, played the timid young Harry who finally has his fill of bullying by two sisters. He concocts a scheme whereby Sister Lettie (Frances Key) poisons sister Hettie.

The cast included Milo Green and Jack McBride, one of Father Williams's television trainees. Ken Wilson filled in for one ailing player, and Mary Lou Starr Wallace took over a role for the last performance. She received a script at eleven that morning and didn't fluff a line.

For the second time, Thomas C. Kennedy came home for an original play. Earlier, he had played John Keats, but his own play, *The Song of the Bridge,* was presented after winning a playwriting competition. A construction engineer, Kennedy drew on his own bridge-building experience to tell a story of workers who risked their lives. Scenes unfold around a tool shed at the bridge site where the job manager deals with a saboteur crane operator (Milo Green, whose dark thin mustache gave him a Don Ameche look).

Somebody must have been counting when *Dream Girl* closed the season in May with a production that required 35 scene changes, 85 light cues and 75 sound cues. The title heroine, played by Nancy Nagl, shifts often from reality to dream scenes, which put a cast of twenty-four into motley settings.

A portrait of Henry Fonda covered an entire tabloid page of the *World-Herald*, which declared him "the toast of Broadway" in *Mr. Roberts*. It was also a season that saw Broadway marvel at young Marlon Brando's shouting "Stella" when he wowed the theater world in *Streetcar Named Desire.* The headline, "Mr. Brando, You Were Born in Omaha," was prompted by his habit of claiming birth in Calcutta, Bangkok or Chicago.

By 1948, though, the Playhouse family felt closer to the young woman they honored at a prenuptial luncheon. Then a wedding photo of Mrs. Daniel O'Connor showed their Lenke, now Lenka on stage, in a beautiful bridal gown by a New York theatrical designer. The new bride was working there with Elia Kazan, recent Oscar winner for *Gentleman's Agreement* and Brando's director in *Streetcar.* Marlon was once their leading lady's baby boy, Hank Fonda and Dorothy McGuire their hero and heroine, but Lenka was fresh from the fold.

Life with Father, Mama, Then Val Teal Play: 1948–1949

A different sort of announcement, in the form of a playbill, greeted the arrival of John Kendrick Wilson in September. Titled, "Their First Born or Thirteen Years A-Waitin'," the event was "produced by Leslie Wilson" and "directed by Kendrick Wilson" with "technical advisor" credit to Dr. Sven Isacson, Lenka's father.

So it seemed fitting that the season opened with *Life with Father,* the Howard Lindsay and Russel Crouse play finally released to community theaters. It had broken Broadway records set by *Tobacco Road.* The new father directed, but the new mother was no longer in charge of makeup. Larry Forsythe played Clarence Day, the title role, and Adelaide Fogg was his wife Vinnie.

A news story called it her first appearance at the Playhouse. Long forgotten were the references to "wee Adelaide" and the "veritable sprite" who won more ink than Mrs. Brando when she danced in the very first Playhouse production, the vaudeville show at Tech High in 1925. Twinkly-toed in tutu, she won more praise performing at those early dinner-dances in the Cooper Studio.

Well, she was still petite at five feet two, and still the apple of critics' eyes. "Adelaide Fogg plays a pleasant, vivacious, shrewd little woman," Rachman wrote, "who understood how to get favors out of her pompous husband." The review simply listed their four boys, including the eldest played by Jerry Venger, a Central High student who remained active in theater for the next half century. New board member Jack Drew, chairman of the "stage-setting committee," furnished antiques for the play set in 1880.

What better encore for Wilson's first season as a father than following with *I Remember Mama* and finding an excuse for two-month-old John to make his stage debut. For the Sunday afternoon matinee, the infant Wilson subbed for the doll wheeled out in a buggy. Irene Henry played John Van Druten's title mother "with an earnest and magnetic quality that made her believable." Jean Berg won a Fonda-McGuire award for her Aunt Trina, a "sniffling, fearful little old maid.

For the second straight season, the Playhouse offered an original play by a local writer. Val Teal had published *With Sirens Blowing* as a serial novelette in the *Woman's Home Companion.* She "was besieged by fan mail," the Prompter said, in reaction to the story of an ordinary Omaha family dealing with rationing, shortages and the like during World War II. "The situations may have been pretty serious then, but they are hilarious today. It could be I'm prejudiced," the Prompter note added, "the author is my wife."

Topper Teal played himself, renamed Pud Andrews, with Maggie Jenkins as the lead character, his mother. The role required that she cook meals for the boys and pass out pie and cookies. Wilson expected the three Andrews lads and some Boy Scouts to put on pounds during the fourteen-day run, which cost $7.50 per show for their food.

Wilson was credited with providing "plenty of sound, bustle and tempo," but Rachman found the plot "so tenuous it almost gets lost in the hurried routine of cooking, washing, baking and other duties." Among the youngsters on stage were several who rose to community leadership—Larry and Jerry Hoberman, and Barry Larson—plus Rifty Fournier, who became an award-winning network television writer-producer. Milo Green played a policeman and Jim Flynn didn't. Between Val Teal's play and the February show, Mrs. Lauritzen again chaired an event now identified as "the annual Playhouse party."

Two of the talented Teals, father Clarence and son Topper, with Echo Guiou in radio play. Jack McBride is on far right.

General LeMay Aids *Command Decision*, *John Loves Mary*

Thanks went to General Curtis LeMay and others at Strategic Air Command for props and advice aiding the March production of *Command Decision*. The film with Clark Gable had recently played Omaha, so Rachman's review made comparisons. The Playhouse treatment "gave ample proof of the heightened power and effect of a stage offering over a screen play." Wilson's direction of the local cast "left little doubt as to which was more effective."

Henry Kelpe, then in radio but soon in television, played the leading role of General Dennis. The all-male cast of sixteen military men and two civilians included Milo Green, who remained in the Army, working in public relations for the recruiting office. A Public Pulse letter seconded the claim that the play was better than the movie, adding that Kelpe "did as well or better than Clark Gable" (who, no doubt, frankly didn't give a damn).

Both *Command Decision* and May's season-ending comedy *John Loves Mary* were publicized with cast caricatures by Bill Spire, son of board president Clarence Spier. His two boys, including son Robert who became Nebraska's Attorney-General, transposed the last two letters of the family name.

Rachman again compared the Playhouse *John Loves Mary* favorably to the movie. Among those joining the ubiquitous Milo Green in the cast was Joel Melcher, whose wife Mimi helped backstage. Listed as Marian, but known as Mimi, she'd make a larger impact in the seasons to come.

A new event billed as the Talent Hunt Annual Fun Frolic offered two free Sunday performances that spring. Directed by Charles Docherty, 65, it promised "an hour of ham, corn and satire that will rock the playhouse." Docherty would soon be hospitalized with a stroke, ending an acting career that began with those pre-Playhouse groups sponsored by the Drama League.

More historic, though, was the notice in the May Prompter: "Do we have among our patrons one or two members ... able to make a sizable contribution toward financing a new theatre building? Our building committee would like to talk to you." It was headed by W. Boyd Jones, owner of a construction company and future Playhouse board president.

They could now regularly sell out their 252-seat theater, a bare fact that made the need for a new building more obvious each year.

Silver Season Sees Milhollin, Opera Hopeful Debut: 1949–1950

Opening in mid-September with *Edward, My Son,* the silver anniversary season saw Charlie Robertson—"Her mother calls her Lois"—become Ken Wilson's technical assistant. She'd later move up to technician Harold Dergen's job. Plays still started at 8:30 p.m., and before the season opener special performances had been sold to three groups—Business and Professional Women, Bell Telephone Pioneers and the Unitarian Women's Club.

Larry Forsythe, often Wilson's first choice for male leads, played "something of a rat," the review said. He was the father who would do anything for his unworthy son. Most notable was the first Playhouse appearance of James Milhollin. His Dr. Parker was "a likable, human kind of medic." Credited with Shakespearean work in California, Milhollin's reputation would grow in Omaha and beyond.

A former *World-Herald* newsman and Nebraska U. grad, William McCleery, wrote the October comedy, *Parlor Story*. Rachman praised the "brisk, brittle and highly humorous dialogue" as his former colleague "blasts forth with some uninhibited opinions of politics, newspapers and ... certain types of Americans in public life." It marked another historic first appearance. Rachman had nothing to say about Alexandra Hunt as the couple's daughter, but the Prompter was prescient: "She aspires to become an opera singer." And that she did.

New Junior Theater Organized, Mrs. Gifford Presides

The 1950 half of the silver season began as usual with the Twelfth Night Party and Libby Lauritzen calling to come dressed as your favorite advertisement. Honors went to Joan Hennecke as "a complexion soap bride," and Harvey Carter, an African-American who helped backstage, as "the breakfast cereal book." The second half of the century brought good and bad news from their favorite alums: Dorothy McGuire Swope stopped at the Blackstone Hotel and introduced Omahans to her ten-month-old daughter, named Mary but known as Topo. Playgoers were promised that *Mr. Roberts* wouldn't play Omaha until Hank Fonda was available for the title role.

Then a chilling headline reported, "Henry Fonda's Wife Ends Own Life in Sanatorium. Farewell Note Discovered After Nurse Finds Actor's Estranged Spouse with Throat Cut." Henry's second wife, the mother of Jane and Peter, was dead and the grim details were kept from her children. Years later, Peter would be getting a haircut in Rome and first learn of his mother's fate by reading a movie magazine.

In local news, trustee Emmy Gifford was identified as M.E. when she painted a prop portrait, but she was Mrs. Harold Gifford in a news story that headlined the interest that became her primary theatrical legacy. She was elected president of "the Omaha Junior Theater, new children's theater group organized last week. She will also be production advisor."

If the organization was new in 1950, the Junior League involvement with children's productions went back before their cooperation with the Playhouse in the 1930s. In 1943, Mrs. Gifford had written and produced a children's movie, *History of a Nutcracker* for the Junior League. (Her first film, two years earlier, captured an eye operation by her husband, Dr. Hal.) Apparently the Junior League would be only one of many groups behind the new Junior Theater, led by a board including Joslyn Museum's Eugene Kingman and Kendrick Wilson of the Playhouse.

Wilson also reported on his latest New York trip to see nine plays. He saw Fonda in *Mr. Roberts* a second time and "during an extremely pleasant conversation" learned he'd bring the Navy drama to Omaha.

Flynn's Last Role, Mrs. Brando Back, Lucy Recalls First Night

First bow-tied and clean-shaven, then fully bearded in gunslinger garb, photos of Jim Milhollin promoted the story of Jesse James in *Missouri Legend*. Much was made of fact vs. fiction, and a headline claimed, "Playhouse Attempts to be Accurate." Milhollin's Jesse, aka Mr. Howard, shared the stage with Milo Green's Pop Hickey and Belle Starr, played by Irene Henry.

"Her matter-of-fact cussing being a highlight," the review said. Rachman seemed skeptical about the outlaw's portrayal as something less than a desperado. "True, he held up a few banks and might have shot a few people who were slow in getting their hands up." It wasn't a musical, but it included that famous ditty about

Emmy Gifford.

"the dirty little coward who shot Mr. Howard and laid poor Jesse in his grave."

Larry David's third appearance of the season raised the old red flag about "a closed group that uses the same 'socialites' in every production. Nothing could be farther from the truth," the March Prompter protested. "Tryouts are open to everyone and Ken Wilson has absolute freedom in his choice of cast members," with his priority being "the best possible cast." More than a hundred participated on and backstage in the first five shows.

Mimi Melcher's title role in *The Heiress* earned a Fonda-McGuire award. The March drama was only the second community production of the play based on Henry James's *Washington Square* novel. Joan Hennecke, now mother of a young daughter, returned to the stage as Mrs. Montgomery while her husband, Robert, helped with lighting.

Some of the theater's grand old players appeared in the season-ending comedy *Two Blind Mice*. Two elderly ladies, played by Edna Dodds and the venerable Mary Murray, continue to run a long-since-abolished government agency, the Department of Medicinal Herbs. It proved to be the final casting of James R. Flynn. When he died a year later at age 71, the obituary said he'd played thirty-four parts, the greatest number by one person in the Playhouse history. The list started in 1931 when he joined Dorothy McGuire and Bernie Szold in *Death Takes a Holiday* and included many politicians. Rachman reminisced about "riding back downtown with him" after plays "and talking show business. His great pleasure was to do a simple subsidiary part," especially the butler.

Before that final play, some familiar faces were seen cutting a big cake to celebrate the birth of the Playhouse in 1925. Clare Mackin, a founding trustee, watched Helen McDonald, widow of Alan, the first board president, wield the cake knife, assisted by L.C. (Brick) Hawley. Looking on was Mrs. Marlon Brando, his co-star in the initial play, *The Enchanted Cottage*. Also present from the first cast were Jayne Fonda Schoentgen and Lucy Updike.

Lucy's birthday note in the Prompter recalled the nervous excitement of the first opening night. "Several of the cast were struggling to overcome stage fright. They were making their debut. Could they utter a word?" Director Foley "was calm (outwardly, at least), reassuring and optimistic. He called, 'On stage,' and we of the cast got there—but with shaking knees. The music stopped … the curtain rose … the play was on! We lived through it and I must admit the audience was wonderfully kind."

Legion: *Born Yesterday* Subversive, Playhouse "Naïve": 1950–1951

Construction contractor W. Boyd Jones had replaced Clarence Spier as president, and trumpets should have sounded at the news that Spire now led the "New Building Committee." Teal again chaired the membership campaign and again set a lower goal before letting season ticket sales climb to 2,784.

Teal was also president of the Playhouse Building Corporation, and in that role announced plans for a one-story steel structure on the 40th and Davenport lot. The separate $4,000 building would be used to build and store scenery. The first addition in twenty-two years, it would move west to the new site in 1959.

All seemed well with the Playhouse world until storm clouds formed nine days before the season opening of *Born Yesterday*. Many know the film version for the Oscar-winning performance by Judy Holliday as Billie Dawn, the tycoon's dumb blonde who gets wise to him. But in September 1950, American troops fought Communists in Korea, and the Red threat would take a growing place in American politics until Senator Joe McCarthy's televised Army hearings led to his censure in 1954.

The play's author, Garson Kanin, was named in "Red Channels," an anti-Communist pamphlet that once listed Lucille Ball because of her father's affiliation. Joseph Vinardi, new commander of American Legion Post No. 1, the nation's largest, called the Playhouse "naïve" for giving "prestige and royalties" to a writer with left-wing ties. Vinardi admitted that he had not read or seen the play.

The board voted to continue, declaring there is "nothing subversive in the play and we feel that it is a good, American comedy." *Born Yesterday* had enjoyed a long, Broadway run before the movie with Holliday and Paul Douglas. Wilson added his view about its "patriotic American theme … make democracy work."

Before the opening, the *World-Herald* reviewed the script. Reporter Lou Gerdes, who later rose through the ranks to become executive editor, emphasized again that the author, not the play, "brought excitement to Omaha last week." He said Americans would find "sharp comedy" with "a lesson in vigilance for democracy. The Omaha audience, like those elsewhere, probably will like the play."

That didn't stop Jack McBride from quitting the cast a few days before opening night. McBride, 24, a World War II veteran, had played the same role in Minnesota summer stock, the part of a journalist who educates Billie to turn against her power-hungry man. He regretted leaving so late in rehearsals and said he saw nothing subversive in the play. He made his decision based on his employment as Creighton University's director of radio, but added that school officials didn't ask him to drop out.

After Wilson discussed Vinardi's statement with the cast, he expected some to withdraw for "personal reasons." A Creighton student on the prop crew also resigned. Creighton president, the Very Rev. William McCabe, said he did not wish "to become involved in the controversy."

So the show went on with Wilson taking McBride's role. Noting that the Legion commander "caused added interest," Rachman's review said "the locally controversial" comedy pleased "an audience that laughed almost continuously." As Brock, the corrupt tycoon, Larry David delivered "a surplus of gusto." Madalyn King, Miss Omaha of 1947, delighted the audience as the decorative, ditzy Billie. She'd won the Miss America talent competition as a dancer and now "gave mounting evidence of becoming a pretty good actress."

The review also praised character roles by Milhollin and Milo Green, and said that "Miriam Shrier got a great deal out of a few brief appearances as the dull maid." A bit player in *Born Yesterday,* Warren Swigart, would play a larger role in Omaha politics, especially as city councilman.

Glass Menagerie, No *Madwoman,* Emergency Shortages

The September Prompter had promised *The Madwoman of Chaillot* next, but perhaps it seemed too radical after the recent flap. Another choice, *The Winslow Boy* , was slipped into the program, but dropped due to casting difficulties.

Instead, *The Glass Menagerie* brought Tennessee Williams to the "temporary" Playhouse for the first and only time.

A cast of only four gave the November Prompter plenty of room to background the actors. It was learned that Mimi Melcher, playing beyond her years as the mother, grew up in Grosse Pointe before doing theater in Detroit. Recently from Chicago, Donna Russell (as the shy daughter who collects the glass animals) taught speech in the public schools after earning an Iowa University Master of Arts degree. Jack Keiner, a Creighton student who worked for radio KSWI, followed his role as the coward who shot Jesse by playing the narrator son.

The Korean War was not mentioned by name, not even as a United Nations police action, but the January 1951 Prompter said, "The national emergency is beginning to be very seriously reflected in our short-handed stage crew." Carpenters, electricians and others were urged to see Charlie Robertson. The item also called for actors, but there were no problems casting *On Borrowed Time* by Paul Osborn.

Veteran Richard Davis took the Lionel Barrymore role of Gramps and two grade school boys, Tom Rosch and Larry Hoberman, split the part of Pud. Claiming the fantasy comedy was only as good as the actor playing Gramps, Rachman said, "If there was ever a better pivotal performance at the Playhouse, we have not seen it." Davis was equal to Barrymore, he added, so it came as no surprise when he later won the Fonda-McGuire award. So did silver-haired Mary Murray as Granny, her twenty-sixth role.

Apparently the Kanin name was not banned after the *Born Yesterday* brouhaha. The February comedy *Goodbye, My Fancy* was written by Garson's sister-in-law, Fay Kanin. Nancy Nagl, back from professional work in New York, played the lead congresswoman. She was paired with Jim Milhollin as her fiancé, a university president sans backbone.

Prices Up, No New Theater, But First Musical in Decade

World and economic conditions plagued Playhouse plans for fund-raising and building. Headed "What About the Future?" a Prompter report from Teal's Building Committee was gloomy. He'd consulted an advertising man and concluded, "Not only is it impossible now to consider building with present governmental restrictions, but at least for the present it is well-nigh impossible" to mount a fund-raising campaign. While "our plans must remain dreams," donations would be gratefully received.

Meanwhile, rising production costs "have finally made it necessary that we raise our prices." For the first time in its history, other than for tax increases, the Playhouse raised its ticket price. Membership would go from $6 to $7.50, the student ticket from $4.50 to $6. Adult single admission would increase to $2.10 with this season's last play.

The trustees heard people were still wondering about the construction on their lot, so added another explanation. "It is simply a large room, 28 by 34, which can be used for work space." Anyone who knew the cramped quarters of the Playhouse wasn't surprised to see the admission that "occasionally we shall use it as an additional dressing room space." The prefabricated building could be dismantled and reassembled as part of a new theater building "when that time comes." Unfortunately, that time was not soon coming.

Many regulars joined young Topper Teal as the title's *The Winslow Boy* when it returned to the schedule with Milhollin as his father crusading for justice when his son is expelled from a

British School. Meanwhile, mother Wilson had returned to her familiar role in makeup.

In May, the Playhouse presented its first musical since *Knickerbocker Holiday* featured "September Song" in 1941. The new effort involved three one-act operas: Kurt Weill again with *Down in the Valley,* Gian-Carlo Menotti's *The Telephone,* and *The Secret of Suzanne* by Ermanno Wolf-Ferrari. Wilson staged the three, but Omaha Symphony conductor Richard Duncan directed the music and Cora Quick provided choreography. Don Nelsen, an eighth-grade teacher who studied music at Omaha University, started as an understudy in one musical, but wound up with the leads in all three. Lucie (Mrs. Paul) Skinner, a lyric soprano, sang the role of Suzanne and shared the Menotti lead with Mrs. Kermit Hansen.

Mary Hansen's opening night performance was reviewed by Martin Bush, the music critic, rather than Rachman. "She both sang brilliantly and gave an arrestingly vivacious impersonation of the feather-brained girl" whose telephone conversations distracted from her suitor's proposals. Nelson's hero and Milo Green's villain were joined in *Down in the Valley* by Don Sarooian as "the Leader." Later spelling his name Saroyan, his acting career would be overshadowed by his marriage to a more successful performer, television great Carol Burnett.

Bush's review claimed the productions removed any "qualms or reservations at the prospect of hearing local amateur talent" doing lyric theater. "Instead of there being any hint of amateurishness about any of the multitudinous major and minor details going into such a project, it sustained a laudable air of professionalism throughout." A twenty-voice chorus sang with *Down in the Valley,* and eight male and female dancers performed with the folk music. Two pianists accompanied all three operas.

By the way, Henry Fonda finally, but barely, made it to Omaha as *Mr. Roberts.* It took forty-three hours, most of it on a snowbound train, to arrive from Minneapolis a day late. A big spread at the Blackstone Hotel was stowed in the refrigerator when the troupe failed to arrive. After the two-day train ordeal, Fonda's brother-in-law Jack Peacock burst into Union Station red-faced with word that his car had broken down. Sister Harriet had slipped on the ice and stayed home with a broken ankle.

Fonda, "haggard and drawn after his 40-hour ordeal in a sleeper," accepted a ride with a reporter. The ordeal wasn't over. They did two shows per night, at 6:30 and 9:30, and performed the first night without scenery, which took eight hours to erect. "Terrific without scenery," Rachman raved, "supercolossal" when the ship was set up for the Navy crew. The cast included Jack Klugman, Lee Van Cleef and Rance Howard, whose son Ron gained greater fame. Hank got a catch in his voice when he thanked the Playhouse for a silver salver proclaiming him the theater's best actor in its first twenty-six years.

First Full-time Designer Hired Away from Ralph Edwards: 1951–1952

Two star players left Omaha before the season got under way. Jack McBride took a teaching job at Wayne University in Detroit, and Jim Milhollin was sent off to try Broadway with the gift of a dollar tree from his Playhouse friends. But the biggest change came with the hiring of Robert Soule, 24, as "our new designer-technician."

Soule's predecessors, going back to Eldon Anspach a decade earlier, had all been hired locally and part-time. All were labeled simply technician while Wilson doubled as set designer. The Prompter described Soule as "a star pupil at the Pasadena Playhouse" who had done set designs for theaters in Phoenix and Santa Fe. He was most recently assistant set designer for Ralph Edwards's *Truth or Consequences* radio broadcast. His work wouldn't be seen until the second show.

Unfortunately, he executed another's design for the season opener, Moss Hart's *Light Up the Sky* and may have shared responsibility for a near-disaster. A rope broke and a 100-pound cast-iron chandelier crashed to the center of the stage. The news story stressed "the show must go on" as actors continued around the fallen prop. But Dolores

Hughes, playing a pretentious trouper, "escaped death or serious head injury when the chandelier missed her by inches." Nancy David "carried on for the balance of the act with blood streaming down her leg." Her husband Larry, known as an ad-libber, was on stage with his wounded wife.

"All I could think of," she said, "was 'Let's see Larry get us out of this one.'" Wilson heard that "few in the audience were aware" the crash was not in the script. As odds would have it, Milo Green was in the cast though clear of the chandelier.

Aside from the crash, "Probably the biggest response," Rachman wrote, "came to Muriel Feltz, who looks and acts like Marie Dressler," known best as Tugboat Annie. She brought Canadian theatrical experience to her Playhouse debut. The show business comedy dealt tongue-in-cheek with a play on its Boston tryout.

Soule won first mention when his single set for *Come Back, Little Sheba* was praised as "particularly interesting." More interesting was the casting of Doc and Lola, the William Inge role associated with Shirley Booth. Wilson brought back two award winners, Mary Peckham and Larry Forsythe. Mary would win her second Fonda-McGuire by dealing with a drunken spouse and calling out the title for her little dog.

The review noted that "other roles are fairly demanding," citing Joe Basilico as the postman who promises Lola a letter if he has to write it himself. Basilico, a packing-house laborer, would come to represent the role of "regular Joes" from "all walks of life" when the new theater arrived in 1959.

Before he could play another lead, Larry Forsythe took his life. News reports made no mention of his final role as the alcoholic Doc. A single man, he was found in his parents' garage, lying near the exhaust pipe of his car, the victim of carbon monoxide poisoning. A memorial fund was established in his name to aid in building the new theater. A Prompter note told of "a feeling of personal loss. We owe him a debt of gratitude."

Another passing was less painful. The Omaha Drama League, founded in 1915, voted to dissolve. The "buxom, high-bosomed ladies," in *Time* magazine's words of yore, had gone "on a standby basis" in 1941. Now a decade later they decided to empty their treasury, giving $2,000 to the Junior Theater and $4,500 to the Playhouse.

New: Lighting Board, Publicist Echo, Player Elaine Jabenis

The High Ground by Charlotte Hastings opened the 1952 portion of the season in January, enjoying a new fashion in press coverage. A full tabloid page of the Sunday Entertainment magazine showed Wilson coaching Nancy David, kneeling before a nun. What separated this from past spreads was color, Mrs. David in red, Wilson in blue and the nun in white habit before a bright stained-glass background. The cover photo was shot across the street at St. Barnabas Episcopal, whose members delighted in seeing their "Te Deum" sanctuary windows. The mystery set in an English convent included four cast members born in England. It also saw the debut of a $6,400 lighting switchboard, the gift of Emmy and Hal Gifford in memory of their son Jonas.

The small size of the board prompted the boast that "one girl can reach and control all 24 units from a sitting position." It took three to operate sixteen dimmers on the old board.

The reviewer liked the atmosphere of *High Ground,* a convent on a bleak hillside. "We have never seen a more appropriate background at the Playhouse" than the one designed by Soule. Another cover photo, on "This Week in Omaha," a motel-hotel entertainment guide, showed the cast's four Englishwomen. Credit for such extensive coverage went to the board's new publicist, Echo Ellick.

That color picture came with a full-page feature on Wilson. Directing the acting, he explained, was only about one-fourth of his effort. "In this business you have to be also a bit of an engineer, carpenter, painter, architect and electrician." What would he like out of life? "A new building."

Ranked among the top twelve theaters in attendance, the Playhouse had the smallest seating capacity of the top twenty-five. "The board has on hand a design for a 491-seat theater. There is a little matter of raising the money to build it, however." (Not reported was the fact that architect F. Merion Mooberry was already drawing up plans for the theater that wouldn't be completed until 1959.)

The story also characterized Wilson's directing style, sans hair-tearing temperament. "He does a lot of running his fingers through his thick curly hair during rehearsal and once in a blue moon he blows his top and the rafters ring with his comments." The writer apparently did not talk to his actors, some of whom argued that his comments, if not volatile, could run on and on a bit. Others went further, complaining to the board of "high-handed" and "rude" treatment.

February's *Father of the Bride* by Caroline Francke brought more new players who would make a lasting impact at the Playhouse. The title bride was Elaine Jabenis, whose radio show,

Bride Elaine Jabenis in 1952.

Elaine's Saturday Scrapbook, ranked as second best woman's show in a national competition. Now raising two children, she had worked for *New York Times* drama critic Brooks Atkinson and traveled widely as the fashion expert for Omaha's Brandeis department store. The review praised Jabenis as "the flighty bride-to-be."

Another new face wore the rugged lines of an Irish pugilist. Gene Driscoll, a collegiate boxing champ, continued in theater and saw his daughter Delaney on stage and in such films as Alexander Payne's Oscar-nominated *Election*, but didn't live long enough to see his son Tim in Payne's *Nebraska*.

Measles, Explanations Delay Fry, Bob Reilly Debuts

Ken Wilson saw ten more Broadway plays on his annual New York trek. He praised *The Moon Is Blue* as "still the funniest play on Broadway." A road company was coming to Omaha and "we might be doing it next fall." He would do it a year later and face the harshest controversy from the Catholic hierarchy since *Family Portrait*.

A new leading man, Frank Andersen who succeeded Jack McBride in the Creighton Drama Department, came down with measles, pushing the opening of *The Lady's Not for Burning* back to April. Further delays were added each night before the first curtain. The review mentioned "a brief introductory narration" by director Wilson to explain the drama by Christopher Fry.

According to historian Dr. Langdon, "The curtain speech which Mr. Wilson gave … became longer every evening. Although the members of the audience were impressed, they couldn't quite decide what was going on." The costume designs by Mrs. Gifford drew attention to her careful research into fifteenth-century style. She was challenged by two hard-to-fit actors—Andersen at six feet five and Dorothy Hume, under five-foot with a size 2 shoe.

Another program change dropped *The Patriots* and closed the season in May with *The Happy Time*, a French family comedy by Samuel Taylor. Tommy Rosch returned as Bibi, a boy with great curiosity about the birds and bees. Ireland's Dympna Sackett plays the mother who tries to shield him from the influence of his father, uncles and grandfather, all "gay, roistering blades" of a romantic, ribald French persuasion.

The father, Robert Reilly, was introduced to playgoers with a flashing smile in the photo accompanying word that he was a former prisoner of war in Germany and now public relations director at Creighton University. He would author a dozen books, run for Congress, and win honors for later roles. The cast included Carol Burnett's future husband, Sarooian, Jean Berg and a villain played by Bill Wiseman, who became a top executive at Mutual of Omaha.

Mary Peckham joined the board now headed by Mrs. Key. Attendance dropped from the previous season's record, but still hovered near 90 percent of capacity. Perhaps a major event in the city's history distracted potential playgoers. The spring of 1952 brought a Missouri River flood that forced evacuation of thousands from the flood plain on the Iowa side and shoring up the Nebraska side to protect downtown Omaha. It brought President Harry Truman and famed journalist Edward R. Murrow to the scene. The CBS icon stood on the sandbagged river bank and reported on the hard-working volunteers in the familiar grave tones that made Murrow and Arthur Godfrey the voices chosen to go on the air if the Cold War flamed into nuclear attack.

High on 40th Street, the Playhouse was always safe from the flood, but no threat had so mobilized manpower since World War II.

Bricks vs. Bouquets Debate Over Critic Koffend: 1952–1953

When rehearsals for *Happy Birthday* by Anita Loos began in mid-August, Soule (that first full-time scenic designer) left, his role now reverting again to Wilson. Anne Connelly, Wilson's former assistant technician, returned full-time for other backstage duties.

The Korean War and early hints of American involvement in Vietnam were barely visible in the life of the Playhouse. A Public Pulse letter warned that "the little theater group is going to miss Sgt. Milo Green," now "cast in the production being staged in the Far East." Put the nostalgia on hold, he stayed long enough for the season's first show.

Another change before the season opening sparked a vigorous exchange of letters to the editor. Reviewer Jake Rachman died "in harness," as the press liked to say when a workhorse fell on the job. His final column, including a plug for singer Julie Wilson, had been typed and illegible corrections added before death came at home. An editor reminded that he could never be persuaded to take a vacation.

Called the "kindest man in show business" by the Hollywood columnist Hedda Hopper, Rachman's passing brought letters with similar thoughts on the bachelor who'd doubled as columnist and drama critic for the past decade. The Playhouse remembered Rachman with a plaque for "a kind drama critic." Too kind, some said.

The controversy came when John Koffend, his successor, returned to the more mixed reviews common in the earlier days of Keith Wilson and Keene Abbott. First a police reporter, Koffend wrote the Stage and Screen column and wrote reviews through 1954 when he left for a *Time* magazine post in Los Angeles. (Later he led a more exotic life on a South Sea island before drowning in the 1970s in a waterfall near Aspen, Colorado.)

Happy Birthday required a variation on the traditional 8:30 p.m. curtain. It went up at 8 to reveal a pantomime of readying a neighborhood bar for the evening trade. The light comedy featured tiny Dorothy Hume as the shy librarian who loosens up as the night wears on and libations flow.

Koffend's first review called Hume "a remarkably poised actress," praised Feltz and Green, and gave Wilson credit "for a well-knit show." All told, he termed it "a sizable success" while elaborating on the passion that goes into performing. "Only love, of course, could suffer them to endure the brutalities of director Kendrick Wilson, ceaselessly honing them down to the drama's razor edge."

The November production of *Abe Lincoln in Illinois* unleashed the round of newspaper letters debating Koffend's criticism. It was a major production involving a cast of 38 and 153 workers. Robert Sherwood's Lincoln was played by tall Frank Andersen, with Nancy David as Mary Todd, the woman who pushed him reluctantly into prominence, Peggy Staley as Ann Rutledge and Bob Reilly as Stephen Douglas. A future Playhouse star, Jim Harker, made his debut.

Koffend found it "ambitious and demanding … over-long to begin with, running nearly three hours without much action." The review praised Andersen, but "the rest of the cast did not equal" his performance.

The flap over Koffend began with a letter from Doris Stevens, drama director at Benson High. She protested "the kind of dramatic criticism" that complained about "one of the most worthy undertakings by the Playhouse in many seasons. Let us have a review that stresses fundamentals and basic virtues rather than trivial details."

Koffend's column used the *Abe Lincoln* production to dramatize the need for a new theater. "Backstage the congestion was something fierce." He cited dimensions that make "everything too small. The stage is woefully inadequate." He reminded that the theater was built under a temporary permit twenty-five years ago to last three years.

Some Praised, Some Panned, *Stalag 17* Most Popular

Bell, Book and Candle, John Van Druten's comedy on modern witchcraft, opened 1953 with a small, experienced cast. Koffend's review gave four reasons to name it the "most successful effort so far this season": the script, the handsome set, the director's "artful hand," and "the truly professional dramatic skill of James Harker." A cat named Pyewacket spent much of the show nestled in Mrs. David's lap.

Stalag 17, the German POW comedy, marked Ken Wilson's fiftieth show, all "without a flop," the February Prompter claimed. Koffend sat in on tryouts, and said, "I am willing to concede that (he) is performing miracles. Almost without exception, the 19 men who showed up that night were incredibly bad readers," his column said. That's no discredit, they weren't actors, but Wilson told them, "Most of you probably will be usable. And therein lies the miracle."

Both a Bill Spire cartoon and a news photo showed Larry David and Jerry Rosen in long johns, dancing barefoot or wearing Hitler mustaches and mock-heiling Cpl. Schultz. Bernie Szold's artist friend, Leonard Thiessen, played the Geneva man inspecting the prison camp. Jack Holley, a high school English teacher who'd become the daily newspaper's editor, "was quite effective" as the youngest prisoner. A packing-house newsletter featured Harvey Carter, more often backstage, as a black prisoner named "Red Dog."

A record 905 nonmembers saw the play, so an extra performance was added on a normally dark Monday. Prompter headlines, "Does Your Organization Need Money?" reminded that a sorority got a cut when it purchased a block of tickets for *Stalag 17*. Boy Scout Explorer Post 42 sold the second Tuesday for *Bell, Book and Candle,* and two groups, A.A.U.W. and Creighton Faculty Wives, did the same for *Abe Lincoln in Illinois.*

A second Van Druten comedy, *The Distaff Side,* was "resurrected" in March, Koffend wrote. His opinion: Director Wilson "should not have performed the exhumation." But "he must have had his reasons for scheduling this rather shallow and vapid comedy," so the reviewer "was sincerely willing to accept them in good faith."

Remains to be Seen by Howard Lindsay and Russel Crouse was "a spirited and noisy way" of saying goodbye to the season in May. "Flashes of gunfire, cymbals and red lingerie" livened the evening. Air Force Maj. Al Lipsey played a lawyer named Stan Kenton who is constantly being confused with the band director of the same name. Two new names would grow more familiar—Edwin Clark, drama department head at Omaha University, and Valerian Kuffel, a young actor destined for many local roles.

Royal Eckert Joins Staff, *Moon Is Blue* Attacked: 1953–1954

Playhouse historian Lucy Updike clipped an item that made passing mention of a new theater on the scene. It recalled the old Council Bluffs Community Players who "just couldn't get the people to buy tickets." A source felt "the whole cultural life of the city is hampered by not having a theater that will seat about a thousand people." But, without such a building, a new group had been born that spring of 1953. Chanticleer presented *The Man Who Came to Dinner* at Thomas Jefferson High, beginning as the Playhouse did in a school auditorium.

The theater founded by a handful of people, including Norman and Louise Filbert, wouldn't have a permanent home for more than a decade, but now the smaller Iowa city across the Missouri River had both the Civic Music Association doing operettas in a movie house (Strand Theater) and Chanticleer doing plays.

So the Playhouse had new competition as it prepared for its next season. There had always been high school and college plays, Ak-Sar-Ben productions, Junior League shows, various performances by groups at the Jewish Community Center and other locations. Outside the schools, however, such theater was sporadic, with nothing approaching the full season of the Playhouse, much less its staff of two full-time and two part-time employees.

Anne Connelly and Harold Dergen were replaced by a more experienced technical director. Royal Eckert came from New York City, where he was stage manager for the Equity Acting Staff of the Actors Union. Perhaps his University of Minnesota background helped his standing with two other alumni, director Wilson and board treasurer Clarence Teal. For the first time in history, the Playhouse had hired a theater man other than the director who would stay to become well established. He joined Wilson, the box office attendant and custodian as staff.

It must have surprised the trustees when their season-opening play, *The Moon Is Blue*, sparked a protest that led to yet another new theater

Eckert honored later by Wilson.

company the following year. Catholics started the Kingsmark Players "out of our concern about that play," said founder Mary Cay Neugent, then a social worker.

Archbishop Gerald Bergan strongly urged Catholics to take no part in the Playhouse. Earlier, he had warned them to stay away from the movie. Then an editorial in the *True Voice* (later renamed the *Catholic Voice*) concluded in all capital letters: "LET NO CATHOLIC BUY ANY TICKET, PURCHASE ANY ADVERTISING, TAKE ANY PART IN ITS PRODUCTIONS OF ANY KIND."

The editorial had argued, "Legally, we suppose, the Community Playhouse has a right to stage 'The Moon Is Blue.' Morally, it shouldn't." The film had been condemned by the Legion of Decency for denying "traditional standards of morality" and dwelling "upon suggestiveness in situation and dialogue." When it stages a play "so rotten that the church must forbid its members to witness it, the Community Playhouse seriously affronts the moral sensibilities of at least one-third of Omaha."

Deja vu for membership chairman Teal, who feared for his job and lost friends after the *Family Portrait* criticism from Bishop Ryan in 1943. The flyer printing the season schedule identified *The Moon Is Blue* as Broadway's leading comedy of the last three years, adding, "Not to be confused with the movie." Teal's membership campaign letter, aiming to match last season's 2,736 members, noted that the stage play received a rating "for adults only" from the Legion of Decency. So the Archbishop's harsh words were not expected. But, just as with *Yes, My Darling Daughter* in 1939, the timing of the film's condemnation seemed to blur the lines between stage and screen.

"You're not going to get me into any morality arguments," Koffend's review began. "No one complained" when it delighted for three years on Broadway, and "no one threw stones" when it played Omaha and Sioux City. Then "the feathers flew" when the movie opened. He finally got around to the point that the small cast did "very well" with a play that is "all clever lines and no action." He particularly admired James Harmon, a newcomer with such roles elsewhere as Caesar, Willy Lohman and Elwood Dowd under his belt. "Just don't come in a contentious mood," Koffend closed.

Perhaps the feathers would have stopped flying sooner if not for those stirring the pot known as the Public Pulse. Mrs. McGill was thankful she had Archbishop Bergan, rather than Koffend, to advise her. Then came the letter from young Jimmy Gleason, "and approximately 300 other signatures." Headlined "Children Say 'Moon' Indecent and Immoral," it began, "We, the children in the Community Playhouse neighborhood, object to the type of play being presented there. Such plays will destroy American youth and then America."

To that, Ed Clark, Omaha U. drama head, voiced fears the boy would grow up bigoted if he learned so young to protest something he hadn't seen. A barrage of counter-attacks labeled the university professor "full of hate, self-exaltation, prejudices and false ideas." Most defended young Gleason, one praised Clark and another offered, "Those who don't want to see 'The Moon Is Blue' don't have to. But do they have the right to say nobody else can see it?" Attendance of more than 3,200 ran second only to the top draw of the season.

Despite strong feelings on all sides of the discussion, the pressure on Catholics must not have been as strict as the upper case warning in the *True Voice* suggested. No dropouts were reported in the small cast or backstage. And the next play, *The Shrike,* included at least one Catholic in a sensitive position, the public relations director for Creighton University, Bob Reilly. He also worked on Playhouse publicity and later agreed to serve on the boards for both the Playhouse and Kingsmark.

It was organized "to provide wholesome activity for Catholics" by such Creighton figures as English professor Ed Corbett and future Coca-Cola chief Don Keough, among others. Miss Neugent recalled that the first meeting was held at the Cathedral, where Archbishop Bergan handed the founders a check for $100. Kingsmark opened the next fall with *Our Town,* a play requiring no royalty payments. Actors with Kingsmark credits soon won Playhouse roles.

The Shrike by Joseph Kamm, set in a mental hospital, opened in November with the approval of Cecil Wittson, director of the Nebraska Psychiatric Institute. He commented as a layman that it was good theater, and as an expert that "we see what is unfortunately true in many hospitals." Attorney Jack Wenstrand played the psychiatric patient, Jose Ferrer's role on Broadway. Wenstrand was "straightforward, restrained and genuine," the reviewer said, in a role that won him a Fonda-McGuire award.

"Keep your eye on Marian Melcher" as his wife, the title's sharp-taloned bird of prey. Koffend may have offended another audience when he described her using "one of the most unscrupulous means ever devised by that unscrupulous animal, woman."

A large, diverse cast included several African-American men and women. The review declared it "the richest collection of amateur talent I've seen so far." Advance photos showed Reilly, Wilkinson Harper and Joe Basilico as mental patients singing a calypso song, and Betty Abbott as a white-uniformed doctor. Then host of a children's television show, she became the first woman on Omaha's city council and fell short in a runoff for mayor.

Davy Crockett Opens Centennial Series, Sets Record

January's Prompter featured the city's centennial logo. It emphasized Omaha's 100th birthday, and the years 1854 and 1954, flanked by a Native American in chief's headdress and a cowboy, both waving. The Playhouse planned to celebrate with a series of six plays tracing the evolution of acting styles. They started with *Davy Crockett,* a melodrama that played Omaha's Academy of Music, a second floor downtown stage, in 1875.

Much like the trappings of *Ten Nights in a Bar-room* in 1929, a long, narrow playbill listed the cast, the full title—"Davy Crockett, or, Be Sure You're Right, Then Go Ahead"—plus olio specialty numbers and such advice as "Ladies Will Remove Their Hats."

Donald Luttrell's title character "wrung his comic-heroic role bone dry. Pure and toothsome ham," Koffend wrote. Crockett entered with "gazelle-like bounds" and froze during exits "to give the audience time to cheer." Jim Harker's villain "plays every stage minute from a feral crouch," and Royal Eckert's Major, guardian of the heroine, used "rotund syllables and windmill gestures" to suggest "better than anyone else the flavor of last century's theater." Patricia Newcomb's heroine, Little Nell, "bats her eyelashes 60 times a minute" to show fondness for Davy.

The review was so enthusiastic about the start of the centennial celebration that it even praised the "offstage manipulators of the wolf heads at the door." John Wilson, son of the director and the makeup artist, played Davy at age five.

The melodrama ran two extra days and "broke all records for attendance" with 3,800, the next Prompter reported.

Cider was served in the lobby for *Crockett,* lemonade for *Secret Service,* circa 1896, and sarsaparilla for April's *Peg O' My Heart*—each drink allegedly the most popular during the time of the play. For *Peg,*

Royal Eckert's design was copied from the 1912 original. Koffend was emphatic about Dympna Sackett's success in the title role. The play, his review said, "is nearly all jewel and no setting," but "fortunately, the Playhouse has the jewel. She's a 21-karat Irish colleen," and "she shines brilliantly without benefit of setting."

For the season-ending *Broadway* in May, Coca-Cola was the mid-1920s drink of choice for the George Abbott and Phillip Dunning play. It wasn't quite a musical, but Cora Quick did the choreography and a news item asked, "Are you fat, female and a piano player?" If so, Wilson wanted you and a half dozen hoofers. The dancers later posed for a leggy chorus line shot. The review dubbed Muriel Feltz as a Sophie Tucker type, "the hit of the evening." Koffend promised, "You should get a bigger bang from the last old-timer than from the earlier three" which had "some of the mustiness of museum pieces."

A new attic fan added comfort for playgoers, but trustees voted to end matinees. "We are forced to admit that not enough patrons care to attend in the afternoon to make the effort worthwhile."

Detective Story Tops Distinguished Season: 1954–1955

The season "might well be termed the most varied and distinguished program in the history of the organization," wrote Harry Langdon. The fact that it was the final year covered in his thesis study may have contributed to that impression, and his role in an elaborate production of *Mary of Scotland* made him a more personal witness.

But Langdon, who went on to a doctorate in theater at the University of Iowa and a drama teaching career that included a time at Creighton University, found support for his claim from two *World-Herald* reviewers, the departing John Koffend and his successor, Glenn Trump. The 1954–1955 season shared with the other twenty-nine its portion of arrivals, farewells and alumni success stories, but most significantly the return of Fonda and McGuire to raise funds for a new theater.

A news photo of a legendary trio—Echo Ellick, Clarence Teal and Emmy Gifford meeting as the play-reading committee—signaled a change in the season program. The Playhouse noted "growing antipathy to the series of dated plays" and dropped the remaining centennial series. That decision pushed *Mary of Scotland* from the opening spot to later in the season and replaced it with a new comedy, *My Three Angels*.

Sam and Bella Spewack's "whimsical idyll of murder" on a French penal colony featured Joe Basilico, Don Dygert and Curt Siemers as the convicts who play guardian angels to the storekeeper's family. The review fashioned Basilico "the most persuasive performer." He won front-page treatment in the *Armour Star* where the South Omaha packing-house reporter identified him as a worker in the "dry salt department." Koffend termed Silvia Egons "promising" in her debut as the storekeeper's daughter. Her Prompter sketch said she "escaped from the Russians on the last ship out of Latvia right after the war." Siemers would still be acting well into the next century.

Langdon's thesis claim for a distinguished season is better backed by reviews of the next

Bob Reilly

two plays, *Detective Story* and *Mary of Scotland*. Sidney Kingsley's drama features a hard-bitten New York detective named McCleod, a role played by Ralph Bellamy on Broadway, Kirk Douglas on film and Bob Reilly at the Playhouse. The reviewer said the play "is one of the solidest all-around acting jobs ... staged in many a season. The overall effect is brilliant ... a shining example of what our local theater can do."

Reilly's detective, hidebound by duty, is "the toughest dramatic assignment," one "fielded with sure and confident skill. I was lost in admiration of him during the final moments of the final act." That ranks among the most enthusiastic critiques from the restrained Koffend, and it was later endorsed with a Fonda-McGuire award.

The reviewer complained that he lacked space to fully credit other choice portrayals—"so many lustrous local jewels." Real-life police sergeant Howard McArdle showed a "natural bent for acting" as Reilly's gentler partner. Jack Reilly, the lead detective's brother, played an "explosive racketeer." He'd worked professionally with Olivier and other greats in the Chicago company of *Mr. Roberts* and was employed in production at KMTV, the dawn of a career that led to senior producer of *Entertainment Tonight* and *ABC's Good Morning, America*.

Another newcomer in the large *Detective Story* cast was Jack Moskovitz, who played several roles in the 1950s, then returned to the Playhouse stage in 2002. Among the detectives was Don Kalal, a noted cabaret performer in later years. For those who weren't counting, the return of Milo Green from Korea brought word his role as an abortionist was number twenty.

A stickler for realism, Green insisted that Bob Reilly pull no punches when the script called for the detective to slug the abortionist. Milo's repeated demands for harder hitting finally inspired a Reilly jab that knocked him cold. As for sensory realism, ex-police reporter Koffend said Eckert's "set was so real I could almost smell the bullpen."

Death came to that grand lady of the stage, Mary Murray, an award-winning actor known as Ethyl Rogers when she worked in the box office.

Sad news, as always, was mixed with success stories. Jim Milhollin, who played Jesse James and other lead Playhouse roles, was appearing in both an off-Broadway play and on television, where he provided "the sinister eyes" that opened and closed Robert Montgomery's *Eye Witness* drama.

Mary of Scotland Soars, *Sabrina Fair* Vivacious

Playhouse directors had turned to Maxwell Anderson so often in the 1930s and 1940s, starting with his *Elizabeth the Queen* in 1932. Now, in the first month of 1955, Anderson's pairing of Elizabeth with *Mary of Scotland* became the ninth of his plays, leading Shaw and Kaufman, both with five.

Writing his last review before leaving for *Time* magazine, Koffend began, "If you want clear proof of how the Omaha Community Playhouse has matured over the past years, by all means see its treatment of a collision between two queens." His earlier complaints and his pending departure added weight to such praise.

The ruling rivals were played by newcomer Nancy Fowler in the title role and the seasoned Kenna Hunt as Elizabeth. The review saw Hunt as "the personification of the devilish queen" in an award-winning performance that outweighed the playwright's sympathy for Mary.

Howard Hall, another of those broadcast announcers who once dominated the Playhouse stage, "turned in a powerful bit" as Protestant reformer John Knox. That portrayal prompted a letter to the editor from Dr. Edward Stimson of Dundee Presbyterian Church, an outspoken student of Scottish history. He praised the overall performance but offered a more generous view of Knox.

Miss Fowler, who studied drama at Carnegie Tech, suffered more than Mary's abdication. She tripped over a stage brace one night and cut her chin. After the final curtain, she went to a hospital for five stitches.

At a time when the full Playhouse budget usually totaled about $25,000, the production cost a record $5,000, including rental of sixty period costumes. The run of *Mary of Scotland* in frigid January added to the call for a new theater. As Lord Huntley, Royal Eckert wore kilts. He recalled that the winter weather gave him a new appreciation for what the women faced when they had to hurry outside the building in short skirts to make entrances on the opposite side of the stage.

That wasn't the year's last weather report. At the opening night intermission for February's *Sabrina Fair,* director Wilson updated the audience on the icy streets outside, as reported by the new reviewer, Glenn Trump. A former sports writer, Trump covered arts and entertainment for less than two years before joining Ak-Sar-Ben civic leaders as public relations director.

In an early Stage and Screen column, he invited readers to describe how they'd spend a million dollars. Milo Green jumped in to say he'd build "a new, spacious, air-conditioned" theater, pay Wilson and Eckert "salaries they could not command elsewhere," sponsor the best plays "with no ceiling on production costs," and fund "at least the minimum Actors' Equity pay scale" for every cast and backstage crew member. No one missed a chance to signal the building campaign ahead.

Sabrina Fair, Trump said, "like many of today's hits contains quite a bit of cursing" and lines "that would never pass Hollywood censors. A little of each at times is cute; when overdone it becomes disgusting."

Behind the scenes, Linda Lou Miller caused an anxious moment. Linda was a greater silver-crested cockatoo valued at $900. She played a French-speaking cockatoo named Maurice and behaved perfectly until escaping the cage one night. David Martin gathered her up expertly while delivering his line: "Mother, don't go off without your new friend."

Caine Mutiny Triumphs, *Mr. Pennypacker* Overshadowed

With *Sabrina* Betty Barker began rendering caricatures in the fashion of those Bill Spire's drawings that had appeared regularly in the *World-Herald*. For *Caine Mutiny Court Martial,* she drew Jim Harmon's Captain Queeg in the witness chair surrounded by profiles of his mutinous officers, including Jim Harker as Lt. Barney Greenwald. Herman Wouk's adaptation of his novel had first starred Henry Fonda as the stage Greenwald, but was best remembered for Humphrey Bogart's film treatment of the paranoid Queeg. The Playhouse became the first community theater to present the just-released drama, and Trump's review added to the claim of a distinguished season.

"The Wilson wonders," he wrote, "not only came off definite winners but enjoyed what this viewer considers one of their greatest triumphs." Let the record show that Trump's alliteration of "Wilson wonders" was not preceded by Foley's phenoms or Szold's zanies. Was Keene Abbott turning over in his grave?

No one shouted "April fool" when that April 1 opening was used to announce that Fonda and McGuire would return to Omaha in June for the leading roles in *The Country Girl*. The back page of the Prompter promised a five-night run at the brand new civic auditorium Music Hall. Members earned first crack at up to four tickets each, ranging from $4 orchestra seats to $1 in the second balcony. The Playhouse's "Most Famous Graduates," the announcement said, would "assist in its drive for new building funds." The Junior League would sponsor $10 patron seating on the main floor opening night.

Perhaps all that overshadowed the regular season's final show, *The Remarkable Mr. Pennypacker* by Liam O'Brien. It was another new release, having recently starred Burgess Meredith in the title role and Playhouse graduate Howard Fischer, future executive Schmad's uncle, as the Sheriff.

Walter Olson played the free-thinking Pennypacker, father of nine children in one city, eight in another. He "handles his part nimbly," the review said, adding praise for Basilico as the Sheriff. Among the youngsters was Jessie Gifford, daughter of Emmy and Hal. She gained more fame as an artist who renamed herself Jessie Nebraska.

May brought the departure of Royal Eckert, "our very excellent designer-technician of the past two seasons." He would stay long enough to execute sets for *The Country Girl* and return after earning a graduate degree at the University of Minnesota.

Country Girl cast, Milhollin, left; director Wilson, George Randol (who played Henry's dresser), McGuire, Henry and Jane Fonda.

Fonda, McGuire in *Country Girl* Open Music Hall, Aid Fund Drive

Measured by income, attendance or publicity, the June 1955 run of *The Country Girl* ranked as the biggest event in the thirty-year history of the Omaha Community Playhouse. A profit of nearly $25,000, five near-capacity crowds in the new 2,500-seat downtown Music Hall and more news clippings than generated by some entire seasons gave momentum to the campaign for a new theater. The keepers of the archives collected *Country Girl* matchbooks, cocktail napkins toasting "The New Playhouse" and invitations to a plethora of opening night parties and gatherings to honor the visiting stars.

Item after item listed guests at lunches, suppers and receptions hosted by the Peacocks and others, with the managing Schimmels hosting the post-performance party at the Blackstone Hotel. A *World-Herald* editorial urged Omahans to turn out, reminding that even the $4 orchestra seats were a bargain compared to $8.80 tickets in New York.

The fund-raising idea came after a campaign committee headed by M. Cooper Smith, a J.C. Penney executive, called for an attention-getting production. Trustee Harriet Peacock called her brother, Henry Fonda. He agreed to perform and then called Dorothy McGuire. Together, director Wilson recalled, they decided upon the play by Clifford Odets, then acclaimed as a film with Bing Crosby and Grace Kelly.

Fonda, McGuire and Jim Milhollin donated salary and travel costs to the building fund, and Jim Harker, the local advertising man who'd played many leading Playhouse roles, returned the $100 he was paid to perform.

Much was made of 17-year-old Jane Fonda's debut as the ingénue, and for young Topper Teal it meant an instant "crush" on Hank's cute daughter. A photo showed her facing papa, his arms folded across the chest, her elbows akimbo with jutting chin. A front-page story explained that Jane had called Ken Wilson, asked for an audition, then read lines over the phone for twenty minutes.

Henry was contacted, and expressed reluctance, but was convinced by Dorothy McGuire who reported him "secretly pleased." In the Teichmann biography, Henry blamed sister Harriet for suggesting her niece and provoking his "Have you lost your mind?" response. Jane's only acting experience came in a few roles at her eastern prep school.

"She's an extremely nice girl," the director said, and "she had the fine sense to admit that she knew nothing and was willing to learn."

Henry said, "Our relationship on stage becomes actor to actress and seems perfectly normal."

Father Fonda had just completed the *Mister Roberts* movie with Jimmy Cagney and Jack Lemmon, and he would next head for Italy to shoot *War and Peace*. Dorothy McGuire's latest film was *Trial* with Glenn Ford. Both brought spouses and children to Omaha, including Topo Swope and Peter Fonda, with the Fondas as usual sharing the house at 5205 Izard with the Peacocks.

A photo spread showed opening-night onlookers waiting behind a rope "for celebrities to arrive," before being driven inside by rain. "As Glittering as Coronation" read a headline. "Mink in all its mutations, except possibly pink, ermine wraps, diamond clips and earrings attested to the importance of the occasion," wrote Evelyn Simpson.

Governor Victor Anderson and other luminaries were "undaunted by the sudden rainstorm" boasted the article. In a reunion with his two stars of *A Kiss for Cinderella,* director Bernie Szold came back to praise the city's "cultural renaissance." Perhaps the $10 patron tickets limited the opening audience to 1,931, but Saturday and Sunday crowds totaled 2,500 and 2,465. It would take ten nights at 40th and Davenport to hold 2,500 playgoers.

And then there was the Odets play, reviewed not by Trump but by an heir from one of the city's pioneer families, Denman Kountze Jr. Omahans had seen a road company's Robert Young play Fonda's lead character, an aging alcoholic actor. The film

McGuire as wife of Fonda's Frank Elgin.

had brought an Oscar nomination for Crosby (Brando won for *On the Waterfront*) and the supporting actress award for Grace Kelly. She and McGuire played the wife coping with a man who fell off the wagon years ago but clings to illusions about his career.

Kountze challenged critics who accused Fonda of repeatedly playing himself: "How then can these people explain the subtle shifts of Frank Elgin (his role), the shaky hands, the uncertain stance, the irritable humor" and so on? How can all this "be conveyed so powerfully? The answer lies in Fonda's consummate skill." As for Elgin's wife, "It is Miss McGuire's particular capacity to live with wavering truth, to make the audience doubt and finally to believe in her."

Harker and Milhollin as the director and producer of the play within the play were praised. The cast also included George Randol, the African-American owner of a real estate company, as Elgin's dresser. (Backstage, Fonda's dresser was thesis author Harry Langdon.) Randol had played the pharaoh on Broadway in *Green Pastures,* the Honeyman in the original *Porgy and Bess,* and toured with Ethel Waters.

The review answered the big question about the teenager playing the ingénue: "Yes, Miss Jane Fonda has a future. It may take some time, but there is no lack of promise. The audience recognized it, too, and she's 17." She raised backstage eyebrows by demanding that Ron Vaad slap her face to help with a tearful entrance. "She surprised the hell out of me," Henry said, "by bursting into tears on cue," but Jane credited the hard slap and the "fear and trembling I had of acting on the same stage with my father."

Eckert watched one night as father Fonda "really chewed out Jane" when a backstage poker game caused her to miss an entrance cue. He found Fonda easy to work with, even when a set door stuck. A local actor blistered Eckert, but Hank didn't complain and gave him a thumbs up when it was fixed. Director Wilson and his star generally worked well together in an atmosphere of deference for Fonda.

"He didn't like Ken's use of a liquor bottle on the table" in a scene where the actor stretched drunk on a cot, Eckert recalled. Fonda said he could convince the audience he was drunk without it, but Wilson wanted it there. Each night, just before the scene began, Fonda dumped the bottle in a waste basket. Nancy Land, who did the lighting, felt that Fonda didn't get close to the crew, but Dorothy McGuire knew most of their names by the run's end.

All in all, considering it was the first play presented in the new Music Hall, the historic production went smoothly and successfully launched the fund-raising campaign. The regular reviewer, Glenn Trump, captured the palpable community pride in his column, The Town Trumpeter. "'Country Girl' Sought in Vain by Theaters on Both Coasts," the headline boasted. Attempts to stage the play "with this same cast, failed despite some lucrative offers." Trump closed, "Omahans will be left with the memories of seeing one of the finest legitimate theater efforts put on anywhere this year."

Fund Kickoff, New Theater Delayed: 1955–1956

With nearly $25,000 profit from ticket sales, the new building campaign was informally under way. The planned fall kickoff was delayed at the urging of civic leaders to avoid conflict with the United Community Chest–Red Cross drive (predecessor of United Way). Fund-raising wouldn't officially start until March 1956. But the souvenir program for *The Country Girl* gave the community a look at plans for the new theater and a brief history with strong evidence of space problems. Noting that the Playhouse had never conducted a financial drive, Val Teal wrote, "For many years we have been bursting at the seams."

The best evidence came from what she identified as "major improvements." One involved cutting a new door on the north side of the prop room. Before, actors went out the east door, ran around the front of the building, then re-entered by the west door to get to the other side of the stage. The "major" improvement? "Now they go outside and circle the back of the theater—a shorter and much less public trip." But it's tempting to scream, "They still had to run outdoors in skimpy costumes."

The other big improvement? That separate steel shop building ended the dangerous mixing of paint in the furnace room. Now the furnace room could double as a dressing room, and they could make coffee in the shop instead of the box office.

Three program pages showed drawings of the proposed new theater, explained alternatives and the pressing need. "The plan is to build ... at the present site at 40th and Davenport, unless a desirably located site with off-street parking space becomes available." The present site would require about $300,000 for the building. An artist's rendering revealed a sweeping glass entry and lobbies with some resemblance to the twenty-first-century plant at 69th and Cass Streets. A 490-seat auditorium almost doubled capacity; and workshop, dressing rooms and two offices for designer and director seemed spacious by comparison to the original theater, though far short of the eventual facility.

The appeal emphasized the growth of other community theaters and the stagnation of the Playhouse. "We've been forced to stop growing," limiting membership to 2,800, while Des Moines grew to 5,000 with a new facility. Trustees found they couldn't enlarge the old "temporary" structure and couldn't ask casts to stretch runs beyond two weeks of performance after four weeks of rehearsal.

When this plea was written, the Playhouse hoped to be in the new building in 1956. Delay of fund-raising made that impossible, but when *King of Hearts* opened the 1955–1956 season, a Prompter call to "Build Me More Spacious Mansions" still hoped "if you all co-operate as magnificently next March as you did last June, we will have a new Playhouse next year."

King of Hearts, Crucible, Dial M for Murder

Glenn Trump said September's *King of Hearts* comedy was not "a touchdown, but at least a near miss" that would score "once some of the opening night flaws are corrected." Julia Burns, cast in the Kingsmark Players' *Our Town* and Jane Fonda's understudy last summer, took the lead role handled on Broadway by the most famous Des Moines Playhouse graduate, Cloris Leachman. She's secretary to a comic strip artist and the object of his assistant's affections.

The review calls 11-year-old Jim Childe and veteran Rudyard Norton, thirty years after his first Playhouse role, the scene stealers. The latter "milks his role as the publisher for every guffaw possible." The bio for Don Shepley, in the minor role of a policeman, claimed a master's degree from the University of Dublin, CBS work in New York and Hollywood, and appearances with the Pasadena Playhouse. Impressive but blatantly false, given his graduation from a Council Bluffs high school just the year before.

The Crucible by Arthur Miller "introduced a dynamic new star," the review noted. He was Leo Hartig, the latest technical director and another Minnesota colleague of Wilson's. He'd been technical director most recently at Stanford. The November play was delayed one week, apparently to accommodate Hartig's late arrival for the lead role.

Trump wrote, "His work as the besieged husband in the witch-hunting story was big league." But the reviewer began his comments with a kiss of death: "It's probably the longest Playhouse effort of its 31 seasons, lasting an over-long 3 hours 5 minutes."

Before the year ended, the Junior League repeated its play, *The Birthday* on WOW-TV. Written by Echo Ellick, the cast included Hartig and such children as the author's son Chuck, Jessica Gifford and, in the lead role, future state senator and congressman Peter Hoagland.

The suspense thriller *Dial M for Murder* opened the 1956 portion of the season featuring a future award winner. Cherie Shaver "gained poise and displayed fine talent" as the tension builds on the telephone. Her husband, Neil. played the Scotland Yard inspector. Keith Homan, in a minor role, began what became more than a half century on the local stage.

See How They Run, *Anastasia*, Then Records for *Cadillac*

You Can't Take It With You was scheduled again, and the Prompter quipped that the title was slightly intentional, given the fund drive. But "many people complained they'd seen the Sycamore family too often," so the English farce *See How They Run* was presented in February. Apparently the fact that it was recently done by Chanticleer in Council Bluffs was no problem. Wilson even cast the director and leading lady from the Iowa production. Chanticleer founders Norm and Lou Filbert paired with those recent arrivals from Southern California, Neil and Cherie Shaver.

Playgoers learned that the Filberts met in a Chicago production of *The Madwoman of Chaillot*, became engaged during *The Male Animal* and married during the run of *The Corn Is*

Audrey and Rudyard in *Solid Gold Cadillac*, 1956.

Green. A photo shows Neil in boxer shorts and Norm leaping over a prostrate actress.

Hartig directed *Anastasia* in April to free Wilson "as the latter busies himself with the building fund drive," Trump reported. The play was noteworthy, he said, for its plot about the identity of the White Russian princess, but "most of all" because it brings Mary Peckham back to the Playhouse stage after a three-year absence with her "Ethel Barrymore-ish touch" as the Dowager Empress Romanoff. He added, "A deep bow is due Rudyard Norton, who has taken part in every Playhouse show this year."

The Solid Gold Cadillac in May would draw more than 4,500 to a record seventeen standing-room-only performances, a fitting achievement for the theater's 200th production. Trump cited the script (Fonda's biographer Howard Teichmann was George Kaufman's latest coauthor), flawless work by Wilson and Marie Jesse's performance as the little lady shareholder who confronts bigwigs. Known as Mrs. John Jesse the book reviewer and as Marie Stewart with the Brandeis Players, she was in good company with Peggy Staley as the romantic lead, Audrey Gloden as the shapely model and a savvy bunch as business tycoons.

Funds Pour In, Downtown Competes for Building Site

"Omaha cannot live by beef alone" was the cover message of the fund-raising booklet. It was the big campaign piece, and an "educational, inspirational dinner" on April 10, 1956, was the kickoff, ten months after *The Country Girl* run. The agenda at the Fontenelle Hotel gave a half dozen speakers pointed topics: Wilson on "the Need," a Tulsa Little Theater director on "the Proof" (he inspected the theater and declared it "obsolete," but was miffed at being limited to five minutes), Chamber president and future mayor Al Sorensen on "What This Means to Business" and so on.

Advance publicity featured Richard Egan, billed as "the next Clark Gable," speaking on "What This Means to an Actor." A photo showed him applying suntan lotion to the bare back of a co-star identified as "the busty" Jane Russell of *The Outlaw* fame. He was chosen to represent ex-Playhouse actor William Dozier, then vice president of RKO Studios. Photos from the campaign booklet showed the "obsolete" conditions, most visibly in a shot of Rudyard Norton bare-legged in slippers and clutching a bathrobe as he ventured out into the winter cold to switch stage sides.

As expected, donors were reminded that the Playhouse "gave to the American stage" the likes of Fonda, McGuire, the lovely Lenka, Milhollin, O'Flynn and Esther Page. If that one rings no bells, she was Evelyn Paeper when she was honored for *The Little Foxes* and she understudied Carol Channing in *Wonderful Town*.

But now the important names were M. Cooper Smith, the campaign committee chairman and his subchairs: Zack Warren, Richard Hiller, Marvin Schmid and, of course, Clarence Teal. Plus 400 volunteers.

Smith had quietly contracted with a New York fund-raising firm to guarantee at least $300,000, roughly $100,000 less than estimates for new construction and equipment. Trustees started it off with $36,000, the banks' clearinghouse added $25,000, and the newspaper where theater-loving Margaret Hitchcock Doorly was still influential gave $22,500. Only when gifts reached $312,000 was the larger need revealed.

Teal told his volunteers, "You have done a wonderful job," then, "We need another $50,000 to do a complete job."

Many made the new theater possible, but Teal not only gave monumental service during those years, but left detailed records of almost everything, including day-by-day reports on fund-raising with copies of correspondence. The list of those designated for the larger "special gifts" category remains a vivid snapshot of civic leadership in the year 1956.

Smaller but generous gifts came in from many of the actors, backstage volunteers and ticket sellers such as Florence Young. Letters report a stock donation from future Mayor and Mrs. A.V. Sorensen, another from Jeannette Newlean. The former Columbian School principal was credited by Teal with steering her student, Dorothy McGuire, to the Playhouse.

A note signed "Hank" came with a $500 check from Fonda, who wrote, "I wish it could be more—but the Peacocks have just licked the platter clean." Teal's reply reminded that, after forgiven expenses, *The Country Girl* finally netted over $27,000.

Norm Sample Jr., son of a trustee, started the Loveland Summer Theatre, presented O'Neill's *Beyond the Horizon,* and donated income to the fund drive.

In hindsight, the dollar amounts seem minor, but doubts about the location of the new building loom large. Recall that Prompter notices had continued to refer to 40th and Davenport. That was still the designated site when the *World-Herald* editorially endorsed the fund drive in April. But in May a tug-of-war seemed likely between two locations—downtown land occupied by Central High and Joslyn Museum, and a western tract at 69th and Cass streets.

A mayor's planning committee spoke on behalf of a downtown cultural center just as the Planning Commission seemed ready to support a proposal by Robert Dillon. He'd buy five acres on 69th Street from Temple Israel in return for approval of rezoning and expansion of his Prom Town House motel, and then give three acres to the Playhouse.

The mayor's committee wanted to include the new theater in a plan that called for conversion of Central High School as the key building in a proposed Cultural Civic Center, an idea similar to one initiated early in the twenty-first century. The downtown committee included building campaign chairman Smith, V.J. Skutt of Mutual of Omaha and other leaders.

Earlier, Clarence Teal was "delighted" by the Dillon offer. But, speaking as president of the Playhouse Building Corporation, he said the downtown plan placed the Playhouse in a "quandary." While either site "would be satisfactory," the downtown plan was a long-range one threatening delay, "and that bothers me tremendously." He later told the Planning Commission that the board "prefers the West Omaha site" because construction could begin soon, and it is "just west of the present center of our membership."

When Teal made that presentation in early June, a pair of actions made the outcome uncertain. The Planning Commission delayed its rezoning decision and the vote by Temple Israel's congregation fell short of the two-thirds needed to sell the land.

Soon they voted again, 91 to 48, to sell, and the newspaper headline asked, "Spring Start on Playhouse?"

Zoning approval followed within days. Dillon would build a parking lot on his remaining two acres, and the Playhouse would build their parking lot south of the building site facing 69th Street. Playgoers had seen drawings of the new theater the previous summer and learned other details. The "rear-most" of the 500 seats would be only 85 feet from the stage—"the maximum distance that an eye in the back row can spot an eyebrow being lifted on stage." Now, in the summer of 1956, they knew where that theater would be built—just north of Dodge, east of Temple Israel, south of the new Methodist church, and west of the gracious homes in Fairacres.

Desperate Hours to *The Great Sebastians*: 1956–1957

Ground would not be broken for the new theater until the following June, but the September Prompter cited advantages for the 69th and Cass site—"plenty of off-street parking," near transportation "in a growing commercial district" (a few blocks from 72nd and Dodge, Omaha's busiest intersection) and ample lot size.

Meanwhile, the season opened with *The Desperate Hours,* about a family held hostage by three escaped convicts. Denman Kountze Jr. had taken over reviewing and the Stage and Screen column from Trump. He'd become a familiar figure with his casual style—tennis shoes, tan slacks and seersucker sports coat. Among other claims to fame, he was the nephew of the second wife of *World-Herald* founder Gilbert Hitchcock and would inherit millions in a few years.

"After a lazy summer," Kountze began his *Desperate Hours* review, "there's an effective way to stimulate audiences—yap at them, snarl at them and wave guns in their faces." He suggested the three thugs needed more restraint. Radio announcer J.P. Mitchell, Joe Basilico and Ron Vaad "looked the part" of the noisy convicts "and undoubtedly in future performances the rough edges will be smoothed."

Architect Mooberry's four-hour meeting with trustees led to some changes in October. "We have definitely decided not to provide for a balcony in the auditorium—it was too expensive for the limited additional seats" and they encountered "some headaches in laying out adequate parking space." The lobby entrance would generally face the corner of 69th and Cass. "We hope to start grading this year," but that hope went unrealized.

The new critic raved about November's *The Rainmaker*, claiming "it would have taken an earthquake to shake its excellence." Royal Eckert, between Minnesota studies and a run at Broadway, returned to play Starbuck, the title con man who bedazzles Lizzie, the plain daughter of the rancher played by Norton.

Time Limit by Henry Denker and Ralph Berkey puts an Army officer on trial for actions in a Korean prisoner-of-war camp. Wilson cast heavyweights Harker and Bob Reilly in key roles. A large cast included historian Harry Langdon, now drama teacher at Creighton University.

Among newcomers: Gary Frazell, head of the Nebraska Humane Society. The daily, still running those social items about Playhouse dinner groups, mentioned a new couple: Warren and Susie Buffett.

Grading for Chanticleer's new theater in Council Bluffs won space in the Kountze column with word that the new Playhouse would now cost $400,000. "May they prosper and build, even in the face of price spirals," he wrote. The Bluffs project fell short of funds and wasn't completed until 1963.

A news item said Wilson "desperately needed" an experienced actor, age 50 or so, to play a mind reader, the male lead in *The Great Sebastians*. At some point, he looked in the mirror and cast himself as the mustachioed Rudi Sebastian opposite Cheri Shaver as his wife Essie. The Sebastians, stranded in communist Czechoslovakia, take their mind-reading act into the Playhouse audience. A newcomer, Beth Gaynes Ginsberg, would become better known as a dancer and choreographer.

Ground Broken as Dressing Rooms, Canopy Deferred

With the June ground-breaking near, a shortage of funds was reported. It seemed $550,000 was needed to complete the original plan, but only $330,000 had been collected. They'd not only forgo the balcony, but "deferred are two floors of a three-floor dressing room wing," various offices, storage space and the soaring, wing-like canopy over the front entrance drive. The latest word was the "the red brick building may be completed," not May 1, but "by the fall of 1958."

Rather than the usual two years, Zack Warren would continue as president through 1960, a four-year span during the building project. At the annual meeting, Milo Green presented his oil painting of the original Playhouse, a 20-by-30 treatment of the theater, done at the request of Director and Mrs. Wilson. It would still hang in the new Playhouse in 2014. And what would become of the old theater?

"I suppose we'll try to sell it," Wilson said, but nothing was yet planned by the June 8, 1957, ground-breaking.

As part of the Second Century Jubilee under way in Omaha, the ground-breaking ceremony won the top spot on the front page of the *World-Herald* with a photo of Julie Wilson singing as Fonda and Mayor Johnny Rosenblatt looked on from the platform.

Henry, now 51, had recently taken his fourth wife, Italian Countess Afdera Franchetti, 24, with Peter, 17, as his best man. Henry made the point that he hadn't dropped work on *Twelve Angry Men* to rush home for the ground-breaking, but its timing came as he planned to pick up Omaha University student Peter from sister Harriet.

For the record, Julie Wilson sang "Omaha" and was joined in the chorus by several hundred onlookers. Speakers included the two neighboring clergymen, First Methodist's Dr. E. Wesley Perry and Rabbi Sidney Brooks of Temple Israel. Warren, Teal and Mrs. Guiou also spoke, the latter incorrectly identified as the first Playhouse president in 1928. The year was right but Alan McDonald and Rev. Ralph Bailey preceded her as earlier presidents.

Fonda praised the trustees and read a congratulatory telegram from Dorothy McGuire. Wilson promised the new facility in time for the 1958–1959 season, or "Sooner, if an angel should appear."

Miller Excavating completed grading in August 1957, and bids of about $550,000 were expected in November. Trustees made a new assessment of their financial situation. They added the $45,000 appraised value of the donated land, the anticipated $32,500 sale price of the old theater, and the $312,000 collected or pledged to claim a total of $390,000. That was well short, even when bids came in lower than expected at $473,000, including black-topping of the parking lot.

The trustees quietly started a second campaign aimed not at the general public, but seeking another $175,000 from foundations and business leaders. They also raised the season membership from $7.50 to $8.50. Raising the season ticket limit to 3,200, the increase added that many dollars to the annual income at a time when budgets were still close to $30,000. They'd always reached ever-higher goals in recent years, and sales came easier with a new theater on the way.

Reluctant Debutante Sets Record, Group Experiments: 1957–1958

Departing technical director Leo Hartig was replaced by Edmund Lynch Jr. He'd just completed a master's degree at the University of Denver and had gained theater experience there and at Trinity College in San Antonio. But Lynch drew more on a background in television production in Washington, D.C., where he helped produce the first Eisenhower inauguration and a tour of the redecorated White House.

Lynch apparently didn't do sets for October's season-opening *The Desk Set,* but its high-tech theme caused a stir in this pre-computer day. The William Marchant comedy centered on the installation of a new machine, Emmavac, that made people outmoded. The Playhouse was proud to borrow a $7,000 Remington Rand Electronic Synchro-Tape typewriter to represent the play's mechanical brain. Of course, the machine was more than fallible, sending out pink slips to everyone, even the firm's president.

Agatha Christie's *Witness for the Prosecution* in November featured Ron Vaad as the husband charged with murder, Cherie Shaver as his wife, and Gregg Dunn as an attorney. Wilson had fun putting trustees in wigs and black robes as British barristers. "They look very dignified and very wise in rehearsals," the director advised.

Dunn, declared "superb" in courtroom battle, was both a radio farm reporter and Captain Ben, a children's host on KMTV. He'd become even better known as Gregor, horror movie host on television, before trying his luck in Hollywood.

Jim Harker and newcomer Jane MacIver won the leads in *The Reluctant Debutante*, which broke records set by *The Solid Gold Cadillac*. The British comedy was extended five nights after standing-room-only crowds swelled attendance over 5,000.

"Drawing room comedy at its lightest and fluffiest," it was the perfect antidote for January blues, and again defied the old pretense that serious stuff sold the most tickets. Harker and MacIver competed for honors. "Just when you thought his performance was absolutely impeccable, Mrs. MacIver stole a march or two." High school senior Nancy Pinkerton, as their daughter, "is possibly the most adept of the junior actresses ... and certainly one of the most attractive."

The Prompter reminded that Pinkerton and other supporting players came to the Playhouse with experience in Junior Theater, Chanticleer and Kingsmark plays. Creighton University students had been appearing at the community theater since the days of Larry and Agnes Krell and William Dozier.

The same was true of Nebraska U. and Omaha University, where a future Playhouse musical star was appearing as nurse Nellie Forbush in *South Pacific*. Sue Ewing Perkins also played in *The Happiest Millionaire* with Peter Fonda, who made his Omaha U. acting debut in *Our Town* while living with Aunt Harriet on Izard Street. Yearbook photos show the slender young Fonda in stiff, ramrod poses, reminiscent of his father's early Playhouse pictures.

Something serious, however, could sell out for a single performance at a dollar a head. The Playhouse revived its earlier attempts at laboratory theater, this time calling it an experimental production of *Electra* by Sophocles. Although billed as a "dramatic reading," a news photo showed Cherie Shaver costumed before a set piece. Neil Shaver, who ran family-owned grocery stores, pushed the idea and directed the production, a forerunner of the Studio Theater. A much-honored cast certainly added to its draw—both Shavers, Harker, MacIver, Mimi Melcher and Norton.

Inherit the Wind brought the Scopes "monkey trial" to the stage with Gregg Dunn as the Darrow-like Drummond and Creighton English professor Edward Corbett as Brady, the William Jennings Bryan character. Dunn made a quaint-looking Darrow, squinting and shuffling, mastering the situation, the review said. Corbett shined as Nebraska's Bryan in his climactic collapse into his wife's arms, moaning, "They're laughing at me, mother."

The cast of forty introduced a new name that would resonate for years, a real trouper named William Bailey, who brought vast stage experience, starting as a vaudeville hoofer. He had helped backstage on an earlier show but soon would become as familiar a character actor as Rudyard Norton.

The season's final show, Thornton Wilder's *The Matchmaker* didn't open until May 30. A week's delay was blamed on casting and rehearsal problems, and its popularity extended the run to mid-June. Cherie Shaver played the conniving Dolly Levi, the role later made famous by Carol Channing in the musical *Hello, Dolly*.

With Dunn as Horace Vandergelder, the play offers all "the lovable characters" that became so familiar. Yvonne Johnson played another African-American servant, but she'd soon land an award-winning role. Another actor bound for major roles, Dudley Sauve, played a waiter.

Now Teal's update on the new theater ran under the headline, "6915 Cass Street," an address that brought the project closer to reality. "We began pouring concrete footings in late March," Teal wrote. "Then we ran into trouble." The problem? Good, solid land on both sides of a "V," but "something like quicksand inside the 'V.'" Work proceeded, all still below the first floor level. Teal didn't make a new prediction on completion, but the season would continue in the "temporary" theater by the Joslyn Castle.

New Theater Rises, Old One for Sale, Shows Go On: 1958–1959

The summer of 1958 wasn't all sidewalk superintending of the construction site. Julia Burns was the latest alum appearing on Broadway, and the movie *No Time for Sergeants* came to Omaha with Jim Milhollin still playing the psychiatrist. Two developments of the past season would soon bear fruit: the success of *Electra* would lead to more dramatic readings referred to as Studio Theater productions, and the Ford Foundation had made an offer the Playhouse couldn't refuse. They'd pay a flat sum subsidy, generally $5,000, to theaters producing works by new American playwrights. Trustees said yes and reserved the opening spot on the 1959–1960 season.

By September, the second fund drive had netted another $65,000, the board took a $75,000 mortgage, and trustees signed a personal note for $35,000 as fund-raising continued. A structural steel skeleton was seen rising against a wooded Fairacres neighborhood background, and readers learned about 70 tons of air conditioning.

"Year around temperature control for its patrons" was no small matter to playgoers who went back to the days when Brace Fonda fielded all those complaints about ventilation. The promised 520 form-fitting and upholstered seats must have sounded heavenly, too.

The last season at the old location, couldn't have started more successfully. *Separate Tables* starred Harker and MacIver, the leads in last year's most popular play, and such favorites as Mimi Melcher, Bill

Bailey, Lucy Jane Baird and newcomer Jean Erdenberger, fresh from Iowa University roles. It was two separate plays, one of "has-beens," the other "never-weres."

Kountze declared *Separate Tables* "one of the more literate and prepossessing dramas of the last decade." Such quality was important to playgoers who now paid $10 for season memberships—the maximum 3,200 were again sold—and $2.50 for single admissions.

The new season was marked by other increases in activity with the return of Royal Eckert. He'd nearly completed an advanced degree and appeared on Broadway and in summer stock while designing sets for several shows. Eckert would now offer classes in stagecraft and basic design, and Leslie Wilson would teach makeup. Principles of acting was promised later in the education program headed by Mrs. Key.

November's *The Happiest Millionaire* gave Dudley Sauve the first of many lead roles in this comedy about the wealthy Biddles of Philadelphia. As his daughter and the author, Julianne Kurtz brought a less memorable name to the Playhouse than the one that gained fame for her cousin, Swoosie Kurtz. Her Air Force officer father drew on the bomber "Swoose Goose" to distinguish his acting-bound daughter. Veteran Jean Berg led a cast including Dick Herre as Angier Duke (Peter Fonda's role at Omaha U.) and Yvonne Johnson once more a black servant.

Before the end of the year, Nancy Pinkerton won rave reviews at the Cleveland Playhouse in the title role of *The Diary of Anne Frank,* a part that would soon bring her back to Omaha. Director Wilson reported on his New York trip. "Our Lenka Peterson has dropped out of 'Look Homeward Angel,'" he noted, "but it's still worth seeing."

The Wilsons mailed one of those dreaded Christmas letters revealing that son John, ten, now stood four feet nine. "His prime joy is climbing the scaffolding to the grid at the new Playhouse."

Then on Dec. 31, 1958, a headline said, "Former Playhouse Building on Sale." Of course, it wasn't yet "former," with much of its last season left, but the For Sale sign was in the yard, and the asking price was

$32,500. It soon sold to a group of doctors, and president Zack Warren sighed, "We are very happy."

The latest Teal update on the building project promised "real progress is being made on the inside." Poor soil forced dropping plans for custodian's quarters on the east side, so they'd go in the ground floor of the dressing room wing, "at least a shell" of which was back in the plans.

Each Prompter carried a report, but Teal had learned to stop making predictions. Ken Wilson bravely told recipients of that Christmas letter, "We believe we'll have our final spring production in the new theatre ... so you see, this is definitely our last season in the little old Playhouse."

Studio Theater Born, Shop Goes West, Muddy Lot Paved

The First Legion by Emmet Lavery got a cold reception from Kountze when it opened the 1959 portion of the season in January. He declared this story of the Society of Jesus as "a rather ponderous succession of precious conversations." But "if wild horses dragged us to this play again it would be to note the absolutely marvelous interaction" of such characters as the blue-nosed Scottish Jesuit played by Bill Bailey or the urbane one played by Edward Corbett. "You could not find, we believe, a more gifted and properly schooled male cast in any community theater," the review concluded. Nor a more aptly dressed one. Creighton Jesuits loaned the real thing.

That wintry month brought something, spawned by Neil Shaver's production of *Electra*, to outlast the old building. The Studio Theater first performed under that name with a weekend presentation of *Under Milk Wood* by Dylan Thomas.

Director Jane MacIver fielded an all-star cast with the likes of Elaine Jabenis, Mimi Melcher, Gregg Dunn, Dudley Sauve, Rudyard Norton and Norm Filbert. They sat on stools, sans costumes but for the women's shawls and the men's tweed jackets, and used only lighting and their voices to bring the Welsh poet to life.

Seventeen actors portrayed sixty-three residents of an imaginary village in Wales, turning backs to the audience when their characters weren't speaking. The villagers ranged from saints to drunkards, doxies to babbits, fishermen to farmers. "Rarely have we been so thrilled with such a deliberate, accurate and sympathetic rendering of a great artist's work in our community theater," Kountze enthused.

The Studio Group's program suggested they'd offer "classical drama and what one might call non-commercial dramatic literature." The use of readings reduced rehearsal time, director MacIver explained, though her troupers leaned only lightly on the scripts held in their hands. In May, they'd do the ancient *Gammer Gurton's Needle* and Christopher Fry's *A Phoenix Too Frequent*.

Later, in the new facility, a formal committee governed this venture and codified its goals: To present plays representative of three modern trends: avant garde; classic, ancient or modern; and contemporary, non-avant garde. In other words, they'd do great plays that might not appeal to the larger Playhouse audience, but that would provide acting plums for the players and not just attract beatniks in berets.

The Teahouse of the August Moon in February sold so many tickets that a three-show extension was needed to meet the demand. The comic lead, Sakini played by Stan Spence, vied with Warren Vickery's Colonel Purdy in a cast including a number of Japanese-Americans, such as Warner Matsuo, whose father was an early Playhouse photographer, and Julie Takechi, whose brother Richard became a city and county office-holder.

She helped maneuver Lady Astor, the goat who climbs in a jeep and guzzles brandy. The goat claimed more stage experience than 9-year-old Julie. Left in Council Bluffs after appearing with the *Teahouse* road company, the goat did *Mr. Roberts* and encored *Teahouse* when Chanticleer did the play in May.

Alas, the bearded goat, though publicized as "the only available member of the New York cast," won no ink, but does here if only because the author was Chanticleer's goat-wrangler in *Mr. Roberts*.

Agatha Christie's *The Hollow* and *The Diary of Anne Frank* would complete the history of the thirty-year-old theater at 40th and Davenport. As the mystery opened in April, the steel shop building was being dismantled for its move to the new site. " 'The Hollow,'" Kountze summarized, "lacks spine-tingling suspense," but he found William Bailey "a thorough delight as the inevitable butler" who didn't do it.

As the Studio Group performed *Gammer Gurton's Needle*, the oldest farce in the English language, they learned that Milo Green, 50, had taken his life in the downtown hotel where he lived. The elderly Asian he played in *Teahouse* had turned out to be the last of his twenty-four roles with the Playhouse, and when one counted his work with Chanticleer and others, he was almost always in a show somewhere.

A Prompter tribute said, "To most of us the theater is only a small but enjoyable part of our lives. To Milo Green, however, the theater was his family, his hopes, in fact his whole life." He'd once played Santa Claus in a store and marveled that "I made the kids happy. They actually believe in me." He had longed for the new theater, but now he wouldn't play there. He left his lovingly painted portrait of the old one.

The May Prompter brought Teal's news that "the front doors are in place," and "the shop has also been erected. It's too bad that we couldn't build it new, too, but we'll hope a paint job makes it fit in with everything else." Spring rains fell. "The mud didn't get very deep, but it was enough that the Trustees authorized paving the parking lot, even though it may make us run over the budget."

When work began on improvements in the year 2002, the original brick wall at the north end of the stage still showed the outline where that steel shop building was attached in spring 1959.

Anne Frank Finale, Name Change, Wilson Interview

The shop was gone, so Eckert's sets for *The Diary of Anne Frank* had been constructed well in advance of its May opening. The play featured the "boisterous, captivating grace" of Nancy Pinkerton in the title role. "Nancy frankly and unabashedly walks off with the part and the entire evening" in what Kountze called "one of the most refreshing performances of the season."

With all facets historic in this final show across the street from Sarah Joslyn's castle, the starting time remained at half past eight. Many aspects of Playhouse life had been the same for years, including Wilson's staff, now that Eckert was back. Only his assistant technician, George Ragan, was relatively new. Mrs. Wilson still applied makeup, Bob Reilly and Morey Landman shared Brace Fonda's old post of house management, and many Omahans still devoted to theater in the twenty-first century could say, "I was there for the last show."

As *Anne Frank* played, they knew the new building would open with the musical *Say, Darling* on August 6. And while preparations for the July move gained momentum, *Community* was dropped from the Omaha Playhouse name. A *World-Herald* editorial called the name change "perhaps as significant as the new building." Trustees told the newspaper they discarded "community" because "it connotes a neighborhood affair … suggests amateurishness and the activities of beginners, and because the community theater had overtones of exclusiveness," that old bugaboo. And, the writer added, "The word suggested something small, and the Playhouse, in line with the swiftly growing city, has become big."

The upcoming census would show that the county had gained 62,000 in population, a 22 percent jump to 343,000 since 1950. A Playhouse supporter, businessman A.V. Sorensen, had moved from Chamber of Commerce president to city council president after leading a charter convention that rejected the old aldermen of Boss Dennison's day for a strong mayor form of city government. Al Sorensen would become mayor by the mid-1960s, and construction giant Peter Kiewit would buy the daily newspaper, keeping it under local ownership rather than part of Samuel Newhouse's New York-based holdings. Interstate highway routes were being debated, and developers sought approval for the Westroads Shopping Center, well west of the new theater site.

One measure of growth was the doubling of the number of cars since World War II, a big factor in the city's westward expansion. But the *Herald* answered its own "How big" question in Playhouse terms: The theater now expected 7,000 to attend each production, and the season ticket campaign was already halfway toward a goal of more than 6,000 memberships. The editorial closed with a historic twist to the name change. Starting as part of the "Little Theater" movement, the Playhouse first outgrew that label to become a "community" theater and now had outgrown that name. Or so it seemed at the time. "Community" would make a comeback.

Another perspective appeared in "Conversation with Kendrick Wilson," a chapter in a 1959 book *Community Theater: Idea and Achievement*. The director called Omaha "very typically Midwestern … so typical it is unique. The greatest advantage in operating the Playhouse is that there's so little other activity, so little competition other than a fine symphony." But "no competition in natural entertainment. We have no lakes; people don't fish or boat in the Missouri River. There's nothing else to do in town." Well, he added, "You can go bowling, drinking, golfing." (Fund-raiser "Coop" Smith made much the same point: "Denver has its mountains, Minneapolis its lakes, but in Omaha diversion must be man-made.")

Maybe one road company a year, a play or a musical, comes to Omaha, Wilson exaggerated. That claim might raise the hackles of Dick Walter, whose promotions alone exceeded that estimate. Perhaps it wasn't plugged as progress, but a third network television affiliate, KETV-7, had joined WOW-TV and KMTV, both nearing their tenth anniversaries on the air. In any case, the director was just getting started in a nine-page article that delivered his "state of the Playhouse" summary as it moved into the new plant.

237

Omaha playgoers, Wilson suggested, have "normal, average American taste. We try to give as much variety in a season as possible … to please at least everyone once a season, and not disappoint them more than once." Any classics? "Every once in a while, yes; not too often. We do keep raising their taste little by little, year by year. But we seldom tell them they are seeing a classic."

Wilson pointed out that the new theater would double seating capacity and predicted that membership would also double as it did when Tulsa, Des Moines and others built theaters with "new comforts." He explained that the fund-raising campaign was falling short at the time of the interview. "We open in August and are in hopes that there will be an angel who will come to our rescue once we get the building. Besides, the Omaha Fire Department is going to kick us out of this building within a year anyway."

Wilson wasn't being prophetic, but the "temporary" theater burned down only months after the Playhouse moved out. Apartments soon occupied the site.

Rental Truck Rolls, Nostalgic Farewells to 40th Street

In the July heat, a rental truck ran back and forth the thirty-two blocks from the old theater to the new one, with Eckert, his assistant and volunteers manning the move. SAC Airman Stan Spence, star of the recent *Teahouse*, had just stepped in as the part-time technician-janitor. He was the tall one with glasses, working alongside the shorter, mustachioed Eckert and teacher Nancy Land, guarding her precious lighting board from the perils of moving.

Wilson had moved his office to the new theater, occupying a backstage space that more than four decades later served as a dressing room for the leading ladies of *Carousel*. But in mid-July, with the grand opening just three weeks away, the director still rehearsed his *Say, Darling* cast in the old theater.

By the end of the month, both the *World-Herald* and the weekly Sun Newspapers ran big spreads of pictures and stories. Readers saw

Emmy Gifford painting the big blue mural covering the 79-by-13-foot foyer wall, and her livelier treatment of the ladies powder room with its semi-clad female figures. Sorry you wouldn't see it, men were told, but then the women wouldn't see Bill Hammon's artwork in the men's room. Symphony conductor Joseph Levine rehearsed a chorus that included Glen Zeisemann, a woman who would play a controversial role in the theater's future.

Most of the publicity looked ahead, but Val Teal took a fond look back at the not-so good old days. She recalled the time when the castle grounds across the street were colorfully gay with costumes drying in the sun, and when her clotheslines "mystified neighbors" who saw everything from pioneer bonnets to clown suits and red long johns hanging there. Such displays came when the Joslyn Gatehouse leaked on the costumes stored there. Gone now were the days when costume girls startled passers-by on 40th Street as they walked "laden with silks and satins, wearing layers of bright vests, coats, shawls and a flopping, beplumed hat topped by several derbies."

Nerve-wracking horrors of the old lighting board, with "two kids straining to hear low spoken lines," then "on cue to pull down 12 levers—gradually and simultaneously." The four hands pulling those twelve levers belonged to Val's son, John Teal, and his future wife, Mildred Mann. "The tired old light board often wearily dropped off unexpectedly, and the plates sputtered rebelliously, biting the hands that touched them."

When the two left for college, a plea went out for "a quick, resourceful octopus to replace them." One night during a mystery, "lights came on suddenly after a blackout to reveal the villain frantically crawling around, groping for the gun" that was supposed to be holding the others at bay.

Mrs. Teal recalled casts huddling under blankets during wartime fuel-saving efforts and problems with sirens and other sounds forcing actors to scream their lines. Noisy plumbing prompted signs forbidding their use after the curtain went up. People were packed so sardinelike in the lobby that "if the outside door were suddenly opened, several fell

Omaha Community Playhouse under construction, 1958.

out." She remembered the parties, especially that jungle affair when a skunk wandered in to impartially spray big-game hunters and pygmies alike. And, as always, she retold the stories of actors running out in the cold winter night to get to the other side of the stage. The good old days? "Don't hanker after them," she concluded.

While Val Teal evoked frosty images of shivering audiences, the new theater was opening in August, so a broadside emphasized "the inaugural production in its new air-conditioned building." And a full-page newspaper ad placed by the contractors dwelled on the comfortable seating. Beyond the creature comforts, the new stage ran 34 feet deep, the old only 24, and the Playhouse now had a rehearsal hall below.

In hindsight, the new facility could be described simply to those familiar with the later, vastly larger quarters: In August 1959, it seemed wonderfully expansive compared to the old theater. But it consisted only of the auditorium, minus balcony and orchestra pit, two backstage offices for Wilson and Eckert, three dressing rooms, a "Green Room" actors' lounge, a makeup room, plus the foyer out front with Emmy Gifford's mural, and the restrooms on the south side.

New Playhouse prior to 1959 opening.

The old steel shop was attached on the north side of the stage; a space above was used for sewing, fitting and costume storage; and a large space below provided four dressing rooms and the rehearsal hall. It became the Studio Theater with a carved door donated by Dorothy McGuire Swope. The basement kitchen remained unequipped due to the lack of funds.

If it all seems small potatoes compared to what it came to be, 6915 Cass was "the fulfillment of a dream" that August. Henry Fonda, home to see Peter, 19, play Elwood P. Dowd in *Harvey* at the university, was "terribly impressed." The preferred phrase was "Omaha's gift to Omaha," the assurance the city "would not live by beef alone."

On Sunday, August 2, the cornerstone was laid, the building was dedicated and Thursday's grand opening was only days away.

Grand Opening "Live" with Blue-Collar Joe and the Swells

Down Dodge Street at the Prom Town House, they dined that opening night on asparagus Polonaise, kumquat garnish and Rock Cornish hen aux sherry with truffle sauce. Apparently $15 for dinner and a seat for *Say, Darling* sounded a bit pricey in August 1959, and the Playhouse reminded that $2.50 or $3 on weekends was still the cost of subsequent tickets.

As Mayor Johnny Rosenblatt and other civic leaders entered the new theater in their formal finest, waiting with microphones in hand were Jim Harker and Elaine Jabenis, co-hosts for a live remote telecast. He wore a black tux with white carnation, she a pale pink off-the-shoulder gown with plunging neckline. But viewers tuned to KMTV at 8:30 p.m. on August 6 did not immediately see her elbow-length white gloves or glittering earrings.

They first saw the round, friendly face of Joe Basilico, sitting at a card table playing solitaire. Just as the founders emphasized on opening night in 1928 that their theater was open to "all walks of life," this regular Joe said he worked at a meat-packing plant and assured, "The Omaha Playhouse is for everybody." He wore a necktie, but his collar seemed to stray, and it looked as if he'd rather free a few chest hairs. Basilico was the last man seen without a tuxedo on a summer night where white was the preferred coat amid all the fashionable floor-length gowns.

Later in the half-hour broadcast, Kendrick Wilson pulled Elaine's microphone toward him to assure, "The formal dress is only tonight." Still, good ol' Joe from Armour's dry salt department wasn't wearing the uniform of the day, as the television audience would soon see.

Basilico was followed by a filmed pep talk from Dorothy McGuire and Henry Fonda and a bear dancing by the sky blue waters for Hamm's beer. Then the cover of the *Say, Darling* program filled the screen as trumpets blared and the doors swung open for "Premiere" sponsored by Omaha National Bank.

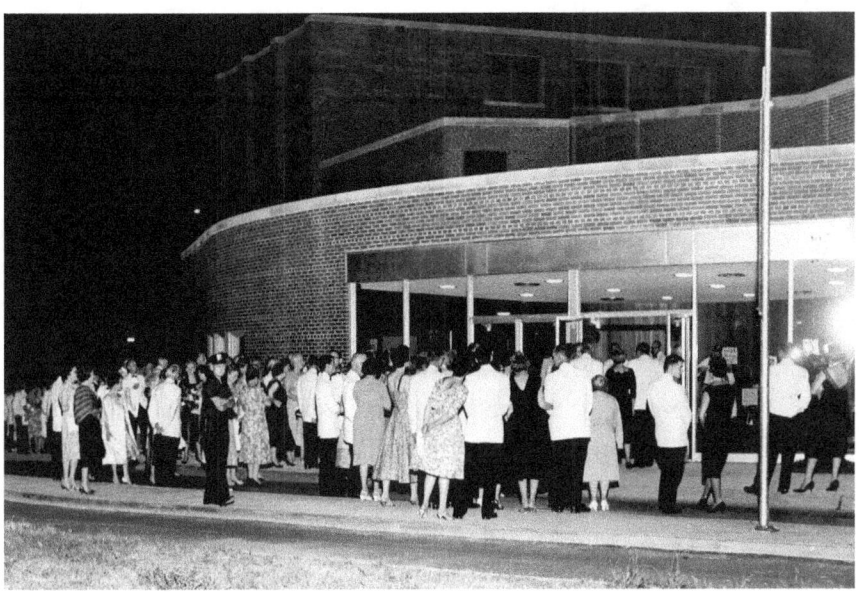

Opening night crowd in white tux coats.

Harker, vice president of Bozell and Jacobs, Omaha's biggest advertising agency, and Jabenis, now an experienced television host, took over. "In 30 minutes the curtain is going to go up," Jim promised, and Elaine in her pink floral brocade enthused about "the true spontaneous excitement and glamour" that awaited viewers. "As far as we know," she said, "TV cameras have never before been permitted backstage just before the opening curtain."

"I've got opening night jitters," Harker confessed, but that didn't stop him from leading the camera down a corridor while clutching great coils of microphone cord. He knocked on the dressing room door, asked if they were decent and started a round of interviews both backstage and in the lobby.

"It's my second Playhouse theater opening," a dapper Rudyard Norton explained, adding "I've lost track—it's in the 30s," when Harker wondered how many shows he'd done. Dick Makousky proved Joe Basilico wasn't the only packing-house employee and others told where they worked. Harker left with, "Let's go see what's going on in the makeup room," quickly realizing the obvious and predicting "makeup."

His co-host took over "in the glamour department," introducing "the first lady of the theater," the director's wife. Leslie Wilson found the new reality even "better than the dream." Jabenis asked, "Don't I see your son John there?" and young Wilson told her he wanted to be an actor or a geologist.

The stars—Maxine Sloan, Bill Bailey and others—also took brief turns in the spotlight before the co-hosts focused on civic leaders and the ribbon-cutting.

Clarence Teal in white tux did the honors "in the name of the board of trustees," inviting everyone to the new Playhouse. With the words, "Here it goes," he snipped the ribbon and couples in formal attire poured into the foyer. Mayor Rosenblatt and others commented on "Omaha's gift to Omaha" with praise for Emmy Gifford's murals and other features. Someone repeated the idea that the theater was "not for a select group, but for all the people."

As curtain time neared, Harker went back to the wings where stage manager Elizabeth Burchard and her assistants, Joan Marx and Bernie Grasso, prepared to call "places." Designer Roy Eckert told him, "We can relax now; all the work's done except shifts."

Then Elaine announced, "Here is the man of the hour," and talked to Ken Wilson, long-faced with black bow tie. He rarely flashed a smile, and his eyes often darted nervously as Jabenis addressed him.

"Tonight, of course, is the biggest thrill of a lifetime," he said. They agreed that the new building gave Omaha the finest community theater in the land.

When the camera went back to Harker, just off stage, he said the time was near, "There's a wonderful hush, people tip-toeing very gently." Actors walked past and he wished them good luck. He told KMTV viewers, "Good night and on with the show."

CHAPTER

6

New Theater Stages Musicals: 1959–1974

Say, Darling Draws Over 7,000 to 69th and Cass: 1959–1960

Who spoke the first line of dialogue in the new theater? The answer to the trivia question was Higgsie. Tall Richard Higgs, who became Eckert's technical assistant in the next season, greets the leading characters at the airport in *Say, Darling*, Richard Bissell's story of the making of his musical *Pajama Game*. Higgs does not ponder whether to be or not to be, nor does he mention his dependence on the kindness of strangers. He simply says, "Hi, Frankie," to Mrs. Jordan (Eileen Boler), and the first event at 6915 Cass is under way. Director Wilson might quibble that son John uttered the first words, an unscripted exclamation as part of the airport crowd.

Soon Schatzie the publicist (Warren Vickery) brings in the first song, an intentionally awful sendup called, "Chief of Love." A song writer is part of a cast complete with music director Joseph Levine's chorus and dancers choreographed by Elfi Hosman. She soloed with

Airport scene opens new Playhouse.

a Russian ballet company before marrying an Omahan. The big production number, "Something's Always Happening on the River," is the one song that received wider play. It winds up with a stage full of performers singing, "Oh, the river is the only life for me."

Three weeks after opening night with one final show to go, Harriet Peacock announced, "We're off to a wonderful start." She reported record attendance of 6,700 at fourteen performances with gross receipts over $21,000.

Reviews critiqued the theater itself. Denny Kountze described "a sparkling showpiece" with "unbelievably fine" acoustics. Norm Filbert praised the building, but summed up *Say, Darling* as "a crisp, smooth and professional three-hour production of mediocre froth with a sophomoric plot and a number of forgettable songs."

Soon the new Playhouse would settle into the September routines of a regular season, only days away. The excitement and publicity had ranged from Mayor Rosenblatt's proclamation of Playhouse Day in Omaha to a feature story about Nancy Land's forty-fourth show on Wilson's lighting crew. Joslyn Museum director Eugene Kingman praised Emmy Gifford's 79-foot murals, and she described her goal, to portray "the intangible, evanescent, dreamlike quality of the theater."

The move to 6915 Cass was complete. The next problem was producing an original play by an unknown.

Ford Funds *Morgan Rock,* Critics Dub It "Melodrama"

The Prompter cover now featured a photo of the new theater's glass entry. The play was new, too. For *Morgan Rock* playwright Philip Pruneau, it was "a little like a New Haven opening." Some 250 scripts were submitted to the Ford Foundation, and his was among eight selected for financing and production. Omaha and Tulsa were the only community theaters chosen to present Ford-supported plays.

Ford money guaranteed financial success, but it was not a critical success. Kountze passed the reviewing baton to colleague Robert McMorris, later a popular columnist, and Dr. Clark, Omaha U. theater director. Their jointly-written review was scathing. "'Morgan Rock' lacks clarity. It's hard to say what the play is about." The second play in the new theater, like the first, was set in eastern Iowa, a town atoning in the 1880s for the past sin of stoning an unwed mother to death. "Dialogue in general is undistinguished. There's hardly a line worth remembering."

A lone sentence refers to "a competent cast" headed by three professionals imported for the premiere. The imports—William Hindman as the preacher, Eugenie Hunt as the offspring of the murdered woman and Bill Alexander as a villain—were joined by such Playhouse stalwarts as Mimi Melcher, Jane MacIver and Jean Berg. Public Pulse writers defended the drama, calling its critics not only "exceedingly harsh and discourteous" but "unfair."

A tradition started with that September Prompter. The Cownie ad on the inside cover featured the ingénue, Eugenie Hunt, in one of their furs. In November, Mary Peckham wore "a natural Norwegian blue fox, a Cownie creation priced at $450." She played a Republican spinster hiding out during the FDR administration as she co-starred with Elaine Jabenis and Lew Kucera in *The Girls in 509*.

FDR on New Year's Eve, Guild Organized, DeMoss in *Gazebo*

Late in 1959, another grand old man of the stage died. Charles Docherty was still present in 2014 on the Playhouse lobby photo wall, the silver-haired gentleman in the iconic photo of little Dorothy McGuire and Henry Fonda as a London bobby.

The Playhouse didn't wait long to offer a counterpoint to the anti-Roosevelt humor of *The Girls in 509*. *Sunrise at Campobello* opened at 8:30 p.m. on Dec. 31. Rita Kersigo wore the Cownie fur as Eleanor, the director's son played FDR Jr., Alison Teal was Anna Roosevelt, and Dudley Sauve clamped the jaunty cigarette holder in his teeth to play the only president elected four times.

Sauve crammed for the part, focused on FDR's coping with polio, by immersing himself in recorded speeches and practicing on crutches and in wheelchairs. Bill Bailey played the president's political intimate, and news anchor Lee Terry was the Happy Warrior, Al Smith. A Republican playing a Democrat, he'd run unsuccessfully for Congress one day and live to see his son, Lee Terry Jr., elected to the House of Representatives.

Why open on New Year's Eve, a Thursday? "With the newness of the Playhouse, I think the idea was for people to attend the 8:30 performance and then go to their parties before midnight," designer Royal Eckert recalled. A news item estimated that revelers would spend an average of eight to ten dollars per couple, but "one popular ballroom is an advance sellout at 15 dollars." The Playhouse had raised single admissions to $2.50, so a couple could spend five bucks there, then head a few blocks west to greet 1960 with the Eddy Haddad orchestra at Peony Park, all for a twenty-dollar bill.

The new year also gave birth to the Playhouse Theatre Guild. A "terrific blizzard" held attendance down to twenty at a January meeting, but the next gathering drew 140 women to hear Dr. Clark on the Broadway season and elect Mrs. Lawrence Shaw as Guild president. Soon to be more famous was her first vice president, Susie (Mrs. Warren) Buffett. Members paid $2 annual dues and vowed to "stimulate greater interest in the Playhouse."

Accompanied by a zither, the Studio players gave a two-night "concert reading" of *Some Loves and Laughs from Shakespeare*. MacIver and Harker directed Jack Reilly and others in passages from the Bard's histories, tragedies and comedies. Kountze called it "one of the genuinely moving experiences this writer has found at the theater."

The Gazebo brought a legendary broadcaster, portly Lyle DeMoss, in a role that would bring him the Fonda award. DeMoss started as a radio pioneer in 1922, was summoned to New York by David Sarnoff to learn about television, hired Johnny Carson at WOW-TV, created a syndicated patio cooking show and in 1960 worked as an advertising executive before returning to talk radio in a career then spanning the entire history of radio and television.

The comedy about an author who buries a body under his gazebo also featured a muscular cop, body-builder Cal Chess, "Mr. Midwest Physical Fitness." For the record, Bob Roberts, a man who'd become a familiar figure on the stage, played the corpse. Surprisingly, the newspaper felt a need to tell readers what a gazebo was—"not a bird or an animal"—and how to pronounce it.

Director Wilson took the stage before the 7:30 p.m. Sunday performance to chide latecomers. The earlier start "gives the cast one evening when they can get home at a somewhat decent hour," the news item explained. That night a third or more came late, holding the curtain about fifteen minutes.

"We must start on time," Wilson warned. "From now on the curtain will go up promptly at 7:30," and those arriving late would wait until the end of the first scene.

Ex-Playhouse Burns, Air Conditioning Stretches Season into Summer

Mrs. McThing by *Harvey* playwright Mary Chase ran a record twenty-seven performances in March and April. The long run accommodated grade schoolers attending as part of the Junior Theater program at Joslyn Museum. Before the play moved to Joslyn, the director told playgoers to avoid 69th Street as "impassable" and Underwood with "too many holes." He recommended coming east from 72nd Street.

Then, before the late May show, the old Playhouse at 40th and Davenport burned. Arson investigators heard that children had been playing "in and around the structure." News pictures showed the night scene "as flames shot skyward" and a daylight view of charred stage and seats. The walls swayed in the wind, so a watchman was assigned to keep people away until the remains were razed.

The Prompter had promised *Once More with Feeling,* but it was replaced by *Strange Bedfellows,* a period comedy on women's suffrage. Jean Berg, the wife of a senator played by Bill Bailey, joins the cause when her favorite son brings home a feminist daughter-in-law.

Before the July run of Norman Krasna's *Who Was That Lady I Saw You With?* White Jacob had taken over as technician after Higgs left to work in summer stock, then landed a role in the TV soap opera, *General Hospital.* Don Schoenbaum and blonde model Karla McKee played a chemistry professor and wife (Tony Curtis and Janet Leigh roles in the movie).

The extended season ended on the last days of July with Arthur Miller's *The View from the Bridge.* A photo showed a taller Connie Hiner kissing stocky Frank DeGeorge on the forehead. As the central character, Brooklyn longshoreman Eddie Carbone, DeGeorge reminded the reviewer of Rod Steiger. Robert McMorris, who now substituted for Kountze on occasion, called DeGeorge "a talented actor" and "excellent" in his first Playhouse appearance. He would go on to play leading roles in musical comedies.

An awed onlooker was Gordon Giffen, returning with his wife and two of their four sons to a different Playhouse than he left as director in 1942. Now manager of a New Jersey radio station, he recalled staging the first musicals such as *Our American Cousin* and *Knickerbocker Holiday*. Other summer news welcomed the film career of Jane Fonda. Henry's daughter, now 21, had signed with Josh Logan, who put her in *A Tall Story* with Tony Perkins. She'd been on the covers of four national magazines after appearing with father Fonda in the Playhouse *Country Girl*. However, the most popular 1960 film with a Playhouse connection starred Dorothy McGuire as the mother in *Swiss Family Robinson*, destined to become a children's classic.

Lively Prompter, Crowd-Pleasing *Kiss Me Kate*: 1960–1961

The first Prompter of the season reintroduced technician White Jacob, who'd worked backstage while stationed at Offutt. Box office manager Mabel Fordyce trained a replacement before she retired, but the job would soon go to Estelle English for more than a decade. Among the items in the Spylight column was word that Glendora Zeisemann had hosted a surprise silver wedding anniversary party for the Wilsons. That would prove an ironic role when she later led to the end of that marriage.

The Guild's Susie Buffett, her husband not yet the Oracle of Omaha, advised, "The dear hardy souls that fairly leaped over snow plows and under icicles" to meet last January "still haven't thawed out their enthusiasm."

Another Ford Foundation play, *Physician for Fools* by Kenneth Cameron, opened the season. It had been the first choice of five theaters, including the Playhouse, the year before, but the author chose the Margot Jones Theatre in Dallas. Now Wilson secured it without Ford support. Creighton's Ed Corbett played the 16th-century doctor who bitterly turns from humans to treating horses. In his second Playhouse role, Dan Lynch, a plumber who became a county commissioner and state senator, played a villain.

The playwright came to see its reincarnation and called it "far better" than the Dallas treatment

Despite flagging season ticket sales, the musical *Kiss Me Kate* in November became the first show to draw 7,000 since *Say, Darling*. Its extended seventeen-performance run was the longest in the new building with its doubled per-night seating capacity. Those extra tickets helped cover the highest royalties, $1,150, yet paid by the Playhouse, and $1,600 for rental of 120 costumes. Costumes, mostly by Emmy Gifford, had cost an average of only $335 per show the previous season.

The Cole Porter music was directed by Joseph Levine, with two-piano accompaniment. William Kellogg, who'd played Curley in Civic Opera's *Oklahoma,* was cast as Petruchio, with another opera star, Dorothy Davitt, as Bianca. The title role went to Glen Zeisemann.

The review emphasized that "Big Bill Kellogg, the Civic Opera pillar, dominated the show by an overwhelming margin" with "his rich baritone voice." The dancing, however, "was often painful to behold."

The chorus included a woman named Miriam and her deep-voiced husband, Richard Boyd. The time would come when he'd create the single most familiar and best-loved character in the history of the Playhouse. He'd play Scrooge in *A Christmas Carol* for thirty years and more than 800 performances.

Torn t-shirts were needed in December for *Streetcar Named Desire*. The Tennessee Williams play ran three nights in the rehearsal hall beneath the stage. Don Schoenbaum played Stanley Kowalski, with his wife, Gerre, as Stella Kowalski and Mimi Melcher as Blanche Dubois. The McMorris review praised her "staggering performance," and said Schoenbaum "makes a great Kowalski. He doesn't mumble like Marlon Brando." Director Ron Vaad staged the drama arena style for the Studio group. Schoenbaum later became manager of the prestigious Guthrie Theater in Minneapolis.

Word came before the end of 1960 that Bernard Szold, director from 1928 to 1935, had died in Texas at age 66. He was remembered "as one of the most vibrant, colorful personalities ever" to grace Omaha. He was pictured with his long, shaggy hair and a coonskin coat that stayed over his shoulders long after he came in from the cold. Despite his hair-tearing, head-banging tantrums, actors called him "a gentle soul."

Longer Runs for Studio Theatre, Wilson's 100th Celebrated

When rights for *J.B.* were withdrawn, *Rashomon* was first chosen to replace it. On reconsideration, the play committee decided to start 1961 with their tenth play from Maxwell Anderson, his *The Wingless Victory*. A review called it "his impassioned sermon against false Christians who use 'the word of God' to defend race hatred." Critics lauded the work of Elaine Jabenis as the Malay princess, Norm Williams as her New England husband and Sauve as his intolerant clergyman brother. It also marked the start of a long friendship for Mrs. Jabenis and actor Frank DeGeorge.

Meanwhile, Dr. Ed Clark reported on his Broadway tour. He saw Playhouse alum Lenka Peterson in *All the Way Home*. Later Lenka would take the lead in the prize-winning play as Colleen Dewhurst dropped out to have a baby. As Mrs. Dan O'Connor, Lenka was now the mother of five.

Peter Fonda would soon land on Broadway in *Blood, Sweat and Stanley Poole*, but first he'd do two Omaha plays, starting with February's *The Golden Fleecing*, a comedy about Navy men on leave in Venice. Eckert designed a luxury suite in the Gritti Palace Hotel, "the most elaborate" set seen at the Playhouse, according to Wilson. Photos again showed a ramrod Fonda, at attention for an Admiral and embracing the Admiral's daughter. He impressed McMorris with his "easy nonchalance" and his "poised, polished movements were fun to watch."

The writer was less generous to Peter's sister Jane who showed up wearing white lipstick, white face makeup and blue eyebrow paint. "Between acts Miss Fonda avoided the crowded lobby by taking uncomfortable puffs on a cigarette while hunched down in her seat … as inconspicuous as a flasher signal on a fire truck."

Jane saw her brother on Saturday, and poppa Hank posed with board president Echo Ellick at the Sunday performance, saying, "I was very proud of his acting." Before the play's run ended, a *Life* magazine photographer arrived and shot dozens of rolls of Peter in his crisp Navy duds but missed his backstage scare. Pranksters put two large catfish in the horse tank used to soak his uniform, simulating his fall in a Venetian canal. If that wasn't excitement enough, a pit bull badly wounded a little mutt owned by a trustee, and poorly parked cars were blocking the steps between the Town House motel and the Playhouse.

The Studio Theatre, now claiming its own committee and basement performance space, tackled *The Beggar's Opera*, the inspiration for *The Threepenny Opera*. Alexandra Hunt, who starred as Polly Peachum, flew off to play in a New York opera, then returned for an encore performance at the Playhouse. To celebrate Kendrick Wilson's 100th Playhouse production, his first Omaha play was repeated. *Ladies in Retirement* again featured Frances Key and Mary Peckham as two murderous sisters.

But the play itself was overshadowed by tributes to the director. A formal dinner drew Governor Frank Morrison, and the Prompter ran Echo Ellick's salute to "Papa Wilson, a man who has given so much of himself." A full-page spread in the *World-Herald* gave an update: "Though 50, he has maintained a deceptively youthful appearance. He still carries a pile of boyish curly hair and the same weight" of his arrival: 153 pounds "distributed over a 5-11 frame." His famous "space shoes" conformed to his combat injuries, and black horn-rimmed glasses, shaped like half-moons, aided his reading.

Another Prompter piece came from the same author who introduced him in 1942. She repeated the earlier claim, "I know him quite well. I've now been married to him for 25 years," Leslie Wilson wrote, "and consider myself lucky, too." The first hint that her husband's luck might be running out came later in the year.

Award Winners Attract Crowd, Director's Behavior Discussed

A news item proposed that Lucy Updike was the most familiar face honoring Wilson because she had seen 95 of his 100 plays. "She was out of town" for the other five. It's doubtful, however, that the Teals and others had missed even that many. More than a decade later, when the theater's golden anniversary was celebrated, attorney Margaret Fischer, aunt of future administrator Tim Schmad, was reported to have seen "every regular show" from the time she sat on folding chairs to watch *The Enchanted Cottage* in 1925 in the Cooper Dance Studio.

A "blue-ribbon" cast was heralded for *The Pleasure of His Company*, and it paid off in another attendance record of over 7,000. With the second appearance of Peter Fonda as a young suitor and Harriet Olson's debut, the witty comedy was a sure thing. Mrs. Olson, whose husband, Mel, was beginning to earn a reputation as a choral

Peter Fonda, Ginny Dyas in *The Pleasure of His Company*, 1961.

director, would soon become an award winner, too, and the host of a noon hour television talk show.

The review called Harriet Olson "superb" as the mother of bride-to-be Ginny Dyas. "Peter Fonda made it plain again that he is a gifted young actor," but the reviewer said "he can't help" his problem in portraying a cattle rancher. "Peter is as skinny as a toothpick and looks like a brisk breeze would blow him down." And he looked "too Ivy League" to be a steer-wrestler.

Julie Wilson came home to enliven the annual awards event. The New York cabaret singer sang in the chorus of *Knickerbocker Holiday* in 1941 and returned for the ground-breaking at the new Playhouse.

The season's end remained a time to revel in the success of Playhouse alumni. Damian O'Flynn was now Dr. Goodfellow on the *Wyatt Earp* show, as Westerns dominated prime-time television. Nancy Pinkerton, 21, was studying under Brando's mentor, Stella Adler, after two years at the Cleveland Playhouse. She'd land a ten-year run as the woman viewers loved to hate on the TV soap *One Life to Live*.

Peter Fonda would head east to learn from Lee Strasburg while supporting Darren McGavin in *Blood, Sweat and Stanley Poole*. He also married at age 21 and wrote a long letter to the Public Pulse proclaiming pride in his Omaha roots: "I keep my Nebraska plates on my car … brought my clothes off the rack in Omaha" and "I'm proud to say I went to Omaha University."

A feature on Dorothy McGuire, "Film Mother Comes of Age," compared her maternal film roles in *Old Yeller, Swiss Family Robinson* and her latest, *Susan Slade,* to raising her own two children.

Something was stirring that summer as the trustees renegotiated Ken Wilson's directing contract. On the surface, the issue was allegedly "high-handed and downright rude" treatment of actors and board members. Or "bad manners" as trustee N.P. Dodge put it. He said the actors on the board agreed that Wilson's "short temper" had alienated many actors. He didn't comment on a critic's shaded reference to "other problems of a personal nature," which "I have no way to credit or evaluate." But Dodge and his committee shared the critic's view that, for the time being, Wilson's accomplishments still outweighed such concerns.

The director's contract would be renewed, and he would finally receive "some sort of retirement annuity or pension," as he had requested. In the future, Dodge's correspondent added, "We might all welcome" a new director with Wilson's directorial skills and one also "warm in his personal relationships" and "a good public relations man in the Omaha community." No open mention was made of an ever-more obvious relationship between the director and Glen Zeisemann, a woman incorrectly identified as "Mr." in a recent Prompter.

Musical Tradition Big Draw, Then First Full Shakespeare: 1961–1962

The "sold out" sign went up in mid-September 1961, halting season ticket sales as the Playhouse bounced back to the peak of two seasons ago, the first in the new theater. When *Pajama Game* opened a week later, it started the tradition of kicking off each season with a big musical, a pattern that continued for more than forty years.

The popularity of the musicals overcame resistance from Wilson who disliked sharing control. *Pajama Game,* their second Iowa-based work by Richard Bissell, became the first show to top 8,000 attendance. The next season opener, *Bye Bye Birdie,* passed the 9,000 mark, then 1965's *The King and I* totaled just over 10,000, and a year later *Guys and Dolls* set a record of 10,212 that would last into the 1970s—all a far cry from the days when Eckert's office door bore the sign, "Help Stamp Out Musicals."

Symphony conductor Levine liked to tell of his first visit to the new Playhouse. He asked, "Where's the orchestra pit?"

Wilson allegedly replied, "We'll never do a musical." Instead, he'd never go a year without one.

Response to "Pajama Game" required two extra shows. One evening a dozen or so patrons showed up in pajamas, causing a weekly columnist to speculate whether it was spontaneous or a publicity stunt.

The *True Voice* writer raised an eyebrow, noting objections from a Catholic group and complaining that the brash dialogue "sometimes became merely smart-alecky and coarse."

But the dancing, panned in *Kiss Me Kate,* now won plaudits for Beth Gaynes, the third new choreographer for recent musicals. The critics liked Louise Filbert in the lead role of the union spokesman tangling and romancing with the shop superintendent. Lou Filbert would form a night club act with two of her supporting players, Eunie Denenberg and Ozzie Nogg, and the Filberts and Denenbergs would later establish the Upstairs Dinner Theater in downtown Omaha.

After such a strong start, what followed might have seemed anticlimactic, but fortunately the second production was also historic. *Julius Caesar* became the first full-scale Shakespeare. It required a cast of eighty-six and two extra weeks of rehearsal. Designer Eckert and technician Jacob took roles. When Marc Antony (Frank Scott, a broadcaster who went on to head the Voice of America) sprained an ankle, Wilson stepped in.

Standing square-jawed and robed in a photo showing Marc Antony bending over the fallen Caesar was "the rough-hewn conspirator Casca," Dick Boyd receiving the first kudos of his Playhouse career.

A tradition much older than the season-opening musical was conjured up on closing night. *Great Caesar's Ghost,* the latest in the run-ending parodies, kept Kountze up late, so readers learned how back-stagers lightened the farewell. A bewildered character in slouch hat and overcoat (Eckert) kept wandering into dramatic scenes, the conspirators couldn't manage to dispatch Caesar, and a petite female swept the steps of the Roman structure, then easily lifted a massive pillar to dust under it.

Roman Candle Fizzles, But Raisin in the Sun Wins Raves

The anticlimax came in early 1962, when *Roman Candle* fizzled, according to the *Sun's* Paul Williams. "Don't go looking for a message

Yvonne Johnson in *A Raisin in the Sun*.

or for thrilling theater," or for "outstanding acting; thus you can avoid disappointment."

The return of Joan Hennecke from California ended her ten-year absence. The venerable trio of Bill Bailey, Rudyard Norton and Lew Kucera conduct a mock trial in *The Deadly Game,* termed "a morality play disguised as a shocker." It puts an American salesman (Al Austin) in the middle of the title game played by three elderly gentlemen in the Swiss Alps. Austin, a radio talk host, followed his role by emceeing the Miss Omaha pageant on the Playhouse stage.

The April drama, Lorraine Hansberry's *A Raisin in the Sun,* gave the thirty-seventh season a third historic highlight. It was based on the Langston Hughes poem that begins, "What happens to a dream deferred? Does it dry up like a raisin in the sun?" The African-American cast won rave reviews and later a McGuire award for Playhouse veteran Yvonne Johnson as Mama Younger. Under a headline, "Finest Dramatic Effort of the Season," the Kountze review called it "a director's dream and a reviewer's delight." Before the season-closing *Blithe Spirit,*

Leslie Wilson told a writer what it was like to be makeup chief for her director husband. "It's a rare privilege for a woman like myself to share as much of my husband's work as I can." Her niche, she explained, brings her close to those directed by Kendrick. "With actors, there are sometimes hurt feelings and misunderstandings. I try to be a leavening influence." That was a telling observation after last summer's take on Ken's rudeness. She also talked about her twelve commandments on her Playhouse wall, including "Thou shalt not take the name of thy director in vain."

The June Prompter ran a feature on Harriet Fonda, suggesting she might have joined her brother on Broadway had she not met a young Englishman named Jack Peacock. The article told of her children and grandchildren, and her "very deep and protective love" for her nephew Peter, who lived with her during his Omaha U. years.

Dorothy McGuire came home in June to present the season's top awards. The new Edith Head award for costuming went to Gloria Johnson. She also designed outfits for comedienne Phyllis Diller who renamed her Omar of Omaha.

Director Added, *Birdie* Soars, *J.B.* Suffers: 1962–1963

The summer of 1962 saw the first associate director added to the Playhouse staff. Going back to Polly Robbins and Henry Fonda in the 1920s, the "assistant" director had been a jack-of-all-trades. The part-time technician-janitor came on board in the 1940s, followed by the scenic designers in the 1950s. Now Gerald Ness, 28, another Minnesota graduate, was welcomed with word that he'd help with the Studio Theater and expanded acting classes.

Like Wilson and Eckert, he brought summer stock experience from the land of 10,000 lakes. He'd also directed the Pensacola (Fla.) Little Theater. With technician White Jacob, Estelle English in the box office, and the day and night custodians, the staff had grown to seven for the first time.

The September run of *Bye Bye Birdie* was extended four days into October for nineteen performances that would draw nearly 9,300, another record crowd.

A new face brought professional polish to the lead role in the fall musical. As Albert Peterson, the Dick Van Dyke role on film and Broadway, Dick Mueller sang, "Put on a Happy Face" with the benefit of six years touring with the Stylemasters quartet. More recently, he was Chanticleer's male lead in *West Side Story*. His character manages Conrad Birdie, the Elvis-like heartthrob who's been drafted into the Army.

Ozzie Nogg co-starred as his amorous secretary, Rose, with Jason Clark as the pelvis who sings "I've Got a Lot of Living to Do" while the teenagers wail, "We love you, Conrad, we really do-ooh."

For the fourth straight musical, a new choreographer stepped in, this time Emaleen Gordon Skinner, recently named director of the new Omaha Ballet Academy.

Elaine Jabenis directed the next Studio drama, three one-acts from *The World of Sholem Aleichem*. Some of his Yiddish works had been performed at the old Labor Lyceum, but the Playhouse presented this play in English on the main stage. The *Sun's* Rosemary Madison saw few dry eyes after "Bontche Schweig" with Dick Makousky in the title role.

Just as the previous season moved from a popular musical to Shakespeare, now a record-breaking *Birdie* was followed with blank verse. *J.B.* by Archibald MacLeish brought the Biblical sufferings of Job to the Playhouse with two past award winners, John Wenstrand in the title role and Sauve as the satanic popcorn peddler, Nickles. Ten children alternated as the five doomed offspring of J.B.

Four reviewers praised the acting, but playgoers were warned it "is not amusing or relaxing." A subsequent Prompter note declared the audience "either fiercely in favor" or "fanatically against it." One of the latter suggested, "a few more lousy plays like 'J.B.' and you'll lose all your friends and customers."

The first play directed by Gerald Ness received a rough welcome from McMorris. He said Stephen Vincent Benet's *John Brown's Body* is "capable of soaring power," but this Studio production "didn't soar to any great height." When it does go "airborne," he credits a capable chorus led by Mel Olson and "delightful interpretations by Jane MacIver." Creighton prof Ed Corbett gestured and talked like Abe Lincoln, but "unfortunately, doesn't especially look like Lincoln" with a tall hat sinking to his eyebrows.

Terry Kiser's Star Rises, Summer Show Season's 10th

A January storm delayed the opening of *Pool's Paradise,* a sequel to Philip King's *See How They Run,* which earlier brought the same characters to the Playhouse. Lou Filbert as Penelope Toop and Rudyard Norton as the Bishop of Lax reprised their earlier roles. Janet Wallace from Paisley, Scotland, moved up from the chorus to a speaking part, and Terry Kiser in his Playhouse debut "showed a remarkable flair for mirth" as the head choir boy.

A new publication, The Callboard, was mailed to all members. Vol. 1, No. 1 in January had promoted *Pool's Paradise,* acting classes, a Guild meeting, and tryouts for *All the Way Home.* It would be directed by assistant director Ness, who also edited the Callboard. A *Sun* profile described him as "tall, dark and a bachelor." Jabenis and MacIver spoke of his "tact" and "approachability," and Wilson said, "He knows how to get along with people."

Ness was blessed to briefly have Mary Peckham in his cast. She broke her leg the day after tryouts. Mary fell at home, but a similar fate for Emmy Gifford was blamed on a skiing accident. Under the circumstances, "break a leg" lost some of its traditional charm.

Come Blow Your Horn, the first Neil Simon work at the Playhouse, closed the regular season with "the most riotously funny" comedy of the year, the *Sun* review claimed. It focused on "two marvelous creations," Libby Sachs as mom and Frank DeGeorge as dad of the two brothers played by Val Kuffel and Terry Kiser. McMorris said

DeGeorge "stomps around shaking his forefinger and shouting 'ya bums!' Mamma is a wailer." Kiser would enjoy success on Broadway before sharing a TV series with Carol Burnett. Then he became the famous corpse in the film *Weekend at Bernie's*.

The new President's Award went to Mrs. Zeisemann for "the greatest contribution in areas other than backstage or on stage." This would also later take on ironic overtones.

The presence of an associate director made it easier to try another summer show, the off-Broadway musical spoof, *Little Mary Sunshine* by Rick Besoyan. Ness, musical director Mel Olson and choreographer Jean Stone staged the "new musical about an old operetta" down below. Moving to the rehearsal hall left room above to prepare for next season's opening musical. One reason for starting each year with a musical, Eckert recalled, was to allow him more time to create the sets.

Think Nelson Eddy and Jeannette MacDonald singing "Indian Love Call," add a hefty Austrian trilling something saccharine, blend in Dudley Do-Right and you catch the spirit of *Little Mary Sunshine*. Instead, Ken Peterson's Forest Ranger and Valerie Stone Thurman's naughty Nancy Twinkle sing "Colorado Love Call," and Christel Pratt Kent sings "In Izzenschnooken on the Lovely Essenzook Zee." Kountze called it "a delightful batch of sure-fire hokum."

When *Sunshine* closed on August 4, the Playhouse had staged ten productions—the six regular shows, three Studio plays and the summer musical. But even ten wasn't enough for Kuffel, Kiser, MacIver, Norton, Filbert, Harriet Olson and others. Calling themselves the Actors Summer Stock Theater, they did three light comedies at the Hill Hotel.

For even lighter fare, *Tammy and the Doctor* played at the Astro, publicized by a photo of Sandra Dee's blondness cuddling up to Peter Fonda's stethoscope. Several films later he summed up his doctor flick: "I didn't know anything could be so awful."

Brigadoon First Twenty-Show Run, *Gideon* Interrupted: 1963–1964

Perhaps the big color news photo of Norton, wearing a tall wizard's hat and long beard while gazing into a crystal ball, conjured the thirty-ninth season's ticket campaign to new heights.

Surely the season-opening musical, *Brigadoon,* helped, too. The fall musicals drew the largest attendance, but didn't always thrill treasurer Teal. *Brigadoon* took in over $19,000 but cost $21,000. *Marriage-Go-Round*, the next summer show, drew by far the smallest audience, 1,889. But as an "extra" show not figured into overall expenses, it netted over $2,600. Such facts of Playhouse life were not generally shared with playgoers, but they influenced decision-making.

Neither the trustees nor their somewhat distant director, however, could have predicted the national tragedy that darkened the second show. First, they had more local mourning to do. They'd lost two of the three honorary board members. Mrs. Guiou survived, but Lucy Updike and W. Boyd Jones were gone. Jones served as trustees' president, then constructed the new Playhouse. Miss Updike had performed in the first play, was elected to the board for thirty years, and still served as historian when she died at 78. Friends toasted her with grasshoppers, her preferred green beverage, at the grave site.

Another change gave the Prompter a new cover design—masks of comedy and tragedy over a Grecian column. The artist, Tom Palmerton, would enjoy popularity and steep prices for his prairie scenes.

Brigadoon emerged from the Highland mists with Jean McCartney as Charlie Dalrymple singing such Lerner and Loewe tunes as "Come to Me, Bend to Me." Janet Wallace, that real Scottish lassie, played Fiona, with Bob Roberts as angry Angus and Bill Bailey as the philosophical village patriarch. J. William Koll, a newcomer with a big voice, would become better known as the Godfather in long-running pizza commercials.   The Studio Theater's October offering of *Cat on a Hot Tin Roof* inspired McMorris to suggest, "Some of the more interesting goings-on at the Playhouse take place in the basement."

Tennessee Williams, though America's leading living playwright, had not yet "gained entry to the upper-level." (How soon they forgot *Glass Menagerie* in 1950.)

Even in the basement, *Cat on a Hot Tin Roof* created such a demand that a second three-show weekend was added to the schedule. Ness led a cast with Deana Grimm as Maggie the Cat, Kiser as Brick, and John Flower as Big Daddy. Tennessee Williams, McMorris concluded, is "powerful below decks," more so thanks to "U-style seating," which allows "an intimate look at the action."

Gideon brought the work of Paddy Chayefsky, best known for *Marty*, his Oscar-winning screen play, to the main stage in mid-November. On the Biblical play's second Friday, the show went on despite the assassination that November day of President John Kennedy. "The cast showed up backstage not knowing whether the show would go on," the daily reported. When a full house arrived, board president Dodge said, "We decided to go on even though we shared a deep sense of loss." The Playhouse then went dark, mourning on Saturday and Sunday, "even though both nights were sell-outs."

Yes to Sartre, No to Ionesco, Bravo to *Bernarda Alba*

Before the year's end, a double bill proved that you can put the avant garde in the basement, but you can't hide theater of the absurd from the critics. "Gem, Gibber in Twin Bill" headlined Kountze's review of the Studio productions of *No Exit* by Jean Paul Sartre and Ionesco's *The Lesson*. The latter, the critic insisted, was "a 50-minute detour into tedium, inanity and gibberish." A whiny pupil drives her professor to homicide, "the only point in the play where the principals make any sense at all."

No Exit, on the other hand, was "a brilliantly executed philosophical drama of man's torment in a hostile world" and "the best thing I've seen at the Playhouse all year." Kountze credited Lew Kucera, Elaine Jabenis and Joan Snyder, "under the inspired direction of Gerald Ness," with "a masterpiece."

The reviewer later applauded the Studio's *House of Bernardo Alba*, the Garcia Lorca tragedy whose cast included four natives of Latin America. January's main stage offering, *The Best Man* by Gore Vidal, featured two broadcast executives, Lew Jeffrey and Jack Coopersmith, as presidential rivals. A photo showed Coopersmith unzipping the dress of his perky blonde wife, played by Nancy Bounds. She wore the fur in the Prompter and later headed her own modeling agency. The review noted the play, "the work of a liberal Democrat playwright," has "its good guys and bad guys"—a Joe McCarthy–like bad guy, an Adlai Stevenson good guy. Walter Olson played a Truman type, "the last of the hicks."

A top choice of the play-reading committee, *Mary, Mary* by Jean Kerr, was still running strong on Broadway, thus not available. So *Breath of Spring* filled its February spot. The Peter Coke comedy was better known as the movie *Make Mine Mink*. Despite the presence of Peckham and Bailey, Kountze gave it his single most negative review of a main floor show. He liked the idea of old ladies stealing furs, led by an aging Army officer. But the headline said, "Talent Can't Liven Feeble Script." Ness directed the play and would later fill in again when Wilson was sidelined by illness.

Sauve as Freud, Illness Delays May Play, Summer Brings *Marriage*

Dudley Sauve had played FDR, Brutus and the satanic Nickles, and now wore the facial hair of Sigmund Freud. Henry Denker's *A Far Country* gives the choice dramatic role to his Viennese patient, played by Louise Nyland. The *Herald* review found it "intriguing," while the *Sun* said Denker's play "is more ponderous than profound, more preoccupied with historical clarity than theatrical sparkle." Both critics applauded the work of Glen Zeisemann as Mrs. Freud and Sylvia Wagner as the psychoanalyst's mother.

Then life really got Freudian at the Playhouse, spawning who knows what sort of night dreams. Earlier, "break a leg" had taken on darker meaning with accidents to Mary Peckham and Emmy Gifford. In April, "Mrs. Freud," who years later became the wife of director Wilson, was involved in an auto accident, and actor-trustee Mrs. Key was injured by her power mower. During *Gideon*, Leslie Wilson had emergency surgery, the first illness for her or Ken in twenty-eight years of marriage, and then an infection hospitalized Wilson before the late May opening of *Take Her, She's Mine*. Ness took over as director only to find his young leading lady hospitalized with an unidentified illness. He found a "quick study," Westside High senior Gail Rowden, to fill the role.

But Jane Rosch made it back for opening night in her off-to-college role. Then on doctor's orders she split performances with Miss Rowden the rest of the way. Gail's special moment came one night when the opening scene, a graduation ceremony, was changed slightly. She wore her school's Westside cap and gown, rather than the gray stage robe, and received her actual Westside diploma. The bio of cast member Chuck Ellick, son of Echo Ellick

Dudley Sauve as Freud.

and grandson of Genevieve Guiou, mentioned that his mother used to write for the Prompter. "Write for it! Ye Gods! She practically invented it," a blurb noted.

Among the new members of the board was attorney Ray Crossman Jr. who would play a key role a decade later in the hiring of director Charles Jones.

In July, Ness directed *Marriage-Go-Round,* billed as "a sophisticated comedy for adults." Sally Kruse, niece of Lucy Updike and the mother of five, played the Julie Newmar role of the towel-clad Swedish sexpot "with tremendous charm," Kountze wrote. Columnist McMorris asked of her towel, "How does it stay up?" The answer, self-sticking nylon tape, provoked a second question which the Playhouse hedged with another question, "Does a Scotsman tell what he's wearing under his kilt?"

Damn Yankees, Shakespeare, New Technician: 1964–1965

White Jacob left for a college post in Ohio, but Allen Cook replaced him as technician in time to help with the season-opening musical, *Damn Yankees.* With degrees from Utah and other university experience, Cook had enjoyed a three-month honeymoon, guiding his bride around Europe on a motor scooter.

A long-suffering Washington Senators fan deals with the devil to become a Yankee-beating slugger. It features "You've Gotta Have Heart," and crowds cheered Jean Stone's cartwheel to cap the big "Heart" number, though few recalled the grandmother's stage debut as 4-year-old Baby Jean. From Benson High's Jimmy Roddy as the dancing batboy to Bill Bailey as the grizzled manager, critics applauded a cast with Carl Oberdorfer reprising his Creighton U. role as Joe Hardy. Ken Wilson continued to work with Mary Levine as musical director, but for the fourth year in a row tried a different choreographer.

It seemed fitting to pair the fortieth Playhouse anniversary with Shakespeare's 400th birthday and *Twelfth Night.* The young heroines,

Viola and Olivia, won less attention than the low comedy types—Sir Toby Belch (John Wenstrand), Sir Andrew Aguecheek (Bob Roberts) and especially Rudyard Norton as Malvolio.

Jack Holley had replaced Denman Kountze as *World-Herald* entertainment editor and reviewer. Kountze, the multimillionaire who didn't need his job, wrote a resignation note after a disagreement with the editor and might have been surprised when it was accepted. (He'd later return.) Holley would soon move up the editing ranks before joining the journalism faculty at Northwestern University.

The street sign outside the Playhouse was widened from three to six feet for the title of *Oh Dad, Poor Dad, Mama's Hung You in the Closet and I'm Feelin' So Sad*. It still wasn't big enough for the subtitle, "A Pseudoclassical Tragifarce in the Bastard French Tradition." The Arthur Kopit play featured Miriam Shrier as the mama who protects her son from a "devouring world."

Amid many Junior Theater activities, including acting classes at the Playhouse, trustee Echo Ellick's children's play, *The Dragon's Curse*, made a national conference appearance.

Mary, Mary Marks 40th Birthday, First Director's Return

The lighter *Mary, Mary* was still not available in January, so a taut drama of the corporate board room, *Calculated Risk*, opened 1965. The wheeling-dealing villain (Roberts) betrayed the executive played by Joe Martin. He was better known as "Jolly Joe," host of countless kiddie and adult shows on radio and television. The review was headlined, "Martin Shines in Playhouse Bow," but Holley added, "The same cannot be said of the Joseph Hayes drama."

The Corn Is Green by Emlyn Williams, a Playhouse "laboratory" drama in the 1940s, gave Wilson a directing respite as Gerald Ness took charge. The cast was praised for authentic Welsh accents. Among the Welsh were that couple from Scotland, Janet and David Wallace, and dancer from London, Barbara Williams. The play "sparkles like sun on dew," the newspaper promised.

After two postponements, Jean Kerr's *Mary, Mary* finally arrived in April with Val Kuffel and Elaine Schaap as the divorcing but still-in-love couple. When "the other woman" came down with mononucleosis, causing some fear that a smooching scene with Kuffel would afflict him with the same "kissing disease," the part was read one night by Mrs. Hart Jenks. Her husband's father of the same name was the Shakespearean actor who guest starred in the early years.

As the comedy coincided with the fortieth anniversary, the Prompter ran a reproduction of the program for the first play in 1925, *The Enchanted Cottage*. The birthday also brought director Greg Foley back for a visit. Foley, 65, toured and declared the new Playhouse "truly wonderful." Among the changes noticed by the founding director: rather than an 8:30 curtain each night, plays started at 7:30 Sundays and 8 p.m. on Tuesdays and Wednesdays, times that would change again.

Associate Ness, Technician Leave, Teal Named "Mr. Playhouse"

The main stage season ended with two one-act plays by Peter Shaffer, *Private Ear, Public Eye*. The leading man in both plays, technician Cook, paired off with Melanie Workhoven and Sally Kruse. He was "so outstanding," Holley wrote, "that it makes me sad." Playing first a nonconformist, then the opposite, Cook transforms so completely "you won't recognize him."

The critic was sad because the technician was taking his talents to the Long Wharf Theater in New Haven, Conn. Don Ferguson, 26, a new Kansas University graduate, replaced him. But Cook's departure after just a year in Omaha was overshadowed by the loss of Gerald Ness to become director of the Columbus, Ohio, Players' Club. His three years as the first associate director and the force behind the Studio Theater won farewell praise for "creating a blossoming and still growing interest in avant garde and theater of the absurd," Rosemary Madison said in the *Sun*. "Ness raised our tank town sights" and did it in "an amiable and unpretentious" way. He'd return in 1974 to head the Nebraska Arts Council and collaborate with director Charles Jones in creation of the Nebraska Theatre Caravan.

Ness directed the Studio's *U.S.A.* before leaving. The cast introduced Melissa Jarecke, destined for many roles in the next half century. New Yorker Frederick Edell, 30, was hired as the next associate director. He had five years' experience as artistic director and director-designer at two Vermont theaters. As Ness had done before him, Edell would direct two Studio productions, another on the main stage and a Junior Theater play. Armed with a prestigious Yale degree, he'd been a drama critic for the *Village Voice*.

The highest honors at the anniversary banquet went to Val and Clarence Teal. She received the annual President's service award and he was cited as "the one person who has contributed the most to the Playhouse in the past 40 years." Trustee since 1940, treasurer since 1947, often membership drive chairman, photographer soon after his 1928

Honors for Clarence "Mr. Playhouse", and Val Teal, 1965.

arrival in Omaha, actor in many plays and singer of "Little Brown Jug," he was designated "Mr. Playhouse" by president J. Alec Merriam, a Northern Natural Gas executive. That President's Award to Val Teal was presented for a final time by Mrs. Guiou. The founder who played such a vital role died at 86 before the next annual meeting.

King and I Confirms Role of Money-Making Musicals: 1965–1966

Tall, bald Bill Koll would gain greater fame as the Godfather of pizza commercials, and Janet Wallace would repeat her lead role of Anna years later. As the season got under way, they were Omaha's Yul Brynner and Deborah Kerr, sharing credit for the first Playhouse production to pass more than 10,000 in attendance.

The financial success of *The King and I* confirmed the now conventional wisdom of opening with a well-established musical. It also justified the decision to start the season earlier in the air-conditioned Playhouse.

And it undermined Ken Wilson's notorious resistance to musicals, which had left the theater with no orchestra pit. Yes, those early musicals, with Mary Levine leading her trio of Elaine Majors on piano and Bill Wakefield percussionist, were pitless. Unless you count a four-inch depression in front of the stage, Wakefield recalled. The young drummer was impressed with "the feistiness of Mary Levine," who always stood up to Wilson on points of artistic disagreement. After the theater-opening *Say Darling* with her husband as musical director, Mrs. Levine served in that role for every Wilson musical.

Not so the choreographers. A new one worked each of Wilson's eight straight musicals. This time it was Valerie Roche, interim director of the Omaha Ballet Academy. The following season, the last of Wilson's long Playhouse run, saw Jean Stone as his eighth dance director. Retired much later at age 84, she reflected on the high turnover in choreographers. "Ken liked women," Jean noted, "but he also needed a whipping boy. He could get ugly." Mary Levine lasted because "he couldn't walk all over her." That put the dance directors directly in the line of Wilson's fire when musicals forced him to share control.

Apparently the problems didn't all stem from the director's personality. After praising the "high quality" of singing and acting, Holley added, "The dancing, frequently a problem in local productions, approaches that level." Koll, a postman and professional bowler when not playing a king, and Mrs. Wallace were especially appealing in their "Shall We Dance?" scene.

A review cited her "beautifully crisp diction," still notable when she reprised the role on the same stage nearly twenty years later. If anyone was type-cast it was Bob Roberts, playing the stern Kralahome, his third villain in recent shows.

Just as each season in the 1960s started with a musical, the second show was always Shakespeare or similar weighty works. This time it was Robert Bolt's *A Man for All Seasons* with Dudley Sauve as the martyr, Sir Thomas More. Roberts was again the villain, Thomas Cromwell, with Ed Corbett the Common Man. Joan Hennecke added another mature role to her long list of credits in a cast including Harry Langdon and Frank Hainey. The latter, a Protestant clergyman, played the ailing Cardinal Wolsey.

"When he comes on stage, shuffling and wheezing," Holley wrote, "you fear that he may die at any moment."

The new associate, dark-bearded Fred Edell, directed his first Studio show, Durrenmatt's *The Physicists,* after explaining his choice of Omaha over New York City. Full-time work in theater attracted him, of course. But he also complained that "off-Broadway is moribund," and both Broadway and off-Broadway "are very commercial." Adding a seventh main stage play meant a third and lighter offering, *Life with Father,* before the end of 1965. Wilson didn't cast anyone from his 1948 version of the popular play, but one of the original children, Jerry Venger, returned as his stage manager. A pretty Westside High sophomore, Sheryl Donnermeyer, debuting as the teenage love interest, became familiar to Omahans as television "weather girl" Donna Meyer.

Lighter Fare Draws Crowds, Criticism; Then Mortgage Burned

Wilson went to New York (his favorite: *Man of LaMancha*) while newcomer Edell directed *A Case of Libel*, a courtroom drama based on one columnist's lawsuit against another, drawn from the acid-penned Westbrook Pegler. The *World-Herald* review compared the overall performance to a recent Nebraska Cornhusker Orange Bowl game—"moments of glory … hurt by fumbles … final score spelled defeat."

Never Too Late in March didn't fare much better with a new daily reviewer, Duane Snodgrass. The story of a fiftyish couple (John Doxon and Ruth Davis) becoming parents again "is a very superficial play, but it's funny." Snodgrass felt it made minimal use of Playhouse talent, thus was "a disappointment."

The age-old debate continued when columnist McMorris complained that *A Man for All Seasons* was "the only stimulating theater upstairs," and the former Playhouse actor and Guthrie Theater manager Schoenbaum urged the theater to "go out on a limb" and do Chekhov and Ibsen. Director Wilson countered, "If we'd do more than two challenging plays we'd go broke." This season, at least, the lighter plays drew the biggest crowds. One of those crowds viewing *Never Too Late* either left early or spent the night down the hill at the Prom Town House when the Blizzard of '66 damaged the front doors and forced playgoers out a side exit.

Arthur Miller's *Death of a Salesman* drew the smallest attendance, but brought the Fonda award for Walter Olson's portrayal of Willy Loman. Loma Livers, who worked with Wilson in those Minnesota summer shows in the 1940s, played Willy's wife, with Warren Zweiback and Barry Larson as their boys.

Ira Wallach's *The Absence of a Cello* is "the presence of a Babbitt," Madison said of the season-ending satire. Cast member Rosalie Ohlinger would marry Playhouse regular Bob Roberts and years later handle publicity for twenty-first–century Broadway shows at the downtown Orpheum Theatre.

The day after *Cello* closed on June 26, the Playhouse held its forty-first annual meeting highlighted by a mortgage burning. After "only seven years," the Playhouse debt was paid on the half-million-dollar building. Congratulations went to treasurer Teal, also head of the building corporation. "We are now in a position," board president Merriam announced, "to reconsider some of the items dropped from the original plans to save money"—a canopy over the entrance and shop space for set construction.

Bob Roberts, right, with Dan Lynch.

Among the new trustees, Mrs. Charles Durham would come to play the largest leadership role. Among honorees not making headlines was the latest to win the President's Award for service—Leslie Wilson. Her service as a theater educator, more than her past work in makeup, was cited. Perhaps the larger reason behind the award was widespread affection and sympathy for the director's wife, feelings soon to play a part in new contract terms that caused his departure.

"Sister" Supplies *Guys and Dolls,* Rudyard Remembers: 1966–1967

The next season would begin and end with staff changes. After just a year as associate director, Edell left to teach at the University of Victoria in British Columbia. His replacement was another in Wilson's long line of fellow Minnesotans, Don Ruble. Most recently with the Paul Bunyan Playhouse in Bemidji, Ruble not only shared an alma mater with Wilson and Eckert, but his father was Ken's classmate. When Wilson and Eckert, now in his twelfth year, would depart at season's end, the only familiar faces remaining on the staff would be box office manager Estelle English and the night custodian.

Treasurer Teal kept scrutinizing balance sheets as *Guys and Dolls* opened the 1966–1967 season. It set records but lost money. The cast of *Guys and Dolls* was also unusual. Those Runyonesque characters— Sky Masterson, Nathan Detroit and his ever-lovin' Adelaide, plus Nicely-Nicely and others—had played the same roles three years before in Council Bluffs. Choreographer Jean Stone had also helped with the Chanticleer production, and her daughter Valerie was among the high-stepping Hot Box Dolls in both shows. Audiences demanded encores when George Heiring's Nicely-Nicely sang "Sit Down, You're Rockin' the Boat." The Prompter applauded "Our Sister, Chanticleer," and urged that "you sample the work … across the river."

Arthur Miller's *Incident at Vichy,* the "serious" October offering, played without intermission "because the action is too powerful" to interrupt, reviewer Madison wrote in a lengthy review. The *World-Herald*'s Snodgrass kept his comments brief after a lead sentence reporting only that the play opened.

Although it was Omaha's first look at the directing of Don Ruble, neither critic took note of his work. The Cownie fur ad on the Prompter's inside cover made history by picking Val Kuffel from the all-male cast to model "a smart black-dyed calfskin car coat," which he did with cigarette in hand. He'd spent the previous year as television movie host Johnny Valerian.

A movie premiere that month put a board vice president in the spotlight. Bob Reilly's book *Red Hugh, Prince of Donegal* became the Disney film *The Fighting Prince of Donegal*. Its opening night in Omaha, declared "Bob Reilly Day" by the mayor, raised funds for Girls Town. Reilly had turned his Playhouse publicist duties over to Helen Moeller, first woman to head the Omaha Advertising Club. She sought a new "trademark." Something "smart, modern and simple," she said, with one restriction: "that the two theater masks not be used." A spotlight design by Milton Wolsky was chosen.

Rosemary Madison, the musician writing *Sun* reviews, continued her crusade for more substantial drama by panning *Any Wednesday*, the comedy moved up in the schedule to precede the film version starring Jane Fonda. The critic loved Eunie Denenberg in the role created by Lincoln's Sandy Dennis on Broadway: She "has a true flair for light comedy, is beautifully relaxed physically and carries off all scenes with aplomb."

Ruble's Studio cast completed the 1966 program by creating a night club atmosphere in the rehearsal hall for *Brecht on Brecht*, a blend of songs, poetry and scenes from the German best known for *Threepenny Opera*. Guild volunteers served coffee and doughnuts at cabaret tables.

Rudyard Norton's role as the voice of Brecht led to a feature story capping his fifty years on stage. Now 66, he recalled his debut as a comic drummer in a Central High road show and his part as Apollinarus, God of Love, in an Ak-Sar-Ben Den show. From studying under Monty Woolley at Yale to his first Playhouse role as Professor Higgins in *Pygmalion*, he regaled the reporter with anecdotes from his silent screen encounter with Sally Rand to his eighty-five roles in Playhouse, Chanticleer and other theaters.

Costume Designer Hired, Actors Guild Organized

During the holiday season, a "costumer" was added to the professional staff. For the first time in its forty-two-year history the Playhouse supported a full-time creative staff of five and a total of nine employees.

Gladys Stuart, who had owned costume shops, created the women's outfits for January's *The Devil's Disciple*. Military uniforms were rented for Shaw's Revolutionary War drama, also staged in the first Playhouse season, but Mrs. Stuart organized a crew of five to sew the other costumes. (The thirty-year-old rentals, by the way, tended to be too small for modern actors.) Her full-time presence would provide training for more volunteers and "expand our modest rental business to schools" and others.

All the reviews praised most facets of the play, from Eckert's "masterfully realistic sets" to C. Richard Draper's "suave speeches" as General Burgoyne. Snodgrass noted, "The period costumes, designed by Mrs. Gladys Stuart, couldn't have been better."

Draper met with others that January to organize the Metropolitan Actors Guild. Orvel Milder, its first president, joined Norm and Louise Filbert, Rudyard Norton, Ozzie Nogg, Harriet Olson, Bob Roberts and Dick Mueller to start MAG, the group that became TAG, the Theater Arts Guild, twenty years later.

Mueller, who hosted the initial meeting, had been paid to perform in the Stylemasters quartet, and he wanted to see more professional treatment of actors. A complaint shared by some organizers was harsh treatment by Ken Wilson. Not only did they feel he was personally abusive, they rebelled against "rehearsals that ran until 1 or 2 in the morning," Filbert recalled.

Other actors also made news. William Marshall, now acting as William Jay, was part of an all-black off-Broadway cast. Ron Vaad had a five-week run in *My Three Angels,* and Terry Kiser was rehearsing a play in New York.

A photo in the *World-Herald* captured the craziness of the next play, *You Can't Take It With You*. Thomson Holtz, a radio and television personality, posed as a portly Roman discus thrower, modeling for Miriam Shrier's Penelope Sycamore. Kaufman and Hart's zanies, including Bill Bailey as Grandpa Vanderhof, seemed dated to the daily's Snodgrass.

A rowdy bunch of teenagers showed up for the April preview of *Picnic*, the William Inge drama set in a small Midwestern town. Snodgrass didn't mention the noisy audience as he complained that the play "dragged through all three acts" and was hard to hear. He praised Frank DeGeorge and his daughter Frances, playing a tomboy, but ignored Elaine Jabenis as the frustrated maiden school teacher.

Rosemary Madison explained that "lines were lost and effects ruined by an audience of noisy teenagers lacking the maturity and background to grasp" the play. A Public Pulse writer was more explicit: "It was bad enough for an audience to laugh through every dramatic scene, but when it became so boorish as to answer back" to an actor's line, "it would be difficult for even a professional group to give a good performance." Mrs. Jabenis, whose Playhouse roles stretched from 1952 to the year 2000, never forgot those teenagers whose laughter left her in tears.

June brought *Barefoot in the Park,* the 134th and last Playhouse show for Kendrick Wilson. Kountze who had returned as the *World-Herald* reviewer paid tribute to both departing veterans, Wilson and designer Eckert, saying, "their deft and no-nonsense touch was outstandingly evident throughout the production." Ozzie Nogg in the Jane Fonda role and Val Kuffel as her newlywed husband "played particularly well together." Norm Filbert in the *Nonpareil* called it the perfect antidote for theater-haters and concluded the final work of Wilson and Eckert "will leave a lasting glow."

Ozzie Nogg, Lyle DeMoss, Val Kuffel in Wilson's last show.

"Unable to Agree," Wilson Goes, Eckert Follows

Ken Wilson's first memory of Omaha was Genevieve Guiou meeting him at the train depot in 1942. As he said farewell in 1967, her daughter, Echo Ellick, took charge of the search for a new director.

Parting may be "such sweet sorrow," in the Bard's words, but this split saw veiled reporting and volatile reactions. Signing herself "Ex Omaha Playhouse actress," Louise Nyland asked, "Omaha—how could you? Ken Wilson leaving the Playhouse. It is inconceivable to me that any theater board could allow this man to get away." Others wondered "what Omaha did in return, as thanks for one of the top community theaters in the country, a mortgage-free building, and an admired nationwide reputation." That came from four in New York City—Connie Danielson, Richard Higgs, Terry Kiser and Ron Vaad—who gave Wilson credit for their success.

If all they knew was what they read in the papers, the parting came by "mutual agreement." The director and the board "were unable to agree on terms of Mr. Wilson's three-year contract." That was true as far as it went. The letter writers wouldn't have known of that exchange during an earlier contract renegotiation. The one that praised his creative talent but wished for a warmer, kinder Ken who could get along with actors and trustees.

His supporters surely knew about the matter mentioned in the board meeting as "the situation." What "situation," a puzzled trustee asked? His highly visible relationship with Glendora Zeisemann. She was the other woman under the same Playhouse roof with Leslie Wilson, who still took charge of makeup and served as Junior Theater treasurer.

So the board imposed its morality on the director? Not according to Bob Reilly, the trustee who agreed to present the contract terms to Wilson. The board said yes to Ken's request for an increase in his $12,000 salary, yes to his call for additional help and yes to more time for his annual New York theater trip. The board promised not to interfere in his "private life."

But they took a stand on complaints that his friend used her intimacy with Wilson to exercise authority over others. They accepted Wilson's demands and added one of their own—girlfriend Glen had to stay away from the Playhouse. As the negotiating trustee and one of the actors on the board, Reilly was relieved when Wilson agreed to the condition.

Then, when Wilson met with the full board in early March, he said, "No. That's not acceptable." He wouldn't ban from the building the woman he'd later marry. As one trustee saw it, "He called our bluff." They still felt his leadership and talent outweighed the negatives, but his rejection of that lone condition ended the Wilson era.

A reporter asked Wilson to explain his disagreement with the board. It involved "policy and other issues," he replied, "but there are too many issues involved. To attempt to explain it would only confuse things." He compared his job to a politician's—"by and by, he'll lose an election. A Playhouse director can't work with 26 bosses over the years without alienating most of them." He noted that only three directors elsewhere in the nation had more longevity.

The *World-Herald* praised his twenty-five-year contribution (not deducting his three-year absence to serve in World War II). And Wilson made it clear that, without the board's cooperation, the Playhouse could not have risen to one of the top three in the nation.

He would teach drama at Southern Illinois University, but wife Leslie and son John, now 19 and an Omaha University student, would stay in Omaha. After the divorce, a brief news item was pasted into the Playhouse scrapbook in late 1968: Wilson would marry Glendora and live in Minneapolis. He died in 1974 at age 69.

Designer Eckert would pursue his doctorate at the University of Nebraska and teach there several years before directing Junior Theater, then joining the faculty at Peru State College. Eckert, after eleven years at the Playhouse, had notified the board of his plans before the director's decision and emphasized his resignation "has nothing to do" with Wilson's departure. President Marvin Schmid said the board was "extremely sorry" to lose "a very talented designer."

Thus the season ended with farewell parties. Stability came from a board with such stalwarts as Echo Ellick, Emmy Gifford, treasurer Teal and corresponding secretary Helen McDonald. The President's Award at the end of that 42nd season went to Morey Landman, recognized for organizing ushers since 1957. He would still be on the volunteer job in the twenty-first century. Only two leaders of membership campaigns, Berdine Urbach and Florence Young, would match his longevity.

Director Cavanaugh, Designer Casker Do *Gypsy*: 1967–1968

The new director was hired in April—ample time to prepare for June tryouts for *Gypsy*, the season-opening musical. Jim Cavanaugh, 35, was born in Omaha but left at an early age and, like Wilson, came to the Playhouse from Minnesota.

A graduate of Brown and Columbia, he had been managing director since 1960 of the Rochester Civic Theater. His flashiest Broadway credit was stage manager for the musical *First Impressions* with Polly Bergen,

Farley Granger and Hermione Gingold. Cavanaugh impressed the board more with his numbers in Rochester, a city of 50,000 population. Under his leadership, theater membership grew from 500 to 3,000 with a staff grown to six in a new facility. He married a board member who'd voted against hiring him. Wife Milles, whose name derived from parents Mildred and Lester, was a silversmith and mother of two preschool children.

Cavanaugh promised he wasn't "coming with a broom to sweep house." Unlike Wilson who arrived with World War II and quickly changed the season schedule, the new director said he'd go with the planned program. His early interviews emphasized, "The big thing I want to do is involve more of the community." He had a rule in Rochester "that at least half of every cast had to be made up" of actors new to the theater. Adding that he wouldn't "bypass the old pros" or strictly follow that rule in Omaha, he stressed the goal of bringing in new people on stage and backstage.

Playgoers found the *Gypsy* Prompter speckled with asterisks, both in cast lists and production staff. They led to the parenthetical explanation—"*Playhouse debut." Another item explained, "A happy blending of old and new faces will keep our Playhouse alive. Of the 60 performers in 'Gypsy,' 34 are new to our stage." Among the debuts: Young Dick Johnson, a ninth grader who'd become Dick Christie, an actor and writer in Hollywood.

Set designer, R. Thomas Casker, arrived in June. Although Cavanaugh would stay only two seasons, Tom Casker would remain for the full "interim," as history would label the seven-year gap between two long-term directors, Wilson and Charles Jones. Casker, another product of Carnegie Tech (Szold's school), came from the Canton, Ohio, Players Guild. "He is slightly skeptical towards so-called amateur little theaters," the Prompter reported, but was impressed enough with the Playhouse to decide that it "could be just a little different from other community theaters."

Cavanaugh's work would raise eyebrows a year later when season sales dropped, and he was questioned when *Gypsy* lost thousands.

But the first effort by the new team won acclaim. Kountze declared, "Any lingering doubts about the prowess" of Cavanaugh "were abruptly dispelled." Rosemary Madison picked up on his promise and noted the "many new performers."

The Rochester newspaper sent a reviewer who got a bit carried away on behalf of their former favorite son. She claimed *Gypsy* won "the first standing ovation anyone can remember at the 43-year-old Omaha Playhouse." And she quoted Harriet Fonda Peacock and Mary Levine on the new director. Mrs. Peacock told her, "He won us immediately. We needed this shot in the arm." Mrs. Levine watched Cavanaugh cast the show "with flawless accuracy" from the 200 who auditioned.

The musical's unsung hero may have been stage manager Suzi Curran. She was stuck with the show's performing monkey. "The cast and crew fell in love with Seymour," Cavanaugh insisted, but Filbert said his wife's feelings for the beast were less than affectionate when it did the nasty things that monkeys do. Mrs. Filbert played the stage mother who sings "Everything's Coming Up Roses."

From Irish Flop to *Little Foxes, Macbeth* and *Odd Couple*

Brian Friel's Irish play *Philadelphia, Here I Come* landed at the bottom of a postseason poll, dooming hope for more from a land so rich in playwrights. *Luv* did even worse at the box office. It featured a love triangle as Cavanaugh directed his first nonmusical and won friendly reviews. Lead actor Gary Frazell headed the Nebraska Humane Society, but reviewers eschewed terms alluding to the city's chief dog-catcher. Audience comments ranged from "funniest in years" to "tasteless and sick." Playgoers were happy on one point: "that lousy orange drink" in the lobby was replaced by Coke and Sprite.

Studio productions continued below in the rehearsal hall, where "smoking is permitted throughout the evening." In November, Ruble directed *Spoon River Anthology* adapted from poet Edgar Lee Masters's village epitaphs. A Tech High youngster who trained under Roy Eckert in Junior Theater, Steve Wheeldon, was listed as lighting designer. He'd gain more experience at the University of Nebraska at Omaha and later join the Playhouse staff before starting his own theater supply and design business.

Ruble had now directed four of the past six shows, including *The Amorous Flea*, the January Studio musical adapted from Moliere. It later ran for twenty weeks at The Twenties night club.

Ruble's heavy duty gave Cavanaugh time to prepare for the Bard in March. He promoted *Macbeth* as if people scorned classic tragedy but might swallow Shakespeare that focused on sword fights. David Haberman, of *The True Voice,* said the battle between Macbeth and MacDuff "becomes an awkward burlesque of the last reel in a dozen Errol Flynn-Tyrone Power-Cornel Wilde flicks still running on the late show." The *Sun's* Warren Francke and author of this book complained, "None of that tragic flaw stuff. Mac just gets winded after a while."

The *Sun* insisted, Only Macbeth's "dagger of the mind" fails to take physical form. When Lady Mac cries, "Out, damned spot," one expected "to see a black-and-white terrier run up the aisle." Haberman noted that when "Birnam Wood comes to Dunsinane," soldiers carried "incongruously insignificant evergreen twigs." And the preview audience laughed. Loud, "you've got to be kidding," laughter.

Maybe it wasn't funny enough for the several who dropped "No more Shakespeare" notes in the Suggestion Box. When all was said and done, it provided a caveat for cast member Al DiMauro's high school drama classes: Be very careful in rigging the harness so you don't really hang Macbeth.

While two-thirds of the audience gave *Macbeth* thumbs up, about 90 percent approved of another classic, *The Little Foxes*. The Playhouse had first presented Lillian Hellman's malevolent Hubbard family in 1944. Elaine Jabenis as Regina brings "the same blood-curdling chill she achieved in Sartre's 'No Exit,'" a review said. Mrs. Jabenis was struck by the contrast between Wilson and Cavanaugh. "There was no comparison. Jim was a very pleasant guy, but I learned so much from Kendrick Wilson. He knew his craft. Jim wasn't as strong."

Cavanaugh's first season ended on a happy note with *The Odd Couple,* the third Neil Simon success at the Playhouse. It not only won the highest approval from playgoers, it drew the biggest adult audience since *Gypsy.*

C. Richard Draper played the finicky Felix Unger, and Cavanaugh was looking for a Walter Matthau type to play the slob, Oscar Madison. He called Elaine Jabenis to ask about her short, stocky friend named Frank DeGeorge. "If you don't cast him, you're making the biggest mistake of your life," she warned. DeGeorge didn't like Ken Wilson, but he found the new director to be both "talented and a very nice man." Reviews used terms such as "exquisite" and "hilariously effective" to describe Draper and DeGeorge.

Margre Durham Heads Board, Season Start Shaky: 1968–1969

Before the season ended, construction was under way on the new scene shop west of the stage. And turnover from the Wilson-Eckert team was completed when Jack Westin, 26, replaced Don Ruble as associate director. Yet another Minnesotan, Westin had founded the Eastside Theatre in St. Paul, a company with aims similar to the Studio schedule.

That summer also brought the birth of the Bellevue Little Theater, joining Chanticleer and Kingsmark as Playhouse "sisters." It started with *Love Rides the Rails,* a melodrama staged at the Bellevue Queen, a riverside restaurant on the Missouri. A decade later this company acquired the Roxie, a downtown movie house, and developed a traditional five-show community theater season.

A more significant change saw Mrs. Chuck Durham become president of the Playhouse board of trustees. Margre would lead the way to even greater physical improvements than the current project. The old shop transplanted from the 40th and Davenport theater was being replaced by a new wing with three times the square footage. Costume storage would more than double, but thirty parking spaces were lost during construction. Latecomers were urged to "drive straight to the Town House lot or one of the adjacent houses of worship" (the next-door synagogue or the Methodist church across the street)—a shorter walk "than from some parts of our own lot."

Margre Durham's board made changes, too. She named an advisory committee of Harriet Peacock, Jack Drew and Zack Warren. New trustees included Mike Yanney, named the most recent "Distinguished Young Man of the Year" by the Junior Chamber of Commerce. Clarence Teal continued as treasurer, but his eventual departure in the mid-1970s stemmed from a disagreement with Mrs. Durham, among others.

Arguably Margre Durham was Omaha's top volunteer in 1968. She had been president of the District 66 school board, chairman of both Clarkson Hospital Fashion Show and the Ak-Sar-Ben Women's Ball committee and other boards. Her daughter Sunny was a recent Queen of Ak-Sar-Ben. With Emmy Gifford, Marge served on Playhouse–Junior Theater merger committee and would be

Margre Durham led trustees.

heavily involved later when the two theaters split. While her husband Chuck amassed a fortune by turning HDR (Henningsen, Durham, Richardson) into an international engineering giant, Mrs. Durham was immersed in community service and joined Chuck in philanthropy.

The 44th season got off to an early, but shaky start. It wasn't the practice of the women who prepared the Playhouse scrapbooks to pen their opinions into the archives, but one of them wrote: "Starting the new season in the middle of summer and with a tragedy was a not too successful experiment."

Instead of the usual opening musical, Cavanaugh led with Jean Anouilh's Joan of Arc drama, *The Lark.* Perhaps the choice of plays and the August 9 start hurt season ticket sales. It didn't help when the word *tedious* appeared in the review headline.

The Studio schedule opened early, too, with *The Blood Knot* by South African Athol Fugard in mid-September. Earlier polling of several thousand playgoers showed that 91 percent "seldom or never attend Studio shows." In other words, director Westin wasn't likely to draw a mob to the basement for a serious look at racial issues.

So, with two shows under their belt, the new creative team looked to a sure-fire musical, the same *Little Mary Sunshine* that was such a summer hit five years ago. But that was below in the rehearsal hall, and this put an off-Broadway parody on the main stage.

The good news was a cast featuring Dick Boyd and Janet Wallace as the Nelson Eddy–Jeanette MacDonald types. It had broadcaster Bill Tombrink as the Dudley Do-Right corporal, and Larry French and Al DiMauro as slapstick Indians. Cavanaugh was aided by Mary Levine and a new choreographer, Marianne Sanders. She'd joined the Omaha Civic Ballet Academy after television dancing on such shows as the *Lucky Strike Hit Parade.* The spoofing fun with "Colorado Love Call" and other songs impressed the critics, but it attracted 4,000 fewer than recent musicals. Worse, it took in almost $13,000 less than expenses.

Hindsight suggests the new team started the season with three ill-timed shows. Everything—from August heat and reduced parking to that "tedious" headline—was stacked against them. Some grumbled about the return to 8:30 curtains on Tuesdays and Wednesdays. And Echo Ellick explained the problem faced by "our hard-working, courageous play-reading committee. Challenged to select new plays, they do, and people don't buy tickets."

Meanwhile, Cavanaugh compiled a ninety-eight-page report on the playgoer responses. Among the criticisms: some plays were "too far-out." Imagine the irony for Clarence Teal and others who suffered through *The Moon Is Blue* controversy to see it mentioned in calls for "a good, clean comedy."

Chekhov at Last, Then Simon Goes Sour, Cavanaugh to College

Uncle Vanya marked the first Chekhov drama in Playhouse history and the premier of Jim Cavanaugh's translation. Westin directed and the *Sun's* Gary Johnson, later an executive producer and question chief for television's *Jeopardy!*, called it "one of the finest offerings" he'd seen, despite the handicaps of the Russian's themes of boredom and ennui. Kountze "was singularly impressed with Tom Casker's split set" and with lighting "uncannily reflecting the changing seasons."

Nebraskans from David City were pleased to see both Martha Peto as an old nurse and her dog Pepi in a walk-on role. They were used to seeing the pair at the town's grain elevator, where Martha was the owner and her half-collie, half-chow pet served as "receptionist."

Attorney Margaret Fischer, who had attended all the plays, waited forty-four years for Chekhov. But she waited only until January 1969 for the Playhouse to present its fourth Neil Simon comedy, *The Star-Spangled Girl*.

Given last season's reception of *The Odd Couple,* how could you go wrong with Simon? Forget the reviews, just read the headlines greeting Cavanaugh's cast of three: "Simon's 'Bomb,'" "You Can't Score Every Time," and "Noise, Gags Don't Jell."

Gary Johnson, who'd win seven writing Emmys, had blamed the actors when the Broadway version "failed to amuse," but now decided, "Simon has finally produced a bomb."

On the plus side, its opening brought the beginning of a series of First Nighter parties featuring social hour and dinner for $5.50 in the basement rehearsal hall. An "angel" donated champagne.

Next up was Westin with an antiwar revue. The Studio musical came in a time when many protested the war in Vietnam. Alison Teal would marry Sam Brown Jr., leader of the Moratorium March against that conflict. The assassinations of Martin Luther King Jr. and Robert Kennedy were still fresh wounds when this Playhouse season got under way. Now Richard Nixon was president and Neil Armstrong would soon walk on the moon.

Photos of the revue, *Oh What a Lovely War,* showed drill sergeant David Wallace barking at recruit Don Noel, and a shaggy Al DiMauro mocking the medals of an overweight general. The headline "Brilliant Indictment of War" meant Johnson loved it. Of course, more saw the headlines than attended the play. It was one part of the larger picture when Cavanaugh resigned.

Then along came Edward Albee. Nebraska's Sandy Dennis and the world's Liz Taylor took home Oscars for Albee's *Who's Afraid of Virginia Woolf?* Not one of his dozen plays had made it to the Playhouse main stage. Now Cavanaugh not only had his Pulitzer Prize drama, *A Delicate Balance,* but what all the newspapers labeled an "all-star" cast of six. Four were Fonda-McGuire winners: Ruth Davis, Harriet Olson, Richard Draper and Walter Olson. And the reviewers that soured on Simon inspired rave headlines—two ranking it "Season Best," another "Superb."

Wait Until Dark proved that "a delicious scare" could pull the season's largest crowd to attend a nonmusical. The Frederick Knott story of a blind housewife menaced by murderous thugs "elicited a deafening shriek" from the audience, one review said. Another swore "it was startling—as evidenced by the hundreds who found themselves jumping, screaming and shouting during the shocking final scene."

Diane Casker, the designer's wife, won honors as the blind woman, but the low-brow hoodlum would go on to greater Playhouse fame. Chicago-trained Tom Wees, father of four boys, made his debut as the crude Carlino. He'd become a frequent Playhouse award winner and be cast in the film *Terms of Endearment*.

After two triumphs, Cavanaugh closed his Playhouse career with Peter Shaffer's one-act *Black Comedy*. The gimmick—a power failure forces the cast to stumble in the dark—wore thin for one critic: "When you've seen your first dozen gropings and pratfalls, you've pretty well seen 'em all."

Associate Westin completed the season with two Studio offerings: three one-acts and *Interview* by van Itallie, which also served as the Playhouse entry in a regional competition with the national winner going to Monaco for the World Amateur Theater Festival. The cast included a couple, journalist Gary Johnson and wife Michele, who would head for Hollywood together and both win Emmys writing for such shows as *Hollywood Squares*. (As senior writer for *Jeopardy!*, Johnson was the reason many Omaha questions confronted contestants.) A Worcester, Mass., company won the national competition, but Westin's cast was awarded a regional commendation.

Executive director Cavanaugh then left after two seasons. "We can only be happy," the Prompter reported, "he has such a fine position" at Mount Holyoke, "one of America's most outstanding colleges for women." He'd direct a laboratory theater and teach in the drama department—a three-play schedule leaving time for his wife and children. And he'd leave "the organized confusion of a community theater" for "a peaceful college campus." He'd shown "marvelous energy, enthusiasm and optimism," not to mention "artistic ability." Not a negative word.

But two daily newspaper headlines told a different story. One said, "Playhouse in Debt $50,000 for Year." Treasurer Teal announced, "We will end the season in the red. We held expenses tight, but not enough to avoid a loss." Cavanaugh talked about empty seats—the best single night was at a performance of *Wait Until Dark,* and it was only 72 percent filled. He blamed a national trend toward a generation gap—older playgoers avoiding the avant garde, younger ones resisting "establishment" plays. "We must concentrate on selling single admissions," rather than season memberships. "Not everyone should see every play."

The second headline, "Puzzled, Dissatisfied," signaled a follow-up editorial. Noting the debt and Cavanaugh's explanation for a shrinking audience, the *World-Herald* complained, "In recent years, the fare has turned markedly toward the obscure and offbeat. Audiences have often left the Playhouse puzzled and dissatisfied." The feeling was compared to searching the library for a book on humor, then "having the librarian insist you take a tome on contemporary social ills." The newspaper hoped the new director would steer the theater toward "understandable, quality entertainment."

Junior Theater, Playhouse Plan Merger, Addition

No one called Omaha a sinking ship, but the departures of Jim Cavanaugh and Junior Theater director Carl Pistilli were overshadowed by farewells to Joslyn Museum director Eugene Kingman and Symphony conductor Joseph Levine. Failure to renew his contract also took Mary Levine, Playhouse music director for the past decade.

Before leaving Omaha, she helped Westin with July's *The Apple Tree,* drawn from Mark Twain and others. Bill Koll played the snake, Bill Kellogg and Ozzie Nogg Adam and Eve. It wasn't just the summer malaise that held attendance down around 3,000, well short of earlier shows. A third of the audience canceled one evening to watch television—Neil Armstrong taking "one small step for man, one giant leap for mankind." They skipped Eden for a walk on the moon.

If that was the biggest world news of 1969, local theater headlines focused on plans for a new Junior Theater addition and that company's merger with the Playhouse. The ties between the two, while unbroken, had varied over the years. Emmy Gifford's involvement with both remained constant, as did the presence of Wilson and now Westin on the Junior board. The Playhouse had done its own children's plays in the early years, and the Junior League had sponsored them until the Junior Theater founding in 1949. Its plays were presented at Central and Tech high schools and Joslyn Museum. This season, more than 12,000 children saw productions of *Androcles and the Lion*, *Rags to Riches* and *Aladdin and the Wonderful Lamp*. The latter won a front-page spread with photos of the Sultan played by newcomer Dave Webber, later known as a television sportscaster and vocalist.

The Playhouse agreed back in 1967 to a merger, provided Omaha Junior Theater could raise $1 million for an addition at 6915 Cass. A fund drive got under way in March 1969. A spokesman said, "We have operated successfully for 20 years on borrowed stages where audiences cannot see and hear as they should, where our materials are stolen, lost, broken and (twice) burned, where we do not have time or space to rehearse, build, light and rig our shows."

A proposed wing at the Playhouse would seat 800 arena-style around a thrust stage. Designed to be divided into a 350-seat space, it would be shared with the three Studio plays. "Under the merger terms, one executive director and one board will supervise policy and personnel, schedule activities, purchase supplies and pay the bills."

The "proposal of marriage ... was solemnized" in late May "during a formal engagement banquet attended by most of the friends and relatives of the prospective groom and bride." So wrote Kountze as the two boards dined together and watched a slide show prepared by Mrs. Gifford. An artist's rendering showed a new west entrance to the wing toward the southwest corner of the existing building.

A fund-raising committee was deep in such leaders as Peter Kiewit, Willis Strauss, Robert Daugherty and Harold Andersen as well as Playhouse president Margre Durham, Mrs. Gifford and reviewer Kountze. A brochure took its theme from *Rumpelstiltskin*, spinning "Straw Into Gold." Kountze devoted a lengthy column to the merger, taking the occasion to once more dispose of an old notion that both theaters "are nothing but the toys of wealthy dilettantes." This, he said, "is nonsense." Both are open to all. "We reach children of all races and backgrounds," Mrs. Gifford added.

Among those attending the "engagement banquet" was the man who'd manage the merger, new executive director Fritz Congdon, 43. Most recently director of the Tulsa Little Theatre, he was president-elect of the American Community Theatre Association. Congdon was a World War II veteran with degrees from Northwestern and Cornell. A football quarterback, helicopter pilot and commander in the Naval Reserve, not to mention a rodeo bulldogger, he was married to Irwin, a fashion designer. They were parents of three children.

But the first point Echo Ellick made in her Prompter introduction was that Fritz had "ethos." So said designer Casker and associate Westin. Others who weren't sure whether to define his "ethos" as attitude or style were "certainly impressed" with "an uncommonly talented man." He'd cast his first show in July.

Congdon Begins with Successful *My Fair Lady*: 1969–1970

The 45th season began with *My Fair Lady*. The Lerner and Loewe musical drew almost 10,000 for the first time since *Guys and Dolls* three years before. The most expensive musical yet mounted by the Playhouse, it came closer to paying its $33,000 costs than any in the past few years.

Choral leader Mel Olson replaced Mary Levine as music director and brought in new pianists, including Claudette Valentine, who'd become musical director for summer shows. Joan White stepped into Mrs. Brando's shoes as the second Eliza Doolittle in a history going back to the original *Pygmalion*. A native of England and a Julie Andrews look-alike, she wowed reviewers as the Cockney changeling. Bob Roberts, an actor known for precise enunciation, was a natural for Professor Henry Higgins, with Bill Bailey as his Colonel Pickering and Tom Wees as the roguish Alfred Doolittle.

Each night, the Queen of Transylvania in the ball scene was played by a different past Queen of Ak-Sar-Ben. They ranged from two granddaughters of Margaret Hitchcock Doorly, the original Mrs. Higgins, to the daughters of president Margre Durham and Libby Lauritzen. Libby recalled her single line in *Stage Door*, the year she was Queen of Quivera: "I sure wish I could git married cuz I'm jist plumb tired of livin' in sin." If Omahans awaited the verdict on the new director, they didn't have to read past headlines that ranged from "Smash" and "Cause to Rejoice" to "By George, They've Got It." Kudos went to Congdon, Casker and Gladys Stuart's costumes. After raves for White's Liza and her wistful "Wouldn't It Be Loverly," reviews favored Wees doing "Get Me to the Church on Time" and "With a Little Bit of Luck."

Wees and White as Alfie and Liza Doolittle.

The Great Sebastians put Bill Koll and Barbara Williams in the title roles played by Ken Wilson and Cherie Shaver in the old Playhouse. Congdon had ended Cavanaugh's practice of marking debuts with asterisks, so newcomers such as Leslie

(Cookie) Hoberman blended with veterans Harry Langdon, the Creighton theater director, and Larry David. The comedy about two mind-reading Czechs coping with Communists made the evening fly by, a review promised.

The year ended with recent success but also a list of losses. Rudge Norton was recuperating from a heart attack, and Bill Bailey's recovery wasn't going well. Death came to Jayne Schoentgen, the Fonda sister who appeared in the first play in 1925, and Harlan Peckham, whose widow Mary would return to the stage in January.

Cactus Flower Caps Season with Top Nonmusical Turnout

Mrs. Peckham played the mother loved by son Earl Katz in *I Never Sang for My Father*. Reviewer Kountze found it "touching yet depressing. You can admire and even laugh with these people, but you wished you hadn't walked in at that time."

It was the second role in a row for Melanie Workhoven, the play's daughter and the real-life daughter of broadcaster Merrill Workhoven. (His footnote in history came as his Omaha mentoring of Johnny Carson was rewarded on a visit to NBC's *Tonight Show* when Carson gave him a new car.)

Westin had directed a "loud, bawdy, funny" Studio version of Aristophanes' *Lysistrata*. He had police officers burst on stage, blow whistles, ban the play and begin taking names. Westin explained the hoax, noting, "The lusty nature of the play" was taking some flak. "Some came expecting to see something obscene," so he staged the raid to break the tension. Now his directing of Woody Allen's *Don't Drink the Water* was his final main stage work.

The associate director wrote a rather philosophical defense of stage nudity under his byline in the *Sun*. A Public Pulse letter suggested if Westin was correct that theater mirrors life and the Playhouse would soon be doing *Hair*, then, "Is it not reasonable to assume that the whole Omaha populace will be going naked in the streets?"

Westin resigned shortly and the MAG newsletter blamed his irritation with "rather arbitrary and insensitive censorship" from members of the board. Both Westin and president Durham "declined to comment." After winding up his Playhouse work with Brecht's *The Good Woman of Setzuan* and a summer musical, Westin joined Houston's Alley Theatre as a stage manager.

The Royal Hunt of the Sun dazzled reviewers and an audience that "burst into spontaneous applause" for the scenic design of Casker and the costumes of Gladys Stuart. She dressed the Inca God-King in white-feathered robe, blue-green feather headdress and a gold mask before Casker's golden sun. Jim Fleming, a Strategic Air Command weather observer, played the role that once won acclaim for director Congdon.

The director's wife, Irwin Congdon, designed costumes for *Cactus Flower,* the French comedy. But comedy more than costumes made this the big hit of many seasons. Tom Wees, Eunie Denenberg and Barbara Ross played a dentist, his nurse and his girlfriend. A reviewer loved the way Denenberg's icy nurse bloomed. First on the Playhouse stage as a 10-year-old in *Inherit the Wind*, Barb Ross went on to a wide range of roles over more than four decades.

Westin wound up his stay with *Your Own Thing*, a musical based on *Twelfth Night*. It was memorable for teaming Dick and MariJane Mueller as the gender-crossed twins and for drawing only 1,600 in midsummer after a season that ended in the black. The planned Junior Theater wing was boosted by Henry Fonda's one-man fundraiser, *Fathers Against Sons,* at the Joslyn Concert Hall. Earlier, he'd seen daughter Jane on the cover of *Time*. The story about "The Flying Fondas" was inspired by her Oscar nomination for *They Shoot Horses, Don't They?* She'd wait two years before winning the best actress award for *Klute*.

On stage, Henry revived his story about Brace Fonda's resistance to his acting. His father's conversion came when Henry's sisters offered mild criticism of his performance in *Merton of the Movies,* prompting Papa to interrupt, "He was perfect."

A newspaper letter complained about Peter Fonda's *Easy Rider* poster that declared, "A man went looking for America and couldn't find it anywhere." The writer urged Peter to leave and "take his spoiled brat sister, Jane, with him." Ahh, there's no place like home.

Sound of Music Opens Tuneful Decade: 1970–1971

"The Sound of the 70s" gave the ticket campaign a slogan for a decade opening with *The Sound of Music*. Large letters promised "TWO BIG MUSICALS," with *The Man of La Mancha* to come, plus four other shows for only $14.63. Unlike the single musicals in the past four years, both made money despite high expenses.

The season also brought new competition for the theater dollar. In early 1971, the popular Miriam Shrier had signed an Equity actors contract to perform at the new Westroads Dinner Theater with Dick Solowicz. A year later, it was joined by Dick Mueller's Firehouse Dinner Theater. Then David Witherspoon (David James when he played in *Hair* on Broadway) started the Talk of the Town theater. And backer Norm Denenberg and director Norm Filbert split from the Firehouse to add a second downtown venue, the Upstairs Dinner Theater. That gave Omaha about 1,200 theater seats for four dinner shows. It also meant paid roles for stars of musicals.

The proposed Junior Theater wing of the Playhouse was still a draftsman's dream, so director Bob Hall was building sets in an empty Taco Grande restaurant. The Juniors would perform at three high schools. Auditions and rehearsals remained at the Playhouse where the director had an office.

After a critic of *My Fair Lady* had asked for "a more lush sound," the Playhouse went well beyond the usual quartet and assembled a seventeen-piece orchestra for Nancy Tuomisto's Maria and Bill Koll's Captain Von Trapp. The new music director Allen Barnard of Bellevue High School called it "half and half," an equal mix of adults and students. When auditions "didn't pan out too well," he made sixty contacts to recruit enough musicians.

Reviews agreed it was a great success, despite its stage and film familiarity. "As you might guess," a reviewer mused, "the children steal the show." The youngest, Gretl played by 6-year-old Loretta Wolf, won the biggest spread in the *World-Herald*. She was feverish and dizzy one night, but had no understudy. So her mother advised, "You've got to fool the audience. Daddy is out there. You've got to fool him." She made Mrs. and Mrs. Joe Wolf proud. Not to mention her nine brothers and sisters.

From *Andersonville Trial* to Triumphant *La Mancha*

The return of Bill Bailey, lean and lined with age after a long illness, and other seasoned players made *The Andersonville Trial* cast better than the play, Kountze claimed. The November production featured Bob Roberts, who "marvelously played" the defendant, a crippled prison commandant. Bailey told a reporter, "I like Fritz (Congdon) best of all the directors. He has a humane approach, and he keeps an even temper and uses tact." The play seemed especially relevant to Kountze, given the My Lai massacre trial and other Vietnam War issues then in the news.

The new associate director, Robert Neu, after directing Studio plays, now tackled the January main stage comedy by Peter Ustinov. His *Romanoff and Juliet* linked Shakespeare's star-crossed lovers to Cold War politics. Marilyn Schooley (Hansen), an interior designer then living in the historic Mercer mansion, and Tom Novotny "threatened to steal several scenes" as an unlikely couple. This comedy and *The Andersonville Trial*, bracketed by musicals, drew the season's smallest attendance.

That second crowd-drawing musical, *Man of La Mancha* by Dale Wasserman, starred Dick Mueller and his wife MariJane. In his last Playhouse role before returning to professional theater at the Firehouse, Mueller sang "The Impossible Dream" and won both the Fonda and Drama Critic's awards, while his wife took the McGuire honor.

The cast included a Benson High student as Quixote's horse Rocinante. Already a veteran of the holiday *Nutcracker*, Wendy Larson would become a principal ballerina with the Omaha Ballet Company. A decision by Congdon to assign Casker the costuming caused Gladys Stuart to resign.

Peter Pan Ends Season in Black

When *Catch Me If You Can* ran on Broadway, billboards demanded, "Don't Reveal the Secret Ending." The Playhouse posted a similar message as audiences exited the theater in April. The Prompter listed the cast without their characters' names to avoid revealing identities. A reviewer said, "Count yourself lucky" if you leave "certain of your own name and with whom you came."

The suspense-comedy involves a Catskills honeymoon. A manic husband reports the disappearance of his bride. Then another woman (Diane Casker) appears, claiming to be the missing wife.

The Studio Theater's spring offering packed the lower level for an original musical revue, *30—Living Scrapbook of a Decade*. Written by George Heiring and Ozzie Nogg, it featured such standards as "Smoke Gets in Your Eyes" and "Puttin' on the Ritz." A reviewer liked Nogg's version of "Ten Cents a Dance." Neu directed with help from two talents whose first Playhouse work preceded the 1930s: costume designer Gifford and the choreographer dating back to the first vaudeville production at Tech High, the woman once known as wee Adelaide Fogg.

The *World-Herald* still ran full-page color photos on the cover of its Sunday Entertainment tabloid, and its style this season took Playhouse performers into outdoor settings. The *Man of La Mancha* leads were posed with Omaha's only sizable windmill, atop the Zuider Zee restaurant. The *30* cast polished a vintage automobile, and the May comedy, *The Captain's Paradise* found David Wallace, in the title role, lounging on the deck of the good ship *Sgt. Floyd* on the Missouri River.

A reviewer warned "anyone whose beliefs in women's rights outweigh his sense of humor" to think twice before catching this "salty saga of the greatest male chauvinist pig to sail the seas." The captain's idea of paradise set him sailing between a British wife in Gibraltar and a temptress in North Africa. Wallace's role had been played by Alec Guinness and Tony Randall. *The Captain's Paradise* joined the ranks of shows forced briefly into the basement by a tornado warning. Scotsman Wallace and others led a capacity crowd in subterranean singing.

The musical *Peter Pan* was not part of the regular season, but reduced ticket prices of $2 for adults, $1 for children helped it draw more than 7,500 in July, a great crowd for midsummer. Designer Casker and technician Schmidt tackled set construction and the ropes used to fly Peter, Wendy and her siblings. "His ulcers will be getting ulcers," Doug Smith wrote of Casker in the *Sun*. But it all worked, his review said.

The daily promised Nancy Tuomisto "could give Mary Martin tough competition for the role of Peter any day." She'd started the season as Maria and returned to sing "Do-Re-Mi" with the Von Trapp children at the June awards night, then capped the year as "a super-spunky Peter Pan."

The big news applauded the season ending $13,000 in the black, just two years after those headlines bemoaning "$50,000 in debt." Treasurer Clarence Teal wrote, "As this is the last time after 25 years that I'll be giving this report, I'm going to go into a little more detail than usual." That turned out to be a false alarm. He'd hold the job nearly four more years. A pillar of the Playhouse, Dee Owen, started a long run as trustee, and Barbara Ford, who'd later lead expansion efforts, headed the Guild. Teal's letter inserted a stage direction—"Burn note"—after announcing, "That debt has been paid off." He also reported "a number of gifts," the largest $5,000, in the last two years.

After decades of boasting that the Playhouse broke even while depending on admissions alone, the time had come to seek an endowment. The next season would bring the slow start of a foundation with gifts totaling under $23,000, well below the $250,000 needed to "function as designed," Teal said. A Prompter item announced a new membership category, "Patrons of the Theatre," for contributions of $100 or more. By the end of August, a list of 80 patron couples, singles and businesses had qualified for the two season tickets offered to donors.

Meanwhile, a news story featured the growth in local competition. Joann Schmidman imported New York friends for the experimental, interactive Magic Theater in the Old Market.

The next year would bring the Nebraska State Repertory Company, which also settled in downtown as the Norton Theatre, named for Rudyard, Omaha's senior thespian. Mueller's Firehouse would soon join the Westroads Dinner Theater, and reporters asked Congdon and Norm Filbert if talent was spreading thin. Filbert's Chanticleer company took a risk by scheduling *Boys in the Band,* forerunner of many gay-oriented plays to come in a time of AIDS awareness and greater acceptance of alternative lifestyles.

After Forty-six Seasons, Change to 8 p.m. Weekday Curtain: 1971–1972

The season brought more changes in personnel. After resigning, Gladys Stuart started Theatrical Costumiers of Omaha across the street from Tech High, and Anna Marie Brooks became Playhouse costume designer. A native New Yorker, she designed costumes for the Globe Shakespeare Festival of Odessa while pursuing a graduate degree at Southwest Texas State. Associate director Neu left and that position remained open for a year, requiring guest direction of Studio plays.

But another change had greater social implications. Since 1925, playgoers had arrived for an 8:30 curtain, and short-lived efforts to change starting times ended in confusion and latecomers. So the Prompter warned, "WATCH IT!" when the weekday time changed again to 8 p.m. (More than two decades later the time changed to 7:30 p.m.) "We had hoped to have only one compromise 8 o'clock curtain, but we bow to the demands of our members and shall try

Oliver's Orphans.

once again the three different curtain times." So Friday and Saturday remained at 8:30, Sunday at 7:30 p.m., dark on Monday. Apparently weekday lifestyles were changing in Omaha. A new teen night policy let teenagers in for $1 on the night between the preview and the opening.

What didn't change was the drawing power of the season-opening musical. Attendance topped 10,000 for the first time in five years for *Oliver*.

Fourth-grader Jay Brooks took the title role and teacher Kent Hanon played Fagin. The most memorable image of Congdon's *Oliver* was Bill Sikes and Bullseye, his faithful bull terrier. John Dennis Johnston wore more beard than the shadow he'd make famous as a shave-headed Hollywood heavy. The dog, one of three to audition, also "won the role due to his sinister appearance." Butch was black with only three legs, making it a scene-stealing amble when he walks up a flight of stairs and across a bridge.

Allen Barnard and Valerie Roche returned as music and dance directors. Marsha Hiner, a member of the orchestra, would later play an offstage role when a recently divorced Congdon would marry her and resign as director.

Critics claimed the mystery of Agatha Christie's *Mousetrap* was how it kept running for years on the London stage. If readers skipped the reviews, headlines were bad enough, panning with title puns such as "'Mousetrap' Spring Badly Rusted." The daily's Jim Bresette ranked it "among the weakest ever dragged across the Playhouse boards."

Absent an associate director and faced with casting problems, the first Studio offering was pushed back to late November with a guest director in charge. Bill Phillips and his cast were treated well by reviewers undaunted by the play's long title—*The Persecution and Assassination of Jean-Paul Marat as Performed by Inmates of the Asylum of Charenton Under the Direction of the Marquis de Sade* (breaking the title record held by *Oh Dad, Poor Dad,* etc.).

As usual, Playhouse members took a New York theater tour that included *Hair*. Val Teal reported, "The majority of those who saw it walked out after the first act or sooner." Mrs. Elton Loucks, past president, skipped it this time. She'd seen it in Las Vegas and "was so bored she slept through most of it." Apparently the Playhouse avoided nudity for fear it would set off an epidemic of yawning.

Subject Was Roses, The Fantasticks Start 1972 Strong

The reviewers who panned *Mousetrap* raved about Congdon's direction of a three-actor cast in *The Subject Was Roses* that "had us eating out of their hands all the way," one wrote. The story of an alienated family won a Pulitzer and other prizes for playwright Frank Gilroy.

The Fantasticks was already a legendary success story when it arrived at the Playhouse in 1972. The off-Broadway musical, produced on a shoestring budget, had grossed millions around the world, and wasn't new to Omaha. Not the usual costly production, it still drew over 10,000 attendance and became the last musical for several years to make money (economics that would lead to recruiting philanthropic sponsors for each show). The only complaint: you can't stop humming "Try to Remember." Rudyard Norton played the Old Actor, a role he'd aged into since his 1926 Playhouse debut.

Indians by Arthur Kopit brought a guilt-ridden Buffalo Bill and Sitting Bull back to demythologize the Old West and satirically reflect on U.S. policy in Vietnam. Dan Brady's casting as Colonel Bill Cody revealed another source of local stage experience in the early '70s—he'd done musicals for the Omaha Parks and Recreation Department. Gene Driscoll was Sitting Bull. Despite upbeat reviews, the politicized play drew the year's smallest audience.

By contrast, a more traditional comedy, *Forty Carats,* closed the membership season (the summer musicals, *The Wizard of Oz* this time, were separate) with the season's largest turnout for a nonmusical. Merle Moores "literally glowed" as the 40-something divorcee tempted by a younger suitor. The cast included David Kalber, whose father Floyd was then an NBC *Today* news anchor.

Honors for Henry Fonda and sister Harriet highlighted the June awards night. It was the year Jane Fonda won an Oscar for *Klute,* and her father was "very proud of the way she handled it," opting not to make a political statement. Engraved theater seats were dedicated in the names of the siblings, Fonda and Mrs. Peacock.

Junior Theater Split Starts Two Years of Transition: 1972–1973

Where did it begin, the little-publicized end of the long partnership between the Playhouse and the Junior Theater? The memories of embattled trustees blend everything from the brouhaha over Emmy Gifford's lobby murals to substantial policy conflicts. The climactic event saw Mrs. Gifford leave the board this season, one that started with her latest cover design gracing the Prompter. It showed more than a dozen rooms busy with Playhouse activities. An explanation included, "The Junior Theater is depicted right next to the kitchen."

An earlier sketch of a Junior Theater wing, adding a large new auditorium, had kicked off fund-raising three years ago. But the time was coming when the board would proceed with the plans or turn away. That meant turning away from a tradition that began in the 1920s and continued with variations through the years.

Their own children's director started it with *Racketty Packetty House* in 1929. Then the Junior League guided youth productions in the 1930s, and Kendrick Wilson served on the Junior Theater board during most of his twenty-five Playhouse years. Emmy Gifford and Echo Ellick served both the Playhouse and Junior Theater for decades. The Junior plays were usually performed in the public schools, earlier at Tech High and more recently at nearby Lewis and Clark Junior High. But auditions and rehearsals often took place in the basement rehearsal hall used for Studio plays, and the Playhouse offered classes for young actors.

The previous season saw sudden changes for the Juniors. William Roundey had arrived from Seward's Concordia College in August 1971 to replace Robert Hall as director. After one play, he scheduled December tryouts in the Studio space and then resigned due to illness. Margaret Shafer, Burke High drama head, directed *Trudy and the Minstrels,* and Steve Regan took over for *Greensleeves Magic.* He became a high school journalism teacher and Omaha school board member who died young; his widow, Georgiann, became Playhouse costume designer. Then a familiar figure returned. Royal Eckert, Wilson's scenic designer, was hired as Junior director. Now 44, he'd earned his master's degree and pursued a Nebraska U. doctorate. He'd remain three seasons.

If the partnership was long-standing, the merger agreement between the Playhouse and Junior Theater reached back only to 1967. The million-dollar fund drive that followed brought a large gift from Chuck and Margre Durham. Such gifts were expected to build that

Junior wing with its 800-seat auditorium, divisible into smaller venues to be shared with the Studio Theatre.

Well, that publicized "proposal of marriage" was heading for a breakup. The board was split, but a majority "didn't want in-house competition," trustee Tom Wees recalled. Mrs. Gifford and Joe Barker led those wanting to merge. Barker felt the question was: "Could the Playhouse grow on its own through the Studio Theatre, as opposed to building its own farm system by merging with the Juniors?" Separation won.

"It was a time," Wees said, "when we worried about competition from the dinner theaters. We talked about doing dinner with the Studio Theatre." The majority wanted to concentrate on the main season and bring the Studio plays out of the basement.

That much is clear. The time frame for hurt feelings may be fuzzier. The Durhams and others considered putting children's theater in the old restaurant space of the Western Heritage Museum, a former train station later to bear the Durham name.

When it was time to repaint the Playhouse lobby after the 1975 tornado, Margre Durham didn't share Emmy Gifford's interest in preserving the murals she painted in 1959. In the years that followed, the Junior Theater became the Emmy Gifford Children's Theater on Center Street, then the Omaha Theater Company for Young People.

Later moved to a Moorish movie house and renamed The Rose for benefactor Rose Blumkin of Nebraska Furniture Mart, the OTCYP grew in the early twenty-first century to America's third largest children's theater. But the historic split in the 1972–1973 season was not reported. The Durham gift was withdrawn, the new wing delayed. Emmy Gifford resigned as trustee and so did Barker. Honored on awards night, Emmy said she left to devote more energy to Junior Theater. Disappointed, like the little girl in an earlier play, she felt her hands were "full of dead birds."

Children's theater would be known by new names in the years ahead, but you'd think the *World-Herald* would master the name of the long-established community theater. Not so, according to a Prompter item.

Three mentions in a recent edition used three different names: "First by our correct name, The Omaha Playhouse, then by our original name, The Omaha Community Playhouse; and finally someone in the Public Pulse paid tribute to The Omaha Public Theatre's production of '1776.'" The commentary suggested "all three names describe us very well. A few years ago we took 'Community' out of our title because some people believed the word suggested 'small town,' or 'neighborhood,' and we now serve not only a big city and its environs but also out-state Nebraska and Iowa."

But, yes, the item went on, "in a larger sense we are a community theater … built by the people of this community and they still run it." Such confusion forecasts the return later to the original name.

Despite "Talent Drain," Awards Go to *1776* Cast

"Will Local Theaters Run Out of Actors?" The headline indicated the Playhouse trustees weren't the only ones concerned with the impact of the dinner theaters in 1972. The news story described "a talent drain" from community theaters, with a fourth venue (the Upstairs) yet to open. Recent Playhouse musical leads were working at the dinner theaters.

"If someone is offering $150 a week," Congdon explained, "and I ask them to do something for nothing, they're more likely to take the paying job." That meant he'd start with less experienced people, train them "to be picked off by one of these groups. I am frustrated by it," the director admitted.

Nearly 9,500 saw the season-opening *1776*, and the founding fathers almost made money. Bob Roberts (John Adams) gave "his finest performance," a critic wrote, and the appearance of Tom Wees as Benjamin Franklin "brought spontaneous applause."

By comparison, though, only 661 made it downstairs for six performances of the Anthony Newley musical, *Stop the World, I Want to Get Off!* It was the debut as Studio director for Pat Rucker from Oklahoma State University.

I Do, I Do Does Better for Star Pegi Than Director Fritz

The Fourposter had been a starring vehicle for Rex Harrison and Lili Palmer in the film. Then *The Fantasticks* team of Tom Jones and Harvey Schmidt turned the story of a fifty-year marriage into the musical, *I Do, I Do,* with Robert Preston and Mary Martin.

In Omaha, it earned Pegi Stommes, who shared the stage with husband, Jerry, critical praise and the 1973 McGuire award. But it drew under 6,500—thousands less than most main stage musicals. And it lost nearly $6,000, by far the largest deficit during Fritz Congdon's three-year stay. His backstage speech before the opening, however, gave clues to the disfavor that would bring his resignation a year later.

It might have been the typical pre-show pep talk, but Congdon told the gathered cast and crew that he had approached several couples to play the leads before settling on Mr. and Mrs. Stommes. Stage manager Ginny Winsor, who'd later manage the Playhouse for two decades, listened in dismay. She later joined two carloads of backstage workers who told the board president that Congdon had driven away volunteers. He had recently divorced his wife, Irwin, and the trustees were again dealing with concerns about a director's love life. (As noted, Congdon would marry Marsha Hiner, a musician in several shows and a Guild member.) The show, of course, went on, and the daily review said, "Mrs. Stommes consistently stole the show from husband Jerry."

Any thievery in the Studio below was done by Gene Driscoll's ominous transformation into Ionesco's *Rhinoceros*. But Bresette's review criticized his romantic interest. Pam Carter, it seemed, had "irritating mannerisms," such as "bouncing from one foot to the other during every tense moment." Pam would become as popular and honored a comedic performer as ever trod the Playhouse stage.

Frank DeGeorge wowed audiences in *The Last of the Red-Hot Lovers*, then with *Butterflies Are Free* in April, another small cast meant Congdon had used only ten actors in the last three shows. But that made it "a community theater director's dream," Bresette wrote: "Small cast, single set and a script" that balances "contemporary irreverent wit with old-fashioned sentiment." Debbie Hike played the kooky Goldie Hawn role. Haberman complained again about "casual sex," but the *Sun* credited the Playhouse for "leaving the little bit of profane reference and the breast-fondling sequence intact."

Associate Rucker promised an "all stops out" and "no holds barred" production of Brecht's epic *Mother Courage*. But he sought a cast of twenty-six with "an overwhelming need for one stupendous actress for the title role." He found Nancy Duncan. She would also be Rucker's successor as Studio director. The lower hall "may seem a rather small arena for 'epic drama,'" the review observed. "But lack of elbow room hasn't deterred" Rucker and cast.

The membership season ended with the farcical *Send Me No Flowers*, starring Jack Frost, an elected utilities board member, as the hypochondriac who mistakenly thinks he's doomed.

Rodgers and Hammerstein's *Cinderella* drew only half the audience of the past summers' *Peter Pan* and *Wizard of Oz*. The made-for-television production lacked "the broad, cross-generational appeal" that made those past summer shows "such a delight."

Anything Goes, But Not All Goes Well in 49th Season: 1973–1974

Helen Gribble, long active in church music and other community activities, turned the board presidency over to Norm Williams, KMTV executive. He'd lead the board during the most dramatic transitions since the departure of Kendrick Wilson. The rise of the dinner theaters and the split from the Junior Theater were well under way. In an arts overview, the newspaper quoted Congdon predicting, "Our future lies in doing the type of plays dinner theaters don't do."

Another 1973 development saw the formation of the Nebraska State Repertory Company, which also promised fare unfamiliar to dinner crowds. Its founders, including Dwayne Ibsen and Howard Swain Jr., set out to perform classics in their Norton Theatre.

They were inspired by big crowds for Chanticleer's *Romeo and Juliet*. The Bluffs theater also did well with the weighty *A Streetcar Named Desire*. The Nebraska Arts Council had contributed to Studio dramas at the Playhouse, so the new company defined its mission with Arts Council funding in mind. Their first season promised Sophocles, Shakespeare and Ibsen plus Sigmund Romberg, Arthur Miller and Thornton Wilder.

The previous Playhouse season had seen new emphasis on patronage. What started as Prompter listing of patrons now added a smaller list of donors. The Durhams, Gribbles, Ed and Dee Owen and the M. Cooper Smiths completed the donor category, indicating gifts of $250 or more. An alphabetical list of seventy-two patrons ($100) began with the daily's Harold and Marian Andersen and included Henry Fonda.

If this seems small potatoes looking back, it marked the start, only in its second year, of something big. Then it grew in the third year to feature a Benefactor—the Kiewit Foundation—and Sponsors, Mr. and Mrs. Webster Pullen, before listing donors and patrons, now numbering 114.

From the same distance, though, the season remains historic because it saw staff changes that brought a heroic charmer, Charles Jones, and others who guided the Playhouse to new heights.

The season started with the worst annual ticket sales since moving to the new theater. The season ended with ambitious plans by the new director, raising issues that would bring a sad farewell for the old treasurer. In between, two musicals averaged just over 6,000 attendance, a contrast to more than 10,000 each just two years before. After the opening musical, treasurer Teal projected a season deficit of $25,000. He later claimed "lumber prices have gone sky high," hurting set building, and complained that recent shows "just haven't been rehearsed long enough." Now "door sales are down," adding to "trouble" noted when season sales fell so short.

Anything Goes opened in September with a benefit. Proceeds aided Equilibria, a drug clinic headed by Dr. Jack Lewis, whose wife Kathy would become a Playhouse trustee. Betty Hudson, an Omaha newcomer

Nancy Duncan.

loaded with stage credits, "was a knockout" on all the Cole Porter hits—from "You're the Top" to "I Get a Kick Out of You." The ocean cruise scripted by the great P.G. Wodehouse, among others, featured Alan Reynolds as Billy Crocker and Gale Madsen as Hope Harcourt.

The Studio Theater claimed a new associate director, Nancy Duncan, for its October offering. *The Night Thoreau Spent in Jail* was billed as an antiwar play with parallels to American involvement in Vietnam. Bresette's review said, "The passion of Thoreau's beliefs fairly radiated from Dick Bakkerud's performance."

Her second play, *The Seeds in the Passes,* dealt with California's ill-fated Donner party. Reviewer Doug Smith, now switched from the *Sun* to the *World-Herald*, called the large cast "talented, if not completely convincing." Mrs. Duncan cast her husband, Harry, a fine arts printer, as George Donner and two of her three children joined the snowbound party. Only 188 turned out in December for the Donner downer.

Attendance Hits Record Low, Adds to Congdon's Woes

Night Watch suffered the fate of that recent mystery, *Mousetrap*. Reviews were scathing, and attendance was the lowest on the main stage since the theater opened in 1959. A review was headlined: "It's No Mystery: Thriller of Year Is a Waste of Time." At least Randy Vest, who'd return years later after working for *People* magazine, seemed to have rehearsed more than once, the review said.

It was the director's last show before he became a "lame duck" midway into his fifth season. Divorced the previous November, Congdon, 47, saw his new marriage reported the day after Christmas. Two days later, a headline declared, "Playhouse Director Closing Career." He'd soon leave for his bride's native Fargo, N.D., "with no plans to get back into theater." Maybe he'd teach, go into broadcasting, or "even decide to become an auto mechanic, who knows?"

A month later, R. Thomas Casker, designer since Eckert left with Wilson in 1967, "didn't want to discuss his reasons for leaving" when his contract expired at season's end. A new director could pick his own designer before the fiftieth anniversary season.

Officially, "The board has been very pleased with Fritz's work," president Williams announced. Unofficially, Congdon was "very much in disfavor" with the board, recalled Berdine Urbach, then Guild president. Treasurer Teal spoke more candidly to the press: "Fritz did a marvelous job when he first came here, but I have a feeling he isn't as interested in the Playhouse as he used to be." No one mentioned those two carloads of volunteers who reported that Congdon was driving workers away.

Ray Crossman, the board's first vice president, would earn a special place in Playhouse history by heading the most successful search committee since the hiring of Kendrick Wilson in 1942. His committee included Mel Quinlan, Margre Durham, Jane Gilmore and Echo Ellick. After the hiring of Greg Foley in 1925, Mrs. Ellick or her mother Genevieve Guiou had taken the lead in recruiting each

313

previous director. For the present, though, Congdon would direct two more shows before guest directors filled out his "lame duck" season.

Congdon's troubles weren't over with his final Simon comedy, the three-part *Plaza Suite*. For unexplained reasons, Joe Moore dropped out and Congdon had to hire New York professional Frank Wells for two of the key roles. Also in dual roles was the popular Miriam Shrier, back from dinner theater.

The review of *Irma La Douce* focused on the director's February exit. It began, "For the first time in what seems like a mighty long time, the Omaha Playhouse deserves to be packed to the rafters. It's ironic," Smith wrote, "that Congdon's last effort for the Playhouse should be such a fine one after several listless productions since the fall of 1972." James Eisenhardt, South High drama teacher and future longtime trustee, played a supporting role. Thus ended Congdon's five years as the Prompter said farewell "with regret."

Hutson Debuts as *Richard III*, Summerfest Follows

A Studio drama put Bill Hutson in the spotlight as Shakespeare's *Richard III*. He was "the brightest spot in an overall fine production, notable for its vastness and complexity." Given the limitations of the basement space, director Duncan "somehow, against all odds, made it work." When Hutson, "the confident young actor," won the Studio award, Echo Ellick said, "It's a pity he stayed in Omaha such a short time. We could use more actors like him."

Then gone to graduate school, Hutson returned first to act in the new Playhouse creation, the Nebraska Theatre Caravan, then as a Creighton drama professor who would play more award-winning roles. His performance helped the Playhouse hire its next director; Hutson impressed Charles Jones on his visit to interview for the job. By 2014, Hutson could claim a record six Fonda awards.

The first guest director was Dr. Jerome Birdman, the new UNO Fine Arts dean. He cast UNO student Bill Koll and two queens in Robert Bolt's *Vivat! Vivat Regina!* Diane Casker, soon to depart with her husband, was Mary, Queen of Scots, and Ann Saville as Elizabeth I would share the year's top Maggie awards with Hutson. "Nearly walking off with the show," Smith said, was Koll as "a torrential raging Knox," the Protestant reformer.

Philip Barry's *Philadelphia Story* (later the musical *High Society*) ended the season with Dr. Edwin Clark, the UNO drama head, as guest director. It outdrew all but *Anything Goes* in this time of transition and poor attendance. Clark's cast included few familiar names with Rose Mealer as Tracy Lord, the Katharine Hepburn role.

After three summers of musical "kid stuff," the Playhouse hooked up with UNO for "its most ambitious summer schedule ever," called "Summerfest '74." Three members of the university faculty and Mrs. Duncan would direct four shows with overlapping runs on four stages.

The fact that one of the productions, the musical revue *Jacques Brel Is Alive and Well and Living in Paris*, would reappear in the next Playhouse season suggests what Smith's review explains. In a cabaret setting, it won "standing ovations and standing-room only crowds." The cast's David K. Johnson would appear often before turning pro.

Overall, the four-show collaboration was viewed as a success, though ticket sales weren't "as high as was hoped."

Long before the final Summerfest curtain fell, the Playhouse knew the name of its new director. Sir Charles. Charlie Jim. The sizable Mr. Jones from Georgia. He'd celebrate the fiftieth anniversary season with a new staff of his own. To some, especially the cautious treasurer, Clarence Teal, the winds of change blew too fast and hard. And then came a real tornado.

CHAPTER

7

Charming Charles Brings *Carol,* Caravan, 1974–1977

Heat, Broken Leg, Blizzard, Tornado Welcome Jones: 1974–1975

It was not a dark and stormy night. That came in January and again in May. It was a "hot, hot, hot day" in July, the start of the most momentous season in the fifty-year history of the Playhouse.

Attorney Ray Crossman had contacted Charles Jones in January, but Omahans first heard of the new director that spring. They later saw him smiling on the cover of the daily's entertainment magazine. Then, on this 104-degree day, he'd come to stay. Omaha had just survived the second coming of Elvis Presley, headlined "10,000 Adore 'Spangled God,'" and Richard Nixon would soon resign as president. The director's wife, Eleanor, and scenic designer Jim Othuse waited at the nearby motel while Charles interviewed choreography candidates.

A reporter identified Jones, 36, first as a Southerner, then as a tall man of 340 pounds. "The Georgian laughs as easily as a magnolia sways in the wind." Othuse, 30, who came north with him, would

Othuse, left, Jones, technician Steve Wheeldon back stage.

be characterized as "a shy, slight man (who) might easily be overlooked were it not for his striking resemblance to comic actor Woody Allen." Othuse would later add a few pounds and escape the comparison.

Joanne Cady, hired that day as choreographer for the upcoming *Music Man*, recalled the July heat as she met "this big gentleman, this perfect Southern gentleman." Underline "gentleman." The courtly charm of Charles Jones comes up again and again in memories of his first season in Omaha. Crossman found him "enchanting."

Back at the motel, Mrs. Jones and the new designer asked Charles, "Who did you hire?" Jones said, "A nice lady, a Council Bluffs housewife." That didn't impress them, so he tried to recall Cady's story about her New York experience. He hadn't mastered the details of her television work with Shari Lewis and Lamb Chop, so he announced, "She was a Rockette." Really? "The short one at the end of the line." Othuse believed it for years. Joanne would join the staff a few years later and stay until 2003. Othuse would continue longer in his design role.

Charlie Jim, as he was dubbed in a *World-Herald* headline, stayed until 1998 after leading the Playhouse to unprecedented success. Rated highly before his arrival, it clearly rose to the top among community theaters by almost any measure—staff, budget, facility, attendance and, arguably, both number and quality of productions.

That half-century anniversary season saw a January blizzard delay a controversial play, a "brutal" decision push the resignation of longtime treasurer Teal, and a roof-raising tornado cancel the celebratory *Golden Follies* production. Othuse was assaulted and robbed that first July in Omaha, heavy rains that fall flooded the Jones condo, and Charles broke his leg days before the historic blizzard.

So how was their second year? Before it ended, the new director began planning the touring Nebraska Theatre Caravan and adapting his highly acclaimed version of Dickens's *A Christmas Carol*. Both *Carol* and the Caravan continued after his retirement—the first a source of both income and goodwill, the other a source of outreach and talent that continued the Jones legacy long after he was gone.

The Georgia house plants Eleanor stowed in the car trunk didn't survive the heat beating down on the motel parking lot that hiring day. And the motel wouldn't survive the next year's tornado. But Jim bounced back from the armed robbery, Charles's leg healed, and Mr. and Mrs. Jones pooh-poohed Georgians who urged them to flee home to gentler climes.

New Creative Team Occupies "Dirty" Playhouse: 1974–1975

The Playhouse now commanded by Charles Jones hadn't changed much since *Say, Darling* opened there in 1959. Emmy Gifford's murals still adorned the lobby and the restrooms. Just inside the main entrance, not yet covered by a canopy, Estelle English ate her lunch of cheese and crackers while managing the box office. Al Perrault lived in his basement apartment. The feisty custodian was often seen with a lady on his arm, but his work "was slowly improving," trustees were told. Jones shocked them at that July board meeting by declaring the Playhouse "dirty."

Freeze this scene. It would soon change. In her sixteenth year on the job that began at 40th and Davenport, Estelle would break her hip, try to return and then retire. Next May's tornado would raise the roof and provide an excuse for painting over the murals. One thing was unchanged: Florence Young, that substitute dancer in the first play, led in season ticket sales as she had before and would in years to come. Those sales dropped to just over 4,000, and later it would be claimed that the total was only 3,000 on Jones's arrival. That was true only because the campaign was then still under way.

Technical director Jack Schmidt didn't leave with Congdon and Casker but resigned in that transitional month of July. Jones replaced him with Steve Wheeldon, not quite a UNO graduate that summer. Wheeldon, who'd stay five years, had trained at Tech High, under Bob Welk at the university and with Mrs. Gifford at the Junior Theater.

Joanne Cady started as a student of Cora Quick, dancing at Ak-Sar-Ben and elsewhere with the Quickettes. She grew up on a Council Bluffs hilltop where she babysat the daughters of Henry Fonda's sister Jayne, and occasionally their visiting cousins, Peter and Jane. She had returned from five years in New York to teach dancing in Lincoln, then her home town, where she choreographed for Chanticleer musicals before signing on with Jones for *The Music Man*.

Jones and Othuse had done the River City musical in Georgia, so they knew what they wanted from the returning staff—technician Tom Johnson, costumer Shirli Frank and her assistant, Harriet Hedrick. Nancy Duncan continued as associate director.

"Our new staff" appeared backstage in a Prompter photo. The unlikely trio eyes a drawing: the shorter Othuse wearing glasses and plaid shirt, the tall, slender Wheeldon with long hair and mustache, flanking Jones with suit coat tossed over a shoulder.

How did Jones of Georgia meet Othuse of Massachusetts? The scenic artist dropped out of Emerson College in Boston and designed his first set in Maine at the Kennebunkport Playhouse. *Marriage-Go-Round* star Kitty Carlisle loved it. Then he studied at the Lester Polakov Studio in New York. There in the mid-1960s he lived in a small brownstone on the lower east side and did scenic design for twenty-six episodes of a Seventh Day Adventist television series.

An ad drew him to Atlanta as assistant designer for a professional repertory theater. A coworker "told me about the Springer," two hours away in Columbus. "I met with Charles, and we hit it off, right off the bat. I was kind of in awe of Charles, the way he spoke so well, his way of getting you to understand what he wanted." Jim's seven-year stay at the Springer Opera House continued after the director left for London, where Jones studied arts administration, adding the business savvy that impressed trustees.

A news story said he was the only candidate that looked into

Joanne Cady.

financial records. Armed with a speech-drama degree from LaGrange College in Georgia, Charles tried acting in New York and Virginia before starting a decade of directing in Columbus in 1962. Describing himself as a "big, showy actor," his humbler memories feature mishaps: "Auditions terrified me," so reticence cost him a chance to understudy Zero Mostel in *A Funny Thing Happened on the Way to the Forum*.

Later, ready to audition for Agnes DeMille, "I was so keyed up that the instant she came on stage I threw up on her shoes." But he turned the Columbus Little Theater into the Springer, Georgia's State Theater Company, before Eleanor and Charles shared the International Arts Career grant that took them to England in 1972.

He'd earned his certification from London Polytechnic and the British Drama League and traveled to Chicago when Crossman found him guest directing *Rosencrantz and Guildenstern Are Dead*. Jones asked a librarian for a history of Nebraska. "The latest one was dated 1907, so she brought me seven Willa Cather books. What a wonderful way to meet Nebraska."

He was sold on Omaha by Ray and Kay Crossman "and, of course, Echo Ellick was just incredible." Charles and Eleanor "liked the idea of raising our boys, then 7 and 11, in a mid-sized city. We knew from living in New York and London that we didn't want to raise them in a big city," and Columbus, Ga., was too small.

As for his own heroic size, it was publicized in Gerald Wade's introductory newspaper feature, "Charlie Jim Moves Up." *World-Herald* columnist Bob McMorris then ribbed his colleague ("a skinny type") for unleashing his "first fat-man joke" only three inches into the story. The sizable McMorris cheered the arrival of "the first non-skinny type ever to direct the Playhouse in its 49-year history." References to Jones's size, board president Williams said, "were forgotten the instant Jones began to answer questions. We were looking only for talent and ability."

Jones reminded several trustees of British character actor Robert Morley as his easy, storytelling charm won hearts and minds. After past episodes, they were pleased that he was a family man. Perhaps they'd found the man mentioned in that 1960s dream: a director with Wilson's talent who could win friends for the Playhouse on and off stage.

Elvis closed his last Omaha concert with "I Can't Help Falling in Love with You." Not a bad anthem for what turned out to be a long romance between Jones and the Playhouse.

Music Man Begins Jones Era, "Community" Back in Name

Othuse and tech director Wheeldon took inventory of all the existing Playhouse scenery. They'd need sixty-five flats and about as many platforms, plus thirty flying batons, for the ten sets and twenty-one scene changes in Meredith Willson's *Music Man*. Wheeldon, "just excited to be there," said, "It's tough to start out new" with the year's biggest sets and a crew of nineteen. Add a cast of forty-eight with newcomer Scott Root as Professor Harold Hill, and the anticipation rising with that mid-September curtain was palpable.

Not that all was spanking new as the season began. Jones had cast seasoned players: Christel Pratt Kent as Eulalie MacKecknie Shinn, the operatic Dorothy Davitt as Mrs. Paroo, and Joan Hennecke, who doubled as props mistress.

Most reviews praised cast, director, designer and choreographer. Critics marveled at the new team's opening scene—the train bouncing in unison with the banter of the traveling salesmen's "You have to know the territory." Attendance, though well below the top opening crowds, beat the past season's musicals. But expenses neared a record $40,000, so it lost over $4,000.

The second show, also a musical, dropped deeper into the red. Last summer's critical triumph, *Jacques Brel Is Alive and Well and Living in Paris*, lost more than $8,000 while drawing fewer than 5,000. None of the season's plays would top 5,000 in attendance. Jones would take the Playhouse to new heights, but it didn't happen overnight.

Not Now Darling wound up 1974 in the December slot soon to be filled by the perennial *Christmas Carol*. Jones said he'd directed 150 plays, but this marked his first British farce. One review likened it to a burlesque dancer's costume: "skimpy, but that's the idea." Debbie Hike bared nearly all in flowered bikini undies, and the daily's James Bresette sniffed, "If a two-hour joke about marital infidelity is likely to make you laugh, then the Playhouse has a play for you."

Another quiet change had taken place that fall with little fanfare. A later Prompter asked, "Have you noticed 'community' is back in our title—on this Prompter cover, on our stationery and in our total operation?" Readers were reminded that the theater couldn't exist without hundreds of volunteers "from the community."

Blizzard of '75 Delays Frank *Championship Season*

Trustees had scheduled *That Championship Season* at arm's length. Fearing a backlash from its frank dialogue, they offered season tickets for "six out of any seven shows, for the first time … a choice to suit your theatrical taste." Those offended by Jason Miller's prize-winning play could skip it. Echo Ellick, who disliked its profanity when she saw it on Broadway, suggested listing it as a Studio play, but staged "in our main auditorium so it will be given a fair test." The Playhouse would become the first community theater to present the gritty story of a basketball team's reunion. The board also kept some distance by not putting it on the new director's plate. The guest director was former associate Gerald Ness, now Nebraska Arts Council executive. The Friday opening fell on January 10.

That happened to be the day Charles Jones visited a doctor to get a cast on his broken leg. The Georgian suffered the fracture playing in the snow with his boys. It was also the day Omaha was hit by the Blizzard of '75, ranked "one of the worst ever" as 18 inches fell and drifted to impassable depths in winds up to 60 miles per hour. Jones's cast hadn't dried and Eleanor needed help from a Samaritan with four-wheel drive to get him home. Ray Crossman called to check on

Bill Koll, left, in *That Championship Season*.

Charles and heard his young son report, "We're roasting his leg in the oven." Drying the cast, that is.

As the storm grew worse, Jones called the Playhouse to cancel the opening and ask Othuse not to leave "until all the women are safely home." Othuse later headed west on Dodge only to add his Buick Riviera to the many abandoned cars and hitchhike back to 69th and Cass. *That Championship Season* wouldn't open until the following Tuesday, but Jim was in luck. The show had an eating scene. He lived that weekend on chicken in the prop refrigerator. Deaths totaled thirty-three, and Jim's car joined more than 2,000 towed.

Schools didn't open until Wednesday, but the play started on Tuesday and won good reviews that led to awards for Bill Koll as the coach and Warren Zweiback as a "sarcastic dipsomaniac." Smith also praised Gene Driscoll's "skirt-chasing strip miner," Tom Wees as the corrupt mayor and Dan Brady as "an ambitious mediocrity."

As for the rough language, the review concluded: "After a few minutes of hearing dialogue laden with obscenities, the tendency is to forget that one is hearing naughty words out of place in a nice place like the Playhouse. The language becomes natural and even appropriate." More than thirty years later that script still contained rougher language than any in an eighty-year history that then included *Hair*.

Jones reported "a few walkouts," but "very good" reaction for the most part from a forewarned audience. Jones told of a theater devotee who "slipped in after the house lights were out because she didn't want anyone to see her. At the end we found her hiding in the light booth. She was weeping and said, 'Oh, it's beautiful.'"

Crown Matrimonial followed, giving Jones his first opportunity to direct Mary Peckham, who'd win her third McGuire award. He cast the empress of the Playhouse as Queen Mary, coping with the abdication of one son (Al DiMauro) to be replaced on England's throne by his weaker brother (Jerry Venger). Decades later, Charles Jones still spoke passionately of "Mah dahlin' Mary Peckham" in that Southern voice redolent of his romance with the theater. It was only his third Omaha show, but he'd already worked with leading players whose credits covered three decades.

One newcomer, Marianne Young, would become his Martha Cratchit for many Christmases to come. The "puckish" Venger, who looked a bit like the real Windsor rather than his Duke of York, credited Jones with guiding his best of several dozen performances.

Back in 1941, Mrs. Peckham had played Annabelle in *George Washington Slept Here,* but Jean Anderson took that role in its April revival. Reviews portrayed the Kaufman-Hart comedy as "an entertaining old chestnut" full of "innocent good fun."

"Mr. Playhouse" Resigns after 27 Years as Treasurer

A tornado would end the season early, postponing the fiftieth anniversary *Golden Follies* variety show, but a more personal storm had already hit the board of trustees. Charles Jones would reflect on his first year and recall, surprisingly, that the worst moment involved a March meeting. Not the broken leg, blizzard or the May tornado, but a meeting when Clarence Teal left the room.

As reported in the *World-Herald*, "A longtime Playhouse board member resigned after a disagreement regarding money collected in a capital improvement fund drive." As reported in board minutes, a large majority voted to separate capital funds from the operating budget maintained by Teal. He then "announced that with regret, after 27 years as treasurer, he was resigning as of this moment." The man called "Mr. Playhouse" ended his fight against red ink. Active since 1928, he'd played perhaps the largest single role in the theater's history— from his photography recording much of the early history, to stage roles, his part in hiring Kendrick Wilson, service as trustee since 1942 and keeping the Playhouse financially afloat during the dark days of World War II.

Teal viewed the vote pushed by Margre Durham as an assault on his integrity. "I didn't think I should go on being a damned fool," working twenty-five hours a week without pay, "if they didn't think I had any integrity."

Mrs. Durham assured, "His integrity has never been challenged. The board is extremely grateful for the many hours he has put in." Tom (Topper) Teal recalled, "Mother took it harder than Dad." Both Clarence and Val were honored at the annual awards dinner, and she wrote a "Dear Margre" letter to Mrs. Durham: Many have given hours and years to the Playhouse, but "Clarence has given his LIFE to it. If it had not been for Clarence and a few others, this 50-year-old institution would not exist."

In 1987, they named the box office for Clarence Teal, the man who for twenty-seven years penciled the attendance for each play in his notebook.

Others saw the Durham-Teal conflict in light of changing times. The treasurer preached for years that the Playhouse should rely only on ticket revenue and believed his insistence guaranteed the theater's survival. Now patrons and benefactors added to the treasury. When Mrs. Durham and others planned improvements, Teal worried about deficits. "He was very conservative," recalled actor-trustee Tom Wees, "and took a hard position on expense in general." The previous fall, Teal had written a memo worrying that "such a large staff" discouraged volunteers. He wondered if what he saw as problems could be solved or should the Playhouse be given to the university.

If others shared Teal's degree of concern, their fears don't surface in board records. It was a time when the board still blamed dinner theaters for declining membership. Trustee Jack Frost was looking into a Class C liquor license, but he bumped into a law requiring 150 feet from church or school. Temple Israel was only 76 feet away at the closest point.

So in March 1975 the traditional Mr. Teal and the modern Mrs. Durham saw Playhouse financing from quite different perspectives. He emphasized ticket sales, she was attuned to the world of grant funding and philanthropy. She won more control of the capital funds account, and Teal stepped down.

If the split was "brutal" in its impact on Teal, he didn't sulk. When Clarence died in 1984, Tom Teal, no longer called Topper, asked himself why his father gave the Playhouse so much time and energy. His answer: "He was having a wonderful time."

When Henry Fonda returned to perform his one-man *Darrow* in May, the newspaper suggested renaming the Playhouse for him. Columnist Bob Reilly countered, "Call it the Teal House. Clarence might go for the idea. If it didn't cost any money." Even that spring of the resignation, Val wrote the Playhouse history for the fiftieth anniversary program, and Clarence promised to sing "Little Brown Jug" one more time.

The Show Does Not Go On: Tornado Raises Roof

Teal's performance had to wait. The May 6 tornado blew the roof off the Playhouse and postponed the *Follies*. Earlier on that stormy Tuesday, an airport press conference attracted a swarm of photographers. They snapped Kitten Natividad, Miss Nude Cosmopolitan. "Her flimsy dress

Tornado-ripped roof, 1975.

fell to the floor, and there she was in all her prize-winning form. 'I like to show why I won,'" she told the press.

More serious news dealt with the first day of the new regime in Saigon as General Ky escaped Vietnam. After surviving the January blizzard and the Teal resignation, the Playhouse took pride in their regional victory in an American Community Theater Association competition. *Interview* later won honorable mention at the national level, a credit to director Steve Wheeldon and his cast.

They'd called the January blizzard "one of the worst ever," and now the tornado that smashed into the Playhouse was labeled "worst since 1913." That earlier fury took more than 100 lives, but this was bad enough: three dead, more than 200 hurt and over $500 million in damage.

The next day's headline said, "Troops Patrol Devastated Sections" and "Destruction 'Unbelievable, Bomb-like.'" Closer to home, a reporter wrote, "After plowing through the Downtowner (the nearby motel known earlier as the Prom Town House) the funnel moved north, ripping off the roof of the Omaha Playhouse." Three other neighbors—Temple Israel, First Methodist Church and Lewis and Clark Junior High—were damaged, but the 6901 Dodge Building, a few feet south, was unscathed.

The storm hit about 4:40 p.m. that Tuesday afternoon. Earlier, Mrs. Durham and others met. "We had a long discussion about cleaning the theater seats. That seems pretty unimportant now," she said the day after. Mrs. Virgil Weisner, a Fairacres resident just east of the theater, saw a steel girder—"it looked as big as an airplane wing"—fly past and land on a neighbor's lawn. After the "all clear," she walked over to check on the Playhouse "and it was heartbreaking. The lobby was full of debris. The costume room and backstage were open to the rain. And there was the caretaker (Al Perrault), all alone, disconsolately sitting out front on a campstool."

Othuse was inside. KMTV anchorman Jeff Jordan called, wanting an eyewitness report. "I told him, I'm looking out from the Green Room window at cars strewn around the parking lot." His Buick Riviera, the same one stuck in the blizzard, was now missing its hood. "I'm seeing the Downtowner Motel leveled," Jim reported.

News photos later showed the lid off the Playhouse, but it looked placid compared to the view south from Temple Israel with motel wreckage everywhere. "Charles came in," Othuse recalled, "and we saw a guy trying to steal the radio out of my car. He was scared off by Charles' size."

Berdine Urbach was filling in at the box office. She had dropped off some new memberships for Estelle English, who still helped from her apartment. "You know, Berdine, there's a tornado warning," she told her friend. Mrs. Urbach made it home before her husband arrived with the windows blown out of his company car. She returned to find the Playhouse box office "a mess. It was hard to find things."

Damage assessments came from directors Jones and Duncan, and Robert Lueder, a longtime Playhouse supporter whose wife, Mary, was board secretary. Chuck Durham had sent a team from his HDR

Engineering to aid in the insurance claims, and Lueder Construction Company would make repairs.

"The biggest worry," Jones reported, "is rain before we get the new roof on. The moment it starts raining, the damage is going to double." Mrs. Duncan told about the tornado sweeping away the roof and trees, flooding the main stage and shattering entry glass. The grid superstructure over the main stage also received heavy damage, Lueder added, "but the building is structurally sound and can be restored." Lueder immediately tackled work across the street at his own church, First Methodist, and the Playhouse.

Among the insurance claims, the Playhouse received over $200,000 to pay Lueder Construction, $22,000 for damage to building contents and $31,000 for loss of income. Gratitude was again owed Clarence Teal, the man responsible for seeing that the theater was solidly insured.

In the aftermath, Jones found papers on his desk that had blown north from the Lueder office miles away. Othuse picked up a book resting on his drawing board. A warning printed inside said, "Don't remove from the sixth floor." He returned the medical dictionary to Bergen Mercy, a hospital many blocks south.

Bug Spray Aids *Godspell*, Ill Wind Blows Some Good

The aftermath of the tornado found Lueder at work both on repairs and the $90,000 renovation previously planned. Within days, a decision was made to delay *The Golden Follies* until September.

Two summer shows were moved to the nearby university. Dick Mueller did a benefit performance of *The Tender Trap* at his Firehouse Dinner Theater, the competition play *Interview* traveled for a benefit at the Lincoln Playhouse, and the Royal Shakespeare Company returned to aid the stricken theater. The English troupe knew about the Playhouse from a March visit to Omaha and now squeezed a *He That Plays the King* benefit into its travels.

The all-black musical, *Lay My Burden Down,* opened only a week late at UNO. A National Endowment for the Arts grant brought choreographer Quincy Edward from New York to work with director Duncan and Harry Eure of the Afro-Academy of the Dramatic Arts. With songs from Bessie Smith, Marvin Gaye and others, *Burden* covered the broad history of blacks in America. The daily assigned a man of color, Titus Fisher, to review.

Cleanup continued as the musical *Godspell* opened outdoors, the stage in the courtyard behind the Playhouse, the crowd on the hillside lawn. In a sign of times that saw lines at gas stations, Smith's review began, "13 young people thumbed their noses at the energy shortage and danced and sang tirelessly for more than two hours. An attractive lion (Eileen Stark) offers to spray the afflicted with insect repellent in return for a kiss."

Among the performers who would remain prominent in community theater was Bill Bohannon. Another player, Kevyn Morrow, capped a musical theater career years later as the London lead in *Ragtime*, a role that would one day bring him home to the Playhouse. The outdoor *Godspell* saw another Playhouse first: publicity from the new community relations director, David K. Johnson, the *Jacques Brel* star hired with grant money.

By now it seemed like the longest of seasons with a new team, a blizzard, a resignation and a tornado. Mid-August, however, brought reports that $300,000 in repairs were halfway completed. And members were reassured that by mid-September they'd enter new doors under a canopy. Those doors and carved ones for the Studio Theater were gifts of actress Dorothy McGuire, their "Cinderella" before movie stardom. They'd find the lobby redesigned, with a cold look replaced by "warm earth and wood tones." If some missed Emmy Gifford's murals, they could drown their sorrows: "A new moveable serving bar has been added."

Golden Follies, 1975.

Golden Follies, Post-Tornado Décor Wow First-Nighters: 1975–1976

The missing murals were overshadowed by enthusiasm for the celebratory *Golden Follies* and renovated lobby. Jones joked, after the season of blizzard, tornado and broken leg, that he'd watched the skies for a plague of locusts. The tornado had even disrupted a telethon for his second membership campaign.

First-nighters arrived under the new entry canopy and entered a lobby featuring floor-to-ceiling mirrors and cylindrical carnival lights. "Are we in the right place?" a playgoer asked as others exclaimed over the warm earth tones of suede-covered walls. They came from a Country Club dinner to see the postponed tribute to the theater's fiftieth anniversary. The musical was worth waiting for, according to Doug Smith, who called it "a show that makes a reviewer ashamed" of past looseness with "superlatives."

It opened with the full company of forty-four singing "The Good Old Days." Under three arches bearing photos of Fonda, McGuire and fifty years of Playhouse memories, such motley characters as Uncle Sam, Marilyn Monroe and the Marx Brothers joined hosts

Janet Wallace and Jean McCartney plus Rudyard Norton as the Old Actor and Ray Williams as the Magician. Norton reprised "Rose of Washington Square," a number he'd done for more than half a century, and the venerable Bill Bailey made "September Song" the sentimental highlight. Nostalgia even ruled backstage where Leslie Wilson once more applied makeup.

Co-writers Echo Ellick and Jones first intended to focus on scenes from past performances until realizing, "We were looking at an eight-hour show." Instead, they mixed fads and fashions of the past with "Songs from the Playhouse." Nearly 10,000 attended and took home a souvenir program complete with Val Teal's fifty-year history and the entire list of plays performed on the main stage. Margaret Fischer, who'd seen them all, said, "What a pleasure it has been."

Boyd as *Galileo*, Bailey's *Sunshine Boys*, and David K. Johnson

The warm glow from the *Golden Follies* lingered, thanks in part to tributes that marked the occasion. Former Playhouse actress Lenka Peterson wrote, "Once I was on the Ed Sullivan Show and while we were standing in the wings he asked me, 'How come so many fine performers come from Omaha?' I said that was easy ... Omaha has one of the best, if not the best, community theaters in the country, so the actors get a head start and high standards."

Alan Ayckbourn's *How the Other Half Loves* brought Eleanor Jones to the directorial rescue when her husband, Charles, "landed in the hospital briefly" with a leg ailment. Pamela Carter furthered her reputation as a leading comedic actress as she "succeeded by attacking her part as the fiery Teresa with the broad comic acting of a Sally Struthers," then starring in television's *All in the Family*.

In the future *A Christmas Carol* would fill December, but the final season without Dickens brought the twists and turns of the year's top drama, *Sleuth*. Don Wright and David K. Johnson engaged in a life-

and-death battle of wits as the protagonists made famous on film by Laurence Olivier and Michael Caine.

February's main stage play, *Galileo*, was blessed with Richard Boyd, "strong and convincing in the title role. But the play overwhelmed most of the large cast," which ranged from "excellent to awful," the review said. The large cast included a pair who would become a popular musical duo in local lounges as Bozak and Morrissey, Lou and Dan.

March might have been declared David K. Johnson month at the Playhouse. First he led an impressive cast in the Studio's *The Passion of Martin Crowne*. Written by Fremont native Margaret Keilstrup, it won the Jane Gilmore playwriting prize. Equity actor Dick Christie returned to play the title character, a man imprisoned for opposing World War I.

Edward Albee's *The Seascape*, the most recent Pulitzer winner, completed the Studio season in April. Smith's mixed review found him impressed with Steven Wheeldon's "painstakingly realistic set complete with three tons of sand" and the portrayal of lizards by Dan Brady and Jill Murphey.

Johnson again had talented company in *Oh Coward!* All reviews applauded the mastery of Barbara Williams doing Noel Coward songs. The London-born dancer had the distinction of being the last living descendant of philosopher Jeremy Bentham. But "teaming impish Darlynn Fellman and the astonishingly talented Johnson may be the best idea Jones ever had," a review said.

The Sunshine Boys in May aired a flap over Bill Bailey's role that ended with the headline, "Quitting Union Pays Off for Actor." Actors Equity refused permission for him to perform, citing "unfair competition" with Firehouse and Westroads dinner theaters. Managers of both gave their okay and Bailey, 76, resigned from Equity, saying, "I'm not living in Russia."

The regular season ended on a high note, but reaction was mixed for the Studio's summer show, *The Kid*. Billed as X-rated, a review warned, "If you scandalize easy, stay home. If you dig dirty words, come on down." Another grumbled it "was less fun than reading the phone book."

Plans for *Carol*, Caravan Pave Road to Top

Associate director Nancy Duncan resigned to lead the homeless Junior Theater. It moved to the cinema house on Center Street where she presented yet another revival of Echo Ellick's *The Dragon's Curse* that fall. The theater would later be re-christened the Emmy Gifford with Mrs. Duncan as director until she moved on as a professional storyteller.

The beloved Estelle English had retired as box office manager, and, after two false starts, was replaced for years by Eileen Stark. Costume designer Shirli Frank left, and Kathryn Wilson took her place. But the personnel change with the most lasting impact saw the hiring of Ginny Winsor as business manager.

Winsor would stay more than twenty years and head the American Community Theater Association during her tenure. A part-time secretarial position was dissolved, and the business manager joined a staff that grew to eleven full-timers during Jones's third season.

Other changes saw Margre Durham leave the board and shift to the President's Advisory Committee. She left another gift, this time $3,000 for furniture. Barbara Ford now headed an expanded effort that recruited 126 patrons donating $25,000. Jones's salary was raised to $22,500. Thanks went Robert Storz (His $5,000 gift improved the tornado-ravaged grounds and parking lot.) and the Guild. Their Santa's Workshop added to Playhouse revenue for several years.

But 1975–1976 also gave birth to a pair of developments that would stand as monuments to director Jones and accelerate the Playhouse rise to number one among community theaters. Both appear first, not in public view, but as minor notations in board minutes. On February 11, trustees heard that Jones planned to offer *A Christmas Carol* in the 1976 December gap. He wouldn't sit down to write it until the eleventh hour in October, "We did not plan to do it for more than one year," and "I didn't have any idea who would be Scrooge," Charles recalled. The rest is history that continued to be written well into the new millennium.

The other landmark development was more complicated. Trustees were told in December 1975 that their Mr. Jones and Gerald Ness, the Nebraska Arts Council executive, were preparing a proposal "to bring together a small group of professional performer-teachers for workshops in Omaha and out-state." It would cost $40,000 for a twelve-week program and "no cash from the Playhouse is involved."

The pilot project would be called "The Nebraska Theatre Caravan from the Omaha Playhouse," the board learned in May. Instead of "no cash," the Playhouse would underwrite $4,500. By the end of the year, they'd be asked to loan the Caravan $3,000 and to hire two of its eight actor-teachers, Carolyn and Christopher Rutherford, as associate artists. Christopher took charge of the Playhouse classes, and Carolyn later became Caravan manager.

Carolyn Rutherford in *Cabaret*.

It grew from conversations between Jones and Ness. They wondered how to respond to the Arts Council goal of spreading theater across the state. Architect Leo Daly, a prime shaker and mover in those years, called for a Nebraska-wide dialogue. "Distance was the thing," Jones explained. "People told us they can't always travel to Denver and Omaha. We want our children to see and know theater. Bring it to us." So the Caravan began cosponsored by the Arts Council and the Playhouse in 1976, then was absorbed by the theater in 1978, when Ms. Rutherford took leadership.

She had played Liesl in *Sound of Music* under Jones's direction in Georgia. He'd been "knocked breathless" by Bill Hutson's performance in *Richard III,* so the future Creighton drama professor, fresh from his Ph.D. studies, joined the Rutherfords. The original eight, paid $175 a week, included Richard Burton Brown, Kenneth Langdon, Jamie Lewis and Marcee Smith, with UNO grad Lynn Broderick on board as technician.

"We tried to get Susie Baer that first year," Jones said, "but she joined later" with husband Carl Beck. If that original twelve-week project had only survived the first three seasons, it could take credit for bringing three future leaders to the Playhouse: artistic director Beck, associate director Susan Baer Collins and music director Jim Boggess.

The first troupe was assembled by Ness, Jones and Nancy Duncan, whose new Junior Theater role left time to share directing with Jones. Described as "a professional workshop and performing company," the Caravan was offered to Nebraska communities and schools from September through November.

A flyer promised plays and workshops ranging from half-day school residency for $300 and full-day school and community residency for $500 to a five-day residency for $1,500. The founding group got rolling in October, playing Offutt Air Base, Omaha high schools and the Playhouse Studio space before traveling 100 miles west to York. By mid-November, they'd gone from Beatrice, Norfolk and other Nebraska stops to Wyoming and Kansas.

Reviews for the Caravan's musical *110 in the Shade,* with Hutson as the rainmaker Starbuck, and three Shakespeare excerpts called *The Boar's Head Tavern*, praised not only the performances but the Caravan concept and the brief tenure of director Jones. The *Sun* review captured the musical's minimalist magic: "Five actors and two actresses. A few planks and a platform for a set." Add piano and banjo, and "that's all (the Caravan) needs to create two delightful hours of entertainment."

The daily's Smith saw the Caravan as "another success in a long string" for Jones. "In a little more than two years, the Georgian has turned the Omaha Playhouse completely around. Memberships are up and so is enthusiasm." When the actors answered questions later in Benson High classrooms, Smith called it "putting the icing on this marvelous living, learning experience."

Shenandoah Launches Season of "Stretching": 1976–1977

When Jones revealed the schedule of plays for the next season, he warned, "We've chosen a very tough season. In fact, we may be stretching beyond our reach." Starting with the Civil War musical, *Shenandoah*, they'd also bring Tennessee Williams (*Orpheus Descending*) and Stephen Sondheim (*A Little Night Music*) to the main stage.

In addition to the six productions, ticket holders could buy half-price $2 seats for the Caravan's *110 in the Shade.* Jones used the Prompter to convince readers that the traveling company "is a remarkable event in the life of our Playhouse," marking the first time the National Endowment for the Arts had allocated funds for amateur theater.

The Southern setting for the opener inspired a reporter to quiz Jones about the fellow Georgian running for president that fall. He talked about his parents' compatibility with Jimmy and Rosalynn Carter, four teetotalers who sought each other's company at parties. Jones spoke most fondly of Miss Lillian, the future president's mother. Just then being discovered by the northern press, the silver-haired matriarch had done five television programs with Jones.

Shenandoah featured Greg Ryerson, whose debut honor introduced a tall vocalist who'd later twice play the Frenchman in *South Pacific*. Others shared praise with music director John J. Bennett, pianist and leader of a seven-piece band. Another debut involved a Creighton professor whose long white beard became familiar to *Christmas Carol* audiences. Robert Snipp won no mention for playing Reverend Byrd, but soon began a long run as a Dickensian ghost.

Christmas Carol Opens with Dick Boyd as Scrooge

Decades later, Charles Jones could still see the snow falling, a surprise in mid-October, a time when "we should have started rehearsals" for his first production of *A Christmas Carol*. He'd carried the ideas "in my mind for a long time." But now he set up a card table in the living room and began to pencil them down on yellow tablets.

"In three days, I popped that script together. I'd call Jim (Othuse) and ask, 'Can we make the bed move?' I wrote the Ghost of Christmas Past and Myrtle Crow (the cackling scavenger) especially for Mary Peckham. But I didn't have any idea who would be Scrooge."

Then he heard Richard Boyd read lines he'd often read to his students in Council Bluffs. The teacher who had recently been Galileo and often sang bass in the opera chorus "just swept me away." Boyd and others expected the role to go to the aging vaudevillian Bill Bailey, who "I thought was the perfect Scrooge."

Jones knew the Dickens novella had been done for several years in Minneapolis, but that version was "so dark." He wanted both the Dickens story and a musical celebration of Christmas. So he worked with Bennett, music director for the season's first shows, to create an eighteenth-century Masque form. Dickens wrote of carolers singing, "God Rest Ye Merry Gentlemen," outside the shop of Scrooge and Marley. Bennett chose old English airs, from "Green Sleeves" to "Good Christian Men, Rejoice."

In his Prompter Director's Notes, Jones cited the hope first offered by Dickens that his little book would "raise a ghost of an idea that would haunt the reader's home pleasantly."

It was, of course, the start of something very big. Not that it opened all that smoothly. "The final dress rehearsal was a disaster," Jones recalled. "The bed swung around and threw the fruit off the top. The Cratchit children were up to their hips in oranges and bananas. Then Topper, blindfolded for a party game, nearly stepped off the stage, "and the big ghost"—Christmas to Come—"fell over." They laughed later, but then "we were in tears."

Jones didn't know he'd be doing *Carol* for decades to come, or sending three road companies to perform it all across the country. Other community theaters in Memphis and Texas would adopt his creation. And, for the next thirty years, Boyd would hear voices on the streets, even miles from Omaha, call out, "Hey, Scrooge."

Boyd and Peckham weren't the only original cast members to remain in roles for years. Tom

Boyd, Peckham as Scrooge, Ghost.

Wees started as Marley's Ghost, was replaced for twenty years by Al DiMauro, then returned to the role. Big Greg Ryerson towered as the Ghost of Christmas Present in 1976, but Professor Snipp took over the second year and continued for more than twenty-five years. Marianne Young, the first Mrs. Cratchit, would bake the plum pudding and worry about Tiny Tim for more than a quarter century.

That youngest Cratchit, the crippled lad who chirps, "God bless us, every one," became the most changeable part. Scott Davis, whose parents Ted and Barbee had both played Playhouse roles, did Tim for two years, and his younger brother Monty later took the role on the road. The original Mr. and Mrs. Fezziwig were drama teacher Tipton Biggs and Becky Noble, who later ran her own Dundee Dinner Theatre. Christopher Rutherford, the Caravan player who'd joined the Playhouse staff, started as Bob Cratchit.

The first *Carol* drew nearly 9,000 for eighteen performances. In January, the board decided to do it again, but not as part of the season ticket. That decision led to the annual production becoming by far the biggest moneymaker in Playhouse history.

From the start, reviews recognized it as a holiday gift to playgoers. The daily's Smith credited Jones with taking "what might have been a routine holiday throwaway … and turned it into an inspired and inspiring experience." Another wrote, "Standing on a London side street as snow begins to fall, or circling a Christmas tree with candlelight, carolers recreate 19th century song and dance."

The critic marveled at Boyd's vocal prowess, and took delight in old Ebenezer "flapping about in his nightgown." His grumpy "Bah! Humbug!" gave way to benevolent joy, and Boyd would come to be seen as a community treasure. Thousands would return year after year to see the snowflakes fall on the London peddlers and Marley's Ghost rise from below in a cloud of smoke.

Sex Fills More Seats than *Orpheus*

Bringing Tennessee Williams up from the basement with *Orpheus Descending* did not fill the seats. So went the "stretching" predicted by Jones. By contrast, the frantic farce, *No Sex, Please, We're British* closed the season with thousands more attending an extended run.

A Little Night Music brought Mary Levine back from Hawaii where Joe Levine now conducted its symphony. Sondheim's music, with Ann Goodwillie singing "Send in the Clowns," also brought opera veteran Mary Hansen back to the Playhouse stage after a twenty-five-year absence.

That season-ending farce opened May 20, but didn't close as planned in early June. When the crowds kept coming, five more performances were added late that month. When two players couldn't return, Jones and Orvel Milder stepped in, joining Chris Rutherford and others. Rutherford stole the show with his "flitting, high-strung, prissified English dandy," the character stuck with hiding Scandinavian pornography that pours into the home of his newlywed friends.

So the season that started by stretching ended with an easy success. It would be remembered for introducing the Caravan and *A Christmas Carol*. The day when the Playhouse could claim both the largest staff and budget of any community theater in America was fast nearing. The day when audiences counted on consistent artistry from Jones and Othuse had already arrived.

CHAPTER

8

Ten-Year Rise to No. 1 Theater, 1977–1986

Cabaret and Texas Trilogy to Future Reflection: 1977–1978

Theaters in Tennessee, Georgia and Iowa were planning productions of *A Christmas Carol,* but Jones worried that it might wear out its local welcome. He didn't want "people saying, 'Ho hum, here it comes again,'" so he predicted its appearance "every three years or so. I really don't want to lock us into an annual production."

Another prediction also missed the mark. He'd stay at the Playhouse "maybe another three years." Noting that designer Othuse was "swamped with job offers," Jones thought Jim would probably leave Omaha even earlier. "It's bad for people in an arts organization to seize on it and refuse to let go."

Any readers who feared sudden farewells were cheered by his list of tasks undone. Jones hoped to adapt some works by Nebraska authors (his versions of Willa Cather's *O Pioneers!* and *My Antonia* would arrive in the 1990s), start a strong summer program and take

Jack Frost, Eleanor Jones, Bailey in *The Oldest Living Graduate*.

Playhouse productions to South Omaha, Florence and other neighborhoods.

Associate director Chris Rutherford assisted Jones with the opening musical *Cabaret*, and they looked no further than Carolyn Rutherford, now manager of the Caravan company. The couple met in Florida when she was playing the role associated with Liza Minnelli. A reviewer praised her performance by claiming, "She nearly does the impossible…making one forget that Liza exists." Another critic found John Harrison "not as sinister as he might be" as the "Vilkommen" emcee. Matt Fonda, a distant cousin of the famous Fondas made his debut.

Memories of the next ambitious production, the Texas Trilogy by Preston Jones, were bittersweet. All three plays won high praise and postseason honors. Jones joined with Chris Rutherford again to present the trilogy both separately and then combined on three marathon Saturday nights. Starting at 6 p.m. and interrupted by a Texas barbecue, the full show ran past midnight. That grand old trouper, Bill Bailey, played the title role in *The Oldest Living Graduate* and also starred in *The Last Meeting of the Knights of the White Magnolia*.

The trilogy opened below in the Studio with *Lu Ann Hampton Lavery Oberlander*. The title character played by Carla Hill goes from cheerleader to divorcee to widow, bravely facing the future after a dashing of early hopes. Director Charles played the imperial wizard when *Knights* moved up to the main stage.

During the run, Bailey lost a daughter to a heart attack, but the show went on. He fell ill the following month, then died in February at age 78. Jones delivered an eloquent eulogy, and an editorial writer alluded to the popular song and declared Bill Bailey "home."

December brought the return of *A Christmas Carol* and an unusual claim from its creator. *World-Herald* reviewer Doug Smith reported that Jones, its adaptor and director, "insists reviewers have gone overboard in their praise of it. He's wrong in that," but "so right" in "everything else." Jones and crew "conjure up enough atmosphere here for everyone in town to cut off a piece and take it home for the holidays."

On the Road Again, Then Caravan Brings *Scapino* Home

The Nebraska Theatre Caravan's second season began with the Rutherfords returning. They'd given 101 performances and held 300 workshops for 45,000 Nebraskans in 37 communities. Four veterans were joined by David K. Johnson and three others. Company manager Carolyn Rutherford and stage manager Ralph Wright, a veteran of the Firehouse Dinner Theater, were aided by four actor-technician interns. They hit the road in October, performing Kipling's *Just So Stories* for elementary schools, repeating their tales from Shakespeare and treating town audiences to *Scapino*, an updating of Moliere's farce.

Before landing at the Playhouse in January, the company learned again that "Touring is never easy," as Ms. Rutherford explained. "But the way Nebraska is laid out makes it even more difficult." The toughest stretch took them from Scottsbluff to Dunning in the central Sand Hills and then southeast to Beatrice. One auditorium stood unused so long that rehearsal lights roused well-established wasps. A custodian sprayed, but the players noticed wasps still stirring amidst the dead ones littering the stage.

Scapino was called "a lot of craziness and clowning around," pulled together by the man "fondly known as David K." Johnson supplies "such a blizzard of insults, sausages and impersonations as you never saw in your life." Directed by Jones, *Scapino* involved the audience before the show began and during the performance with the cast cavorting in the aisles and through the rows of seats.

The musical *How to Succeed in Business Without Really Trying* completed the season by awarding performances by radio's "morning mouth" Dave Wingert and pioneer broadcaster Lyle DeMoss as his boss. And Darlynn Fellman "sets the stage ablaze" as the antic Smitty. A July production of *Peter Pan* featured the Caravan's Marcee Smith in the title role and its David K. Johnson as Captain Hook. Their work underlined the cooperative effort involving the Playhouse, the Caravan company, Westside Community Schools and the Nebraska Arts Council.

Costs/Sales Rise, *Carol* Tops *Kismet*: 1978–1979

Reports warned of economic woes of performing groups as the Jewish Community Center "abandoned its season" and the Westroads Dinner Theater folded. On the plus side, the Filberts and Denenbergs started the Upstairs Dinner Theatre downtown and Joann Schmidman's Magic Theatre would send an original play to the Winter Olympics better known for the hockey team's "miracle on ice."

His "state of the Playhouse" interview that summer gave Charles Jones, who'd signed a three-year contract renewal, a chance to review the recent past and speculate on the future. He noted that the theater and its traveling company "now constitute a $500,000-a-year arts agency." It operated "well in the black" the past season but "cannot possibly operate that way in the future without greatly increased support." He called for more than 6,000 members "just to keep pace." Cost increases "are eating us alive."

He emphasized the growing role of the Caravan as it entered a third season with plans to spend four weeks in nearby states. Perhaps its most significant impact would come from three new members of the touring company—Carl Beck, Susan Baer and Jim Boggess, all destined for key roles on the Playhouse staff. Beck, who'd succeed Jones as artistic director, came from Louisiana, then college in Oklahoma. Baer was a University of Nebraska undergraduate when she met Beck in the Nebraska Repertory Company in 1972. .

Another measure of growth came with the hiring of Jay Cady as promotional and educational coordinator. Son of the choreographer, he took a job held briefly by David K. Johnson, but the position had been dropped when Johnson headed for the Alley Theatre in Houston. Cady stayed for a season, then Brooke Ann Benscoter replaced him with a new title, director of community relations.

Any questions about the wisdom of a third straight run of *A Christmas Carol* were answered by its success. *Carol* now required a twenty-two-show run to accommodate demand from more than 10,300 playgoers. Both musicals, the spring's *Robber Bridegroom* and the opening *Kismet*, drew fewer than 9,000. But both also made Playhouse history.

Kismet, the theater's 350th production, was co-directed by Jones and Cady. It starred newcomers Tom Shomaker and Lee Chelminiak. A television news reporter off stage, Lee sang "Stranger in Paradise" in a time when Baghdad still meant the romance of Arabian nights. Shomaker, a young attorney, played the poet. It was his first in a long line of musical leading men for the Playhouse, including the title role in the upcoming *Robber Bridegroom*. The daily review exclaimed over the costumes and the expanse of uncovered female flesh.

Before adding Kansas, Iowa and Cheyenne, Wyoming, to its Nebraska tour, the Caravan visited the Studio Theatre to perform Shakespeare's *Twelfth Night*. Beck was Sir Andrew Aguecheeck, Baer Viola and Boggess Feste the Fool. Beck and Baer, sporting a dark, thin

Susie Baer, Carl Beck in Caravan's *Twelfth Night*.

mustache in her male disguise, can still be seen in their first roles on the theater's photo wall. The Studio was still subterranean, but comfortable enough for the Caravan, which had performed in such venues as the Bassett, Neb., barn where cattle were auctioned.

The Harper Lee classic, *To Kill a Mockingbird,* brought lawyer Atticus Finch to the main stage in October. The Gregory Peck role was played by Joel Knutson, a future staff member. But the actor who'd gain the widest fame was John Beasley, cast as the falsely accused Tom Robinson. Beasley would take larger Playhouse roles and appear in such films as *Rudy* and Robert Duval's *The Apostle,* then the television series *Everwood.*

Loretta Wolf "is a wonder" as Scout, the daughter of Atticus, "giving a performance that is both convincing and polished." Todd Brooks was "very good" as her brother Jem, the review added. Brooks would later play musical leads and direct Omaha productions. Playhouse veteran Bertha Davis was cast as Calpurnia the maid, and the Calvin Memorial Presbyterian

The Robber Bridegroom, 1979.

Church choir added its voices to suggest an indomitable black spirit. A debut in a minor role brought Matt Kamprath to a stage where he'd later win many honors.

Hutson Does *Hamlet '79*, *Robber Bridegroom* Goes Abroad

Before *Hamlet '79* opened in March, a reporter wrote that director Jones "two, three times now has called it an oddball project." One review deemed it "a splendid blend of quality and novelty." The daily said, "On paper, Jones's devices might seem pure gimmickry: dressing Hamlet and friends in sweatsuits and Adidas, having characters boogie to disco music, arming the king's guards with machine guns, signaling alarms with siren blasts." Not to mention the final showdown in white fencing outfits.

A review praised Bill Hutson in the title role, but another headlined "Hamlet Mocked" that his soliloquy "in a red jogging suit" approaches "blasphemy." Ophelia was Kelly Hitch, then a high school senior but later wife of Hutson's Creighton colleague, actor Alan Klem.

Audiences attending *The Robber Bridegroom* in April knew it would represent not only the Playhouse but the entire Western Hemisphere when it traveled abroad that summer. An invitation to the International Amateur Theater Festival in Bulgaria was "something of a feather in the cap for the community," Jones said. It would be accepted if fundraising could help pay the way. Shomaker played the title bandit, with Andrea McCall-Tynan as his love interest and Sue Perkins as a money-and-man-hungry stepmother. Perkins, oft-compared to Ethel Merman, had played musical leads at the University of Omaha, but now launched an illustrious Playhouse career.

Before taking *Bridegroom* abroad, the Playhouse presented *The Royal Family* with honors for Pam Carter while a review declared the Barrymore-like clan "a bit talky." A mid-May variety show at the Orpheum Theatre raised about $12,000 to guarantee the Bulgarian trip. Julie Wilson, the Playhouse alum turned cabaret singer, headlined a cast with everyone from Peckham and Norton to the young Rizzuto sisters. Donors and a performance in Columbus brought the travel purse to over $16,000, a total still requiring twenty-three cast members to pay a portion of their expenses to Blagoevgrad, while Jones and others paid their way.

Their festival performance had sold out, so even run-throughs drew crowds. Villagers heard the rehearsal music begin, and soon filled the seats, Joanne Cady recalled. With a rooster as alarm clock, the cast sweated out their stay with no air conditioning or even ice. And the Cold War was still being waged in 1979, so these Omaha capitalists faced a standing-room-only Communist crowd in stifling heat.

"It was a little frightening," Jones reported. Lee Perkins, the educator husband of singer Sue, had been snapping pictures one day, then his camera disappeared. But *Robber Bridegroom* won a standing ovation, and many in the cheering throng brought flowers to the stage. The cast later partied with Soviets who sang along with Shomaker's guitar. When word came that President Carter and Leonid Brezhnev had signed the second SALT (Strategic Arms Limitations Treaty) agreement, the Playhouse troupe joined the Russians in a toast.

Near No. 1 and Climbing with *Camelot*, *Shadow Box*: 1979–1980

With *Camelot* coming up as the season opener, Lancelot (Paul Tranisi) and Guinevere (Lee Chelminiak) posed against the backdrop of Joslyn Castle. Their color photo decorated the latest state-of-the-Playhouse article. It said Jones, "a large man, sat with an ailing leg on a chair for comfort and looked at seasons past and the season ahead," which saw a record 8,000 members.

"The Omaha Community Playhouse may not be No. 1," wrote Steve Millburg, the new *World-Herald* reviewer, "but it's no worse than No. 5." Jones noted larger memberships in Memphis and Albuquerque, a better building in Midland, Texas, and several other comparisons. The operating budget of $400,000, plus another $400,000 for the Caravan also placed the Playhouse in the top ranks.

Summing up, Jones promised to "stick around as long as he feels useful." He proclaimed his *Camelot* "a thousand times better than the production of 'Music Man' we did as my opening show five seasons ago." And, for the first time, the music swelled from a new orchestra pit. In the year that death came to ex-director Kendrick Wilson, long reluctant to do musicals, the Playhouse ended two pitless decades.

Digging 34 feet deep, a construction crew feared hitting the underground stream said to flow beneath the floor. It ran into air ducts and wiring that had to be relocated. Dirt was moved by hand and wheelbarrow, then up a conveyor belt to the main stage before being hauled out the stage door. The Guild, the Millard Foundation and Ak-Sar-Ben gave the largest of $72,000-plus in gifts.

Conductor John Bennett and an eighteen-piece orchestra became the first pit-dwellers as they struck up the overture, and then accompanied Bill Hutson's Arthur as he sang. Tranisi's Lancelot marked his Playhouse debut, the first of musical roles stretching into the next century. He accidentally christened the orchestra pit when Lancelot's sword blade separated from the hilt and clattered down on ducking musicians. Unharmed, they donned yellow hard hats the next evening.

Reviewers agreed that Lee Chelminiak's Guinevere had the best voice in the show. Joe Miloni, identified as a "perennial local favorite," doubled as Merlin the magician and the evil Mordred. "No one in town skulks better than he, and he seems to ooze malevolence by the quart." Don Kalal's comical Pellinore was praised, but won less ink than his dog, dubbed "the most written-about mutt in the history of Omaha journalism." (The sheep dog belonged to entertainment columnist Peter Citron.)

In sharp contrast to the splendor of *Camelot*, the next drama, *The Shadow Box*, came wrapped in warnings. Fearing some "may be scared away" by the story of three terminally ill patients, Jones assured that it was more about living than dying. It would bring a record fourth Fonda-McGuire award for Mary Peckham, breaking her tie with the late Bill Bailey. One reviewer couldn't resist singling out Peckham, "who was able to wrench the audience from helpless laughter to helpless despair and back again."

The Shadow Box attracted the season's smallest audience and largest number of acting awards. It would, for many, be ranked among the great moments in Playhouse history.

Scrooge Draws Home Crowd, Caravan's *Carol* Tours the Midwest

For the first time that November, the Playhouse bustled with preparations for two *Christmas Carol* companies—one on the main stage and another that would travel the Midwest as the Nebraska Theatre Caravan. At home, four asterisks by Dick Boyd's name meant he was playing Scrooge for the fourth straight year. The same four marked Peckham's ghost, Wees's Marley, and Merritt Stinson's Mr. Fezziwig. Three asterisks sufficed for Bob Snipp's ghost and Hennecke's

Nell and Mrs. Dilber, the crone who joins Mary Peckham's Mrs. Crow in stripping Scrooge's bed.

Nearing 80, Mrs. Peckham rolled up her sleeve one night to show Joan the bruises from their bedside tussles. But the play went unbruised by critics who showered it once more with superlatives. Millburg, raving about the "ridiculously high standards" of designer Othuse, said, "The production is worth seeing for the scenery alone. Literally."

Music director John Bennett jotted scores for each instrument at home and on the road. An eleventh-hour decision was made to send him packing. "We'd hired four musicians for each stop," Bennett recalled, "and a Caravan conductor and keyboard player." But they switched roles. It made more sense to send Bennett, the man behind the music, to work with ever-changing instrumentalists each night, and leave the less-experienced hire at home, directing the same musicians for all performances.

So Bennett boarded the bus with about three dozen who doubled as performers and everything else, including the driver of the 24-foot truck. Othuse had created the tour scenery folded as cargo. Jim Boggess, who toured as The Beggar the second year, remembers those travels as "very, very hard, but fun." After a preview show in Bassett, they rolled from Illinois to Iowa and Illinois again for one-night stands. Later, one-nighters took them from Whitewater to Neenah to Oshkosh, Wisconsin, before going all the way to Columbus, Ohio, for a full weekend. And so went the first tour: a night in Muncie, then four in Indianapolis and four more in Des Moines.

"Setting up was very difficult," Boggess notes. "And we had lots of accidents—a flat fell on somebody, and so on." His fellow Caravan regulars, such as David K. Johnson as Marley, were joined by Joseph Young, a Dallas professional, cast as Scrooge. Costume designer Kathryn Wilson, a jolly Mrs. Fezziwig, and her successor Denise Ervin acted and helped maintain costumes. It wasn't easy keeping everything intact for a fast-moving month across a dozen Midwestern cities.

The four "always charming" Rizzuto sisters, three still in grade school, shared the offstage responsibility for the Cratchit family

Christmas tree. By late December, it was so road-weary that Allison, Heather, Jaymie and Rachel finally despaired of making it presentable and sat sobbing around the pathetic tree. Their mother and DeDe Laughlin chaperoned a cast including three Laughlin youngsters, with Melissa, 6, hiding enough hair to play Tiny Tim.

It was a memorable experience for 13-year-old Mark Laughlin, later a trustee. He was impressed by the gentle grace of Charles Jones in coaxing the best from everyone. Then came Mark's accidental dressing room peek at voluptuous Andrea McCall in dishabille: "It doesn't get much better than that for an eighth grader." Any doubts about the road-worthiness of the Jones-Dickens collaboration, however, would be settled by its history: the Midwest tours continued, joined three years later by an East Coast company, in 1987 by a third Caravan tour of the West Coast and, later, the first trip through the Southeast.

Back in town after a brief break, the Caravan opened *Diamond Studs* at the Playhouse January 10. A reviewer liked McCall "as a buxom Belle Starr, as talented as she is gorgeous" and Boggess as a wisecracking train robber. But he mourned that Beck and Baer had left for New York, not knowing they'd return to stay.

Studio's Short Season, Then *Dracula*, *Cole*, *Mr. Roberts*

The Studio season had thrived in the days when it was the primary responsibility of an associate director. That position remained vacant. The first and last Studio event of the season brought two plays on alternate nights. As the Playhouse grew, so did resistance to scheduling the less marketable productions in the basement.

Dracula was welcomed in March with mixed headlines: "Saved by Special Effects" and "Fun, But for Wrong Reasons," that is, the audience laughed at the wrong times. One review called it the worst version of the Bram Stoker story. "The real star is technical director Dennis Richardson," the *Sun* wrote, "for when 'Dracula' succeeds it is because of his little stunts. Bats fly out into the audience, rats scurry across the stage, and the count goes through baffling disappearing acts that are truly exciting." The audience verdict: it was held over four extra days.

A stage full of vocalists sang forty-six Cole Porter hits in *Cole*, the spring musical, a revue with little story, lots of song and dance. Sue Perkins "is a wow," a review raved, whether solo on "I Get a Kick Out of You," or in a duet with Phyllis Noble.

The crew hitting the deck of a Navy cargo ship completed the season with *Mr. Roberts*. Their officers were Joel Knutson in Henry Fonda's title role, Frank DeGeorge as the banty bully of a captain and debut award winner Patrick Coyle as Ensign Pulver, the comedy role that launched the career of Jack Lemmon.

My Fair Lady Wins Applause for Othuse, Wees: 1980–1981

Years ago in Georgia, Jim Othuse had impressed colleague Charles with "gorgeous drawings" for *My Fair Lady* sets. Back then, Jones feared they'd run out of construction time, and he was right. Now Othuse could complete the job when the musical opened the 1980 season. The result, a review explained, found a fine cast led by Tom Wees as Alfred Doolittle competing with Othuse's "astounding scenery and lighting."

Sets "elicited oohs and aahs. An outburst of applause greeted the embassy scene" a full ninety minutes into the play. As for Wees, his "mugging and comic dancing" nearly stopped the show twice, and he repeated the postseason honors won when he first played Liza Doolittle's father at the Playhouse a decade before. Dawn Buller, a name popping up in a servant role, would become a familiar one in future Playhouse musicals. Playhouse secretary Valerie Thorson was Liza Doolittle. The staff had grown from seven to seventeen since Jones arrived, adding choreographer Cady full-time as class coordinator and Betty Davis as the first community relations director with extensive experience.

Jones and Othuse had taken the fall assignment of directing and designing the Ak-Sar-Ben coronation. The significance of their service to the leaders behind the civic organization may have been underestimated at the time. It helped bond Jones to many with great resources.

So Bill Hutson and Steve Wheeldon stepped in to direct and design the next play, *Of Mice and Men*. The dramatization of the Steinbeck novel featured Don Fiedler as the large, child-like Lenny and Patrick Coyle as George, a pair of drifting ranch hands who dream of owning their own farm. "Lumbering about the stage like some hayseed Frankenstein, Fiedler gives the very best performance of his career," one critic wrote. Terry Doughman played a laconic ranch foreman but would develop an ongoing community role in fight choreography. Reviews took detailed note of Wheeldon's use of 25,000 leaves strung on 5,000 feet of piano wire.

In its fifth season, *A Christmas Carol* drew well over 11,000 with familiar names now followed by five asterisks. A news photo showed "a brand new Marley," Al DiMauro, shrouded in smoke. The Caravan's touring *Carol* company gave forty-two performances in six Midwest states.

Outreach '80, Fonda Tribute Bring Henry, Improvements

The 1980 Ak-Sar-Ben Coronation Ball gave Jones and Othuse the opportunity to create a "sprawling pageant" depicting the Trans-Mississippi Exposition of 1898. Instead of their usual full house of 514, the arena capacity was 8,000. Jones promised a cast of 300, counting performers and other participants, "and I know only a few of them."

His first crack at the coronation saw University of Nebraska at Omaha president Ronald Roskens crowned king and featured dozens of Playhouse regulars plus new names that would grace the stage for years to come: Rob Baker, Gordon Krentz, dancer Kerry Ecklebe and stand-up comic Pat Hazell, among others.

Jones employed *My Fair Lady* costumes, and Othuse worked his usual scenic magic. His only disappointment: he couldn't quite justify a version of the Exposition's half-mile lagoon, squelching his hope for floating the king and queen on a gondola. Their Scrooge, Dick Boyd, donned Cardinal's robes and crowned the monarchs. Playhouse booster Ed Owen chaired the ball and wife Dee served as the theater board's secretary.

While the Ak-Sar-Ben connection continued for the Playhouse staff, that autumn's OutReach '80 campaign paid for major improvements and paved the way for historic expansion a few years later. Starting with a $200,000 matching gift from the Kiewit Foundation, the fund drive aimed for a $500,000 goal. The Kiewit money was confined to capital improvements.

Henry Fonda was named honorary chairman for the drive, but it was headed by telephone executive Jerry Hargitt, aided by Sue Shipley in her second year as board president. Jones said the Playhouse, despite operating in the black for several years, wanted to retire nearly $77,000 in accumulated debt and use another $122,000 to start an endowment fund and reestablish a foundation. The most expensive improvement required more than $100,000 for a new stage lighting system.

"An Evening with Mr. Fonda" was set for Jan. 10, 1981. It promised to bring the actor, his wife, Shirlee, his son Peter and wife with grandson Justin, to join Henry's sister, Harriet Warren, at the Playhouse. About the time the tribute was announced in October, Henry stopped by the Playhouse with Howard Teichmann to research their co-written autobiography. Publicist Betty Davis called the *World-Herald* to exclaim, "You're never going to guess who's here!"

Unfortunately, December found Fonda, 75, in a Los Angeles hospital. Problems with the pacemaker in his heart had placed him in intensive care for ten days and seemed to threaten both his future and the January tribute. But he made it home once more. Fonda arrived at the Eppley air terminal, grimly scanned a crowd of press and onlookers, and then "broke into a smile, raised a clenched fist and shouted, 'Omaha!'"

The love-fest continued that evening with filmed interviews and clips paying tribute to his career. First, though, he faced a stiff schedule of back-to-back press conferences, starting with *Time*, followed by local media. Mrs. Davis saw Fonda in a waiting room, looking gaunt, pale and weak, his head down. As he walked out to meet the press, he seemed to draw on inner resources, standing tall again as the years fell away.

That evening, he told stories and answered questions. He repeated a point he'd often made before, "I really feel that I was a lucky boy to have grown up in Omaha." A man in the audience was called on to ask a question, but commented instead: "Anyone who remembers his roots and his friends is a hell of a guy. I think you're a hell of a guy."

Fonda called Dorothy McGuire to the stage to learn that a theater chair now bore her name. Noting that his children, Jane and Peter, made early appearances for the Playhouse, he called his grandson, 14, to join him. "I thought it might be appropriate that Justin take his first bow at the Omaha Community Playhouse." The lad bowed and the crowd applauded a third generation.

Marge Quinlan, the board member coordinating the tribute, survived a few crises—the right film reel replaced the wrong one in the nick of time—and then they ran out of liquor. "To the rescue came a Time Magazine reporter who went out for more."

It ranked among the grander evenings since that televised opening night in 1959. The final question came from Peter Fonda: "Mr. Fonda, this is your son. We've really enjoyed this evening with you, and we were just wondering: Would it be possible for us to have dinner with you now?" It would be remembered as a fitting farewell.

In a few months, the Playhouse would present *On Golden Pond*, the stage version of the film that would soon win Hank his long-awaited Oscar. In a few more months, life would end for the man who went on from his Playhouse debut in 1925 to become a film legend.

Musketeers, 70 Girls, Golden Pond and Studio Finale

A week later, the Caravan brought an Old West musical, *Gold Dust*, to the main stage, introducing Jerry Longe. He'd stay in Omaha as an Equity actor and play many roles before replacing the original Scrooge. The Caravan's *Romeo and Juliet* survived an evening when their Juliet was ready to end it all but couldn't find her dagger.

How big was March's *The Three Musketeers?* Jones promised "a whale of a story, a big elephant of a production." It was so big the stage expanded past the orchestra pit and the first row of seats. So big the Playhouse rented seventy-five, count 'em, seventeenth-century French costumes and made another nineteen pieces in house. And those Anne Winsor designs were elaborate—20 yards of brocade for 10-pound gowns worn by the Queen and Milady.

Othuse eyed the script calling for forty-two scenes and declared it "a madhouse." Jones quipped, "You're right. I want a complete madhouse and don't forget the Hall of Mirrors at Versailles." Praise for the costumes was a nice parting nod to Winsor, who'd soon head to Hollywood and win a television Emmy for costume work on a hospital show, *St. Elsewhere*.

70, Girls, 70 saw Sue Perkins, Frank DeGeorge, Phyllis Noble and Don Kalal blend musical talents in a grouping that continued decades later as a cabaret troupe. With John Bennett directing music and a veteran cast, Jones might have expected an easy interlude that April. No such luck. The headlines, "Playhouse Plagued" and "Cast Casualties Rattle Director," led the claim that "it's never happened to him before." And he prayed it wouldn't happen again. First the male lead, DeGeorge, threw out his back. Then Tom Adams, who'd just turned 80, was hospitalized with pneumonia. Thus began a last-minute game of musical chairs. As many as four actors read from scripts some nights.

On Golden Pond paired Dick Boyd and Mary Peckham in the Fonda-Hepburn roles. The *Sun* review suggested, "This sentimental and inspiring little show is so well done that it should silence those detractors of Jones who charge the director is only good with overstuffed musical extravaganzas." The director, armed with a new four-year contract, managed to get Mary, his favorite leading lady, into blue jeans, "reason enough to buy a ticket to this play."

The Studio Theater waited until March to begin its family-themed three-show season. They first re-staged a one-hour version of *The Shadow Box* with its original award-winning cast. Then *Children* was followed by *Joseph and the Amazing Technicolor Dream Coat* with Jerry Longe as Joseph. It packed the Studio space and required an extended run. The daily's Roger Catlin declared it "the best argument to keep the Studio Theater going."

Chairman Joan Hennecke had tried to do that, but the Tim Rice and Andrew Lloyd Webber creation, borrowing its cast from the Caravan, marked the end "for at least a year" of the smaller-scale, often experimental productions with a twenty-year history.

"Jones said success forced the decision," a news story explained. The nearly 9,000 members require longer runs on the main stage. "You don't want to be seeing 'On Golden Pond,'" Jones added, "and be hearing the score of 'Joseph' coming up through the floor." The Caravan often needed that same space for rehearsals. The Playhouse board, Jones said, "is just beginning to talk about adding space" to allow two simultaneous performances. "We certainly are not abandoning either that space or the idea of a studio," he emphasized. But that alternative season would be re-born five years later in a new space with a different name.

Controversy, Honors for *Whose Life Is It?*: 1981–1982

Auditions for the fall musical found Jones seeking someone with an "indomitable, 'I will survive' quality" to play *The Unsinkable Molly Brown*. He cast Darlynn Fellman in Meredith Willson's title role with Paul Tranisi as the lucky Colorado miner, Johnny Brown. Fellman, a review said, "storms about the stage with the energy of a tiny twister."

It took a few more months to reach the $500,000 goal of OutReach '80, but the orchestra pit lift, the new sound system and parking lot resurfacing had been completed.

One facet of the new sound equipment caught a critic's ear. "When leading men got too close to (Mrs.) Fellman's bodice, their voices boomed ominously" from a hidden microphone.

Controversy preceded the October start of *Whose Life Is It, Anyway?* Metro Right to Life protesters objected to right-to-die treatment of euthanasia for a quadriplegic sculptor played by Dave Wingert. Letters "insist we withdraw the play and not produce it," Jones reported. "Of course we will produce the play. It is a very timely, important play." Although two Creighton professors, including the reviewer for the *Catholic Voice*, criticized it, Jones could point to the play's director, Creighton drama professor Hutson, and a Jesuit cast member, the Rev. Tony Weber. For added buffers, the Prompter listed a medical advisor and a legal advisor.

Unsinkable Darlynn Fellman.

The sixth cast of *A Christmas Carol* was speckled with a still longer list of asterisks. Boyd was joined by his daughter Lynne Boyd as Mrs. Fezziwig with high school teacher Jim Eisenhardt as Mr. Fezziwig. "After five years," though, "a new wardrobe was an absolute necessity," Jones emphasized. He'd decided to put the story back in the 1840s, when Dickens wrote it, rather than the 1880s used previously for the Playhouse production. So newcomer Denise Ervin looked back in history to design new costumes "that can be both laundered and look authentic." She found velvet on sale at $12 a yard, the sort of economizing necessary when outfitting forty-six cast members times three changes.

Pond Premiere Starts Expansion Drive, *Chicago* Wins Raves

The focus was on Fondas in 1982 for the second straight January, though Henry was again hospitalized in Los Angeles. His new movie was coming to the Orpheum Theatre for a premiere, two weeks before its general release. Jane Fonda had joined her father and Katharine Hepburn in the cast of *On Golden Pond,* and she came to Omaha with co-stars Dabney Coleman and young Doug McKeon for the premiere.

Jane had apologized to the Playhouse after failing to mention the event in an appearance with Johnny Carson on the *Tonight Show*. She'd inked reminder notes on her hands but didn't get a chance to plug the Omaha premiere. No matter. More than 2,000 tickets were sold. The movie plus a buffet on the Playhouse stage netted nearly $85,000, thanks to tickets ranging up to $100.

That meant about $55,000 "start-up money for the Henry Fonda Theater project," Jones noted. "It will allow us to do the appropriate studies to determine what kind of theater to build and how best to go about fund-raising." He promised a performing and educational wing costing between $2 and $4 million. When that came about in the mid-1980s, Fonda shared the recognition with his co-star from *A Kiss for Cinderella*. The plays scheduled on the new stage became the Fonda-McGuire Series, an alternative season that replaced the Studio Theater.

Omahans praised the film but had divided reactions to Jane Fonda, mixing protests with applause. Public Pulse letters took sides, regretting her antiwar activities or urging her critics to get over it and appreciate her talent. First Henry won a Golden Globe, then both Hepburn and Fonda won Oscars as locals exclaimed, "It's about time." Jane received a special trustee's award in June. Then, on August 12 came the long-expected headline: "Fonda, 77, Dies; Heart Gives Out." The story topped the front page of the *World-Herald*.

Joining in tributes were such Playhouse stalwarts as Echo Ellick, Emmy Gifford and Rudyard Norton. "I remember his performance in 'Merton of the Movies' more vividly than any theatrical production I've seen in my life," Norton said. Mrs. Gifford recalled Hank's help in establishing the children's theater, and Mrs. Ellick recalled his visit for dinner one evening

Henry's last visit to Playhouse.

after portraying Clarence Darrow. "He was completely exhausted. He put his whole self into the performance."

The family asked that "in lieu of flowers contributions be made to the Henry Fonda Memorial Wing of the Omaha Community Playhouse." Within days, more than sixty gifts and letters had arrived with touching notes. Comments ranged from, "My earliest memory was when I was 14 and saw you in 'The Trail of the Lonesome Pine,'" and "Thank you, Mr. Roberts" to "'On Golden Pond' has brought us much closer in our aging years."

It was fitting, then, that James Allison Flynn returned to the Playhouse stage for Shakespeare's *As You Like It* that same January. The retired *World-Herald* artist had appeared with Fonda in *Merton* in 1926. Flynn was not only an early Playhouse actor, but did memorable scenic designs for *The Hairy Ape* and other dramas in the 1930s.

Sweet Bird of Youth in March reminded *Sun* reviewer Gary Schweikhart of the days when Tennessee Williams was confined to the basement Studio. The daily critic, though, complained that "the plot that shocked in the late 1950s is now the stuff of daytime dramas." He argued that the leading players, Elaine Jabenis and Joel Knutson, "perform competently but are hampered by their very niceness."

Then came *Chicago*. Catlin called it "the best musical I've seen on the Playhouse stage." Carolyn Rutherford and Janet Ratekin played the murderous chorines, Roxie Hart and Velma Kelly, and Frank DeGeorge was a memorable Amos Hart singing "Mr. Cellophane." The "achievement in Charles Jones' staging is that one show-stopper follows another." As the razzle-dazzle lawyer Billy Flynn, "Tom Shomaker must be having the time of his life." Photos showed him surrounded by "long-legged lovelies," including his future wife, Lori Ecklebe and her sister Kerry.

New Lighting, Beck as *Merton*, Profit from *Carol*: 1982–1983

The absence of well-known musicals was blamed when season sales declined for the first time in the Jones era. The Playhouse, now with a staff of nineteen, opened the season with its own Gershwin creation, *Fascinating Rhythms* and followed in the spring with the unfamiliar *Ballroom*. And it didn't help that the season-ender was titled *Suicide Farce*.

For perspective, a news story spelled out the single-ticket cost of theater in Omaha. Dick Walter had delivered Broadway shows to the Orpheum for $11 to $17 a seat—"still less than half the Broadway prices." The Playhouse got up to $10 per ticket, Chanticleer $7, the Norton $6 for its operettas, the new Center Stage $5, down to $3 for the Magic Theater and university productions.

At the Playhouse, the Gershwin revue drew over 13,000, only about 500 below the past season's musicals. Jones, et al., created the "splashy musical revue after extensive homework, including consultation with and special permission from lyricist Ira Gershwin, 86."

"Stringing together nearly 50 great songs" by the Gershwins "almost guarantees a special evening," a review promised. It was no surprise to read, "The biggest show-stopper was irrepressible Sue Perkins, who belted out her numbers like no one else in the cast."

Merton of the Movies returned in October, billed as Henry Fonda's first leading role in 1926. A fund-raiser for the proposed Fonda Theatre Center featured artwork by such celebrities as Burt Reynolds, Peter Falk, Dinah Shore and Red Skelton. There was even a needlepoint pillow by Tab Hunter. Plans for the addition, a news item said, included a 350-seat auditorium. That number would change. So would the total of gifts in memory of Fonda. By October, more than 300 donations exceeded $23,000, including $5,000 from Dorothy McGuire.

Carl Beck, the former Caravan performer, had returned from Atlanta to guest-direct for the Caravan. He also accepted the challenge of re-creating Merton Gill, Fonda's title role, and was rewarded with

Carl Beck.

this review: "Beck's a spitting image of young Fonda—high cheekbones, gaunt face, thin and wiry. His nasal Midwestern twang and phrasing make the transformation complete. It's no cheap imitation" but "an astounding performance—probably better than the 1926 Fonda doing Fonda doing Merton. All the mannerisms are there and the comic pratfalls are splendid."

In a supporting cast that included Mary Peckham and Dave Wingert, the review called Pam Carter and Jesse Perlman the standouts. But time had taken its toll on the drama, reviewer Catlin noted. "When the biggest walk-on response goes to a pair of Afghan hounds, you know there is a problem. And the problem lies mostly in the hoary script."

Was *A Christmas Carol* as good as ever in its seventh (count the asterisks) season? "Yes," wrote the *Catholic Voice* reviewer. There was always something new. The latest Tiny Tim, Clark Lauritzen, 6, would be told that Grandma Libby had starred in *Green Grow the Lilacs* forty years before.

By now, the Caravan's two touring companies brought *Carol*

as far as Pittsburgh, Penn., and Burlington, Vt. While the Caravan did sixty shows on the road, the home cast led by Dick Boyd again drew nearly 12,000. Trustees were told to expect the three to gross over $370,000, with the travelers earning a $35,000 profit. That was the good news. The bad news in late 1982 was that season ticket sales were down.

Immediate Money Problems, But Promising Plans Unfold

Carl Beck would soon join the staff as associate director. But first he joined Charles Jones in co-directing *Strider*, the Caravan adaptation of a story by Tolstoy with Longe as the title horse. "Fails to Hit Its Stride," a headlines warned. It didn't help that playgoers meet the horse "just before his throat is to be slit."

The Playhouse board learned of a weak box office for *Strider* and the companion children's play, *Treasure Island*. The shortfall would require briefly borrowing $15,000 from their Foundation. Who to blame? *World-Herald's* Catlin wrote that "any other play would be more welcome" than this "strangely joyless" one. The trustees discussed telling the newspaper's publisher, Harold Andersen, about their "displeasure and frustrations with poor, prejudiced and unfair reviews" by Catlin. When late season shows also fared badly, trustees were told of a morale problem among ticket sellers for the next season. "Because some of this season's plays were not too popular, some existing season membership holders are losing their enthusiasm," it was reported.

The timing could have been better. Plans were unfolding for the expansion still identified as the Fonda Center. That February the cost was estimated at $4,675,000. The breakdown: $199,000 for land to add parking for 200 cars, $1.5 million for rehearsal and education space, and $2,371,000 for Phase III, the new theater addition.

When completed, the expansion would permit the Playhouse to claim the nation's outstanding community theater facility and two program schedules, adding the Fonda-McGuire Series in 1986–1987. Ed Owen, whose wife, Dee, continued as board secretary, would lead the building effort as head of the Development Council. He'd work with

Barbara Ford, the new board president. The city promised to widen 69th Street to four lanes, boosting access to the expanded Playhouse.

If the future was bright, the present posed problems. In March, the new United Arts/Omaha agency delivered the first checks from combined corporate giving. Arts groups asked for $930,000, but would receive only $700,000. The first installment brought only $55,000 to the Playhouse, though it had requested "a significantly higher" amount at a time when only 13 percent of a $1.2 million budget came from donors.

The Adventures of Sherlock Holmes boosted morale in March when more than 8,000 made it the season's most-attended drama. Don Wright as Holmes and Bill Koll as the arch-criminal Moriarty were joined by Don Kalal as Dr. Watson. Then the Russian play *A Suicide Farce* lost $7,000 despite adding *farce* to its real name.

The spring musical, *Ballroom,* was adapted from a television movie, *Queen of the Stardust Ballroom.* A sentimental story of senior romance on the dance floor, it won good reviews and a McGuire award for Sue Perkins, a widowed grandmother paired with a lonely mailman played by Frank DeGeorge. Perhaps the absence of familiar show tunes explained the low turnout.

An on-stage bandstand featured fourteen musicians with vocalists Don Kalal and Laura Beth Leacox, an ex-big band singer, at the microphones. But the big musical event that season combined the talents of Othuse with symphony and ballet artists for a massive Opera/Omaha production of *Aida* at Ak-Sar-Ben. A runaway elephant nearly trampled the *Aida* audience.

Expansion Drive Begins, *King and I* Fills Seats: 1983–1984

The Playhouse was still planning an expanded building to surpass any community theater in the land as the next season opened. That required the greatest fund-raising effort in its history and for added staff, now totaling twenty-three with Carla Hill as development coordinator.

A matching grant of $275,000 from the Kiewit Foundation got the fund drive rolling in September, followed by gifts of $500,000 each from the Owen Foundation and Robert Storz. The latter added a gift of land south of the Playhouse property and bought two 69th Street houses that stood in the way of growth. By spring, the initial corporate gifts campaign would collect $2,775,000 toward its $3.2 million goal.

The largest donation came from Kiewit, a $1 million supplement to its earlier gift. InterNorth (later Enron) provided $150,000, and $100,000 amounts came from the *World-Herald* and First National Bank. A new player was heard from when ConAgra, not yet the global food giant it became, gave $50,000. Omaha's corporate world was changing a year after a court decision split the companies once owned by AT&T, and a year before the landslide reelection of President Ronald Reagan. Sandra Day O'Connor became the first woman appointed to the Supreme Court, and Sally Ride the first woman in space.

If times were changing, the Playhouse could still count on a season-opening musical to draw a crowd. *The King and I* returned with the same Anna, Janet Wallace, who played the role in 1965. Unlike Broadway's Yul Brynner and Omaha's Bill Koll, Paul Tranisi didn't shave his head to play the king. Director Jones noted that the real king was not bald, but "about 5-1 and looked like a frog," thus not tempting imitation. It ran a month, then added three extra performances.

Tranisi's "booming voice and gruff demeanor made him well-suited for his role." Mrs. Wallace "still comes off as fresh and determined, which is exactly what the role demands." A cast of fifty-eight backed by John Bennett's twenty-piece orchestra, Othuse scenery and Ervin's costumes "weaves its magic well," the review noted. Speaking of weaving, it was reported that 525 yards of silks, satins, brocades and exotic prints were transformed into costumes with 2,000 hours of labor by Ervin, five full-time aides and fifteen volunteers.

Mary Peckham blew out the candles on her birthday cake and then celebrated her 80th by starring in *The Gin Game*. She'd win her record fifth McGuire. Beck directed Peckham and David Rosenberg in the Pulitzer-winning two-character play. They were Fonsia and Walter, residents of a state-run retirement center. A review noted, "Determined but slightly dotty Fonsia gives her punch lines an extra kick by throwing down her cards and proclaiming "Gin!" to the frustration of the bombastic, foul-mouthed Walter." One fewer review ran as the *Sun* weeklies, no longer owned by Warren Buffett, folded.

The eighth version of *A Christmas Carol* brought back Boyd and the other favorites, but an asterisk-free Prompter suggested that someone decided seven were enough. Instead, the number of years in the role followed actors' names. The local *Carol* brought in $400,000, and the two Caravan companies promised to net more than $300,000. Both tours ventured into Canada for the first time.

See How They Run Big Hit, Then Ground-Breaking for Addition

The Dining Room opened in February with a cast of eight, but one stood out. A memorable photo showed Susan Baer Beck in pigtails as she stuck out her tongue and hugged a teddy bear. She'd been seen before and won praise in Caravan casts, but now the reviews were unanimous. One called her "outstanding, moving from a credible depiction of a teddy-bear toting brat" to a "heart-tugging domestic" to an elderly aunt. If timing is everything, the Playhouse got lucky when reviving *Inherit the Wind* in April. An Iowa school board was debating evolution versus creationism in a science textbook, while Nebraska found itself in the national spotlight with a court battle over the Rev. Everett Sileven who fought state certification of his Christian school teachers.

"'Inherit' Theme Still Controversial" one headline proclaimed, and another said the Playhouse "Offers Stimulating Drama" with its treatment of the Scopes "Monkey" trial. A review credited veteran actor Bob Roberts with "one of his finest performances" as the character representing attorney Clarence Darrow. As his Bryan-like rival, John Flower "has the stature and Midwestern stuff" but "fell short of being the silver-tongued orator from the Platte."

Then *See How They Run* was the hit of the season. First seen at the old Playhouse in 1956, the British comedy revival featured a familiar cast directed by Beck. Joan Hennecke and Joe Miloni won awards for her snoopy gossip and his blustery bishop. Scenes between Miloni and Dave Wingert "are priceless," Catlin wrote. When it gets rolling, *See How They Run* provides "the kind of continuous laughter that's such very good medicine, you might expect a doctor's bill."

Perhaps something more than the healing power of laughter stirred interest in the season-ending show. A review declared it "well worth the harrowing maze through closed roads to see it." The long-awaited widening of 69th Street was finally under way, and summer construction of the expanded Playhouse was at hand.

A June news story promised, "The largest community theater in the country," but not one named for Henry Fonda. "We feel it's important to retain the Omaha Community Playhouse name," explained the spokesman. A formal statement outlined the theater's needs, primarily space problems that led to halting the Studio season and even overcrowded restrooms as attendance grew.

The three-phase plan had already begun with the acquisition to the south for 210 added parking spaces. Phase II, scheduled for completion in August 1985, would add 12,200 square feet of rehearsal and education facilities. Phase III, due in 1987, was projected as a 300- to 350-seat theater and other improvements.

The June 1984 announcement that promised the nation's largest community theater put the plans in sharper focus with Jones emphasizing "a crying need for added rehearsal and educational space." The main auditorium ceiling would be raised to allow a 92-seat balcony and an acoustical canopy. Due in 1985 were a new main entrance facing the southeast, a two-story glass-walled lobby and box office, and a three-level wing on the south. It would house rehearsal space, classrooms, offices and a costume shop.

"Right now it's crippling," Jones said, because the Playhouse can't build sets and do shows at the same time. So the Fonda Theatre was on hold, but a new performing space promised a "second season." For now,

Phase II ground-breaking coincided with the annual awards program. It was no coincidence that the trustees' awards went to Charles Jones, marking his tenth year with the Playhouse, and to Dee and Ed Owen, the longtime board secretary and the man heading the fund drive.

So much was changing, but one award winner dated back to their first play in 1925. For the umpteenth year, Florence Young, now 75, led ticket sales. She'd keep selling tickets and live another thirty-one years.

From "Dust and Junk," Blocked Street, to "Sure Bet": 1984–1985

"Luck be a lady tonight." Gambler Sky Masterson rehearsed Frank Loesser's lyrics as opening night neared for *Guys and Dolls*. He wasn't the only one keeping his fingers crossed. With the sixtieth season's preview performance just two days away, the chaos of construction still clogged the theater. "It's going to be right down to the wire," spokesman Rick Brayshaw warned. "We have people working around the clock—I mean that literally! The seat crews are working midnight to dawn."

Mayor Mike Boyle had assured that the barricades blocking 69th Street would be removed by Friday. All summer a sign—"Temporary Exit … Caution"— had directed Playhouse traffic past piles of earth and concrete. Now a blue-and-white circus tent sheltered pre-show party guests on the lawn, but hard hats, ladders and tools still littered the interior. When trustees met before the mid-September opening, they heard promises: "Restrooms to west ready by Sept. 14, parking next week. Need city to open 69th" and so on. Lobby wall coverings were rejected, so painting sufficed for the time being. "Having problems with chairs in auditorium, but most will be in place." Seats weren't numbered until weeks later.

None of that seemed to matter much at the gala preview night. For the first time, the 510-seat auditorium had a 92-seat balcony. Parking and restrooms were ready. A news photo showed president Barbara Ford, director Jones and Governor Bob Kerrey smiling before a bright Broadway setting. Kerrey, whose friendship with actress Debra Winger had made recent headlines, saw the improved theater and said, "Wow—this is great." Development leader Owen observed, "This was all just dust and junk a week ago … and now look at this. I'm just delighted."

The Playhouse "placed a sure bet," a review said, by starting with *Guys and Dolls* in the expanded and refurbished theater. "Especially delectable were those elements in which the Playhouse has always excelled since Jones took over 10 seasons ago"—Othuse's revolving sets, Bennett's energetic music, Cady's exuberant choreography. But "the best things" were Christopher Crotty's "perfect" Sky Masterson and Frank DeGeorge as Nathan Detroit. Dawn Buller won a big response as Sarah Brown as did Jim Eisenhardt as Nicely-Nicely on "Sit Down You're Rockin' the Boat." An added performance would have boosted attendance over 14,000, but its 600 tickets were stolen and the extra show was canceled.

Sue Shipley left the board to become development director, and she also served as chairman of the community fund drive. The slogan, "Hit Us With a Brick!" promoted gifts from $5,000 ("Ton of Bricks") to $100 ("One Brick By Itself"). Donors would find their names permanently in bricks at the entry to "America's finest community theater."

During September's construction turmoil, death came to Clarence Teal, the longtime treasurer and Playhouse photographer. Survived then by his wife, Val, he would be memorialized later when the box office bore their names.

As work progressed on the second phase of expansion, the "Brick" campaign gained momentum, growing from $61,000 in October to $150,000 in March. All pledges grew from $3.4 million in October to $4.5 million in February. By then, expansion costs had risen to $5.6 million, but soon another $500,000 matching grant from Kiewit, the lead contractor on the expansion, would put the higher figure within reach.

Honors for Hutson, Mrs. Beck; Record Crowd for *Auntie Mame*

The expanded Playhouse was still on its shakedown cruise when *Caine Mutiny Court Martial* opened in late October. Problems with the lobby, a brass rail, doors and the concession area were being corrected. Trustees, looking to reduce costs of the next phase by $1 million, were told "rehearsals halls and classrooms are too important to cut."

Word came that flu and a virus had hit the touring Caravan company, but rave reviews for the *Caine* cast were cheering, and so was high attendance for a serious drama. DeGeorge was Captain Queeg, the Bogart role, and Hutson took Fonda's role as Lt. Barney Greenwald under Beck's direction.

The use of director Beck and Zuby as scenic designer for the second show followed a pattern that permitted Jones and Othuse to focus on *Christmas Carol* and the Ak-Sar-Ben coronation after the opening musical.

The top Associated Press feature writer of her day, Tad Bartimus, gave the Playhouse national exposure in a story crediting the role of *Carol* in its rise to prominence. She noted the work of Mary Peckham, now 81, and Dick Boyd, while citing the theater's $1.2 million budget and staff of twenty-one (not counting three custodial employees).

If anyone feared that its popularity was fading, the ninth version of the Dickens classic drew a new high of 13,346 for what was the 400th production in Playhouse history. It saw the only two men to play Marley's Ghost, Tom Wees and Al DiMauro, alternating.

And two Priesmans appeared in the cast, starting a family tradition. Marion Priesman, in the ensemble, and son Brian as a schoolboy would be followed by her husband, Steve, as stage manager. Jennifer Priesman, like her mother and brother, would play various roles, on both the main stage and the Caravan. Steve became a trusted stage manager, not only for *Carol* but on two international outings.

The Caravan brought *Cyrano* to the Playhouse in January. After a year off, Jerry Longe returned for a fourth year of touring but with a new stage name, Jerry McLean. Letters to the Caravan, printed in the Prompter, gave glimpses of its impact elsewhere. An Illinois woman wrote about driving 100 miles to see *Carol* for a second time, and a Sand Hills teacher doubted that the players could "imagine the good you do … unless you have lived in an area this remote."

The new year also brought the first unused computers to the Playhouse. Other additions included fifteen sets of headphones for the hearing-impaired and security officers patrolling the parking lot. Plans to present the Caravan's *Candide* in the old Studio space while *Look Homeward Angel* played on the main stage were stopped by sound leaking from the auditorium. As fund-raising and construction continued, a $300,000 gift from the Hitchcock Foundation led to the naming of a rehearsal hall for the founding publisher of the *World-Herald*.

The next musical inspired some wariness even before its April opening. Blame one word in the title, *The Best Little Whorehouse in Texas*. Trustees were told "as

Jones as side-stepping Texas Governor.

much rough language as possible" was cut. The Playhouse had labeled it "for the mature only," and a review told readers they'd like the show "so long as four-letter words and suggestive choreography do not offend you greatly." Director Jones himself played the Texas Governor, the savvy politico who does "The Sidestep."

The season was extended in mid-June for extra performances of *Auntie Mame,* the popular story of an eccentric sophisticate and her 13-year-old nephew. A record audience for a nonmusical reduced an earlier $70,000 deficit. Sans Roz Russell, director Beck was blessed with a tall, elegant Mame, Janet Maddux Traub, who was born to don Ervin's sixteen lavish costumes. When Traub missed a few shows due to illness, Pam Carter stepped into the role. Agnes Gooch, Mame's screwball aide, won supporting honors for Darlynn Fellman. A debut award went to Angela Ankenbauer, a teacher who would return for many Playhouse roles. Reference to a "sparkling" second act came uncomfortably close to the backstage mishap that burned ten costumes. The cause: sparks from construction.

Weathering Chaos on Way to Doubling Space: 1985–1986

As *Barnum* opened the next season, Charles Jones thanked the audience "for finding your way through the construction and debris." A drawing of the new southeast entrance and the glass-walled lobby accompanied his invitation to "share the excitement of the season as dreams and drawings become realities 'One Brick at a Time.'"

It was exciting, but it was also the second season to begin under trying conditions. Trustees gave their okay for borrowing $1.5 million "if and when necessary." They discussed cutting the size of the Caravan company and canceling its spring tour "unless bookings indicate" at least breaking even.

Before dreams became realities, there was a whole lot of coping going on. Kiewit equipment occupied some spaces, so First Methodist Church permitted parking across the street. Joanne Cady could rehearse *Barnum* dancers in the "dungeon," a subterranean area without windows, ventilation or air conditioning. "After 15 or 20 minutes, it smelled like a locker room," the choreographer recalled. But the staff looked forward to the future "and we decided we might as well have fun" with the temporary horrors. She took her dancers out on the north lawn where it was cooler than the dungeon.

A whole wall was missing on the second floor that September, replaced by a sheet of plastic. The Playhouse now operated on three floors, but its elevator wouldn't be running until spring.

Jones and administrator Winsor kept seeing plans for the box office spread on the floor and saying, "No, that's not what we want," then settling on a curved counter. Jones began his eleventh season "up to his elbows in construction chaos," the daily reported. "Workers in yellow hardhats kick up dust nearly everywhere you look" and "getting from parking lot to lobby might be an adventure." But it all meant doubling the size of the Playhouse.

So the season began with a stage version of *The Greatest Show on Earth*. Fred Garbo was hired from the Broadway cast and Ringling Bros. to teach circus stunts. He taught State Senator Dave Landis as P.T. Barnum to walk a tight rope and had others juggling everything from clubs to cleavers. Landis slipped once on preview night, but gave the crowd a thrill when he "teetered on one foot as the tension mounted." The senator's wife, Melodee Landis, played his stage wife.

From Double-cast *Evita* to Building Dedication

Before *Crimes of the Heart* in October, the box office moved to a trailer in the parking lot. For the first time, credit cards could be used to buy single tickets, including some at only $3 during "student rush." That applied to high schoolers and collegians who showed up fifteen minutes before curtain. Vague references were made to a "new space" or rehearsal hall, later to be named the Howard Drew Theatre. "We want the people of Omaha to know we're getting better, not just bigger," Jones stressed.

A Christmas Carol brought its attendance record and all that single-ticket revenue, which had become a lucrative habit. Meanwhile, the Playhouse looked in new directions for income. The Foundation headed by Ed Owen established by-laws. Rental rates were set for use of the new facilities as negotiations began with the ballet and the Choral Arts Society. Young Brad Finkle built the Playhouse a Stone Castle of Terror, a haunted house that took in over $1,200. And Sue Shipley organized a sixteen-night telemarketing campaign that collected over $15,000.

By December, the earlier hints of a double season were spelled out. In addition to the six main stage productions, the 1986–1987 program would offer a four-show season in what was still being called a "rehearsal hall." In January, staff and trustees began sorting out new ticket prices as the "new hall" and "new space" briefly became the Fonda-McGuire Hall "for pursuit of excellence in amateur theater."

By the time *Terra Nova* was playing in March, the Owen Lobby and the new boardroom (later named to honor founder Genevieve Guiou) were near completion and other work was on schedule.

Terra Nova, a drama of rivals racing to the South Pole, seemed "very timely" to reviewers. It opened just a month after the perils of exploration shocked a world that watched the space shuttle *Challenger* explode, killing six astronauts and teacher Krista McAuliffe.

Evita arrived in April, the first Andrew Lloyd Webber–Tim Rice musical on the main stage. Jones cast both Sue Perkins and Camille Metoyer-Moten as Eva Peron, calling it "necessary because of the tremendous vocal demands" of the rock opera. They alternated, a practice also used on Broadway.

The May finale, *Tom Jones*, joined *Evita* in grabbing the lion's share of awards as the Metropolitan Actors Guild held its final event before becoming TAG, the Theatre Arts Guild, adding backstage workers. Joe Miloni, honored for his role in *Tom Jones*, started seventeen years as Playhouse costume designer, and the board honored Robert Storz for donating the parking lot.

Jones had announced the climactic moment in the Prompter: "At long last! Our expansion is complete." At the preview of *Tom Jones* he had asked the audience to "please stand. Now give yourself a number of good pats on the back," the executive director said. "You have given us a hell of a theater."

Most of the 400 on hand had been significant donors to the $5.5 million effort. He urged them to "live long enough to fulfill your pledges."

CHAPTER

9

Nation's Top Community Theater, 1986–2006

Launch Fonda-McGuire Series, Stake Historic Claim

It was easy to slip into superlatives. A staff now totaling twenty-eight could mount the curving staircase in the glass-walled lobby or ride the elevator to spacious offices. Such space loomed large, 66,000 square feet, when compared to the old cramped quarters beneath the stage.

And the expanded program required promotion. Brochures promised, "Twice the Action! Twice the Fun!" Not just the six main stage shows, but "a complete season of four high-quality productions, staged in our astounding and versatile new space." It would later take the name of donor Howard Drew, but for now the home of the first Fonda-McGuire Series was simply a space that was new. The time had come, however, to stake a significant claim for the house that Charles built with a lot of help from his friends.

The memorable words appeared as a message from Barbara Ford, in her fourth and final term as president of the board. The soft-spoken Mrs. Ford was not given to such exclamations as "eye-popping grand

Expanded Playhouse (Don Quixote sculpture was added later).

entrance," but that boast wasn't the historic part of the public letter above her signature. It came in the first official claim that the Omaha Playhouse was no longer just one of the best. Now, it was declared, "The nation's largest and finest community theatre."

PR and Marketing director Sue Shipley recalled, "We absolutely believed it." The Playhouse had the best facility, largest staff, biggest budget and was producing three groups of plays—main stage, the new series and the touring Caravan. And it was now approaching the highest membership.

Thus was launched its "most ambitious season in 62 years." Jones, Othuse, Cady and Beck were joined by a full-time music director. John Bennett wasn't new, of course. He'd directed and conducted most of the musicals since Jones's arrival in 1974, including their collaboration on *A Christmas Carol*. The staff of this brave new Playhouse even added a computer programmer, Mac Beaver, who'd served as house manager.

Even at the founding of the Fonda-McGuire Series, planning began for something more called Showcase Productions. The concept called for anything from one-act plays and one-man performances to variety shows and readers' theater. The first offering revived "His Name Is John," the papal solo by Tom Wees. "Staff would not be needed," the proposal promised. Tickets would cost only $4 (single admission to the new space was generally $10).

The new support group, ACT II, was ready to aid the fund-raising that fell under the marketing roles of Shipley and Carla Hill. ("I'd like to take credit," Shipley confided, "but Charles was the master of fund-raising.") President Ford took Sue Scott and Barbara Call to lunch, launching the group. The long-established Guild became the educational branch of ACT II, which was seen as the fruit of Jones's Ak-Sar-Ben connections.

One measure of such efforts was seen in the first Prompter of 1986–1987. More than 300 firms and individuals were listed as contributors. The bottom line: The role of philanthropy, first emphasized by Margre Durham in the early 1970s, had grown into a significant source of income. The Playhouse once kept afloat by season memberships and the frugality of Clarence Teal now also flourished through benevolence and the income from *A Christmas Carol*.

A year later, a third Caravan company would tour *Carol* on the West Coast, and two more Caravan alums would join the staff. Susan Baer Beck and Bill Hutson, who'd left Creighton University to perform in Texas, were added as associate artists. Most of the key ingredients and creative leaders who'd take the Playhouse into the twenty-first century would soon be in place.

Here's the trivia question: What was the first show in the new space? For two weekends before the mid-September opening of the Fonda-McGuire Series, Wees reprised his film role as Pope John XXIII. It sold out most nights and raised several thousand dollars.

Colorful *Can-Can,* Then *Hunchback* in New Space: 1986–1987

A black tie gala invited first-nighters for pre-*Can-Can* dining on "brace de quail veronique," a touch of the style seen at earlier milestones. Moving into their own theater for the first time in 1928, playgoers in mink and ermine were pleased simply to have a sloping floor. The celebration of the new Playhouse in 1959 brought gowns and tuxedoes to 69th and Cass for that live telecast hosted by Elaine Jabenis.

Black tie formality on Sept. 4, 1986, was brightened by period posters on loan from the French consulate in New York City. A color photo showed a red-gowned Pamela Carter propping a shapely leg on a chair. Playing Pistache, a Parisian cabaret proprietor, she posed to reflect the 1890s Toulouse-Lautrec poster in the background. A cousin of composer Cole Porter was present to declare it all "a wonderful experience." Reviews praised everything but the French accents. Carter shared the spotlight with tall Tom Shomaker, whose wife Lori and her sister Kerry were high-kicking the can-can.

New lobby art dedicated to Ed and Dee Owen was soon installed. Milt Heinrich's Opening Night, a sculptural collage, was dedicated when The Hunchback of Notre Dame opened in mid-September. The artist combined wood, metal, and found objects in a 16-by-16-foot construction. The theater was still awaiting a liquor license, and desserts were served in the lobby.

Hunchback was special for more than the debut of the Fonda-McGuire Series. Director Beck was rehearsing the Caravan in Crete when he "stumbled onto a copy of the Victor Hugo novel" in the school library. He searched but found no published plays, though the novel had been adapted for films three times. He collaborated with former Caravaner Chris Kliesen to boil 500 pages down to a stage-able story of eleven key characters.

The first Fonda-McGuire audience sat on three sides in canvas-backed directors' chairs, many hauled up from the old Studio. They watched Quasimodo, the hunchbacked bell ringer, prowl the catwalk above and swoop down on his bell rope. And they got their first look at talented Bridget Wiley. She played Esmeralda, the Gypsy dancer, and later joined the staff as Bridget Robbins. Those canvas chairs would survive several seasons, rarely toppling the unsuspecting from the risers.

Tryouts for the next two shows brought a call for "new blood, new faces." The opening musical and *A Christmas Carol* always required their share of warm bodies, but another three dozen or so were needed for the next two, including the first Fonda-McGuire musical without a Caravan cast.

The call for new faces was answered by Rhonda Hall, whose role as a *Witness for the Prosecution* juror didn't forecast her future as ubiquitous props-wrangler for many theater companies.

Prompter notes from Mrs. Jones added a capsule look at the busy new Playhouse. She pictured volunteers squeezing fast food meals between duties as "kids from ballet classes flit through, and choral singers make wondrous sounds. … zealous stagehands transform empty space into the cathedrals and bistros of Paris, a courtroom in London, or a radio studio in a bygone era somewhere in America. I can't think of a better place to visit than backstage at the Omaha Community Playhouse."

Meanwhile, husband Charles prepared *The 1940s Radio Hour* with Sue Perkins singing "That Old Black Magic" and "A Merry Little Christmas." Her salty chanteuse and others populated the radio variety hour with John Morrissey as the klutzy, easy-going emcee. Theresa Cassady did a ditzy girl who parks her gum on the microphone while jingling "Pepsi Cola hits the spot" and still managing to play "the other woman" in *Witness for the Prosecution* across the building.

Then a May fund-raiser netted $4,300 to help send the *Radio Hour* cast to Austria's international theater festival. Jones encouraged sending the show overseas as "a good American piece that was both recognizable and traditional."

This most active of years ended with *A Christmas Carol* again selling more than 13,000 tickets and adding profits to Playhouse coffers.

A formal announcement of the re-established Foundation headed by Ed Owen promised "to ensure the future" of programs and activities "that make the Playhouse unique to the nation."

Three At Once, Then Brits Come, OCP to Austria

The autumn bustle of performance and preparation described by Eleanor Brodie Jones was impressive as two shows ran while three companies geared up for *A Christmas Carol.* January cranked it up a notch. The Caravan returned with *Man of La Mancha* in the main auditorium. *The 1940s Radio Hour* came back to the space still identified at times as "the large rehearsal hall." And the Showcase with Joan Hennecke as Sister Mary Ignatius occupied the smaller Hitchcock Rehearsal Hall.

Even trustees' minutes caught the spirit, calling "three performances at once," all "successful and exciting." And all three made money. If that wasn't productive enough, the Playhouse got ready to host four performances of *King Richard the II* by the National Theatre of Great Britain … while working out details of May's Austrian trip for the *Radio Hour* cast.

A stark, stripped-down version of *Richard II* didn't fill the Playhouse. Seven actors sans props and scenery put the focus on the title king played by the lavishly named Nigel Le Vaillant. A discussion was led by Rick Scott, the British company's American representative. He would return later to head the Caravan staff.

Prior to the next main stage production, some hoped that controversy was sidestepped when *The Execution of Justice* was replaced by *Children of a Lesser God.* The former story of the city hall shooting of San Francisco's Harvey Milk, the first openly gay elected official, was promoted in preseason brochures, then dropped. The ostensible reason was a shortage of the men required for it and *Paint Your Wagon*. Its replacement had earned an Oscar for deaf actress Marlee Matlin and a Tony for the stage version..

Janna Sweenie, a dark-haired woman who worked for the Iowa School for the Deaf, and the Rev. Kevin Williams, a minister to the hearing-impaired, took the lead roles. Williams had "shadowed" Scrooge and done other signing for Playhouse shows. *Children of a Lesser God* was called "thought-provoking" in Millburg's review. Then the board supervising Rev. Williams' deaf mission work objected on moral grounds and Williams withdrew from the role. The main characters enter a sexual relationship that leads to marriage, but their behavior displeased the minister's boss. The show closed for two nights while the director prepared another cast member for the lead role.

Noises Off inspired near-continuous laughter and a standing ovation on preview night. It stopped only for a few March snow days until 8,500 saw for themselves why reviewers confessed to spending two hours in hysterics. Director Beck claimed it was the first show he'd directed "wearing a whistle around my neck." Eleven actors did Michael Frayn's British farce, spoofing a spoof within a spoof, at breakneck speed. They juggled countless props, including plates of sardines and an ax that slips crazily from hand to hand.

Paint Your Wagon featured Dick Boyd as the leader of rough-hewn gold miners. The cast included a couple, Bradley and Roxanne Nielsen. She'd danced in the *Wizard of Oz* in the summer of 1972 and later became Playhouse choreographer and education coordinator. Stan Lassegard, in his twenty-first role, sang "They Call the Wind Maria." *Quilters* became the second Fonda-McGuire production so successful that it was quickly revived. Carolyn Rutherford directed a memorable cast led by Mary Peckham as Sarah, the pioneer mother figure created by Playhouse alum Lenka Peterson on Broadway. Sarah's daughters on the 1860s prairie included Susie Baer Beck and Laura Marr, who'd act professionally then head the Circle Theater with playwright husband Doug.

"Mary was a wonderful Sarah" in *Quilters* rehearsals, Susie Baer Beck recalled. But she collapsed on stage during a Tuesday dress rehearsal. She was taken to a hospital and treated for a heart blockage. First reports offered hope that she'd come back, but the 82-year-old

Mrs. Peckham did not return. Rutherford recruited a friend from Kansas City, Nancy Marcy, who rehearsed on Wednesday and played the preview performance on Thursday.

The daily's Millburg said he spent half the play with tears in his eyes. He pronounced Marcy "superb. I would have thought so even had I not known she was a last-minute replacement." Joan Hennecke became Sarah in the summer revival and a trip to the Soviet Union. And Mary Peckham recovered from heart surgery to play the Ghost of Christmas Past again at 83.

When *Brighton Beach Memoirs* closed on the first day of summer, it ended the busiest season in Playhouse history. The Austrian adventure of *The 1940s Radio Hour* had gone well in May. The travelers, ages 22 to 69, discovered that their musical was the most conventional offering among more avant garde and political entries.

If the Playhouse could say, "We're No. 1," before the season began, the claim now had even greater credibility. And the city council finally awarded that long-awaited liquor license.

Staff Adds Hutson, Susie Baer; More Records Set: 1987–1988

The season solidified status as the nation's top community theater. Two musicals set attendance records, the staff grew to thirty-five, including two associate artists, and traveling productions reached beyond Nebraska's borders. Three Caravan companies toured with *A Christmas Carol,* and *Quilters* visited Gorbachev's Soviet Union.

Original plays premiered again at the Playhouse amidst a flourishing metropolitan theater scene. Shakespeare on the Green was born in Elmwood Park that summer, a marriage of UNO and Creighton universities as The Nebraska Shakespeare Festival. Doug Marr, who wrote plays for his own Circle Theater and the Emmy Gifford Children's Theater, would soon create another original for the Playhouse. The Center Stage planned an all-black *Arsenic and Old Lace,* while Chanticleer scheduled a thirty-fifth anniversary retrospective.

The Nebraska Repertory Company at the Norton Theatre in Dundee tackled Victor Herbert and Sondheim. Two downtown dinner theaters, the Firehouse and the Upstairs, continued to emphasize musicals and comedies.

For the first time, Charles Jones could cast three staff professionals. He'd used Carolyn Rutherford, his Caravan manager, on stage. Now the addition of Bill Hutson and Susan Baer Beck as associate artists put two more award-winning actors at his fingertips. The opening musical, *Sugar Babies,* saw Rutherford join Frank DeGeorge in roles that would bring them acting honors.

Hutson directed the first play in the Fonda-McGuire Series, *Animal Farm,* then co-starred with Susan Beck in the second one, the premiering *Qualities.* Hutson then played Scrooge in the West Coast *Christmas Carol,* directed *Tenderloin* and took the male lead in *Lion in Winter.*

Mrs. Beck played in *House of Blue Leaves* and reprised her role in *Quilters.* Donald Craig Lee, hired as assistant to designer Othuse, soon became scenic artist, a post he held for a dozen years.

Hutson would later join the Creighton University faculty but continue to play roles at the Playhouse. Susan would become associate director. That first year, "Bill and I taught a master class with some of the best actors in the city," including Amy Kunz, she said. "It was a great experience." She evolved into more directing and became a big note-taker. Called the research queen, Susan said, "My strongest suit is communicating with actors."

With the fullest staff since his arrival in 1974, Jones mounted a *Sugar Babies* that accentuated the "tease" in burlesque's "strip tease." Nobody could do double takes and baggy-pants comedy like DeGeorge as the Top Banana. And Ms. Rutherford's prima donna fit perfectly with the director's goal: Make the show "innocent, fresh and wonderfully wicked."

By mid-September, that new liquor license was also paying off. With three portable bars, an early report had alcohol earning $70 a night, matched by the candy called *Sugar Babies* while desserts and soft drinks took in more.

George Orwell's *Animal Farm* had never toured in the United States until performed that autumn by the Caravan. Hutson directed a cast combining new and old Caravaners with others. One nontouring addition was Brian Priesman, 10, who'd first traveled with *Carol* at age 7.

October brought *Corpse*, the original *Qualities* and another haunted house while rehearsals began for all four *Carol* companies. Director Beck applauded State Senator David Landis for agreeing "in a moment of personal insanity" to tackle the roles of twins in *Corpse*.

Omaha-born J. Ruth Gendler's *Book of Qualities* fell into the hands of Eleanor Jones who shared it with husband, Charles. Among those joining the two associate artists was newcomer Julie Huff, who'd later play as the Ghost of Christmas Past in *Carol*.

When *A Christmas Carol* first traveled, local casting supplied all but Scrooge. Now the fourth company headed west with only a handful of Omahans, including Hutson as Scrooge, DeGeorge and Phyllis Noble as Mr. and Mrs. Fezziwig. A troupe of forty-one, ages 9 to 66, started in Boise, Idaho, with such stops as Walla Walla, Wash., and Malibu before long hauls to St. Louis and Denver. An Oklahoma blizzard stopped their progress from California to St. Louis, but they made it to nine sold-out performances at the 4,600-seat Fox Theatre.

The previous year, one of the Cratchit kids broke a leg, so manager Greg Morales was keeping closer watch than usual on the youngsters. The home company, with Boyd and Peckham back, drew more than 14,600.

South Pacific Sets All-Time Records for Run, Attendance

Over Here! (subtitled "America's Big Band Musical") brought World War II tunes to the main stage in another Caravan show. Written for the Andrews Sisters, it takes place on a cross-country train. Characters named Mitzi, Lucky and Utah sang "Buy a Victory

Bond" and "Don't Shoot the Hooey to Me, Louie."

It was described as "rousing vaudeville-style" by a new *World-Herald* reviewer. Jim Delmont, a history major from Minnesota, was writing editorials for the newspaper when he began sharing theater assignments. He'd soon become the lead film and drama critic and continue in that role into 2004, longer than any of his predecessors. April's weightier *Lion in Winter* outdrew both *The House of Blue Leaves* and the earlier *Corpse*. Carolyn Rutherford directed Hutson as the king and Elaine Jabenis as Eleanor of Aquitaine, one of Katharine Hepburn's Oscar-winning roles.

It seemed fitting to bring the season to a historic climax with *South Pacific*. Almost forty years after its Broadway opening, the Rodgers and Hammerstein musical had never been performed at the Playhouse. Greg Ryerson, the tall blond with an even bigger voice, had appeared in *Shenandoah* and the first *Carol* in 1976. Most recently, he'd been singing opera in Australia. He returned as the Frenchman while Janice Arington was nurse Nellie

Big Greg Ryerson in *South Pacific*, 1988.

Forbush, washing that man "right outta my hair."

Ryerson was identified as "the first paid performer," whose success promised more guest professionals. Henry Fonda, of course, was paid when he returned in 1930 to star with Dorothy McGuire in *A Kiss for Cinderella*. But few, other than instrumental musicians, had been paid in the previous sixty-five or so years. (Joy Hodges Doorly, for example, guest starred in *Knickerbocker Holiday* in 1942.) Some grumbling grew from paying Ryerson, but Joanne Cady recalls audible sighs from women each night when the big guy began singing "Some Enchanted Evening."

Reviews agreed that it was, indeed, "an enchanted evening." With its run extended five extra days, the musical set records: thirty-six performances, nearly 20,000 in attendance, and the first production, other than *Carol*, to earn more than $100,000. Single-ticket prices were raised to $17 on weekends, the level approved for the next season.

The return of *Quilters*, Jones might have added, also illustrated the creative reach of the expanded

Joan Hennecke hugs a Quilters 'daughter'.

Playhouse. It became the third show in a decade to travel abroad. Most of the original cast reprised their roles on the Fonda-McGuire stage before touring in the Soviet Union. Joan Hennecke joined the "daughters" as mother Sarah, and director Rutherford explained why she was such a fitting choice. Her great-grandfather McCague came to Nebraska in 1860, and she grew up with knowledge of the pioneer heritage represented by the quilts.

The Soviet jaunt was "a disaster," Jones recalled. Lacking a word for "quilters," the translation came out "women who sew little pieces of cloth together to make blankets." Russians shrugged. A mix-up in booking found Crimean tenants being evicted in the wee hours to house the troupe. Tough trip but they saw the magnificent Hermitage.

New Role For Sponsors, Record Crowd for *Rocky Horror*: 1988–1989

Led by Margre Durham and others in the mid-1970s, Playhouse backers had learned that ticket sales couldn't cover the cost of a large staff and superior program without corporate and individual gifts. The past season had also seen growing effort to recruit sponsors. ConAgra backed the Caravan, and the not-yet-infamous Enron sponsored *South Pacific*.

Looking ahead to the coming season, the board formalized sponsorship by setting standard amounts: $25,000 for *A Christmas Carol*, $20,000 for main stage musicals, $10,000 for main stage dramas and "new space" musicals, and $5,000 for new stage dramas. First National Bank took *Carol*.

Between seasons, trustees were reminded that expenses often exceeded the usual royalties, salaries and upkeep. New technical rigging cost $60,000 and the entry canopy needed repairs after a mishap. Either the school bus was too high or the canopy too low. But a gift started the fall season on a happy note. Thanks to $94,000 from Ed and Dee Owen, the opening night for *Of Thee I Sing* featured a mortgage burning on stage. The Owen gift saved thousands in future interest payments.

Director Jones prefaced the performance with a reminder: It "was written and produced in 1931, and history has moved fast since then. It is hoped that the audience will remember this." Time didn't tarnish such Gershwin tunes as the title rouser or "Love Is Sweeping the Country." And it certainly didn't diminish "But Not for Me," which made it back to Broadway a few years later in *Crazy for You.*

Critics liked the political farce, with John Morrissey as a "hammy, but likable" president, and Frank DeGeorge as Throttlebottom, the befuddled vice president. Newcomer John Gibilisco became a long-term addition as electrician and sound engineer.

The first Fonda-McGuire production of the 1988-89 season, *The Diviners,* marked the Playhouse directing debut for Susan Baer Beck. She'd guided the Caravan's *Arkansaw Bear* for student audiences, but now she directed Bill Hutson, Jim Devney, Roxie Versaci and others in a folksy, Depression-era story of a boy with water-witching powers. The director observed, "I never thought that I'd be curious enough to cut a forked willow stick and go in search of buried water in my own back yard. But I was." What followed also made history. In the third Fonda-McGuire season, a production in the new space nearly matched attendance for a main stage drama. A record Fonda-McGuire crowd saw the campy cult musical *The Rocky Horror Show,* while even more caught *A Pack of Lies* in the larger auditorium. Ray Means and Melissa Jarecke played a pair who think their neighbors are spies. *Rocky Horror* required four extra performances. In it, Carl Beck directed Equity actor Holland Hayes as Frank N. Furter. He's the flamboyant transsexual who opens his castle to a very straight couple.

The review warned, "Some might find the show a bit sick, which it is. But that's the point" of its self-satire, which Beck delivered as "sugar-coated decadence." Adding to the spectacle was the costumed fan club, veterans of countless midnight *Rocky Horror Picture Show* viewings. They served as ushers and occasional on-stage performers. *Rocky Horror* observed its cinema tradition with a midnight Saturday

Boyd and Sue Perkins as new Ghost, 1988.

showing. The first late show sold out and the run was under way toward a record that lasted.

There was nothing unlucky about the thirteenth time around for *A Christmas Carol*. Its 16,000-plus audience would be the season's largest at the Playhouse, and three Caravan companies would travel with Hutson, Cork Ramer and Matt Kamprath as their three Scrooges, with the latter two continuing their roles well into the next millennium.

A memorable absence from the home cast was Mary Peckham, now in her mid-80s and declining in health. Sue Perkins took the role of the Ghost of Christmas Past for the next seven years. Perkins knew audiences had seen only Mrs. Peckham as Scrooge's cheerful tour guide, so she quickly recovered when a well-dressed dowager stopped by her dressing room and announced, "You're no Mary Peckham."

Talent Flows from Caravan, "Fest '89" Brings Brits, Soviets

Thornton Wilder's *Our Town* and that long-running little musical, *The Fantasticks,* revived successes from the 1939 and 1972 seasons, and their drawing power was still strong in the winter of 1989. Tipton Biggs was "superb" in the *Our Town* Stage Manager role, and R.H. Fanders made his Playhouse debut after thirty-five years directing high school drama. *The Fantasticks* brought two who'd become key staff members: music director Jonathan Cole and technician Greg Scheer, who remained in 2014.

Then the recent Playhouse penchant to go global saw it host The Fest of Theatre 1989. The Caravan's *Fantasticks* and *Julius Caesar* combined with the National Theatre of Great Britain and the Moscow Studio Theatre of the Southwest for three weeks of performances and workshops starting in mid-February. A *World-Herald* editorial underlined the significance of housing six productions and forty other events—possible only because "strong community support" has given Omaha the expanded Playhouse facility.

Julius Caesar, first performed at the Playhouse in 1961, continued on the main stage after its Fest appearances. Jones set Shakespeare's drama in a modern totalitarian state and dared to cast Mrs. Beck as a female Cassius. She gave "a first-rate performance in a fascinating part," a review said. She prepared by visiting female officers at the Strategic Air Command and found the role "empowering."

On the Verge got a lukewarm reception in the new space despite such talents as Pam Carter, Phyllis Doughman and Rob Baker. By contrast, *Gigi* was described as "a sheer delight from start to finish" with Joe Miloni singing "Thank Heaven for Little Girls." *The Musical Comedy Murders of 1940,* a review warned, was so "delightfully loony" that nearly 10,000 playgoers would spend more time laughing than solving murders. Darlynn Fellman, as a feisty German maid, jutted her chin into the chest of sinister-looking John Durbin. Beck directed Durbin's Playhouse debut. The Council Bluffs actor would be seen in films and on television, and as John Jackson he did casting for Alexander Payne movies from *Election* to *Nebraska*.

Jones had toured Russia with the *Quilters*, returned to direct *Gigi* and then was sidelined with a leg infection. He could look back at a season that found new funds coming from varied sources. The Playhouse applied for $20,000 from a new county lodging tax, the Foundation reported $66,000 in income (aiming for a goal of $2 million by 1993), and ACT II, now headed by Kathy (Mrs. Jack) Lewis, gave $76,000, including money for a new sign.

Charles had recently reflected on the fifteen years that began with his "trial" day in Omaha before his hiring in 1974. On that introductory occasion, he sat in on an evening meeting focused on a $150,000 renovation. In walked the project co-chairs, just home from an African safari and wearing knee-high jungle bush outfits. He asked his host, Ray Crossman, about the exotic couple in short khaki britches.

Crossman informed him they were Margre and Chuck Durham, "respected citizens who, like their neighbors and friends, wanted Omaha to be the best community in the country for their families." Then, the Durhams reported that the $150,000 had been pledged.

Charles would gladly keep working in a community with such a generous spirit, and with a staff that filled in capably when he was out of action. He'd been hospitalized for five weeks, before resting at home for three more weeks, recovering from that leg infection. Jones would continue his battle with weight that exceeded 400 pounds at times, but a greater health crisis was looming.

Farewell to Three Giants, Welcome Brass Actors: 1989–1990

Solemn tributes marked farewells for three who'd left great legacies. Gone in September was Rudyard Norton. He'd done his "Rose of Washington Square" at Central High in 1918, then revived it for the *Golden Follies* in 1975. In between, he'd done some forty roles at the Playhouse, starting before *Pygmalion* with Dodie Brando and Mrs.

Doorly, and lent his name to a nearby theater. Rudge Norton embodied acting for a generation that grew up watching his work.

Then death came to Echo Ellick, daughter of the founding Mrs. Guiou and a coauthor of the fiftieth anniversary *Follies*. She'd acted in the earliest children's plays in the late 1920s and written others, including her oft-produced *The Dragon's Curse*. Board president, longtime trustee and longer member of the advisory committee, she'd served the Playhouse most of her 72 years. Jones wrote a Eulogy for Echo that repeated her given name and underlined its meaning in her life—echoing back to the community and giving to "the love of her life," the Playhouse. An award for continuing acting excellence was established in Norton's name, joining others, including the Echo Ellick Production award.

The third loss came early in 1990 and left a more immediate vacancy. The trustees stopped for a moment of silence after hearing a tribute to the contributions of Ed Owen. He'd headed the Omaha Community Playhouse

Ed and Dee Owen.

Foundation since its formal organization in the mid-1980s. His wife, Dee, still served as board secretary at the time of his death. Their names were given permanence in the Owen Lobby, and now the Edward F. Owen Award would honor key donors.

The Owens had served in all facets of the theater's life. A few even remembered Ed's initial appearance at the Playhouse in 1941: he was a soldier in *Knickerbocker Holiday*, the first production billed as a musical comedy, and the chorus debut of future cabaret queen Julie Wilson, then a teenager calling herself Mary Lou.

Three giants were gone, but three larger-than-life figures arrived at the Playhouse early in the 1989–1990 season: Don Quixote, lance pointing to the south entrance, led "The Actors' Procession." The Man of La Mancha was trailed by a Japanese kabuki player and a Greco-Roman in laurel wreath and half-mask. Stretching up to 20 feet high and 75 feet long, the full-relief, sheet-brass figures drew eyes to "Omaha Community Playhouse" in the same metal.

Robert Storz, his name on the parking plaza, had complained that the nameless building it bordered "looked like a warehouse" from the south lot. He commissioned Milt Heinrich, the Dana College artist who'd created Opening Night in the Owen Lobby. Heinrich huddled with Storz and Jones before settling on the final concept. The Greco-Roman testifies to the historic longevity of theater, the Asian with fan (Madame Butterfly or Yum-Yum) affirms the female contribution and cultural breadth, and Quixote pursues his noble quest. Before Storz died in 1992 at age 93, he had also commissioned the Actors' Quest, the athletic metal figures on the north exterior wall.

Gypsy, with music and lyrics by Styne and Sondheim, got the new season rolling with good attendance and great reviews. Sue Perkins "belted out—in Ethel Merman style—all the memorable songs." Equity actor Delaney Driscoll, already active in films, played Gypsy Rose Lee, the overshadowed daughter who transforms into a glamorous stripper. Dancers included a rare find, Brendan Buchanan, a high school freshman built like a football player. The hoofer would perform in more musicals before devoting his time to a band.

The new space opened with an original, *Bunk Bed Brothers* by Matt Goldman and Pat Hazell, who played the title roles. Omahans had seen Hazell rise from performing street corner magic in the Old Market to warm-up comic for television's *Seinfeld*. He paired with Goldman to pen what the review termed "a daffy" script, "a running gag about two grown-up brothers" returning to their childhood bedroom of the 1970s. Carl Beck's cast included a pizza delivery man. Each night a different local celebrity, such as former mayor Mike Boyle, took the role.

Original *Starkweather* Drama Based on "True Story"

The smaller stage made room again for innovation, another original but more controversial play, *Starkweather*. Dee Owen noted in board minutes that "hopefully the play will negate the negative attitude" expressed by a letter writer who called the yet unseen play "abnormal and macabre." Reviews praised the work of playwright Doug Marr. He'd written several dozen original plays for children's theater and his own Circle Theatre. Meanwhile, the Blue Barn Theatre had been formed in the Old Market by three young actors from New York—Kevin Lawler, Hughston Walkinshaw and Nils Haaland. After working with Marr on the script, Carl Beck would cast Haaland as Starkweather, the "punk" whose 1958 killing spree terrorized Nebraska.

Fleeing Lincoln with his 14-year-old girl friend, Caril Fugate, Starkweather set off on a lethal rampage that left eleven dead as Nebraskans loaded guns and locked doors. Marr didn't recreate the murders, but studied the killer, the girl and reporters in a multimedia production. Joanne Cady's sister, journalist Ninette Beaver, had interviewed and written a book about Miss Fugate, who heard about the play and wrote to Marr. "Here is the true story," she scribbled, adding three exclamation points plus an audio tape.

Director Beck and Marr listened to Fugate's recording, heavy with sobbing while under hypnosis. Marr drew on many sources, including Starkweather's jailhouse journal. "It is not a play you'd want to see over and over," Delmont wrote, "but it is a fascinating psychological examination of a disturbing subject." Its style was captured by a review that read, "Four reporters guide the play's action. The AP wire goes wild as reporters run to the machine. 'Oh my God! He's killed in Western Nebraska. Take a plane. Get out there!'"

It didn't hurt that the *World-Herald* ran a full-page spread revisiting "Starkweather's Reign of Terror." For director Beck, the experience was fascinating, but he was relieved when it was over. Marr often wrote on tamer subjects such as *A Brady Bunch Halloween* and a series set in "Phil's diner."

The 1990 half of the season began as usual with a Caravan musical, *The Pied Piper*. Kamprath was the pompous mayor with a loud Yiddish accent, and the long-legged Ramer romped in shorts and beanie as his brattish son. Thirty children wound through the aisles as rats following the piper of Hamelin.

Then South African playwright Athol Fugard's *The Road to Mecca* marked the first time, other than Caravan casts, that all players were paid professionals. That record crowd for *South Pacific* seemed to prove that paying a guest star could be profitable. The Fugard drama sold only a few more tickets than the equally serious *All My Sons,* but a crazy show called *El Grande de Coca-Cola* drew the season's biggest crowd in the Fonda-McGuire Series. Delmont's review labeled it a "wild, comic, vulgar Latino musical satire," adding "tacky is not a strong enough word to describe the outrageously sleazy and sloppy goings-on." It's all emceed by one Pepe Hernandez (Joe Miloni), who speaks only Spanish. Such gifted character actors as Darlynn Fellman, Dawn Buller and Gordon Krentz joined the "nonstop pandemonium" flanked by two giant Coca-Cola bottles, with live chickens clucking under foot. "Raisa Gorbachev" is introduced from the audience, but soon mud-wrestles "Nancy Reagan."

The next Fonda-McGuire offering, *Steel Magnolias,* was almost as popular, inspiring Delmont to call it "probably the best play this reviewer has seen at the Playhouse."

A $10,000 grant was available to bring Lenka Peterson home to star in *Social Security* on the main stage. That didn't work out, but Jones cast a Playhouse favorite, Elaine Jabenis, as the neglected Jewish mother who moves in with her sophisticated yuppie offspring. Romance blooms between the 90-somethings when she meets a painter. For Jabenis, it meant Playhouse honors in a fifth decade, starting with *Father of the Bride* in 1952.

Good news on the financial front saw the Foundation's endowment climb to $111,000. And an anonymous grant of $125,000 over five years was later credited to the Criss Foundation, linked to Mutual of Omaha founders. Jim Eisenhardt started a new volunteer group, Stage Door, for backstage volunteers. He was its first president, followed by Brad Finkle, who'd brought in another $5,000 from his annual haunted house.

Equity actor Jerry Longe, the former Caravaner, played President Teddy Roosevelt and Patton Campbell returned to do the costume designs for *Teddy and Alice*. Thanks to a $10,000 grant, the Central High grad who had costumed the Fondas and Dorothy McGuire in *The Country Girl* took time from his duties as a professor of theater and costume design in New York.

Longe, who'd done fifteen shows at the Firehouse Dinner Theatre, gave "a robust and delightful impersonation of T.R.," and Janie Foley won a Mary Peckham award for her Alice Roosevelt (Longworth). She's the daughter who prompts Teddy to declare, "I can either be President of the United States or attend to Alice—I can't do both."

New Sign, Staff Changes and Milestone for *Carol*: 1990–1991

On the corner of 69th and Cass Street, a larger, brighter sign promoted the musical *Big River* at the opening of the sixty-sixth season. Manager Ginny Winsor had promised city planners, "It will be tasteful" and won the approval needed for an electronic message board in what was defined as "a primarily residential area." Winsor noted, "For years, "we've been trying to find the right kind of sign." The board settled on a three-sided one, permitting electronic messages instead of the old manual marquee. An improved model would replace it a decade later.

New marketing strategies more aggressively pursued younger playgoers, publicist Curt Ratliff reported, citing more membership options, such as choice cards to select any six of ten plays. Carl Beck emphasized that the Fonda-McGuire Series provided space for "plays with stronger themes and stronger language."

The two staff artists were gone. Hutson had returned to Creighton

Brooks, Brown in *Big River*.

University, and Susan Baer Beck had joined her husband and Joanne Cady as associate directors. Production and administrative staff, plus a half dozen Caravan employees, had reached a new high of forty-four. At the time, only one other community theater employed as many as thirty-five. When season memberships climbed again to a few short of 11,000, trustees were told that number was "the most here or anywhere in the nation."

As *Big River* and *The Last Stand of the Polish Sharpshooters* opened in late summer 1990, Omahans were buying tickets to a touring company's *Les Misérables* at the Orpheum. Two dinner theaters were still active but that didn't keep *Big River* from drawing more than 15,000 to see Roger ("King of the Road") Miller's treatment of Mark Twain's *Huckleberry Finn*. Frank-Douglas Brown, a professional from the Boulder Dinner Theatre, played Jim, the black slave who rafts down the river with Huck, played by Todd Brooks. The set design by James Othuse, praised as "a distinctive achievement," used lighting and billowing smoke to "create the rippling water and fog of the Mississippi."

The Polish Sharpshooters brought a new play by Joe Palka, former WOW radio deejay, to the small stage. A weekly reviewer named Joe Dejka matched ancestry with the playwright and declared it "a side-splitting slice of Polish culture that's as satisfying as hot kielbasa with sauerkraut on rye." Palka told a reporter, "You don't have to be Polish to enjoy it," and Jim Delmont agreed. But his review noted, "It helps to be Catholic to appreciate the humor here." It focused on a stagnant Polish-American Club planning their parade float featuring the Polish pope.

The Playhouse joined Nebraska Citizens for the Arts that October in fighting a 2 percent lid on school spending. Its opposition was broadly based, but included concern about public school participation in Caravan offerings.

Eleanor Brodie Jones directed *Death Trap*, the tangled mystery by Ira Levin. The lead character, a writer played by Don Wright, described "a disease, thrilleritis malignis, the fevered pursuit of the one-set five-character moneymaker." With Diana Andrade as his wife and R. Stephen Kuhn as the young playwright, the play won praise as "gloriously contrived" and "delightfully creepy."

A smaller audience saw *The Boys Next Door,* directed by Carl Beck in the new space. His wife, Susie, who had taught part-time for the Greater Omaha Association for Retarded Citizens, brought cast members playing impaired characters together with a GOARC team. A review gave "kudos to a gifted group of performers in a finely-tuned" story set in a group home.

When the Playhouse board met during those two runs, a toast was given for Charles Jones, "who is ill at home." The following November those words would seem more ominous, but now his version of *A Christmas Carol* celebrated its fifteenth season with the originators still in charge. The 1990 *Carol* drew a record audience and a profit of $42,000 plus its annual bonus of good will and Christmas spirit.

Charles honored the anniversary by reflecting on that long ago October when, with a fire blazing and his creative juices flowing, "I filled our living room with my imagined version" of Dickens's tale. He asked Jim Othuse, "Can you design a snowstorm and a huge bed that could whirl around the stage?" The designer said, "Yes, I think so," and Jones went to Joanne Cady. He wanted dances to look like children's games. She quickly offered "London Bridge, Red Rover" and so on.

Jones recalled frantic rehearsals that first year. "Tom Wees is stuck in the Marley lift, the wind machine has yards of gauzy curtains around Mary Peckham's neck, and … "opening night—the bells begin to jingle, and I know everything will be all right because on stage it begins to snow."

From Rainy *Shade*, to *Ladies* and *Hello, Dolly* Hits

Jones began rehearsing the Caravan's *110 in the Shade* as Operation Desert Storm brought the first Gulf War from Kuwait to Iraq. He gave the cast a break when the tensions of the evening blended with the emotions of their characters to bring his actors to tears. Combat was over before the musical opened, and tears gave way to the rain that fell from an elaborate creation of Jim Othuse and technical director Steve Thompson.

The story of Starbuck, the title *Rainmaker* of the play that inspired the musical, and Lizzie's romance on the parched plains demands a downpour. It took more than hole-riddled tubing and feeder hoses. They had to slant a false stage to keep water from drenching the orchestra pit. First-nighters "were squinting and buzzing," a columnist wrote, "about whether that was real water" raining down.

Another sign of the times prefaced *The Mystery of Irma Vep*. A tribute to its author, Charles Ludlam, explained that at age 44 he was a victim of AIDS, a threat that later would strike closer to home. He called his comedy "a penny dreadful," and a review said it was "filled with rollicking, fast-paced mirth." Two cast members, pros Susan Baer Beck and Jerry Longe, played a "fantastic array of characters," working at "breakneck speed." The mixed roles confused the newspaper, which misidentified a photo with Jerry as red-wigged damsel and Susie as the Englishman in monocle and mustache.

The British farce, *A Bedfull of Foreigners*, took time to get going, Delmont's review said, then romped in a door-slamming game of musical beds. Full of sight gags and double entendres, it features British tourists who land at a French inn run by the German Helga (Angela Ankenbauer) and her English husband who has a French girlfriend on the side.

Next *The Prime of Miss Jean Brodie* boasted Pam Carter in the title role and introduced eighth-grader Christina Belford, a future Playhouse star. Director Beck touted the virtues of the Fonda-McGuire space as he staged *Sophisticated Ladies,* a Duke Ellington tribute that nearly broke record attendance set by *Rocky Horror*. Beck explained the flexible seating system that allowed experimentation in the new space. And the "total intimacy" brings audience and actors together so "you're going to see it all," even a hair out of place. Reviews praised the orchestral work of Jonathan Cole and the vocals of Kathy Tyree, who sang, "It Don't Mean a Thing" (if you ain't got that swing). Fortunately, they had it.

"*Hello, Dolly* capped the season with a third Fonda-McGuire award for Sue Perkins in the title role. The largest crowd to see a musical since *South Pacific* three years before, nearly 17,000 cheered Perkins's Dolly. A review credited Jim McKain with "energy and strong comedy skills," but reminded that the dominant figure was Dolly, played "with a sure sense of character" by Perkins.

The Best of Times, Worst of Times for Charles Jones: 1991–1992

The season would be remembered for the catastrophic blow that put Charles Jones in the hospital. Reflecting years later, he noted that the worst year of his life was in many ways another triumphant one for the Playhouse. The stroke that hospitalized him from late November into May was the greatest setback, but it wasn't the first problem faced by the staff. What was reported as "positive cash flow" disappeared with the discovery of accounting errors. Entries totaling about $30,000 had somehow been dropped back in March, and costumes for *Hello, Dolly* cost $6,000 more than budgeted.

A bookkeeper resigned and trustees heard recommendations for cost controls. They'd also learned earlier that United Arts Omaha would allocate less to the Playhouse. The cutbacks hit all the arts groups, providing nothing to thirteen arts organizations that received funds the year before. UAO fund-raising had fallen $500,000 short of the past period.

The good news in September 1991 was that tickets were going fast for the season-opening *Forty-Second Street,* and membership sales promised to reach a new peak of close to 12,000, much higher than No. 2 Theater Memphis with 8,000. The nation's leading community theater now showed both expenses and income nearing $3 million.

Demand overloaded phones in the box office where Lanelle Poole became manager. Jonathan Cole had replaced Bennett as music director. A profile of Tom Shomaker stirred interest in *Forty-Second Street*. The tall attorney played Julian Marsh, the director who whips the Broadway show into shape during the Depression. Columnist Mike Kelly contrasted the lead character, part tyrant, with Jones who makes "please" and "thank you" part of every sentence. Janet Williams as the upstart Peggy Sawyer and Carolyn Rutherford as the fading diva led the dance-heavy production studded with such songs as "Lullaby of Broadway," "Shuffle Off to Buffalo" and the title show-stopper. Crowds packed the seats to see "those dancing feet."

On Borrowed Time in October gave Susan Baer Beck the opportunity to direct her first main stage drama. Originally presented at the Playhouse in 1950, it had a *Twilight Zone* charm, the director said. Barb Ross, as the grandmother, returned to the Playhouse after a twenty-year absence, and Tim Siragusa made his debut.

A Funny Thing Happened on the Way to the Forum arrived that November, almost thirty years after its Broadway debut with Zero Mostel. Since Greg Ryerson's success in *South Pacific,* more guest professionals took leading roles, thanks to foundation gifts. Equity actors Jerry Longe and Greg Fellows played slaves Pseudolus and Hysterium, a pair that supply much of the musical's promised "Comedy Tonight." It moved up to the main stage on its return a decade later.

Before Thanksgiving, Charles Jones had launched his sixteenth version of *A Christmas Carol* and put three Caravan companies on the road again. The director had been working eighteen-hour days. At the age of 53, he weighed 440 pounds and suffered from phlebitis. When *Carol* opened to fill a record 18,000-plus seats, Jones was in Methodist Hospital being treated for pneumonia and a congestive heart condition. Five days later, preparing to leave the hospital, he leaned over to tie his shoes. That was all he'd remember for days to come. A blood clot had raced from heart to brain. He suffered a paralyzing stroke.

He'd come to call it the worst year of his life. When trustees met in early December, they heard Joanne Cady report that "therapy has begun." Doctors predicted "a long but complete recovery." Dee Owen wrote in the minutes, "Please keep him in our prayers." He'd go home briefly at Christmas, tearful with gratitude, then return to the Immanuel Rehabilitation Center.

The show, of course, went on, with productions directed by Charles's wife, Eleanor, Carolyn Rutherford, Carl and Susan Beck. After the early days of despair—"I was so depressed, so unbelievably angry"—Eleanor's determination and his growing sense of gratitude for the many devoted to his recovery gave him hope. When the Playhouse board met in January, they heard "his attitude is wonderful." They took action to set up his office in the hospital room. It helped that the board president, L.B. "Red" Thomas of ConAgra, had learned from a heart attack suffered by his boss, Mike Harper. "If Mr. Harper could run ConAgra from his hospital bed," Thomas said, "then Charles can run the Playhouse from his."

Thus began three months of days with therapy until 3 p.m. Then came visits from the staff and meetings with the play-reading and other committees. By April Jones would spend a few hours each day at the Playhouse, still in a wheelchair. By May he was directing *Brigadoon*. The time when the board had to consider replacing him had passed for now. Charles was back in charge.

Eleanor Jones Directs, Then Charles Returns for Musical *Brigadoon*

Meanwhile, the year that would bring the election of Bill Clinton as president began with the Dickensian musical, *The Mystery of Edwin Drood* in what a reviewer described as the Nebraska Caravan's "smooth professionalism" under "the flawless direction of Carl Beck." Familiar faces—Kamprath as a loquacious narrator and Ramer as a lanky vicar blended with newcomers. The audience voted each night on alternative endings to the melodramatic comedy.

When she wasn't encouraging her husband's rehab, Eleanor Jones was directing *Mountain* in the Fonda-McGuire Series. Dick Boyd dominated the stage with "a terrific performance" as liberal Supreme Court Justice William Douglas.

The practice of paying guests for distinctive roles brought James Harbour to play Salieri, the role in *Amadeus* that won F. Murray Abraham an Oscar. The Whitmore Foundation supplied his $6,500 salary. Director Beck knew his work as Scrooge on *Carol* tours. Delmont's review said of his "bravura" portrayal, "If ever an actor deserved a standing ovation, it was Harbour … after an exhausting, fascinating, charming and gripping performance." Keith Hale's bratty Mozart earned a postseason award after a critic wrote that Hale "energizes the 'obscene child,'" playing the composer "like a Stradivarius."

Both the main stage farce, *Lend Me a Tenor*, and a more dramatic comedy, *Other People's Money*, opened in mid-April as Jones became more active again. *Money* author Jerry Sterner was feted with Jones on hand as Rutherford directed his play. "Two wonderful performances" were cited: Jeff Taxman as Garfinkle, the colorful corporate raider, and Phyllis Doughman as the mother of the woman lawyer fighting him on behalf of a benevolent businessman.

Lend Me a Tenor prompted critic Delmont to warn that viewers might wear out "laugh muscles." The madcap antics, full of door-slamming and mistaken identities, left Carl Beck with "a battered cast" led by Joe Miloni as the Italian opera star.

Those "laugh muscles" were tested again in *Greater Tuna*, the year's best turnout for the Fonda-McGuire space. Susie Beck directed Jim Boggess and Dennis Collins, her future husband, as a motley crew from Tuna, Texas. A review said both had "consummate timing and showmanship" as they raced through rapid transformations, from radio announcers and grannies, to squirrelly rednecks and even a dog. The critic suggested, "The proceedings are so aggressively mad that a stiff drink before curtain might help." If so, margaritas were on sale in the lobby.

The worst of times for Jones got better as he mounted a popular revival of *Brigadoon*. Tom Shomaker and Becky Jones, the director's daughter-in-law, landed the lead roles. The "lovely" musical, set in "a misty, darkish, fairy tale glen" by Jim Othuse, left "no doubt that Charles Jones is back at the helm," a review said.

The Playhouse that weathered blizzard and tornado the season of Jones's arrival in Omaha had survived the trauma of his absence. Other problems seemed minor by comparison. The city's long hassle with cruising on Dodge Street had spilled into the theater parking lot, so the Playhouse posted "Closed Property" signs. The generous Robert Storz died, but his latest gift provided a companion piece to Quixote and the other south wall figures. The new Heinrichs sculptures, The Actors' Quest, now enhanced the curved north exterior wall. Metal figures, 45-feet wide and 12-feet high, represent actors "endeavoring to get ready to perform," Jones said.

Tom Teal, familiar as Topper in the Playhouse past, visited. Senior editor of the *Harvard Business Review,* he recalled his role in the controversial *A Family Portrait* in 1943 and other moments from the years his father, Clarence, served as the theater's treasurer. Tom's adventures included work for the late comedian Lenny Bruce, writing for the *New Yorker* and speech-writing for President Jimmy Carter.

Jones Directs *The Wiz* and His Own *O Pioneers!*: 1992–1993

The executive director walked with a cane and cradled a limp right hand in the left one. But he opened what promotions called "A Season of Ahhs!" by directing *The Wiz* (of Oz) while writing *O Pioneers!*

Charles Jones's adaptation of the Willa Cather novel reminded that he'd read her Nebraska stories to prepare for his move to the Playhouse in 1974. The racially mixed cast of *The Wiz*, with Equity actor Clyde McNeal in the title role, gave Jones "a wonderful, happy experience" to start the season.

Jones's approach was inspired by the set design. Othuse created tornado-swept mounds of colorful debris, which Jones felt represented the bright clutter of Omaha's busiest streets. A review called the "cheerful, black-oriented" version of Frank Baum's story "a delight

Baker, Krentz, Nielsen as Marx Brothers.

to eye and ear." DeeDee Ellis was honored for her portrayal of Dorothy.

As the election of President Bill Clinton neared, the stage version of Richard Condon's *The Manchurian Candidate* offered the political intrigue of brainwashing but drew by far the season's smallest audience. Jim Delmont's review called the plot unbelievable, noting that the Korean War concept of an assassin controlled by posthypnotic suggestion had been debunked by psychologists. He liked the performance of Cathy Wells Venta as an "incomparably wicked" woman. As Cathy Kurz, she founded the Brigit St. Brigit Theatre, where she directed classics and Irish plays.

Beck's next Fonda-McGuire offering, the farcical *The Foreigner*, won critical raves. Its "inspired lunacy" and Jerry Longe's "superb performance" as the comic visitor who pretends to speak no English were emphasized in a cast including Karl Rohling's cringing simpleton.

The adaptation of Cather's *O Pioneers!* by Jones brought a "stark, classical" quality to the stage, a review noted. Jones explained that his effort to bring the novel to life "frequently requires the actors to speak descriptive Cather passages directly to the audience. Thus the entire cast joins Cather as storytellers." One review bowed to the noble intentions but said dramatic flow suffered as players went in and out of character to become narrators. The enduring image of *O Pioneers!* came from treatment of the Nebraska prairie by Othuse. Using a sloped stage, he created "a vast canvas of sky," isolating actors against the distant horizon.

Big Crowds for *Rumors* and *Fiddler*, Hopes for *Les Misérables*

As membership reached a new high close to 12,300 early in 1993, added excitement came from the "verbal promise" of *Les Misérables* for spring 1994. "We don't have permission to announce it," trustees were told, but word would get out. A season profit of $52,000 was also forecast, welcome news after a "frightening" financial report a few months before.

Patrons complained about smoking in the lobby and on stage. They were reminded that the Scott lobby was smokefree, but smoking was allowed in the larger Owen Lobby. It had been years since smoking was permitted in the auditorium of the original Playhouse.

The Caravan sang the lilting "Love Makes the World Go Round" with *Carnival* on the main stage while *A Day in Hollywood/A Night in Ukraine* brought the Marx Brothers to the smaller room. Carl Beck had Rob Baker as Groucho, Gordon Krentz as Chico and Roxanne Nielsen as Harpo.

Still recovering from his stroke, Jones was assisted in directing *Cat on a Hot Tin Roof*. The Tennessee Williams drama featured an award-winning performance by John Billings as Big Daddy.

Neil Simon's *Rumors* scored the season's biggest comedy hit. Ads termed it a farce of the "wham-bam-doors-slam" type. It quickly reached a high pitch of hysteria after guests arriving for a couple's anniversary find the host shot in the ear and the hostess missing.

Jones presented the resilient villagers of Anatevka to complete the season with *Fiddler on the Roof.* Delmont nominated the "swirling, boisterous, sentimental" show as one of the best seen in his six years of reviewing. Paul Tranisi's Tevye netted him a Fonda-McGuire award.

As *Fiddler* closed, the next season's ticket sales were still climbing. But the box office wouldn't mail a sixth main stage ticket for the coming year, still hoping for rights to *Les Misérables.* Promotion promised a "Jubilee Production" marking the seventieth anniversary season and the twenty-year artistic partnership of Charles Jones, James Othuse and Joanne Cady. The title of "the biggest musical in Playhouse history" could not be announced at this time, the flyer said, "because of its extended engagements in New York and London."

Meanwhile, three new theater companies arrived on the local scene, and they'd still be active when the Playhouse celebrated its ninetieth season. The Nebraska AIDS project gave birth to SNAP! Productions focused on gay-lesbian themes. The Shelterbelt Theater was launched in October 1993 by playwright Scott Working and others. Their motives matched those early companies that preceded the Playhouse in the 1920s—they wanted a place to produce their own original plays. SNAP! used the Firehouse and other venues but in 2001 joined the Shelterbelt in the former Kilgore's sandwich shop and jazz joint near 33rd and California. Cathy Wells (later Kurz) opened her Brigit Saint Brigit Theatre, a company that settled at College of St. Mary for much of its history, with Ibsen's *A Doll's House.*

Box Office and Artistic Triumphs Mark Season: 1993–1994

Season ticket sales fell only a little short of a record without Jean Valjean to spur newcomers. But the season broke single run records for both musicals and drama. Jones adapted another Willa Cather novel, and his *My Antonia* drew 14,478, a lasting record for a nonmusical.

And thanks in part to the use of revolving children's choirs, *Joseph and the Amazing Technicolor Dream Coat* broke the musical record held by *South Pacific* when it sold 19,677 tickets, also a total that would not be surpassed.

As the staff also peaked at fifty, two were added who would stay more than twenty years—technical director Don Hook and Georgiann Regan, starting in the costume department she would later head.

The season started strong, with *Funny Girl* and *M. Butterfly* proving an artistic triumph in the smaller space. Charles Jones cast *Funny Girl* and began working with the musical but was then hospitalized for three months with circulatory problems. Joanne Cady took over directing the story of Fanny Brice with Camille Metoyer-Moten honored for her title role. A review credited Cady with "a big, confident, glossy production—of the type only the Playhouse can do." Tom Shomaker played Nicky Arnstein, Fanny's gambler husband.

When Kevin Camp, as hoofer Eddie Ryan, became ill, a Tuesday night performance suffered a rare cancellation. The next day Tom Neumann, an experienced actor with no major Playhouse roles to his credit, filled in with script at his side. One of the Ziegfeld girls, Andrea Lang, whispered cues from time to time, and Neumann came through like a trouper. After the final curtain, he was teary-eyed as the cast surrounded him with applause, embraces and back-slapping. "It took a lot of guts," Shomaker said.

Eleanor Brodie Jones directed David Henry Hwang's *M. Butterfly* as Bill Hutson and Don Nguyen brought audiences to their feet. Hutson, ineligible for honors as a paid actor, delivered a performance that would long be cited as among the most memorable in Playhouse history. The Prompter listed his co-star only as D. Nguyen to avoid gender identification. Nguyen had played the Peking Opera star earlier at Creighton University. His character becomes mistress to Hutson's French diplomat, who didn't know his lover was a man and a Chinese Communist spy. The Playhouse warned audiences about frank sexual dialogue and a male nude scene. Delmont credited a beguiling mood that reduces shock to "Hutson's sincerity and Nguyen's disarming charm."

A Few Good Men, the Aaron Sorkin drama, arrived on the main stage a year after the film's Jack Nicholson as the Marine officer snarls, "You can't handle the truth." Ron Chvala handled that heavy while comedian Pat Hazell returned as Lieutenant Caffee. At the time, Hazell was studio warm-up comic for television's hit *Seinfeld* show.

With Jones still ailing, Susan Baer Beck took over as director of *The Member of the Wedding.* For Jones, back to work half-days, it was to have been a sentimental journey back to the time in Georgia when the playwright Carson McCullers died suddenly at age 50. He'd also been prepared then to direct one of her plays, but her passing changed plans and he staged a tribute instead. Her story tells of 12-year-old Frankie and a 45-year-old black cook who served as the only mother she'd known. Christina Belford (later Christina Rohling) and Lanette Metoyer-Moore "were so memorable," the reviewer wrote, "that they dominate the yet-young theater season."

When the Caravan came to the Playhouse in January, its treatment of *Joseph and the Amazing Technicolor Dream Coat* attracted a record crowd. It helped that Delmont's review advised, "Run, don't walk, for tickets to this one. It may sell out." And it didn't hurt that various young choirs, 157 "Dreamcoat Kids," inspired parents, grandparents and others to see the Andrew Lloyd Webber and Tim Rice musical.

Add a handsome Joseph (Joseph Cassidy), a winsome narrator (Laura Freeman) and an Elvis-like pharaoh (Dan Rodden), and what else could director Carl Beck need? A sexy Mrs. Potiphar (Tracy Arnold) and three all-time favorite Caravan comics: Kamprath, Longe and Ramer.

My Antonia Called "Magnum Opus" for Charles Jones

As health problems limited his mobility, Charles Jones found the creative resources to write his version of Willa Cather's *My Antonia.*, "I never really trusted that I could write," he recalled a decade later.

"It was so frustrating to not have my physical freedom. I needed to express that somehow."

So in his twentieth anniversary season, he penned the words to bring Cather's masterpiece to the Playhouse stage. He introduced that indomitable Nebraskan with a quotation from the book: "The eyes that peered anxiously at me were, simply, Antonia's eyes. She was there in the full vigor of her personality, battered but not diminished." Thanking many, Jones emphasized his indebtedness to another woman who had willed his recovery—"the most indomitable person I have ever known, Eleanor Brodie Jones." As his monumental contribution to the Playhouse neared an end, he believed it had been extended by her pioneer determination.

A review declared *My Antonia* his "magnum opus, a miracle of condensation from the huge, sprawling novel." Three Antonias at different ages—Marie Ellis, Christina Belford and Julie Huff—charmed the record crowd. Othuse summoned a simple setting of changing prairie skies, and music director Cole arranged a moving score of folk melodies. Children dominated early scenes, but then Joan Hennecke as Grandmother Burden became a central character.

"She is wonderful," Delmont wrote, with "dignity, humor, strength and a genuine feeling for the role." Authenticity called for eight language coaches to help with Czech, Russian and other tongues. Thus it unfolded, the story of the Burdens, Cuzaks and Shimerdas, of immigrant pioneers on the plains. To underline such roots, Prompter bios listed "ancestral origins" of the cast.

This time of triumphs continued in a lighter vein with *A Little Shop of Horrors*. The popular musical's man-eating plant named Audrey II, featured R. Stephen Kuhn as the nerdy, plant-tending Seymour and Jill Anderson as his sweetheart singing "Suddenly, Seymour."

Marvin's Room dealt bravely with dying and the human spirit, a subject understood by playwright Scott McPherson, a victim of AIDS. It found Susan Baer Beck directing her grade school son Ben, who'd debuted two years earlier in *Carol*. Young Beck as "a goofy bookworm" and teenager Josh Perilo as a "rebel loner" were praised by critics. Linda

Mead's happy-go-lucky aunt and Connie Lee's selfish sister helped playgoers laugh through the story's sorrows.

Billed as the 70th Jubilee show, *Most Happy Fella* brought vocalist Charles Karel to Omaha as Tony the Napa Valley vintner, before starting his first season with the Metropolitan Opera. One critic had recently seen the Broadway revival accompanied by two pianos and pronounced the Playhouse version with its fourteen-piece orchestra and cast of forty "vastly superior." It capped a season that drew 125,000, a full 11,000 higher than past totals.

Jones's Role Changes, New Staff for Caravan, Playhouse: 1994–1995

They'd already staged that Jubilee show, but the entire 1994–1995 schedule was billed as the Jubilee season. The festivities began in August with *Tribute to Our Stars,* honoring twenty years of service by Jones, Othuse and Cady, and the seventieth anniversary of the Playhouse.

Film and musical tributes entertained a crowd of 400, which heard that $420,000 had been raised by selling bronze and granite stars, a "Walk of the Stars" at the south entrance. They also heard a favorite fiction—the claim that the theater was founded at a meeting held in the home of Dodie Brando. The story of Marguerite Beckman, that *Gypsy Rover* dropout, who brought Alan McDonald and others to the Burgess-Nash Tea Room in 1924 had long been forgotten.

The season finale would revive *The Music Man,* the show that introduced Jones and his aides to Omaha.

Before those "76 trombones" would lead the big parade, a difficult transition led to the end of that triumphant era of Sir Charles. The trustees would deal with dramatic changes in personnel, but not before hearing other bad news. Memberships dropped. Most reasons for nonrenewal were customary—too busy, too costly, didn't like the shows. Others said they bought tickets expecting *Les Misérables.* A few mishaps troubled the first musical. Then the day before the mid-October opening of *Black Comedy,* the second main-stage production,

Jones, 56, fell and broke a hip. Wife Eleanor took over and promised, "Charles has been prepping me," so "we're forging ahead full tilt."

In the late days of October, the board reached a decision. Encouraged by word that insurance would provide Jones with long-term disability benefits, it was announced that he'd become executive/artistic director emeritus. He'd head the Foundation and remain chair of the play-reading committee. The death of Al Ellick left the Foundation vacancy. Joanne Cady became interim director, assisted by Carolyn Rutherford and business manager Ginny Winsor. A search began for an administrator.

Within days, Rutherford informed that she was leaving to head the Midwest Arts Alliance. The program located at William Jewell College in Kansas brought her closer to her ailing mother. In January, Rick Scott was welcomed as Caravan director. For Rutherford, in charge soon after its founding in 1976, it meant leaving the post to a friend from her London studies.

Earlier, the departure of Jack Mahaffey brought Betsye Paragas as director of marketing. Most recently a fund-raiser for the Children's Museum, Paragas had studied at the famed Pasadena Playhouse, while living with her great-uncle. His name was William Frawley, but more knew him from television as Lucille Ball's neighbor, Fred Mertz. Other changes waited for the new administrator.

Sweet Charity opened the season with its great credentials—a Neil Simon comedy with music by Cy Coleman and original choreography by Bob Fosse. But a headline, emphasized "Long, Repetitious First Half," as Delmont added "a very long show—fully three hours with intermission and much of the long first act is a jumble of episodes."

Jones and crew attacked the problem. "We labored all Labor Day weekend and trimmed the show down," the director explained. After cutting twenty-five minutes, Sunday audiences saw "a more streamlined show." The damage was done. It drew the smallest audience for a season opener in seven years. Janet Ratekin Williams played the title role associated with Gwen Verdon and Shirley MacLaine. One of her sidekicks, Sue Gillespie Booton, left the show for a professional role, so

Marsha Kaye returned to the Playhouse. She'd done Jones's first show, *Music Man,* twenty years before, then signed a Nashville recording contract at age 14.

The Fonda-McGuire space also opened with a musical, Sondheim's *Sweeney Todd: The Demon Barber of Fleet Street.* The daily's review praised its "sheer viewing satisfaction." It noted the strong voice of Paul Tranisi's barber, then suggested that Susie Beck's "blissfully nitwitted" portrayal of the pie-making Mrs. Lovett was the show's "most enjoyable aspect." Othuse created a collapsing barber chair that dumped victims swiftly into Mrs. Lovett's oven.

As Eleanor Jones subbed for her husband with the broken hip, *Black Comedy* reversed light and dark. It opens in blackness, which the cast treats as normal lighting. Then a fuse blows, and lights go on for the audience while the players cope with darkness. Critics couldn't complain about length: It ran 83 minutes with no intermission and drew well. Joe Miloni takes a beating during the lights-out illusion, prat-falling all over the place. Praise also went to a "charming" turn by young Christina Belford and a farewell triumph by Carolyn Rutherford.

The home company of *A Christmas Carol* drew its smallest turnout in seven years. The original costume designer, Denise Ervin, joined Miloni in updating costumes for the cast.

Frankenstein Sizzles, *Music Man* Returns, Hunt Hired

January 1995 was a time of transition for more than the Playhouse. Mary Roberts, artistic and general director of Opera Omaha since 1981, announced her pending departure. Bruce Hangen, Omaha Symphony music director and conductor since 1984, was completing his final season. And Ballet Omaha had not renewed the contract of Robert Vickrey, its artistic director since 1985. None, however, matched the twenty-year tenure of Charles Jones.

The Playhouse, in the middle of its seventieth season, had dominated local theater since its early decades. Chanticleer was founded across the river in the 1950s, the Bellevue Little Theater in 1968, but now the daily newspaper counted sixty-five plays reviewed in 1994 at seventeen theaters, including the senior-oriented Grande Olde Players.

The reviewers, Delmont and Jim Minge, picked their best of the past year, topped by *My Antonia*, and then Minge asked, after listing the seventeen theaters, "Is it too much?" And could Omaha handle even more? Answers were mixed. Norm Filbert, the Chanticleer cofounder, said the number of productions spread thin the pool of experienced performers. Susan Baer Beck expressed gratitude for some of the new theaters, but doubted the city could stretch to encompass more.

All that competition didn't stop 11,412 from seeing *Into the Woods*, with Kamprath as Sondheim's main storyteller and Ramer, the other seven-year veteran of the Caravan, as the Big Bad Wolf. Red Riding Hood fared well enough, but it was a rough trip for Cinderella. Terry Ince dislocated her shoulder in an in-line skating portion of the Caravan children's show, *Ozma of Oz*, so Rapunzel (Melissa Lewis) subbed for a few days.

Gary Bosanek with Tom Shomaker in *The Music Man*, 1995.

Dan Prescher as Frankenstein's Monster.

Mrs. Jones then directed *Breaking Legs,* a comedy about Mafia dons backing a professor's off-Broadway play. Delaney Driscoll plays the prof's sweetie who urges her gangster pop (real-life father Gene Driscoll) to be the show's angel. Other mobsters? Dick Boyd and big Don Fiedler. Then came a remarkable success that epitomized the Playhouse creative capacity.

Frankenstein, a play that failed on Broadway, drew nearly 14,000, as director Carl Beck smiled each night to hear them scream in terror. One reviewer wrote that the audience knows what to suspect, even "titters self-consciously as the lovely Elizabeth (Christina Belford) nears her ominous wardrobe, then draws back. So we're guarded, alert, then GOTCHA. There's the monster, the music swells and we're all screaming, then quickly laughing at ourselves."

Beck was aided by 6 foot 3 Dan Prescher's award-winning performance as the monster, sizzling special effects from the UNO physics department, and a 24-foot castle laboratory by designer Othuse. Even with crackling coils and shock effects, poignant and pathetic moments were beautifully realized, especially when the monster meets the blind man (R.H. Fanders). Andrew Donavan played Victor Frankenstein, who delivers that chilling line from Mary Shelley: "I have reason to believe I am capable of reanimating life."

Then four directors prepared twenty-three couples, a new pair each night, to perform *Love Letters,* the epistolary play by A.R. Gurney. The letters span a half century, and the actors ranged from university chancellor Del Weber and philanthropist Margre Durham to TV anchorwoman Carol Schrader and zoo director Lee Simmons, mixed with such veterans as Elaine Jabenis and Frank DeGeorge. A review noted, "People will pay to see their friends fail bravely."

The ever-changing cast, scripts in hand, got "minimalist" direction from Mr. and Mrs. Jones and the Becks. Gurney gave them a captivating couple, the stuffier preppy and his spunky Melissa, and the spare

Playhouse approach kept the focus on their lifetime of letters. The closest anyone came to disaster was newspaper columnist Bob McMorris, who tumbled off the stage with his chair. It happened during rehearsal, spoiling the fun for those who hoped to see the famous falter.

Neil Simon's *Lost in Yonkers* had Carl Beck directing wife, Susie, as the simple Aunt Bella and Linda Mead as the stern Grandma Kurnitz. Two boys, their mother dead and their father off on extended sales trips, grow up in grandma's forbidding apartment. *Shadowlands*, the drama of love and loss in the life of author C.S. Lewis, gave Eleanor Jones the chance to direct Bill Hutson again as that famous Oxford professor. Sara Flores played the American divorcee who falls in love with the Christian apologist.

The season of transition ended triumphantly with the return of *The Music Man* drawing a season-high attendance. It starred Tom Shomaker as Harold Hill and Dawn Buller-Kirke as Marian the librarian.

Before *Music Man* opened in June, the Playhouse announced the hiring of its managing director, Duwain Hunt. Jones, who had not directed a new production during the season, "will continue to guide Playhouse on-stage activities" as artistic director, marketing director Paragas explained. Hunt would manage the administrative and business side. He'd guided a theater complex in a suburb of Kalamazoo, Michigan.

Armed with a range of experience, he said, "I am filled with excitement, apprehension and a sense of challenge here." He knew he was leading "the finest community theater in America," with a budget of $3.4 million. When Hunt went to work on July 1, he faced deficits, declining membership and both staff and community loyal and deeply indebted to Charles Jones. He bowed to Jones as "a legend … the spirit, the artistic soul of the Playhouse. I feel perfectly comfortable working with him."

From Will Rogers to Original *Glory Years, Godspell*: 1995–1996

So another time of transition was under way when *Will Rogers Follies* opened the season's offerings. A new flyer urged playgoers to "get ready for a high-stepping, lariat-twirling" opener, while promising something new called *Curtain Calls,* nine evenings of late-night cabaret-style entertainment featuring musical director Jonathan Cole and other talents.

Administrator Hunt would later add his most significant innovation, theater technology apprenticeships that would not only train young Nebraskans but spread nationwide under the leadership of Steve Bross. Early on, however, the new leader gave some the impression that he expected employees to clock in on regular hours. That concerned Cole, known for doing his best composing and arranging after midnight.

As usual, stability trumped change. Familiar names topped the list of ticket sellers, but none reached as far back into Playhouse history as Florence Young and Val Teal. And *Will Rogers Follies* drew more than 15,000 and a review revealing, "The audience loved it and gave it a roaring standing ovation." Earl Bates, a popular folk singer and guitar player, "was made for the role of humorist Will Rogers," the Oklahoman who never met a man he didn't like. Leggy showgirls paraded in lavish costumes designed by Denise Ervin. The only fly in the ointment was a bat that fluttered around the piano during a Sunday matinee. Rare at the Playhouse, resident bats were so routine at Chanticleer that the Council Bluffs theater used them as a fund-raising symbol.

Another original work by Jones opened the Fonda-McGuire season. His *Glory Years* told the civic story of Ak-Sar-Ben and was co-produced by the Knights of Ak-Sar-Ben, who'd been spelling Nebraska backwards for 100 years. Led by Travis Walker as Richard Cornhusker, a large cast played a host of prominent citizens, such as Dick Boyd as Peter Kiewit, Mike Harper, and others; Al DiMauro as V.J. Skutt and Willis Strauss; Gene Driscoll as John Brandeis and Leo Daly. The homage to civic leadership drew the season's smallest audience.

The Metoyer sisters, Camille Moten and Lanette Moore, attracted a few more to *The Queen of Bingo*, thanks perhaps to publicity in *The Bingo Caller* newspaper. Someone was counting, so the twentieth anniversary of *A Christmas Carol* marked 500 performances for Boyd as Ebenezer Scrooge. Nobody multiplied the times he muttered, "Bah, humbug!"

The Caravan also marked its twentieth year by bringing *Godspell* indoors in January. An earlier version of the musical had been performed outside a roofless Playhouse after the tornado blew through in 1975.

Sing "Do Wah Diddy" as Fonda-McGuire Space Named for Drew

The largest single gift yet recorded by the Playhouse led to naming the smaller theater for businessman Howard Drew. Shows in that intimate setting would continue to be identified as the Fonda-McGuire Series as they had since its inception in 1986.

Jabenis, Beasley in *Driving Miss Daisy*.

Leader of the Pack became the first presentation under the new name. Renovation plans began with acceptance of $1 million from Drew, a retired real estate man, and work would be completed by the start of the 1996 season. *Leader of the Pack* got the Drew Theater off to a good start, drawing the season's best turnout there with nearly 5,000 rocking to "Do Wah Diddy" and other music from pop composer Ellie Greenwich, played by Kathy Wheeldon. The cast included Terry Berner as pop guru Phil Spector with Kathy Tyree, Ginny Hermann and Tiffany White as rock icons, similar to their long run in the Old Market production of *Bee Hive*. Designer Othuse had ordered new seating, but the *Pack* audience still sat in those wobbly canvas director's chairs.

The Grapes of Wrath wasn't helped when a headline followed "Impressive" with "but Depressing." One review credited director Carl Beck and his cast for treating the audience as adults, noting it was John Steinbeck's story of Okies escaping the Dust Bowl in the Great Depression, "not *Annie* where the sun comes out tomorrow." The play retained the novel's language deleted from the Henry Fonda movie. Tall Dan Prescher's Tom Joad sounded like Fonda as he topped a strong cast. The audience held its breath and a spectator gasped, "Oh, my God!," as Rose of Sharon delivered her baby with flood waters rising.

The casting of Elaine Jabenis and John Beasley as her chauffeur in *Driving Miss Daisy* was promising enough to bring the season's biggest crowd for a drama. An award-winning player for more than forty years, Elaine told director Jones, "I know that old lady, Charles, believe me." Beasley had enjoyed stage, film and television credits, including the popular Notre Dame football movie *Rudy*. Add the fact that Jones, the ailing native of Georgia, was directing a play set in Atlanta, and his creative vision led to unique visual enhancement: artist Craig Lee's 14-by-32-foot treatment of Georgia O'Keefe's "Apple Blossoms."

Jabenis worried that her accent would sound phony to the Southerner, but Jones assured, "Honey, you're right on." She'd recall that he didn't miss a rehearsal, telling the cast as one ended, "Ah just enjoyed that so much I can hardly wait for tomorrow night." An audience likely familiar with the Oscar-winning movie gave Jabenis and Beasley. standing ovations.

Tennessee Williams and Leonard Bernstein completed the season with *Glass Menagerie* and *West Side Story*. Nearly 17,000, a season high, saw Dave Jackson as Tony and the Caravan's Melissa Lewis as Maria. Music director Cole promised, "Something's coming, something good," as the Playhouse first tackled the classic thirty years after its Chanticleer premiere. Carl Beck's treatment of *Menagerie* won praise for Phyllis Doughman as the Southern mother of a shy daughter (Kaitlyn Byrd) and restless son Tom (Steven Barron).

Another new effort was called "Classical Conversations," linking the Playhouse and the Omaha Symphony in hybrid events combining refreshments, performance and discussion. President Steven Olson continued to lead the trustees as the season ended with expenses approaching $4 million.

Techies Come, Canvas Chairs Go, Charles Does It Again: 1996–1997

Time and events add weight to words that may fall more lightly when first written. When *Oliver* opened the season, a review praising "the big, boisterous, colorful" musical said, "Charles Jones has done it again." It wasn't known then that the Southern gentleman would do it only once more before leaving the Playhouse for what was termed "a sabbatical." That August opening was well-received as *Oliver* marked the debut of Jim Boggess as music director, replacing Cole.

With Jones, 58, and in his twenty-third season at the creative helm, his likely departure became more apparent in December. A newspaper column headed, "Jones: I'm Not OCP's Future," reported that his contract ended in August 1998, "but I might exit sooner." He said his health was better, and he believed he'd done some of his "best directing" since his stroke, "But it would be helpful for the Playhouse if I could find a way to step aside."

When the season promoted as "Hot Stuff" opened, though, he was still on the job. And the fall musical had competition for the attention of the season members, now fewer than 10,000. The French comedy *My Three Angels* with Rob Baker, Tom Bertino and Gordon Krentz as the title's comical convicts opened the renovated Howard Drew Theatre. The million-dollar gift from its namesake provided new risers, lighting and sound systems. They were all welcomed, but overshadowed by the new seating.

Patrons who'd wobbled on canvas director's chairs now settled into burgundy seats fashioned by "the noted Italian designer" Giancarlo Piretti. Director Carl Beck moved the action "at such a pace," a review suggested, "you could sit on a bed of nails and still be smiling when it's over."

The project's coordinator, Othuse, reminded that the canvas chairs had been a temporary solution when the Fonda-McGuire Series began a decade before. If that brought memories of that "temporary" Playhouse that housed the theater from 1928 to 1959, so did the final day before the Drew reopened. In 1928, seats were still being bolted down as people arrived.

This time the customized labels numbering the 225 chairs didn't arrive until the Thursday morning of preview night. "Luckily that was the only thing that came down to the wire."

A less visible but significant addition to the Playhouse was initiated by managing director Hunt. Northwest High teacher Steve Bross was hired to head the theater technology apprenticeship program Hunt first launched in Kalamazoo. Explaining that hundreds of theater technician jobs go unfilled, he described a cooperative program with Metropolitan Community College.

From twenty-five to thirty-five apprentices would take classes, earn college credits and gain hands-on experience with sound, lighting, rigging, scenery, construction, props, costumes and stage management. They also learn, "you know you're a techie when you really believe you can fix anything with Gaff tape and a glue gun" and when "you have a permanent mark above your ears from the headset." Later, Bross created a curriculum marketed to schools and theaters.

Graduates of the Playhouse training soon worked in university theaters, Shakespeare festivals in Omaha and Utah, television and filmmaking. "When the city's new Qwest Center opened," Bross said, its technical needs made his students "gold."

Wendy Wasserstein's ethnic comedy, *The Sisters Rosensweig,* and the Dale Wasserman stage treatment of Ken Kesey's *One Flew Over the Cuckoo's Nest* took the main stage and the Drew in the fall. Pam Carter hobbled on high heels and conversed with hands flying freely from suspended wrists as Gorgeous Tietelbaum. A review called her "possibly the strongest and most entertaining actor in the metro area."

The director, now identified as Susan Baer again after her divorce from Carl Beck, called it "really a treat to do a play with such great writing and such great roles for women. Beck directed *Cuckoo's Nest* with "The Rockett," morning radio jock G. Rockett Phillips, in the role played on stage by Kirk Douglas and in the Oscar winning film by Jack Nicholson. With Sara Flores as the nasty nurse Ratched and a mental ward full of "eccentric and compelling characters," the cast inspired superlatives.

For the final time, Charles Jones directed *A Christmas Carol.* As usual, the Jones collaboration with Charles Dickens lured the season's largest attendance, nearly 17,000. Jones would direct just one more show, and a vital volunteer would pass from the scene shortly before the end of 1996.

Al Ellick, chairman of the Playhouse Foundation for five years, died and received tributes from Jones and others for his community work. His service to the Playhouse continued the contributions of his late wife, Echo Guiou Ellick, and her mother, Genevieve Baldwin Guiou, stretching back to the founding year of 1925. A week before his death, Ellick had signed hundreds of fund appeal letters "with notes of affection and appreciation."

A Foundation portfolio appraisal a few months later showed what he'd built for successor John Gottschalk, publisher of the *Omaha*

World-Herald. The total of $1,850,579 included an artistic endowment of $387,000, a building endowment of $659,000 and the Drew endowment of $745,000.

Cranes Grace Caravan, Drew Used Flexibly, Jones Leaves

After one of its three touring *Carol* companies set an attendance record in St. Louis, the Nebraska Theatre Caravan brought the musical *Pippin* to the Playhouse in January 1997. The troupe arrived home in the middle of a season that also featured an original play, *Songs of Myself,* and a production of *A Thousand Cranes*. It filled the theater with paper cranes (birds) and led to a trip to Japan.

The Caravan's education coordinator since 1992, Marya Lucca-Thyberg, won a grant from U.S. West and others through the Nebraska Arts Council and journeyed to Japan with Caravan director Rick Scott to connect with Omaha's sister city, Shizuoka, and visit the Hiroshima memorial.

The play tells of the young survivor of the atomic bombing of Hiroshima who created the use of cranes to honor those memories. It would continue on national tours the next three seasons. *Songs of Myself* by Peg Sheldrick of Lincoln offered junior and senior high school students a dramatic treatment of a young Everyman encountering genius in the form of famous figures from the arts and sciences. *Pippin*, the story of Charlemagne's son, gave Baer a chance to direct "the first show I ever saw on Broadway."

Harper Lee's *To Kill a Mockingbird*, the comedy *Don't Dress for Dinner* and *Oklahoma* successfully completed the main stage season. Reviews praised the performances of Hilary and Spencer Williams as Scout and Jem Finch. Dan Prescher's work as Atticus Finch, the noble lawyer portrayed by Gregory Peck in the film, won a Peckham award.

In sharp contrast, director Susan Baer billed *Don't Dress for Dinner* as aimed at "the theatergoer who insists, 'I don't want to think, I just want to be entertained.'" The adapted French farce featured such burlesque fun as the on-stage ripping of a French maid outfit into a chic cocktail dress, plus the usual door-slamming and mistaken identities. A review asked, "Will Robert sleep in the cow shed with Suzanne or in the piggery with Suzette rather than in the hay loft with Jacqueline?"

The most surprising fact about the May production of *Oklahoma* was that the 1943 Rodgers and Hammerstein musical hadn't been performed at the Playhouse. In 1942, they'd done a lively version of *Green Grow the Lilacs*, the play that inspired it, but not the famous show that begins with a cowboy named Curley singing, "Oh, what a beautiful morning." Director Baer was blessed with Michael Zaller as Curley, Becky Jones as Laurey and Brian Barratt as the menacing Jud Fry.

Two Howard Drew productions proved the flexibility of the renovated Howard Drew stage. First, Charles Jones directed his final Playhouse show *The Boy Friend* in the round. Angela Balderston, as a scene-stealing maid, quickly showed the audience that theater-in-the-round can play all angles. She exploited her French maid getup (ruffled pink panties and a plunging neckline) by

Sarah and Brendan Buchanan in Jones' finale.

bending deeply while dusting all four corners of the stage. Sarah Buchanan gave heroine Polly a peachy Doris Day innocence. Add Dawn Buller-Kirke as a drunken battleax, plus Sue Perkins and Tom Shomaker as show-stopping vocalists, and Jones left on a high note.

Demand for the next Drew show, *Tony n' Tina's Wedding*, required extra performances and would have set an attendance record if not for reduced seating. It helped that many wanted to see it two or three times. They entered through the back loading dock, strolled past tables laden with wedding gifts, and took seats in the Hitchcock Rehearsal Hall, set up as a chapel. Then the "guests" moved to tables in the Drew Theatre, renamed Vinnie's Pompeii Gardens, for the "reception" and a wild evening of "structured improvisation."

From Rob Baker as Vinnie the caterer to Andrea Lang as the overheated maid of honor, more than two dozen cast members make up a zany wedding party, often chatting up playgoers at their tables. Dutch Haling as mobster Tony Nunzio, the groom's father, put arriving men up against the wall and patted them down for weapons—uneventful until he patted a big hogleg packed by a lawman.

A Marilyn Monroe impersonation and a summer Caravan show, *Schoolhouse Rock LIVE!* rounded out the schedule. Former music director Cole accompanied the Monroe look-alike, Katie LaBourdette, as the Drew provided the venue for her professional production of *Marilyn, Sleepless Nights* in April.

Then board president Olson announced in August that Charles Jones would take a sabbatical followed a year later by his retirement at age 60. Jones had been hospitalized again in the spring. His retirement, Olson said, had been long planned after "a very successful career." Later in August, a Delmont column reported that Jones would direct the musical *Mame* at the Dundee Dinner Theater. One of his Playhouse favorites, Sue Perkins, would play the title role.

Fuller profiles would follow, giving Jones primary credit for the community theater's rise to the top. In September, the Omaha Press Club honored him as the first member of the arts community to become their ceremonial "Face on the Barroom Floor." At his departure, the

Playhouse budget had reached $4 million and the staff, including eight with the Caravan, had reached a peak of fifty-three. No other community theater came close to those numbers, nor, later, would the Playhouse.

Growing Awareness of New Competition: 1997–1998

As the next season began, Jones was listed as artistic director emeritus, Beck as acting artistic director, Baer and Joanne Cady as associate directors. "Acting" would soon drop from the title, and Carl Beck would lead the company that he joined as a member of the Caravan. Hunt continued as managing director with Ginny Winsor still serving as general manager.

Season memberships fell. The musicals, as always, did better than nonmusicals, but even the colorful opener, *La Cage aux Folles*, fell well short of the opening crowds in previous years. When Hunt resigned three years later, he attributed the drop-off largely to the opening of the riverboat gambling casinos in Council Bluffs in the mid-1990s, an unlikely culprit. Others noted the presence of fifteen theater companies in the metropolitan area and Broadway tours.

The Grande Olde Players had just moved to a new home, but another event signaled that the Playhouse not only shared its audience with others but competed for philanthropy. An $8 million fund-raising campaign was under way to transform a downtown theater into The Rose. The Rose Blumkin Performing Arts Center, named for the centenarian entrepreneur who created the market-dominating Nebraska Furniture Mart, had once been an ornate movie house as the Paramount and Astro. Now it would become home to one of the leading youth theaters in the country with a professional staff, including a full-time troupe of actors. The company known as the Junior Theater when still connected to the Playhouse had become the Emmy Gifford Children's Theater and now the Omaha Theater for Young People.

Boggess and Miloni in *La Cage*.

La Cage Aux Folles had been presented by other metro theaters, but the Playhouse waited until broad acceptance of the gender-bending musical was proven by the film version, *The Birdcage*. It centers on a future in-law, leader of the decency league, meeting the drag queen "mother" of their daughter's fiancé. The leading men received rave reviews. Costume designer Miloni played the "plain homosexual" Georges and music director Boggess was Albin, the flamboyant cross-dressing Zaza. Delmont described "the pleasure of seeing Miloni—this wonderfully sly and clever performer—on stage again." He credited the "astonishing" Boggess with "the very essence of maturing womanhood."

Fans of A.R. Gurney's *Love Letters* returned to the Drew for his *Sylvia* with newcomer Kim Clark-Kaczmarek as the title pooch. Headlines ranged from "Comedic Gem" to "Love at First Woof" and "Down, Sylvia, Down."

The next Fonda-McGuire drama, *Scotland Road,* arrived in November, too soon to benefit from the record-breaking popularity of the James Cameron film treating the same historic event, the sinking of the *Titanic*. The play directed by Bridget Wiley dealt with the mystery of an alleged survivor, portrayed by Kay Vivian. It didn't help that the opening came a few days after an October ice storm. It blocked streets with fallen trees and downed power lines, leaving thousands without electricity for up to nine days.

Promotion for *The Woman in Black* warned "prepare for sleepless nights" and "go if you like being scared out of your wits." A weekly newspaper waxed even more enthusiastic, promising "one of the most exciting, gripping and successful theatre events ever staged at the Omaha Community Playhouse." Burdened with such forecasting, it also arrived during that October ice storm, causing some cancellations, and didn't inspire enough word of mouth to bring attendance up.

A Christmas Carol appeared for the first time without Jones in charge. Beck and Baer shared in preparing all four companies. Perhaps the crowd of 16,963, largest in five years, sought

Ramer's Adams and Kamprath's Franklin.

assurance that the holiday tradition survived intact. Reviews for Boyd and the rest of the continuing cast members remained as impressive as the revenue. Never fear, *Carol* was still here.

First Season Without Jones Since '74 Ends with Two Hits

As America learned in January 1998 of sexual allegations against President Clinton and "that woman," the Founding Fathers forged a nation on the Playhouse stage. The Caravan returned with the musical *1776* featuring veterans Ramer and Kamprath as John Adams and Ben Franklin and drawing over 11,000. A few years later, David McCullough's book about Adams confirmed that the third president deserved a starring role.

The Heiress, drawn from the Henry James novel *Washington Square,* earned Jacque Camperud, playing the title character, credit from Delmont for "perhaps the performance of this theater season." Alexandra Hunt, a former opera star performing on the Met, La Scala and other stages, returned as Aunt Lavinia, a foolish romantic. The audience responded with "oohs" and "aahs" to the 1850 setting designed by Othuse. The actors retained poise when one of the 8,227 attending was far too audible when whispering of Bernie Clark's character, the cruel, demanding father, "He's a mean one."

The smallest main stage audience in years saw the April production, *Camping with Henry & Tom.* President Warren Harding met Henry Ford and Thomas Edison at a campsite in 1922, an event suggesting this fiction. "You know the age of heroes is really over when the tradition-bound Playhouse's production dumps three icons of the past off their pedestals," wrote a new *World-Herald* reviewer, Bob Fischbach. A copy editor born on a South Dakota farm, he would replace Delmont as the daily's main theater critic on the latter's retirement in 2004.

The Fonda-McGuire Series contrasted comedy, from the cerebral *Picasso at the Lapin Agile* to the spacey *Return to the Forbidden Planet*. A reviewer would have renamed the former, "Steve Martin Ushers in the 20th Century with a Pretentious Yet Appealing 90-minute comedy." *Forbidden Planet* drew almost double its audience with its sci-fi spoof of Shakespeare's *The Tempest* as a meteor shower has the cast singing "Great Balls of Fire."

Top kudos went to a pair from the season-closing main-stage musical *Camelot*. First directed in 1979 by Jones, Baer brought the Lerner and Loewe hit back. Fischbach's review focused on the elaborate costumes created by Georgiann Regan and the "scenery and lighting miracles" performed by Othuse, an upbeat ending to the first schedule without Charles Jones.

"We're the Top" Claim Backed by Bigger Crowds: 1998–1999

Cole Porter's *Anything Goes* opened the season and gave the Playhouse a good reason to remind the world that "the largest community theatre in the nation belongs to Omaha." Porter's "You're the Top" was borrowed to proclaim "We're the Top" and the response to productions backed the boast.

The "acting" was gone from Beck's title of artistic director, and for the first time in twenty-five years Charles Jones did not lead the play selection process. *Anything Goes,* dating back to 1934, drew nearly 15,000 thanks to the songs that "have kept it afloat for 64 years," Delmont wrote. J. Laureen Pickle brought her big voice to the Ethel Merman role of Reno Sweeney, with dancer Brendan Buchanan as Billy Crocker, the male lead. The shipboard set designed by Othuse provided a playground for "two of the best character actors in the area," Kamprath as gangster Moonface Martin and Jerry Longe as Sir Evelyn Oakleigh. Choreographer Roxanne Nielsen subbed as a late replacement for the gangster's moll. She was in the middle of a three-generation family now serving on the Playhouse staff with her mother France Bennett as executive secretary and daughter Sarah Nielsen as receptionist.

Grace and Glorie started the Drew series with the story of a country woman dying of cancer and her city-woman caregiver. "A friendship warily develops," a review noted, "and is celebrated throughout in the richest humor," thanks especially to Lanette Metoyer-Moore's "deeply felt and fully realized performance as the abrupt, cackling, scolding old girl" paired with Julie Huff.

A Tuna Christmas then filled the small space to a season-high 92 percent of capacity as playgoers laughed at the antics of Stuart Stenger and Karl Rohling. Backstage dressers rushed them through costume changes for twenty-two roles as Texas zanies. "Stenger goes from broadcaster in bib overalls to redhead Bertha Bumiller in green pants suit, then returns as R.R. Snavely, a drunk in blue coveralls who sees UFOs." The set design added to the fun with a crazy conveyor belt carrying oddities and a wall that opened into the Tasty Kreme Drive-in window.

The Cemetery Club, the play that inspired television's *The Golden Girls,* cast Barb Ross, Merrilyn Stephens and Lois Nemec as three widows gathering at their husbands' graves. It was Judith K. Hart's directing debut in the fall slot when Playhouse directors and designer Othuse were busy again with the Ak-Sar-Ben coronation and preparing four *Christmas Carol* companies.

A Christmas Carol not only soared to attendance of 17,493, highest since 1992, but surprised Boyd in his twenty-third year as Ebenezer Scrooge. Mayor Hal Daub declared December 20 "Dick Boyd Day" and presented him a key to the city with Governor Ben Nelson on hand for the tribute. Advance word of the day in Boyd's honor raised suspicions that it marked his last run in the classic role. Unwarranted fear did wonders for the box office.

Secret Garden Sweeps Honors, Report Sums Season

A third show with a country theme, the Caravan's *Smoke on the Mountain* treated more than 13,000 to such familiar gospel songs as "Rock of Ages." Now identified as Susan Baer Collins after her marriage to lawyer-actor Dennis Collins, the director had Ramer as the head of the Sanders Family Singers and Elizabeth Loos as his comical daughter.

Adding to the country flavor was the fiddling of Heather Kolbrek, who had worked at Nashville's Opryland U.S.A.

The setting for that February's Fonda-McGuire musical changed to the Caribbean for *Once on This Island*, the poetic story of an orphan peasant girl seeking help from Haitian voodoo gods. Archetypal gods were played by Camille Metoyer-Moten (love goddess), Julie Valentine (earth mother) and D. Kevin Williams (demon of death). The season's top Drew crowd saw a show dominated by Neilsen's "joyful choreography," featuring "head-rolling, shoulder-shaking, rhythmic-stepping and foot-stomping."

Director Beck promised a *Dracula* complete with seductive eroticism and "buckets of blood." Fischbach's review began, "Thunder clapped. From a stage bathed in red light, fog rolled so thick people in the audience coughed. And the blood: dripping from lips, oozing from a slashed chest, spurting into the faces of men pounding wooden stakes."

The season's largest audience for a drama, saw the new version

Carter, Longe in *Moon Over Buffalo*.

of Bram Stoker's story. Dan Prescher added the blood-sucking Count to his earlier triumph as Frankenstein's monster, inspiring a review to "swear he was the blood relative of Bela Lugosi." Fischbach called Kamprath "exceptional" as Van Helsing and praised Teri Fender as Dracula's sexy victim. The review noted that the horrific climax drew laughter rather than screams of fear.

The hilarious *Moon Over Buffalo* gave Longe and triple Fonda-McGuire winner Pam Carter freedom to ham it up. They played fading stage stars whose hopes for movie fame depend on a visit by director Frank Capra. Longe got great mileage from drunken scenes and bawdy misplacement of Cyrano de Bergerac's prodigious nose. Beck also cast such comedic talents as Stenger and Theresa Sindelar.

Lillian Hellman's *The Little Foxes* proved again that even a well-performed classic can't easily fill the seats, even with Connie Lee as Regina Giddens. She was "simply delicious," directed by M. Michele Phillips, a review said, "as the hottest cold-blooded villain imaginable."

When *The Secret Garden* opened at the end of May, Delmont began, "Wow! The Playhouse saved the best for last." He went further when the musical won 13 of 28 TAG awards, along with Paul Tranisi's Fonda-McGuire award, a Mary Peckham award for young Hilary Williams and others to make it the most-honored show in many a season, declared "one of the finest productions of the decade." Nearly 16,000 watched a cast directed by Baer Collins and featuring the powerful voice of Dawn Buller-Kirke. The story from Frances Hodgson Burnett tells of a young girl sent to the English mansion of a brooding uncle after her parents die of cholera.

The board, headed by Kathy Lewis, provided a sixteen-page annual report, one of the few published in seventy-four years. Facts cited in the report ranged from that attendance total of nearly 115,000 to figures on revenue and expenses. Admissions and contributions ($524,000) were up, Caravan touring fees and grants were down. Overall revenue dropped some $600,000 to about $3,864,000. Expenses, however, also declined to just over $4 million. The Caravan cost more than home productions, while Playhouse shows accounted for 38 percent of revenue, the Caravan 28 percent.

Toasting 75th Anniversary Season: 1999–2000

The diamond anniversary season began under a tent on the Playhouse lawn, but, unlike the golden anniversary, the seventy-fifth wasn't forced outdoors by a roof-raising tornado. It was a festive "thank you" to supporters, minus fund-raising or other appeals. After a trumpet fanfare, champagne glasses were raised and honorary chairman Dee Owen joined Carl Beck in toasting the anniversary.

The gathering of past and present, with Charles Jones joining Hunt and others, heard songs from the Caravan's *Forever Plaid* and the season-opening musical *Crazy for You*. Later, *The Enchanted Cottage*, the play that launched the Playhouse in 1925, was revisited with a new script. Anniversary hoopla may have helped boost season memberships. For the first time in seven years, two productions,

Simpson with Ecklebe sisters, Lori and Kerry, and Ann Marie Metzger (front).

A Christmas Carol and the season-ending *My Fair Lady* sold more than 17,000 tickets.

The Gershwin songs of *Crazy for You* also drew the best opening crowd since *Funny Girl* six years before. A review began, "If 'I've Got Rhythm,' music and my gal, the Gershwins argue, 'who could ask for anything more?'" That number alone, another said, "is worth the price of admission." The lasting image landed on the photo wall that came later in the lobby: leading man Michal Simpson framed by smiling showgirls.

Nearly 12,000 saw *The Miracle Worker* on the main stage in October after a Bob Fischbach review urged those familiar with the story of Annie Sullivan teaching the deaf and blind Helen Keller, "Treat yourself again. You haven't seen it with Jill Anderson and Rachel Lien." It has, he added, "inspired direction by Susan Baer Collins, and all the little Playhouse touches that elevate a show to something a notch above." Anderson, a former Caravan Equity actor, and the preteen Miss Lien, wore padding in rehearsals, protection against the struggles to tame the wild child.

The Playhouse was reminded again that it wasn't alone on the local theater scene. When *Clue—The Musical* took the Drew stage in November, it had been performed the previous May by a new company, Stages of Omaha, at a new venue, the downtown Millennium Theatre. The company primarily presented musicals until it folded five years later. Another guest director, ex-Caravaner Brandon Higdem, guided the spin-off of the board game, featuring such colorful suspects as Professor Plum, Miss Scarlet and Mrs. Peacock. Gordon Krentz led a cast dominated by Playhouse debuts.

Meanwhile, *A Christmas Carol* drew record crowds for the second year in a row with the familiar cast. A year that saw Republicans fail to convict an impeached President Clinton and shocked Americans with the Columbine School massacre in Colorado ended with the Dow Jones industrial average at a record high. However, the bull market that rewarded not only investors but the nonprofit groups that benefited from their philanthropy was near an end. Fears of a midnight disaster as computers turned from 1999 to 2000 were unfounded, and the year ahead would see a second George Bush elected as President of the United States.

Though experts couldn't quite agree if 2000 was the start of a new century or the end of an old one, the Playhouse started with the usual Caravan musical. *Forever Plaid,* a dinner theater favorite, hit Omaha with word from director Collins that "I don't remember a show as challenging musically as this one." Music director Mitch Fuller would wince when reminded of the show years later, but reviews were varied. The consensus: a mixed bag as four young men sang standards and joked about their death in a car crash. Brian Whisenant sang Johnny Ray's "Cry" well enough to be invited back for an award-winning role in the season-closing *My Fair Lady.*

Three touring *Carol* companies were cut to a pair, minus the West Coast tour. For the next three seasons, however, the Caravan musical did not appear in its usual January slot, forecasting larger changes yet to come.

The Enchanted Cottage brought the Playhouse back to its origins. The play was the theater's first when Dodie Brando played the lead in spring 1925. Later, it was a Hollywood movie with Dorothy McGuire, adding to its significance for the Playhouse.

In February, as rewritten by Larry B. Williams and directed by Collins, unfortunately, it received a tepid reception.

A Sherlock Holmes spoof, *The Mask of Moriarty,* gave Longe and Stenger the chance to play Holmes and Dr. Watson, followed by *The Last Night of Ballyhoo,* another Southern story by the author of *Driving Miss Daisy.* The Fonda-McGuire Series closed with *Gross Indecency, The Three Trials of Oscar Wilde,* directed by Beck. Delmont's review declared it "neither gross nor indecent," though dealing with "a troubling theme—the clash of public standards with private conduct." That was the conduct of author Wilde, "a rather bold and frivolous bisexual" of the Victorian age, as played by Nils Haaland. Norman Filbert's portrayal of Wilde's adversary, the Marquis of Queensbury, won a cameo award.

My Fair Lady became the first musical to grace the Playhouse stage for a third time. Julie Harper was Liza Doolittle and Matt Kamprath played her father Alfie. A weekly headlined it as "Perhaps Playhouse's All-Time Best." Delmont settled for "perfect," adding that it offered "an extravagance of costumes rarely, if ever, seen there before." Miloni and Georgiann Regan collaborated on the Edwardian outfits. Director Collins had another Caravan veteran, Ramer, as Professor Henry Higgins, and two favorites, Elaine Jabenis and Rob Baker, as mother Higgins and sidekick Pickering.

Manager Hunt Departs, New Executive Schmad Arrives: 2000–2001

The season borrowed its theme from the opening musical *A Funny Thing Happened on the Way to the Forum*. It formed the greeting from the "Managing Director's Corner" where Duwain Hunt wrote, "A hearty welcome to the 'Something for Everyone' season."

A summary history looked to the future by noting that Beck and Hunt together were "focusing on artistic excellence and solid business management." The theme came from the show-opening "Comedy Tonight," but soon the "something" for Hunt wasn't so funny. A few weeks later "Exit, Stage Left" ran over an item announcing his resignation and return to Kalamazoo. He declined to comment, the item reported, but the board president complimented his five years at the Playhouse.

The news story used the occasion for a status report on the theater, noting fifty on staff and a $4 million budget. As usual in such farewells, the real story was more complicated than statistics and varied with sources and their relationships with Hunt. The board apparently became aware that he had lined up a new opportunity. Undoubtedly, he paid a price for being the first administrator who didn't wear the artistic hat so gallantly donned by Jones. Stories persist that the sound of applause followed his exit from the building.

In any case, he was replaced on an interim basis by the board's executive vice president, Betsy Moran. A University of Nebraska graduate, her volunteer service included the presidency of ACT II. Ginny Winsor remained as general manager. As for Hunt who attributed a drop in season tickets to the Council Bluffs casinos, skeptics doubted that Playhouse supporters had fled to the slots. Fonder memories of that time featured *Forum* with Kamprath as Pseudolus and Kirsten Kluver as the skimpily clad courtesan.

It was tempting to multiply as twenty women played forty roles in eighty costumes when *The Women* by Clare Boothe Luce graced the Drew stage. Reviews hinted that it might be dated, but Delmont found enough universalism in the 1930s satire, and he praised performances by Connie Lee as the idealist, Amanda Link as the brassy blonde and Kathy Wheeldon as the cheating wife of a cheating man. This was the play scheduled when the men went off to war in 1942. Then it was deemed too "obstetrical."

Kirsten as courtesan with Brian Whisenant.

New executive Tim Schmad

November brought *Inspecting Carol,* a parody of the Dickens's Christmas story to the Drew. Tim Siragusa, ready to tour with a Caravan *Carol* cast, reviewed for a weekly and applauded the Playhouse willingness to make sport of its "cash cow," now running "longer than many of those reading this review have been alive." Rob Baker played a Scrooge fed up with the role and urging a new ending where Ebenezer does not reform. Tiny Tim (Tim Agnew), grown too large to perch on shoulders, is lost in his Game Boy while surrounded by chaos.

The real thing drew over 19,000, again boosted by unfounded rumors that Dick Boyd would call it curtains for his beloved Scrooge, and the parody did well in the Drew.

The William Inge drama, *The Dark at the Top of the Stairs,* brought Susan Clement-Toberer from the Blue Barn Theatre in Omaha's Old Market to direct the story of a 1920s Oklahoma family. Julie Huff won an award as the mother whose dispute with her husband (Earl Bates) drives the action.

The final Drew offering, *Our Country's Good*, arrived with an admission from director Collins that the play-reading committee worried that it might be too risky. "The behavior and language is a little rougher than most Playhouse productions." It's the story of British convicts shipped to Australia, and, yes, a reviewer agreed, "It borders on the unbearable and yet finally revels in the nobility that allows human beings to rise above the meanest circumstances."

An all-star cast with such talents as Hutson, Kamprath and Ankenbauer kept such good company that lesser-knowns Paul Thelan and Suzanne Withem joined three former Caravan members (Hutson, Kamprath and Jamie Lewis) on awards night. Its late May opening added weight to a reviewer's claim "as perhaps the season's finest theatrical offering."

The spring musical *Mack and Mabel* added to Theresa Sindelar's growing reputation as the theater's top comedic female. She played Mabel Normand, the waitress turned into a star by Keystone Kops creator Mack Sennett (Jerry Longe). The custom of ending the main stage season with a big musical was discarded for a rare June opening of *The Sunshine Boys*. Beck directed Dennis Collins and Bernie Clark as those cantankerous old vaudevillians.

The comedy's late run left time for the Prompter to introduce Hunt's replacement, Tim Schmad as executive director. Schmad came to the Playhouse from an executive role with the charitable Knights of Ak-Sar-Ben, the venerable organization of civic leaders that until recent years had run thoroughbred racing. The horses once attracted crowds of 20,000-plus on weekends, but the arrival of casino gambling in Council Bluffs and other alternatives brought its decline. Schmad had also worked in sports public relations, but came from a family familiar with theater. His uncle Howard Fischer had performed at the Playhouse as a professional actor. His aunt, attorney Margaret Fischer, was the only person to attend every Playhouse production from its origins in 1925 until the 1990s.

Schmad introduced himself in that Prompter "as a guy who vaguely remembers the old 40th and Davenport Playhouse," and called his new position "an honor."

Fund Drive, Then Belt-Tightening Staff Cuts: 2001–2002

The Playhouse launched a $7 million drive for capital improvement and endowment funds. About $3.5 million had been raised before the announcement, and a decision was made to reduce the original $10 million goal to a figure "more realistic in the current economic climate." The end of the bull market and the Sept. 11, 2001, terrorist attacks were being felt by the Playhouse and other arts organizations. The Enron bankruptcy added to market jitters.

Board president Dennis O'Neal told a reporter, "We were reasonably happy with phase one of our fund-raising, but phase two has been a little disappointing." Schmad joined O'Neal in describing the theater's needs. "Visitors are impressed with our lobby," Schmad noted, "but they don't realize the roof leaks." The original 1958 boiler needed to go, 1986 carpet needed replacement and other remodeling included a women's restroom and the box office.

They spelled out Playhouse finances, including a deficit in the past season. A $4 million budget, more than double the next largest community theater, was met 70 percent by ticket sales, with the other 30 percent from giving and grants. O'Neal emphasized that the Playhouse had no debt and assets valued at about $10 million.

In March 2002, "Contributions lag, local groups trim budgets and jobs to keep the arts alive" ran the headline over a news story focused on "belt-tightening" in the arts. The Playhouse showed a drop in contributions and season ticket sales. Schmad, still new on the job, confessed, "I wouldn't kid you that we haven't been affected" by the stock market decline. "We need to run a tight ship to be able to continue the way we want to."

The first big change greeted his arrival when trustees cut the Nebraska Theatre Caravan back to two *Christmas Carol* tours and dropped its Nebraska tours of student and community offerings. "We are absolutely not ending the caravan," emphasized operations director Betsy Moran. "The caravan is very much part of what the Playhouse is—an essential part."

Marya Lucca-Thyberg, who had been promoted to Caravan director, left the post, and former director Rick Scott returned. The interim was reported to be a time of evaluation, as the headline said, while the Caravan "seeks out direction." Moran cited the rising costs of touring, and the need for "new sources of revenue."

The Caravan would return to its traditional offering of three productions in the next season. The number of actors and technicians on tour had been trimmed from twelve to six. It would bring its treatment of *My Way*, a musical revue of Frank Sinatra songs, back to its familiar January slot in 2004. That was the good news.

The bad news was that even the gentle reviewing of Jim Delmont complimented only one of the four singers, and another review reported its audience grumbling about voices that lacked the Sinatra style. But costs, not the generally well-received performances, would end the Nebraska touring in 2005. An April 7 news story put it bluntly: "After 29 years of taking theater on the road across Nebraska, the Nebraska Theatre Caravan will tour the state no more."

Artistic director Beck called the board decision "extremely difficult" and one not made quickly. "It's the culmination of many years of effort to make a program we love work." The words were convincing, coming from a former Caravan player. The time had come, he explained, to refocus on the Omaha program. Tour manager Lara Marsh stayed on to arrange the two surviving *Carol* tours.

The scope of the Caravan loss couldn't be avoided by anyone reading a summary in the Prompter:
- toured 81 productions in more than 160 Nebraska communities and 446 other cities in 49 states and four Canadian cities.
- rented 48,420 hotel rooms and produced 64 *Carol* tours.
- taught 3,756 workshops and employed 2,750 company members and staff.

DeGeorge, Buller-Kirke in *Sugar Babies*.

Layoffs hadn't been avoided during a second round of "belt-tightening" in 2003. Four staff members had lost jobs the year before, and then 10 more were laid off, including scenic designer Keith Hart and the senior costume designer, Joe Miloni. His artistry was not an issue, but years earlier Miloni had left supervision of the costume department to Georgiann Regan, so she remained as supervisor and designer. The retirement of associate director and choreographer Joanne Cady left scenic designer Jim Othuse the only remaining member of Charles Jones's original creative team. Roxanne Nielsen had already taken the lead in choreography when health caused Cady's absence, and she joined in saying farewell to the woman once described by Jones as "a nice housewife from Council Bluffs" who'd danced with the Rockettes.

Show Goes On After 9/11, *I Love You* Proves Perfect

Performers and playgoers were shaken by the events of Sept. 11, 2001. Had it happened at midweek, the enormity of terrorists hijacking planes and crashing them into the Twin Towers and the Pentagon, performances would have been delayed. But by Wednesday for *Sugar Babies* and Thursday for *Ancestral Voices,* the show went on.

Sugar Babies had opened in August, well before the attacks. So it was easier then to applaud "a lollapalooza of a burlesque musical with … plenty of energy and humor." Award-winning Frank DeGeorge was back as the top banana he first played in 1988. Dawn Buller-Kirke "dominates every scene she is in with her amazing energy."

Dual casts of *Ancestral Voices* included the final Playhouse appearance of Norm Filbert, the Chanticleer founder. The family play by A.R. Gurney of *Love Letters* fame gave director Collins the opportunity to work with Filbert and Tom Wees as the grandfather, plus Alexandra Hunt and Lois Nemec as the grandmother. The misfortune of opening the weekend after the 9/11 horror meant fewer saw the nostalgic drama about a son coping with the elderly couple's breakup.

The rest of the season ranged from risky to sure things, from average audiences to near-record crowds. And it would be followed by a remarkably popular run of shows the next season. Nearly 10,000 saw a well-received *The Diary of Anne Frank* on the main stage, while *You Should Be So Lucky* in the Drew inspired this weekly newspaper headline: "I See Gay People/The Playhouse Takes a Risk with Charles Busch Farce."

Beck cast such comedic favorites as Stenger, Baker and Sindelar with Bernie Clark as the accidental victim of Stenger's gay electrologist. For such skeptics as the weekly reviewer, it was a breakthrough to schedule anything by Busch, better known for the likes of his *Vampire Lesbians of Sodom.* The daily's Delmont dubbed *Lucky* a "rip-roaring farce" and praised Beck for brilliant staging of "the wildest comic scenes."

The sure things included *A Christmas Carol,* still starring Boyd as Scrooge and still bringing more than 17,000 back to refresh their holiday spirit. And the spring musical *Carousel* lured over 13,000 to see the Playhouse "do what it does best," Delmont wrote, presenting a classic Rodgers and Hammerstein production. Michael Zaller as Billy Bigelow was paired with Julie Harper as his young wife. Dawn Buller-Kirke sang, "You'll Never Walk Alone."

In between *Carol* and *Carousel,* the main stage featured the familiar *The Man Who Came to Dinner* with Ramer in the title role and *Over the River and Through the Woods.* That folksy drama featured Eric Griffith as a young man with two doting pairs of grandparents (Kay Clark and Okley Gibbs, Melissa Jarecke and Jack Moskovitz, a fifty-year veteran of the Playhouse stage). Griffith won a Peckham acting award after surviving perhaps the worst on-stage accident in the theater's history. Entering a second or two late, he ran into the sharp corner of a free-hanging portrait and suffered a bloody wound requiring stitches. As he received first aid, guest director Susan Clement-Toberer advised the audience that she might have to take his place.

Sound designer John Gibilisco called Griffith's cut "gruesome," and the scene "tension-packed." Backstage, Griffith coaxed the director, "Let me go back in, coach," and his bandaged return prompted thunderous applause. The crowd roared at his first line, "Sorry I'm late. I had a special session with my psychia—er, my head doctor." Many assumed it was an ad lib, but the script supplied his timely line.

The *Over the River* author, Joe DiPietro, soon brought a bigger hit to the Drew stage. His musical *I Love You, You're Perfect, Now Change* neared the *Rocky Horror* attendance record and then came back for an encore a year later. The episodic take on courtship, sex, marriage and parenthood featured two couples, Michael Zaller and Jane Noseworthy, and a pairing of Angela Jenson and Christopher Stephens. Delmont described it as "the best valentine show imaginable," and another review was headlined, " 'I Love You' proves perfect, needs no changes." All but Noseworthy, later a Miss Nebraska pageant winner, had performed with the Caravan.

Buddy Sets Sales Record, *Wonderettes* Sells All Seats: 2002–2003

Buddy, the story of rocker Buddy Holly (and "the night the music died" when an Iowa plane crash took Holly, Richie Valens and the Big Bopper), set a Playhouse record for single-ticket sales of $210,670. It was a record with an asterisk because *A Christmas Carol* regularly netted more.

Rave reviews and word of mouth about the title performance of Billy McGuigan, the son of an Offutt airman, and co-stars not only made it a sellout, but led to a popular follow-up revue. McGuigan and his band wound up a holiday run of *Rave On* on New Year's Eve in subsequent seasons. Later, with two younger brothers, he'd do a popular Beatles tribute to their late father.

A Public Pulse letter captured the original excitement when a woman wrote that she'd enjoyed many Playhouse shows, but "I had never seen a production that moved the audience so much that people were dancing in the aisles." Delmont wrote, "Never in my 14

Billy McGuigan as Buddy.

years of reviewing had I seen on audience as hyped up as this one." And that came after a half-hour delay and evacuation below for a tornado warning. Director Beck knew he'd found some stage magic when he joined music director Boggess months before at Dub's Pub in Benson. They heard McGuigan, Boggess recalled, and Carl said, "He's it. He's the guy we want."

Another sellout plus three added shows rocked the Drew stage with *The Marvelous Wonderettes*. Attendance fell short of earlier hits only because of reduced seating to meet staging demands for rock 'n' roll nostalgia. All four "Wonderettes"—Buller-Kirke, Ginny Hermann, Kathy Tyree and Tiffany White-Welchen—shared Peckham awards for best actress in a musical.

Game Show, starring Rob Baker as the title host, gave the audience a chance to compete and win prizes. The Drew season had started with popular treatment of *The Elephant Man*, which won honors for Daniel Dorner who "acted" the deformity of the title character without special makeup or costuming. Its historical footnote: the first breasts bared by a woman sympathetic to the deformed man. The main stage closed with *The Sound of Music* and Emily Griebel as Maria.

The impact of *Buddy* and the season's other revenue successes led to a report headlined, "Omaha Playhouse a hit with audiences, not donors." Once again a drop in giving was noted, but this time the good news involved an all-time record of $807,000 in single-ticket sales, a lasting trend that balanced lower season ticket sales. That meant the Playhouse would finish in the black after dealing with conditions that led to staff cuts. Nonmusicals on the main stage were led by the comedy classic *Arsenic and Old Lace* and the return of *No Sex Please, We're British*. *Arsenic* brought a debut award for Cliff Radcliff as the Teddy Roosevelt character.

But Neil Simon's *Broadway Bound* captured more postseason honors for Andrew Neary as Eugene, Stacie Lamb as his mother and Frank DeGeorge as the grandfather. Reviewers agreed, but also credited Don Noel as the father with a performance "among the best of the season."

Once more the season stretched into summer as *More Fun Than Bowling* drew a small house, but two additions to the schedule—*Sing-Along Sound of Music* and the return of *I Love You, You're Perfect, Now Change*—proved profitable. The sing-along not only had the audience joining in the familiar songs, but some came in Tyrolean attire.

That capital fund drive had brought changes. If renovated restrooms were the most functional, the new photo wall could be seen even by passers-by on the street. An earlier display of black-and-white photos had deteriorated and been moved. Othuse and others prepared 110 images for Renze Display, and the Bekins Foundation financed the illuminated wall. Photos were backlit on glass-like panels.

From Henry Fonda and Dodie Brando to Charles Jones and Dick Boyd, the visual history shined brightly in the lobby. Fonda dressed as a London bobby seems to be admonishing 13-year-old Dorothy McGuire. The smiling trio, Jones, Cady and Othuse. Old favorites Peckham, Norton, Bailey, Jabenis and DeGeorge shared the wall with a mustachioed Susan Baer Collins and a straw-hatted Beck when the current directors were disguised for Shakespeare. For Jabenis, it displayed dramatic scenes starting with *Father of the Bride* in 1952, roles that led to her selection as the fourth recipient of the Dick Boyd award for a career that reached to *My Fair Lady* in 2000.

Zombie Prom Scores Hit, Flap Over *Allergist's Wife*: 2003–2004

The excitement over the Oscar-winning film version of the Bob Fosse musical *Chicago* made it a natural to open the season. But a week after announcing that choice came word that its recent success led to making the rights unavailable.

Instead, *The Will Rogers Follies,* performed eight years before, would return. America was at war against terrorism, so marketing director Betsye Paragas reminded, "It's all-American, patriotic, uplifting. People have been begging us to do it again." So Earl Bates was back in the title role, and the Follies showgirls reprised a popular number,

"Our Favorite Son," with a seated chorus line flashing hand and leg action in show-stopping rhythm.

While season sales were only a little short of the year before, the overall attendance fell further from matching that banner year, just over 90,000 compared to 100,000. (The 1993-94 season topped attendance with nearly 125,000. That total included record crowds for a musical, *Joseph and the Amazing Technicolor Dream Coat* and a drama, *My Antonia*.) Adding to the exterior appeal of the Playhouse facility was the Drew Foundation plaza just north of the canopied entrance.

The surprise hit of the season was *Zombie Prom*. Delmont's review credited director Beck for "another home run" with "the happily demented 1950s comedy-musical." A new medium, the website Performance Omaha, described the audience leaping "to its feet" for "a thunderous round of applause" and reported that the same reaction occurred the night before. Opposite a cherub-faced Carrie Beth Stickrod as his prom date, Seth

Fox as teen zombie.

Fox played a rebellious teenager who returns as a zombie after his suicidal dive into nuclear waste.

Playgoers had an unusual opportunity to compare stellar performances earlier in the season when the Shelterbelt Theatre and the Playhouse both scheduled *Visiting Mr. Green*. Two of the community's most accomplished actors, Norm Filbert and Bill Hutson, played the title role, an elderly Jewish widower. For Filbert, it triumphantly ended a half century on stage. Death came a half year later as he directed *La Cage Aux Folles* for the Council Bluffs theater he cofounded.

Barb Ross provoked more response than she bargained for as a blunt grandmother in *The Tale of the Allergist's Wife*. On awards night, she accepted a Barbara Ford honor, but earlier her character's language and an implied ménage a trois stirred the most complaints of recent years. And they came as the Playhouse announced *Hair* with its nude scene as the next season's opener.

The only criticism that appeared in print reflected others that came in phone calls or letters. "The last thing we need to hear is a cussing, grandmotherly type spouting the 'F' word. You can hear that for free most anywhere." A cover story headlined "Hair and Hairier" in *The Reader* took the occasion to recall how such controversies had arisen from the earliest years of the Playhouse to present.

From Dodie Brando's roles in *Liliom* and *Anna Christie* in the 1920s to *The Moon Is Blue* in 1953 and *That Championship Season* in 1975, playgoers took offense at times. For artistic director Beck, the response to *Allergist's Wife* was a reminder that advance warning is vital in preparing the audience.

Cheers and Farewells in the 80th Season: 2004–2005

The Playhouse didn't act like an octogenarian. Not with a schedule that opened with *Hair* and closed with 195 little girls auditioning for *Annie*. When the season ended, after mourning major losses, Playhouse talent dominated TAG awards for shows, talent and direction. Death

Musical *Hair*, 2004.

came to Charles Jones and significant loss to one of his theatrical offspring, the Nebraska Theatre Caravan.

Also mourned were Joan Hennecke and Pam Carter, whose final performance in *Wonder of the World* took the featured actress award. Her sudden passing, caused by an aneurysm, was a shocking loss of a shining star, a triple Fonda-McGuire winner long seen as the community's outstanding comedienne. Mrs. Hennecke first appeared on a Playhouse stage in 1943 and served graciously in roles ranging from trustee and Studio Theatre chair to prompter and oft-honored actor. The theater community turned out for Carter and Hennecke funerals, and both services gave friends the opportunity to reminisce about great moments on and off stage, from Pam's first role to Joan's competition with the great Mary Peckham. The tributes to Jones recognized his singular contribution to the theater.

A 20-foot tie-dyed shirt covered the east side of the Playhouse in August and colorful tie-dyed billboards beckoned, "Join us for the Re-dawning of the Age of Aquarius." Nearly 12,000 accepted the invitation and were greeted by cast members in hippy garb assembled by costume designer Regan. Director Beck had noted that "the curiosity factor" focused on the nude scene, but "if people come waiting and watching" for nudity, "it will be a disappointment to them." He promised a visual treat and reviews applauded the "spectacle" rather than a thin script.

Not for Nightingales, an early, seldom-seen Tennessee Williams drama, started the Drew season with a brutal story of prison life in the 1930s. "Ensemble theater doesn't get much better than this," began a review that said many actors richly deserved accolades but Hutson dominated as a prison warden. "Not easy to watch," it drew the second smallest audience in the twenty-year Drew history.

The season lightened up with *Over the Tavern* on the main stage and *Wonder of the World* in the Drew. Middle-school student David Kalis played Rudy, an inquisitive Polish-Catholic schoolboy who lived above his father's tavern. Under the direction of Judith K. Hart, he stole the show that was later named as the season's best comedy.

Niagara Falls, as seen through an Othuse-created Viewmaster, was the *Wonder of the World* where "laughter poured all night long," noted a review. "Everybody in the show is pretty wigged out," Fischbach wrote, and, "Pam Carter brings down the house in six outrageous character roles." Jane Noseworthy, the main zany, is shocked by hubby's perversity, so sets forth with a to-do list topped by "finding a sidekick."

A Christmas Carol drew nearly 16,000 for what would be the penultimate performance by Dick Boyd, and *Spitfire Grill* became the final January visit by the Nebraska Theatre Caravan. Word came in April that the touring would end, except for two *Carol* companies. "We will continue to be leaner and meaner and tighten our budgets" as other arts groups are doing, Beck said.

Productions that dominated the season's awards ran on the two stages in March. Lois Nemec swept honors for *A Trip to Bountiful*, which went dark one night for Pam Carter's memorial service. Jim McKain matched her success as a Dublin bus conductor in *A Man of No Importance*, also a triumph for Moira Mangiameli as his sister.

Dirty Blonde allowed Theresa Sindelar as Mae West to invite Rob Baker, "Why doncha come up and see me some time?"

Auditions for *Annie*, making its Playhouse debut found the place swarming with 195 little girls eager to be orphans. Director Collins, aided by Boggess and choreographer Nielsen, picked nine, from Caroline Iliff for the title role to Charlotte Hedican, 8, plus two dogs to share the role of Sandy. The girls "are so cute," said Judy Radcliff as the bossy and boozy Hannigan, "it's hard to be mean to them." Some 13,600 saw award-winning performances by Iliff, Radcliff, Kenny Glenn as Daddy Warbucks, Seth Fox as Rooster and Dennis Collins as FDR.

It showcased the scenic artistry of Mike Bristol and the work of Othuse, who celebrated his thirty-first year as scenic designer. The lobby exhibited scale models of sets he'd designed.

The Show Goes On after Farewell for Scrooge: 2005–2006

The season soon spoke volumes about the state of the Playhouse. Did declining memberships mean lower turnouts for productions? Not when shows such as *Swing* and *The Graduate* were followed by a record-breaking thirtieth run of *A Christmas Carol*. The season would close with Kevyn Morrow, who'd performed in the post-tornado *Godspell*, returning to star in the musical *Ragtime*, as he did in London.

It was nonstop song and dance, from Boggess banging the keyboard on "It Don't Mean a Thing If It Ain't Got That Swing," to what a review called "the no holds barred finale of 'Sing, Sing, Sing.' Directed by Roxanne Nielsen, and dominated by the music of Count Basie, Duke Ellington and Benny Goodman, *Swing* brought in over $206,000, second only to the income generated by another night of musical nostalgia, *Buddy*, taking advantage of the appeal of vintage music. "If there's a trend," Carl Beck observed, "look for small shows that are extremely successful that can be remounted in the summer."

In the Drew, a headline said, "'The Graduate' captures sexiness, humor of '67 film." Connie Lee, who wowed earlier as a dance teacher in *Stepping Out*, didn't disrobe, like Broadway's Kathleen Turner, but her Mrs. Robinson was "a revelation," Fischbach wrote, "and the play exudes sexiness just the same, while steadily building a wave of humor."

Other offerings were soon overshadowed by all that led up to *Carol*. It was announced in August that Dick Boyd, 83, had decided to make his thirtieth year as Ebenezer Scrooge the final one. The weeks before his farewell were a time for reflection. A year that began with the passing of Charles Jones, who adapted the Dickens story and chose so well its star, would end with eyes turned toward his creation and the actor at the heart of its appeal.

Boyd was featured on the network news as ABC's Person of the Week, and *USA Today* devoted a full page and five photos to "Beloved Scrooge takes his final bow." The story began with a question: "Who knew there would come a time when thousands would stand in

Connie Lee as sultry Mrs. Robinson.

Boyd's Last Scrooge.

line to give Scrooge a hug?" The 443,000 who saw him redeemed 818 times knew.

Opening night was named Dick Boyd Day by Mayor Mike Fahey and Governor Dave Heineman made him an Admiral in the mythical Nebraska Navy. Two days later, another candidate for governor, former Cornhusker football coach and then Congressman Tom Osborne, gave Boyd a signed football.

And so it went up to the last performance on December 22 when artistic director Beck took the stage. He drew attention to others who'd shared in the love and longevity of *A Christmas Carol*. Bob Snipp, whose deep voice and long white beard, were absent only in the first season, would retire as the Ghost of Christmas Present after twenty-nine years. In the orchestra, Jan Bogardus had been playing English horn for twenty-eight years. Beck spoke of the *Carol* family, of the bonding among those who'd shared the stage with Boyd, and others present in the audience.

Members of the Charles Jones family, including his wife, Eleanor, looked on in what some called the house that Jones built. Miriam Boyd would soon appear once more on stage with her husband. Laine Swanger, 2, handed her great-grandpa a rose during the closing ovation. As reported in the next morning's paper, "Dry-eyed, he waved the crowd silent after two solid minutes and had a final word. Turning to his cast: 'You were wonderful, and I love you all.'"

Then Boyd stood in line until the last well-wisher gave a hug or shook his hand. He'd join trustees for a reception, then head home to Council Bluffs in the wee hours of the morning. That didn't stop the octogenarian from making his annual post-run appointment with his barber. And it didn't end three decades of memories that began with his improbable casting at age 53 and included such moments as Tiny Tim throwing up on Scrooge and his white nightshirt showing through his open zipper. Offered keepsakes, he took his coin purse, top hat and long red scarf. He left behind the affection of a community and a Playhouse stronger for his contributions.

Kevyn Morrow as Coalhouse Walker in *Ragtime*.

Boyd, right, with the two touring Scrooges, Matt Kamprath above, Cork Ramer below.

The season ended with a performance of the musical *Ragtime* with Kevyn Morrow, an ex-Omahan who'd started with the Caravan, returning to play Coalhouse Walker, the role that won him an Olivier nomination in London. At intermission and after the final standing ovation, playgoers buzzed with exclamation points. They couldn't wait to tell friends that the Playhouse was still "the place to be."

CHAPTER

10

Living the Legacy and Looking Ahead, 2006–2014

New Scrooge, Redesigned *Carol*: 2006–2007

Talk about tough acts to follow: the celebration of Dick Boyd's three decades as Ebenezer Scrooge and a prize-winning production of the musical *Ragtime*. The season had no more daunting task than continuing the success of *A Christmas Carol* in the absence of a beloved Scrooge. But before that bridge could be crossed, an opening musical lured its audience with such teasing headlines as "Nudity Plan Kept Under Wraps."

Fans of *The Full Monty* film knew the title referred to the male anatomy sans fig leaf, so the daily asked, "Will these average Joes have the guts to take it all off?" Earlier, a touring company at the Orpheum handled the climactic strip by blinding the crowd with glaring spotlights behind the six male strippers, and that's how the Playhouse spared viewers too intimate a view.

Designer Jim Othuse recalls that the woman responsible for the super-bright lights worried that she'd miss her cue and leave the men exposed. Director Beck and choreographer Neilsen tackled transforming nontrained dancers from awkward to confident, but it was up to costume designer Georgiann Regan to make sure they shed outfits with ease. Seth Fox and Cameron Van Cleave, as his bulky buddy, led the steelworkers turned Chippendales.

The Talented Mr. Ripley in the Drew and *King o' the Moon* on the main stage preceded arrival of a redesigned *Carol*. Susan Collins directed Brandon Rohe as the title's twisted con man, hired by a dying mother (Connie Lee) to find her missing son. *King* brought back the Polish-Catholic Pazinski family in a sequel to *Over the Tavern*. Rudy, the focus of the earlier play, is no longer a boy but a seminarian (Stephen Shelton) who protests the Vietnam War—troubling his brother (Andrew McGreevy), a tough Marine.

Anyone bah-humbugging the annual Christmas classic could go to the Drew where once more the Playhouse boldly spoofed its most valuable tradition. Theresa Sindelar took the title role in *Mrs. Bob Cratchit's Wild Christmas Binge*. She tells Tiny Tim (Bailey Newman) to shut up and quit being a martyr. Ghosts and the angel from *It's a Wonderful Life* try to prevent her drunken plunge in the Thames. Scrooge lusts after her, but nothing bothers a mindlessly cheery Bob (Tom Neumann).

When the annual production of *A Christmas Carol* neared, Boyd's absence inspired references to "big shoes to fill." No auditions were needed to cast a new Scrooge. Equity actor Jerry Longe got the role. "He's one of the premier character actors in Omaha," director Beck said. "We jumped at the chance to get him." Like Beck and others, Longe came to Omaha with the Playhouse's own Nebraska Theatre Caravan and toured as Bob Cratchit and Marley's Ghost. He'd done everything from comedy leads at the Playhouse to heavy roles at the Blue Barn, from network cartoon voice work to the Fruit of the Loom apple singing with Warren Buffett at Berkshire-Hathaway annual meetings.

At 52, near Boyd's age when he began in the 1970s, Jerry's virgin Scrooge had him marveling over Boyd's endurance at age 83. With his predecessor in the second row, an exhausted Longe heard applause from an opening night audience and thought "a 30-year run would be terrific."

November 2006 brought more than a new Scrooge to cheer. It saw the lobby dedication of a bust of Charles Jones, sculpted by James T. Olsen and seasonally wrapped in a red scarf. And a complete redesign of his creation kept the crowd from focusing only on Scrooge comparisons. White-bearded Bob Snipp, retired as the Ghost of Christmas Present, was replaced by longtime Fezziwig Mike Farrell who suddenly grew taller rather than perching atop the canopied bed. That spared a harnessed Scrooge flying to the bed-top.

Fiber optics made a black sky twinkle with stars and conjured a new Ghost of Christmas to Come instead of the old robed giant pointing to the grave. Marley's ghost came roaring out of a split fireplace wall instead of rising through the floor, and he was joined now by raggedy little minions. And, as the review reminded, it didn't just snow as usual on the stage, "It snowed on

Longe as new Scrooge.

the entire audience." At least flakes fell on the front rows. Amidst all those changes, young Spencer Newman completed his record four-year run as Tiny Tim. And it still scored about $360,000.

The holidays also brought the first of what became annual offerings from Billy McGuigan, who had wowed crowds in 2002 by starring in the musical *Buddy.* He reprised those Buddy Holly songs and others in *Rave On! A Tribute to the Day the Music Died,* performed from early December to New Year's Eve in the Drew.

Billy, with his brothers Ryan and Matthew, returned in July with *Yesterday and Today,* billed as "A Concert Celebration of Beatles Music." It sold out and was extended into August. After one more holiday run for *Rave On!* they performed the Beatles songbook each December, charming audiences that requested the likes of "Yesterday" or "Yellow Submarine" by describing how they became personal favorites.

Three musicals, a comedy classic, a tribute to President Harry Truman, and a dysfunctional family with a rapidly aging daughter made up the 2007 half of the season. The latter show, *Kimberly Akimbo* in the Drew, was headlined "funny and foul" in the daily. It featured Melissa Jarecke as a 16-year-old looking sixtyish and afflicted with dysfunctional parents. Her hugely pregnant mother boozes and pops pills. Don't worry, she promises, she did the same with Kimberly "and she turned out all right."

The classic *You Can't Take It With You,* first staged at the Playhouse in 1942, gave Susie Collins the chance to direct husband, Dennis, to an award-winning role as the grandpa who dropped out of the rat race and won't pay taxes. And he's one of the saner members of the Sycamore family.

History with humor took the main stage when Matt Kamprath starred as the president from Missouri in *Give 'Em Hell Harry.* Guest director Hughston Walkinshaw, a Blue Barn Theatre founder, researched it in Truman's town of Independence. Footage of the atomic bomb, the victory over Tom Dewey, and the Korean War firing of General MacArthur added authenticity to a script narrated by Derrick Crawford as Truman's butler. When the Nebraska legislature debated a bill exempting performing arts materials from taxes, Kamprath appeared as Truman to testify.

Those three musicals ranged from country legend Patsy Cline to all-time family favorite *Peter Pan* and an offering introduced by advising, "Of course you're not supposed to like the title." It's part, the ad continued, "of the good-natured and remarkably successful joke that is *Urinetown*," a city plagued by drought and a public rebellion against its pay-toilet monopoly. Press played with the people's "pee free" protests.

Carl Beck had radio's Dave Wingert as a nasty corporate boss, Theresa Sindelar as Penelope Pennywise who runs Public Urinal No. 9, and Tom Shomaker as a police officer-narrator.

Erika Hall starred as the country singer in *Always, Patsy Cline,* with Judy Radcliff as her real-life fan Louise. Their award-winning performances and those twenty-seven songs from "Crazy" and "Sweet Dreams" to "True Love" were popular enough to command a summer remounting of the musical two years later.

The season ended with Christina Rohling as the crowing

Erika Hall as Patsy.

Christina Rohling as *Peter Pan*.

and flying *Peter Pan*. As Christina Belford, whose father Tom became a theater trustee, she was a teenage star then and now sang, "I Won't Grow Up." The Playhouse hired Flying by Foy to help her soar with their apparatus used first by Mary Martin on Broadway and later by Sandy Duncan and Cathy Rigby. Director Collins also cast Bill Hutson as Captain Hook and newcomer Amy Schweid as an agile Tiger Lily.

Reach Out with *Crowns*, Musical After Labor Day: 2007–2008

Playhouse seasons, since the new theater opened in 1959, began with a big musical, and that posed a few problems. Huge productions with large casts got rolling in July to open in late August, squeezing vacation times for staff and volunteers. Summer runs in recent years added to logistical burdens. And playgoers complained that main stage shows started before they'd returned from summer travel. So why not start with a smaller show in the Drew?

The choice of *Crowns* also helped with the goal of greater outreach to less-served audiences. Director Collins hired guest artists to help her bring authenticity to a musical drama drawn from a book subtitled, "Portraits of Black Women in Church Hats." She added gospel pianist/vocalist Janet Ashley as musical director with Sondra McSwain, a veteran of the Center Stage black theater, and her two dancing daughters, Mia and Michelle, as choreographers.

"Millinery designed by Lynne Ridge" was a credit not usually found in the show's Prompter. Her creations included "The Queen Mother hat with attitude" for Lanette Moore. A young woman's grandmother takes her to church to meet "the hat queens," who teach her about "faith, hat-wearing, love and life." One writer dubbed it "a hand-clapping, foot-stomping, dancing-in-your-chair celebration of gospel music" that inspired more than one "Amen!"

Collins called the change "sort of an experiment" that allowed holding the fall musical until after the Labor Day weekend. That meant opening *Thoroughly Modern Millie* in mid-September and treating Omaha to Jill Anderson, the Equity pro who made any role memorable. Her Millie heads from Kansas to New York, planning to marry wealth, but she winds up with Jimmy, played by Seth Fox, another pro. A hotel proprietor (Kim Jubenville) livens the action by luring girls into white slavery with the aid of two hilarious Chinamen played by the director's son, Ben Beck, and Drew Vamosi. For blonde innocence, there's Angela Jenson-Frey and for a show-stopping song, Tiffany White.

The musical was now the only main stage show before *Carol*, leaving a single play, *Matt and Ben*, in the Drew before McGuigan's return. The title characters, Damon and Affleck, won fame and an Oscar with their script for *Good Will Hunting*. Playwrights Mindy Kaling and Brenda Withers decided that the script for *Matt and Ben* must have dropped intact from the ceiling as the boys failed to adapt J.D. Salinger's *Catcher in the Rye*. Two women, Sindelar and Shannon Jackson, as Ben and Matt, skewer male bonding with glee.

The major changes in *A Christmas Carol* were completed the previous season, but a Prompter credit for "Flying by Foy" wasn't just a leftover from its work on *Peter Pan*. Now Julie Huff, who'd played the grown-up Wendy in that musical, would enter Scrooge's bedroom by flying for the first time in her fourteen years as the Ghost of Christmas Past.

While the Playhouse remained a community theater committed to volunteers, paying Jill Anderson to star in *Thoroughly Modern Millie* was followed in 2008 by hiring Seth Fox as Bobby in Sondheim's *Company* as well as Brigit players Scott Kurz and Amy Kunz, leads for Arthur Miller's *The Crucible*.

The quality of the volunteer actors showed up as usual in January with award-winning performances by Connie Lee and Ben Birkholtz in *Same Time, Next Year*, playing the couple having a twenty-five-year affair confined to a brief annual rendezvous. Hutson won his record fifth Fonda award for *Shakespeare in Hollywood*, fantasizing his Oberon in twentieth-century movietown.

If anyone wondered why big Greg Ryerson was hired to play the Frenchman in the spring musical *South Pacific*, they could check what happened when he sang the role at the Playhouse thirty years before: record attendance of nearly 20,000 and the first show other than *A Christmas Carol*

Theresa Sindelar, Bernie Clark in *Shakespeare in Hollywood*.

to take in over $100,000 beyond season subscriptions. Then the blonde basso, who also played the Ghost of Christmas Present in the first *Carol*, inspired sighs when he sang "Some Enchanted Evening."

This time a review upped that to "swooning." His co-star, Angela Jenson-Frey was nurse Nellie Forbush, with Judy Radcliff as Bloody Mary and Jim McKain as Luther Billis.

Moving Forward after Resignation Storm: 2008–2009

The experiment continued with *Intimate Apparel* opening in August and the musical *Cocoanuts* starting in September. *Apparel* again reached out to a diverse community in a nation that elected Barack Obama president. This time the drama dominated by an African-American cast featured Denise Chapman as a 1905 seamstress, sewing intimate garments for wealthy white women and prostitutes. "Everyone in this play," director Susie Collins, emphasized, "is a victim of their times."

Jim and Angela as Luther and Nellie.

It could be argued before the season was over that the Playhouse briefly fell victim to the economic times of 2008. All went well enough early on, greeting playgoers with "Welcome to the House That We All Built," an expansion of the familiar "house that Charles (Jones) built."

The Groucho Marx musical *Cocoanuts* on the main stage was director Beck's adaptation of the George Kaufman script with music by Irving Berlin. It starred Rob Baker as the Groucho character. Then *Stones in the Pocket* about Irishmen involved in a Hollywood movie being filmed in Ireland ran in the Drew with some audience confusion over Nils Haaland and Nick Zadina playing all fifteen characters.

But the year's financial troubles were reflected when Bob Fischbach's *Christmas Carol* review in the daily began, "Stock market. Bah. Economic recession. Humbug." He invited readers to escape worrisome headlines and be transported by the Dickens classic. Times may have been changing, but Jerry Longe was back as Scrooge, promising to play the role for thirty years under two conditions, "If I'm alive and they'll let me." Joseph O'Connor II was Young Scrooge, a role that didn't fully reveal the voice that would wow audiences later when he'd play Marius in *Les Misérables*.

Veteran actor Doug Blackburn, was the new Marley, and he'd play a minor part in the tempest to come. Then a major role would be played by Mark Laughlin, president of the trustees, who'd performed in *Carol* as a youngster and now saw his son Graham as one of the *Carol* schoolboys.

Before the storm, 2009 began unremarkably with the Noel Coward favorite *Blithe Spirit,* returning after a quarter-century absence from the Playhouse, and continued serenely with *Glorious*, a period comedy starring Diane L. Jones as a caterwauling vocalist blissfully unaware of her shortcomings. In between, Beck directed, *Bat Boy—The Musical,* the tabloid sendup. It became the surprise hit of the season, thanks especially to Tim Abou-Nasr, hanging batlike in the title role.

Suddenly, on April 10, seven days before the opening of the play *Moonlight and Magnolias,* a front-page headline warned that the show might not go on after actors "quit over a cost-cutting move targeting the artistic director." That threat came to pass. For the first time in Playhouse history, a show was canceled.

No Jeff Taxman as David Selznick or Dave Wingert as Ben Hecht in the making of *Gone with the Wind*. Eventually, the apt title for the conflict changed from *The Tempest* to *All's Well That Ends Well*. But before calm was restored, dire prophecy filled the air. Eleanor Jones, widow of Charles, dramatically despaired "the end of the Playhouse." What actually occurred wasn't completely clear at first, given variations in the early news reports.

Budget problems due to the troubled economy had earlier led to voluntary pay cuts for executive director Schmad, artistic director Beck and other top staff. But now the board's executive committee, conscious that no other community theater paid two full-time directors, authorized Schmad and board president Laughlin to seek Beck's resignation. He reportedly declined a generous financial offer to remain as director on a contract basis. His title was offered to his ex-wife, associate director Collins. She turned it down while agreeing to direct two more shows, the spring musical *Gypsy* and the summer remount of *Always, Patsy Cline,* before also resigning.

Soon Susan Clement-Toberer, guest director for the season's final Drew play, *12 Angry Men,* said she wouldn't continue directing in the future, and Jerry Longe vowed not to return as Scrooge. Beck, artistic director since 1997, said his decision to leave was influenced by a shift in power to the management side depriving the artistic side of a voice in decisions.

Laughlin pointed out in a radio interview that no other theater paid two full-time directors. His critics countered that no other theater was as large as the Playhouse, noting especially the challenge annually of preparing three productions of *A Christmas Carol,* the show generating 20 percent of the theater's revenue. Laughlin praised Beck as a director and assured critics that the board wanted him to continue, but added that hard choices were necessary "to keep the Playhouse healthy long into the future."

Then came the forum in the main stage auditorium, packed heavily by actors supporting the two directors who had resigned the week before. Before the floor opened to comments, the tension that had been building for days was lifted when board president Laughlin and administrator Schmad were joined on stage by Beck and Collins. Some still spoke in harsh terms, demanding the resignations of Laughlin and Schmad. Others were more conciliatory.

But the worst fears faded when the crowd heard that the four had been talking at length to resolve differences and would soon talk again. Collins said, "We've already aired a lot of dirty laundry … I'm elated we're here talking today." Progress seemed assured when Beck, who had missed the last staff meeting, promised, "I expect to be at many, many more." And Schmad, praised as a hard worker by board member Tom Belford, urged, "You've got to believe me when I say I'm trying to do my darnedest to do what's best for the Playhouse and keep these doors open."

So, call it a storm or just a dust-up, the forum ended with optimism and Laughlin's call to move forward without dwelling on past differences. Later, the same four appeared together at a press conference emphasizing that Beck and Collins had withdrawn their resignations and job titles were being put aside for now to aid in the ongoing dialogue about decision-making. The crowd at the forum and the outpouring of other responses had reminded of how much the community treasured its Playhouse.

Dave Kirkwood, who would succeed Laughlin as board president, sat next to a staff member who was crying. "And it hit me when I saw her and I knew this would turn out all right. It was the passion for the Playhouse. She felt it, everyone did."

Schmad admitted, "It's a painful way to unite people." He wound up as the only person to report to the board. Collins felt both sides gained more respect for the other side—artists for the administrators, the business side for the artists. Beck vividly remembered the blunt words of Jeff Jones, saying in the voice of his father, Charles: "Fix it."

The next Prompter ran "A note to our patrons," signed by Schmad, Beck and Collins, all sans titles, including Schmad's relatively new one of president. Yes, the past weeks were stressful, they agreed, but the episode underlined that the theater "truly does hold a special place in peoples' hearts." And the people were called on for financial support, both by buying season tickets and joining the donors that supply about a fourth of annual income.

Tickets for *Moonlight and Magnolias* were honored for its replacement, Billy McGuigan's *Rock Legends* musical revue, or the closing musical, *Gypsy*.

New Hawks Auditorium: 2009–2010

The "save the Playhouse" fervor of those stormy days in April made an impact in September. The season opened solidly with nearly 5,500 revisiting *The Quilters*, the pioneer saga so popular in its earlier appearances. Both it and the musical that followed required extended runs.

The preview performance of the fall musical, Andrew Lloyd Webber's *Joseph and the Amazing Technicolor Dream Coat*, revealed a renovated main auditorium and other good news. Thanks to an unspecified gift from Howard and Rhonda Hawks, the space bearing their names featured new seating with more leg room, new aisle carpeting over a new floor of Brazilian mahogany and other improvements.

Hawks, president of Tenaska, an energy company, added an endowment donation to the couple's auditorium gift. Schmad said a $3.1 million influx would bring the endowment near $5 million with more millions needed to maintain the present level and permit future improvements. More leg room meant fewer seats, dropping capacity from 601 to 562. The spring musical, a revival of *Fiddler on the Roof*, did better than *Joseph* with Mark Thornburg as Tevye who ponders "If I Were a Rich Man," while conversing with God. Even potential problems turned positive: Before opening as the lead mother in *Quilters*, Kim Jubenville needed emergency surgery, but Judy Radcliff

Thornburg as Tevye.

Radcliff in *Quilters*.

filled in smoothly after only four days of rehearsal. The Arthur Miller classic *Death of a Salesman* won honors for Lois Nemec, Bernie Clark and Anthony Clark-Kaczmarek as the Lohmans and son Biff.

Add 21 & Over Alternative, Resident Director: 2010–2011

Again, the Playhouse imported a one-man show, *Defending the Caveman,* to fill the summer gap between seasons, then opened in the fall season with its first one-woman show, *The Lady with All the Answers.*

Progress led by the renovated auditorium the previous September continued. The recent storm argued that directing for the nation's largest community theater wasn't a one-man or one-woman show, and now a part-time resident director was added to the mix. Amy Lane, adjunct professor at the University of Nebraska–Omaha, had directed *Almost, Maine* in the Drew and next directed *A Thousand Clowns* on the main stage in October. She'd also take charge of the new

21 & Over series, promoted as "21st Century Plays for a 21st Century Audience…contemporary works for a mature audience."

Lane, who'd attended Creighton University, earned an MFA in Memphis and a Ph.D. in Detroit. She credited artistic director Beck with the idea for "alternative programming," reaching out to new playgoers, "especially younger audiences." The free staged readings ran for only a single Monday performance, but three proved worthy of a longer look. The opener, *boom*, and the final show, *August: Osage County*, would both be added to the theater's 2012 season, and *In the Next Room, or the Vibrator Play* was produced by the Blue Barn Theatre. All three contained either language or situations that might offend more traditional playgoers, and all three won raves with their one-night stands.

In short, the new series quickly pumped new life into a program sometimes accused of sticking with the tried and true. The following June, the last in the eight-show series, the award-winning *Osage County*, won such a response that it was moved from the Drew to the larger auditorium. Even when the three-hour play was interrupted to send the crowd below for a tornado warning, many felt the reading by Lane's all-star cast headed by Collins topped the season's best full productions.

Other changes mixed gains and losses. Two of Omaha's most-honored performers, Matt Kamprath and Phyllis Doughman, fell victim to cancer, and Eleanor Jones passed away. She had arrived in Omaha when her husband, Charles, took the helm of the Playhouse in 1974 and served not only at his side but as an accomplished director. A staff change saw Betsye Paragas leave her post as director of marketing, replaced by Katie Wortmann (later Broman), Betsye's former intern.

The fall musical *Footloose*, chosen for its popularity in a poll of playgoers, featured teenagers who rebelled against a preacher's ban on dancing. As usual, *A Christmas Carol* brought both the biggest audience and the most income. It also said farewell to its stage manager for twenty-four years, Steve Priesman. He reminisced about couples who met during the performances and eventually got married,

Hutson as Morrie.

including his son Brian and his daughter-in-law.

More familiar shows, *The Odd Couple, Nunsense, Steel Magnolias* and *Guys and Dolls,* shared the 2011 schedule with two new ones, *The 25th Annual Putnam County Spelling Bee* and *Tuesdays with Morrie.* The latter saw veteran actor Bill Hutson win a record sixth Fonda as the dying Morrie with Chris Shonka as writer Mitch Albom. Awards also went to Connie Lee, Charleen Willoughby and Jennifer McGill as beauty shop friends in *Magnolias,* as well as Jennifer Tritz and Eric Micks in *Bee,* the season's biggest draw in the Drew. Kirsten Kluver's Adelaide in *Guys and Dolls* swept honors that she'd soon repeat for *Chicago.*

Fantasticks Promises More Touring for Caravan: 2011–2012

That August experiment was now a well-established pattern: A summer import to fill the "down time," followed by a play, this time *Becky's New Car,* opening the Drew, and the fall musical, a revival of *Chicago* in September.

Schmad explained the importance of a large, well-staffed facility being busy, renting spaces, holding classes, and running the apprentice program. Denise Chapman replaced Melanie Walters as direction of education/outreach as both also played leads on the two stages. Denise was the homesteader in all-black Nicodemus, Kansas, in *Flyin' West* while Melanie was Velma to Kluver's Roxie in *Chicago*. That outreach to the minority community came when the John Beasley Theatre had become inactive due to a heavier acting schedule for its namesake.

While other shows shared critical acclaim, *Hairspray* won the most honors, especially for Jim McKain as the larger-than-life mother of the girl who integrates a take-off on Dick Clark's American Bandstand show.

Altar Boyz was the only other new show among familiar favorites: the sentimental *On Golden Pond*; the popular door-slamming, bed-hopping *Lend Me a Tenor*; the powerful *Streetcar Named Desire*; and the world's longest-running musical, *The Fantasticks*.

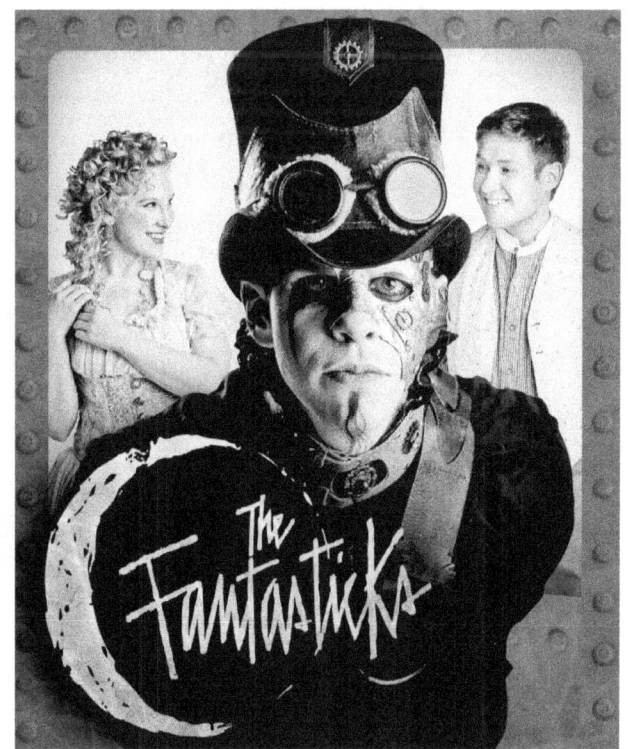

Steampunk style for *Fantasticks*.

Pond brought Dennis Collins a Fonda-McGuire in the role played by Henry Fonda on screen. *Tenor* won recognition for lead actor Anthony Clark-Kaczmarek and director Beck among others, and *The Fantasticks,* the season's best-attended show in the Drew, led to a revival of the Nebraska Theatre Caravan.

Carl Beck told Prompter readers, "We were looking for a fresh approach" to the traditional production, when the costume shop supervisor, Paula Clowers, "innocently uttered the words, 'Ever heard of steampunk?'" It was new to Beck who jumped at the chance for an edgy mix of Victorian-era steam machinery and '80s punk. A cast led by Seth Fox who sings "Try to Remember," plus husband and wife Rick and Jennifer Tritz as the Boy and Girl, scored with audiences and sparked plans to mount the show for touring.

Since conceived by Charles Jones in 1975, the Caravan had annually toured Nebraska and nearby states, but that ended in fall 2004, confining it to the two *Christmas Carol* companies. Staff and trustees had talked about returning to the road with the right marketable show.

The Fantasticks travels easily with only seven in the cast, and the steampunk treatment gave a new look to a proven show. When the tour was announced the following January, Caravan producing director Beau Bisson reported that bookings already assured a profit when it hit the road in 2014. Jennifer Tritz would encore her role as the company traveled first to Rapid City, S.D., on its way through twenty-eight states. It's not just the revenue, managing director Greg Scheer reminded, but the talent drawn to Omaha. He arrived with the Caravan long ago like Beck, Collins, Boggess, Longe and others.

The return to the road was especially encouraging to the Caravan's artistic coordinator, Lara Marsh, and even greater blessings were headed her way. She'd lived with cystic fibrosis and needed a double lung transplant. The theater community had shared in many fundraisers to support that need, and in 2013 she'd travel to Colorado to receive new lungs that allowed her to breathe more easily.

Directors Beck, Collins Reveal Two-Year Farewell: 2012–2013

Entering August, the big news of the season spread with a slogan, "Find Your Stage," promising "innovative programming" in the Drew for what president Schmad termed "our theatre adventuresome patrons."

It was a new twist on the never-ending struggle to find the right balance between the more traditional shows that pleased faithful subscribers and edgier shows that might bring new playgoers. And the Playhouse couldn't have found a better play to meet that challenge. *August: Osage County* first won raves on Broadway, then brought playwright Tracy Letts a Pulitzer Prize and Tony awards. The laugh-filled treatment of a dysfunctional family lived up to expectations, later sweeping postseason honors.

But before it opened, even bigger news came with the headline, "Playhouse retirements mean end of an era." Directors Carl Beck and Susan Baer Collins, then 63 and 61, announced they'd retire after the 2013–2014 season, allowing two years for a smooth transition.

"It's hard to express the gratitude the board and I have for their service," noted board president Dave Kirkwood. Both arrived with the Caravan in the 1970s. Beck joined the home staff in 1983 and became artistic director in 1997; Collins became full-time in 1987. They directed seven of ten shows most seasons and shared the annual mounting of all three *Carol* companies, a task now joined by resident director Amy Lane.

"I'll still be in Omaha and I'm not literally retiring," Collins explained. "I just want a little more control of my time." The rave reviews she received for her lead role in *Osage County* reminded of triumphs acting in such shows as *Sweeney Todd,* and offered hopes that she'd be seen again on stage.

Beck, also a gifted actor, was busy rehearsing the fall musical, *Legally Blonde,* when their future plans were announced, and Ben Beck, their son, would soon star in *boom* in the Drew. The doomsday comedy was set to star Bill Grennan, but in the process of earning Equity status he opted for a professional role in Florida, so Ben Beck filled in as the young scientist waiting for the world to end with a bang. Attendance-wise, the new "Find Your Own Stage" concept worked better for *Osage County* and *Evil Dead: The Musical*.

A fourth play in the Drew was neither edgy nor aimed at the "21 & Over" types. *Recommended Reading for Girls* became the first creation of an Omaha author staged at the Playhouse since Doug Marr's *Starkweather* more than twenty years before. Playwright Ellen Struve had also showcased it in staged readings, both at the Playhouse and the Great Plains Theater Conference.

Even in early drafts, as director Lane put it, "The heart of the play was already so deeply felt." A young woman, played by Christina Rohling, returns to the home of her cancer-stricken mother and encounters young storybook heroines such as Heidi and Anne of Green Gables. The spring musical *The Wizard of Oz* came closest to the financial boost of *Carol* while *Osage*

Moira Mangiameli, Susie Collins in *August: Osage County*.

County brought the most honors to director Lane, Collins and Moira Mangiameli among others.

Les Misérables Sells Out, New Director Arrives: 2013–2014

The season would have been momentous enough as the final one for Beck and Collins, plus the naming of the first new artistic director since Charles Jones arrived almost forty years ago. But it was predictable when auditions began in March for *Les Misérables* that the long-awaited musical would rank as the most memorable production in Playhouse history.

When Charles thought he'd won the rights to do it twenty years before, anticipation led to season ticket sales of over 12,000. Now more than 350 hopefuls flocked to auditions, and many who'd starred as leads in other musicals willingly took places in the ensemble. Yet it wasn't an easy decision for the trustees. Chairman Tom Belford called it "the biggest question" of his two-year term: "Can we afford to put on *Les Misérables*? We sat and debated, and even when we voted for it, some thought it would take the Playhouse down."

Any hesitation came from the cost: Beck and Collins, planning to co-direct, submitted a wish list totaling $200,000 in expenses, more than twice the cost of any previous musical. The turning point in swaying trustees came when Schmad could report that he already had $115,000 from three sponsors, HDR, Kiewit and Valmont. "I didn't think we were taking a risk," he recalls.

The foundation, while under the leadership of Dennis O'Neal, was still in the process of building the endowment from only $1 million five years before to nearly $7 million by 2014. And the foundation had promised to stand behind the needed funds, which finally reached $225,000 from donors.

So Collins, who eventually became lead director, had the dollars and almost the entire cast. All she needed was a proven professional to play John Valjean, the key role with its double-octave demands. Enter

Star-studded *Les Misérables* ensemble.

Timothy Shew, who'd portrayed Victor Hugo's ex-convict on the run to redemption more than 1,600 times on Broadway and elsewhere.

Les Misérables would run an extended twenty-eight performances and the usual seven weeks of rehearsal grew to ten. The results, under the baton of music director Jim Boggess, were stunning. From Shew singing, "Bring Him Home," to Julie Crowell as Fantine on "I Dreamed a Dream," to "A Heart Full of Love" with Joseph T. O'Connor II, Jennifer Tritz and Abigael Stewart, and on through the score, packed houses were transported by the musical that had drawn 66 million worldwide.

"It was so exciting," Belford says, "when all of a sudden the place sold out." Income exceeded $350,000, a figure topped only by *A Christmas Carol*. Among those who watched and found it "glorious," as the audience stood and cheered, was Hilary Adams, who would soon serve as the new artistic director.

There was more to come, of course, before the transition in May when she would begin to share two overlap months with her predecessors. Susie Collins was busy in January directing two sisters, Camille Metoyer-Moten and Lanette Moore in *Having Our Say,* the story of two African-American siblings who've survived past the century mark. She'd follow with the incomparable Kathy Tyree in *Ella,* celebrating the life and music of jazz great Ella Fitzgerald. Beck was preparing *The Fantasticks* for the road and directing the comedy *Boeing Boeing* before joining Collins again to co-direct their final spring musical, *Young Frankenstein.* Beck, a native of the South, planned to move to Florida, but "final" was likely not the conclusion for Collins. She'd stay in Omaha with husband, Dennis, and expected to do some guest directing and acting. But the "transition" meant passing of the torch handed by Jones to Beck and now to Adams.

When Adams arrived from New York, David Mamet's *Race,* with black lawyers defending a white man accused of raping a

Carl Beck and Susie Baer Collins.

Metoyer sisters in *Having Our Say.*

black woman, played in the Drew and *Young Frankenstein* ran on the Hawks main stage. As always, the Playhouse buzzed with classes and meetings.

The ninetieth season had been announced, and it promised more of the revived Caravan with the musical *Little Women* playing first at the Playhouse before going on the road. Thus began the decade that would take the nation's top community theater to its centennial. The leaders who welcomed Adams defined the challenge she'd share with Schmad, the trustees and others in a varied ways.

For Dennis O'Neal, any fears for the future had shifted. O'Neal, who'd led the successful endowment campaign before retiring to Arizona, was coaxed by Kim Lauritzen, wife of Bruce, his boss at First National Bank, to try the Playhouse for ninety days. He stayed to serve as trustee for eighteen years. "Until a few years ago," he explained, "I would have said the biggest challenge was financial, but now I'd say artistic."

The careful recruitment process and Adams's enthusiastic reception diminished doubts about the transition. The process began with a thirty-page plan from Dave Kirkwood, then funds were raised for the search. The top four candidates came to Omaha after a field of seventy-eight was narrowed to nine for Skype interviews. Lloyd Meyer, a Leo Daly executive who'd soon replace Belford as chair of the trustees, headed the search committee—a mix of members like John Mock with human resources experience and artistic backgrounds, longtime board member Jim Eisenhardt, who'd been a high school drama teacher, and Melanie Walters, former Playhouse staffer and award-winning performer.

Beck and Collins watched the winnowing with more than casual interest. Beck observed, "We couldn't have made the cut." They shared the enthusiasm for Adams that was unanimous with the search committee and others who met her. Ask a dozen of those boosters and you seldom heard much about her impressive eighteen years of experience, her college degrees, the Drama Desk nomination for directing *Moby Dick*, the Manhattan Theatre Club directing fellowships or the long list of plays directed in regional theaters or New York City. The many credits as director compete for her heart with other assignments, such as assisting with the musical *Titanic*.

But the staff and trustees raved about the personal qualities, from her preparation for the visit to her creativity and intelligence. Schmad marveled at "her total interest in everything. It was unbelievable how prepared she was, she really did her homework."

Search chair Meyer told the daily, "We're not just happy, we're thrilled." Beck called her "charming, very intuitive" and commended her "very cautious, respectful approach." Kirkwood spoke of coffee with Adams and others downtown, lasting "a couple of hours with everybody hitting on all cylinders, starting to brainstorm. Wouldn't it be wonderful," he mused, "if every search led to such a clear choice."

For Adams, it came close to love at first sight. "I'd heard of the Playhouse and when I read the description, it was a perfect match," her dream job. "The further I got into my research, the more excited I got," and "I can't

Dennis O'Neal with auditorium donors Rhonda and Howard Hawks.

New director Hilary Adams

wait to get started." While visiting, she watched the rehearsals for three companies of *Carol*, the "glorious madness, unlike anything I've ever experienced."

Building on the Past, Looking Toward a Century of Excellence

If re-creating the Christmas magic looms as a specific challenge in the season to come, she'll hear broader takes on the challenges ahead. The business and the artistic sides may have dealt with differences in the past, but now Schmad, Beck and Collins agreed on job one: fill the seats in the main auditorium. In Beck's terms, that requires "cultivating a new audience."

Kirkwood, like the others a member of the crucial play-reading committee, talks about "getting the right scripts." Collins emphasizes that selection used to feature plays for the main stage but now demands musicals "to make the nut." And O'Neal, when he elaborates on the artistic challenge, joins Kirkwood in noting the competition from the Broadway shows at the Orpheum. He stresses "superior theater at terrific values" to protect people who "can't afford to pay $90 and buy parking downtown."

Adams hears these voices and promises "to listen a lot and ask a lot of questions." She "honors and embraces" the legacy of those who've gone before her and values their institutional memories. She already shares the excitement of that production of *Les Misérables* and can appreciate it when others recall their favorite moments on the Playhouse stages.

Beck was around long enough to see "kids grow up, and then their kids come along," and he'll never forget how "it overwhelmed me night after night" to hear the audience scream when the monster of *Frankenstein* burst from the wardrobe.

Collins could still smile about taking bows after her performance in *House of Blue Leaves,* only to have a woman walk up, tear the program and toss it her way saying, "You want trash? Here's some trash." But she carries happier memories that begin with a Caravan musical, *Taking the Sky* and extending to *The Secret Garden* and many others.

Schmad loves the scene in *Buddy* where the rocker's lone guitar stands in the spotlight before the stage comes alive as Billy McGuigan "cuts loose" as Buddy Holly. But, like the two directors, his list of favorites runs long, from Jim McKain dancing as Luther Billis in *South Pacific* to the late great Matt Kamprath as Harry Truman, to the thunder, lightning and rain in the Drew as the jury met in *12 Angry Men*.

The keepers of the ninety-year legacy also agree about how the Playhouse grew in the 1970s and 1980s to become the nation's leading community theater. They credit Charles Jones and, of course, his creation of *A Christmas Carol* and the Nebraska Theatre Caravan.

Schmad mentions the way Jones connected to community leaders, and Beck cites the way "he established a standard of excellence" and the talent that he brought to the Playhouse, starting with scenic designer Jim Othuse. Then employment at the Playhouse was "an intermediate job," Beck explains. Now "we're no longer a transitional place where people work two or three years." Othuse remains forty years later.

John Gibilisco started as a volunteer "bed bug," maneuvering Scrooge's bed in *A Christmas Carol* and remains nearly four decades later as master electrician and sound designer. John and others "get frequent job offers but they stay," Beck observed. So a newcomer can understand when some call the theater "the house that Jones built." But another version of that proclamation impressed itself on Dave Kirkwood when he sat at the back of the auditorium and witnessed the passion during the storm over those resignations.

"What it told me," he recalls, "is this is YOUR community Playhouse. It's who we are." The house, many could say, we all built.

The torch that was passed from Alan McDonald and Genevieve Guiou to her daughter Echo Ellick and such stalwarts as Clarence Teal had been passed to Jones and others. Now Beck and Collins passed it on to Hilary Adams. It all started with the rise of movies and the decline of road companies in 1924. It grew with those stars of that first decade—Dodie Brando, Henry Fonda and Dorothy McGuire. It nearly stopped during World War II and faced new challenges in the years that followed. It not only survived, but grew and flourished so that many could share what Dorothy McGuire felt as her stage and film career blossomed. Asked what the Playhouse experience meant to her rise, she said, "Why, everything!"

90 Years of Theatre Productions

1925-26
The Enchanted Cottage
You and I
The Devil's Disciple
Mary the Third
Liliom
The Romantic Age
Outward Bound
Captain Applejack
The Swan

1926-27
Merton of the Movies
Anna Christie
The Youngest
He Who Gets Slapped
Lady Windermere's Fan
The Guardsman
R.U.R.
March Hares
Pygmalion

1927-28
The Potters
Secrets
The School for Scandal
Beyond the Horizon
Seventeen
The Enemy
Rip Van Winkle
You Never Can Tell

1928-29
Aren't We All
They Knew What They Wanted
Fashion
Dear Brutus
Torchbearers
Arms and the Man
Grumpy

1929-30
An Ideal Husband
Ten Nights in a Bar Room
Sun-Up
Escape
The Hairy Ape
The Queen's Husband
A Kiss for Cinderella

1930-31
Cock Robin
Ned McCobb's Daughter
Behold This Dreamer
The Criminal Code
The Intimate Strangers
Death Takes A Holiday
Alice-Sit-By-the-Fire

1931-32
Berkeley Square
Jealousy
Once in a Lifetime
What Every Woman Knows
Mister Antonio
The Royal Family
The Last Mile

1932-33
The First Mrs. Fraser
Elizabeth The Queen
The Devil Passes
East of Suez
The Perfect Alibi
Brigham Young
Engaged

1933-34
Both Your Houses
June Moon
A Doll's House
Springtime for Henry
Uncle Tom's Cabin
Counselor-at-Law
Three Cornered Moon

1934-35
The Good Fairy
Dear Brutus
Inheritors
A Thing of Beauty
Wet Paint
One Sunday Afternoon
Louder Please

1935-36
Her Master's Voice
Kind Lady
The Return of Peter Grimm
Yellow Jack
The Far-Off Hills
As You Like It
Macbeth (Shorter Form)
Post Road

1936-37
Libel!
The Senator's Husband
Winterset
Personal Appearance
Pride and Prejudice
Night of January 16th

1937-38
Excursion
Night Must Fall
High Tor
Storm Over Patsy
Stage Door
Blind Alley

1938-39
Tonight at 8:30
The Masque of Kings
George and Margaret
Street Scene
Yes, My Darling Daughter
Our American Cousin

1939-40
Our Town
Candida
The Roof
Bachelor Born
The Petrified Forest
The Gondoliers

1940-41
Margin for Error
My Heart's in the Highlands
Happy Journey
Air Raid
Rarely Fatal
The Gentle People
The Great Adventure
Knickerbocker Holiday

1941-42

The Male Animal
Brief Music
George Washington Slept Here
Green Grow the Lilacs
Mr. and Mrs. North
You Can't Take It With You

1942-43

Ladies in Retirement
The Women
Dark Tower
Family Portrait
The Eve of St. Mark
Aaron Stick from Punkin Creek

1943-44

I Killed the Count
Papa Is All
Let Us Be Gay
The Guardsman
Janie
Dark Eyes

1944-45

Suspect
Hay Fever
The Little Foxes
The Lady Who Came To Stay
Pursuit of Happiness
Over 21

1945-46

Kiss and Tell
The Silver Cord
The Skin of Our Teeth
Old Acquaintance
The Hasty Heart
First Lady

1946-47

The Late George Apley
My Sister Eileen
Soldier's Wife
The Time of Your Life
Joan of Lorraine
I Like It Here

1947-48

The Great Big Doorstep
The Importance of Being Earnest
Years Ago
Uncle Harry
The Song of the Bridge
Dream Girl

1948-49

Life With Father
I Remember Mama
With Sirens Blowing
An Inspector Calls
Command Decision
John Loves Mary

1949-50

Edward My Son
Parlor Story
The Bat
Missouri Legend
The Heiress
Two Blind Mice

1950-51

Born Yesterday
The Glass Menagerie
On Borrowed Time
Goodbye My Fancy
The Winslow Boy
The Secret of Suzanne
Down in the Valley
The Telephone

1951-52
Light Up the Sky
Come Back Little Sheba
The High Ground
Father of the Bride
The Lady's Not for Burning
The Happy Time

1952-53
Happy Birthday
Abe Lincoln in Illinois
Bell, Book and Candle
Stalag 17
The Distaff Side
Remains To Be Seen

1953-54
The Moon Is Blue
The Shrike
Davy Crockett
Secret Service
Peg O' My Heart
Broadway

1954-55
My Three Angles
Detective Story
Mary of Scotland
Sabrina Fair
The Caine Mutiny
Court Martial
The Remarkable
Mr. Pennypacker

Extra Production - June 1955
Country Girl-Playhouse Benefit

1955-56
King of Hearts
The Crucible
Dial "M" for Murder
See How They Run
Anastasia
The Solid Gold Cadillac

1956-57
The Desperate Hours
The Rainmaker
But Not Goodbye
Time Limit
The Chalk Garden
The Great Sebastians

1957-58
The Desk Set
Witness for the Prosecution
The Reluctant Debutante
Inherit the Wind
Therese
The Matchmaker

1958-59
Separate Tables
The Happiest Millionaire
The First Legion
Teahouse of the August Moon
The Hollow
Diary of Anne Frank

1959-60
Say Darling
The Morgan Rock
The Girls in 509
Sunrise at Campobello
The Gazebo
Mrs. McThing
Strange Bedfellows
Who Was That Lady I Saw You With?

1960-61
Physician for Fools
Kiss Me, Kate
Wingless Victory
Golden Fleecing
Ladies in Retirement
The Pleasure of His Company

1961-62
Pajama Game
Julius Caesar
Roman Candle
The Deadly Game
A Raisin in the Sun
Blithe Spirit

1962-63
Bye, Bye, Birdie
J.B.
Pool's Paradise
All The Way Home
Write Me A Murder
Come Blow Your Horn

1963-64
Little Mary Sunshine
Brigadoon
Gideon
The Best Man
Breath of Spring
A Far Country
Take Her, She's Mine

1964-65
Marriage Go Round (Summer Prod)
Damn Yankees
Twelfth Night
Calculated Risk
The Corn Is Green
Mary, Mary
The Private Ear and the Public Eye

1965-66
The King and I
A Man For All Seasons
Life With Father
A Case of Libel
Never Too Late
Death of a Salesman
Absence of a Cello

1966-67
Guys and Dolls
Incident at Vichy
Any Wednesday
Devil's Disciple
You Can't Take It With You
Picnic
Barefoot in the Park

1967-68
Gypsy
Philadelphia, Here I Come
Luv
Generation
Macbeth
The Little Foxes
The Odd Couple

1968-69
The Lark
Little Mary Sunshine
Uncle Vanya
Star Spangled Girl
A Delicate Balance
Wait Until Dark
Black Comedy
The Apple Tree (Summer Prod)

1969-70
My Fair Lady
The Great Sebastians
I Never Sang for My Father
Don't Drink the Water
Royal Hunt of the Sun
Cactus Flower
Your Own Thing (Summer Prod)

1970-71

The Sound of Music
The Andersonville Trial
Romanoff and Juliet
Man of LaMancha
Catch Me If You Can
The Captain's Paradise
Peter Pan (Summer Production)

1971-72

Oliver!
The Mousetrap
The Subject Was Roses
The Fantasticks
Indians
Forty Carats
The Wizard of Oz (Summer Production)

1972-73

1776
Child's Play
I Do! I Do!
The Last of the Red Hot Lovers
Butterflies are Free
Send Me No Flowers
Cinderella (Summer Production)

1973-74

Anything Goes
Night Watch
Plaza Suite
Irma La Douce
Vivat! Vivat Regina!
Philadelphia Story
6 Rms Riv Vu

Summerfest, 1974

Produced in cooperation with the Department of Dramatic Arts, University of Nebraska at Omaha
Taming of the Shrew
Jacques Brel Is Alive and Well and Living in Paris
The Me Nobody Knows

1974-75

The Music Man
Jacques Brel Is Alive and Well and Living in Paris
Not Now Darling
That Championship Season
Crown Matrimonial
George Washington Slept Here
Godspell

1975-76

The Golden Follies
How the Other Half Loves
Sleuth
Galileo
Oh, Coward!
The Sunshine Boys
The Kid (Summer Prod)

1976-77

Shenandoah
The Veldt and The Wonderful Ice Cream Suit
A Christmas Carol
Orpheus Descending
A Little Night Music
No Sex Please, We're British (Held over for a summer run)

1977-78

Cabaret
Last Meeting of Knights of the White Magnolia
A Christmas Carol
Scapino-A Long Way from Moliere
St. Joan
How to Succeed in Business without Really Trying
Blithe Spirit
Peter Pan (Summer Prod in cooperation with District 66-Westside Schools, Nebraska Arts Council and the Nebraska Theatre Caravan)

1978-79
Kismet
To Kill a Mockingbird
A Christmas Carol
Something's Afoot
Hamlet '79
The Robber Bridegroom
The Royal Family

1979-80
Camelot
Shadow Box
A Christmas Carol
Diamond Studs
Dracula
Cole (Cole Porter)
Mr. Roberts

1980-81
My Fair Lady
Of Mice and Men
A Christmas Carol
Gold Dust
The Three Musketeers
70, Girls 70
On Golden Pond

1981-82
Unsinkable Molly Brown
Whose Life Is It, Anyway?
A Christmas Carol
As You Like It
Sweet Bird of Youth
Chicago
Bedroom Farce

1982-83
Fascinating Rhythms
Merton of the Movies
A Christmas Carol
Strider
Treasure Island
Sherlock Holmes
The Suicide Farce
Ballroom

1983-84
The King and I
Gin Game
A Christmas Carol
TinTypes
Robin Hood
The Dining Room
Inherit the Wind
See How They Run

1984-85
Guys and Dolls
The Caine Mutiny Court Martial
A Christmas Carol
Cyrano
Look Homeward, Angel
The Best Little Whorehouse In Texas
Auntie Mame

1985-86
Barnum
Crimes of the Heart
A Christmas Carol
Pump Boys & Dinettes
Terra Nova
Evita
Tom Jones

1986-87
Can-Can
Witness for the Prosecution
A Christmas Carol
Man of LaMancha
Noises Off
Paint Your Wagon
Brighton Beach Memoirs
The Hunchback of Notre Dame
The 1940s Radio Hour
Children of a Lesser God
Quilters

1987-88

Sugar Babies
Animal Farm
Corpse
Qualities (World Premiere)
A Christmas Carol
Over Here
Tenderloin
House of Blue Leaves
Lion in Winter
Creation
South Pacific
Arkansas Bear
Quilters (June '88)

1988-89

Of Thee I Sing
Diviners
Pack of Lies
Rocky Horror Picture Show
A Christmas Carol
Fantasticks
Our Town
On the Verge
Julius Caesar
Gigi
Musical Comedy Murders

1989-90

Gypsy
Bunk Bed Brothers
All My Sons
Starkweather
A Christmas Carol
The Pied Piper
Road to Mecca
El Grande de Coca Cola
Social Security
Steel Magnolias
Teddy & Alice

1990-91

Big River
Polish Sharp Shooters
Deathtrap
Boys Next Door
A Christmas Carol
110 in the Shade
Irma Vep
Bedful of Foreigners
Prime of Miss Jean Brodie
Sophisticated Ladies
Hello, Dolly

1991-92

42nd Street
On Borrowed Time
A Funny Thing Happened...
A Christmas Carol
Edwin Drood
Mountain
Amadeus
Other People's Money
Lend Me A Tenor
Greater Tuna
Brigadoon

1992-93

The Wiz
O Pioneers
Carnival
A Christmas Carol
Cat on a Hot Tin Roof
Rumors
Fiddler on the Roof
Manchurian Candidate
Foreigner
A Day in Hollywood/ Night in Ukraine
Skin of Our Teeth

1993-94
Funny Girl
A Few Good Men
Joseph & The Amazing Technicolor® Dreamcoat
A Christmas Carol
My Antonia
Sly Fox
The Most Happy Fella
M. Butterfly
Member of the Wedding
Little Shop of Horrors
Marvin's Room

1994-95
Sweet Charity
Black Comedy
Sweeney Todd
A Christmas Carol
Into the Woods
Breaking Legs
Frankenstein
Love Letters
Lost in Yonkers
Shadowlands
The Music Man

1995-96
The Will Rogers Follies
Glory Years (Ak-Sar-Ben History)
Wait Until Dark
The Queen of Bingo
A Christmas Carol
Godspell
Leader of the Pack
The Grapes of Wrath
Driving Miss Daisy
The Glass Menagerie
West Side Story

1996-97
Oliver!
My Three Angels
The Sisters Rosensweig
One Flew Over the Cuckoo's Nest
A Christmas Carol
Pippin
The Boyfriend
To Kill A Mockingbird
Don't Dress for Dinner
Oklahoma!
Tony 'n Tina's Wedding

1997-98
LaCage Aux Folles
The Woman In Black
1776
The Heiress
Camping With Henry and Tom
Camelot
A Christmas Carol
Sylvia
Scotland Road
Picasso At The Lapin Agile
Return To The Forbidden Planet

1998-1999
Anything Goes
The Cemetery Club
Smoke On The Mountain
Dracula
Moon Over Buffalo
The Secret Garden
A Christmas Carol
Grace & Glorie
A Tuna Christmas
Once On This Island
The Little Foxes

1999-2000

Crazy For You
The Miracle Worker
Forever Plaid
The Mask of Moriarty
The Last Night of Ballyhoo
My Fair Lady
A Christmas Carol
Tons of Money
Clue – The Musical
The Enchanted Cottage
Gross Indecency

2000-2001

A Funny Thing Happened on the Way to the Forum
Communicating Doors
Beau Jest
Dark at the Top of the Stairs
Mack and Mabel
The Sunshine Boys
A Christmas Carol
The Women
Inspecting Carol
Violet
Our Country's Good

2001-2002

Sugar Babies
The Diary of Anne Frank
A Christmas Carol
Over the River and Through the Woods
The Man Who Came To Dinner
Carousel
Art
Ancestral Voices
You Should Be So Lucky
I Love You, You're Perfect, Now Change
The Complete History of America (Abridged)

2002-2003

Buddy
The Bad Seed
A Christmas Carol
Arsenic and Old Lace
Broadway Bound
No Sex Please, We're British
The Sound of Music
The Elephant Man
Game Show
The Marvelous Wonderettes
More Fun Than Bowling

2003-2004

Will Rogers Follies
Misery
A Christmas Carol
My Way
The Tale of the Allergist's Wife
Noises Off
Annie Get Your Gun
Visiting Mr. Green
The Importance of Being Earnest
Rave On! special event
Zombie Prom
Stepping Out

2004-2005

Hair
Over the Tavern
A Christmas Carol
The Spitfire Grill
The Trip to Bountiful
The Nerd
Annie
Not About Nightingales
Wonder of the World
Rave On! (special event)
A Man of No Importance
Dirty Blonde

Summer 2005

The Marvelous Wonderettes (remount)
Lost in the 50's (show brought in)

2005-2006

Swing
The Battle of Shallowford
A Christmas Carol
Das Barbecü
Bus Stop
The Underpants
Ragtime
The Graduate
Pride's Crossing
Rave On! special event
Ruthless! The Musical
Biloxi Blues

Summer 2006

Jukebox Journey (Show brought in)

2006-2007

The Full Monty
King O' the Moon
A Christmas Carol
Always...Patsy Cline
Give 'em Hell Harry!
You Can't Take It With You
Peter Pan
The Talented Mr. Ripley
Mrs. Bob Cratchit's Wild Christmas Binge
Rave On! special event
Urinetown
Kimberly Akimbo

Summer 2007

Yesterday and Today (Billy McGuigan)

2007-2008

Crowns
Thoroughly Modern Millie
Matt and Ben
A Christmas Carol
Rave On! Special event
Same Time, Next Year
Company
Cliffhanger
Shakespeare in Hollywood
The Crucible
South Pacific

Summer 2008

Late Night Catechism

2008-2009

Intimate Apparel
The Cocoanuts
Stones In His Pockets
A Christmas Carol
Yesterday & Today (Special Event)
Blithe Spirit
Bat Boy – The Musical
Glorious
Rock Legends
Twelve Angry Men
Gypsy

Summer 2009

Late Night Catechism
Always...Patsy Cline (remount)

2009-2010

Almost Maine
A Christmas Carol
Yesterday & Today (Special Event)
Cheaper by the Dozen
Death of a Salesman
All Shook Up
Mr. Roberts
Awesome 80s Prom
A Fiddler on the Roof

2009 2010 cont.

Quilters
Joseph and the Amazing Technicolor® Dreamcoat
Rave On: Living Legends Edition

Summer 2010

Rock Legends
Defending the Caveman

2010-2011

The Lady with All The Answers
Footloose – The Musical
A Thousand Clowns
A Christmas Carol
Yesterday and Today (Special Event)
The Odd Couple
The 25th Annual Putnam County Spelling Bee
Nunsense
Steel Magnolias
Tuesdays with Morrie
Guys and Dolls
Rave On

2011-2012

The Blues Brothers Revue
Becky's New Car
Chicago
Flyin' West
A Christmas Carol
Yesterday and Today
On Golden Pond
The Fantasticks
Altar Boyz
Lend Me a Tenor
A Streetcar Named Desire
Hairspray
Rave On

2012-2013

August: Osage County
Legally Blonde
Boom
A Christmas Carol
Yesterday and Today
Deathtrap
Evil Dead: The Musical
All Night Strut
A Night with the Family
Recommended Reading for Girls
The Wizard of Oz
Late Nite Catechism 3

2013-2014

Sirens
Les Miserables
Freud's Last Session
A Christmas Carol
Yesterday and Today
Having Our Say
Next to Normal
Ella
Boeing Boeing
Race
Young Frankenstein
Pat Hazell's The Wonder Bread Years

Other Studio Theatre and Nebraska Theatre Caravan productions are noted in the context of this book.

Acknowledgments

Gratitude goes to many, especially Earl and the late Grace Riley Leinart for their generous gift to support the research and writing. The long list of helpful sources starts with the keepers of the scrapbooks from 1925 to the 1990s, and to those many journalists who wrote feature stories, columns and reviews: from Keene Abbott, Keith Wilson and Jake Rachman up to Denman Kountze Jr., Jim Delmont and Bob Fischbach at the *Omaha World-Herald*; from the *Bee*, the *News* and the *Bee-News*, the scribes for those long-gone dailies, to the more recent weeklies, the *Sun* Newspapers of Dave Blacker and Warren Buffett to *The Reader* and some short-lived others; from the Theatre Arts Guild *TAGlines* newsletter to the *Catholic Voice*; the memorabilia of such giants of Playhouse history as Echo Ellick and Rudyard Norton.

I am grateful for the countless interviews with many still living and others I was fortunate enough to reminisce with before their final farewells: Joan Hennecke who first performed at the Playhouse in the 1940s; Royal Eckert who arrived as scenic designer in the early 1950s, my writing colleague Bob Reilly who began acting in the 1950s and later served on the board as publicist, and Charles Jones and Jim Othuse who arrived in the mid-70s and took the Playhouse to the top. Often helpful in connecting the Playhouse to its neighbors was

Norman Filbert Jr., co-founder of Chanticleer Theatre in Council Bluffs, the second oldest community theater in the metro area. The single most consistent source for the Playhouse story was the *Prompters*, starting in 1929, not only rich in cast bios and director's notes but other news on and off-stage.

Special thanks to Betsye Paragas and her successor as director of marketing and public relations, Katie Broman and the Omaha Community Playhouse staff for their help in gathering information from the more recent years, a time when I attended most of the shows each season.

Much of this history was read by Reilly, longtime trustee Bob Lueder and Dr. Paul Lundell before their passing. Dr. Harl Dahlstrom and Larry Dwyer read much of the book and offered useful advice. Among the many contributors from the Playhouse staff, their leader, president Tim Schmad, kept the faith in bringing this book to publication with the backing of the Playhouse Foundation and the expertise and hard work of Lisa Pelto and her staff at Concierge Marketing Publishing Services, and my editor, Sandra Wendel.

About the Author

For more than a half century, Dr. Warren T. Francke has worked for daily and weekly newspapers, taught journalism and written as a freelance theater reporter, columnist, feature writer and media critic. After degrees in journalism and literature at the University of Nebraska at Omaha, he earned a Ph.D. in Mass Communication with a minor in American intellectual history at the University of Minnesota. While teaching at UNO for 35 years, he wrote for academic journals, newspapers and television, especially "Watching the Watchdogs" media commentary on WOWT, and contributed a biographical entry to the Oxford English Dictionary. His publications include *The Way Was Clear: the Centennial History of Dundee Presbyterian Church, 1901-2001.*

As co-author of *Lucky: the Story of the Durhams and HDR*, he wrote about engineering entrepreneur and philanthropist Chuck Durham from birth to graduation from Iowa State University.

Born in Council Bluffs, Iowa, Dr. Francke is a member of that city's Abraham Lincoln High School Hall of Fame. At UNO, he was the recipient of the University's excellence in teaching award and the School of Communication's Lifetime Achievement Award. He was named

Ralph Wardle Diamond Professor at the school's 75th anniversary. He also taught at the University of Minnesota and, through UNO, for a half-year in Germany. He is Professor Emeritus in the School of Communication at UNO, and won the Omaha Press Club Educator Award. He has reviewed theater for the Council Bluffs *Daily Nonpareil*, the *Sun* Newspapers of Omaha and *The Reader*. An Omaha resident and summer resident of Colorado, he is the husband of Carol Burnett Francke and the father of two children.

INDEX

Numbers

12 Angry Men, 477, 493
21 & Over series, 481
The 25th Annual Putnam County Spelling Bee, 482
30—Living Scrapbook of a Decade, 300
70, Girls, 70, 361
110 in the Shade, 339, 407
1776, 308, 438
The 1940s Radio Hour, 387–388, 390

A

Aaron Slick from Punkin Creek, 162
Abbey Players (Dublin), 123
Abbott, Avery, 27
Abbott, Betty, 206–207
Abbott, George, 208
Abbott, Keene, 6, 22–23, 27–29, 34–36, 39, 41–42, 44, 50, 53–55, 57, 59, 66, 68, 74–75, 79–80, 86–87, 90, 92–93, 98, 103, 106–107, 111–112, 115, 120, 200
Abe Lincoln in Illinois, 201–202
Abie's Irish Rose, 97
Abou-Nasr, Tim, 476
Abraham, F. Murray, 412
The Absence of a Cello, 274–275
Academy of Music, 207
ACT II, 385, 399, 447
Actor's Company, 116
Actors Guild, 121–124, 132
Actors Summer Stock Theater, 263
Adams, Hilary, 488–493
Adams, John, 308, 437–438
Adams, Maude, 139
Adams, Tom, 361
Adler, Anabel Shotwell, 176
Adler, Stella, 256
The Adventures of Sherlock Holmes, 370
Aesop's Fables, 70
Affleck, Ben, 473
Afro-Academy of the Dramatic Arts, 332
Agnew, Tim, 448
Ah, Wilderness!, 113
Aherne, Brian, 128
Aida, 370
Air Raid, 148–149

Aitchison, Lee, 34
Ak-Sar-Ben, 5, 14, 61, 106, 148, 212, 287, 295, 320, 353, 357–359, 370, 376, 385, 426, 440, 449
Aladdin and the Wonderful Lamp, 92, 96, 112, 293
Albee, Edward, 290, 335
Albom, Mitch, 482
Aldrich, Bess Streeter, 27
Alexander, Bill, 247
Alice in Wonderland (film), 111
Alice in Wonderland (play), 124
Alice-Sit-By-the-Fire, 87
All My Sons, 403
All the Way Home, 253, 262
Allen, Woody, 296, 318
Alley Theatre (Houston), 297, 349
Almost, Maine, 480
Altar Boyz, 483
Always, Patsy Cline, 471, 477
Amadeus, 412
American Community Theater Association, 329, 336
The Amorous Flea, 285
Anastasia, 222
Ancestral Voices, 453
Andersen, Frank, 198, 201
Andersen, Harold, 293, 311, 369
Andersen, Marian, 311
Anderson, Jean, 326, 444
Anderson, Jill, 419, 473–474
Anderson, Maxwell, 11, 97, 105, 125–127, 132, 135, 137, 150, 161, 177, 211, 253
Anderson, Victor, 216
The Andersonville Trial, 299
Andrade, Diana, 407
Andrews Sisters, 392
Andreyev, Leonid, 53
Androcles and the Lion, 293
Animal Farm, 391–392
Ankenbauer, Angela, 378, 408, 449
Anna Christie, 1, 48, 50, 52, 54, 74, 77, 459
Annie, 459, 462
Anouilh, Jean, 288
Anspach, Eldon, 138, 154, 158, 165, 194
Any Wednesday, 277
Anything Goes, 142, 311–312, 315, 439
The Apostle (film), 350

The Apple Tree, 292
Aren't We All?, 63, 66–67
Aristophanes, 296
Arksansaw Bear, 396
Arlen, Harold, 142
Arlington, Janice, 393
Arms and the Man, 72
Armstrong, Louis, 41
Armstrong, Neil, 290, 292
Arnold, Tracy, 418
Arsenic and Old Lace, 456
Arthur, Evelyn Paeper, 167–168, 223
Arthur Murray dancers, 149
As Thousands Cheer, 142
As You Like It, 123, 366
Ashburn, Virginia, 157
Ashley, Janet, 473
Astaire, Adele, 11
Astaire, Fred, 11, 87
Astro movie house, 435
Atkinson, Brooks, 198
August: Osage County, 481, 485–487
Auntie Mame, 378
Austen, Jane, 126, 129
Austerlitz siblings, 11
Austin, Al, 259
Ayckbourn, Alan, 334
Ayers, Erna Reed (Mrs. Philip), 92, 152, 157
Ayers, Philip, 152

B

Babes in Arms, 142
Bachelor Born, 146
Baer, Mabel Mahoney (Mrs. Lesem), 91, 93, 97–98, 108–109, 114, 123, 138, 152
Baer, Susan, 91, 338, 349–350, 356, 372, 385, 389, 391, 396, 398, 406–408, 410–412, 418–419, 422–425, 431–433, 435, 437, 439–440, 442, 444–446, 449, 453, 457, 462, 468, 470, 472–473, 475, 477–479, 481, 484–487, 489–490, 492–493
Bailey, Bill, 230–233, 235, 244, 248, 250, 259, 264, 266, 268, 279, 294, 296, 299, 334–335, 340, 346–347, 354, 457

511

Bailey, Ralph E., 20–21, 39, 45, 56–57, 59, 228
Baird, Lucy Jane, 232
Baker, Rob, 358, 398, 414–415, 430, 434, 446, 448, 453, 456, 462, 476
Baker, Russell, 99, 125, 147
Bakkerud, Dick, 312
Balderston, Angela, 433–434
Baldridge, Letitia (Tish), 72, 134–135
Baldwin, Caleb, 60–61
Baldwin, Genevieve. See Guiou, Genevieve
Baldwin, John, 60–61
Ball, Lucille, 127, 189, 421
Ballard, Fred, 125–127
Ballet Omaha, 422
Ballroom, 367, 370
Bandle, Guy, 134
Bankhead, Tallulah, 10
Barbara Ford award, 459
Barefoot in the Park, 279
Barker, Betty, 212–213
Barker, Joe, 307
Barlow, Frank, 38–39, 52, 58
Barnard, Allen, 298, 304
Barnum, 378–379
Barr, Betty, 73
Barratt, Brian, 433
Barrie, Elaine, 144
Barrie, J.M., 33, 70, 78–79, 87, 91, 111
Barron, Steven, 429
Barry, Philip, 2, 32–34, 52, 175, 315
Barrymore, Ethel, 8, 10, 87
Barrymore, John, 9, 92, 144
Barrymore, Lionel, 191
Bartimus, Tad, 376
Basie, Count, 462
Basilico, Joe, 195, 206, 209, 213, 226, 242
Bat Boy—The Musical, 476
Bates, Earl, 426, 448, 457
Baum, Frank, 413
Baxter, Ellinore, 53
Baxter, Mrs. William F., 16, 20, 67
Beasley, John, 350, 427–429
Beatles, 455, 470
Beaver, Mac, 384
Beaver, Ninette, 402
Beck, Ben, 419, 473, 485–486
Beck, Carl, 338, 349–350, 356, 367–369, 371, 373, 376, 378, 384, 386, 389, 392, 396, 398, 402–403, 405–408, 411–412, 414–415, 418, 424–425, 428–431, 435, 437, 439, 441–443, 445–446, 449, 451, 453, 456–459, 461–462, 464, 468, 471, 476–479, 481, 484–485, 487, 489–493
Beck, Susan. See Baer, Susan
Beckman, Marguerite, 2–3, 9, 15, 17–18, 21, 25, 42, 420
Becky's New Car, 482
A Bedfull of Foreigners, 408
Bee Hive, 428
The Beggar's Opera, 254
Bekins Foundation, 457
Belasco, David, 4, 121
Belford, Tom, 472, 478, 487–488, 490
Belford (Rohling), Christina. See Rohling, Christina Belford
Bell, Book and Candle, 201–202
Bellamy, Ralph, 210
Bellevue Little Theater, 286, 422
Benchley, Robert, 131, 140
Benet, Stephen Vincent, 262
Benner, Van Wyck, 131
Bennett, France, 439
Bennett, Joan, 174
Bennett, John J., 340, 353, 355, 361, 371, 375, 384, 409
Benolken, Irving, 45
Benscoter, Brooke Ann, 349
Benson High School (Omaha), 14, 58, 91
Bentham, Jeremy, 335
Berg, Jean, 182, 199, 232, 247, 250
Bergan, Gerald, 204–206
Bergen, Polly, 282
Bergman, Ingrid, 177
Berkeley Square, 90
Berkey, Ralph, 226
Berlin, Irving, 11, 142, 476
Berner, Terry, 428
Bernstein, Leonard, 429
Berryman, Edward, 150
Berryman, Warren, 150
Bertino, Tom, 430
Berwanger, Jay, 126
Besoyan, Rick, 263
The Best Little Whorehouse in Texas, 377–378
The Best Man, 266
Beyond the Horizon, 57, 224
Big Bopper, 455
Big River, 405–406
Biggs, Tipton, 342, 398
Billings, George, 51
Billings, John, 415
Biography, 94, 108
The Birdcage (film), 436
Birdman, Jerome, 314
The Birds' Christmas Carol, 91
Birkholtz, Ben, 474
Birmingham Little Theater, 62
The Birth of a Nation, 8
The Birthday, 220
Bissell, Richard, 245, 257
Bisson, Beau, 484
Black Comedy, 291, 420, 422
Blackburn, Doug, 476
Blind Alley, 134, 145
Blithe Spirit, 259, 476
Blood, Sweat and Stanley Poole, 253, 256
The Blood Knot, 288
Blue Barn Theatre, 402, 448, 468, 470, 481
The Blue Bird, 75
Blumenthal, Russell, 114
Blumkin, Rose, 307
The Boar's Head Tavern, 339
Bodeen, DeWitt, 112
Boeing Boeing, 489
Bogardus, Jan, 464
Bogart, Humphrey, 11, 127, 147, 213
Boggess, Jim, 338, 349, 355–356, 412, 429, 436, 456, 462, 484, 488
Bohannon, Bill, 332
Boler, Eileen, 245
Bolt, Robert, 273, 314
Book of Qualities (Gendler), 392
boom, 481, 485
Booth, John Wilkes, 143
Booth, Shirley, 11, 195
Boothe Luce, Clare, 148, 156, 158, 447
Booton, Sue Gillespie, 421
Borglum, August, 109, 147–148
Borglum, Gutzon, 109
Borglum, Jean, 109
Born Yesterday, 189–192
Bosanek, Gary, 423
Both Your Houses, 105
Boulder Dinner Theatre, 406
Bounds, Nancy, 266
Bowman, Lee, 75
The Boy Friend, 433–434
Boyd, Lynne, 364
Boyd, Miriam, 252, 465
Boyd, Richard (Dick), 252, 258, 288, 335, 340–342, 354, 359, 361, 364, 369, 372, 376, 389, 392, 397,

411, 424, 426–427, 438, 440, 448, 453, 457, 461, 463–465, 467–468
Boyer, Charles, 137
Boyer, Virginia Skinner, 99, 145
Boyle, Mike, 374, 402
Boys in the Band, 302
The Boys Next Door, 407
Bozell, Bess, 113
Bozell, Leo, 104, 113
Braddock, Earl, 169
Bradford, Dana, 92
Brady, Dan, 305, 325, 335
Brandeis, Emil, 8
Brandeis, John, 426
Brandeis Players, 222
Brandeis Theater, 7–8, 10–11, 16, 37, 80, 87, 90, 96, 127, 139
Brandes, Adolph, 86, 97, 99, 103
Brando, (Big) Marlon, 42–43, 54, 56, 81–84
Brando, Dorothy (Dodie), 1–2, 4, 22, 25–30, 34, 37, 40–41, 46, 52, 54, 57, 68, 71, 74, 81–84, 104, 115, 188, 399, 420, 445, 457, 459, 494
Brando, Jocelyn, 54–55, 84
Brando, Marlon (Bud), 2, 42, 81–84, 115, 145, 174, 181, 217
Brayshaw, Rick, 374
Breaking Legs, 424
Breath of Spring, 266
Brecht, Bertolt, 297, 310
Brecht on Brecht, 277
Breci, Sebi, 177
Bresette, Jim, 304, 309–310, 312, 324
Brezhnev, Leonid, 352–353
Brice, Fanny, 11
Brief Music, 152
Brigadoon, 264, 411–413
Brigham Young, 94–95, 100–104, 109, 125, 127
Brighton Beach Memoirs, 390
Brigit St. Brigit Theatre, 414, 416
Brink, Palmer, 164–165
Brinkema, Bernice, 105
Brinkema, Robert, 97, 105, 109, 120–121, 127, 137
Bristol, Mike, 462
Broadway, 158, 208
Broadway Bound, 456
Broderick, Lynn, 338
Brokaw, Frances, 125, 186
Brooks, Anna Marie, 302
Brooks, Sidney, 228
Brooks, Todd, 350, 405–406

Bross, Steve, 426, 430–431
Brown, Alfred, 46
Brown, Frances, 114
Brown, Frank-Douglas, 405–406
Brown, Mrs. Alfred J., 42–44, 66, 97, 158
Brown, Richard Burton, 338
Brown, Sam, Jr., 290
Brown (Pyper), Frances, 97
Browne, Maurice, 18, 62
Brownell Hall (school), 91–92
Bruce, Lenny, 413
Bryan, William Jennings, 21, 230, 372
Brynner, Yul, 272, 371
Buchanan, Brendan, 401, 439
Buchanan, Sarah, 434
Buddy, 455–456, 462, 470, 493
Buffett, Ernest, 58
Buffett, Howard, 135
Buffett, Mrs. Howard, 135
Buffett, Susie, 226, 249, 251
Buffett, Warren, 135, 226, 372, 468
Bulldog, 123
Buller-Kirke, Dawn, 357, 375, 403, 425, 434, 442, 452–454, 456
Bunk Bed Brothers, 402
Burchard, Elizabeth, 244
Burnett, Carol, 193, 199, 263
Burnett, Frances Hodgson, 442
Burns, Julia, 220, 231
Burns, Mrs. Sam, 34
Busch, Charles, 453
Bush, George W., 445
Bush, Martin, 193
Butler, Dan, 132, 139–141
Butterflies Are Free, 309
Bye Bye Birdie, 257, 261
Byrd, Kaitlyn, 429

C

Cabaret, 337, 346
Cactus Flower, 297
Cady, Jay, 349
Cady, Joanne, 75, 318–321, 352, 357, 375, 378–379, 384, 394, 402, 406–407, 410, 416–417, 420–421, 435, 452, 457
Caffrey, Juliann (Julann), 129, 137, 174
Cagney, Jimmy, 116, 215
Caine, Michael, 335
Caine Mutiny Court Martial, 212–213, 376

Calculated Risk, 269
Caldwell, Erskine, 139–140
Caldwell (Morsman), Julie, 69
Call, Barbara, 385
The Camel with the Wrinkled Knees, 134
Camelot, 353–354, 439
Cameron, James, 437
Cameron, Kenneth, 251
Camp, Kevin, 417
Campbell, Mrs. Patrick, 8
Campbell, Patton, 404
Camperud, Jacque, 438
Camping with Henry & Tom, 438
Can Can, 386
Candida, 106, 145, 174
Candide, 377
Canton Players Guild (Ohio), 283
Capek, Karel, 48
Capra, Frank, 131, 442
Captain Applejack, 43
The Captain's Paradise, 300–301
Carlisle, Kitty, 321
Carnival, 415
Carousel, 39, 238, 453
Carpenter, Elizabeth Reed (Mrs. I.W., Jr.), 36–37, 84–86, 91–92, 106, 112, 124–126, 130–131, 136, 152–153
Carson, Johnny, 149, 249, 296, 364
Carter, Harvey, 186, 202
Carter, Jimmy, 339, 352–353, 413
Carter, Lillian, 339
Carter, Pamela, 309, 334, 352, 368, 378, 386, 398, 408, 431, 441–442, 460–461
Carter, Rossalynn, 339
Carver, Rosemary, 92
A Case of Libel, 274
Casey, Frank, 93
Casker, Diane, 291, 300, 314–315
Casker, R. Thomas, 283, 289, 294–295, 297, 300–301, 313, 315, 320
Cassady, Theresa, 387
Cassidy, Joseph, 418
Cat on a Hot Tin Roof, 264–265, 415
Catch Me If You Can, 300
Catcher in the Rye (Salinger), 473
Cather, Willa, 27, 322, 345, 413–416, 418–419
Catlin, Roger, 362, 366, 368–369, 373
Cavanaugh, Jim, 282–286, 288–292, 295

Cavanaugh, Milles, 283
The Cemetery Club, 440
Center Stage theater, 367, 390, 473
Central High School, 14, 224, 293
Chaney, Lon, Jr., 165
Channing, Carol, 223, 230
Chanticleer Theater (Council Bluffs), 203, 221, 226, 229, 234–235, 261, 276, 286, 302, 311, 320, 367, 390, 422–423, 426, 429, 453, 459
Chapman, Deloris, 168
Chapman, Denise, 475, 483
Chase, Mary, 250
Chayefsky, Paddy, 265
Chekhov, Anton, 274, 289
Chelminiak, Lee, 349, 353–354
Chesebrough, Bea, 113
Chess, Cal, 249
Chicago Drama League, 4
Chicago (film), 457
Chicago Little Theatre, 4
Chicago (play), 366, 457, 482–483
Chicoine, Martin, 96, 122, 124–125
Childe, Jim, 220
Children, 362
Children of a Lesser God, 388–389
Chodorov, Edward, 119
Choral Arts Society, 380
Christiansen, Jack, 127
Christie, Agatha, 229, 235, 304
Christie, Dick, 335
A Christmas Carol, 91, 252, 319, 324, 334, 336, 340–343, 345, 347, 349, 354–356, 358, 364, 368, 372, 376–377, 380, 384–385, 387–388, 390–395, 397, 407, 410, 412, 419, 422, 427, 431–432, 437–438, 440, 444–445, 448, 450–451, 453, 455, 461–465, 467–470, 473–477, 481, 484–486, 488, 492–493
Chvala, Ron, 418
Cinderella, 310
Circle Theater, 389–390, 402
Citron, Peter, 354
Civic Music Association (Council Bluffs), 142, 203
Civic Opera Society, 252
Civic Theatre Guild of Omaha, 170
Clark, Bernie, 438, 449, 453, 474, 480
Clark, Dick, 483
Clark, Edwin, 202, 205, 247, 249, 253, 315
Clark, Jason, 261

Clark, Kay, 454
Clark, W. Dale, 40
Clark-Kaczmarek, Anthony, 480, 484
Clark-Kaczmarek, Kim, 436
Claudia, 95, 162–163
Clement-Toberer, Susan, 448, 454, 477
Clements, Colin, 149
Cleveland Playhouse, 4, 44, 62, 136, 232, 256
Cline, Patsy, 471
Clinton, Bill, 411, 438, 444
Clizbe, Harold, 143
The Clod, 41
Clooney, Rosemary, 150
Clowers, Paula, 484
Clue—The Musical, 444
Coca, Imogene, 11
Cock Robin, 85
Cocoanuts, 475–476
Cody, Mildred, 92
Cohan, George M., 11, 33, 113, 150
Cohn, Esther, 20
Cohn, Frederick, 4, 20, 24, 32, 39
Coke, Peter, 266
Cole, Jonathan, 398, 408–409, 419, 426, 429, 434
Coleman, Cy, 421
Coleman, Dabney, 364
Collins, Dennis, 412, 440, 449, 462, 470, 484, 489
Collins, Judy, 150
Collins, Susan. See Baer, Susan
Columbus Little Theater, 322
Come Back, Little Sheba, 195
Come Blow Your Horn, 262
Comegys, Kathleen, 90
Command Decision, 184
The Community Playhouse of the Air, 165
Community Theater: Idea and Achievement (Gard and Burley), 237
Company, 474
Condon, Richard, 414
Congdon, Fritz, 294–297, 299–300, 302–304, 308–309, 313–314, 320
Congdon, Irwin, 294, 297, 309
Conklin, Grace Lennon, 28, 43
Connelly, Anne, 199, 203
Connelly, Marc, 11, 33, 48
Cook, Allen, 268, 270
Cooper, Mary F., 22–23, 46, 48–49, 75

Cooper Dance Studio, 24–25, 27, 30, 32, 35, 38, 43, 45, 48–49, 56, 58, 182, 255
Coopersmith, Jack, 266
Corbett, Ed, 206, 230, 233, 251, 262, 273
The Corn Is Green, 221–222, 269
Cornell, Katharine, 11, 80, 114, 121, 174
Corpse, 392–393
Council Bluffs Community Players, 96, 100, 203
Counsellor-at-Law, 108
The Country Girl, 116, 213–218, 224, 251, 404
Coward, Noel, 11, 33, 137, 167, 335, 476
Cowdery, Ben, 106
Coyle, Patrick, 357–358
Craig, Gordon, 31
Craik, Oscar Wilder, 6–8
Crawford, Derrick, 470
Crawford, Robert, 76
Crazy for You, 396, 443–444
Crimes of the Heart, 379
The Criminal Code, 86
Criss Foundation, 404
The Critic, 6
Crosby, Bing, 215–216
Crossman, Kay, 322
Crossman, Ray, Jr., 268, 313, 317–318, 322, 324–325, 399
Crothers, Rachel, 39, 164
Crotty, Christopher, 375
Crouse, Russel, 182, 202
Crowell, Julie, 488
Crown Matrimonial, 326
Crowns, 472–473
The Crucible, 220, 474
Cunningham, Glenn, 122–123, 131, 138, 146
Curran, Suzi, 284
Curtain Calls, 426
Curtis, Tony, 250
Cyrano, 376

D

Daddy Long Legs, 90
Dahlman, Jim, 10
Dalrymple, Charlie, 264
Daly, Leo, 338, 426, 490
Damn Yankees, 268
Damon, Matt, 473
Danielson, Connie, 280

The Dark at the Top of the Stairs, 448
Dark Eyes, 166
The Dark Tower, 158–159
Darling, Milton, 80, 139
Darnell, Edward, 146
Darrow, 328
Darrow, Clarence, 20, 230, 366, 372
Daub, Hal, 440
Daugherty, Robert, 293
David, Larry, 188, 190, 195, 202, 296
David, Nancy, 195–196, 201
Davidson, Dorothy, 38, 52–53
Davis, Barbee, 342
Davis, Bertha, 350
Davis, Bette, 127
Davis, Betty, 357, 359–360
Davis, Elmer, 72
Davis, Monty, 342
Davis, Mrs. Herbert, 82
Davis, Richard, 191
Davis, Ruth, 274, 290
Davis, Scott, 342
Davis, Ted, 342
Davis (Lauritzen), Elizabeth Ann. See Lauritzen, Libby Davis
Davison's Louisville Loons, 11
Davitt, Dorothy, 252, 323
Davlin, Rita, 143
Davy Crockett, 207
A Day in Hollywood/A Night in Ukraine, 415
de Bergerac, Cyrano, 442
The Deadly Game, 259
Dean, Alexander, 137
Dear Brutus, 70, 74, 111–112
Death of a Salesman, 274, 480
Death Takes a Holiday, 87, 188
Death Trap, 406–407
Dee, Sandra, 263
Defending the Caveman, 480
DeForest, Lee, 9
DeGeorge, Frances, 279
DeGeorge, Frank, 250, 253, 263, 279, 286, 309, 357, 361, 366, 370, 375–376, 391–392, 396, 424, 452–453, 456–457
Dejka, Joe, 406
A Delicate Balance, 290
Delmont, Jim, 28, 393, 403, 406, 408, 412, 414, 416–419, 421, 423, 434, 436, 438–439, 442, 445–447, 451, 453–456, 458
DeMille, Agnes, 322

DeMille, Cecil B., 68
DeMoss, Lyle, 149, 249, 280, 348
Denenberg, Eunie, 258, 277, 297, 348
Denenberg, Norm, 298, 348
Denker, Henry, 226
Dennis, Sandy, 277, 290
Dennison, Tom, 10, 13, 86, 236
Densmore, Wess, 171–172
Dergen, Harold, 180, 185, 203
Des Moines Playhouse, 220
Desert Song, 143
Desire Under the Elms, 11
The Desk Set, 228–229
The Desperate Hours, 225–226
Detective Story, 210
The Devil Passes, 99
The Devil's Disciple, 32–33, 36–38, 278
Devney, Jim, 396
Dewhurst, Colleen, 253
Dial M for Murder, 220
Diamond Studs, 356
The Diary of Anne Frank, 232, 235–236, 453
Dick Boyd award, 457
Dickens, Charles, 319, 340–341, 356, 364, 376, 407, 411, 431, 448, 463, 476
Diller, Phyllis, 260
Dillon, Robert, 224–225
DiMauro, Al, 285, 288, 290, 326, 342, 358, 376, 426
The Dining Room, 372
DiPietro, Joe, 454
Dirty Blonde, 462
The Distaff Side, 202
The Diviners, 396
Docherty, Charles, 6, 161, 176, 184, 248
Dock Street Theater (Charleston), 151, 154
Dodds, Edna, 188
Dodge, Grenville, 61
Dodge, Mrs. N.P., 32
Dodge, N.P., 61, 256–257, 265
A Doll's House, 105–107, 416
Donavan, Andrew, 424
Donnell, Cliff, 164
Donnermeyer, Sheryl (Donna Meyer), 273
Don't Dress for Dinner, 432–433
Don't Drink the Water, 296
Doorly, Gilbert, 150
Doorly, Henry, 5–6, 35, 106, 130

Doorly, Joy Hodges, 150, 394
Doorly, Katherine, 40, 44
Doorly, Margaret Hitchcock (Mrs. Henry), 5–7, 25, 33, 35, 40, 54–55, 81, 96, 103, 106, 138, 223, 295, 400
Doorly (Cowdery), Peggy, 106, 124
Dorner, Daniel, 456
Doughman, Phyllis, 398, 412, 429, 481
Doughman, Terry, 358
Douglas, Kirk, 210, 431
Douglas, Paul, 190
Douglas, William, 411
Down in the Valley, 193
Doxon, John, 274
Doyle, David, 83
Doyle, Fitzy, 83
Doyle, John (Dugie), 83
Doyle, Lom, 83
Dozier, William, 54, 69–70, 223, 229
Dracula, 356–357, 441–442
The Dragon's Curse, 269, 336, 400
Drama Critic's award, 299
Draper, C. Richard, 278, 286, 290
Dream Girl, 181
Dressler, Jane, 165–166
Drew, Howard, 383, 427–428
Drew, Jack, 182, 287
Drew Theatre. See Howard Drew Theatre
Driscoll, Delaney, 198, 401, 424
Driscoll, Gene, 198, 305, 309, 325, 424, 426
Driscoll, Tim, 198
Driving Miss Daisy, 427–428, 445
The Duenna, 90
Dulles, John Foster, 125
Dunbier, Auguste, 75
Duncan, Harry, 312
Duncan, Nancy, 310, 312, 314–315, 320, 330–332, 336, 338
Duncan, Richard, 193
Duncan, Sandy, 472
Dundee Dinner Theatre, 342, 434
Dunn, A.D., 136
Dunn, Gregg, 229–230, 233
Dunning, Phillip, 208
Durante, Jimmy, 150
Durbin, John (John Jackson), 398–399
Durham, Chuck, 288, 306–307, 311, 330–331, 399

515

Durham, Margre (Mrs. Charles), 275, 286–288, 293, 295, 297, 306–307, 311, 313, 327–328, 330, 336, 385, 395, 399, 424
Durham, Sunny, 287
Durrenmatt, Friedrich, 273
Duval, Robert, 350
Dyas, Ginny, 255–256
Dygert, Don, 209

E

Earl Carroll's Vanities, 11
East Lynne, 113
East of Suez, 99
Eastside Theatre (St. Paul), 286
Easy Rider (film), 298
Eaton, Joseph, 72
Eckert, Royal, 203–204, 207–208, 210, 212–213, 217, 226, 232, 236, 238, 240, 244, 248, 253, 257–258, 260, 263, 276, 278–279, 282, 284, 306, 313
Ecklebe, Kerry, 358, 366, 386, 443
Ecklebe, Lori, 366, 386, 443
Eckstrom, Fred, 56, 96
Eddy, Nelson, 150, 263, 288
Edell, Frederick, 271, 273–274, 276
Edison, Thomas, 438
Edith Head award, 260
Edward, My Son, 185
Edward, Quincy, 332
Edwards, Ralph, 194
Egan, Richard, 222–223
Egons, Silvia, 209
Eisenhardt, James, 314, 364, 375, 404, 490
Eisenhower, Dwight D., 125, 228
El Grande de Coca-Cola, 403
The Eldest, 113
Election (film), 198, 399
Electra, 230–231, 233
The Elephant Man, 456
Elizabeth the Queen, 97–98, 211
Ella, 489
Ellick, Al, 66, 421, 431
Ellick, Chuck, 220, 267
Ellick, Echo Guiou, 2, 24, 42, 66, 71, 73, 80, 126, 128, 138–139, 146, 149, 176, 183, 196, 208, 220, 254, 267, 269, 280, 282, 289, 294, 306, 313–314, 322, 324, 334, 336, 365–366, 400, 431, 493
Ellick, Robert, 66
Ellington, Duke, 408, 462
Ellis, DeeDee, 414
Ellis, Marie, 419
Emmy Gifford Children's Theater, 307, 390, 435
The Emperor's Physician, 100
Empress Theatre, 11–12
The Enchanted Cottage (film), 170
The Enchanted Cottage (play), 23–30, 32, 42–43, 95, 114, 143, 188, 255, 270, 443, 445
Engaged, 103–104
English, Estelle, 251, 260, 276, 319–320, 330, 336
English, James, 44
Enslin, Berne, 167–170
Enslin, Merrily Ann, 167
Eppley, Eugene, 100
Erdenberger, Jean, 232
Ervin, Denise, 355, 364, 371, 378, 422, 426
Escape, 76
Eure, Harry, 332
Evans, Mary Joan, 149
The Eve of St. Mark, 161
Evil Dead: The Musical, 486
Evita, 380
Excursion, 131
The Execution of Justice, 388

F

Fahey, Mike, 464
Falk, Peter, 367
A Family Portrait, 159–161, 198, 205, 413
Fanders, R.H., 398, 424
The Fantasticks, 304–305, 309, 398, 483–484, 489
A Far Country, 266
The Far-Off Hills, 123
The Farmer Takes a Wife (film), 114, 117
Farrell, Beatrice Hoel, 73–74, 158, 160, 163–164, 166, 168–170, 173, 178–179
Farrell, Mike, 469
Fascinating Rhythms, 367
Fashion, 68–69, 74, 103, 114, 142
Father of the Bride, 197–198, 404, 457
Fathers Against Sons, 297
Fauchois, Rene, 113
Fellman, Darlynn, 335, 348, 362–363, 378, 398, 403
Fellows, Greg, 410
Felton, Harold, 74, 105
Feltz, Muriel, 195, 200, 208
Fender, Teri, 442
Ferber, Edna, 11, 33, 92, 133
Ferguson, Don, 270
Ferrer, Jose, 206
The Fest of Theatre 1989, 398
A Few Good Men, 418
Fiddler on the Roof, 416, 479–480
Fidler, Jimmy, 146
Fiedler, Don, 358, 424
Field, Eugene, 17
Fields, W.C., 11
The Fighting Prince of Donegal (film), 277
Filbert, Louise, 203, 221, 258, 262–263, 278, 284, 348
Filbert, Norman, 203, 221–222, 233, 246, 278–279, 284, 298, 302, 348, 423, 445, 453, 459
Finkle, Brad, 380, 404
Fintel, Frances, 70–71, 73, 87, 96, 112
Firehouse Dinner Theater, 298–299, 302, 331, 335, 347, 391, 404, 416
First Impressions, 282
First Lady, 173
The First Legion, 233
The First Mrs. Fraser, 96–97
Fischbach, Bob, 28, 438–439, 441–442, 444, 461, 463, 476
Fischer, Howard, 114, 121, 125, 127, 213, 449
Fischer, Margaret, 255, 289, 334, 449
Fisher, Titus, 332
Fiske, Minnie, 8, 126–127
Fitch, Clyde, 33
Fitch, Lois, 174
Fitch, Louise, 127
Fitzgerald, Ella, 489
Flapper Wives (film), 12
Flavin, Martin, 86
Fleming, Jim, 297
Flores, Sara, 425, 431
Flower, John, 265, 372
Floyd, Robert, 177
Flyin' West, 483
Flynn, Catherine, 87, 92, 111–112, 159
Flynn, Damian, 58, 70, 74, 90, 94–96, 99, 104–106, 108, 113, 127, 138, 177, 223, 256
Flynn, James Allison, 40, 51, 54, 58, 77, 87, 95, 109, 146, 366

Flynn, James R., 112, 176, 183, 188
Flynn, Mary Emilie, 112
Fogarty, Edward F., 22
Fogarty, Frank, 22
Fogarty, Hugh, 22, 160
Fogg, Adelaide, 22–23, 68, 182, 300
Foley, Evelyn Sarrell, 49–50
Foley, Greg, 2, 16, 21, 23–27, 30, 32–34, 36–38, 40–41, 43–45, 48–49, 52–53, 57, 59–60, 63, 67–68, 85, 87, 94, 109, 133, 135–136, 189, 270, 313
Foley, Janie, 404
(Folio) Shakespeare Company, 33, 81, 106, 138
Folk Theatre, 6–9
Fonda, Douw (Dow), 59, 127, 131, 137, 151, 176–177
Fonda, Harriet, 34, 41–42, 51, 53, 70, 106, 114, 117–118, 124, 194, 214–215, 227, 230, 246, 260, 284, 287, 305, 359
Fonda, Henry, 2, 4, 7, 34, 36–37, 41, 43–44, 48–60, 67, 70, 72–73, 78–81, 84, 91, 94–95, 105, 108, 110, 114–118, 120, 125, 131, 136, 145, 151, 181, 186–187, 193, 208, 213–218, 223–224, 227–228, 241–242, 248, 251, 254, 260, 297, 305, 311, 328, 333, 359–360, 364–368, 394, 428, 457, 484, 494
Fonda, Herberta, 2, 51, 84, 118
Fonda, Jane, 34, 125, 137, 186, 214–215, 217, 220, 251, 253–254, 277, 279, 297–298, 305, 320, 360, 364–365
Fonda, Jayne, 25, 29, 34, 53, 72–73, 100, 117, 188, 296, 320
Fonda, Justin, 359–360
Fonda, Matt, 346
Fonda, Peter, 70, 125, 186, 215, 227, 230, 232, 241, 253–256, 260, 263, 298, 320, 359–360
Fonda, Shirlee, 359
Fonda, W. Brace, 7, 50–51, 58, 63, 72, 88–89, 114, 118, 231, 236, 297
Fonda-McGuire awards, 149, 151–152, 162, 182, 188, 192, 195, 206, 210, 249, 259, 274, 290, 299, 309, 314, 326, 354, 370–371, 409, 416, 442, 460, 474, 482, 484
Fonda-McGuire Hall, 380
Fonda-McGuire Series, 365, 369, 383–387, 389, 391, 395–396, 403, 405, 408, 411–412, 414, 422, 426–427, 430, 436–438, 441, 445
Fonda Theatre Center, 364–365, 367, 369, 373
Fontaine, Joan, 128
Fontanne, Lynn, 11, 132
Footlights Across America (MacGowan), 4, 80
Footloose, 481
Ford, Barbara, 301, 336, 370, 374, 383–385
Ford, Glenn, 171, 215
Ford, Henry, 438
Ford Foundation, 231, 247, 251
Fordyce, Mabel, 251
The Foreigner, 414
Forever Plaid, 443, 445
Forsythe, Lawrence, 92, 99, 145, 149, 165, 170, 173, 177, 182, 185, 195
Forty Carats, 305
Forty-Second Street, 409–410
Fosse, Bob, 421, 457
Fournier, Rifty, 183
The Fourposter (film), 309
Fowler, Nancy, 211
Fox, Seth, 458–459, 462, 468, 473–474, 484
Fox Theatre, 392
Franchetti, Afdera, 227
Francke, Caroline, 197
Francke, Warren, 285
Frank, Shirli, 320, 336
Frankenstein, 424, 492
Franklin, Benjamin, 308, 437–438
Frawley, William, 421
Frayn, Michael, 389
Frazell, Gary, 226, 284
Freeman, Laura, 418
French, Larry, 288
French, Samuel, 32
Freud, Sigmund, 266–267
Friel, Brian, 284
Friml, Rudolf, 11, 142
Frost, Jack, 310, 328, 346
Fry, Christopher, 198, 234
Fugard, Athol, 288, 403
Fugate, Caril, 402
The Full Monty (film), 467
Fuller, Mitch, 445
Funny Girl, 417, 444
A Funny Thing Happened on the Way to the Forum, 322, 410, 446–447
Furman, Bess, 72

G

Gable, Clark, 99, 184
Galileo, 335, 340
Gallagher, Paul, 99
Gallagher, Rachel, 98–99, 111, 115, 117–120
Galsworthy, John, 145
Galt, Robert, 25
Gamble, John, 20, 37
Game Show, 456
Gammer Gurton's Needle, 234–235
Garbo, Fred, 379
Garrett, Sue, 90, 97
Gast, Russell, 149, 151
Gaye, Marvin, 332
Gayety Theatre, 11
Gaynes, Beth, 258
Gaynor, Janet, 114
The Gazebo, 249
Gendler, Ruth, 392
Gentle People, 149
Gentleman's Agreement (film), 181
George and Margaret, 138
George Washington Slept Here, 151–152, 326
George White's Scandals, 10
Gerdes, Lou, 190
German Grand Opera company, 86
Gerow, Maude, 56
Gershwin, Ira and George, 11, 142, 367, 396, 444
Gibbs, Okley, 454
Gibilisco, John, 396, 454, 493
Gideon, 265, 267
Giffen, Gordon, 136–137, 143, 145, 147–149, 151–154, 162, 251
Giffen, Peter Thomas, 136
Giffen, True, 136, 139, 143, 148, 152, 154
Gifford, Harold, 186, 196, 213
Gifford, Jessie (Jessie Nebraska), 213, 220
Gifford, Jonas, 196
Gifford, M.E. (Emmy), 91, 124, 129–130, 147, 165, 186–187, 196, 198, 208, 213, 239–240, 244, 247, 252, 262, 267, 282, 287, 292–294, 300, 305–307, 319–320, 332, 336, 365

Gifford, Mrs. Sanford, 57
Gigi, 398–399
Gilbert, Lauren, 97, 105
Gilbert and Sullivan, 103, 143, 147–148
Gilmore, Jane, 313, 335
Gilroy, Frank, 304
The Gin Game, 371–372
Gingold, Hermione, 283
Ginsberg, Beth Gaynes, 227
The Girls in 509, 248
Gish, Dorothy, 90
Give 'Em Hell Harry, 470
Glaspell, Susan, 111
Glass Menagerie, 265, 429
The Glass Menagerie, 191
Gleason, Jimmy, 205
Glenn, Kenny, 462
Gloden, Audrey, 221–222
Glorious, 476
Glory Years, 426
Godfrey, Arthur, 199
Godspell, 332, 427, 462
Gold Dust, 361
The Golden Fleecing, 253
The Golden Follies show, 16, 319, 326, 328, 331, 333–334, 399–400
The Golden Goose, 106
Goldilocks and the Three Bears, 125
Goldman, Matt, 402
Goldwyn, Sam, 164
The Gondoliers, 143, 147
The Good Fairy, 111
Good Will Hunting (film), 473
The Good Woman of Setzuan, 297
Goodbye, My Fancy, 192
Goodman, Benny, 462
Goodman, Johnny, 132
Goodwillie, Ann, 343
Gordon, Ruth, 180
Gottschalk, John, 431
The Grab Bag, 10
Grable, Betty, 127
Grace and Glorie, 439–440
The Graduate, 462–463
Graham, Walt, 162
Grande Olde Players, 423, 435
Granger, Farley, 283
Grant, Heber, 101
The Grapes of Wrath, 428
Grapes of Wrath (film), 145
Grasso, Bernie, 244
Gray, Carl Raymond, 101
Gray, Charles, 161
Great Caesar's Ghost, 258

The Great Sebastians, 226–227, 295–296
Greater Tuna, 412
The Greatest Show On Earth, 379
Green, Milo, 173, 176, 180–181, 183–184, 187, 191, 193, 195, 200, 210, 212, 227, 235
Green Grow the Lilacs, 153, 368, 433
Green Pastures, 217
Greenberg, Sam, 91
Greenhouse, Bertha, 70
Greenleaf, Miles, 130
Greensleeves Magic, 306
Greenwich, Ellie, 428
Grennan, Bill, 486
Gribble, Harry Wagstaff, 54, 311
Gribble, Helen, 310–311
Griebel, Emily, 456
Griffith, D.W., 8
Griffith, Eric, 454
Grimes, George, 36
Grimm, Deana, 265
Griswold, Dwight, 162
Groh, Abe, 22
Gross Indecency, The Three Trials of Oscar Wilde, 445
Grumpy, 72
Grunwald, Bing, Jr., 44
The Guardsman, 11, 53, 165
Guinness, Alec, 301
Guiou, Arthur, 2, 60–61
Guiou, Genevieve Baldwin, 2, 4, 7–8, 15, 18, 24, 32, 43, 45, 59–62, 70, 88, 96, 110, 116, 124–125, 132, 135, 138–139, 144–145, 154–156, 228, 264, 268, 272, 280, 313, 380, 400, 431, 493
Guiou, Sarah, 71
Guiou (Ellick), Echo. See Ellick, Echo Guiou
Gurney, A.R., 424, 436, 453
Gurney, Melissa, 424
Guthrie Theater (Minneapolis), 252, 274
Guys and Dolls, 257, 276, 294, 374–375, 482
Gypsy, 282–284, 286, 401, 477, 479
The Gypsy Rover (road company), 3, 9, 15, 420

H

Haaland, Nils, 402, 445, 476
Haas, Ted, 150
Haberman, David, 285, 310

Hainey, Frank, 273
Hair, 296, 298, 304, 326, 459–460
Hairspray, 483
The Hairy Ape, 73, 76–77, 366
Hale, Keith, 412
Haling, Dutch, 434
Hall, Bob, 298, 306
Hall, Erika, 471
Hall, Howard, 211
Hall, Jerry, 41, 44
Hall, Rhonda, 387
Hamlet, 37
Hamlet '79, 351
Hammerstein, Oscar, 153, 310, 393, 433, 454
Hammon, Bill, 239
Hangen, Bruce, 422
Hanon, Kent, 303
Hansberry, Lorraine, 259
Hansen, Kermit, 148
Hansen, Mary (Mrs. Kermit), 193, 343
Hansen, Nels, 100
Hanson, Howard, 56–57
The Happiest Millionaire, 229, 232
Happy Birthday, 199–200
Happy Journey, 148
The Happy Time, 198–199
Harbour, James, 412
Harding, Warren, 438
Hargitt, Jerry, 359
Harker, Jim, 201, 207, 213, 215, 217, 226, 229–231, 242–244, 249
Harmati, Mrs. Sandor, 53
Harmati, Sandor, 35, 40, 63, 85
Harmon, James, 205, 212–213
Harms, Ruth, 6
Harper, Julie, 446, 454
Harper, Mike, 411, 426
Harper, Wilkinson, 206
Harrison, John, 346
Harrison, Rex, 309
Hart, Judith K., 440, 461
Hart, Keith, 452
Hart, Lorenz, 142
Hart, Moss, 33, 71, 90, 112, 152, 194, 279, 326
Hartig, Leo, 220, 222, 228
Harvey, 241
Hastings, Charlotte, 196
The Hasty Heart, 172–173
Haugh, Dorothy, 148
Having Our Say, 489
Hawks, Howard, 479, 491
Hawks, Rhonda, 479, 491

Hawley, L.C. (Brick), 22, 25, 28–30, 44, 188
Hawn, Goldie, 310
Hay Fever, 167
Hayes, Holland, 396
Hayes, Joseph, 269
Hazell, Pat, 358, 402, 418
He That Plays the King, 331
He Who Gets Slapped, 53
Hearst, William Randolph, 29, 130
The Heart Buster (film), 12
Hedda Gabler, 84
Hedican, Charlotte, 462
Hedrick, Harriet, 320
Heidi, 87–88
Heineman, Dave, 464
Heinrich, Milt, 386, 401, 413
The Heiress, 188, 438
Heiring, George, 276, 300
Helga and the White Peacock, 87
Hellman, Lillian, 168, 285, 442
Hello, Dolly, 230, 409
Hellzapoppin, 142
Hembree, Joe, 171
Heming, Violet, 80
Hennecke, Joan McCague, 159, 170–172, 186, 188, 259, 273, 323, 354–355, 362, 373, 388, 390, 394–395, 419, 460
Hennecke, Robert, 188
Henry, Irene, 182, 187
Hepburn, Katharine, 145, 315, 364–365, 393
Her Master's Voice, 119–120
Herbert, Hugh, 171–172
Herbert, Victor, 391
Hermann, Ginny, 428, 456
Herre, Dick, 232
Herrick, Mrs. Lester, 16
Higdem, Brandon, 444
Higgs, Richard, 245, 250, 280
The High Ground, 196
High Society, 315
High Tor, 132
Hike, Debbie, 310, 324
Hill, Carla, 347, 370, 385
Hiller, Richard, 223
Hindman, William, 247
Hiner, Connie, 250
Hiner, Marsha, 304, 309, 313
Hiram, 11
History of a Nutcracker (Gifford), 186–187
History of Drama in Omaha (Brown and Guiou), 43

History of the Omaha Playhouse from 1924 to 1963 (Nelson), 24
Hitch, Kelly, 352
Hitchcock, Gilbert, 4, 55, 225
Hitchcock, Margaret. See Doorly, Margaret Hitchcock
Hitchcock Foundation, 377
Hixenbaugh, Mrs. Walter, Jr., 16
Hixenbaugh, Walter, Jr., 31
Hoagland, Peter, 220
Hoberman, Jerry, 183
Hoberman, Larry, 183, 191
Hoberman, Leslie (Cookie), 295–296
Hoel (Farrell), Beatrice. See Farrell, Beatrice Hoel
Hoffman, Aaron, 13
Holiday, 175
Holland, E.L., 25, 33
Hollenbeck, Don, 130
Holley, Jack, 202, 269–270, 273
Holliday, Doreene, 168
Holliday, Judy, 189–190
Holliday, Virginia, 25, 27, 34, 36, 48
The Hollow, 235
Holly, Buddy, 455, 470, 493
Holmes, Stella, 123
Holtz, Lou, 10–11
Holtz, Thomson, 279
Homan, Keith, 220–221
Hook, Don, 417
Hope, Bob, 63, 116
Hopper, Edna Wallace, 12
Hopper, Hedda, 159, 200
Horne, Lena, 150
Hosman, Elfi, 245–246
House of Bernando Alba, 266
The House of Blue Leaves, 391, 393, 492
How the Other Half Loves, 334
How to Succeed in Business Without Really Trying, 348
Howard, Rance, 194
Howard, Ron, 194
Howard, Sidney, 68, 122, 172
Howard Drew Theatre, 379, 427–428, 430–431, 433–434, 436, 439, 441, 444, 447–449, 453–454, 456, 461, 463, 468, 470, 473, 476, 480–482, 484–486, 490, 493
Howell, Alice, 95
Howell, Rosemary, 78
Howes, Marguerite, 38
Huckleberry Finn (Twain), 406
Hudson, Betty, 311–312

Huff, Julie, 392, 419, 448, 473–474
Hughes, Dolores, 194–195
Hughes, Langston, 259
Hugo, Victor, 386
Hume, Dorothy, 198, 200
The Hunchback of Notre Dame, 386–387
Hunt, Alexandra, 185, 254, 438, 453
Hunt, Duwain, 425–426, 430, 435, 443, 446–447, 449
Hunt, Eugenie, 247
Hunt, Kenna, 211
Hunter, Tab, 367
Huston, Virginia, 166, 174
Huston, Walter, 11, 137
Hutson, Bill, 314–315, 338–339, 351–353, 358, 363, 376, 385, 391–393, 396–397, 405–406, 417–418, 425, 449, 459, 461, 472, 474, 482
Hwang, David Henry, 417

I

I Do, I Do, 309
I Killed the Count, 163
I Like It Here, 178
I Love You, You're Perfect, Now Change, 454, 457
I Never Sang for My Father, 296
I Remember Mama, 172, 182
Ibsen, Dwayne, 310
Ibsen, Henrik, 11, 33, 84, 105–107, 115, 274, 311, 416
I'd Rather Be Right, 150
An Ideal Husband, 73, 86
Idiot's Delight, 132, 140
Iliff, Caroline, 462
I'll Say She Is, 11
The Importance of Being Earnest, 179
In the Next Room, or the Vibrator Play, 481
Ince, Terry, 423
Incident at Vichy, 276
Indians, 305
Inge, William, 279, 448
Inherit the Wind, 230, 297, 372
The Inheritors, 111–112
Inspecting Carol, 448
International Amateur Theater Festival, 352
Interview, 291, 329, 331
Intimate Apparel, 475
Intimate Strangers, 86

Into the Woods, 423
Ionesco, Eugene, 265, 309
Irma La Douce, 314
Irving, Washington, 150, 170
Isaacson, Jake, 35
Isacson, Lenka. See Peterson, Lenka
Isacson, Sven, 181
It's a Wonderful Life, 468

J

Jabenis, Elaine, 197–198, 233, 242–244, 248, 253, 261–262, 265, 279, 285–286, 366, 386, 393, 404, 424, 427–429, 446, 457
Jack and Jill Playhouse, 55
Jack and the Beanstalk, 86, 143
Jackson, Dave, 429
Jackson, John (John Durbin), 398–399
Jackson, Shannon, 473
Jacob, White, 250–251, 258, 260, 268
Jacques Brel Is Alive and Well and Living in Paris, 315, 323, 332
James, Henry, 188, 438
James, Jesse, 187
Janie, 165, 174
Jarecke, Melissa, 271, 396, 454, 470
Jazz Singer (film), 9
J.B., 253, 261
Jealousy, 90
Jeffrey, Lew, 266
Jelen, Josephine, 123
Jenkins, Maggie, 183
Jenks, Hart, 73–74, 81, 91–92, 96, 106, 133
Jenks, Mrs. Hart, 270
Jenson-Frey, Angela, 454, 473, 475
Jesse, Marie Stewart (Mrs. John), 222
Jewish Community Center, 203, 348
Jiggers of 1923, 38
Jim Dandy, 152, 173
Jitney Players, 90
Joan of Lorraine, 177–178
John Beasley Theatre, 483
John Brown's Body, 262
John Loves Mary, 184
John XXIII (Pope), 385
Johnson, David K., 315, 332, 334–335, 347–349, 355
Johnson, Dick (Dick Christie), 283

Johnson, Gary, 289–291
Johnson, Gloria, 260
Johnson, Mary T., 69
Johnson, Michele, 291
Johnson, Tom, 320
Johnson, Yvonne, 230, 232, 259
Johnston, Anne, 29
Johnston, John Dennis, 303
Johnston (Marshall), Sally, 94, 120, 138–139
Jolson, Al, 9, 63
Jonas, Carl, 91
Jonas, Mary Elizabeth. See Gifford, M.E. (Emmy)
Jones, Becky, 412, 433
Jones, Charles, 268, 271, 283, 311, 314–315, 317–326, 330–331, 333–343, 345–349, 351–354, 356–359, 361–364, 366–367, 369, 371, 373–381, 383–385, 387, 391–392, 394–396, 398–401, 404, 407, 409–422, 424–426, 428–431, 433–435, 437, 439, 443, 446, 452, 457, 460, 463–465, 469, 476, 478, 481, 484, 487, 489, 493
Jones, Eleanor Brodie, 317–319, 322, 324, 334, 346, 387–388, 392, 406, 411, 417, 419, 421–422, 424–425, 464, 477, 481
Jones, Jeff, 478
Jones, Jennifer, 116
Jones, Preston, 346
Jones, Slim, 14
Jones, Tom, 309
Jones, W. Boyd, 185, 189, 264
Jonson, Ben, 113
Jordan, Jeff, 330
Joseph, Leon Edward, 57
Joseph and the Amazing Technicolor Dream Coat, 362, 417–418, 458, 479
Joslyn, Sarah, 19, 32, 41, 55, 63, 66, 94, 110, 146
Joslyn, Violet, 19
Joslyn Museum, 19, 95, 101, 105, 146, 152, 178, 224, 250, 292–293
Jubenville, Kim, 473, 479
Judd, Franklyn, 120, 125
Julius Caesar, 258, 398
June Moon, 105
Junior League Players, 112
Junior Theater, 55, 186, 196, 229, 250, 269, 271, 292–294, 298, 305–308, 310, 336, 435
Just So Stories, 347

K

Kahn, Otto, 45, 52
Kalal, Don, 210, 354, 361, 370
Kalber, David, 305
Kalber, Floyd, 305
Kaling, Mindy, 473
Kalis, David, 461
Kamm, Joseph, 206
Kamprath, Matt, 351, 397, 403, 411, 418, 423, 437–439, 442, 446–447, 449, 470–471, 481, 493
Kanin, Fay, 192
Kanin, Garson, 189, 192
Karel, Charles, 420
Katz, Earl, 296
Kaufman, George S., 11, 33, 48, 71, 90, 92, 105, 112, 133, 152, 175, 211, 222, 279, 326, 476
Kaye, Marsha, 422
Kazan, Elia, 181
Keats, John, 112, 138, 180
Keilstrup, Margaret, 335
Keiner, Jack, 191
Keller, Helen, 444
Kellogg, William, 252, 292
Kelly, George, 32–33
Kelly, Grace, 215, 217
Kelly, Jean, 165
Kelly, Mike, 410
Kelpe, Henry, 184
Kennebunkport Playhouse, 321
Kennedy, Jackie, 135
Kennedy, John, 265
Kennedy, Robert, 290
Kennedy, Thomas C., 112, 138, 147, 180–181
Kent, Christel Pratt, 138, 143, 154, 263, 323
Keough, Don, 206
Kern, Jerome, 142
Kerr, Deborah, 272
Kerr, Jean, 266, 270
Kerrey, Bob, 374–375
Kersigo, Rita, 248
Kesey, Ken, 431
Key, Frances McChesney, 129, 157, 159, 166, 170, 173, 177, 180, 199, 232, 254, 267
Key, Walter, 166
The Kid, 335–336
Kiewit, Peter, 71, 236–237, 293, 426
Kiewit, Ralph, 70–71
Kiewit Foundation, 311, 359, 371, 375

Kimball, Arabell, 5–6, 35
Kimball, Mrs. T.L., 35, 52
Kimball, Thomas, 4–6, 19, 34, 42
Kimberly Akimbo, 470
Kind Lady, 119, 121
King, Madalyn, 190
King, Martin Luther, Jr., 290
King, Philip, 262
King and I, 257, 272, 371
King o' the Moon, 468
King of Hearts, 219–220
King Richard the II, 388
Kingman, Eugene, 186, 247, 292
Kingsley, Sidney, 210
Kingsmark Players, 204, 206, 220, 229, 286
Kipling, Rudyard, 347
Kirkwood, Dave, 478, 485, 490–493
Kiser, Terry, 262–263, 265, 278, 280
Kismet, 349
Kiss and Tell, 170–172
A Kiss for Cinderella, 72–73, 78–80, 84, 145, 216, 364, 394
Kiss Me Kate, 252, 258
Kit Kat Klub (London), 92
Klammer, A.A., 140
Klem, Alan, 352
Kliesen, Chris, 386
Klugman, Jack, 194
Klute (film), 297, 305
Kluver, Kirsten, 447, 482–483
Knickerbocker Holiday, 150–151, 170, 193, 251, 256, 394, 401
Knott, Frederick, 290
Knox, John, 211
Knutson, Joel, 350, 357, 366
Koch, Harry, 63
Koffend, John, 200–202, 205–211
Kolbrek, Heather, 441
Koll, J. William (Bill), 264, 272–273, 292, 295, 298, 314–315, 325, 370–371
Konecky, Eugene, 8–9, 76–77
Kopit, Arthur, 269, 305
Kountze, Denman, Jr., 28, 216–217, 225–226, 232–236, 246–247, 249–250, 258–259, 263, 265–266, 268–269, 279, 284, 289, 293–294, 296, 299
Krasna, Norman, 114, 250
Krell, Agnes, 123, 131, 134, 154, 229
Krell, Lawrence, 72, 114–115, 122, 151, 154, 229
Krentz, Gordon, 358, 403, 414–415, 430, 444

Kruse, Sally, 268, 270
Kucera, Lew, 248, 259, 265
Kuffel, Valerian (Johnny Valerian), 202, 262–263, 270, 276, 279–280
Kuhn, R. Stephen, 407, 419
Kunz, Amy, 391, 474
Kurtz, Julianne, 232
Kurtz, Swoosie, 232
Kurz, Cathy Wells, 414, 416
Kurz, Scott, 474

L

La Cage aux Folles, 435–436, 459
Laboratory Group, 69, 87, 151–152, 230, 269, 291
LaBourdette, Katie, 434
Ladies in Retirement, 156–157, 254
Ladies of the Jury, 127
Lady Astor (goat), 234
Lady Be Good, 11
The Lady Who Came to Stay, 168
Lady Windemere's Fan, 48
The Lady with All the Answers, 480
The Lady's Not for Burning, 198
Lamb, Stacie, 456
Land, Nancy, 218, 238, 246–247
Landis, David, 379, 392
Landis, Melodee, 379
Landman, Morey, 176, 236, 282
Lane, Amy, 480–481, 485–487
Lane, Mary, 14, 76
Lang, Andrea, 417, 434
Langdon, Harry, 103, 135, 198, 208–209, 217, 226, 273, 296
Langdon, Kenneth, 338
LaPlante, Laura, 11
Lardner, Ring, 105
The Lark, 288
Larsen, Wendy, 300
Larson, Barry, 183, 274
Lassegard, Stan, 389
The Last Meeting of the Knights of the White Magnolia, 347
The Last Mile, 90, 93, 107
The Last Night of Ballyhoo, 445
The Last of the Red-Hot Lovers, 309
The Last Stand of the Polish Sharpshooters, 406
The Late Christopher Bean, 113
The Late George Apley, 175–176
Lauder, Harry, 22
Laughlin, DeDe, 356
Laughlin, Graham, 476–478
Laughlin, Mark, 356, 476

Laughlin, Melissa, 356
Lauritzen, Bruce, 490
Lauritzen, Clark, 368
Lauritzen, Kim, 490
Lauritzen, Libby Davis, 133, 153, 180, 183, 186, 295, 368
Lavery, Emmet, 152, 233
Lawler, Kevin, 402
Lawrence, Gertrude, 137
Lay My Burden Down, 331–332
Le Vaillant, Nigel, 388
Leachman, Cloris, 220
Leacox, Laura Beth, 370
Leader of the Pack, 428
Lee, Connie, 420, 442, 447, 463, 468, 474, 482
Lee, Craig, 428
Lee, Donald Craig, 391
Lee, Harper, 350, 432
Legally Blonde, 485
Lehman, Joseph, 85
Lehman, Mrs. Joseph, 119
Leigh, Janet, 250
LeMay, Curtis, 184
Lemmon, Jack, 215, 357
Lend Me a Tenor, 412, 483–484
The Leopard Lady, 59
Lerner, Alan Jay, 264, 294, 439
Les Misérables, 406, 415–416, 420, 476, 487–488, 492
The Lesson, 265
Lester Polakov Studio, 321
Let 'Er Go Gallagher, 59
Let Us Be Gay, 164–165
Letts, Tracy, 485
Levin, Ira, 406
Levine, Joseph, 239, 245, 252, 257, 272, 292, 343
Levine, Mary, 268, 272–273, 284, 288, 292, 294, 343
Levings, Mark, 2, 6, 16–17, 32, 36, 41, 51, 121, 131, 149
Levings, Mary, 16–18, 25
Lewis, C.S., 425
Lewis, Jack, 311
Lewis, Jamie, 338, 449
Lewis, Kathy (Mrs. Jack), 311, 399, 442
Lewis, Klea Orschel, 21
Lewis, Melissa, 423, 429
Lewis, Shari, 318
Lewis and Clark Junior High School, 306
Libel, 125–126
Liberman, Cappy, 114

Lien, Rachel, 444
Life with Father, 182, 273
Light Up the Sky, 194–195
Lilienthal, David, 116
Liliom, 15, 30, 32–33, 38–41, 77, 459
Lillie, Bea, 11, 80
Lincoln, Abraham, 141, 155, 262
Lincoln Playhouse, 331
Lindsay, Howard, 182, 202
Link, Amanda, 447
Lion in Winter, 391, 393
Lipsey, Al, 202
Littau, Joseph, 86
Little Black Sambo, 130
The Little Foxes, 168, 223, 285, 442
Little Mary Sunshine, 263, 288
A Little Night Music, 339, 343
Little Post Theatre, 5
The Little Princess, 73
A Little Shop of Horrors, 419
Little Women, 490
Livers, Loma, 274
Lloyd Webber, Andrew, 362, 380, 418, 479
Loesser, Frank, 374
Loewe, Frederick, 264, 294, 439
Logan, Josh, 251
Long, Almon, 103
Long Wharf Theater (New Haven), 270
Longe, Jerry, 361–362, 369, 376–377, 404, 408, 410, 414, 418, 439, 441–442, 445, 449, 468–469, 476–477, 484
Lonsdale, Frederick, 33, 63, 66
Look Homeward Angel, 232, 377
Loos, Anita, 199
Loos, Elizabeth, 440
Lorca, Garcia, 266
Lord, Pauline, 10–11
Los Moros y Christianos, 3
Lost in Yonkers, 425
Loucks, Mrs. Elton, 151, 304
Louder, Please, 114–115
Louis, Mrs. Karl, 66–67
The Love Duel, 87
Love 'Em and Leave 'Em (film), 9
Love Letters, 424, 436, 453
Love Rides the Rails, 286
Love Song (film), 117
Loveland Summer Theatre, 224
Lu Ann Hampton Lavery Oberlander, 347
Lucca-Thyberg, Marya, 432, 451
Luce, Henry, 148

Ludlam, Charles, 408
Lueder, Mary, 330
Lueder, Robert, 330–331
Lugosi, Bela, 442
Lunt, Alfred, 11, 132, 137, 140
Luttrell, Donald, 145, 207
Luv, 284
Lynch, Dan, 252, 275
Lynch, Edmund, Jr., 228
Lysistrata, 296

M

M. Butterfly, 417–418
Macbeth, 123, 285
MacDonald, Jeannette, 263, 288
MacGowan, Kenneth, 3–4, 23, 32–33, 80
MacIver, Jane, 229–231, 233–234, 247, 249, 262–263
Mack and Mabel, 449
Mackin, Clare, 2, 16, 20, 59, 188
Mackin, Marie, 2, 16, 25, 40, 90
MacLaine, Shirley, 421
MacLeish, Archibald, 148, 261
MacLeod, Bernice, 96
Madison, Rosemary, 261, 270, 276–277, 279, 284
Madsen, Gale, 312
The Madwoman of Chaillot, 191, 221
Maeterlinck, Maurice, 75
Maggie awards, 315
Magic Theater, 302, 348, 367
Mahaffey, Jack, 421
Mahoney, Mabel. See Baer, Mabel Mahoney
Majors, David, 162
Majors, Elaine, 272
Make Mine Mink (film), 266
Makousky, Dick, 243, 261
The Male Animal, 151–152, 221
Mame, 434
Mamet, David, 489
A Man for All Seasons, 273–274
Man of La Mancha, 274, 298–300, 388
A Man of No Importance, 461
The Man Who Came to Dinner, 203, 454
The Manchurian Candidate, 414
Mangiameli, Moira, 461, 486–487
Manhattan Theatre Club, 490
Mann, Mildred, 239
Mansfield, Richard, 67

Manso, Peter, 81
Mantell, Robert, 37
March Hares, 54
Marchant, William, 229
Marchbanks, Eugene, 145
Marcy, Nancy, 390
Margin for Error, 148
Margot Jones Theatre (Dallas), 251
Marilyn, Sleepless Nights, 434
Marked Woman (film), 127
Markham, Edwin, 20
Marquand, John P., 175
Marquis De Sade, 304
Marr, Doug, 389–390, 402–403, 486
Marr, Laura, 389
Marriage-Go-Round, 264, 268, 321
Marsh, Lara, 451, 484
Marshall, John, 139
Marshall, Sally Johnston. See Johnston (Marshall), Sally
Marshall, William (William Jay), 278
Martin, David, 212
Martin, Joe, 269
Martin, Mary, 309, 472
Marty (film), 265
The Marvelous Wonderettes, 456
Marvin's Room, 419
Marx, Groucho, 476
Marx, Joan, 244
Marx Brothers, 11, 333, 414–415
Mary, Mary, 266, 269–270
Mary of Scotland, 208–212
Mary Peckham award, 404, 432, 442, 454, 456
Mary the Third, 38–39
The Mask of Moriarty, 445
Mason, Myrtle, 37, 39–40
Masque of Kings, 137
Masters, Edgar Lee, 284
Masters, Helen, 7, 16, 18
Masters, J.G., 7
The Matchmaker, 230
Matlin, Marlee, 388
Matsuo, Warner, 234
Matt and Ben, 473
Matthau, Walter, 286
Maugham, W. Somerset, 99
May, Foster, 129
Mayerling (film), 137
McArdle, Howard, 210
McAuliffe, Krista, 380
McBride, Jack, 176, 180, 183, 190, 194, 198
McCabe, William, 190

McCague (Hennecke), Joan. See Hennecke, Joan McCague
McCall, Andrea, 356
McCall-Tynan, Andrea, 352
McCarthy, Joe, 189
McCartney, Jean, 264, 334
McChesney (Key), Frances. See Key, Frances McChesney
McCleery, William, 185
McConnell, Frederick, 18, 62, 136
McCrea, Joel, 118
McCullers, Carson, 418
McCullough, David, 438
McDonald, Alan, 2, 16, 18–21, 23, 25, 30, 35, 40–41, 49, 53–56, 58, 63–64, 85, 88–89, 93, 104, 136, 140, 146–147, 178–179, 188, 228, 420, 493
McDonald, Donald, 20, 71
McDonald, Helen Scobie (Mrs. Alan), 18–20, 24, 99, 180, 188, 282
McDonald, John, 19, 55, 58, 64, 146
McDonald, Wallace, 20, 71
McEvoy, J.P., 57
McGavin, Darren, 256
McGee, Fibber, 143
McGee, John, 100, 103–104, 125
McGill, Jennifer, 482
McGill, Mrs., 205
McGorrisk, Dora Sass, 21
McGreevy, Andrew, 468
McGuigan, Billy, 455–456, 470, 473, 479, 493
McGuigan, Matthew, 470
McGuigan, Ryan, 470
McGuire, Dorothy, 2, 4, 73, 75, 78–80, 84, 87–88, 92, 94–95, 116, 119, 133, 138, 144–145, 151, 162–163, 170, 177, 181, 186, 188, 208, 213–218, 223–224, 228, 241–242, 248, 251, 256, 260, 332–333, 360, 364–365, 367, 394, 445, 457, 494
McGuire award. See Fonda-McGuire awards
McHugh, Kate, 4, 6–7
McIntyre, George, 40, 54, 72, 78, 92
McIntyre, Molly, 58
McKain, Jim, 409, 461, 475, 483, 493
McKee, Karla, 250
McKeon, Doug, 364
McLean, Jerry. See Longe, Jerry

McMorris, Robert, 247, 250, 252–253, 262–265, 268, 322, 424–425
McNeal, Clyde, 413
McNichols, Eloise West, 68, 143, 145
McNichols, Larry, 145
McPherson, Scott, 419
McSwain, Mia, 473
McSwain, Michelle, 473
McSwain, Sondra, 473
M'Cullough, T.W., 115
Mead, J.F., 43
Mead, Linda, 419–420, 425
Mealer, Rose, 315
Means, Ray, 396
Medders, Ruth, 68
Melcher, Joel, 184
Melcher, Marian (Mimi), 184, 188, 191, 206, 230–231, 233, 247, 252
The Member of the Wedding, 418
Menard, Orville, 10
Menotti, Gian-Carlo, 193
Mercer, Nancy, 113
Mercer, Nelson, 113
Mercer, Samuel, 113
Meredith, Burgess, 213
Merman, Ethel, 352, 401, 439
Merriam, J. Alec, 272, 275
Merrily We Roll Along, 71, 112
Merton of the Movies, 48–50, 73, 297, 365–367
Metoyer-Moore, Lanette, 418, 427, 440, 489
Metoyer-Moten, Camille, 380, 417, 427, 441, 489
Metropolitan Actors Guild (MAG), 278, 380
Metropolitan Opera Company, 45, 420, 438
Metzger, Mary Ann, 443
Meyer, Lloyd, 490–491
Mick, Phil, 37, 39–40
Micks, Eric, 482
Midsummer Night's Dream, 123
Midwest Arts Alliance, 421
Milan, Henri, 40–41
Milder, Orvel, 278, 343
Milhollin, James, 185, 187, 191–192, 194, 211, 214–215, 217, 223, 231
Military Theater, 87
Milk, Harvey, 388
Millard Foundation, 353
Millburg, Steve, 353, 355, 389–390
Millennium Theatre, 444

Miller, Ann, 116
Miller, Arthur, 220, 250, 274, 276, 311, 474, 480
Miller, Jason, 324
Miller, Kathleen Shaw, 148
Miller, Linda Lou (cockatoo), 212
Miller, Morris, 75
Miller, Roger, 406
Milne, A.A., 33, 41
Miloni, Joe, 354, 373, 380, 398, 403, 412, 422, 436, 446, 452
Minge, Jim, 423
Minnelli, Liza, 346
The Miracle Worker, 444
Misner, Ernest, 7
Misner School of the Spoken Word, 7–8
Missouri Legend, 187
Mister Antonio, 92
Mister Roberts (film), 215
Mitchell, J.P., 226
Mix, Tom, 12
Moby Dick, 490
Mock, John, 490
Moeller, Helen, 277
The Mole, 25
Moliere, 33, 285, 347
Molnar, Ferenc, 11, 32–33, 39–40, 43–44, 53, 63, 111, 165
The Money-Changers, 96, 100, 148
Monroe, Marilyn, 333, 434
Monsieur Beaucaire, 67
Montgomery, Robert, 211
Mooberry, Eleanor, 178
Mooberry, F. Merion, 197, 226
The Moon Is Blue, 198, 203–206, 289, 459
Moon Over Buffalo, 441–442
Moon Theater, 12
Moonlight and Magnolias, 476, 479
Moore, Charles, 38
Moore, Joe, 314
Moore, Lanette, 473
Moores, Merle, 305
Morales, Greg, 392
Moran, Betsy, 447, 451
More, Thomas, 273
More Fun Than Bowling, 457
Morehouse, Rex, 2, 6, 15–18, 40, 48
Morgan, Ed, 165
Morgan Rock, 247
Morley, Robert, 322
Morrill, Dean, 179–180
Morris, Kenyon, 27
Morrison, Frank, 254

Morrissey, John, 387, 396
Morrow, Fred, 100
Morrow, Kevyn, 332, 462, 465–466
Morsman, Julie Caldwell, 69
Morton, Donald, 93, 107
Moscow Studio Theatre of the Southwest, 398
Moskovitz, Jack, 210, 454
Most Happy Fella, 68, 420
Mostel, Zero, 322, 410
Mother Courage, 310
Motherwell, Robert, 43
Motion Picture Relief Fund, 164
Mountain, 411
Mousetrap, 304, 313
Mowatt, Anna Cora Ogden, 68
Mr. and Mrs. North, 153–154
Mr. Pepys, 56
Mr. Roberts, 84, 181, 186–187, 193, 210, 234, 366
Mrs. Bob Cratchit's Wild Christmas Binge, 468
Mrs. McThing Harvey, 250
Mueller, Dick, 261, 278, 297–299, 302, 331
Mueller, MariJane, 297, 299
Murphey, Jill, 335
Murray, Mary (Ethyl Rogers), 133, 164, 176, 188, 192, 210
Murrow, Edward R., 199
Muse Theater, 12
Music Hall, 213, 218
The Music Man, 241, 318, 320, 323, 353, 420, 422, 425
The Musical Comedy Murders of 1940, 398–399
My Antonia, 345, 416, 418–419, 423, 458
My Dear Children, 144
My Fair Lady, 54, 142, 294–295, 298, 357–358, 444–446, 457
My Heart's in the Highlands, 148
My Life (Fonda), 34, 215
My Sister Eileen, 176
My Three Angels, 209, 278, 430
My Way, 451
The Mystery of Edwin Drood, 411
The Mystery of Irma Vep, 408

N

Nagl, Nancy, 181, 192
National Art Players, 90
National Endowment for the Arts, 331, 339
National Theatre of Great Britain, 398
Natividad, Kitten, 328
Neary, Andrew, 456
Nebraska Arts Council, 271, 311, 325, 337, 348, 433
Nebraska (film), 198, 399
Nebraska Repertory Company, 302, 310, 349, 391
The Nebraska Shakespeare Festival, 390
Nebraska Theatre Caravan, 29, 271, 314, 319, 337–339, 343, 346–350, 353–356, 358, 361–362, 367–369, 372, 376–378, 384–386, 388, 390, 392, 396–398, 403, 406–407, 410–411, 415, 418, 421, 423, 427, 432, 434–435, 438, 440, 442–443, 445, 448–451, 454, 460–461, 466, 468, 484–485, 490, 493
Ned McCobb's Daughter, 85
Neihardt, John, 27
Nelsen, Don, 193
Nelson, Ben, 440
Nelson, Robert Martin, 24, 30
Nemec, Lois, 440, 453, 461, 480
Ness, Gerald, 260, 262–263, 265–271, 324, 337–338
Nethaway, Lulu, 149
Neu, Robert, 299–300, 302
Neugent, Mary Cay, 204, 206
Neumann, Tom, 417, 468
Never Too Late, 274
New Faces of 1934, 94–95, 105, 108
Newbranch, Harvey, 77
Newbranch, Myrtle, 77
Newbranch, Nancy, 107
Newcomb, Patricia, 207
Newhouse, Samuel, 237
Newlean, Jeannette, 223
Newley, Anthony, 308
Newman, Bailey, 468
Newman, Spencer, 470
Newmar, Julie, 268
Nguyen, Don, 417–418
Nicholson, Jack, 418, 431
Nielsen, Bradley, 389
Nielsen, Roxanne, 389, 414–415, 439, 441, 452, 462, 468
Nielsen, Sarah, 439
Night Must Fall, 131
Night of January 6th (play), 126, 129
Night of January 6th (Rand), 126, 129
The Night Thoreau Spent in Jail, 312
Night Watch, 313
Nightengale, Helen, 41
The 1940s Radio Hour, 387–388, 390
Nixon, Richard, 290, 317
No Exit, 265, 285
No Sex, Please, We're British, 343, 456
No Time for Sergeants (film), 231
Noble, Becky, 342
Noble, Phyllis, 357, 361, 392
Noel, Don, 290, 456
Nogg, Ozzie, 258, 261, 278–280, 292, 300
Noises Off, 389
None So Blind (film), 174
Norton, Dorothy, 38–39
Norton, Kenneth, 38
Norton, Lewis J., 42
Norton, Rudyard, 38–39, 54, 59, 66, 97–98, 104–105, 107, 133, 139, 175–176, 178, 220–221, 223, 226, 230, 233, 243, 259, 262–264, 269, 277–278, 296, 302, 305, 334, 352, 365, 399–400, 457
Norton Theatre, 302, 310, 367, 391
Noseworthy, Jane, 454, 461
Not for Nightingales, 461
Not Now Darling, 323
Novotny, Tom, 299
Nunsense, 482
Nutcracker, 300
Nyland, Louise, 266, 280

O

O Pioneers!, 345, 413–415
Obama, Barack, 475
Oberdorfer, Carl, 268
O'Brien, Liam, 213
O'Casey, Sean, 119
O'Connor, Daniel, 152, 173, 177, 181, 253
O'Connor, Joseph, II, 476, 488
O'Connor, Sandra Day, 371
O'Dare, Bobbie, 59
The Odd Couple, 286, 289, 482
Odets, Clifford, 117, 119, 215–216
Of Mice and Men, 358
Of Thee I Sing, 142, 395–396
Of Them We Sing, 88–89
O'Flynn, Damian. See Flynn, Damian
Oh Coward!, 335

Oh Dad, Poor Dad, Mama's Hung You in the Closet and I'm Feelin' So Sad, 269, 304
Oh What a Lovely War, 290
Ohlinger, Rosalie, 274
O'Keefe, Georgia, 428
Oklahoma, 142, 153, 252, 432–433
Old Acquaintance, 172
Old Yeller (film), 256
The Oldest Living Graduate, 346–347
Oliver, 303, 429
Olivier, Laurence, 335
Olsen, James T., 469
Olsen and Johnson (comedy team), 142
Olson, Harriet, 255–256, 263, 278, 290
Olson, Mel, 255–256, 262–263, 294
Olson, Oscar, 64–65
Olson, Steven, 429, 434
Olson, Walter, 213, 266, 274, 290
Omaha Ballet Academy, 261, 272
Omaha Ballet Company, 300
Omaha Civic Ballet Academy, 288
Omaha Drama League, 2, 4, 15, 196
Omaha Junior Theater. See Junior Theater
Omaha Society for the Grand Opera, 70
Omaha Symphony, 53, 86, 136, 422, 429
Omaha Theater Company for Young People (OTCYP), 307, 435
On Borrowed Time, 191, 410
On Golden Pond (film), 360–361, 364–366
On Golden Pond (play), 360–362, 483–484
On the Verge, 398
On the Waterfront (film), 81, 217
Once in a Lifetime, 90
Once More with Feeling, 250
Once on This Island, 441
One Flew Over the Cuckoo's Nest, 431
One Sunday Afternoon, 114
O'Neal, Dennis, 450, 487, 490–492
110 in the Shade, 339, 407
O'Neill, Eugene, 1, 3, 11, 33, 39, 48, 52, 57–58, 73, 76, 99, 113, 115, 224
Ong, Eugenia, 96
Opera Omaha, 422
O'Rourke, Sally Ann, 44

Orpheum Theatre, 10–11, 20, 25, 27, 117, 274, 352, 364, 367, 406, 467, 492
Orpheus Descending, 339, 343
Orson Welles Mercury Theater of the Air, 147
Orwell, George, 392
Osborn, Paul, 191
Osborne, Tom, 464
Othello, 91
Other People's Money, 412
Othuse, Jim, 317–321, 323, 325, 330–331, 340, 343, 345, 355, 357–358, 361, 371, 375–376, 384, 391, 406–408, 413, 415–416, 419–420, 424, 428, 430, 438–440, 452, 457, 461–462, 467, 493
Our American Cousin, 141–144, 251
Our Country's Good, 449
Our Town, 133, 138, 145, 206, 220, 230, 398
Ouspenskaya, Maria, 165
The Outlaw (film), 223
Outward Bound, 42–43, 45
Over 21, 170
Over Here!, 392–393
Over the River and Through the Woods, 454
Over the Tavern, 461, 468
Owen, Dee, 151, 153, 301, 311, 359, 369, 374, 386, 395–396, 400–402, 410, 443
Owen, Ed, 151, 153, 311, 359, 369, 374–375, 380, 386, 388, 395–396, 400–401
Owen Foundation, 371, 380
Ozma of Oz, 423

P

A Pack of Lies, 396
Page, Esther, 167–168, 223
Paint Your Wagon, 388–389
Pajama Game, 245, 257
Palka, Joe, 406
Palmer, Lili, 309
Palmerton, Tom, 264
Papa Is All, 164
Paragas, Betsye, 421, 425, 457, 481
Paramount movie house, 435
Parlor Story, 185
Parsons, Louella, 110
Pasadena Playhouse, 4, 18, 43–44, 59, 69, 96, 146, 194, 220, 421
The Passion of Martin Crowne, 335

Patrick, John, 172
The Patriots, 198
Patton, James, 140
Paul Bunyan Playhouse, 276
Payne, Alexander, 198, 399
Peacock, Harriet Fonda. See Fonda, Harriet
Peacock, Jack, 193–194, 214–215, 260
Peacock, John Blanchard, 70
Peck, Gregory, 116, 350, 432
Peckham, Harlan, 296, 326
Peckham, Mary, 151–152, 157, 161, 172, 175–176, 195, 199, 222, 247–248, 254, 262, 266–267, 296, 340–341, 352, 354–355, 361–362, 368, 371, 376, 389–390, 392, 397, 407, 457, 460
Peg O' My Heart, 207–208
Pegler, Westbrook, 274
Pennington, Penny, 154
Pensacola Little Theater, 260
Perilo, Josh, 419
Perkins, J.R., 100
Perkins, Lee, 352
Perkins, Marlin, 171
Perkins, Sue, 229, 352, 357, 361, 367, 370, 380, 387, 397, 401, 409, 434
Perkins, Tony, 251
Perkins, William, 100
Perlman, Jesse, 368
Peron, Evita, 380
Perrault, Al, 319–320, 330
Perry, Antoinette, 11
Perry, E. Wesley, 228
The Persecution and Assassination of Jean-Paul Marat as Performed by Inmates of the Asylum of Charenton Under the Direction of the Marquis de Sade, 304
Personal Appearance, 126, 128
Peter Pan, 301, 310, 348, 471–473
Peterson, Ken, 263
Peterson, Lenka, 135, 149, 152–153, 159, 161, 170, 172–174, 177, 181, 223, 232, 253, 389, 404
Le Petit Theatre du Vieux Carre, 115
Peto, Martha, 289
The Petrified Forest, 147
Philadelphia, Here I Come, 284
Philadelphia Story, 315
Phillips, Bill, 304
Phillips, G. Rockett, 431
Phillips, M. Michele, 442

A Phoenix Too Frequent, 234
Physician for Fools, 251
The Physicists, 273
Picasso at the Lapin Agile, 438
Pickford, Mary, 164, 174
Pickle, J. Laureen, 439
Picnic, 279
The Pied Piper, 403
Pierpoint, Mrs. Walter, 68
Pilkington, America, 161
Pilkington, George, 161
Pinero, Arthur Wing, 10, 23, 27, 32–33
Pinkerton, Nancy, 229, 232, 236, 256
Pinocchio, 85, 124
Pippin, 432
Pirandello, Luigi, 33, 119
Piretti, Giancarlo, 430
Pistilli, Carl, 292
Plantation Playhouse (Minnesota), 173
Players Club (Columbus, Ohio), 270
Players Club (Omaha), 5–6
Players' Guild (San Francisco), 48
Playhouse Foundation, 55, 66, 301, 359, 369, 388, 399–401, 404, 421, 431, 487
Playhouse Theatre Guild, 249
Plaza Suite, 314
The Pleasure of His Company, 255–256
Podrok, Narodni, 53–54
Pons, Lily, 117
Poole, Lanelle, 409
Pool's Paradise, 262
The Popular Sin, 15
Porgy and Bess, 142, 217
Porter, Cole, 11, 142, 252, 357, 386, 439
Portmanteau Theater, 6
Post Road, 124
Potter, Francis, 22
The Potters, 56–57
Powell, Eleanor, 171
Prairie Playmakers, 96, 122, 138
Pratt (Kent), Christel, 138, 143, 154
Preminger, Otto, 144
Prenez Garde a la Peinture, 113
Prescher, Dan, 423, 424, 428, 432, 442
President's award, 263, 271–272, 275, 282
Presley, Elvis, 317, 323
Preston, Robert, 309

Pride and Prejudice (Austen), 126, 129
Pride and Prejudice (play), 129
Priesman, Brian, 376, 392, 482
Priesman, Jennifer, 376
Priesman, Marion, 376
Priesman, Steve, 376, 481
The Prime of Miss Jean Brodie, 408
Prinz, George, 16, 19
Prinz, Mrs. George, 16, 67
Private Ear, Public Eye, 270
Prologue to Glory, 155
Prompter (playbill), 69–70
Provincetown Players, 3–4
Pruneau, Philip, 247
Pullen, Mr. and Mrs. Webster, 311
Pursuit of Happiness, 169
Pygmalion, 1, 8, 47, 54, 277, 294, 399
Pyper, Frances Brown, 97
Pyper, Walt, 97

Q

Qualities, 391–392
The Queen of Bingo, 427
Queen of the Stardust Ballroom (film), 370
The Queen's Husband, 73, 75
Quick, Cora, 75, 193, 208, 320
Quigley, Scampy, 162
Quilters, 389–391, 394–395, 399, 479–480
Quinlan, Margaret, 55–56, 94, 360
Quinlan, Mel, 313

R

Race, 489–490
Rachman, Jake, 28, 153, 159, 161, 163–164, 166–169, 172, 177, 182–185, 187–188, 190–191, 194–195, 200
Racketty Packetty House, 70, 107, 306
Radcliff, Judy, 462, 471, 475, 479–480
Radcliff, Cliff, 456
Ragan, George, 236
Raggedy Ann and Andy, 71–72, 134–135
Rags to Riches, 293
Ragtime, 332, 462, 465–467
The Rainmaker, 226, 408
A Raisin in the Sun, 259
Ramer, Cork, 397, 403, 411, 418, 423, 437–438, 440, 446, 454

Rand, Ayn, 126, 129
Rand, Sally, 277
Randall, Tony, 301
Randol, George, 214, 217
Rarely Fatal, 149
Rashomon, 253
Ratekin (Williams), Janet, 366, 410, 421
Rathbone, Basil, 11, 164
Ratliff, Curt, 405
Rave On! special event, 455, 470
Ray, Johnny, 445
Reagan, Ronald, 371
Rebecca, 164
Recommended Reading for Girls, 486
Red Hugh, Prince of Donegal (Reilly), 277
Reed, Byron, 3, 36, 125
Reed, Marian, 27
Reed, Walter, 122
Reed (Ayers), Erna, 92, 152
Reel, Jack, 103, 109, 111, 115, 130
Rees, Henrietta, 7
Reese, Paul, 92
Reeves, Jack, 180
Regan, Georgiann, 306, 417, 439, 446, 452, 461, 468
Regan, Steve, 306
Reilly, Bob, 199, 201, 206, 209–210, 226, 236, 277, 280, 328
Reilly, Jack, 210, 249
Reisser, Donald, 150
The Reluctant Debutante, 229
The Reluctant Lady, 96
Remains to be Seen, 202
The Remarkable Mr. Pennypacker, 213
The Return of Peter Grimm, 121
Return to the Forbidden Planet, 438–439
Reynolds, Alan, 312
Reynolds, Burt, 367
Reynolds, Sam, 42
Rhinoceros, 309
Rhodes, Betty, 168
Rhodes, Dusty, 132
Rialto Theater, 12
Rice, Elmer, 139
Rice, Tim, 362, 380, 418
Richard and Mary Holland Performing Arts Center, 25
Richard III, 314, 338
Richardson, Dennis, 356
Ride, Sally, 371

Ridge, Lynne, 473
Rigby, Cathy, 472
Riley, Whitcomb, 17
Rip Van Winkle, 58–59
Ritz Theater, 113
Rizzuto sisters, 352, 355–356
The Road to Mecca, 403
The Robber Bridegroom, 349, 351–352
Robbins, Bridget Wiley, 387, 437
Robbins, Polly, 41, 48, 53, 55, 133, 260
Roberts, Bob, 249, 264, 269, 273–275, 278, 294, 299, 308, 372
Roberts, Mary, 422
Robertson, Lois (Charlie), 185, 191
Robinson, Lennox, 123
Robson, May, 40
Roche, Valerie, 272, 304
Rochester Civic Theater (Minnesota), 282
Rock Legends, 479, 505
Rockefeller, John D., 21
Rocky Horror Picture Show (film), 396
The Rocky Horror Show, 396–397, 408, 454
Rodden, Dan, 418
Roddy, Jimmy, 268
Rodgers, Richard, 142, 153, 310, 393, 433, 454
Rogers, Ethyl (Mary Murray). See Murray, Mary (Ethyl Rogers)
Rogers, Mrs. Edward, 129
Rogers, Will, 11, 426
Rohe, Brandon, 468
Rohling, Christina Belford, 408, 418–419, 422, 424, 471–472, 486
Rohling, Karl, 414, 440
Roman Candle, 258
Romanoff and Juliet, 299
The Romantic Age, 41–42
Romberg, Sigmund, 311
Romeo and Juliet, 84, 95, 114, 311, 361
The Roof, 145
Roosevelt, Eleanor, 72, 83
Roosevelt, Franklin Delano, 168, 170, 248, 462
Roosevelt, Teddy, 404, 456
Roosevelt (Longworth), Alice, 404
Root, Scott, 323
Rosch, Jane, 267
Rosch, Tom, 191, 198–199
Rose, Charles, 176

Rose, Echo Guiou. See Ellick, Echo Guiou
Rose, Halleck, 42, 139
Rose, Hudson, 42
Rose Blumkin Performing Arts Center, 435
Rose-Marie, 142
Rosen, Jerry, 202
Rosenberg, David, 371
Rosenblatt, Johnny, 227, 242, 244, 246
Rosencrantz and Guildenstern Are Dead, 322
Rosenthal, Henry (Harry), 63, 89
Roskens, Ronald, 358
Ross, Barbara, 297, 410, 440, 459
Rostand, Edmond, 33
Roundey, William, 306
Rowden, Gail, 267
Rowsey, Elwood, 160
Roxie movie house, 286
The Royal Family, 92, 352
The Royal Hunt of the Sun, 297
Royal Shakespeare Company, 331
Ruble, Don, 276–277, 284–286
Rucker, Pat, 308, 310
Rudy (film), 350, 428
Ruggles, Charles, 127
Rumors, 415–416
Rumpelstiltskin, 293
R.U.R., 48, 53–54
Rush, Angeline, 128
Russell, Donna, 191
Russell, Jane, 223
Rutherford, Carolyn, 337–338, 346–347, 366, 389–391, 393, 395, 410–412, 421–422
Rutherford, Christopher, 337–338, 342–343, 346
Ryan, Belle, 111
Ryan, James Hugh, 160, 205
Ryan, Robert, 174
Ryerson, Florence, 149
Ryerson, Greg, 340, 342, 393–394, 410, 474–475

S

Sabrina Fair, 212
Sackett, Dympna, 199, 208
Salinger, J.D., 473
Same Time, Next Year, 474
Sample, Norm, Jr., 224
Sanctuary, 96
Sanders, Marianne, 288

Sarnoff, David, 249
Sarooian (Saroyan), Don, 193, 199
Saroyan, William, 148, 152, 177
Sarrell (Foley), Evelyn, 49–50
Sartre, Jean Paul, 265, 285
Sauve, Dudley, 230, 232–233, 248, 253, 261, 266–267, 273
Savage, John, 73
Saville, Ann, 315
Say, Darling, 236, 238, 242–247, 252, 272, 319
Scapino, 347–348
Schaap, Elaine, 270
Scheer, Greg, 398, 484
Schildkraut, Joseph, 40
Schmad, Tim, 114, 213, 255, 448–450, 477–479, 483, 485, 487, 490–493
Schmid, Marvin, 223, 282
Schmidman, Joann, 302, 348
Schmidt, Harvey, 309
Schmidt, Jack, 301, 320
Schneider, Adolph, 132, 137
Schoenbaum, Don, 250, 252, 274
Schoenbaum, Gerre, 252
Schoentgen, E.P., 100
Schoentgen, Jayne Fonda. See Fonda, Jayne
Schoentgen, John, 117
The School for Scandal, 56–57
Schooley (Hansen), Marilyn, 299
Schoolhouse Rock LIVE!, 434
Schrader, Carol, 424
Schweid, Amy, 472
Schweikhart, Gary, 366
Scotland Road, 436–437
Scott, Frank, 258
Scott, Martha, 138
Scott, Rick, 388, 421, 432, 451
Scott, Sue, 385
Scribner, Mrs. Arthur, 124
The Seascape, 335
The Second Mrs. Tanqueray, 10
The Secret Garden, 442, 493
The Secret of Suzanne, 193
Secret Service, 59, 207
Secrets (film), 12
Secrets (play), 56
See How They Run, 221, 262, 373
The Seeds in the Passes, 312
Segur, Fred, 143, 150, 169–170
The Senator's Husband, 125, 127
Send Me No Flowers, 310
Separate Tables, 231–232
Seventeen, 58

1776, 308, 438
70, Girls, 70, 361
The Shadow Box, 354, 362
Shadowlands, 425
Shafer, Margaret, 306
Shaffer, Peter, 270, 291
Shakespeare, William, 33, 37, 80, 84, 119, 123–124, 135, 164, 258, 268, 273, 285, 311, 314, 339, 347, 349, 366, 398, 439, 457
Shakespeare in Hollywood, 474
Sharpe, Virgil, 93, 138
Shaver, Cherie, 220–221, 227, 229–230, 295
Shaver, Neil, 220–222, 230, 233
Shaw, George Bernard, 1, 8, 11, 32–33, 36, 47, 54, 59, 72, 106, 131, 135, 145, 174, 211
Shaw, Irwin, 149
Shaw, Mrs. Lawrence, 249
Shearer, Norma, 99
Shedd, Harry, 27, 34, 59, 70, 86, 88–89, 99, 121
Sheldrick, Peg, 432
The Sheik (film), 12
Shelley, Mary, 424
Shelterbelt Theater, 416, 459
Shelton, Stephen, 468
Shenandoah, 339–340, 393
Shepley, Don, 220
Sheridan, Richard Brinsley, 6, 33, 56, 90
Sherwood, Robert, 33, 75, 147, 201
Shew, Timothy, 488
Shipley, Sue, 359, 375, 380, 384–385
Shomaker, Tom, 241, 349, 352, 366, 386, 410, 412, 417, 423, 425, 434, 471
Shonka, Chris, 482
Shore, Dinah, 367
Shotwell, Hudson, 94, 105, 108, 114, 176
The Show-Off, 32
Showcase Productions, 384–385, 388
Shrier, Miriam, 191, 269, 279, 298, 314
The Shrike, 206
Shubert brothers, 11
Siemers, Curt, 209
Sikes, Bill, 303
Sileven, Everett, 372
The Silver Chord, 172
The Silver Thread, 77, 87
Simkins, Cleveland, 154

Simmons, Lee, 424
Simon, Neil, 262, 286, 289–290, 314, 415, 421, 425, 456
Simpson, Evelyn, 216
Simpson, Michal, 443–444
Sinatra, Frank, 451
Sindelar, Theresa, 442, 449, 453, 462, 471, 473–474
Sing-Along Sound of Music, 457
Siragusa, Tim, 410, 448
The Sisters Rosensweig, 431
Skelton, Red, 367
The Skin of Our Teeth, 172
Skinner, Emaleen Gordon, 261
Skinner, Lucie (Mrs. Paul), 193
Skinner, Otis, 8
Skinner (Boyer), Virginia, 99, 145
Skutt, V.J., 224, 426
Sleeping Beauty, 134
Sleuth, 334
Sloan, Maxine, 244
Slocum, Cecil, 165
Smetana, L.W., 42, 45
Smith, Bessie, 332
Smith, Doug, 301, 312, 314–315, 325, 332–333, 335, 339, 342, 347
Smith, H.A., 53
Smith, Joseph, 102
Smith, M. Cooper, 215, 223–224, 237, 311
Smith, Marcee, 338, 348
Smoke on the Mountain, 440–441
SNAP! Productions, 416
Snipp, Robert, 340, 342, 354, 464, 469
Snodgrass, Duane, 274, 276, 278–279
Snow White and the Seven Dwarfs, 85
Snyder, Joan, 265
Social Security, 404
Society of Liberal Arts, 146–147
Sokol Auditorium, 170
Soldier's Wife, 176
The Solid Gold Cadillac, 221–222, 229
Solowicz, Dick, 298
Some Loves and Laughs from Shakespeare, 249
Sondheim, Stephen, 339, 343, 391, 401, 422–423, 474
The Song of the Bridge, 180–181
Songs My Mother Taught Me (Brando), 82
Songs of Myself, 432

Sophisticated Ladies, 408
Sophocles, 230, 311
Sorensen, Al V., 222–223, 236
Sorkin, Aaron, 418
Soule, Robert, 194–196, 199
Sound of Music, 338
The Sound of Music, 298–299, 456
South High School, 14, 91
South Pacific, 229, 340, 393, 395, 403, 409–410, 417, 474–475, 493
Sparks, C.A., 69–70
Spector, Phil, 428
Spence, Stan, 234, 238
Spewack, Bella, 209
Spewack, Sam, 209
Spier, Clarence, 184, 189
Spire, Bill, 184, 202, 212
Spire, Robert, 184
Spitfire Grill, 461
Spoon River Anthology, 284
Sprecher, Emma, 87
Springer Opera House, 321
Springtime for Henry, 106
St. Denis, Ruth, 22
St. Paul Little Theater, 156
St. Paul "Y" Players, 156
Stage Door, 133–134, 295
Stage Door volunteers, 404
Stages of Omaha, 444
Stalag 17, 201–202
Staley, Peggy, 201, 222
Standard Oil Dramatic Club, 72
The Star-Spangled Girl, 289
Stark, Eileen, 332, 336
Starkweather, 402–403, 486
Starr, Belle, 356
Starr (Wallace), Mary Lou, 169, 180
Stastny, Olga, 40
The Steadfast Soldier, 99
Steel Magnolias, 403, 482
Steinbeck, John, 358, 428
Steinmetz, Edward G., Jr., 118–119, 124–125, 127–128, 131, 133–135, 145, 173
Stenger, Stuart, 440, 442, 445, 453
Stephens, Christopher, 454
Stephens, Merrilyn, 440
Stepping Out, 463
Sterner, Jerry, 412
Stevens, Doris, 201
Stevens, Thomas Wood, 18, 62, 123
Stewart, Abigael, 488
Stewart, Jimmy, 63, 116, 125, 163
Stewart, John, II, 104–105, 110
Stewart, Marie Jesse, 222

Stickrod, Carrie Beth, 458
Stilphen, Ben, 105–106
Stimson, Edward, 211
Stinson, Merritt, 354
Stoker, Bram, 356, 442
Stommes, Jerry, 309
Stommes, Pegi, 309
Stone, Jean, 263, 268, 272, 276
Stone, Valerie, 276
Stones in the Pocket, 476
Stop the World, I Want to Get Off!, 308
Storm Over Patsy, 133
Storz, Robert, 336, 371, 380, 401, 413
Stowe, Harriet Beecher, 107
Strahl, Mary, 131
Strand Theater (Council Bluffs), 203
Strand Theater (Omaha), 12, 58
Strange Bedfellows, 250
Strange Interlude (film), 99
Strasburg, Lee, 256
Strauss, Willis, 293, 426
Street Scene, 139
A Streetcar Named Desire, 2, 81, 181, 252, 311, 483
Strider, 369
Strindberg, August, 33
Struthers, Sally, 334
Struve, Ellen, 486
Stuart, Gladys, 278, 295, 297, 300, 302
Student Prince, 143
Studio award, 314
Studio Theater, 230–231, 233–235, 241, 254, 260, 264–266, 270–271, 273, 277, 284–285, 288, 290–291, 293, 296, 299–300, 302, 306–312, 314, 324, 332, 335, 347, 349–350, 356, 362, 365–366, 460
Styne, Julie, 401
Suber, Ray, 66, 113, 138, 228
The Subject Was Roses, 304
Sugar Babies, 391–392, 452–453
A Suicide Farce, 367, 370
Sullavan, Margaret, 91, 110
Sullivan, Annie, 444
Sun Theater, 12
Sun-up, 74
Sun-Up, 33, 163
Sunrise at Campobello, 248
The Sunshine Boys, 335, 449
Susan Slade (film), 256
Suspect, 167
Swain, Howard, Jr., 310

Swan, John, 59
The Swan, 40, 43–46
Swanger, Laine, 465
Sweeney Todd, 422, 485
Sweenie, Janna, 389
Sweet Bird of Youth, 366
Sweet Charity, 421
Swigart, Warren, 191
Swing, 462
Swiss Family Robinson (film), 251, 256
Swope, Dorothy McGuire. See McGuire, Dorothy
Swope, John, 163
Swope, Mary (Topo), 186, 215
Sylvester, B.F., 133
Sylvia, 436
Szold, Bernard, 18, 62–64, 66–69, 71–73, 75–80, 83–88, 90, 92, 94, 96–97, 99–116, 122, 124, 130–131, 135, 165, 188, 202, 216, 252–253, 283
Szold, Elizabeth Stephanie, 109
Szold, Elizabeth Woolworth, 73, 75, 78, 85, 91, 96, 109, 113

T

Take Her, She's Mine, 267
Takechi, Julie, 234
Takechi, Richard, 234
Taking the Sky, 493
The Tale of the Allergist's Wife, 459
The Talented Mr. Ripley, 468
Talk of the Town Theater, 298
A Tall Story (film), 251
Talmadge, Norma, 12
Taming of the Shrew, 84
Taminosian, Florence, 42
Tammy and the Doctor (film), 263
Tandy, Jessica, 81
Tarkington, Booth, 86, 92
Taxman, Jeff, 412
Taylor, Liz, 290
Taylor, Samuel, 198
Taylor, Tom, 141
Tea Theatre (Boston), 4
The Teahouse of the August Moon, 234–235, 238
Teal, Alison, 248, 290
Teal, Clarence, 24, 65, 74, 105, 121, 128, 134, 138, 142–143, 145, 147, 150–151, 155–156, 159–161, 163–165, 167, 169–171, 174–175, 183, 189, 192, 203, 205, 208, 223–225, 228, 231, 233, 235, 244, 264, 271–272, 275–276, 282, 287, 289, 291, 301–302, 311, 313, 315, 319, 327–329, 331, 375, 385, 413, 493
Teal, John, 159, 161, 169, 178, 239
Teal, Peter, 159
Teal, Tom (Topper), 159, 161, 183, 192, 215, 327–328, 341, 413
Teal, Val, 24, 65, 90, 159, 171, 182–183, 218, 239–240, 271–272, 304, 327–328, 334, 375, 426
Technical High School (Omaha), 7, 23–25, 49, 79, 85, 91, 113, 144, 182, 293, 300, 306
Teddy and Alice, 404
Teichmann, Howard, 34, 215, 222, 359
The Telephone, 193
The Tempest, 439
Ten Nights in a Bar-room, 73–76, 81, 103, 142, 207
The Tender Trap, 331
Tenderloin, 391
Terms of Endearment (film), 291
Terra Nova, 380
Terry, Lee, 248
Terry, Lee, Jr., 248
Texas Trilogy, 346–347
That Championship Season, 324–326, 459
Theatre Arts Guild (TAG), 278, 380, 442, 459
Thelan, Paul, 449
Thelen, Janis, 123
They Knew What They Wanted, 10, 67–69
They Shoot Horses, Don't They? (film), 297
Thiessen Leonard, 202
A Thing of Beauty, 112
30—Living Scrapbook of a Decade, 300
Thomas, Dylan, 233
Thomas, L.B., 411
Thomas Jefferson High School (Council Bluffs), 203
Thompson, Edward, 43
Thompson, Steve, 408
Thornburg, Mark, 479–480
Thoroughly Modern Millie, 473–474
Thorson, Valerie, 357
A Thousand Clowns, 480
A Thousand Cranes, 432
Three-Cornered Moon, 108

The Three Musketeers, 361
The Threepenny Opera, 254, 277
Thurber, James, 152
Thurman, Valerie Stone, 263
Thurmond, Jess, 40
Tide's End, 116
Time Limit, 226
The Time of Your Life, 177
Titanic, 491
To Kill a Mockingbird, 350, 432
Tobacco Road, 140, 182
Tolle, Miriam, 115
Tolstoy, Leo, 33, 369
Tom Jones, 380–381
Tombrink, Bill, 288
Tonight at 8:30, 137
Tony n' Tina's Wedding, 434
The Torchbearers, 71
The Town Musicians of Bremen, 86
Toyland Circus, 125
Trail of the Lonesome Pine (film), 118, 366
Tranisi, Paul, 353–354, 362, 371, 416, 422, 442
Trapp, Andy, 162
Traub, Janet Maddux, 378
Treasure Island, 75, 369
Trial (film), 215
Tribute to Our Stars, 420
Trifles, 22
A Trip to Bountiful, 461
Tritz, Jennifer, 482, 484, 488
Tritz, Rick, 484
Trudy and the Minstrels, 306
Truman, Harry, 199, 470–471, 493
Truman, Nevajo, 86
Trump, Glenn, 208, 212–213, 218, 220, 222, 225
Tucker, Forrest, 116
Tucker, Sophie, 11
Tuesdays with Morrie, 482
Tulsa Little Theater, 222, 294
A Tuna Christmas, 440
Tunnicliff, Mrs. Minette, 154, 164
Tuomisto, Nancy, 298, 301
Turner, Kathleen, 463
Turner, Kenneth W., 163
Twain, Mark, 292, 406
Twelfth Night, 164, 268–269, 297, 349–350
Twelve Angry Men (film), 227
12 Angry Men, 477, 493
The 25th Annual Putnam County Spelling Bee, 482
21 & Over series, 481

Two Blind Mice, 188
Tyree, Kathy, 408, 428, 456, 489

U

Uncle Harry, 180
Uncle Tom's Cabin, 104, 107–108, 113
Uncle Vanya, 289
Under Milk Wood, 233–234
University of Nebraska Theater, 167
University Players, 91, 95
The Unsinkable Molly Brown, 362–363
Updike, Lucy, 27, 29, 42, 57, 74, 111, 188–189, 203, 255, 264, 268
Updike, Mary, 111, 115
Updike, Nels, 29
Updike, Nelson, Jr., 40
Upstairs Dinner Theater, 258, 298, 348, 391
Urbach, Berdine, 282, 313, 330
Urinetown, 471
U.S.A., 271
Ustinov, Peter, 299

V

Vaad, Ron, 217, 226, 229, 252, 278, 280
Valens, Richie, 455
Valentine, Claudette, 294
Valentine, Julie, 441
Valentino, Rudolph, 12
Vamosi, Drew, 473
Vampire Lesbians of Sodom, 453
Van Cleave, Cameron, 468
Van Cleef, Lee, 194
Van Druten, John, 172, 182, 201–202
Van Dyke, Dick, 261
van Itallie, Jean-Claude, 291
Vane, Sutton, 33, 42
A Vaudeville Entertainment, 21
Venger, Jerry, 182, 273, 326
Venta, Cathy Wells, 414
Verdon, Gwen, 421
Versaci, Roxie, 396
Vest, Randy, 313
Vickery, Warren, 234, 245
Vickrey, Robert, 422
Vidal, Gore, 266
The View from the Bridge, 250
Vinardi, Joseph, 189–190
Visiting Mr. Green, 459
Vivat! Vivat Regina!, 314–315

Vivian, Kay, 437
Vollmer, Lulu, 74
Volpone, 113

W

Wade, Gerald, 322
Wagner, Sylvia, 266
Wait Until Dark, 290–291
Waiting for Lefty, 117, 119, 127
Wakefield, Bill, 272
Walker, Harriet, 177–178
Walker, Travis, 426
Walkinshaw, Hughston, 402, 470
Wallace, David, 269, 288, 290, 300–301
Wallace, J. Laurie, 19, 101
Wallace, Janet, 262, 264, 269, 272–273, 334, 371
Wallace, Lula, 33
Wallace, Mary Lou Starr, 169, 180
Wallace, William Henry, 22
Wallach, Ira, 274
Walter, Dick, 142, 237, 367
Walters, Melanie, 483, 490
War and Peace (film), 215
Warren, Harriet Fonda. *See* Fonda, Harriet, *see also* Peacock, Harrie
Warren, Zack, 223, 227–228, 233, 287
Washington Square (James), 188, 438
Washington Square Players (New York), 4
Wasserman, Dale, 299, 431
Wasserstein, Wendy, 431
Waters, Ethel, 217
Webber, Dave, 293
Weber, Del, 424
Weber, Tony, 363
Weber (Webber), Rose, 68, 127
Weekend at Bernie's (film), 263
Wees, Tom, 291, 294–295, 297, 307–308, 325, 327–328, 341–342, 354, 357, 376, 385, 407, 453
Weichel, Beverly, 158, 162
Weill, Kurt, 150, 193
Weisner, Virgil, 330
Welcome Strangers (film), 12–13
Welk, Bob, 320
Wells, Frank, 314
Wells (Kurz), Cathy, 414, 416
Wenstrand, John (Jack), 206, 261, 269
Werndorff, Mrs. Karl, 27

West, Belle, 27, 82
West, Mae, 62, 462
West Side Story, 261, 429
West Sisters String Quartette, 6, 27, 143
Western Heritage Museum, 307
Westin, Jack, 286, 288–294, 296–297
Westroads Dinner Theater, 298, 302, 335, 348
Wet Paint, 113
Wharton, Edith, 15
What Every Woman Knows, 91–92
Wheeldon, Kathy, 428, 447
Wheeldon, Steve, 284–285, 320, 323, 329, 335, 358
Whisenant, Brian, 445, 447
White, Joan, 294–295
White Lies, 6
White-Welchen, Tiffany, 428, 456, 473
Whitmore Foundation, 412
Who Was That Lady I Saw You With?, 250
Who's Afraid of Virginia Woolf?, 290
Whose Life Is It, Anyway?, 363
Wilde, Oscar, 33, 48, 53, 73, 179, 445
Wilder, Thornton, 145, 148, 172, 230, 311, 398
Wiley (Robbins), Bridget, 387, 437
The Will Rogers Follies, 426, 457–458
Willard, Patty, 172
Williams, Barbara, 269, 295, 335
Williams, D. Kevin, 441
Williams, Emlyn, 269
Williams, Hilary, 432, 442
Williams, Janet Ratekin, 366, 410, 421
Williams, Kevin, 389
Williams, Larry B., 445
Williams, Lena May, 16
Williams, Norm, 253, 310, 313, 322
Williams, Paul, 258
Williams, Ray, 334
Williams, Roswell, 180
Williams, Spencer, 432
Williams, Tennessee, 191, 252, 265, 339, 343, 366, 415, 429, 461
Willoughby, Charleen, 482
Willson, Meredith, 323, 362
Wilson, John Kendrick, 181–182, 207, 232, 244–245, 248, 282

Wilson, Julie (Mary Lou), 150, 200, 227, 256, 352, 401
Wilson, Kathryn, 336, 355
Wilson, Keith, 15, 28, 120, 122–123, 129–133, 135, 137–139, 143–150, 152–155, 157–158
Wilson, Kendrick, 62, 155–159, 161–162, 165, 167, 171–173, 175, 177–181, 183, 185–188, 190, 193–204, 208, 212–215, 217, 220–222, 226–229, 232–233, 236–238, 240, 242, 244–245, 247, 249, 251, 253–258, 260, 262, 266–268, 272–274, 276, 278–283, 285–286, 292, 295, 306, 310, 313, 323, 327, 353
Wilson, Leslie, 156, 159, 170–172, 176, 181, 193, 227, 232, 236, 244, 251, 254, 260, 267, 275, 280, 282, 334
Wilson, Mary Lee, 111–112
Winger, Debra, 374
Wingert, Dave, 348, 363, 368, 373, 471
The Wingless Victory, 253
The Winslow Boy, 191–193
Winsor, Anne, 361
Winsor, Ginny, 309, 336, 379, 405, 421, 435, 447
Winterset, 126–127
Wiseman, Bill, 199
With Sirens Blowing, 182
Withem, Suzanne, 449
Withers, Brenda, 473
Witherspoon, David (David James), 298
Witness for the Prosecution, 229, 387
Wittson, Cecil, 206
The Wiz, 413–415
The Wizard of Oz, 73, 112, 115, 305, 310, 389, 486
Wodehouse, P.G., 312
Wolf, Loretta, 299, 350
Wolf, Mr. and Mrs. Joe, 299
Wolf-Ferrari, Ermanno, 193
The Wolfman, 165
Wolsky, Milton, 277
The Woman in Black, 437
The Women, 156, 158, 162, 447
Women's Home Companion (novelette), 182
Wonder of the World, 460–461
Wonderful Town, 223

Wood, Grant, 62, 88, 94–95, 100–101, 103–104, 116
Woolley, Monty, 277
Woolworth, Elizabeth. See Szold, Elizabeth Woolworth
Woolworth, Gilbert, 75
Workhoven, Melanie, 270, 296
Workhoven, Merrill, 296
Working, Scott, 416
The World of Sholem Aleichem, 261
World Theater, 12
Wortmann (Broman), Katie, 481
Wouk, Herman, 213
Wright, Don, 334, 370, 406
Wright, Ralph, 347
Wynn, Ed, 10
Wynne, Chet, 43

Y

Yanney, Mike, 287
Years Ago, 180
Yellow Jack, 94, 108, 122–123
Yes, My Darling Daughter, 139–141, 143, 205
Yesterday and Today, 470
You and I, 2, 32–36
You Can't Take It With You, 154, 221, 279, 470
You Never Can Tell, 59
You Should Be So Lucky, 453
Young, Brigham, 101–103
Young, Florence, 42, 223, 282, 320, 374, 426
Young, Joseph, 355
Young, Marianne, 326, 342
Young, Richard, 40
Young, Robert, 216
Young Frankenstein, 489–490
Young Mr. Lincoln (film), 145
The Youngest, 52–53
Your Own Thing, 297

Z

Zadina, Nick, 476
Zaller, Michael, 433, 454
Zeisemann, Glendora, 239, 251–252, 257, 263, 266–267, 280–282
Zevitz, Eileen, 145
Zombie Prom, 458–459
Zuby (scenic designer), 376
Zweiback, Warren, 274, 325

www.ingramcontent.com/pod-product-compliance
Lightning Source LLC
Chambersburg PA
CBHW081156230426
43666CB00016B/2833